Foreword to the Fourth Edition

Competition law is a major part of Community law measured, not so much by the proportion of cases involving Articles 85 and 86 of the Rome Treaty which are decided by the European Court of Justice in relation to the total volume of litigation before it, as by reason of the economic, financial and intellectual interest of the issues which are at stake and by reason of the considerable attention which decisions receive in legal literature.

It is a field in itself, which requires a very special skill in sorting out and analysing the facts, an understanding of pricing mechanisms, a knowledge of how business actually operates and, last but not least, policy evaluations. It is often argued that cartel agreements can never last very long and that, unless based on statutory measures, single-firm monopolies are almost invariably subject to challenge and will soon be unable to keep their stronghold upon the market. But the practical questions are: how long and how soon. For, meanwhile, consumers and competitors may be badly hurt.

Hence the importance of competition law, which is designed to do away with all artificial barriers erected through collusion or unilateral exclusionary tactics. The need for it will soon be discovered by central and eastern European countries which, after the collapse of their centrally-planned economic systems, are trying to turn to a market economy at the same time as they start enjoying basic political freedoms.

Whether, in the EEC, competition law is really 'about the legal enforcement of competition' or merely 'about who is to decide whether industrialists shall on a particular occasion be free to act non-competitively and in what way they are going to be free not to act competitively'[1] is still a matter open to debate. I shall not discuss it here. Part of the answer will be found in Valentine Korah's book. But what is certain is that, although the EEC Commission is not making many more than ten decisions a year, the case law is now very abundant—especially if one adds the Court's judgments under Article 173 or 177 [now Articles 230 and 234] of the Rome Treaty—and has grown enormously in complexity. And case law is not the only thing to look at. Apart from the transport regulations, there are no fewer than eight EEC Commission group exemption regulations which businessmen and their advisers have to take into account before drafting their co-operation, distribution or licensing agreements. It has become a risky venture to find one's way through that forest of cases and regulations, for paths are as yet not always clearly marked. Moreover, some institutional changes, such as the creation of the Court of First Instance, are not going to make that task easier. Although whole libraries have been devoted to competition law, a concrete and concise

---

1 Jeremy Lever, 'Enterprise Law of the 80s', in Frederick M Rowe, Francis G Jacobs and Mark R Joelson (eds), *ABA*, p 97.

guidebook was needed to provide students and businessmen with a survey of this complex field. This has been the purpose of Valentine Korah in writing what she calls her 'Little Yellow Book.'

No-one is better qualified for that job. Valentine Korah has written extensively and expertly about both the UK law of restrictive trade practices and EEC competition law, has wide experience in economics, has taken part in, and even organised, innumerable conferences for practitioners, maintains contacts with civil servants responsible for law enforcement, knows the case law extremely well and never gets tired of reading the decisions prepared by DGIV of the Commission, even the most obscure ones.

Readers will not only find a description of the law in Valentine Korah's book. I am sure that they, and especially EEC civil servants, will greatly benefit from her critical views. I myself am very much inclined to agree with her when she criticises the legalistic and formalistic approach often taken by DGIV officials, and when she stresses that, by not relating specific facts to its legal appraisal, the EEC Commission misses a wonderful opportunity to educate people dealing with competition law—including its own officials. But Valentine Korah is not altogether pessimistic. She regards DGIV officials as more open to outsiders' views than any national administration she knows of (see chapter 12.0). I hope very much that the future will prove her to be right. Meanwhile, I am very pleased to wish the fourth edition of her 'Little Yellow Book' all the attention and success it deserves.

Judge René Joliet
Court of Justice of the
European Communities
August 1990,

Foreword to the Seventh Edition

Sir Christopher Bellamy QC

As one who has greatly profited from the first six editions of this work, it gives me very great pleasure to write a forward to the seventh edition of *An Introductory Guide to EC Competition Law and Practice*.

In the period of over 20 years since the first edition, competition law has moved centre stage. Unlike the position in the 1970s, when there were still relatively few decisions under Article 81 (ex Article 85) and hardly half-a-dozen under Article 82 (ex Article 86), there are now a mass of decisions under both Articles, as well as many decisions under the Merger Regulation, a substantially increased number of block exemption regulations, and a very considerable case law of decisions of both the Court of First Instance (which did not then even exist) and the Court of Justice. In addition, in contrast to the position in the 1970s when only a few national competition laws existed, almost all Member States and aspiring Member States have now created national competition regimes, the majority of which are closely modelled on Articles 81 and 82. The most recent example of reform is of course in the United Kingdom itself, where the Restrictive Trade Practices legislation has been repealed and replaced by the new prohibitions under the Competition Act 1998, which are taken directly from Articles 81 and 82. As if all these developments were not enough, there is now also the Commission's own White Paper on Modernisation of the rules implementing Articles 81 and 82 of the EC Treaty which envisages a much wider role for national authorities and courts in enforcing those Articles.

There is thus more need than ever for a clear, authoritative yet simple introduction to the why and the wherefore of EC competition law, written primarily for the non-specialist or student. The seventh edition amply fulfils this need, and guides the uninitiated and initiated alike through all the main aspects of this complex subject in a most clear and comprehensive fashion.

But *EC Competition Law and Practice* has always fulfilled a second, no less important, role: that of constructive criticism of the way in which EC competition law has been developed and implemented over the years. With extraordinary consistency over more than a quarter of a century, Valentine Korah has urged the Commission, among other things, to adopt a less legalistic and more economically orientated approach in its decisions, to give better reasoning, to improve its procedures and to achieve greater consistency of approach. Now, at last, it seems that the Mountain has come to Mohommed. There is now widespread recognition of the need to refocus competition law away from a 'catch all' approach (which sweeps into the net of prohibition many innocuous or pro-competitive agreements) towards the more selective prosecution of seriously anti-competitive price fixing and market sharing

cartels, and serious cases of abuse of market power. This new approach rein-
forces the need to concentrate on economic effects. If the White Paper is
adopted, the system of pre-notification and the Commission's monopoly over
the grant of exemption under Article 81(3) will be abolished. These developments should, if properly implemented, lead to a more flexible and effective
EC competition policy than has sometimes been the case in the past. If the
Commission's new initiatives meet many of the objectives raised in earlier editions of the *Guide*, as the author herself acknowledges in Chapter 13, the fact
remains that it is in large part Valentine Korah who has been proved right all
along.

   All competition law regimes pose inherent challenges: how to deliver legal
certainty with an effects based test; how to catch the sharks but not the minnows; how to combine fair procedures with speedy decision making; how to
ensure effective competition without undue regulatory burdens; and so on.
However formidable such challenges may seem, we could not wish for a better *Introductory Guide* to help us meet them.

Christopher Bellamy
President of Appeal Tribunals
Competition Commission
London, 15 August 2000

Preface

Businessmen, large and small, are increasingly operating in more than one Member State of the European Communities. Even those whose activities are confined to a single Member State or who export to Europe from outside the common market may find that the EC competition rules apply to them, as any substantial restriction of competition within even a single Member State may have repercussions on trade between Member States and infringe the competition rules. A contract made by foreigners outside the common market is subject to the competition rules if it is implemented and foreseeably restricts competition directly and substantially within the common market.

Firms may be heavily fined or unable to enforce important provisions in their contracts if they do not take account of the EC competition rules. The maximum fine is 10% of the undertaking's turnover for the previous year, and in *Pioneer*[2] the Court of Justice of the European Communities held that this relates to the total turnover of the whole group of companies, all products, worldwide. The maximum has never been reached, and is limited by the doctrine of proportionality. If only a small part of the undertaking's activities is affected, the infringement is less grave than if all its activities are. It was arguable that the fine should be based on the turnover of the subsidiary that infringed and the product affected, but this limit was exceeded in the *Pre-insulated Pipe Cartel* (1.7 below). The fine exceeded 10% of its turnover in pre-insulated pipes.

Agreements fixing prices and allocating markets have been subject to very heavy fines. A fine of 462 million euros was imposed on *Hoffmann La Roche*[3] for participating in the *Vitamin Cartel* and a fine of 497.2 million euros on *Microsoft,* for what was not clearly an infringement of Article 82 at the time the conduct took place, was even higher. Heavy fines can also be expected for anything that is considered by the Commission to deter new entrants to the market from growing. Most large firms are well advised by in-house lawyers or those in private practice, but small firms may not know when to seek advice and may be tempted to save this expense, which is likely to be proportionately higher for them.

This book was originally written to help businessmen to comply with the EC competition rules, or at least to know when to consult a lawyer. It may also help them to collect their thoughts and the relevant information before seeking advice and thereby reduce the cost of obtaining it. In fact, however, lawyers and law students have also been buying the book. Consequently, in the third edition, I added short sections on price theory, which few lawyers in Europe

---

2 (100–103/80) [1983] ECR 1825, since confirmed in several of the appeals from the vitamins cartel decision.
3 OJ 2003, L6/1, [2003] 4 CMLR 1030.

used to learn about at University, although the position is changing. Readers familiar with how markets work can skip these sections. For the convenience of lawyers who may not have access to the official reports, multiple citations to the cases and legislation mentioned in the text are to be found in the tables.

My students are advised to read the book in conjunction with selected pages from my casebook. Otherwise the terse language that I have tried to use is difficult to follow. Law teachers are advised to refer their students to at least some of the cases in addition to this book.

Throughout, I have tried to explain the rules critically in the light of the objectives they are intended to achieve. It is important to understand the problems of policy, partly because it helps one to argue a case before the Commission or a court and partly because I hope that the book may help to educate those who may later become officials or work at one of the Community Courts. In the fourth edition, I added a final critical chapter. Recently, there have been so many important changes in the attitude of both courts and Commission that very substantial changes were required for this edition.

I have supported the text with short bibliographies at the end of most chapters, as well as a more general bibliography and a glossary at the end of the work. The tables and appendices are fuller than is usual. Clearly, those practising substantially in the field will need to progress to a larger book including more legislation. Nevertheless, my book is intended to be practical and consider controversial issues.

Judge Joliet wrote a foreword to the 4th edition of this book. Most of the problems now current in competition law are dealt with in his comparative books on Articles 81 and 82, published in 1967 and 1970. He was the first person to criticise the practice of finding any important restriction of conduct anti-competitive even if without protection some kind of investment would not have been forthcoming. I have learned a great deal from the books and articles he wrote while he was teaching at Liège. They are very easy to read, because he took the trouble to analyse clearly before he started to write. He also had the gift of the vivid phrase. I would prefer to read his work in French than that of most people in my own tongue.

I am most grateful for Judge Joliet's support and the interesting things that he said in a foreword to this book. His death eight years ago has not only saddened me personally, it has deprived the European Court of Justice of a brilliant and lucid analyst of problems of competition law and policy and all of us of the results of his wise advice and careful drafting.

I am doubly fortunate in that Sir Christopher Bellamy, now President of the UK Competition Appeals Tribunal and formerly a member of the Court of First Instance in Luxembourg, wrote a foreword for the seventh edition. With Graham Child, Sir Christopher wrote one of the first excellent books in English on EC competition law, now in its fifth edition, vastly expanded into a major practitioners' work. After his extensive practice in the UK, he contributed to many important judgments in Luxembourg, of which my favourite is *European Night Services* (13.2.2.2 below). It went close to adopting a rule of reason under Article 81(1) and is one of many judgments extending the traditional jurisdiction of the CFI from judicial review towards a new trial on the merits on the basis of defects in reasoning and, on one point, manifest error of assessment.

This year I have also been lucky in that my colleague at UCL, Joshua Holmes, currently working for Advocate General Jacobs at the ECJ, kindly read through a draft of several chapters of this edition. His comments and support have been invaluable. He has saved me from many errors and persuaded me to consider several interesting issues. I learned much from our discussions, especially on the control of government intervention under Article 86 and how to reconcile conflicting Community policies.

I am indebted to Fordham University School of Law. Since 1991 I have taught courses there each spring semester on EC competition law and on technology licensing. Fordham has supported me in many ways, provided library facilities, an office with a fast computer and help with its use. It also made available funds for research assistance.

I am grateful also to University College for keeping on a retired professor part time, letting me take seminars and supporting me in ways similar to those in which I have been helped by Fordham.

I would also like to thank the librarians at Fordham Law School and the Institute of Advanced Legal Studies in London for help given cheerfully and going far beyond what could reasonably be expected. Both libraries are blessed with extremely knowledgeable and constructive people. Mary McKee at Fordham checked the bibliography against publishers' websites to ensure that I included the latest editions and supplements as well as ensuring that I was able to consult all the recent books on the subject.

I am indebted to two very able research assistants, Mattan Meridor and Andrej Fatur. They were studying for their LL.M. degrees, Mattan at University College and Andrej at Fordham. Both helped me competently with problems relating to the use of computers and web sites. Each has helped me to keep my citations accurate by checking the more recent ones. Both have become friends and, undoubtedly, will go far. Nelson Jung, another of my best students, kindly helped check the table of cases and legislation at short notice.

I like small publishers, who can make rapid decisions on the phone or using email and take more care over each book. Hart Publishing has grown prodigiously both in reputation and the number of books published annually in less than eight years from its formation, but it can still take decisions and produce a work fast. Whoever answers its phone responds constructively to almost any enquiry.

I am grateful to Richard Hart for undertaking the copy editing himself, bit by bit as I completed a chapter, so as to make up time when I was unable to submit my script at the beginning of May. He has been very flexible and constructive. I should also like to thank Hope Services, who have now type-set three editions of this book, and who continue to do so accurately and quickly. Typesetters such as Hope are a rare breed, and I hope they continue to flourish.

My thanks to all these people and to my students round the world who cope so well with my difficult questions! Without them, I would not have taken the trouble to write my books.

The cut off dates have been April or May depending on when the particular chapter was finished.

Valentine Korah
University College London,
valentine.korah@ucl.ac.uk,
and
Guildford Chambers, fax 44 1483 300 542
Richard Moore, Chief Clerk
May 2004

Contents

Table of Cases

References in bold type are to discussions in the text.

I. THE COMMISION AND COURTS

II. EUROPEAN COURT OF HUMAN RIGHTS

III. AUSTRALIA

IV. FRANCE

V. GERMANY

VI. UNITED KINGDOM

VII. UNITED STATES

Table of Legislation

Legislative titles in bold type are the more important ones; section references in bold refer to discussions in the text.

II. SUBORDINATE LEGISLATION

1 TABLE OF LEGISLATION

III. NATIONAL LEGISLATION

1. Introduction

1.1 The Common Market

Many economic advantages were expected to flow from the establishment of the European common market embracing an area that had been divided by national customs duties and quotas for over a century. Goods and services should be produced in the areas most suited to each and sold in the areas where they were wanted. Opportunities for specialisation leading to automatic production lines and substantial cost savings would be possible in larger geographic markets. In many industries, firms might be able to grow to a size at which they enjoyed economies of scale and scope in production and distribution, while leaving room for other producers to compete with them.

Under the EEC Treaty, which I shall usually call 'the Treaty,' or 'the Treaty (EC)' the European Economic Community (EEC) was formed by the six original Member States from 1958. The various objectives of the Community were set out in Article 2. These included an accelerated raising of living standards and a continuous and balanced expansion of economic activity to be achieved through the establishment of a common market.

The Treaty of Maastricht, which came into force on 1 November 1993, supplemented the earlier treaties and created a European Union when it added a common foreign policy, as well as co-operation in the environmental and social areas and the aim of achieving a monetary union between the Member States. The Treaty of Maastricht changed the name of the EEC to the European Community (EC).

The Treaty of Amsterdam, which came into force on 1 May 1999, amended and renumbered most of the Articles of the EC Treaty.[1] After the Treaties of Maastricht and Amsterdam, the European Union consists of three pillars: first, the European Community created by the original EEC Treaty, secondly, Police and Judicial Cooperation in Criminal Matters and thirdly, the Common Foreign and Security matters.

The Treaty of Nice, signed on 26 February 2001, came into force on 1 February 2003 and, inter alia, provided the mechanism for voting when 10 new Member States acceded to the European Union.

From January 2002, most Member States have operated a single currency—the euro. Sweden, Denmark and the UK still retain their own currencies as do the ten new member states. It was hoped that the ability easily to compare prices in different countries would help to integrate the market. It is still expensive to change sterling for euros and vice versa through banks, even when there is no risk because the other currency is credited only after a cheque has been collected.

---

1 I shall use the new numbers throughout this book, even in quotations from before that date and I shall refer to the Articles as amended. A table of derivations from the former numbers is appendix III.

In the common market all economic resources should be free to move throughout, unimpeded by national boundaries. Consequently, the EC Treaty provides for the free movement of goods, services, workers and capital as well as the right to establish a business in other Member States. It would, however, be of little use to abolish government restrictions such as customs barriers and quotas between Member States if traders in different countries were allowed to replace them by cartels, under which they agreed reciprocally to keep out of each other's home market. Agreements having the object or effect of restricting competition are, therefore, controlled under the competition rules in the Treaty.

Herr von der Gröben, the first Member of the Commission responsible for competition policy, believed that these rules also had a longer term function—to encourage the expansion of efficient firms and sectors of the economy at the expense of those less good at supplying what people want to pay for. This view is receiving greater acceptance, although some concern remains that the rules have been applied so as to protect smaller firms at the expense of larger, irrespective of efficiency (1.3.2.2–1.3.2.7 below). This view has led to the geographic spread of competition law and over 80 countries have now adopted rules intended to control anti-competitive conduct, even when there was no need to support rules for integrating markets.

1.2 The competition rules

The main competition rules governing undertakings in the public and private sectors were set out in Articles 81 and 82 of the EC Treaty (reproduced in Appendix I.) They were renumbered from Articles 85 and 86 by the Treaty of Amsterdam, but not amended.

Article 81 forbids, as incompatible with the common market, collusion between undertakings that may affect trade between Member States and has the object or effect of restricting competition within the common market. Article 82 forbids as incompatible with the common market the abusive exploitation of a dominant position. Article 81 controls agreements between undertakings and Article 82 the conduct, unilateral or otherwise, of firms that are subject only to remote competitive pressures.

Conduct may infringe both Articles and citizens are required to comply with both. In *Vitamins*,[2] the European Court of Justice, (hereafter called 'the ECJ') confirmed the Commission's decision that Hoffmann-La Roche had infringed Article 82 by granting discounts to large buyers who had bought or who agreed to buy a large proportion of their requirements from it, making it difficult for its smaller suppliers to compete. Such a contract might also be forbidden by Article 81.

---

2   *Hoffmann-La Roche & Co. AG v Commission (Vitamins)*, Case 85/76, [1979] ECR 461.

In *Tetra Pak I*,[3] the Court of First Instance (hereafter called 'the CFI') upheld a decision condemning under Article 82 the acquisition by a dominant firm of a potential competitor that had an exclusive licence to the main alternative technology although the licence had been exempted from the prohibition of Article 81(1).

Articles 81 and 82 are enforced not only by the Commission's intervention under Regulation 1/2003[4] with prohibition orders and fines or commitments offered by the parties (chapter 7 below), but also by national competition authorities and national courts. Making a prohibited agreement gives rise to a non-contractual duty under Community law and anti-competitive provisions in contracts may be void and the victim entitled to damages (7.3.4 and 7.3.4.1 below). The prohibitions of Articles 81 and 82 have direct effect in national law. National courts are required to protect the victims of infringement by granting adequate remedies (7.2 below). In *Courage v Crehan*,[5] the ECJ held that the owner of a small chain of pubs, which probably had no opportunity to negotiate the terms of its contract, could not be deprived of its rights under Article 81 by the English rule that the party to an illegal contract cannot seek the assistance of the courts.

National competition authorities (NCAs) may impose penalties under national law to deter infringement of the competition rules (7.3.1 below) and the Commission may impose fines and penalties under Regulation 2001/03 (7.6–7.6.3 below).

1.2.1 *Article 81—collusion that restricts competition*

Article 81(1) (chapter 2 below) provides that:

> (1) The following shall be prohibited as incompatible with the common market: all agreements between undertakings, decisions by associations of undertakings and concerted practices which may affect trade between Member States and which have as their object or effect the prevention, restriction or distortion of competition within the common market, and in particular those which . . .

There follows a list of examples of conduct assumed to be anti-competitive, without any express distinction being drawn between agreements between competitors and those between firms operating at different levels of trade or between restrictions that are necessary to make some legitimate transaction viable and those that are not (8.1–8.1.3 below).

Article 81(2) provides that agreements that infringe the Article are void (7.3.4.1 below). The ECJ ruled[6] that the nullity applies only to the provisions having the object or effect of restricting competition: it is for national law to

---

3   Case T–51/89, [1990] ECR II–309, paras 23–25 and 37.
4   OJ 2003, L1/1
5   C–453/99, [2001] ECR 1–6297.
6   In *Société La Technique Minière v Maschinenbau Ulm GmbH* (56/65) [1966] ECR. 235.

decide whether what remains can be enforced. In deciding whether trade between Member States may be affected, however, the agreement as a whole is appraised and not only the provision in issue.

National courts will not be able to order parties to fulfil their contracts if the provisions in question infringe Article 81. This can have far reaching consequences. When enforcing an exclusive agreement one may be met by a Euro-defence that, in its legal and economic context, parts of the agreement infringe Article 81 and are void.

Article 81(3) provides for exceptions from the prohibition. Until May 2004 these could be adopted only by the Commission, the executive body of the EC, and not by national courts or competition authorities. This has changed.[7] The Commission initiated reform by adopting a white paper on modernisation.[8] It examined various options for reform and proposed a fundamentally different system of enforcement based on the direct applicability of Article 81(3), enabling national competition authorities and courts to apply Article 81(3). The Council adopted the Commission's proposal in Regulation 1/2003[9] after making some changes.

In *Pronuptia*,[10] it was argued in the German Supreme Court that a franchise agreement for three cities in the Federal Republic was contrary to Article 81(1) and void, and that, consequently, the franchisor in France could not recover the agreed royalty payments. Meeting such a defence may require an analysis of the market, which may be expensive and difficult for both counsel and judges or the establishment that the provisions that restricted conduct were necessary to make viable a transaction that was not, in itself, anticompetitive. Such an analysis may increase the cost of litigation and make it more difficult to obtain advice on whether contracts can be enforced. Consequently, it may be more difficult to settle disputed cases.

1.2.2   *Article 82—the abuse of a dominant position*

Article 82 (chapters 4 and 5 below) prohibits the abusive exploitation of a dominant position:

> Any abuse by one or more undertakings of a dominant position within the common market or in a substantial part of it shall be prohibited as incompatible with the common market in so far as it may affect trade between Member States. Such abuse may, in particular, consist in: . . .

The examples relate to exploitation, to conduct that oppresses buyers and sellers dealing with a dominant firm: charging too much, paying too little, restricting production or markets, discriminating against some firms and so

---

7   Regulation 1/2003, OJ 2003, L1/1, 1.5–1.5.4 and chap 7 below.
8   [1999] 5 CMLR 208.
9   OJ 2003, L1/1, [2003] 4 CMLR 551.
10   (161/84) [1986] ECR, 353 (9.5.1 below).

making it difficult for them to compete downstream, and refusing to supply the monopolised product without some other product the buyer would prefer to obtain elsewhere.

'Abuse' is a poor authentic translation of the double concept of 'abusive exploitation' used in most Community languages. It was thought that the Article forbids the exploitation of market power to harm customers or suppliers, providing for regulation of prices and conditions imposed by firms with market power. This is not practicable in view of the tiny resources the Community devotes to enforcing the competition rules. More importantly, it would be inconsistent with the liberal spirit in which the Community was created.

In *Continental Can v Commission*,[11] the ECJ held that the acquisition by a dominant firm of a potential competitor might infringe Article 82, although the shareholders in the target company had not been harmed; nor was it alleged that they had been forced to sell their shares because Continental Can enjoyed a dominant position. Buyers may be harmed indirectly by the reduction of competition.

So the ECJ construed the words 'abusive exploitation of a dominant position' to include conduct that affects the structure of the market by absorbing a potential competitor, and not only conduct that exploits the lack of competition. The increased concentration of the market might lead to higher prices to the detriment of consumers later. This has been extended in many later cases to conduct of a dominant firm that makes it more difficult for other undertakings to compete.

It is difficult to advise firms on the application of Article 82, as it has been held that even firms that have little market power may be dominant, and it is not clear what conduct is forbidden. The Community Courts have had difficulty distinguishing conduct that excludes others through efficiency, by giving better value for money, from methods of exclusion not based on the merits. They have used a formula suggesting that competition on the basis of performance is lawful, but it is not clear what is included in this category (5.1 below). Consequently, conduct that would not infringe US antitrust law may infringe that of the EC.

Moreover, until fairly recently, the Community courts and Commission seem to have been concerned about the interest of a trader entering a market of his choice. Recently, there have been welcome signs that they are more concerned with the interests of consumers, although there is some concern that the Commission sometimes perceives efficiency—providing what consumers want to buy—as excluding those less good at doing so.[12]

---

11   (6/72) [1973] ECR. 215, paras 26–27 (5.2 below).
12   *E.g.*, Commissioner Monti in XXXI *Report on Competition Policy 2001*, (2002), p 3.

1.2.3 *Regulation 4064/89—the control of concentrations*

Merger control under Article 81 is unsatisfactory. Nullity by virtue of Article 81(2) is a poor sanction if it results in the acquiring firm not owning the assets of the target company. If it were to sell them, whether or not in the course of business, a *bona fide* purchaser would get no title. An order to sell some of the overlapping assets or activities would be far less disruptive of commerce than invalidity.

In *Continental Can*,[13] the ECJ gave the Commission power under Article 82 to forbid an acquisition by a firm already dominant of an actual or potential competitor when this would virtually eliminate competition. The Commission, however, wanted to be able to monitor mergers before they were consummated and was concerned by mergers that might lead to a dominant position. In 1973 it proposed that the Council should adopt a regulation requiring the parties to a merger between companies with large turnovers to notify it in advance and giving the Commission power to restrain mergers. Eventually, in 1989, the Council adopted Regulation 4064/89[14] giving the Commission such powers. The Council of Ministers has recently revised the merger regulation.[15]

The parties to a merger of firms with large turnovers are required to notify it in advance to the Commission. The Commission is required to decide whether it

> would significantly impede effective competition, in the common market or in a substantial part of it, in particular as a result of the creation or strengthening of a dominant position[.]

It is required to make decisions under the merger regulation far faster than under Article 81 or 82, and has nearly always met its deadlines. Most mergers were permitted within a month, (now 25 working days) sometimes subject to undertakings given by the parties. Where the merger gives rise to substantial doubts as to its validity it may be appraised over a further 4 months (now 90 working days).

1.2.4 *The interpretation of the competition rules and the integration of the common market*

Both Articles 81 and 82 and the regulations that implement them as well as the merger regulation must be read in the light of the objectives of the Treaty. Article 2, as amended, provides that:

---

13   (6/72) [1973] ECR, 215, paras 26–27 (5.2 below).
14   Text as amended by Regulation 1310/97, [1990] 4 CMLR 859, described in chapter 12 below.
15   Regulation 139/2004, OJ 2004, L 24/1 (chapter 12 below).

The Community shall have as its task, by establishing a common market and an economic and monetary union and by implementing the common policies or activities referred to in Articles 3 and 4, to promote throughout the Community a harmonious development of economic activities, sustainable and non-inflationary growth respecting the environment, a high degree of convergence of economic performance, a high level of employment and of social protection, the raising of the standard of living and quality of life and economic and social cohesion and solidarity among Member States.

One might think that the common market is the mechanism by which the expansion, stability and so forth are to be achieved, but market integration has been elevated in competition cases to an aim in itself,[16] and has been pursued in a mechanical way, even when this leads to reduced competition and may delay the integration of the market (1.3.2–1.3.2.7 below).

Article 3 provides that:

For the purposes set out in Article 2, the activities of the Community shall include, as provided in this treaty and in accordance with the timetable set out therein:

(a) the elimination, as between Member States, of customs duties and of quantitative restrictions on the import and export of goods, and of all other measures having equivalent effect;. . .

(g) the institution of a system ensuring that competition in the internal market is not distorted; . . .

The ECJ has held more than once that both Articles 81 and 82 should be construed in the light of these provisions, even when there is a fairly clear literal interpretation to the contrary. In *Continental Can*, for instance, the ECJ interpreted Article 82 not only as a provision under which the conduct of firms already dominant which harmed consumers directly could be regulated but also as one forbidding the weakening of any remaining potential competition by a firm already dominant, as this might harm consumers in the longer term.[17]

1.2.5 *The treaty covers all sectors of the economy*

The competition rules apply to services as well as goods and to licences of incorporeal property such as patents, but there are some sectors receiving special treatment.

Most coal and steel products were subject to the Treaty of Paris which established the European Coal and Steel Community (ECSC) and not to the EC Treaty. The ECSC Treaty contained somewhat similar competition rules in Articles 65 and 66,[18] but the Commission had greater power to intervene over these two products and the competition rules could not be enforced in the

---

16 *Consten & Grundig v Commission* (56 & 58/64) [1966] ECR 299 (2.3.1 and 2.4.1 below).
17 See also 1.2.2 above and 5.2 below.
18 The Articles of the ECSC Treaty have not been renumbered.

courts of Member States until the Commission had found an infringement.[19] Agreements affecting coal and steel products might infringe the old rules even if there was no effect on trade between Member States. The older coal and steel precedents must therefore be applied to the EC only with caution.

On June 23 2002, the ECSC Treaty expired by virtue of Article 97 thereof, and coal and steel products fell automatically into the EC Treaty (Article 305). For some years the Commission has been adopting a similar policy to coal and steel as to the EC products, and all it did to accommodate coal and steel products to the EC Treaty was to issue a notice explaining the position.[20] It was not necessary to preserve the validity of exemptions granted under the earlier treaty. The Commission does not intend to impose fines for making or implementing agreements that were exempt under the ECSC Treaty, although provisions contained in them may be void as a consequence of the direct effect of Articles 81 and 82 (EC).

Many of the agreements exempted individually or by a general decision under the ECSC Treaty will be full function joint ventures and if the event triggering the merger regulation occurred after 23 June 2002, those where the turnover exceeds the thresholds should be notified under the merger regulation.

The law relating to coal and steel will be ignored in this book, as will the provisions of the Euratom treaty which relates to nuclear energy, another sector to which, by virtue of Article 305 (EC), the EC Treaty does not apply to the extent that there are special rules for Euratom.

Council regulations have made special provision modifying the competition rules as regards agriculture.[21] Moreover, for products that can be stored, such as corn, skimmed milk powder and butter, elaborate protection has been created through intervention authorities which are required by Community law to buy any intervention products offered to them at the prices fixed by the currently applicable regulations. For some products—mainly those grown in Northern Europe—this floor is supported by Community levies on imports from outside the common market. For other agricultural products, such as olive oil, there is less protection.

These provisions were adopted to ensure an adequate living standard for farmers, especially small, part-time farmers, but they are highly anti-competitive and have angered the governments of non-Community countries who would like to compete in Europe. There is little temptation for private firms to agree on common prices or quotas for some of the products subject to the common agricultural policy. In the early days, agricultural policy trumped competition policy.

Even when there is no such protection, national common rules for the agricultural products listed in annex 1 to the EC Treaty are treated more

19   *HJ Banks & Co v British Coal Corporation* (C–128/92) [1994] ECR. I–1209, paras 15–23. Contrast EC products.
20   O.J. 2002, C152/5, [2002] 5 CMLR 1036.
21   Regulation 26/62, adopted under Article 34, OJ Spec Ed, 1962, 129.

favourably than other industries.[22] Nevertheless, in principle, agriculture is also subject to the competition rules. In *Frubo v Commission*,[23] for example, the ECJ upheld the Commission's decision that some of the rules of membership of associations of importers and wholesalers taking part in a fruit auction infringed Article 81.

Regulation 17 has been replaced as from 1 May 2004 by Regulation 1/2003.[24] Under Regulation 17, the Commission had less power to enforce the competition rules against transport. Regulation 141/62 (since repealed) disapplied Regulation 17 from transport and specific regulations applied the various kinds of transport. It was not clear that transport was subject to the competition rules in 1962, so the Commission was not very aggressive in taking power. Now its powers in relation to transport[25] will be the same as for other sectors (Article 43(2) of Regulation 1/2003).

The ECJ ruled in *Albany*[26] that social policy was not consistent with competition policy and that Article 81 could not be applied to collective labour agreements. It is not clear how far this goes. Cynics allege that the ECJ was not prepared to take on the unions!

1.3 The economics of market power

Resources in the world are limited, but demand for them is not. In socialist economies or wartime, resources have been allocated by officials and rationing. The free market solution, however, is to ration resources through price. On the supply side, firms good at producing things that people want to buy will flourish and have more to invest than those less good at doing so. This has the advantage that the market encourages firms to produce efficiently what people want to buy. The consumer is king.

Even if one firm is so successful that it expands and produces most of a particular product, its profits may be noticed or guessed at by other firms, which are encouraged to produce something similar and enter the market. So the successful firm is not likely to go on enjoying market power for long unless it remains more than usually efficient or, for some reason, other firms cannot enter the market freely and those already in the market are unable to expand. Competition works also on the demand side of the market. If the cost of fish increases, some people who used to eat fish may eat more meat or eggs.

Even the only seller will not be profitable unless there are both barriers to entry on the supply side of the market and no adequate substitutes for the product supplied on the demand side (4.3–4.3.5 below). In the short term,

22   *French New Potatoes* [1988] 4 CMLR, 790.
23   (71/74) [1975] ECR, 563.
24   OJ.2003, L1/1 (chapter 7 below).
25   Other than tramp shipping and flights between one EC and one non-EC airport.
26   *Albany International BV v Stichting, Bedrijfspensioenfonds Textielindustrie and others*, (C–67/96, C–115–117 and 219/97) [1999] ECR I–5751 (paras 59 & 60).

many firms appear to have market power: they can raise their prices without losing much trade. Economists, however, frequently assume a period of time long enough to build new production facilities. Consequently, in the absence of regulation or state ownership, they tend to perceive most markets as competitive.

Most economists welcome the 'invisible hand' of competition to allocate scarce resources in accordance with consumer choice, to avoid waste in acquiring market power and to stimulate efficiency in other ways. The Community lacks the governmental resources to regulate many markets, so it is particularly important that resources be allocated by the market.

1.3.1 *Welfare economics—efficiency*

It may be argued that an unduly high price for products that people continue to buy is not necessarily undesirable: who is to say that sellers do not welcome high prices as much as buyers dislike them? Most monopolists are large firms, most of whose capital is owned by institutions such as life assurance and pension funds. A pensioner may enjoy the extra income yielded by the monopoly profit as much as the monopolist's customers dislike the extra charge. These issues relate to how wealth should be distributed in the Community. They are of political and philosophical concern, better resolved through tax and welfare systems.

Since Adam Smith,[27] however, it has been clear that if prices are raised above cost, some people who would buy the product if it were available at cost (including a normal profit on the resources committed, adjusted for risk) will not be prepared to pay the higher price and will spend their money on something else. A firm exercising market power to raise prices above cost will be able to sell less than it would otherwise have done.

Consumers will be worse off: the loss in their welfare, when the money is spent on other things they value less in terms of the value of the resources used to produce them, is the demand for the monopolised product foregone less what it would have cost to supply. No one benefits from this loss. So, it is sometimes called 'the deadweight loss.'

Richard Posner goes further and alleges that a more important cause for concern over high prices is the waste of resources spent on acquiring and maintaining market power.[28] Competitors have to organise and enforce an agreement to keep prices up, persuade politicians to regulate the industry and keep others out, and so forth. These resources could be better spent on producing more goods and services for consumption.

---

27   *The Wealth of Nations* vol 1 (1st ed, 1776).
28   *Antitrust Law: An Economic Perspective* (Chicago, University of Chicago Press, 1976), chap 1.

A third objection to market power is that it reduces the incentive to increase efficiency. In a competitive market, firms that do not efficiently produce what buyers want to pay for may go out of business. This helps to ensure that only the more efficient survive and there is pressure on firms to prune their costs or provide better bargains in other ways.

If efficiency be the only goal of competition policy there will be little need for officials to intervene. In the absence of government regulation, few industries are protected by significant barriers to entry preventing competition from equally efficient firms.

In the early days, EC competition policy was greatly influenced by the theory of perfect competition. In a perfectly competitive market supply is likely to increase until marginal revenue equals marginal cost. If all markets are perfectly competitive, the resources of society will be allocated according to the ability and willingness of consumers to buy.

Unfortunately few markets are perfectly competitive, although some commodity markets and stock exchanges may get close. The theory assumes that in a particular market there is

1) a very large number of buyers and sellers independent of each other and none of them enjoying a significant market share,
2) each producing identical (homogenous) products,
3) it is easy for traders to ascertain the prices at which the product is traded,
4) it is easy to enter the market or leave it so resources can move easily to or from other activities.

These conditions are strict and if any of them does not prevail it is not clear that making other conditions apply more precisely will increase efficiency. In some markets the minimum efficient scale of production results in it being productively inefficient for there to be many suppliers (1.3.3.2.1 below). If any market is not perfectly competitive, it is not clear that making other markets approximate more precisely to the concept will improve efficiency.

There are other limitations to the theory of perfect competition. Most firms are managed by professional managers who do not own all the shares. Their interests may not coincide with those of the shareholders. Their position in society may depend on their managing a large company—they may prefer to maximise growth subject only to a slight constraint based on the need to earn sufficient profit to finance the growth. Not all managers are profit maximisers. If their objective is to maximise growth, shareholders may not maximise their interests, but consumers may—more will be produced at lower prices.

Other managers may prefer a quiet life to maximising profit. It is unpleasant to have to combat a strike to keep costs down, or to dismiss workers who do not work effectively. Both shareholders and consumers may suffer.

1.3.2   *Other reasons for controlling market power*

Efficiency is not the only objective of the EC competition rules.

1.3.2.1   *Market integration*—Competition in the common market is also intended to further market integration, an overriding aim considered by some to be more important than efficiency. Articles 81 and 82 are intended to support the rules for free movement (1.1 above) by preventing firms from replacing protection enjoyed for over a century as a result of state action by agreements to keep out of each other's markets. Hence, export bans or deterrents are likely to be condemned under the competition rules. It may be surprising that many officials still give such priority to this objective 44 years after the Treaty came into force, but there have been a succession of new Member States, now 25, with ten countries in Eastern Europe acceding in 2004 (1.1 above). Negotiations with Bulgaria, Rumania and Turkey continue.

1.3.2.2   *Fair competition*—Some Europeans desire competition also to help to achieve fairness within the economy. 'Fair competition' is listed as desirable in the preamble to the EC Treaty. The meaning of the term is not clear. Should small firms be helped to compete against supermarkets, even if they are less efficient in providing what consumers want to buy and have to charge more? Where one firm has invested in promotion for the benefit of a brand as a whole, is it fair or desirable to let other firms take advantage of this investment for free?

1.3.2.3   *Small and medium-sized firms*—Integration brings with it the risk that small and medium-sized firms, formerly protected from imports by national customs duties and quotas, may find it difficult to compete successfully with larger firms operating from other Member States. To mitigate this risk, the Commission has encouraged collaboration between them, especially where the parties carry on business in different Member States.

The Commission has also shown concern for foreclosure of firms that would like to enter a market, whether or not their possible entry would benefit consumers.

Another populist view is that small is beautiful and workers are entitled to be their own bosses. Many difficulties face a small business trying to enter a market or to expand, such as the lack of capital, managerial expertise and so forth. If the concern of the law be to protect small and medium-sized firms, market power will be perceived as far more pervasive than if the sole concern is with efficiency, and this may account for the Commission's view that any exclusive rights are highly suspect.

Efficiency has been taken more seriously recently, and the Commission has recognised that contractual restraints may be justified by free rider arguments. A better way to help smaller firms may be to free them from bureaucratic controls that fall more heavily on them than on their larger competitors.

1.3.2.4 *Political freedom*—Another strand of thought, enshrined in the German constitution and also reflected in the preamble to the EC Treaty, is the ordo-liberal view that every citizen should have a chance to enter a market as part of his or her political freedom. Some may fail and go under, but should have a chance to try. This view is less important than it was in the early days.

The notion of competition at Community level has also been influenced by the different policies in Member States, particularly in Germany and France. Although it has largely been based on liberal ideas of free markets, competition policy has not been oblivious of social demands, a reference to which has been added to Article 2 (EC) (6.2 below).

1.3.2.5 *Workable competition*—Article 81(1) is concerned not only with price competition, but also with competition in ambience for glamour products and in services offered by retailers of technical products. Consequently, traders may be required by a brand owner of consumer electronics to sell only to consumers or to qualified retailers[29] (9.4 below).

1.3.2.6 *Cultural, environmental and social policy*—Other Community objectives include the special cultural role of books,[30] the environment[31] and social policy.[32] Rules imposed to protect the environment usually restrict competition, and a requirement that insurance bodies should ensure that the rich or healthy should subsidise the poor or disabled is not viable if the insured can turn to the public sector to obtain better terms. The exclusivity necessary to make the insurance funds viable infringes the competition rules. Rules designed to further culture may also be excluded. There must be some way to reconcile the different policies.

In *Albany*[33] the ECJ held that when Community policies are hard to reconcile, the policy other than competition will be narrowly construed (in that case only 'collective agreements about conditions of work and employment')

---

29 *Metro I,* case 26/76, [1977] ECR 1875, paras 20–22. See selective distribution (9.4 below).
30 See Art 151(4) and Council resolution 1999/C 42/02 on fixed book prices in homogenous cross-border linguistic areas, OJ 1999, C42/02.
31 See Art 3(l). In *Arge Bat, ZVEI and HDE,* OJ 1998, C172/12, [1999] 4 CMLR 526, the Commission announced its intention to take a favourable view of a scheme entered into between competitors to ensure that used batteries were disposed of in a way that would not harm the environment. In *CECED,* OJ 2000, L187/47, [2000] 5 CMLR 635, the Commission also exempted an industry plan to reduce the use of electricity when television sets are on standby.
32 Art 3(j) and (k) *Albany* (C–67/96 and others), [1999] ECR I–5751, opinion of AG Jacobs, para 437.
33 *Ibid* judgment, paras 59–70.

and to that extent Article 81 will give way. The Court is speaking of Article 81(1), not Article 81(3).

In *AOK and others v Ichthyl-Gesellsschaft Cordes and others*,[34] Advocate General Jacobs thought it might be better to consider policies other than competition, in that case social policy, under Article 86 (6.2 below). He considered that the sickness funds required by national law to join a buying cartel infringed Article 81(1) and that the act of state defence should be considered under Article 86(2). This had the advantage that competition law gives way only to the extent necessary to enable the insurance funds to perform the general interest task entrusted to them. The Court disagreed and held that the funds were not undertakings because of the considerable element of solidarity. Consequently the funds were not subject to the Community competition rules at all.

The Court has not been entirely consistent. Sometimes, as in Albany, it construes the other policy narrowly and leaves some scope for competition policy. In AOK it held that the competition rules did not trump the other Community policy even when this is not inconsistent with the task of the social body; sometimes it uses Article 86(2).

The Commission, however, has been applying Article 81(3) to except agreements on environmental grounds (3.1.1.1 below). The problem with this approach is that under Article 81(3) a fair share of the benefits must be passed on to consumers of the product, not to consumers generally.

1.3.2.7 *Objectives of national law*—The ECJ has been unwilling to override the protection of smaller retailers conferred by national law. In *Metro* (paras 28–30), the ECJ also considered the separation of functions between wholesalers and retailers that is protected by German law and it approved restraints on wholesalers selling to the public and earning a double margin. In other countries, such as the UK, the confusion of these functions by supermarket chains has led to large cost savings and a reduction in margins. In Regulation 1/2003,[35] national courts and competition authorities are expressly permitted to forbid infringements of national fair competition rules, even if they do not amount to the abuse of a dominant position.

This may explain the judgment of the ECJ in *Wouters, Savelbergh and Price Waterhouse v Algemene Raad Van de Nederlandse Orde van Advocaten*,[36] where it ruled that rules in the ethical code of the Dutch Bar did not infringe Article 81, although they restricted competition and might affect trade between Member States (2.4.5 below).

1.3.2.8 *Conflict of goals*—How far competition law is capable of furthering all these goals without a considerable loss in efficiency is controversial. Small

---

34   C–264, 306 & 355/01, opinion 22 May 2003.
35   Art 3 and Recital 9.
36   C–309/99, [2002] ECR I–1577.

firms that are efficient need no special treatment. Help required for those that are not reduces efficiency as it consumes resources and encourages the creation and growth of firms that are less efficient.

The ability to trade across national frontiers has strengthened competition within the EC and increased efficiency immensely, but when Member States have different laws, for instance those relating to patents or maximum prices, it may not be possible to sell at all in some Member States and still less to sell at the same price and subject to the same conditions throughout the common market. Many of these different measures have been harmonised under the 1992 programme for market integration, but some differences in laws remain, especially for pharmaceutical products, the maximum price of which is fixed, directly or indirectly, at different levels in each Member State. Nevertheless, export bans and geographic price discrimination have been prohibited without any analysis of the reasons for imposing them.

The British firm, *Distillers*,[37] charged some £5 a case of 12 bottles more for whisky that was to be exported from the UK at a time when, contrary to Community law, France was discriminating against the kinds of alcohol that were not produced in France. It prohibited the advertising of whisky but not of alcohol distilled from fruit which was produced in France. Moreover, like several other Member States, it taxed whisky more heavily than the locally produced liquor.

Distillers claimed that differential prices were necessary because on the Continent, owing to high and discriminatory taxes, demand had to be increased through the promotional efforts of its exclusive dealers. These would not be able to afford to keep three months' stock and perform other promotional activities if at popular times, such as Christmas, local supermarkets, which did not bear these expenses, were able to import large quantities from the UK and undercut them. Yet in the United Kingdom, because demand was very sensitive to price differences, Distillers would lose sales to other brands if it were to charge the extra £5.

The Commission did not address this argument, but adopted a decision condemning the extra charge for exports.[38] Consequently, Distillers divided its brands, ceasing to supply 'red label' in the United Kingdom and raising the prices of two other brands. These brands continued to be promoted on the Continent but virtually ceased to be bought in the UK, whereas distributors on the Continent ceased to invest in promoting the other brands, which could be bought cheaply by parallel importers from the United Kingdom.

I have been told that Distillers' sales of the three brands, which could not be bought cheaply in the UK, increased on the Continent more than those of its other brands, presumably because they continued to be worth promoting on the Continent.

---

37 *Distillers Co. Ltd. v Commission* (30/78), [1980] ECR 2229.
38 *Distillers* [1978] 1 CMLR 400 (see 8.6.1 below).

Demand in the United Kingdom was very responsive to price; that on the Continent to promotion. There was no way in which the same brands could be sold at the same prices in the two markets. This was recognised by Advocate General Warner when the case was appealed, but for procedural reasons the ECJ did not address the issue.[39]

In this case, the Commission's simple view that an extra charge for the whisky exported to other Member States divided the common market must have delayed its integration. When the illegal discrimination on the Continent against whisky ended, Distillers had different brands known in the two areas. The Commission objected to the symptom of differential prices before the cause, the illegal discrimination in taxes, was removed.

Moreover, it is more difficult to introduce a foreign product than to continue to sell that to which the local population is accustomed. The Commission failed to analyse the transaction *ex ante*, from the time when Distillers was trying to persuade its distributors to spend money promoting its brands, but looked only *ex post*, to competition at the time the decision was adopted from the firms that wanted to take a free ride on that promotion and undercut the distributors without having to make the same investments. It did not consider whether, without the investment induced by the territorial protection, parallel importers would have wanted to stock Distillers' products.

The Commission has recently been stressing an efficient allocation of resources for the benefit of consumers and market integration as the important objectives of Article 81(1) and (3). In its notice on the application of Article 81(3) of the Treaty,[40] the Commission states that

> 13. The objective of Article 81(1) is to protect competition on the market as a means of enhancing consumer welfare and of ensuring an efficient allocation of resources. Competition and market integration serve these ends since the creation and preservation of an open single market promotes an efficient allocation of resources throughout the Community for the benefit of consumers.

At paragraph 33 it used very similar language in relation to Article 81(3). At paragraph 46 it added that it was for national law to protect conditions of fair competition. There is some inconsistency between market integration and the benefit of consumers, but far less weight is currently being placed by the Commission on the other goals.

At a political level the choice of objectives is unclear. At the Lisbon Summit,[41]

39   *Distillers v Commission* (30/78) [1980] ECR 2229, paras 26–27.
40   OJ 2004, C101/97, [2004] CMLR 000.
41   Presidency Conclusions, Lisbon European Council, 23 and 24 March 2000, http://www.europa.eu.int/comm/off/index_en.htm.

5. *The Union has today set itself a **new strategic goal** for the next decade: to become the most competitive and dynamic knowledge-based economy in the world, capable of sustainable economic growth with more and better jobs and greater social cohesion. . . .'* (italics and bold in the original)

At paragraphs 14–15 the Council concluded that it should create a climate favourable to small and medium sized firms. It continues to urge divergent aims.

1.3.3 *Barriers to entry and substitutes may define the relevant market*

Where there are many suppliers to whom buyers can turn, a firm that offers bad bargains will soon lose business. Consequently, competition both acts as a spur to efficiency and determines price levels. Market power—power over price and other components of bargains—assumes, therefore, first, that there are entry barriers on the supply side preventing new firms from entering a profitable market on a sufficient scale as prices rise and that few firms have, or can, overcome them. Secondly, it assumes a lack of substitutes to which buyers can turn.

Even if they collaborate, existing pear growers are unlikely to have much market power unless there is government regulation excluding new fruit growers, limiting the number of fruit trees that may be planted or providing a minimum price at which the government will buy up surplus pears. Market power also presupposes, on the demand side, that there are no substitutes to which buyers can turn. If the price of pears rises, some fruit eaters will eat more grapes or apples.

Competition from substitutes on the demand side of the market often operates more rapidly than the entry of new firms into the market or the expansion of existing firms—it takes time to build a plant or for a fruit tree to become sufficiently mature to bear much fruit, but each mechanism controls market power for most products. Substitutes on both sides of the market, the ease with which suppliers can enter or expand and that with which consumers can turn to other products are considered by some economists to define the market relevant to assessing whether a firm or firms enjoy market power. It is not irrelevant to the definition of the relevant market under EC and US law, but the concept is less clear (4.3.1–4.3.1.5 below).

1.3.3.1 *Substitutes on the demand side*—In *United Brands*[42] the ECJ confirmed the Commission's view that bananas were in a separate market from apples, oranges and other summer fruit, partly because the very young, old and infirm could not manage other fruit, although there was no way of discriminating against the dentally challenged, since they rarely shop for themselves. They were protected from high prices by the loss of sales to healthy people

42   (27/76) [1978] ECR 207.

that would result if the price of bananas were raised. In total they eat far more bananas than do the young, old and sick. It is thought that *United Brands* will no longer be followed.[43]

1.3.3.2 *Barriers to entry*—In *Michelin*,[44] the ECJ excluded from its consideration the possibility of other firms entering the market to supply heavy tyres because it takes too long to build a factory. Most economists, in Europe as well as in the United States, think that competition works mainly in the long term, which is often defined to mean the time needed to build the necessary production facilities.

If the only goal of competition policy is efficiency, there are few entry barriers that matter. Entry of equally efficient firms is obstructed only by something that is more difficult or expensive for the new entrant than for the old. The fact that I have a factory and you do not is no entry barrier, because I had to invest resources to acquire mine, and you are no worse off having to pay for yours.

Many economists, especially those associated with the University of Chicago, assert that there are only two kinds of entry barriers that exclude equally efficient firms: a minimum efficient scale of operation that is large in relation to the demand or its growth and government regulation of all kinds. One might add that the first suppliers of a product may have acquired the resources for making it, and this would be an entry barrier if there were no other equally good resources for others to acquire or produce. There are few firms in the world with mines from which platinum can be extracted.[45] So, the few existing owners have some market power.

The more traditional view is that entry barriers are far more common. An established firm may adopt practices, such as a discount structure, or raising rivals' costs, which make it hard for smaller firms to compete successfully (chapter 5 below).

Much of the current debate is concerned with problems of information, including reputation. Where the product is difficult for clients to assess, they may tend to deal with the firm with the established reputation. The Commission and ECJ have considered that the need to invest in technology, a well-developed marketing system and other benefits for which the incumbent had to provide resources may increase market power even if they would not keep out equally efficient firms. EC law has been concerned to protect not only efficient firms, but also competitors who may want to enter the market

---

43   Doubt was cast on the judgment in *United Brands* in *Commission v Italy* (184/85), [1987] ECR 2013, where the ECJ held that 'bananas must be regarded as being in partial competition with [Italian soft] fruit' within the meaning of Art 90. See also the Commission's notice on market definition, paras 13–24 [1998] 4 CMLR, 177 (4.3.1–4.3.5 below).
44   (322/81) [1983] ECR 3461, para 41.
45   See the Commission's decision on the merger *Gencor/Lonrho* M619, OJ 1997, L11/30, [1999] 4 CMLR 1076, confirmed by CFI *Gencor v Commission*, (T–102/96) [1999] ECR II–753.

whether or not the possibility of entry may help consumers. There are signs recently that this may be changing[46] (Guideline 13 and 33 of the Commission's notice on Article 81(3))

1.3.3.2.1 *Minimum efficient scale*—If a single plant can reprocess all the spent nuclear fuel in Europe substantially more cheaply than could smaller plants, it would be unprofitable for a second firm to establish a smaller plant.[47] Consequently, the first firm to enter the market on an efficient scale may have considerable power over price. It can charge at a level that merely covers its costs, including a return on capital and compensation for unusual risks, or it could make a higher charge up to the point where it pays someone to enter the market on a smaller scale.

There are few products for which the minimum efficient scale of operation does not permit several plants in the common market, after allowance has been made for the higher costs of delivery from a single plant, customers' desire to have more than one source and so on. Moreover, scale economies at the level of the firm, such as spreading investment in R & D over a large turnover, may be outweighed by the problems of running a large organisation.

Large capital requirements, in themselves, are not now treated as important barriers to entry by Chicago economists and some others.[48] If a market looks profitable, there are usually enough large firms that can raise the finance to enter it. An existing supplier will not be able to maintain high prices for long. If, however, one is concerned, as some are in Europe, with the welfare of small firms, which can raise capital only at greater cost than a larger incumbent, the need for capital may constitute a barrier to entry.

On the other hand, even if one is concerned only with efficiency for the benefit of consumers, quite small amounts of capital may be a barrier to entry into small markets. Once there is a baker in a remote village, it may not pay another to install a large oven, or transport the bread from a distance, even if a loaf is a cent or two dearer than in the neighbouring town. It is not the amount of capital that is relevant, but whether there is likely to be sufficient demand for the product to yield a normal return once a new entrant has invested his capital.

There is not much that can be done about local market power, apart from improving the infrastructure of roads, canals, postal services, telecommunications, email and so forth. In nineteenth century England, local market

46 See. *e.g.* the opinion of Jacobs AG in *Oscar Bronner* (5.2.5.4 below).
47 The facts in *KEWA* [1976] 2 CMLR D15.
48 Oliver E Williamson, *Markets and Hierarchies, Analysis and antitrust implications: a study in the economics of internal organization*, (New York, Free Press, 1975), 11–113 and 'Delimiting Antitrust', 76 *Georgetown Law Journal*, 271.
   Some economists and others believe that if significant investment is required it may be many years before anyone undertakes it. Moreover, only very large firms or joint ventures will be potential entrants.

power was undermined by the development of rail and canal systems. Sometimes such power is eroded by new entry at a point between the existing suppliers. When capital can easily be withdrawn from the market, the possibility of hit and run entry may constrain the incumbent. Unfortunately, the new entrant often has sunk costs that cannot be withdrawn without significant loss and this constitutes an entry barrier.

1.3.3.2.2 *Contestable markets*—Sunk costs are investments that cannot be used for anything else if the project fails. Where significant costs have to be sunk, the investment is more risky than where the resources have other uses, such as an office building. If the investment is risky, it will not be made unless high profits are expected if it is successful.

Theory suggests that even a route between two towns supplied by a single transport operator may be contestable if others could bring in a vehicle and compete. In practice, sunk costs are required more often than was realised. It is expensive for an airline to set up a hub.

1.3.3.2.3 *Network markets*—Network markets are those where the more customers there are, the more each customer is pleased. There would be no point in having the only phone in the world, as there would be no people with whom to communicate. Each time someone else acquires a phone line, the value of your phone increases.

Network industries are not necessarily those with a fixed network, but natural monopolies. The first firm to enter such a market and acquire customers has a significant advantage over subsequent entrants and may enjoy market power, even if it is not more expensive for a newcomer to supply a similar product.[49]

Sometimes, network effects 'tip' the market so that the less efficient technology may oust a better product, which the supplier was less successful in marketing first.

There are ways of partially combating such power. Several subsequent smaller entrants may adopt protocols enabling them to communicate with each other and together enjoy more subscribers, but that may not lead to as large a customer base as the first mover. A subscriber to BT is able to phone a Deutsche Telecom subscriber through protocols made available by the two phone companies.

Incumbents are induced not to charge excessively, because of the race to be the largest supplier. Many of the dot.com companies failed to cover their costs, because they tried to get ahead of their competitors through rapid expansion. Nevertheless they must expect to charge considerably more than average variable cost, or they would not undertake the initial investment.

---

49   See Christian Ahlborn, David S Evans and Atilano Jorge Padilla,'Competition Policy in the New Economy: is European Competition Law Up to the Challenge?' [2001] *European Competition Law Review*, 156.

Moreover, network markets often require the latest technology, and are characterised by a race to be the first developer of new technology and get an advantage in the next generation of equipment. One monopolist may succeed another. There is competition for the market rather than within it.

The question arises whether we should be concerned by the first mover advantage, when the market power it confirms is likely to be short lived. Twenty years ago, we all wanted IBM compatible word processors, but its market power gave way to that of Microsoft with its windows operating systems. Will we all turn to Linux with its open architecture and middle ware by the end of this decade? Should we be concerned by Microsoft's high profit levels now, or earlier with the low or negative profits it earned in its race to get ahead of the competition in technology? Competition authorities may want to prevent the incumbent foreclosing potential competitors and prolonging its natural advantage.

In its decision on *Microsoft*[50] the Commission's main concern was that if Microsoft's dominant position over operating systems was allowed to extend to parts of the IT market that were capable of being competitive, such as the media player and low end servers, it might become impossible for any other firm to challenge its dominance over any part of the network.

1.3.3.2.4 *Government regulation*—A prevalent entry barrier is government regulation. If town planning authorities will allow only one fish and chip shop or launderette in an area, few local inhabitants will go to the trouble and expense of going further for a cheaper source of supply. Even so, the fish fryer or organiser of the launderette may not make undue profits—it is the owner of the land who can earn a monopoly rent by charging more for occupying licensed premises.

A pub in the United Kingdom that loses its licence to sell alcohol for consumption on the premises without a meal suffers a dramatic loss of capital value. The prospect of monopoly profits may be capitalised. If the barrier to entry is removed by deregulation, the incumbent may suffer a reduction in the value of its premises.

The ECJ and Commission have intervened to liberalise some of the markets where Member States granted exclusive rights (6.2 below). The public sector in some Member States has shrunk considerably during the 1990s. There have been significant directives freeing firms to supply telecom services.

1.3.3.2.5 *Intellectual property rights*—Patents, copyright and other intellectual property rights confer an exclusive right by law, so are an example of government regulation, although they may be justified as pro-competitive.

Perceived *ex post*, after the investment in innovation has been made, important intellectual property rights may well constitute entry barriers. The

50   March 24, 2004, (5.7 below).

exclusive right of the holder keeps other firms out and enables the holder to charge high prices.

Perceived *ex ante*, when an undertaking is deciding whether to invest in innovation, art or reputation, however, the expectation of such rights may increase competition. The hope of monopoly profits resulting from an exclusive right creates an incentive to invest. If exclusive rights were not obtainable, some sorts of innovation that can be easily copied might not take place at all.

1.3.3.2.6 *Free riders*—Pharmaceutical firms spend a substantial part of their turnover on research and development and on the trials medicines must undergo before they can legally be released to the public. Yet often it is easy to copy a drug after its therapeutic and side effects are known. Little research and development would be financed for products that can be reverse engineered if anyone could undercut the inventor by copying the invention without incurring the costs of research, development and testing. Such people are often called 'free riders'. They take a 'free ride' on the investment of the innovator.

Whether an exclusive right for 20 years from application for a patent, provided the invention is novel and not obvious, is the protection that yields the best amount of investment in research and development cannot be known, but almost everyone now recognises that patent protection is required if the common market is to compete in developing, disseminating and using advanced technology.

'Free riders' create major difficulties for firms investing in many contexts. In the short term free riders increase competition and reduce prices, but in the longer term the possibility of free riders may discourage the very investment that creates the competition. When parallel importers were enabled to take advantage of the promotion paid for by Distillers' dealers on the Continent (1.3.2.8 above), the dealers ceased to promote and the brands became less attractive even to parallel importers.

This has not always been the prevailing view of economists. In the 1950s economists and lawyers associated with Harvard were concerned by many factors that would not now be treated in the United States as serious entry barriers. As a reaction to Nazi domination, West German economists and politicians just after the Second World War were so concerned about entry barriers that patents, copyright and other intellectual property rights were distrusted.[51] Many countries still reduce the value of patents by providing for compulsory licensing, price control or limiting the disbursements which health schemes will reimburse.

---

51   David Gerber, *Law and Competition in Twentieth Century Europe*, (OUP, 1998), chap VII, 232–65.

This distrust of exclusive rights may account for the Community policy of reducing the benefits of holders of such rights (chapters 10 and 11 below).

If one of the goals of competition policy is to enable small firms to enter markets, then entry barriers are pervasive. Many markets can be supplied only after considerable capital investments are made or technology developed. These are not barriers to the entry of an equally efficient firm unless the firm already in the market acquired these assets more cheaply, which is rarely the case after allowance has been made for general inflation.

The ECJ has treated many costs as if they were entry barriers, such as a good distribution system, a technological lead or capital requirements. It should be realised that a firm protected only by such resources is not in a position to hold its customers or suppliers to ransom except in the short term. To control the conduct of firms with such fragile protection may discourage large European firms from making investments to enable them to compete aggressively with firms from outside Europe.

1.4 The institutions of the EC

1.4.1 *The Council*

For the competition rules, the legislative body of the EC is still the Council of Ministers which can enact subordinate legislation by virtue of Article 83 on a proposal by the Commission, provided it consults the European Parliament. By virtue of the Treaty of Amsterdam, the Parliament, which used to be little more than a debating chamber, has powers of co-determination on most matters. Article 83, however, enables the Council to implement the competition rules by regulations and directives on consulting Parliament, but the latter has no veto.

The principal regulations implementing the competition rules have been made by the Council, which consists of ministers of Member States. It has delegated more detailed administrative legislation to the Commission.

1.4.2 *The Commission—the executive of the Communities*

The Commission is the executive arm of the EC In practice each Member State appoints one or two members to the Commission, but they are required to act entirely independently of their national interests. The Commission is now composed of 30 members (two each from the five largest Member States and one each from the remainder).[52] From 1 November 2004, the new Commission will be composed of one national from each Member State, currently amounting to 25 Commissioners.[53]

---

52   Article 45 of the Act of Accession, OJ 2003.
53   *Ibid.*

Each member of the Commission is responsible for specified policy areas. They are served by a small secretariat, divided into Directorates General— DGs—each responsible for one policy area. Currently Mario Monti is responsible, *inter alia*, for competition. The Competition DG (DG Comp) assists him on competition matters. Important decisions, however, must be taken collegiately by the Commission as a whole, although less important matters of management may be delegated to one of their members.

DG comp is divided into directorates. Directorate A deals with policy, new legislation, international affairs and coordination with other institutions. The Commission has disbanded the merger task force and spread its officials amongst the other directorates in an attempt to widen the influence of officials who have met the challenge of short deadlines in complex cases involving difficult economic issues. Directorates G and H deal with state aids, a highly political activity to which the Director General devotes much of his attention.

An advisory committee consists of officials from the national competition authorities. They comment on new draft legislation as well as on draft individual decisions. It has become more important now that Regulation 1/2003 is in force and a network to coordinate enforcement between the Commission and national competition authorities is crucial (7.3.3 below).

There are fewer officials working for the Commission in all departments than are employed by any one of the major departments of the UK civil service. There is not the manpower for much regulation, which is one reason for reliance upon market forces. An attempt is made to appoint officials from each Member State according to the size of its population. The tradition of the EC secretariat is very open. Members and their officials consult with business, national officials, academics and practising lawyers on proposed legislation and welcome a dialogue with those interested.

In the early days there was less horizontal consultation between different departments than in the British civil service. Originally, officials reported to their boss and he to his until matters were sorted out by the Members of the Commission. There is a growing tendency, now, for officials in one department of the Commission to consult informally and formally with those from another before initiatives reach formal decisions by the Commission.

There used to be a tendency for some officials not to spell out the reasons for their decisions cogently, for fear that this would give the ECJ an opportunity to quash them. Now some chambers of the CFI are quashing decision for not adequately stating the reasons on which they are based contrary to Article 253. This encourages the Commission to prepare more cogent reasons and makes it easier to advise clients on the law.

1.4.3 *The Community Courts*

Originally there was a single Community Court, the ECJ, which heard appeals under Article 230 from the Community institutions, including the

Commission. In 1989 the CFI, started to operate in competition and staff cases.[54] Its jurisdiction was significantly increased in 1993 and 1994.[55] It now includes state aids, dumping and many other matters. Indeed it hears all direct actions save for those brought by or against Member States. An appeal lies to the ECJ only on points of law. At that stage the factual issues have been decided and far less preliminary reading by the judges is required.

The ECJ also has jurisdiction under Article 234 to interpret the treaty and subordinate legislation and decide whether the latter is valid at the request of national courts.

1.4.3.1 *Membership of EC courts*—The courts consist of judges appointed collectively by the Member States. In practice each state nominates one judge for each court and the others accept him or her. The judges operate completely independently of their national governments, although they are appointed for a renewable term of only six years, half retiring each three years. There were 15 judges in each court. These resources were inadequate but now there are ten more judges in each court as the new Member States acceded to the treaties.

Each judge is assisted by three legal secretaries: most of them are bright young lawyers who took a master's degree including significant amounts of Community law, and many of whom have also practised in Community law for several years.

The ECJ started by being both the supreme constitutional court and the ultimate court of appeal, yet many of its decisions were also at first instance. Advocates General were, therefore, appointed to provide a basis for the ECJ. They have equal status with the judges but operate a little like a judge at first instance, reading and hearing the arguments of the parties and delivering an unbiased opinion.

Nevertheless, the analogy should not be pressed too far: there is normally no further hearing and after the opinion is delivered the ECJ proceeds automatically to judgment after some delay. There are no separate Advocates General in the CFI, and it is some years since it appointed one of the judges to act as an Advocate General. Its case-load is too great to spare the resource. The CFI usually holds its first deliberation immediately after the hearing, but the ECJ has to wait for the opinion of the Advocate General, by which time the issues may be less freshly in the minds of the judges.

The office of Advocate General works well when individuals attempt to analyse the problems rationally. It works less helpfully when an individual

---

54   Acting under Decision 88/591/ECSC/EEC/Euratom OJ 1988, L319/1.
55   Council Decision, OJ 1993, L 144/21 and Council Decision, OJ 1994, L 66/29. Also in 1994 the Council Regulation (EC) 40/94 on Community trade mark, OJ L 11/1 gave CFI jurisdiction to hear appeals from decisions on trade mark matters.
Recently it has been enabled to sit in chambers of one, but this power is unlikely to be used in competition cases, Council decision 1999/291/EC, ECSC, Euratom, OJ 1999, L114/52.

Advocate General tries to find out which way the ECJ will go, and leans that way. I regret that some assess their success by how often they are followed by the ECJ. Five of the eight Advocates General in the ECJ are appointed by the larger Member States and their office may be renewed, but the smaller Member States take turns to appoint the other three. The new Member States from Eastern Europe do not appoint Advocates General. Some of the smaller ones have found it difficult enough to spare two qualified people to be judges. The ECJ and CFI do not deliver dissenting or individual judgments, only a single collegiate judgment. Naturally, independent judges of high standing, coming from different cultural and legal traditions and caring about the development of Community law, do not always perceive issues in identical fashion. They have to agree on the words of their judgment, if not its substance.

The need to compromise may lead to obscurity. Sometimes, inconsistent statements are left in, or at least statements with a very different emphasis. Sometimes, a wide principle is followed by a narrower proposition, sufficient to deal with the facts before the ECJ. Sometimes, key paragraphs are left obscure, again probably in an attempt to achieve a consensus. Many judgments now express conclusions, with very little reasoning. The ECJ has been loath to overrule its earlier case law.

Recently, the ECJ has tended to address only the minimum issues necessary rather than to develop broad principles of law, as it did in the early days. Often it declines jurisdiction, for instance by treating questions of mixed law and fact as factual and outside its jurisdiction. Moreover, the courts have no jurisdiction to consider points of substance not argued in the pleadings.[56]

A full court in the ECJ often consists of 11 or 13 judges these days, although competition appeals to the CFI from the Commission or from the CFI to the ECJ are usually heard by a chamber of three or five. The CFI never sits in plenum even in very important cases. It is difficult for the ECJ to be radical on anything that is politically sensitive and it is unwilling to reverse its earlier judgments unless there is a large majority.

In my view, it is unfortunate that the ECJ frequently fails clearly to articulate the reasons of policy for its decisions. In the view of some, it is time that the ECJ and CFI started to allow dissenting and separate opinions, so that the judgments can become more comprehensible and principled. Others consider that the Advocates General perform the function of separate and dissenting judgments. The confidentiality of policy reasoning is in line with tradition in some civil law Member States, such as Denmark or France. Some judges think it leaves them more freedom to change their minds.

---

56   Codified version of the Rules of Procedure of CFI, OJ 2003, C 193/2, [2003] 3 CMLR 823, Articles 48(2) and 76a and Codified version of the Rules of Procedure of ECJ, OJ 2003, C 193/1, [2003] CMLR 769, Articles 42(2) and 62a.

The ECJ's backlog increased over the years but the CFI has taken some of the pressure off the ECJ and, although some of its decisions have been appealed, the appeal must be confined to points of law, so the files to be examined by the ECJ are far less massive than those before the CFI. The President is very keen to reduce the ECJ's backlog and the majority of cases to obtain a preliminary ruling take over two years (1.4.3.2 and glossary).[57]

Both courts lack sufficient resources, and they have to seek them from the Council. The Council agreed to the appointment of two further judges, but has not been able to decide from which country they should come. So this initiative seems to have died.

The accession of ten new states from May 2004 has added ten judges to each court. New functions still continue to be given to the courts, such as decisions on appeal from the new trade mark office in Alicante.

Under the Treaty of Nice further changes may be made to the jurisdiction of the courts, with the CFI being empowered to give preliminary rulings in selected areas, which might well start with trade marks and then competition. There is also a possibility of attaching to the CFI panels dealing with particular areas of law. The back log of cases on trade marks coming from the trade mark office is so great that the first new panel is likely to be for intellectual property. Competition may then follow.

1.4.3.2 *The Jurisdiction of CFI and ECJ*—By virtue of Article 230 of the treaty, the parties to whom a decision is addressed and others to whom it is of direct and individual concern (3.1.1.2) have the right to appeal. Such an appeal now lies to the CFI. It is not a rehearing of the merits, but the court is required to consider whether the Commission has violated the Treaty in substance or procedurally. Seldom did the ECJ go far in investigating the facts found by the Commission but, as was hoped, in several cases involving horizontal cartels and mergers the CFI has gone very far in re-examining the evidence on which the Commission's decision was based. It does not have to decide whether the decisions are correct, but rather whether they are manifestly inconsistent with the Treaty or based on inadequate reasoning. It has quashed some Commission decisions for not being adequately based on reasons expressed in the decisions, and this puts pressure on the Commission to improve the quality of its reasoning. Recently the CFI has more frequently quashed decisions by the Commission on both grounds.

In merger cases the CFI has said that the Commission must get the facts right, although the CFI recognises that the Commission has a margin of discretion in appraising complex economic matters such as a dominant position.

In *European Night Services (ENS) and others v Commission*,[58] the CFI quashed a Commission decision for not defining the relevant market or giving

---

57   2002 Annual Report, 'Statistics on the judicial activity of the ECJ,' p 164; also available on: http://www.curia.eu.int/en/instit/presentationfr/index.htm, p10.
58   (T–374/94 and others), [1998] ECR II–3141.

reasons, as required by Article 253 (ex Article 190) of the Treaty, for finding that a joint venture restricted competition appreciably, contrary to Article 81(1). It also quashed the decision for failing to give sufficient reasons for holding that an exemption could last for less time than would warrant the huge and risky investment in the joint venture.

In several cases, including those relating to mergers,[59] the CFI has required the Commission to get simple facts right, although it has allowed the Commission a considerable margin of appraisal for complex questions such as the existence or likely existence of a dominant position. Where the Commission has invoked an economic theory, the CFI has required it to establish the facts necessary to its application.

Under Article 232, the Commission may also be sued in the CFI for failing to take action required by the Treaty, but few such actions have succeeded under the competition rules, largely because many of the Commission's powers are discretionary and the Court considers that competition policy is primarily a matter for the Commission. Nevertheless, if there is undue delay such an action may lie.[60]

Under Article 234, a national court may request the ECJ for a preliminary ruling on the interpretation of Community law or the validity of subordinate legislation. Judgments given under Article 234 are, by and large, less helpful than those given on an appeal from a decision of the Commission. The ECJ is required to give an abstract ruling rather than apply it to the facts, although, on occasion, it has applied the law.

Between the 1960s and the 1980s, with political stalemate on many matters in the Council, the ECJ often took an active role in furthering the integration of the common market. Many of its judgments, such as *Continental Can*,[61] have changed what most people thought was the law, and it is misleading to study Community legislation without becoming familiar with the Court's work.

Now that legislation can more easily be adopted by the Council often with the co-determination of the European Parliament, however, the ECJ develops the law less vigorously. On two or three occasions, it has deliberately reversed its earlier judgments. Usually it merely distinguishes or fails to mention judgments which it no longer thinks good. It is now loath to depart from earlier judgments.

The procedure before both Courts is mostly written, a feature made necessary by the linguistic difficulties caused by multiple official languages, now 20.[62] There is a short oral hearing, but each party is restricted usually to half

59   *Airtours PLC v Commission*, T–342/99, [2002] 5 CMLR 317, para 64, *Tetra Laval/Sidel*, T–5/02, [2002] 5 CMLR 1182, and *Schneider/LeGrand* (310/01) [2002] ECR II–4071, [2003] 4 CMLR 768 (12.2.6.1.3 below).
60   *JCB Service v Commission*, T 67/01, 13 January 2004, paras 36–46.
61   (6/72) [1973] ECR 215 (5.2)
62   Czech, Danish, Dutch, English, Estonian, Finnish, French, German, Greek, Hungarian, Italian, Latvian, Lithuanian, Maltese, Polish, Portuguese, Slovak, Slovenian, Spanish and Swedish. In theory Irish is a further community language, and the EC treaty was translated into Gaelic, but the Irish have never insisted on its further use.

an hour or less to meet new points or go over the salient features of its case. Perhaps the most important function of the hearing is to enable the members of the court to ask questions of counsel. Both courts frequently give advance notice of their questions to enable counsel to take instructions. Many of their questions are well conceived and searching.

1.5 Enforcement of the competition rules

1.5.1 *Regulation 1/2003*

The enforcement of Articles 81 and 82 is being radically altered by Regulation 1/2003 (chapter 7 below). Until recently, they have been enforced mainly by the Commission. Its exclusive power under Regulation 17 (now repealed) to grant individual exemptions discouraged national courts and authorities from using Community law.

The Commission wanted to devote its scarce resources to controlling international cartels, since national institutions might have problems obtaining evidence from abroad and enforcing their orders. Moreover only the Commission had power to control state aids that have been notified to it and has exclusive powers to control the conduct of undertakings granted special or exclusive rights by government licensing requirements. It wanted national courts and authorities to play a larger role under Articles 81 and 82.

The Commission proposed legislation, which became Regulation 1/2003, to the Council, which came into force in May 2004.

It provides that Articles 81 and 82 have direct effect. National courts are required to give effect to them (7.2 below) and national authorities and the Commission may do so. The notification system and the Commission's exclusive power to apply Article 81(3) have been ended. National courts and competition authorities will be able to decide whether an agreement infringes Article 81 as a whole and will no longer have to adjourn if one of the parties requests an exemption from the Commission as they did under Regulation 17 (now repealed) when only the Commission was empowered to grant an individual exemption.

1.5.2 *Enforcement by national courts*

The competition rules, like many others in the Treaty, were incorporated into the law of the six original Member States—Belgium, France, Germany, Italy, Luxembourg and the Netherlands—on the establishment of the common market, although the first implementing regulation[63] was adopted only in 1962.

The rules became part of the law of the first three new Member States (the United Kingdom, Denmark and the Republic of Ireland) by reason of their

---

63   Reg 17, OJ Spec Ed, 1959–62, 87, JO 1962, 204.

accession to the Community at the beginning of 1973. They applied to Greece on its accession at the end of 1980, to Spain and Portugal from 1986 and to Austria, Finland and Sweden from the beginning of 1995. Similar rules also apply throughout the EEA—Norway, Iceland and Liechtenstein—as well as the members of the European Union.

The new Member States from Eastern Europe and the Mediterranean (1.3.2.1 above) have already introduced laws based on Article 81 and 82, and became subject to those Articles when they acceded to the EC Treaty.

The prohibitions in Articles 81 and 82 have direct effect in the law of Member States and give rise to actions in tort in national courts.[64] It is for national law to establish procedural rules such as which court has jurisdiction, but the remedy must be efficacious, and no worse than that available for infringement of national law. In the UK the House of Lords held in *Garden Cottage Foods v Milk Marketing Board*[65] that the appropriate action would be for breach of statutory duty.

In *Peterbroeck*,[66] the ECJ ruled that a national court could not be prevented by domestic rules of procedure from considering of its own motion whether a measure of domestic law is compatible with a provision of EC law.

In *Leclerc v Commission*,[67] the CFI stated that according to consistent case law, national courts could apply Article 81(1) as a result of its direct effect. Consequently, a dealer wrongly excluded from a selective distribution system can bring an action before national courts or before national authorities.

There are, however, many difficulties in the way of a plaintiff that deter such actions (7.3.4 below). Under Article 81, the plaintiff would have to establish collusion, but it cannot use the Commission's powers to obtain information under Regulation 1/2003, nor can it obtain information on discovery under English law, as there is privilege against disclosing information that may render a person liable to penalties such as those the Commission can impose under Regulation 1/2003.[68]

Contractual provisions with the object or effect of restricting competition are void and national courts should not enforce them.[69] This gives rise to considerable difficulty, as it may be necessary to analyse the market in order to assess the effect of an agreement or the conduct of a dominant firm on competition. Frequently, it may not be simple to tell whether a provision infringes Article 81 or may be enforced. There is considerable concern about the ability of many national judges to appraise matters of economic law.

---

64   *Courage v Crehan* C–453/99, [2001] ECR 1–62976 (7.2 & 7.3.4.1 below).
65   [1984] AC 130.
66   *Peterbroeck, Van Campenhout & Cie v Belgian State* (C–312/93) [1995] ECR. I–4599 and *Van Schijndel*, (C–430&431/93, [1995] ECR I 4705.
67   (*Yves Saint Laurent*) (T–19/92), [1996] ECR II–995, [1997] 4 CMLR 995, para 128 and (*Givenchy*) (T–88/92), [1996] ECR II 1961, 4 CMLR 352, para 122.
68   *Westinghouse Electric Corporation* [1978] AC 547.
69   *Société la Technique Minière v Machinenbau Ulm* (55/65) [1966] ECR 235, at 250.

1.5.3 *Enforcement by national authorities*

By virtue of Articles 1 and 5 of Regulation 1/2003, national authorities will also be empowered to apply Articles 81 and 82 and will no longer be permitted to apply national competition rules where an agreement may have an effect on trade between Member States unless they also apply Community law (7.3.1 below). A network of competition authorities will decide which national authority or the Commission will handle a case.

1.5.4 *Enforcement by the Commission*

The Commission also has power to make final or interim decisions requiring an infringement of Article 81 or 82 to be terminated, accepting commitments from the infringer imposing fines and daily penalties. If it starts proceedings, the jurisdiction of national authorities is terminated, and it is likely to do so only if there is a novel and important point of law to be determined, the conduct affects more than three Member States, or the circumstances make national enforcement difficult. It may, nevertheless, maintain considerable control over competition policy through the network of competition authorities and the advice it is empowered to give to them and to national courts.

The Commission's exclusive power under various Council regulations to grant group exemptions (3.1.2 below) to specified kinds of agreements, such as vertical distribution agreements or patent licences, remains. Under Regulation 1/2003, it may withdraw the benefit from an individual exemption where an agreement does not merit exemption.

Mergers involving undertakings with large turnovers are required to be notified in advance to the Commission which alone has power to forbid them under the merger regulation (chapter 12 below). National authorities may control mergers between undertakings with smaller turnovers under national law.

The Commission operates formally through the decisions of its members, which must be adopted collegiately.[70] When it acts informally by administrative letter from a senior official, the persons addressed are not bound, although a national court may take such 'comfort letters' into account.

1.6 Extraterritorial competence

The Commission has long assumed that any agreement having a prohibited effect in the common market is caught, even if the agreement be made outside the common market by foreigners who carry on no activities within the

---

70   Treaty, Art 219 and *AKZO Chemie BV and AKZO Chemie UK Ltd v Commission*, case 5/85, [1986] ECR 2485.

common market. In *Wood Pulp*,[71] the ECJ adopted the traditional territorial theory of international law. It held that if a contract made by non nationals outside the common market is implemented within it, the Commission is competent. It was not clear whether a foreigner could be fined for making an agreement to keep out of the common market. Would the agreement be 'implemented' by a collusive decision not to trade within the Community?The 'implementation' theory was criticised on the ground that it was not expressed to be subject to the limitations traditionally placed on the 'effects' doctrine: that the effects in the country exercising jurisdiction must reasonably be foreseen to be immediate and substantial. In *Gencor v Commission*,[72] The CFI confirmed the Commission's decision[73] forbidding a merger between two firms producing platinum in South Africa, although the merger had been cleared by the South African competition authorities.

The merger, which would lead some two years later to two firms, each producing 40% of the platinum in the world, would affect world prices. The CFI did not stress that the firms were selling through brokers in the common market.

The CFI pointed out that the merger regulation impliedly embraced such a situation. To claim jurisdiction when substantial and immediate effects were reasonably foreseen as likely was not contrary to public international law. The South African authority had not required the parties to complete the merger, but merely permitted them to do so, so there was no conflict with South African law. Whether a doctrine of comity should go further than avoiding conflicting orders was not considered. It remains to be decided whether the ECJ accepts the doctrine of the CFI. It is not inconsistent with Wood Pulp and limits its application.

There is now considerable cooperation between DG Competition and the US antitrust agencies, especially when monitoring cartels or mergers that have effects in both jurisdictions. In order to avoid inconsistent undertakings being required, the parties to mergers frequently provide each agency with all the information given to the other and authorise officials in each country to discuss confidential matters with those in the other. There is less incentive for the parties to release the obligation of confidentiality in relation to cartels, but the leniency programmes in the US and EC have induced considerable whistle blowing. A new Treaty has been concluded permitting collaboration with the Canadian authorities.[74]

---

71   (89/85 etc) [1988] ECR. 5193, para 143. See Theofanis Christoforou and David B Rockwell, 'European Economic Community Law: The Territorial Scope of Application of EEC Antitrust Law—The *Wood Pulp* Judgment' (1989) 30 *Harvard International Law Journal*, 195.
72   (T–102/96) [1999] ECR II–753.
73   *Gencor/Lonrho* M 619, [1999] 4 CMLR 1076.
74   Competition Laws, Cooperation Treaty, 1999 CEC/ECSC/Canada, [1999] 5 CMLR 713.

1.6.1 *Free Trade Agreements*

There are provisions similar to Articles 81 and 82 in Free Trade Agreements—the treaties entered into between the Communities and various other countries, such as those with the members of EFTA. Before Finland's accession to the EU, the ECJ in *Wood Pulp*[75] added, in relation to the Finnish firms involved, that enforcing Articles 81 and 82 is the method whereby the Community gives effect to its obligations under the Free Trade Agreements to prohibit agreements that restrict trade between the Community and the other party. The EC competition rules can, therefore, be applied to implement the Free Trade Agreements.

There are also provisions similar to the rules on free movement and competition in the Europe Agreements made with countries from Eastern Europe, but they do not have direct effect and are not of great importance, although most East European countries have developed national competition rules modelled on those of the European Community. Ten countries acceded to the EU in 2004 and the EC competition rules have direct effect in their national courts (1.3.2.1 above).

1.6.2 *The European Economic Area (EEA)*

In January 1994, the EEA treaty entered into force and replaced the Free Trade Agreements for most of the members of EFTA. Austria, Finland, and Sweden joined the EU shortly afterwards, while Iceland, Liechtenstein and Norway joined the Member States of the common market in closer relations than in a free trade area. Switzerland put the proposal to a referendum, which was negative, and had to withdraw. The EEA treaty has provisions corresponding to Articles 81 and 82 of the EC treaty, but the institutional provisions are different. The EEA has become less important since the accession of its three largest members to the European Union.

The EFTA members of the EEA have accepted the case law and practice of the Communities and the Treaty will largely be enforced through the Commission of the European Communities, but in specified cases by the EFTA Surveillance Authority (ESA), the administrative body of the EEA. The decisions of the ESA are subject to appeal to the EFTA Court but those of the Commission relating to the EEA are subject to appeal to the CFI in Luxembourg.

Articles 53 and 54 of the EEA treaty correspond to Articles 81 and 82 of the EC treaty and Article 57 enables the EC Commission to control mergers that may create or strengthen a dominant position as a result of which competition is impeded within the European Economic Area.

---

75   (89/85 etc) [1988] ECR 5193 (1.6 above).

Annex XIV of the EEA Treaty incorporates the various regulations adopted by the Communities in relation to competition, and protocol 28 incorporates the doctrine of exhaustion of intellectual property rights developed in the EC (10.4 below) in relation to the whole EEA. New EC regulations, such as those granting group exemptions from the competition rules, have to be adopted by the ESA and then expressly incorporated into national law of the Member States.

The EFTA court has taken great care to interpret and apply the EEA Treaty in the same way that the EC Treaty is applied. Officials of the ESA worked with DG Competition at first in order to gain experience of its practice, and there are provisions for the Commission and ESA to communicate with each other. They send each other copies of notifications and so forth. The importance of the EEA treaty was, however, greatly reduced when Austria, Finland, and Sweden joined the Community in 1995. It will hardly be considered in this book.

1.7 The importance of the competition rules

It is very important to consider the EC competition rules when planning a firm's production and marketing policy. The Commission and EFTA Surveillance Authority have power to impose on undertakings that have intentionally or negligently infringed the competition rules fines of up to 10% of their turnover for the previous year (7.6–7.6.3). Ignorance of the law is no excuse if the firms ought to have known that their conduct was anti-competitive.

In *Pioneer*,[76] the ECJ confirmed that the 10% limit may be based on the turnover of the entire group of companies, worldwide and for all products. On the other hand, when the infringement has affected only a small part of a large firm's activities, the fine may be reduced in accordance with the doctrine of proportionality. In its decision on the *Pre-insulated Pipe Cartel*,[77] however, the fine on the ringleader exceeded 10% of ABB's annual turnover in the product affected, but was confirmed by the CFI.

The Commission has recently issued two sets of guidelines on its fining policy. For a grievous infringement, such as a cartel or export ban, the calculation will start at 20 million or more euros. This was multiplied in the *pre-insulated pipe cartel* by 2.5 because of the gravity of the offence and ABB's role as leader. It may also be multiplied if the infringement lasts over a year, although less than proportionately. It may be increased or decreased by other aggravating or mitigating factors (7.6.1 below).[78]

---

76 (100–103/80) [1983] ECR 1825, paras 118–19.
77 [1999] 4 CMLR 402. Confirmed on appeal to the CFI by several firms that were fined, e.g., *LR AF 1998 AS v Commission* T–23/99, [2002] 5 CMLR 571. Appeals to the ECJ have been lodged.
78 Notice on the method of setting fines imposed pursuant to Art 15(2) of Reg 17 and Art 65 of the ECSC Treaty, OJ 1998, C9/3, [1998] 4 CMLR 472 (7.6.1 below).

The leniency notice, or whistle-blower's charter,[79] (7.6.2 below) encourages firms to tell the Commission about their infringements by indicating very substantial discounts on the fines that would otherwise be imposed to those who give it information about a cartel which provides significant added value to what the Commission already knows and help it to proceed against the others. The first whistle blower will now be forgiven the whole fine in specified conditions.

Where the cartel extends to the US or Canada, it is usual for the parties to inform all the relevant agencies as soon as possible. Each grants complete amnesty only to the first to give it information. It may be dangerous to delay informing the authorities abroad until sufficient information is collected for the Europeans.

Another difficulty in claiming amnesty is that if the US authorities use the information to prosecute an international cartel, even the first whistle-blower in all jurisdictions will be at risk of actions in the US for treble damages by those harmed by the cartel. The EC used to require a memorandum with more information than initially required in North America, but now accepts oral information, which is recorded only in the Commission's minutes, to save the whistle-blower from having to surrender it in North America in discovery proceedings in treble damage actions. Whether this protects the whistle-blower from private damage actions in the US is unclear.

Formerly, when a lawyer discovered that his client had agreed with its competitors about the level of prices, he used merely to say 'stop it' and ensure that employees who cartelise are dismissed or at least not promoted. Now he warns his client of the danger of one of the other members of the cartel blowing the whistle first. Each carteliser now has a huge incentive to be disloyal to the cartel. The Commission is devoting more of its resources to punishing cartels these days. Agreeing with competitors about minimum or fixed prices has become far more dangerous.

Heavy fines have been imposed on members of a cartel (7.6.1 and 7.6.2 below), 661 million euros on Hoffmann la Roche in *Vitamins*.[80] On appeal to the CFI, fines have been reduced by the CFI only a little, where it was not satisfied that some of the fringe firms had been party to the cartel throughout the period alleged. It has confirmed the Commission's ideology.

Fines can be imposed on firms with their seat outside the common market and for conduct outside, if substantial and immediate effects within the common market are reasonably foreseeable (1.6 above).

A firm taking over a company that has infringed the rules takes over the target's liability to be fined, and the fine will not be reduced solely because the

---

79   Commission Notice on immunity from fines and reduction of fines in cartel cases. OJ 2002, C45/3, [2002] 4 CMLR 906.
80   *Hoffmann-La Roche & Co AG* (vitamins cartel) OJ 2003, L6/1, [2003] 4 CMLR 1030. The fine on Hoffmann-La Roche alone for various cartels relating to different vitamins was 296.16 million euros, the largest imposed on a single firm for a single series of infringements.

acquiring company was innocent,[81] although, if it informs the Commission before the Commission knew of the infringement, it may benefit from the leniency notice. It is important, when advising on mergers, to ensure that there is no liability of the target company to fines or to obtain a reduction in price to compensate for the risk.

Another important sanction is that provisions, which restrict competition within the common market contained in contracts, which affect trade between Member States, are automatically void by virtue of Article 81(2). Consequently, a manufacturer suing its exclusive dealer in a national court for selling outside his territory may be met with the defence that an export restraint is contrary to Article 81(1) of the Treaty and does not meet the criteria of Article 81(3). If the brand the dealer is appointed to sell has a significant impact on the market, parts of the agreement may be void—a total ban on exports almost certainly would be, as well as being subject to a hefty fine.[82]

A third sanction is that Articles 81 and 82 have direct effects in the law of Member States and the victim must be able to recover adequate redress.[83]

Some territorial protection is exempted under various regulations applying to vertical exclusive dealing agreements and technology licences, but export restrictions that go further than permitted prevent the group exemption from applying even to clauses whereby the dealer agrees not to handle competing products and the manufacturer agrees not to sell directly to any other dealer within the dealer's territory, in which case those clauses may also be void.

It is not sufficient to ensure that the contract itself is legal, and then by a nod or a wink make it clear that one will not compete with a friend. Concerted practices may be illegal as well as contracts, and the contract itself may be tainted if it is the means whereby an illegal concerted practice is to be implemented.

The EC competition rules are of wide application and enforced by important sanctions. It may be costly to remain ignorant of them.

1.8 The plan for the book

In this book it is intended first to analyse the substantive law enacted by Articles 81 and 82, then the main implementing regulation. This will place the reader in a position to understand the case law on the extent to which agreements and other conduct that infringe the competition rules may be void and illegal.

---

81   *British Sugar and others* OJ 1999, L76/1, [1999] 4 CMLR 1316.
82   In *Volkswagen*, OJ 1998, L124/60, [1998] 5 CMLR 33, the fine on a single firm for discouraging exports from Italy to Germany exceeded 100 million euros.
83   *Courage v Crehan*, C–453/99, [2001] ECR 1–6297 (7.2 below).

In chapters 8–13 various kinds of agreements and other conduct will be considered, mainly under Article 81, but occasionally Article 82 is relevant to agreements. Merger control is described in chapter 12. I shall start in chapter 6 to analyse conduct that almost certainly infringes Article 81 and should be abrogated forthwith; then, from chapter 7, permissible kinds of agreements, such as bilateral exclusive dealing, technology licences and other forms of collaboration such as specialisation agreements and joint ventures. Chapter 14 will contain more general comments, many of them controversial.

While this book is intended to be introductory, the basic controversial problems are addressed. It is hoped that sufficient citations of authority have been made, in the footnotes and bibliographies, for readers to refer easily on particular points to more detailed analysis. Some of the larger practitioners' books are listed and described in the main bibliography at the end. Shorter, more specialised works are listed at the ends of most chapters. The table of cases at the beginning of the book gives multiple citations, as readers may have access to different series of reports, and the glossary may be helpful when the meaning of technical terms is not precisely known.

Some beginners have complained that this book is not easy to understand, because the writing is condensed. My students read it in combination with the cases, often as edited with many accompanying questions in my *Cases and Materials on EC Competition Law*, 2nd ed (2001), also published by Hart Publishing.

1.9 Bibliography

Anthony Arnull, *The European Union and its Court of Justice*, (Oxford, OUP, 1999), Chapter 12, 394–458, 'the Law of Competition.' (*Oxford EC Law Library*).

Paul Craig and Gráinne de Búrca, *EU Law, Text, Cases and Materials*, 3rd edn (Oxford, OUP, 2002), chapters 20–23.

David Gerber, *Law and Competition in Twentieth Century Europe*, (Oxford, Clarendon Press, 1998), 232–65.

PJG Kapteyn and P Verloren Van Themaat, *Introduction to the Law of the European Communities from Maastricht to Amsterdam*, 3rd edn by Laurence Gormley (The Hague, Kluwer Law and Taxation Publishers, 1998).

KPE Lasok and D Lasok, *Law and Institutions of the European Union*, 7th edn (London, Butterworths, 2001).

Frank McDonald and Stephen Dearden, *European Economic Integration*, 3rd edn (Harlow, Longman Group, 1998).

Takis Tridimas, *The General Principles of EC Law*, (Oxford, OUP, 1999) *Oxford EC Law Library*.

Bo Vesterdorf, '*The Community court system ten years from now and beyond: challenges and possibilities*' (2003) 28 *EL Rev*.

2. Analysis of Article 81(1)

2.1 Introduction

Article 81(1) prohibits as incompatible with the common market collusion that may affect trade between Member States and that has the object or effect of restricting competition. It provides:

1. The following shall be prohibited as incompatible with the common market: all agreements between undertakings, decisions by associations of undertakings and concerted practices which may affect trade between Member States and which have as their object or effect the prevention, restriction or distortion of competition within the common market, and in particular those which:

(a) directly or indirectly fix purchase or selling prices or any other trading conditions;

(b) limit or control production, markets, technical development, or investment;

(c) share markets or sources of supply;

(d) apply dissimilar conditions to equivalent transactions with other trading parties, thereby placing them at a competitive disadvantage;

(e) make the conclusion of contracts subject to acceptance by the other parties of supplementary obligations which, by their nature or according to commercial usage, have no connection with the subject of such contracts.

2. Any agreements or decisions prohibited pursuant to this Article shall be automatically void.

3. The provisions of paragraph 1 may, however, be declared inapplicable in the case of:

— any agreement or category of agreements between undertakings;

— any decision or category of decisions by associations of undertakings;

— any concerted practice or category of concerted practices;

which contributes to improving the production or distribution of goods or to promoting technical or economic progress, while allowing consumers a fair share of the resulting benefit, and which does not:

(a) impose on the undertakings concerned restrictions which are not indispensable to the attainment of these objectives;

(b) afford such undertakings the possibility of eliminating competition in respect of a substantial part of the products in question.

The kinds of agreements between competitors that were common before the Second World War, whereby all the producers in an industry fixed minimum prices and allocated markets by quota or otherwise, are clearly forbidden. Economic theory predicts that they are likely to lead to prices being raised and less being sold than when competition determines the price of goods and services (1.3 and 1.3.1 above and 2.2.4.1 below).

Other agreements may restrict competition between one of the parties and other persons, as in the case of protection given by a brand owner to an exclusive dealer against other dealers in the same brand. This may be commercially sensible in order to persuade the protected dealers to invest in risky pre-sales services, which may increase competition between different brands or result in other benefits to the economy. If such agreements are caught by Article 81(1), they may be justified under Article 81(3).

The introductory words to the Article 'as incompatible with the common market' are as important as what follows. Both Court and Commission have been concerned about agreements that divide the common market or discriminate between Member States, even when this is economically efficient.

To infringe Article 81(1), three conditions must be satisfied. There must be:

(1) some form of collusion between undertakings,
(2) which may affect trade between Member States, and
(3) which has the object or effect of restricting competition within the common market.

Each of these three elements will be examined in some detail in this chapter. In chapter 3, it is intended to describe shortly Article 81(3), which provides for the prohibition of Article 81(1) not to apply to agreements that benefit consumers and satisfy other conditions and Article 81(2), which provides that agreements infringing the Article as a whole shall be void. It is, however, difficult to understand the problems created for firms by automatic nullity until procedure has been explained in chapter 7, so nullity and other sanctions will hardly be considered until chapter 7.

2.2 Collusion between undertakings

Article 81(1) prohibits as incompatible with the common market

> all agreements between undertakings, decisions by associations of undertakings and concerted practices . . .

The various elements in this part of the definition must be considered separately.

2.2.1 *Undertakings*

'Undertaking' is a broad concept, which has the same meaning in Articles 81, 82 and 86.[1] In *Höfner and Elser v Macrotron GmbH*,[2] an employment office owned and organised by the state was held to be an undertaking when headhunting for clients, even though it made no charges. Such activities can be

---

1   See 6.2.1 below for some cases under Arts 82 and 86 in combination. In *Kali und Salz/MdK/Treuhand* (IV/M.308) [1995] EEC Merger Control Reporter B178, however, the merger task force treated former state enterprises in East Germany as a single undertaking only if they were supervised by the same administrative division of the Treuhandanstalt. More generally, for the position under the merger regulation, see C J Cook and C S Kerse, *EC Merger Control*, 3rd edn (London, Sweet and Maxwell, 2000). 22.4.1.
2   (C–41/90) [1991] ECR I–1979, [1993] 4 CMLR 306, paras 21 and 22.

carried out in the private sector, although it would have been illegal under German law. The ECJ said that

> The concept of an undertaking encompasses every entity engaged in an economic activity regardless of the legal status of the entity and the way in which it is financed.
>
> 22. The fact that employment procurement activities are normally entrusted to public agencies cannot affect the economic nature of such activities. Employment procurement has not always been and is not necessarily, carried out by public entities. This finding applies in particular to executive recruitment.

The concept embraces a company, partnership, sole trader or an association, whether or not dealing with its members. A trust company authorised to police a cartel was held by the Commission to be an undertaking.[3]

In *Aeroports de Paris v Commission*,[4] the ECJ held that fact that ADP operated under official powers and occupied government land did not prevent the application of Article 82, which also applies only to undertakings. The CFI had distinguished purely administrative activities, in particular, supervisory activities, from the management and operation of the Paris airports. The CFI had not been wrong in treating ADP as an undertaking in relation to the management of the Paris airports.

Whether or not exercising official authority, however, an entity does not always amount to an undertaking. In *Christian Poucet v Assurances Generals de France (AGP.)*[5] the ECJ held that a French regional office administering a compulsory social security scheme was not an undertaking because the contributions were based on social solidarity and proportional to income. They bore no relationship to risk and could not have been carried on the private sector.

In *FFSA v Commission*,[6] however, the principle was limited in relation to a voluntary scheme, where the elements of solidarity were far more limited, although some members could have found better terms in the private sector (para 20). CCMSA, a non-profit making body, which managed the statutory scheme was held to be an undertaking, despite its social purpose and the public law nature of its constitution.

Public sector buying power is now important and in *FENIN*,[7] the CFI confirmed the Commission's rejection of a complaint on the ground that hospitals buying from the private sectors were not undertakings when acting in the exercise of public activities, even if they bought large quantities on

---

3   *Italian Cast Glass* [1982] 2 CMLR 61, para 40. See also 6.2.1 below for the wide concept of 'undertaking' in recent judgments.
4   (C–82/01 P), paras 75–83, appeal from the CFI, (T–128/98), [2000]ECR II–3929, para 109.
5   (C–159 & 160/91) [1993] ECR I–637.
6   (C–224/94) [1995] ECR I–4013, paras 15–22.
7   (T–319/99), [2003] ECR 000, an appeal has been lodged. See Lauro Montano and Jane Jellia, 'The Concept of Undertaking in Competition Law and Application to Public Bodies: can you buy your way into Article 82?' (2003) 2 *Competition Law Journal*, 110.

favourable terms and enjoyed substantial market power. They did not resell what they bought, but used it to perform a public function.

This judgment is contrary to the UK judgment in *Better Care*,[8] which closely analysed the older Community case law. The CFI stated that in principle the act of purchasing in itself is not sufficient to turn a public body into an undertaking when the product is not acquired for an economic activity (para 37). Somewhat surprisingly, the CFI held that procurement activities are not economic activities. In *Fenin*, however, the element of solidarity was even stronger than in *Poucet*: hospital treatment was free under the Spanish health service.

The judgment in *Fenin* is very important as in most Member States the public sector is large. The rules on public procurement are concerned with the integration of the common market, rather than competition. The sector has been left free of the competition rules to extort favourable treatment from suppliers. The CFI did not address the issue where a public body buys partly for its own use and partly for sale.

A federation of public authorities for water supply was fined as an undertaking for helping to exclude parallel imports of washing machines into Belgium,[9] but in *Bodson v Pompes Funèbres des Régions Libérées*,[10] the ECJ ruled that concessions granted by communes acting as public authorities were not agreements between 'undertakings.' The local authorities were not carrying on an economic, but an administrative, activity. The ECJ also stressed that the enterprise entity theory applies only where the parent dictates the market strategy of the subsidiary.

The liberal professions were once thought to be sufficiently outside commerce not to be undertakings, but this is now clearly wrong. World class opera singers were treated as undertakings by the Commission in *RAI/Unitel*.[11]

Customs agents in Italy are classified by Italian law as liberal professions, but are still undertakings:[12] they provide services for pay and accept commercial risks. So their activities have a commercial character. Lawyers have been held in *Wouters*[13] to be undertakings and the Dutch Bar to constitute an association of undertakings. Patent agents entitled to work with the European Patent Office and their trade associations qualify.[14]

---

8   [2002] Comp AR 226.

9   *Anseau* [1982] 2 CMLR 193.

10   (30/87) [1988] ECR 2479, para 18.

11   [1978] 3 CMLR 306, para 6.

12   *CNSD*, OJ 1993, L203/27, [1995] 5 CMLR 495, confirmed in *Commission v Italy*, (C–35/96) [1998] ECR I–3851. See also *CNSD v Commission*, T–513/93, [2000] ECR II–1807.

13   *Wouters, Save Bergh and Price Waterhouse v Algemene Raad Van de Nederlandse Orde van Advocaten*, C–309/99, [2002] ECR I–1577.

14   *EPI Code of conduct*, [1999] 5 CMLR 540, largely confirmed in *Institut des Mandataires Agréé v Commission* (T–144/99) [2001] ECR II–1087.

In their relations with their employer, employees are not undertakings—they act for their employer and are part of its undertaking, even if employed on a very temporary basis.[15]

Nevertheless, trades unions and employees may also carry on a business independently of their employer and in connection with that business are undertakings: in *Reuter/BASF*,[16] an employee selling shares in a company he had created and of which he was managing director was treated as an undertaking.

The Community's social policy relating to collective agreements concluded between unions and employers and relating to working conditions would, however, be seriously compromised if they were subject to the competition rules and in *Albany*,[17] the ECJ held that such agreements fall outside the competition rules. The basis for this conclusion is unclear. Social policy as well as competition are derived from the EC Treaty. It would, however, be difficult to compromise between them. While allowing social policy to trump competition policy, the ECJ defined social policy narrowly to relate only to collective agreements about pay and conditions for work. Perhaps the ECJ hesitated to antagonise the unions.

Are in-house counsel undertakings? In *P Pavlov and Another v Stichting Pensioensfond Medische Specialisten*,[18] Advocate General Jacobs observed that professions differ from each other and from the sellers of most goods and services in that their clients often cannot assess the quality of their service in advance and often not even after receiving the service. In many Member States the professions are regulated. Consequently, they should be appraised on a case-by-case basis. The judgment avoided the issue, since the doctors, whose pension funds were in issue, were all self-employed (paras 76 and 77).

The ECJ has held that whether an agent is treated as part of its principal's undertaking depends on whether it is integrated into it (9.7.1 below)—a difficult concept to apply, as many independent dealers are also closely integrated into their supplier's undertaking. The Commission is now looking mainly to risk. If the agent bears significant risk it is likely to be independent and its agreement with its principal subject to Article 81.[19]

A group of companies is treated as a single undertaking when acting under common control. In *Hydrotherm v Andreoli*[20] the Community ECJ held that a man and both the company and the partnership that he controlled were but one undertaking.

---

15   *Bécu and others*, (C–22/98) [1999] ECR I–5665, para 26.
16   [1976] 2 CMLR D44.
17   (C–67/96, C–115, –117 and 219/97) [1999] ECR I–5751. AG Jacobs discussed many of the cases in his opinion at paras 310–14.
18   (C–180/98) [2000] ECR I–6451, from para 83.
19   Commission's Guidelines 12–20 on vertical restraints, OJ 2000, C291/01, [2000] 5 CMLR 1074. *DaimlerChrysler, re Mercedes Benz* [2001] 4 CMLR 2001.
20   (170/83) [1984] ECR 2999, para 11.

Commission regulations and notices which apply only to undertakings below a certain size, whether adopted before or after that judgment, contain provisions for aggregating the turnover of all the companies within the group, and each has a definition of 'connected undertakings.' The definitions adopted earlier included affiliated companies that were only one quarter owned, but the more recent ones have referred to a link of over 50%. In *Gosmé/Martel-DMP*,[21] the Commission decided that a 50/50 joint venture did not constitute a single undertaking with either parent because it was subject to control by more than one parent. In *Irish Sugar*,[22] the ECJ held that a 51% subsidiary was jointly dominant with its parent, from which one might infer that they were not a single undertaking. The point, however, does not appear to have been pleaded. Consequently, the ECJ had no jurisdiction to consider it (1.4.3.2 above).

In *Viho v Commission*,[23] the ECJ confirmed the view of the Commission and the judgment of the CFI[24] that agreements within the corporate group fell outside Article 81(1), whether or not they allocated tasks between the various subsidiaries. Even export bans imposed on a subsidiary did not infringe Article 81, although those imposed on dealers independent of Viho had been held to do so and attracted a fine. The case law has been about wholly owned subsidiaries, and the position of partly owned companies has still to be worked out. Control under the merger regulation has been assessed *de facto*: in *Arjoumari*,[25] less than 50% of the shares was held to give control, as the other share holdings were small.

Most of the ECJ cases have been concerned with the imputation of a subsidiary's conduct to the parent, and in *Commercial Solvents*,[26] the conduct of a 51% subsidiary was attributed to its parent when the subsidiary had followed the policy decided by the parent. A fine was imposed jointly and severally on the Italian subsidiary and its US parent. Where, however, a subsidiary disobeyed instructions not to discourage exports, the parent had done nothing wrong and the ECJ confirmed in *BMW Belgium v Commission*[27] that it was the subsidiary that should be fined.

Irish Sugar,[28] held just over 51% of the shares in SDL and they had the power to adopt a common policy. The Commission, confirmed by the CFI, treated the companies as jointly dominant. Should one infer that a parent and an affiliate more than half owned that it does not control from day to day is not a single undertaking?

21   [1992] 5 CMLR 586, para 30.
22   (C497/99R), [2001] ECR I–5332.
23   (C–73/95P) [1996] ECR I–5457.
24   (T–102/92), [1996] ECR II–17, paras 47–55.
25   *Arjoumari-Prioux/Wiggins Teape Appleton Plc* (IV/M 025), [1991] 4 CMLR 854.
26   (6 & 7/73) [1974] ECR 223, para 41.
27   (32 & 36–82/78) [1979] ECR 2435, para 24.
28   (T–228/97), [1999] ECR II–2969, paras 44–68.

Where the subsidiary of a state-owned company is privatised and no longer subject to control by its former parent, agreements between them may become subject to Article 81[29] and, where a subsidiary is sold by a company in the private sector, a geographic restriction of competition between it and another member of the former group of companies may start to infringe Article 81(1).[30]

A parent company may be fined for the conduct of a subsidiary which was acquired later,[31] at least where it continued to pursue the same policy after acquisition.

'Decisions of associations of undertakings' are considered at 2.2.3 below. Their recommendations may also be treated as agreements between their members, and fines have been imposed on individual members. Members of a trade association are not treated as a single undertaking. Judgments and decisions as to the meaning of undertaking are also considered at 6.2 below.

2.2.2 Agreements

The concept of agreement clearly includes a contract, but is broader. In *ACF Chemiefarma NV v Commission*,[32] a contract fixing prices and quotas for supplying quinine to much of the world expressly excluded the common market, but the parties entered into a written 'gentlemen's agreement,' enforceable by arbitration, to extend its application to the common market. This and the implementing oral and written arrangements were held to amount to 'agreements' within the meaning of Article 81(1), even after they were put into mothballs by the parties, since they intended the prices fixed previously to continue in the common market.

The Commission added that, even if this suspension ended the legally binding character of the agreement, it would remain a 'concerted practice' and a fine was imposed.

In *BP Kemi*,[33] an agreement that had never been signed was held by the Commission to be part of an 'agreement' since it had been implemented by the parties. The Commission also held that two separate contracts, one signed and the other implemented, each dependent on the other, formed part of the same agreement. It is thought, but not established, that when a later contract is dependent on the first but the first is made without any assurance that the second will be made, they form separate agreements: that an option and its exercise, for instance, are not parts of the same agreement.

The exact scope of the term 'agreement' is seldom important because the category of 'concerted practices' catches less formal agreements. Cartel

29   *Austin Rover Group/Unipart* [1988] 4 CMLR 513, para 25.
30   *Quantel International-Continuum/Quantel SA* [1993] 5 CMLR 497.
31   *Sugar Cartel* (40/73 etc) [1975] ECR 1663, paras 76–88.
32   (41/69) [1970] ECR 661, paras 110–114 and 163–169.
33   [1979] 3 CMLR 684, para 45.

arrangements may involve multiple meetings over a period. The courts have confirmed in *Anic Partecipazioni*[34] that an undertaking which attended only some of the meetings, and did not abide by the prices fixed, may be fined. The Commission easily infers an agreement and/or concerted practice from conduct and might do so from the exercise of an option.

In *Polypropylene*,[35] the CFI approved the Commission's finding of a single infringement consisting of an agreement and concerted practices where it would have been artificial to split a single course of conduct to raise prices collusively into separate agreements and concerted practices.

In the appeals from the *PVC cartel*, the ECJ confirmed much of the case law of the CFI in various cases. In *Enichem v Commission*,[36] for instance, it confirmed that in the context of an international cartel, there is no need to establish anti-competitive effects, as the object was to restrict competition (para 508). It added:

> 509. The liability of a particular undertaking in respect of the infringement is properly established where it participated in those meetings with knowledge of their aim, even if it did not proceed to implement any of the measures agreed. . . .

> 513. the frequency of an undertaking's presence at the meeting does not affect the fact of its participation in the infringement but rather the extent of that participation.

In the appeals from the *cartel in pre-insulated pipes*, the CFI said:[37]

> 45. The mere fact that there is identity of object between an agreement in which an undertaking participated and a global cartel does not suffice to render that undertaking responsible for the global cartel. It is only if the undertaking knew or should have known when it participated in the cartel that in doing so it was joining in the global cartel that its participation in the agreement concerned can constitute the expression of its accession to that global cartel.

2.2.2.1 *Unilateral conduct in the context of a long term contract with selected dealers*—The Commission and courts have extended the concept of collusion. In *AEG Telefunken v Commission*,[38] it was argued that even if AEG had consistently refused to supply dealers operating on narrow margins in order to maintain resale prices for the legitimate trade, it would be unilateral conduct on its part. The ECJ held that:

> 38. . . . On the contrary, it forms part of the contractual relations between the undertaking and resellers. Indeed, in the case of the admission of a distributor, approval is based on the acceptance, tacit or express, by the contracting parties of

---

34   (C49/92P) [1999] ECR I–4125, para 96.
35   See, *e.g.*, *Hercules v Commission* (T–7/89) [1991] ECR II–1711, paras 262–64.
36   (C–251/99), 15 October 2002, not yet reported.
37   *Sigma Tecnologie v Commission,* (T–28/99) [2002] ECR 1845.
38   (107/82) [1983] ECR 3151. Contrast the US Supreme Court in *Monsanto v Spray-Rite*, 465 US 752 (1984).

the policy pursued by AEG which requires inter alia the exclusion from the network of all distributors who are qualified for admission but are not prepared to adhere to that policy.

The Commission and ECJ have long treated conditions of sale as forming part of the long term contract on which sales are regularly made to a dealer. In *Sandoz*,[39] the maximum prices of pharmaceutical products were controlled in Italy, so Sandoz had an interest in deterring parallel exports to countries where prices were not so tightly controlled. Its invoices bore the words 'export prohibited.' The ECJ held that this was not a unilateral act outside Article 81(1) on two grounds: the invoices contained other important terms, so were not merely accounting documents and the ECJ held that they:

> . . . formed part of the general framework of commercial relationships which the firm undertook with its customers.
>
> [Paragraph 10, my translation from the French. The case was never fully reported in the ECR.]

The ECJ went on to suggest that when Sandoz first appointed a distributor and the latter received these invoices after every order, the distributor tacitly accepted Sandoz' normal method of distribution by settling its accounts on the basis of the invoices, whether or not the distributor actually abided by the term. The distributors were not condemned for infringing Article 81 in this decision. The ECJ's use of the concept of 'tacit acceptance' may explain the term 'tacit' in *AEG*. The ECJ seems not be treating the parties as if they had made an agreement when they had not, but rather to be inferring agreement from conduct, which is less worrying.

In several cases, such as *AEG* and *Ford Werke AG and Ford of Europe Inc v Commission*,[40] the ECJ went further and in the absence of any express export ban, treated apparently unilateral action as collusive in view of the underlying selective distribution agreement between the supplier and approved dealer, under which the dealers were required to promote its products by providing technical services, and the fact that the dealers had implemented the conduct required.

The Commission went further in *Adalat*,[41] a decision relating to Bayer's best selling drug. In most Member States, the maximum price of Adalat is fixed directly or indirectly by health authorities. It was illegal to sell in Spain and France at prices as high as permitted in England. Between 1989 and 1993, Bayer's sales of Adelat in the UK were halved because of the impact of parallel trade, first from Spain and later also from France.

Bayer refused to supply dealers in the countries where Adelat was cheap with as much as they wanted. Although the dealers did everything they could

---

39   (277/87), para 10, reported only in summary [1990] ECR I-45.
40   (228–229/82), [1984] ECR 1129.
41   [1996] 5 CMLR 416.

to obtain additional Adelat and export it, the Commission found a concerted practice in view of the long term relationship with each distributor and to Bayer's system for identifying wholesalers which exported and by progressively reducing the volume supplied to them.

On appeal to the CFI,[42] Bayer denied imposing an export ban, although it admitted that the purpose of rationing was unilaterally to restrain parallel trade (para 76). The CFI considered the cases cited to it by the Commission, and was able to distinguish them on the facts. It was not alleged that there was an agreement between Bayer and the English dealers being protected and the CFI looked very carefully at the evidence alleged to establish an agreement between Bayer and each of the Spanish or French wholesalers and found it insufficient.

The dealers were obtaining all the Adelat they could and encouraging their customers to acquire Adelat independently so as to have more to export to the UK. The CFI accepted that conduct that was apparently unilateral has been treated by the ECJ as constituting an agreement (para 70); but considered that the unilateral nature of Bayer's rationing was not merely apparent. It is not enough to allege a long-term relationship, unless the Commission can establish the acquiescence of the dealers. This it had not done to the requisite standard, whatever that may mean. It had not established a concurrence of wills (para 173).

On appeal to the ECJ, Advocate General Tizzano recommended that the ECJ should uphold the CFI.[43] He observed that the earlier judgments were concerned with a situation where the dealer had entered into a selective distribution agreement with supplier. They were approved dealers, relied upon to promote the supplier's products by providing ambience or technical advice to customers with whom the supplier enjoyed a close on going relationship. He added, in note 49, that there was no need to consider the judgments of the CFI. It is the judgments of the ECJ that matter.

The ECJ observed that the Commission's only allegation was that Article 81 had been infringed; possible infringements of other provisions, such as Article 82 were not in issue. It confirmed at para 61 that the burden of proof rests on the Commission. The CFI had found that the Commission was wrong in stating that Bayer had systematically monitored the final destination of the product it had supplied (para 81):

> 88. The mere fact that the unilateral policy of quotas implemented by Bayer, combined with the national requirements on the wholesalers to offer a full product range, produces the same effect as an export ban does not mean either that the manufacturer imposed such a ban or that there was an agreement prohibited by Article 85(1) (now Article 81(1) of the Treaty).

42   *Bayer v Commission* (T–41/96), [2000] ECR II–3383.
43   C2 & 3/01, *Bundesverband der Arzneimittel-Importeure eV and Commission v Bayer* (C–2 & 3/01P) [2004] 4 CMLR 653.

At para 97, the ECJ stated that:

> the CFI set out from the principle that the concept of an agreement within the meaning of Article 81(1) of the Treaty centres around the existence of a concurrence of wills between at least two parties, the form in which it is manifested being unimportant so long as it constitutes the faithful expression of the parties' intention. . . . for there to be an agreement within the meaning of Article 81(1) . . . it is sufficient that the undertakings in question should have expressed their common intention to conduct themselves on the market in a specific way.

The CFI had not required proof of an express export ban. The ECJ confirmed that the decision should be quashed.

Bayer's success may be difficult to copy. It is not easy to ensure that no salesman discourages customers from engaging in parallel trade. Moreover, the wholesalers had not implemented any discouragement by Bayer: they had circumvented the quotas in every way they could. The burden of proof is clearly on the Commission.

Meanwhile in *Sifait*,[44] The Greek Competition Commission has made a reference to the ECJ asking whether there is a per se rule against a dominant firm acting unilaterally with the intention of limiting the export activities of dealers. It asks various other interesting supplementary questions, such as the relevance of governmental distortions to the market.

The Commission's decision against unilateral resale price maintenance for the Passat model by Volkswagen[45] was also quashed by the CFI. The Commission alleged that the instruction to its dealers amounted to collusion in the light of the long-term relationship with selected distributors and alternatively, when the dealers agreed to abide by instructions on joining the network, they agreed to those instructions. The CFI followed its judgment in *Bayer* and held that there must be evidence of acquiescence by the dealers and there was none. Moreover, even if an agreement to abide by subsequent instructions might amount to the necessary element of collusion when the instructions were legal, it certainly did not do so when they were illegal.

Commissioner Monti was concerned about the judgment of the CFI in *Bayer* and said that unless he won the appeal he would use Article 82 against dominant firms that bar parallel trade. The Commission treats each group of medicines with a particular function as a separate market, so patentees of break through medicines may be treated as dominant.

In *Glaxo Wellcome*,[46] the Commission refused an exemption to a firm that had not argued the non-existence of an agreement to reduce parallel trade in a different medicine. Most economists accept that price discrimination is not always undesirable, especially where overheads form a large part of total costs and different prices are obtainable in different markets. Provided that

---

44   C–53/03, OJ 2003, C101/18, [2003] 4 CMLR 925.
45   *Volkswagen Passat*, OJ 2001, L 262/14, [2001] 5 CMLR 1309, T–208/01.
46   OJ 2001, L302/1, [2002] 4 CMLR 335, [2002] CEC 2107, judgment of CFI awaited.

the lower price covers the variable cost, everyone is better off. Those in the low priced market can get the product and may make some contribution to the overhead cost for the benefit of those in the higher priced market (5.2.2 below). For such discrimination to be possible export deterrents may be necessary. The Commission has never accepted the argument in justification of export bans.

2.2.2.2 *Tenuous evidence on which collusion is sometimes found*—There is concern that the Commission may sometimes find an agreement or concerted practice on somewhat unsatisfactory evidence. The CFI has been taking great pains to ensure that the Commission takes care to prepare its cartel decisions properly. The Commission, however, lacks sufficient resources.

The Commission's decisions in *Italian Flat Glass*[47] were quashed in part and the fines reduced or quashed[48] when the CFI, of its own motion, read several hundred handwritten notes in Italian. It found that, when transcribed by the Commission as part of its evidence, a significant part of one document that favoured one of the parties had not been included and that not all the conduct alleged had been established. It is not possible for the over-stretched legal service to check that case handlers do not do this in future: the competition department has had to put its own house in order. In *Polypropylene*,[49] too, the evidence against some of the fringe participants was held to be inadequate at least for part of the period.[50]

More recently the Commission has taken greater care and few of its decisions have been upset on this ground, save in relation to fringe firms, whose membership of the cartel had not been established for the full period alleged by the Commission.

Three merger decisions were, however, quashed by the CFI in 2002: *Air Tours/First Choice*,[51] *Schneider/Legrand*[52] and *Tetra Laval BV v Commission*.[53] The ECJ held that the Commission should get clear facts, such as the contents of a letter, right, although it enjoys a margin of discretion on more complex matters such as whether a merger would result in a dominant position as a result of which competition would be substantially lessened. The Commission seems to have overreacted and is currently loathe to pursue a complaint unless it can establish all the facts with complete assurance.

47 [1990] 4 CMLR 535.
48 (T–68, 77 & 78/89) [1992] ECR II–1403.
49 *Petrofina* (T–2/89) [1991] ECR II–1087, paras 73–80; *BASF v Commission* (T–4/89) [1991] ECR II–1523, paras 64–73; *Enichem Anio SpA v Commission* (T–6–8/89) [1991] ECR II–1623, paras 69–73.
50 (2.2.4.2 below).
51 (T–342/99) [2002] ECR II–2585, [2002] 5 CMLR 317.
52 (T–310/01) [2002] ECR II–2387.
53 (T–5/02) [2002] ECR II–4381.

2.2.3 *Decisions by associations of undertakings*

In *Vereeniging van Cementhandelaren v Commission*,[54] the ECJ held that the words include recommendations by a trade association to its members, even if they are not binding. Such recommendations have also been treated by the ECJ as agreements between the members who implemented them after attending general meetings where they were discussed, for instance in *Belasco*, where the ECJ confirmed the Commission's decision fining the members and not just the association.[55]

In *Compagnie Maritime Belge v Commission*,[56] the CFI confirmed at para 232 that the Commission was entitled to address the statement of objections and decision to the members of a shipping conference that had no legal personality. The fines were based on the turnover of each member.

Sometimes all the members of a trade association are themselves trade associations, but in *BNIC v Clair*,[57] the ECJ treated recommendations of the federal association as coming within the phrase. Although the association had been established on ministerial instigation and was supervised by the minister's delegate, its conduct was condemned under Article 81 in combination with Article 10. The minister had reinforced the effect of the private agreement and jeopardised the objectives of the Community (see 6.1.2 below). In *FRUBO*,[58] two trade associations made an agreement which was not enforceable except by each association requiring its members to comply. Nevertheless the ECJ upheld a finding that there was an agreement between undertakings.

Some trade associations organise exclusive trade fairs for their members and, in a series of cases, the Commission has treated as contrary to Article 81(1) the restriction on exhibiting elsewhere, but has exempted the rules under Article 81(3) where the conditions of participation were altered so as to enable undertakings from abroad to participate and members to exhibit elsewhere for part of the period between the big international fairs.[59]

Professional disciplinary bodies are associations of undertakings, even when their members are technically qualified professionals.[60] The rules may well contain restrictions of competition. For instance a restraint on all advertising clearly infringes Article 81, but a restraint on comparative advertising may be permitted for a transitional period when an association has traditionally allowed no advertising and is amending its rules to limit the restraint to misleading advertising. A restraint on deceptive advertising is unlikely to infringe Article 81(1).

---

54   (8/72) [1972] ECR 977, paras 18–22.
55   (246/86) [1989] ECR 2117.
56   (T–24/93 & others) [1996] ECR II 1201.
57   (123/83) [1985] ECR 39 (6.1.1 below).
58   (71/74) [1975] ECR 563, paras 28–32.
59   *E.g. SMM&T Exhibition Agreement* [1984] 1 CMLR 611.
60   *EPI Code of conduct*, T–144/99, [2001] 5 CMLR 97.

2.2.4 *Concerted practices*

2.2.4.1 *Economic considerations*—Hard core cartels between competitors fixing prices or allocating production or sales have long been thought by classical economists to be anti-competitive and contrary to the public interest because, if they are successful, prices are likely to be higher than they would be under free competition (see 1.3.1 above). Consequently, some people who would have bought at the competitive price, and would have liked to pay at least as much as the costs of production and distribution including a normal return on capital, will be forced to spend their money on other things which they want less. Scarce resources are misallocated.

Cartels have to exclude outsiders from the market if they want to raise price, so usually erect entry barriers restricting the freedom of others to enter the market, a concern of the Ordo Liberals (4.2 below).

Moreover, cartels tend to be inefficient. Even ill-equipped firms must be accommodated within the cartel to reduce price cutting.

Such cartels seldom work effectively unless the number of participants is very small, or they are backed by state intervention, since it pays each participant to cheat and expand its production by selling at less than the agreed price to a few large customers who can be relied upon to keep quiet. Once this is suspected, the others may cut prices even further and cartels often break down.[61]

Moreover, the higher price charged by a cartel may induce new producers to enter the market. Even OPEC (the Organisation of Petroleum Exporting Countries) has to ensure that the price of oil does not rise too far or too many third parties may start or increase exploration and production. OPEC managed to raise prices in its early years and to cause a worldwide recession for a decade. It was again sufficiently disciplined in 1999/2000 to double the price in a year.

In industries with only a very few producers, whether worldwide or in a small local market protected by the cost of freight and other entry barriers, suppliers may be able to raise prices above the competitive level without making any price-fixing agreement.

If firm A sells at above its long run incremental costs,[62] including a return on the capital employed, firm B may find that it pays it to sell at the same price when there is spare capacity in the industry. Unless B expects to be able to force A out of the market, it will not increase its share of the market at A's expense if it undercuts A: A would have to reduce its prices to B's level or lose as much of its market as B could supply. Each will have some market power, as long as the other does not act competitively.

---

61   But not always: see Jonathan B Baker, 'Recent Developments in Economics that Challenge Chicago School Views' (1989) 58 *Antitrust Law Journal,* 645.
62   See the Glossary at the end of the book.

The same argument applies to some extent even if there are four or five suppliers in the market. If there are dozens, it would be difficult to find out what secret discounts competing firms were giving. Owing to the lack of transparency, the oligopolistic interdependence would probably break down. If the industry were very concentrated, each firm taking its own independent decisions over a period of time would realise that these would affect its competitors' decisions. If it were to reduce prices, the others would be forced to do so too unless there were a shortage of capacity.

Most economists argue that oligopolists are unlikely to keep prices high unless there is some mechanism for disciplining those who cut prices. This was accepted by the CFI in *Air Tours v Commission*[63] in the context of a merger.

If A were to announce a price rise, its competitors would know that A would not be able to maintain the rise unless most of them were to follow it. So the others would be under pressure to respond rapidly to such an announcement. Even if there were no collusion, the firms might act as if there were and follow any price rise announced by A within a day or two. They are likely to compete only in ways that cannot be imitated rapidly, such as research and development.

The question arises whether parallel conduct that is not collusive, such as that described above, but which has much the same effect as a price fixing agreement infringes Article 81(1). Is market behaviour, adopted in the knowledge and hope that competitors will follow it, a concerted practice if, in fact, competitors do follow? Enabling competitors to learn of a price rise plus the hope that they would follow or maintain it might be treated as an offer to collude accepted when competitors follow.

The difficulty for an enforcement agency is that it would be silly to prohibit such behaviour. As costs rise in times of inflation, one firm after another would have to leave the industry if it could not raise prices without the risk of substantial fines. At the very least, they would not build new capacity as old plant becomes obsolete or worn out or when demand is expected to increase.

The sensible remedies to restrain conscious parallelism are, first, to ensure that without a strong justification nothing is done by the government or by the existing suppliers to prevent other firms entering the industry so that the number of suppliers becomes too great for cheating to be controlled; secondly, to forbid facilitating devices that make it easier for firms not to compete, such as announcing price rises months in advance, so that the price leader can see whether the other firms are going up before it implements its rise (2.2.4.2 below).

A major problem in the common market is that many entry barriers are created by national or local licensing requirements and other action by Member States which there is little power to control under the EC Treaty,

---

although some progress has been made under the rules for the free movement of goods and services in combination with Article 86 (6.2 below).

Where there are substantial entry barriers, it would be sensible to control mergers which lead to more concentrated markets. The Commission's power to do this is limited.[64] There has been pressure on the Commission to extend the concept of 'concerted practices' in order to control parallel behaviour under Article 81. The unfortunate result has been that in concentrated markets it may be difficult to raise prices, even if costs increase, without incurring a risk of being fined. The problem is significant because many markets for intermediate products, such as raw materials or components are concentrated.

2.2.4.2 *Legal precedents*—In *Dyestuffs*,[65] the ECJ observed that Article 81 distinguishes concerted practices from agreements and decisions in order to bring within the competition rules

> 64. . . . a form of co-ordination between undertakings which, without having reached the stage where an agreement properly so-called has been concluded, knowingly substitutes practical co-operation between them for the risks of competition.

This passage may have been intended to distinguish the German practice at that time, according to which only a binding written agreement infringed the earlier sections of the German cartel law. In both *Dyestuffs* and the *Sugar Cartel*,[66] the ECJ said that for the few firms in a concentrated market to take account of each other's market behaviour does not amount to a concerted practice. In *Dyestuffs*, for instance, it said:

> 118. Although every producer is free to change his prices, taking into account in so doing the present or foreseeable conduct of his competitors, nevertheless it is contrary to the rules on competition contained in the treaty for a producer to co-operate with his competitors, in any way whatsoever, in order to determine a co-ordinated course of action relating to a price increase and to ensure its success by prior elimination of all uncertainty as to each other's conduct regarding the essential elements of that action, such as the amount, subject-matter, date and place of the increases.

This passage raised concern that the ECJ's phrase, 'co-ordinated course of action,' might be broader than collusion. It was feared that facilitating devices, acting in a way that makes it easier for suppliers or buyers not to compete, for instance by giving considerable notice of price increases in a trade journal, might amount to a concerted practice if competitors followed the rise.

---

64   Chap 12 below.
65   *ICI (Imperial Chemical Industries Ltd) and Others v Commission* (48/69 & others), [1972] ECR 619, (appeal from Commission decision in *Dyestuffs*) [1969] CMLR D23.
66   *Re the European Sugar Cartel: Cooperatiëve Vereniging 'Suiker Unie' UA v Commission* (40/73 & others), [1975] ECR 1663, paras 173–74.

There are other facilitating devices that make it easier for suppliers not to compete in concentrated markets, such as promising many customers that they will receive any discounts given to anyone else. This makes it less attractive to give secret discounts to other buyers as they would have to be matched. Secret discounts are the only kind of price competition likely in a concentrated market.

It is not clear that the ECJ understood the way that prices may be set without collusion in concentrated markets. At paragraph 66, it said:

> Although parallel behaviour may not by itself be identified with a concerted practice, it may however amount to strong evidence of such a practice if it leads to conditions of competition which do not correspond to the normal conditions of the market, having regard to the nature of the products, the size and number of the undertakings and the volume of the said market.

The ECJ went on to refer to stabilising prices at a level different from that to which competition would have led. This is unknowable. In the absence of collusion, prices might be at the competitive level, the level that maximises the profits of a monopolist in the short term, or anywhere in between. A firm can set the prices anywhere it wants within that range and, unless some of the others charge less, it can profitably maintain them at that level.

If the market be oligopolistic, over time it is likely that market power will lead to higher prices than if there were more suppliers even in the absence of collusion. One cautious feature of the judgment in *ICI* is that at paragraph 68 the ECJ referred to the factual evidence on which the Commission had found the concertation.

In the *Dyestuffs* decision,[67] the Commission had found (paragraphs 7–10) that the price increases on three occasions were 'concerted,' partly because the producers had met and discussed price and partly because of various other items of circumstantial evidence of collusion.

On the first occasion, six out of the ten firms which were fined and which supplied about 85% of the dyestuffs in the common market had sent notices of increases to their subsidiaries and dealers in Italy by telex on the same evening (ICI used the telephone, Francolor did not sell much outside France and ACNA had no need to communicate since it was already in Italy). They had used much the same wording to give similar detailed instructions, for example to refuse to backdate invoices.

The ECJ placed less weight on these circumstances, but pointed out that the three increases showed progressive co-ordination, which consisted mainly of the leader announcing its intended price rise for a particular country further in advance.

The final increase was announced three months in advance by Geigy at a meeting of the producers. This gave time for the largest supplier in France to

67 [1969] CMLR D23.

announce a rather larger increase there, as prices had previously been frozen by the government and so had not been increased when those in other countries had been. The others had time to follow this and each announced the larger increase for France before the smaller increase originally intended was implemented.

The price increases on all the Community markets (except Italy, where the Italian producer had refrained from following the increase announced by the others on the second and third occasions) came into effect on the same day.

In *The Sugar Cartel*,[68] there was plenty of evidence of concertation, but on appeal. The ECJ used wide language when confirming the fines:

173. The criteria of coordination and cooperation laid down by the case-law of the Court, *which in no way require the working out of an actual plan*, must be understood in the light of the concept inherent in the provisions of the Treaty relating to competition that each economic operator must determine independently the policy which he intends to adopt on the common market including the choice of the persons and undertakings to which he makes offers or sells.

174. Although it is correct to say that this requirement of independence does not deprive economic operators of the right to adapt themselves intelligently to the existing and anticipated conduct of their competitors, it does however *strictly preclude any direct or indirect contact between such operators*, the object or effect whereof is either to influence the conduct on the market of an actual or potential competitor or to disclose to such a competitor the course of conduct which they themselves have decided to adopt or contemplate adopting on the market. [Author's italics]

From these judgments there was concern that merely announcing one's price increases to customers or in the trade press would amount to a concerted practice if competitors made similar price increases.

In the *Polypropylene* cases, the question to be answered by the CFI was not whether parallel conduct on the market was the result of collusion. The Commission had found ample documentary evidence that 15 petrochemical companies had worked out a complex scheme of arrangements with the purpose of setting and implementing target prices and quotas. There was clear evidence of collusion, but there were hardly any effects on the market. As one expert stated, the initiative had 'no more than a placebo effect on nervous branch managers.'[69] The CFI held that the existence of an intent to concert is sufficient to establish a concerted practice, even if there are no actual effects.[70]

In *Rhône-Poulenc*, the CFI also confirmed that:

126. Those schemes were part of a series of efforts made by the undertakings in question in pursuit of a single economic aim, namely to distort the normal

---

68   (40/73 etc) [1975] ECR 1663.
69   As cited by Judge Vesterdorf, acting as Advocate General [1991] ECR II–869, 946.
70   *Shell v Commission* (T–11/89) [1992] ECR II–757, 881, para 299. *Rhône-Poulenc v Commission* (T–1/89) [1991] ECR II–867, 1073, paras 120–24.

movement of prices on the market in polypropylene. It would thus be artificial to split up such continuous conduct, characterized by a single purpose, by treating it as consisting of a number of separate infringements. The fact is that the applicant took part—over a period of years—in an integrated set of schemes constituting a single infringement, which progressively manifested itself in both unlawful agreements and unlawful concerted practices . . .'

The concepts of agreement and concerted practice are fluid and overlap. The CFI added that:

the Commission was also entitled to characterize that single infringement as "an agreement and a concerted practice," since the infringement involved at one and the same time factual elements to be characterized as "agreements" and factual elements to be characterized as "concerted practices".

In its judgment in *Wood Pulp*,[71] the ECJ significantly limited the concept of 'concerted practices.' The pulp producers announced maximum prices quarterly in advance to their customers. The ECJ said:

64. In this case, the communications arise from the price announcements made to users. They constitute in themselves market behaviour which does not lessen each undertaking's uncertainty as to the future attitude of its competitors. At the same time when each undertaking engages in such behaviour, it cannot be sure of the future conduct of others.

65. Accordingly, the system of quarterly price announcements on the pulp market is not to be regarded as constituting in itself an infringement of Article 81(1) EEC.

While the ECJ has frequently said that consciously parallel behaviour by itself does not amount to a concerted practice, concerting has easily been inferred by the Commission as in the *PVC* and *LdPE* decisions (especially that against Shell[72]), if the parties have been in communication with each other.

There were several appeals against cartel decisions of the Commission to the CFI. In the *Cartonboard* judgments[73] the CFI confirmed most of the fines along the lines of its earlier judgments in *Polypropylene*. The producers who, without objection, attended meetings which they knew were intended to reduce price competition and impose quotas, were liable to fines, even if they said nothing, missed some of the meetings and cheated on the cartel.

It is still not entirely clear whether the announcement of price changes well in advance to customers, or in a trade journal, constitutes the necessary element of co-ordination. Advance warning makes it easier for other producers to decide how far to follow the announced rise, and for the original leader to resile wholly or partly if its lead is not fully followed.

71   *Wood Pulp—A Ahlström OY and others v Commission* (C–89/85 etc), [1988] ECR 5193.
72   (T–11/89) [1992] ECR II–757, from p 793.
73   Appeals from the Commission decision OJ 1994, L243/1, [1994] 5 CMLR 547, *e.g.*, *Sarrio v Commission*, (T–334/94) [1998] ECR II–1439, *SCA Holdings v Commission* (T–327/94) [1998] ECR II–1373.

On the other hand, there may be sensible commercial reasons for announcing price rises in advance. Customers may make fixed price contracts and want notice of a change in their costs; a temporary glut may be cleared; in markets where there are few suppliers, price competition may take the form of tough negotiations for individual discounts and time may be needed for these to take place.

Where there is another reasonable explanation for parallel conduct, collusion will not be inferred. In *SACEM*,[74] the various national copyright collection societies in the EC had entered into reciprocal licences, so the rights of their copyright holders to royalties resulting from public performances in other Member States were enforced by the local collection society. Although each society remained entitled to license public performances of music in other Member States, none of them was willing to license the operators of discotheques in France.

The discotheque operators used little other than Anglo-American music and would have liked licences confined to such music at the lower royalty charged by the collecting societies outside France. They argued that the refusal of each society to grant licences of their rights in France was a concerted practice. SACEM replied that it would be onerous for each of the copyright societies to grant such licences abroad, as they would have to negotiate them and check what was being played. Since there was another explanation of parallel conduct, the ECJ ruled that it was not collusive.

The ECJ referred to *Dyestuffs* and said that:

> However, concerted action of that kind cannot be presumed where the parallel behaviour can be accounted for by reasons other than the existence of concerted action. Such a reason might be that the copyright-management societies of other Member States should be obliged, in the event of direct access to their repertories, to organise their own management and monitoring system in another country.

I hope that recognition that price cuts are likely to be copied by competitors would be treated as a sufficient reason to explain identical lists of prices.

2.2.4.3 *Agreements to exchange information*—Since it is illegal to agree with competitors about prices, firms have adopted practices that tend to make strong competition less likely. Agreements between competitors to exchange detailed information about price or output changes may well be treated as having the object or effect of restricting competition.[75] If competitors will immediately know of orders obtained by discounts they may retaliate and there may be no incentive to make the cut. Usually there are clear agreements

74   *Lucazeau v SACEM* (110/88), *SACEM v Debelle* and *SACEM v Soumagnac* (241 & 242/88) [1989] ECR 2565, para 18 and *Ministère Publique v Tournier* (395/87) [1989] ECR 2565, para 24.
75   (8.2.2 below).

to exchange information, but the actual exchange without prior agreement was treated in *COBELPA*[76] as a concerted practice.

2.3 'Which may affect trade between Member States'

The condition that trade between Member States be affected is easily satisfied. Even an agreement confined to activities in a single Member State may infringe Article 81(1). The concept of trade is very broad, and covers all economic activities relating to goods or services, even the right of a trader in one Member State to set up business in another.[77] The Commission analysed the case law in its guidelines on effect on trade[78] in connection with Article 3 of Regulation 1/2003 (7.3.1 below).

Since May 2004, the condition has been more important, as NCAs are not allowed to apply national competition law without also applying Community law where trade between Member States may be affected. The double barrier doctrine will continue to apply to Article 82: citizens must comply with national and Community law. It will not, however, apply to Article 81.[79]

2.3.1 *Market integration*

The condition that trade between Member States may be affected has been construed in the light of the need to establish and maintain a single market: export boosters distort trade as much as import deterrents. In its first judgment on appeal from the Commission, *Consten and Grundig v Commission*,[80] the ECJ said:

> The concept of an agreement "which may affect trade between Member States" is intended to define, in the law governing cartels, the boundary between the areas respectively covered by Community law and national law.

In itself, this does not help us to draw the line. Moreover, in *Wilhelm v Bundeskartellamt*,[81] the ECJ ruled that some agreements may be subject to both national and Community law. The condition about trade between Member States limits the scope of Community law. It limits that of national law only to the extent that if Community law conflicts with it Community law takes precedence.

The next paragraph of *Grundig* was more helpful in deciding where Community law ceases to apply:

---

76 [1977] 2 CMLR D28.
77 (2.3.3 below).
78 OJ 2004, C101/81, [2004] CMLR 000.
79 Reg 1/2003, OJ 2003, L1/1, Art 3 and recitals 8 & 9, (7.3.1 below).
80 (56 & 58/64), [1966] ECR 299, at 341.
81 (14/68), [1969] ECR 1.

[W]hat is particularly important is whether the agreement is capable of constituting a threat, either direct or indirect, actual or potential, to freedom of trade between Member States in a manner which might harm the attainment of the objectives of a single market between states. Thus the fact that an agreement encourages an increase, even a large one, in the volume of trade between states is not sufficient to exclude the possibility that the agreement may "affect" such trade in the above-mentioned manner.

This broad concept results in few agreements that significantly restrict competition escaping the prohibition of Article 81(1).

In 1957, Grundig decided to start exporting from Germany to France and agreed with Consten that Consten should be its exclusive dealer there. It agreed to supply no one else in France, and Consten agreed not to handle competing brands, to promote Grundig products, to arrange for an after-sales service, to buy minimum quantities, order regularly in advance and make sales forecasts.

Incurring these costs would be worthwhile for Consten only if it could reap where it had sown. The investment was risky, in that the costs were 'sunk': the effort would be wasted unless it could be recovered through the sale of Grundig products at a time when a licence from the French government was required to import them and might not be granted.

To encourage Consten's commitment to this expenditure, Grundig tried to confer absolute territorial protection on Consten by isolating the French market. Its distributors in other Member States and dealers in Germany were forbidden to export, as was Consten. Moreover, all Grundig machines of that period bore the mark 'Gint' (Grundig International) as well as the Grundig mark. Consten was allowed to register 'Gint' as a trade mark under French law, and so was able to sue for trade mark infringement anyone importing commercially or selling without its consent a machine bearing that mark.

When a third party, UNEF, started to buy Grundig apparatus in Germany and sell it in France at prices lower than those Consten's dealers charged, Consten and Grundig sued it for trade mark infringement, and also for the French tort of unfair competition, on the ground that UNEF knew that sales by the German dealers were in breach of their contracts with Grundig and would undermine Consten's exclusive distributorship.

Not only did the ECJ uphold the Commission's decision that the agreement infringed Article 81, it upheld its order that neither party should make it difficult for dealers and other buyers to obtain Grundig apparatus elsewhere. Of this limitation to the market sharing function of trade marks, patents etc. far more will be said in chapter 10.

To return to the concept of affecting trade between Member States, the ECJ added that:

[T]he contract between Grundig and Consten, on the one hand by preventing undertakings other than Consten from importing Grundig products into France, and on the other hand by prohibiting Consten from re-exporting those products to other countries of the common market, indisputably affects trade between Member States.

The insulation of the French market from the lower-priced German one clearly affected trade between the countries, but the second passage I have quoted from the ECJ's judgment is far broader. The ECJ refrained from considering linguistic points in the four Community languages as to whether the 'effect' must be harmful, but returned to the basic principle of the free movement of goods, the treatment of the whole Community as a single market.

In fact, sales of Grundig's products in France increased substantially between 1957 when the contract was made and the Commission's decision in 1964, but the ECJ stated that this did not prevent there being an effect on trade between Member States. One might think that the increase was due to other factors, such as the expansion and final abrogation of national quotas and the reduction of customs duties between Germany and France under the transitional provisions of the treaty, but the Court did not use this argument.

In *Commercial Solvents*,[82] a case involving the prohibition in Article 82 which is subject to the same condition about affecting trade between Member States, the ECJ stated that any abuse of a dominant position leading to the elimination of a competitor downstream in Italy was prohibited, but it went on to refer to the possibility of Zoja, the competitor, exporting to Germany and France. It may be that different members of the ECJ favoured different tests.

In *Groupement des Fabricants de Papiers Peints de Belgique v Commission*, Advocate General Trabucchi suggested a third possible meaning for the condition as the common market matures[83]:

> Moreover, as has been brought out in legal writings, . . . in a unified multinational market, within which there are no longer any national frontiers impeding the movement of goods, the . . . criterion ["may affect trade between Member States"] must assume a significance to match the new situation which has come into being; it must be interpreted in such a way as to bring within the prohibitions of Article 81 agreements in restraint of competition which affect the attainment of the objectives for which the common market was established. In this sense, the criterion relating to the effect of the restriction of competition on trade between Member States serves to define that restriction itself by requiring that, in order to come within the purview of Community law, it must be of importance within the ambit of the Community system in respect of the objectives pursued.

Even unimportant cartels in a small Member State are likely to have effects outside the country; quite major restrictions in a large Member State may not. The effects on cross-frontier trade may be the first problems faced by a new common market, but as it becomes mature, the criterion should become the importance of the restriction of competition.

---

82   (6 & 7/73) [1974] ECR 223. See also the quotation at 2.3.4 below.
83   (73/74) [1975] ECR 1491, at 1522–23.

In *Groupement des Papiers Peints* the ECJ did not take up the idea invoked by its Advocate General. Nevertheless, in *Consten and Grundig*, the ECJ started by stating that the function of the condition was to define the relative spheres of national and Community law. On that basis, Advocate General Trabucchi's view has much to commend it.

There is no need to prove an actual effect on trade between states: a potential effect is enough. The goods immediately subject to an agreement may not move between Member States, but if there is or may be trade between Member States in the products of which they form part, the condition is fulfilled. In *BNIC v Clair*,[84] an agreement relating to *eaux de vie* was held to infringe Article 81, although little was exported, since the cognac made from them was sold throughout the Community.

Nor is it necessary to show that the effect is adverse. In *Cimbel*,[85] the agreement was intended to increase exports from Belgium, but it discriminated along state boundaries and infringed Article 81(1). In *Consten and Grundig* stress was laid on the isolation of the French market.

Some kinds of agreement are particularly likely to affect trade between Member States. Export bans and deterrents are condemned virtually per se. International cartels almost always affect trade, as the parties have to keep out imports if they are to raise prices. Single branding usually prevents a dealer from importing rival brands. Exclusive distribution for a whole Member State prevents competition within the territory from other distributors.

2.3.2 Condition often fulfilled even if agreement is confined to a single Member State

An agreement confined to activities in a single Member State may infringe Article 81(1). In *Vereeniging van Cementhandelaren v Commission*,[86] a Dutch trade association, of which most Dutch cement dealers were members, recommended the prices at which its members should sell in the Netherlands. It was argued that, as this did not apply to exports, it did not 'affect trade between Member States,' but the ECJ answered:

> 29. An agreement extending over the whole of the territory of a Member State by its very nature has the effect of reinforcing the compartmentalization of markets on a national basis, thereby holding up the economic inter-penetration which the treaty is designed to bring about and protecting domestic production.

> 30. In particular, the provisions of the agreement which are mutually binding on the members of the applicant association and the prohibition by the association on all sales to resellers who are not authorized by it make it more difficult for producers or sellers from other Member States to be active in or penetrate the Netherlands market.'

84   (123/83) [1985] ECR 391, paras 28–29.
85   *Re La Cimenterie Belge SA* [1973] CMLR D167.
86   (8/72) [1972] ECR 977, paras 29–30.

In the light of the facts of the case, this was a particularly strong statement. What seems to have kept imports out of the Netherlands, at least until very shortly before the Commission's decision, was an agreement, the subject of separate proceedings,[87] between the cement producers in neighbouring states under which they agreed how much each might export to the Netherlands.

The more the Cement Dealers' Trade Association restrained price cutting in the Netherlands by established dealers, the more other dealers there would be encouraged to import cement and undercut them. The agreement in issue must have increased imports rather than restrained them. That was irrelevant. The ECJ was concerned that the common market should be treated as a unit, and price fixing throughout the Netherlands affects the pattern of trade by creating a distortion along the Dutch border.

The judgment is explained in *Belasco v Commission*,[88] where Advocate General Mischo and the ECJ observed that cartels confined to a single Member State have to take measures to restrict imports, and that is why national agreements may normally be prohibited. Where the barriers to cross frontier trade are not created by the parties, it may be argued that a national agreement does not infringe Article 81.

Where there are direct restrictions on imports or exports between Member States, the conditions of application for the prohibition are usually satisfied. Nevertheless in *Hugin v Commission*,[89] despite the presence of an export ban, the ECJ quashed a decision that Article 82 was infringed by refusing to supply Liptons, a small firm that operated only within a radius of 30 miles of London. The judgment makes sense, however, if the condition about trade between Member States is meant to distinguish important agreements, subject to Community competence, from minor ones to be dealt with only by national authorities.[90] No such argument was articulated in the judgment.

In other cases where only one Member State is directly affected it used to be impossible to foretell the outcome. Sometimes the ECJ asked the Commission to spell out the mechanism restraining imports or exports; yet in other cases, such as *FRUBO*,[91] and most of the later cases, it observed that currents of trade are appreciably affected and confirmed an infringement even if no mechanism restraining trade across frontiers was indicated.

Sometimes, as in *Tepea*,[92] the ECJ quashed the Commission's condemnation, observing that there were no appreciable effects on trade between Member States. Yet in *Société de Vente de Ciments et Bétons v Kerpen & Kerpen*,[93] the ECJ ruled that a restriction accepted by a buyer in one part of

---

87 *Cimenteries* (8–11/66) [1967] ECR 75.
88 (246/86) [1989] ECR 1–2117, at 2174 (opinion of Mischo AG) and paras 33–35 (judgment).
89 (22/78) [1979] ECR 1869.
90 (2.3.1 above).
91 (71/74) [1975] ECR 563, para 38.
92 (28/77) [1978] ECR 1391, paras 46–48.
93 (319/82) [1983] ECR 4173, para 9.

the Federal Republic of Germany on selling in another part of it might infringe Article 81, and that the effect on inter-state trade was perceptible, because the contract related to 10% of the cement exported from France to the Federal Republic of Germany. It is thought that this may be an unreliable precedent. Where an insignificant part of the demand in state A is satisfied by imports from state B, it is thought that effects on inter-state trade are not necessarily appreciable whatever the restriction.

In *Bagnasco*,[94] the ECJ found that uniform conditions for opening current accounts agreed between all the Italian banks did not appreciably affect trade between Member States, since current accounts had limited effects on inter-state trade. Agreements covering a whole Member State may not automatically infringe. Some market analysis may be required.

Some practices are likely to foreclose foreign firms. Collective aggregated rebates—a rebate given to customers who bought a fixed quantity of ceramic tiles from the members of a German producers' trade association—was found to deter buyers from buying a proportion of their requirements from Italy and so to affect trade between Member States.[95] The organisation of trade fairs by national trade associations has been exempted by the Commission only when members were allowed to exhibit elsewhere for part of the period between fairs and sellers from other Member States were able to exhibit.[96]

The concept of 'appreciable' effect (2.4.9 below) increases the unpredictability. The concept is, however, sometimes invoked by the Commission to increase its discretion to ignore a complaint, and enables the parties to enforce agreements that do not significantly restrict competition without the Commission having to proceed to a formal exemption.

2.3.3 *The condition has been further narrowed*

In the last two decades several propositions have been established by the ECJ which have further reduced the importance of the condition that trade between Member States must be affected. In *Windsurfing v Commission*,[97] the ECJ stated that, although it is only the particular provisions that restrict competition that are void under Article 81(2), if the agreement as a whole affects trade between Member States, Article 81 may be infringed even if the restrictions of competition do not affect such trade.

In *Pronuptia*,[98] the ECJ included the possibility of a firm becoming established in another Member State in the concept of effect on trade between Member States. Trade is not confined to the movement of goods or services, but extends also to the right of establishment and the free movement of the

94   [1999] 4 CMLR 624.
95   *German Ceramic Tiles* JO 1971, L10/15, [1971] CMLR D6.
96   *SMM&T Exhibition Agreement*, OJ 1983, L376/1, [1984] 1 CMLR 611.
97   (193/83) [1986] ECR 611, paras 96–97.
98   (161/84) [1986] ECR 353, para 26.

suppliers. It applies also to the other freedoms of movement, such as that for capital.[99]

In *Fire Insurance*,[100] the ECJ observed that foreign insurance companies were allowed to operate in the Federal Republic of Germany only if they set up a branch there. This, however, did not prevent an arrangement limited to the insurance of fire risks in the Federal Republic being found to affect trade between Member States. The minimum premium recommended by the trade association must have affected the financial relationship between the foreign head office and its German branch and made it harder for foreign firms to enter by competing on premiums.

2.3.4 *Commission's notice*

There is a new notice on the effect on trade concept contained in Articles 81 and 82 of the Treaty.[101]

2.3.5 *The comparable provision in Article 82 is similarly construed*

The construction of the term 'may affect trade between Member States' in Article 82 has been similar. In *Commercial Solvents v Commission*,[102] the ECJ, referring expressly to Article 81 as well, said that the condition should be applied in the light of Articles 2 and 3(1)(g) of the treaty. The abuse of a dominant position alleged in that case consisted of refusing to supply raw materials to a small pharmaceutical producer which competed downstream. It was argued that this did not affect trade between Member States, since 90 % of the final product was exported to non-member countries and most of the rest was sold in Italy, where the complainant manufactured it. The ECJ responded:

> 33. The Community authorities must therefore consider all the consequences of the conduct complained of for the competitive structure in the common market without distinguishing between production intended for sale within the market and that intended for export. When an undertaking in a dominant position within the common market abuses its position in such a way that a competitor in the common market is likely to be eliminated, it does not matter whether the conduct relates to the latter's exports or its trade within the common market, once it has been established that this elimination will have repercussions on the competitive structure within the common market.

This all-embracing statement, which almost read the condition about interstate trade out of the competition rules, was followed by the observation that the victim of the abuse had in fact been exporting part of its production to

---

99   *Zuchner* (172/80), [1981] ECR 2021, and Commission notice on trade between Member States g 19.
100   *Verband der Sachversicherer v Commission* (45/85) [1987] ECR 405, para 49.
101   OJ 2004, C101/81.
102   (6 & 7/73) [1974] ECR 223, para 32.

France and the Federal Republic of Germany. These paragraphs may represent a compromise, some members of the ECJ wanting to establish the broad principle, while others were prepared to go no further than was required by the facts of the case.

2.3.6 *The EEA*

Articles 53 and 54 of the EEA treaty forbid the same sorts of conduct as Articles 81 and 82 of the EC treaty when 'they may affect trade between the Contracting Parties.' Article 2(c) EEA provides that the term 'Contracting Parties' sometimes refers to the EC and sometimes to its Member States. This is not very helpful. It is thought that for the EEA to apply there must be at least one non-EC Member State affected. When only EC Member States are affected their conduct will remain subject to the EC competition rules.

2.4 'Have as their object or effect the prevention, restriction or distortion of competition within the common market'

To be caught, arrangements must have 'as their object *or* effect' the prohibited effects on competition. Although the phrase is followed by a list of examples, the list is not exhaustive. The Italian authentic text of the treaty refers to 'object *and* effect', but in *Ferrière Nord v Commission*,[103] the ECJ held that it should be construed in the light of the other language versions to read 'object *or* effect' even when applied to the Italian participant in a cartel. Community law must be consistent throughout the common market.

Whether an agreement has the object of restricting competition depends not so much on the purpose of the parties. They may have had a legitimate purpose, but have taken steps that went further than necessary.

The ECJ uses the term 'by its very nature' in cases involving deterrents on trade between Member State and price fixing, vertical or horizontal.

In *NVIAZ International Belgium and others v Commission*,[104] the manufacturers of washing machines were concerned that the public supply of drinking water should not be contaminated by the waste from washing machines returning to the public water pipes. They arranged for type testing of the models sold in Belgium resulting in the supply of conformity labels. They also arranged that only the manufacturer or exclusive distributor of each brand should be able to obtain these labels, making it costly for parallel importers to operate, as they would need type testing for small quantities to obtain conformity labels.

The parties objected that the Commission had not established that their object was to restrict competition. The ECJ said:

---

103   (C–219/95P), [1997] ECR 1–4411, paras 13–16, following AG Léger, paras 15–21.
104   (96/82 etc) [1983] ECR 3369, paras 23–25.

... the agreement, regard being had to its content, its origin and the circumstances in which it was implemented, clearly expresses the intention of treating parallel imports less favourably than official imports with a view to hindering the former.

Although, there was evidence that their intention was clearly to exclude parallel trade, the judgment is cited by two officials of the Competition department,[105] for the proposition that agreements that 'by their very nature' restrict competition are treated as having that object. They suggest that this applies almost only to horizontal or vertical price fixing or market sharing, and to provisions that deter parallel trade.

Frequently, the Commission has said merely that certain kinds of conduct are restrained and asserts that this has *the object* of restricting competition even if, without the restriction, no one could sensibly have entered the market.

Often, it has found that an exclusive territory given to a dealer or licensee restricts the supplier or licensor from appointing another dealer or licensee and has the object of restricting competition contrary to Article 81(1) without investigating whether it is intended to induce investment. Nevertheless, it states when granting an exemption under Article 81(3) that, without an exclusive territory, no one could have been found to develop the market or tool up.[106] If this is so, competition must have been increased. So this practice of the Commission, which became less common in the late 1990s, seems to me to be contradictory.

The Commission's notice on agreements of minor importance (2.4.9 below) treats vertical as well as horizontal price fixing and territorial limitations as hard core restraints which are outside the safe harbour for agreements between parties with small shares of the relevant market.

There is no general possibility of exemption from the prohibition in the US Sherman Act, so the judges early recognised the absurdity of treating every contract as being in restraint of trade and illegal. They were able to limit the prohibition to agreements that were unlikely to have significant pro-competitive benefits.

The possibility of exemption under Article 81(3) of the EC Treaty has caused difficulty. It has encouraged Commission and Court to interpret the prohibition widely. Some say that if the increase in inter-brand competition caused by the entry of Grundig into the French market were to take the exclusive agreement outside Article 81(1), there would be no function for Article 81(3). It would probably have to be used only when consumers benefit from non-competitive advantages, such as a cleaner environment (3.1.1.1 below).

---

105   J Faull and A Nikpay, (eds) *The EC Law of Competition*, (Oxford, OUP, 1999) 82–3.
106   *E.g., Davidson Rubber* [1972] CMLR D22.

2.4.1 Consten & Grundig

In *Consten and Grundig v Commission*,[107] it may not only have been the effects of the absolute territorial protection on the allocation of markets that had the object of restricting competition and so fell within the prohibition but, possibly, also the exclusivity provisions whereby Consten agreed not to handle competing equipment and Grundig directly to supply no one in France other than Consten, although these do not figure in the list given in Article 81(1). In chapter 9, however, it will be seen that such restrictions are frequently exempted and do not always infringe Article 81(1).[108] Moreover, the ECJ quashed the Commission's decision in part for failing to give reasons for condemning the exclusivity.

The ECJ held in *Consten and Grundig* that there is no need to examine the effects of an agreement if its object is to restrict competition. Consten and Grundig asked the ECJ to quash the Commission's decision for not having made an analysis of the market for the kinds of equipment affected by the agreement; the Commission had not stated even that Grundig was an important brand name. The ECJ stated that the brand was important, but perceived the issue *ex post* from 1964 when the Commission adopted a decision and not *ex ante* when the agreement was made and Consten had still to establish the name in France.[109]

In 1957, when Consten undertook to incur costs promoting the product, before the common market had removed quotas, it incurred significant risks. It might not be able to obtain import licences for many or even for any items of equipment. Even if Consten managed to obtain a licence, the expenditure would have to be spread over a limited number of items and would be wasted unless Consten were able to sell enough of the Grundig product. The costs were sunk: the investment had no value save for promoting the Grundig brand. Consequently, Consten would need to expect unusually high profits if it was to be successful.

A high margin would attract imports from Germany, where there was no need for an import licence and average costs and risk would be less. Such traders from Germany would take a free ride on Consten's investment in making the product acceptable. Unless Consten could be protected sufficiently from these parallel imports, it might well have found the risk unacceptable.

If Grundig could not have found someone to promote its product in the early days, Grundig products might have been less attractive to the parallel importers. The Commission never investigated how much protection was necessary to induce the optimal amount of investment in promotion. Nor was the question raised whether Grundig, which backed its judgement as to the

---

107   (56 & 58/64) [1966] ECR 299, at 341 (discussed at 2.3.1 above).
108   *Société La Technique Minière v Maschinenbau Ulm GmbH* (56/65), [1966] ECR 235.
109   Contrast 9.5.1 below.

amount of protection needed with its expectation of profit, was better able to judge than officials in the Commission.

On appeal from the Commission, the ECJ said that the Commission had found that the object of this agreement was to restrict competition between Consten and Grundig's other dealers. The Commission had properly taken into account not just the agreement in issue but the whole network of Grundig distribution agreements, which clearly attempted to insulate the national markets from competition from other distributors of the same brand. It confirmed the Commission's condemnation of the agreement.

2.4.2 *Restrictions by object*

In the early days, the ECJ and Commission tended to say that almost any restriction on conduct had the object of restricting competition if it had appreciable effects on the market. As the ECJ held in *Consten and Grundig* (2.4.1 above) absolute territorial protection has the object of restricting competition and there is no need to make a market analysis.[110] The same has been held of price fixing agreements, whether between competitors or imposed on supplier or customer, licensor or licensee. All that needs to be established is collusion and that the agreement may affect trade between Member States appreciably.

These 'restrictions by object' are now often referred to by the Commission as hard core restraints. Very early, a distinction started to be drawn between horizontal or vertical price fixing or export bans, which had the object of restricting competition, and other restrictions on conduct which did not infringe Article 81 unless an appreciable restrictive effect on competition was established.[111]

To see whether an agreement has 'the effect'[112] of restricting competition, an agreement should be appraised in its legal and economic context. In *Société La Technique Minière v Maschinenbau Ulm*[113] an exclusive distribution agreement was infringed, and the defence was that the exclusive provisions infringed Article 81. Unlike *Consten and Grundig*, there were no export bans. The ECJ stated that if an agreement, considered in its economic and legal context, does not have the object of restricting competition:

> the consequences of the agreement should then be considered and for it to be caught by the prohibition it is then necessary to find that those factors are present which show that competition has in fact been prevented or restricted or distorted to an appreciable extent.

---

110   Confirmed in *Miller International Schallplatten GmbH v Commission* (19/77), [1978] ECR 131 and followed in many Commission decisions.
111   See the Commission's guidelines on the application of Art 81(3) of the Treaty, OJ 2004, C101/97, Gs 20–22.
112   *Ibid*. Gs 24 *et seq*.
113   (56/65) [1966] ECR 235, at 247, 249–50.

The competition in question must be understood within the actual context in which it would occur in the absence of the agreement in dispute. In particular, it may be doubted whether there is an interference with competition if the said agreement seems really necessary for the penetration of a new area by an undertaking.

The ECJ continued that to decide whether an exclusive dealing agreement is:

prohibited by reason of its object or of its effect, it is appropriate to take into account in particular the nature and quantity, limited or otherwise, of the products covered by the agreement, the position and importance of the grantor and the concessionaire on the market for the products concerned, the isolated nature of the disputed agreement or, alternatively, its position in a series of agreements, the severity of the clauses intended to protect the exclusive dealership or, alternatively, the opportunities allowed for their commercial competitors in the same products by way of parallel re-exportation and importation.

The judgment in which, under Article 234 of the EC Treaty, the ECJ interpreted Community law for a national court to apply, uses two concepts that may possibly exclude the application of the prohibition of Article 81(1).

The first doctrine—'ancillary restraints'—is expressed in more than one way. One is that the competition excluded was not possible without the restraint, for instance, that the firm could not have penetrated another Member State without co-operation from a local exclusive dealer who would need some protection from other dealers taking a free ride to induce investment. Alternatively an ancillary restraint may be one that is 'directly related and necessary to the implementation of the main operation' (2.4.5 below).

The second concept is that agreements should be appraised in their economic as well as their legal context: only if the agreement substantially foreclosed other dealers—only if there was little inter-brand competition, would the agreement infringe Article 81(1).

2.4.3 *Legal and economic context*

The relevance of the legal and economic context was reaffirmed by the ECJ in 1991 in *Delimitis v Henninger Bräu*[114] in relation to the situation where a tenant agreed to acquire from its landlord all the beer to be consumed in its bar. The ECJ pointed to the benefits to both parties and at paragraph 13 concluded that the restriction did not have the 'object of restricting competition'.

It then required a national court to make a full analysis of the market to appraise its effects: was it easy to enter at the retail level and, if not, were so many outlets tied to one or other of the brewers for so long that insufficient free outlets remained or came on the market to take the supply of a new brewer of a viable size for distribution entering the market or for existing

114 (C–234/89) [1991] ECR I–935.

brewers to expand.

The Chicago school of economics observed that the parties to vertical agreements—those between suppliers at different levels of trade and industry, that did not compete with each other, such as a supplier and its customer or a technology licensor and its licensee—contributed complementary products rather than substitutes. Each would benefit from increased demand if the other were to lower its price and increase its output. Collaboration between competitors should be judged more harshly, since each would benefit if the other produced less rather than more.

Some officials have treated vertical agreements more harshly than those between competitors, because they perceived vertical agreements as dividing the common market. Often an exclusive territory bounded by national frontiers was granted to the firm downstream. Moreover, under the Ordo Liberal influence (4.2 below), some officials have been worried about excluding citizens from the market, even when this does not harm consumers. Agreements to handle the products only of a particular supplier or to buy exclusively or nearly exclusively from it may foreclose other suppliers. Recently, views are changing, and vertical restraints are likely to be treated more leniently (2.4.7 & 8.1.3 below).

2.4.4 *Market definition*

It is now quite clear that in order to appraise the economic context of an agreement, it is necessary to analyse the market and, therefore, to define it. The CFI quashed the Commission's decision in *European Night Services*,[115] for failing to give adequate reasons in its decision for its selection of the relevant market in proceedings under Article 81(1). This clearly applies also to proceedings before national courts or national authorities.

The concepts of dominant position and the relevant market are considered more fully at 4.3-4.3.1.6 below. A market is where competition operates. A supplier competes not only with suppliers of identical products, but also suppliers of products to which its customers might turn if it were to raise its price. It also competes, although usually less immediately, with suppliers who might start to supply the same or substitute goods if it were to raise its price.

For economists, a market is defined in terms of substitutes on both the demand and supply side. In other words, a market includes potential competition. This is the view of the American enforcement officials and was adopted by the Commission in its notice on market definition, although the courts in Luxembourg continue to use older, more concrete tests based on demand side substitution as has the Commission in some of its non-merger cases.

---

115   *European Night Services (ENS) and others v Commission* (T–374/94) etc, [1998] ECR II–3141, paras 90–101 (see also 2.4.7 above & 13.2.2.2 below).

2.4.5 *Ancillary restraints*

The doctrine of ancillary restraints was also developed from the first passage in the judgment of the ECJ in *Société La Technique Minière v Maschinenbau Ulm GmbH*[116] quoted at 2.4.2 above. The ECJ implied that if the dealer would not have made the investments necessary to organise distribution without being promised protection from free riders, then that protection would not infringe Article 81(1). A restriction of conduct that is necessary to make the main transaction viable does not infringe Article 81(1) if the main transaction does not.

Brand owners sometimes want to control the retail outlets where their products are sold in order to compete not only on price, but also on pre-sales service, location or ambience, for which it may be difficult to make a separate charge to consumers. They may authorise only those dealers who provide such services, and require them to sell only to the general public or to other authorised dealers, thereby preventing their goods being sold from unauthorised outlets. This is sometimes called 'selective distribution.'

In *Metro v Commission*,[117] at a time when Commission decisions often treated any restriction of conduct that was important on the market as a restriction of competition, the ECJ referred rather to 'workable competition'

> that is to say the degree of competition necessary to ensure the observance of the basic requirements and the attainment of the objectives of the Treaty, in particular the creation of a single market achieving conditions similar to those of a domestic market.

It accepted that selective distribution did not infringe Article 81(1) even though it restricted the conduct of dealers. It was legitimate to compete not only on price, but also on service, provided that the brand owner applied specified, qualitative criteria without discrimination. The criteria must not include limitations of quantity, such as only one dealer in an area with a particular population, must be proportionate—appropriate to the product being sold—and no wider than necessary.

The courts in Luxembourg continue to uphold the concept of ancillary restraints which may not infringe Article 81(1), although there are a few judgments, such as *Windsurfing*,[118] where, by a chamber of three, the ECJ has treated any important restrictions on conduct as having the object or effect of restricting competition.

There is more than one definition of ancillary restraints which do not infringe Article 81(1) provided that they are reasonable and proportionate and no wider than necessary to support the basic transaction.

116   (56/65), [1966] ECR 235.
117   (26/76) [1977] ECR 1875.
118   (193/83) [1986] ECR 611, paras 45–46, 57, 74, 81, 93 and many decisions of the Commission.

1. The term may embrace provisions that make viable a transaction not in itself inherently anti-competitive, such as one leading to the penetration of a new market.

2. The Commission treats 'any restriction which is directly related and necessary to the implementation of a main operation'[119] as an ancillary restraint and the CFI in *Métropole Télévision (M6) and Others v Commission II*,[120] used the same definition, saying that the analysis had to be somewhat abstract.

3. According to Enrique Gonzalez Diaz,[121] the ancillary restraints doctrine is 'used to justify restrictions that are necessary for the full preservation or full transfer of value in certain types of transaction.'

The judgments of the courts in Luxembourg have not always made it clear which definition is being applied, and they are not entirely consistent.

In *Nungesser v Commission*,[122] the ECJ held that an open exclusive licence of plant breeders' rights, one not granting absolute territorial protection, did not in itself infringe Article 81(1) because it was needed to induce the investment of both parties and, in *Coditel (II)*,[123] it held that in the light of the practice of the industry, exclusive licences of performing rights did not do so, even though in the circumstances, they conferred absolute territorial protection. These judgments seem to be based on the first definition.

In *Pronuptia*,[124] the ECJ ruled that many restrictions on conduct do not infringe Article 81(1) where they are necessary to make a distribution franchising network viable, since franchising, in itself, does not restrict competition. Nevertheless, the ECJ ruled that the effect of two clauses in combination—an exclusive territory, coupled with an obligation to sell only from the franchised outlet—may confer absolute territorial protection and infringe Article 81(1) once the network is widespread. Absolute territorial protection is a restriction by object.

The Advocate General stressed the economic context of the agreement and advised the ECJ that competition policy is concerned only with the horizontal effects of vertical agreements: that in the absence of substantial market power or restrictions on cross border trade, franchise agreements do not infringe Article 81(1).

The ECJ adopted a different line of reasoning. In clearing clauses required to maintain a uniform image for the network as outside the prohibition of 81(1): at paragraph 15, the ECJ referred to the provisions being necessary to make distribution franchising work. This seems to be an application of the

---

119   Commission notice on ancillary restraints (mergers) guidelines, [2001] 5 CMLR 787.
120   (T–206/99) [2001] ECR II–1061, para 104–14.
121   'Some Reflections on the Notion of Ancillary Restraints under EC Competition Law,' [1995] *Fordham Corporate Law Institute* 325, 328.
122   (258/78) [1982] ECR 2015, paras 56–58 (and 11.3 below).
123   (262/81) [1982] ECR 3381, paras 15–19 (and 11.3 below).
124   (161/84) [1986] ECR 353 (and 9.5.1 below).

first definition of ancillary restraint; on the other hand, the analysis was abstract. Certain provisions in the franchising contract are always valid, irrespective of market power, although few franchised networks, if any, have much market power.

In *Metropole II*,[125] the CFI clearly adopted the second definition, which it took from Commission guidelines. It stated that there should be no balancing between competitive benefits and detriments under Article 81(1): any benefits should be considered under Article 81(3). It construed the concept of ancillary restraints narrowly, to be applied in a relatively abstract manner.

The second concept of ancillary restraints 'directly related' to a transaction and 'necessary for its existence' has drawbacks. It lacks precision. Moreover, the inducement to investment by both parties in *Nungesser* was not directly related to the open exclusive licence. It seems to me that the relationship was indirect; the chain of causation was broken by the investment induced by the protection from free riders.

American courts treat as ancillary a restriction on conduct that is '*reasonably* related' to the main transaction and *reasonably* necessary, rather than 'directly related'. Can the Commission and CFI requirement of a direct relationship be so construed? I hope so.

The CFI's judgment in *Metropole II* may be difficult to reconcile with the later judgment in *Wouters*,[126] where ECJ seems to have adopted an unlimited balancing of anticompetitive effects against non-competitive justifications under Article 81(1). It did not refer to the judgment of the CFI in *Métropole II*. It held that a rule of the Dutch Bar forbidding lawyers to enter into multidisciplinary partnerships with accountants amounted to a decision of an association of undertakings and restricted competition because clients might want a single firm to advise them on the accounting as well as legal aspects of a transaction. It might also affect trade between Member States (paragraphs 86–90 & 95–97).

Nevertheless, the ECJ considered that the Bar might reasonably have wanted to exclude the conflicts of interest that might arise from lawyers being in partnership with accountants and ensure the independence of the bar (paragraphs 97–110). The ECJ, therefore, cleared the rule as not infringing Article 81(1) The refusal to balance pro- and anticompetitive effects in *Metropole II*, may have been overruled by the ECJ in *Wouters*.

The judgment is highly controversial. The ECJ might have invoked Article 86(2) (1.3.2.8 and 6.2 below) and excepted the rules of ethics as being necessary to the task entrusted by statute to the Dutch Bar Council, but it did not refer to Article 86.

The ethical rule in *Wouters* was clearly not an example of an ancillary restraint. It was not directly or reasonably necessary for the establishment of

125   (T–206/99) [2001] ECR II–1061.
126   (C–309/99), [2002] ECR I–1577.

the Dutch Bar, as the ECJ stated that multidisciplinary partnerships might be permitted in other countries.

The concept used in *Wouters* has not been fully classified. Some consider that the judgment was wrong. How can a court decide whether the public interest in avoiding conflicts of interest outweighs the loss of efficiency in enabling a 'one-stop-shop' to be provided? Is the issue appropriate for a court?

Many commentators consider, however, that *Wouters* is to be explained as a separate exception to Article 81(1), based on national public interest (2.4.6 below).

The advantage of the narrow interpretation of ancillary restraints is that it is easier for officials and lawyers to apply Article 81(1), but the certainty required by businessmen relates to the validity of the contract under Article 81 as a whole and that is not enhanced.

The main objection to a narrow interpretation of the concept of ancillary restraint was that only the Commission used to be able to grant exemptions, and it did not have the resources to adopt many decisions. Since May 2004, however, national courts and competition authorities have been able to apply Article 81(3) (7.2 below). So, this objection has disappeared.

There remains the problem that the burden of proof under Article 81(3) is on the parties wanting an exemption, while the burden of establishing an infringement of Article 81(1) is on the party alleging it.[127] Many contracts that do not have either anti-competitive object or effect will have to be justified when enforcing them, and this may make it harder to persuade the defendant to abide by its contract without going to court.

There is a growing series of articles in the law reviews advocating a more flexible approach to Article 81(1) (bibliography 2.6 below). The concept of ancillary restraints is explained further at 6.2 below.

2.4.6 *National public interest*

National public interests have been recognised under Article 86(2) (6.2 below). Article 86 provides:

> 1. In the case of . . . undertakings to which Member States grant special or exclusive rights, Member States shall neither enact or maintain in force any measure contrary to the rules contained in this treaty and in particular to those rules provided for in . . . Articles 81–91.

Paragraph (2) provides a derogation for undertakings entrusted with the operation of services of general economic interest in so far as the rules obstruct the particular task assigned to the undertaking.

---

127   Council Reg 1/2003, OJ 2003, 1/1, [2003] 4 CMLR 551, Art 2.

In *Albany*,[128] the ECJ was concerned with a sectoral supplementary pension scheme. The basic state pension in the Netherlands is low and, in the context of employment or self- employed activities, is topped up by hundreds of schemes for different professions, which may be made compulsory by the minister for social affairs.

Albany runs a textile business and wanted to leave the compulsory scheme for textile workers and subscribe to a private scheme offering more generous payments.

The ECJ seems to have considered that it would be inappropriate to expose labour markets to the full discipline of competition and treated collective bargaining about terms and conditions of work between organisations representing employers and employees as outside Article 81 altogether. The national interest in social policy, which is also a Community policy, trumped Article 81 when competition policy was incompatible with it.

It interpreted Article 86(2) as enabling Member States:

> to take account of objectives pertaining to their national policy or from endeavouring to attain them by means of obligations and constraints which they impose on such undertakings.' (para 102)

The supplementary pension scheme made binding by the Dutch minister 'fulfils an essential social function within the Dutch pension system,' which had been recognised in a Community directive (paragraphs 105 & 106). The ECJ then held that the national social objective trumped Article 81. Unless the exclusive right given by the Dutch government was respected the scheme would not be viable, as the good risks would leave the scheme.

Is this an example of the ancillary restraint doctrine, according to the first definition, or of the overriding effect of national public policy? Some experts explain *Wouters* as being another example of a national interest trumping competition law.

2.4.7 *The Commission's view*

Despite the clear rulings by the ECJ, the Commission has rarely taken into account under Article 81(1) the economic context of the agreement or whether, without the protection from competition agreed, the basic activity would have been commercially attractive. Often it has found that an agreement is caught by the prohibition of Article 81(1) and granted an exemption or sent a comfort letter on the ground that, without an exclusive territory, no dealer or licensee could have been found. Although if this were the case, one would have thought that the agreement should have been cleared rather than exempted on the first definition of 'ancillary restraints' (2.4.5 above).

---

128   *Albany International BV v Stichting, Bedrijfspensioenfonds Textielindustrie and others*, (C–67/96 etc) [1999] ECR I–5751, paras 103–23.

It has usually refused to analyse markets carefully under Article 81(1). In accordance with the second definition of ancillary restraints, it has often taken the view that competition constitutes freedom from significant contractual restraints, even when these are necessary to induce investment. There have, however, been occasional decisions taking another view, such as *Odin*,[129] where a joint venture was cleared despite restraints on the parties who were considered by the Commission not to be actual or potential competitors. The Commission's views began to change.

In *Langnese*,[130] the Commission postponed its appraisal of the market until considering Article 81(3), but the CFI held that it should have done so under Article 81(1). More recently, however, in *Whitbread*,[131] the Commission appraised an exclusive purchasing obligation taking many market factors into account under Article 81(1).

The Commission's recent decisions on joint ventures, technology licences and franchising have found that many important clauses do not infringe Article 81(1), although it has usually exempted, and not cleared, exclusive territories.

In *European Night Services*,[132] the CFI quashed a decision granting an exemption to a joint venture subject to conditions. The parties, the incumbent railway companies in four different Member States, set up a joint venture to run long distance train services at night under the English Channel. The CFI emphasised that the Commission must give good reasons for deciding that an agreement infringes Article 81(1) and must define and appraise the market properly. For lack of such reasoning, the decision was quashed.

If the agreement did not infringe Article 81(1) it would need no exemption. Nevertheless, the CFI spelled out also the faulty reasoning about the exemption. The Commission had not shown the need for the conditions requiring the joint venture to make available to third parties paths under the Channel,[133] special locomotives and crews. Nor had it established an appropriate criterion for the duration of the exemption. It is clear that the Commission must now make far fuller analyses of the market under Article 81(1) than it used to do. This must apply equally to other bodies finding infringements—national courts and authorities.

Many joint ventures are now dealt with under the merger regulation rather than Article 81,[134] although coordination between the parties will be monitored

---

129   *Odin—Elopak/Metal Box-Odin Developments Ltd*, [1991] 4 CMLR 832 (13.2.2.1 below).
130   *Langnese-Iglo GmbH & Co KG*, 93/406/EEC, OJ 1993, L183/19, [1994] 4 CMLR 51; on appeal, *Langnese-Iglo GmbH & Co KG v Commission*, (case T–7/93), [1995] ECR II–1533. The judgment of the ECJ was confined to procedural matters.
131   [1999] 5 CMLR 118, paras 108–27.
132   (T–374, 375, 384 & 388/94) [1998] ECR II–3141 (13.2.2.2 below).
133   A Commission directive provided for these.
134   Those that are 'full function', by virtue of Council regulation 4064/89—Control of concentrations, Art 2(3), OJ 1990, L157/14, [1990] 4 CMLR 286, analysed at 12.2.2 below. There are hundreds of formal decisions on joint ventures under the merger regulation, but more of the joint ventures created are subject to Article 81.

according to the criteria of Article 81 (12.2.2 below). So the construction of Article 81(1) is less important to joint ventures than it used to be.

At last, in its notice on Article 81(3),[135] guidelines 17–18, the Commission cited *La Technique Minière*. It is now prepared to consider whether an agreement or its restrictions limits any competition that would have been possible without them. This is a major change of view.

2.4.8 *De facto restrictions*

For competition to be restricted, it is not necessary that any obligation should be accepted. In *Kali und Salz/Kali Chemie v Commission*,[136] the ECJ treated an option to require Kali und Salz to buy any potash not required by Kali Chemie itself as if Kali Chemie were bound to sell it to Kali und Salz, since Kali Chemie was giving up its distribution network for the product and its declining sources of supply would not warrant the expense of re-establishing one. It was, therefore, clear that it would exercise its option and the option restricted competition contrary to Article 81(1).

2.4.9 *'Appreciable' effects*

The ECJ has confirmed an implied condition that to infringe Article 81, the restriction of competition and the possible effect on trade between Member States should be appreciable. In *Völk v Vervaecke*,[137] Völk made less than 1% of the washing machines produced in Germany and the ECJ ruled that even absolute territorial protection granted to its exclusive distributor for Belgium and Luxembourg would not infringe Article 81(1) if it did not appreciably restrict competition and appreciably affect inter-state trade.

The Commission tried to reduce the uncertainty surrounding this *de minimis* rule by issuing a notice on Minor Agreements in 1970. The notice has been reissued with alterations several times, most recently at the end of 2001.[138]

Formerly, there was a ceiling of turnover, at 300 million ecus since 1994. This has now been abrogated. Large firms with small shares of particular markets may be able to come within the notice. The older notices applied to both concepts, trade between Member States and competition. The current one deals only with the second criterion. The Commission's views on trade are in its guidelines on effect on trade, which describe the case law.[139]

---

135   OJ 2004, C101/97.
136   (19 & 20/74) [1975] ECR 499, paras 8–9.
137   (5/69) [1969] ECR 295, para 3.
138   2001 OJ, C368/13, [2002] 4 CMLR 699.
139   OJ 2004, C101/81.

The current notice states that:

7. The Commission holds the view that agreements between undertakings which affect trade between Member States do not appreciably restrict competition within the meaning of Article 81(1):

  (a) if the market share held by the parties to the agreement does not exceed 10% of the relevant markets affected by the agreement, where the agreement is made between undertakings which are actual or potential competitors on any of these markets (agreements between competitors) or

  (b) if the market share held by each of the parties to the agreement does not exceed 15% on any relevant markets affected by the agreement, where the agreement is made between undertakings which are not actual or potential competitors on any of these markets (agreements between non-competitors).

Recital 8 provides that where there is a cumulative foreclosing effect like that in *Delimitis*[140], the ceiling for agreements between competitors or non-competitors is 5%. This limitation of the notice would remove most of its benefit from small suppliers. They are most likely to be concerned in distribution or franchising agreements, and likely to be part of a network, competing with other networks.

Recital 3, however, provides that:

3. Agreements between small and medium-sized undertakings, as defined in the Annex to the Commission recommendation of April 1996, 96/280 EC141 are rarely capable of appreciably affecting trade between Member States. Small and medium-sized undertakings are currently defined in that recommendation as undertakings which have fewer than 250 employees and have either an annual turnover not exceeding EUR 40 million or an annual balance-sheet total not exceeding EUR 27 million.

The Commission explains in its guidelines on effect on trade para 50 that the activities of small and medium-sized enterprises are normally local or regional. Paragraph 9 provides some marginal relief for the ceilings in paragraphs 7 and 8.

Recital 2 makes it clear that the current notice deals only with effects on competition, not on trade between Member States. Agreements that fail to qualify under the notice may not have an appreciable effect on Member States and may escape the Community rules.[141]

The notice on minor agreements does not apply at all to hard core restraints, those restricting prices or output or conferring strong territorial protection, whether between competitors or not (recital 11). The exclusion of hard core restraints between non-competitors with an aggregate market share

---

140   (C–234/89), [1991] ECR I–935 (2.4.3 above).
141   OJ 1996, L107/4, [1997] 4 CMLR 510.
142   *Völk v Ets Vervaecke Sprl* (5/69), [1969] ECR 295.

not exceeding 15% is hard to reconcile with *Völk v Vervaecke*,[142] where markets were partitioned and territorial protection was absolute. It is also questionable on economic grounds, since competition will constrain suppliers in competitive markets not to restrict production to raise price.

Commission notices are not binding on the Community or national courts. In *Suiker Unie' UA v Commission*,[143] the ECJ quashed a fine on the ground that the parties might have misinterpreted the agency notice and thought their agreement escaped the prohibition. Several Advocates General have told the ECJ to ignore the notice on minor agreements and it has not mentioned it.[144] In *European Night Services*,[145] the CFI refused to follow the notice blindly. *Völk v Vervaecke* laid down a *de minimis* rule at a level that was not determined. Nevertheless, there are political constraints encouraging the Commission to abide by its notices when deciding whether to investigate or take action.

Notices stating how the Commission intends to exercise its discretion, however, do give rise to legitimate expectations, and bind the Commission unless withdrawn before the conduct referred to took place (7.6.2 below).

2.5 Nullity

Article 81(2) provides that 'any agreements or decisions prohibited by this Article shall be automatically void.' Nevertheless, it is not the whole of an agreement that is rendered void by Article 81(2). In *Société La Technique Minière v Maschinenbau Ulm*,[146] the ECJ ruled that only those provisions that have the object or effect of restricting competition are void. In *Consten and Grundig*,[147] the ECJ quashed the decision for not specifying how much of the agreement was contrary to Article 81. Whether the rest of the agreement can be severed and enforced is a question for the national law (7.3.4.1 below).

It used to be important to distinguish between agreements that are not caught by Article 81(1) and those that are caught but merit exemption. Until exemption was granted, whether individually or through a group exemption, some provisions in an agreement that infringed Article 81(1) could not be enforced in national courts. This has changed pursuant to Regulation 1/2003. National courts and competition authorities can declare the prohibition of Article 81(1) inapplicable by virtue of Article 81(3). Nevertheless, the parties will bear the burden of providing evidence that the agreement merits exemption.

It is difficult to explain the developments in the case law about nullity until

---

143   (40/73 etc), [1975] ECR 1663, paras 555–57.
144   *E.g.*, AG Dutheillet de Lamothe in *Cadillon v Höss*, case 1/71, [1991] ECR 351, 361. See also AG Warner in *Miller International Schallplatten v Commission*, case 19/77, [1978] ECR 131, at 156–58.
145   (T–374, 374, 384 & 388/94) [1998] ECR II–3141, para 102.
146   (56/65) [1966] ECR 235, at 250.
147   (56 & 58/64) [1966] ECR 299 (and 2.3.1 and 2.4 above).

the implementing Regulation, no 1/2003, has been briefly analysed, so this will be postponed until chapter 7.

2.6 Bibliography

Jonathan B Baker, 'Recent Developments in Economics that Challenge Chicago School Views' (1989) 58 *Antitrust Law Journal* 645.

Christopher Bright, 'Deregulation and EC Competition Policy: Rethinking Article 81(1)' [1994] *Fordham Corporate Law Institute* 505.

Commission's guidelines on the effect on trade OJ 2004, C101/81.

Commission's guidelines on the application of Article 81(3) of the Treaty, OJ 2004, C101/97.

John Daltrop and *John Ferry*, 'The Relationship Between Articles 85 & 86: *Tetra Pak*' [1991] *European Intellectual Property Review* 31.

Jonathan Faull, 'Effects on Trade between Member States and Community-Member State Jurisdiction,' [1989] *Fordham Corporate Law Institute*, 485.

Ian Forrester and *Christopher Norall*, 'The Laïcization of Community Law: self-help and the rule of reason: how competition law is and could be applied' (1984) 21 *CML Rev*, 11.

Enrique Gonzalez Diaz, 'Some Reflections on the Notion of Ancillary Restraints under EC Competition Law' [1995] *Fordham Corporate Law Institute*, 325.

Luc Gyselen, 'Vertical Restraints in the Distribution Process: strength and weakness of the Free Rider Rationale under EEC Competition Law' (1984) 21 *CML Rev*, 648.

Barry Hawk, 'System Failure: Vertical Restraints and EC Competition Law,' (1995) 32 *CML Rev* 973.

Frédéric Jenny, 'Competition and Efficiency' [1993] *Fordham Corporate Law Institute*, 185.

René Joliet, 'La Notion de Pratique Concerte et l'Arrêt *I.C.I.* Dans une Perspective Comparative' [1974] cde 251.

—— *The Rule of Reason in Antitrust Law* (see main Bibliography).

Valentine Korah, 'Concerted Practices' (1973) 36 *Modern Law Review*, 220.

—— 'EEC Competition Policy—Legal Form or Economic Efficiency' [1986] *Current Legal Problems*, 85.

Georgio Monti, 'Article 81 and public policy,' (2002) 39 *CML Rev*, 1057.

Patrick Ray and James S. Venit, 'Parallel Trade & Pharmaceuticals: a Policy in Search of Itself', (2004) 29 *ELR* 153.

MC Schechter, 'The Rule of Reason in European Competition Law' (1982) *Legal Issues of European Integration*, 1.

M. Waelbroeck, 'Antitrust Analysis under Arts 85(1) and 85(3)' [1987] *Fordham Corporate Law Institute*, 693.

3. Analysis of Article 81(3)

3.1 Article 81(3)

Not all agreements that perceptibly restrict competition and may affect inter-state trade are prohibited. Some forms of collaboration restrictive of competition may have beneficial effects and by virtue of Article 81(3), reproduced in Appendix I below, the prohibition in Article 81(1) may be declared inapplicable to any agreements with certain characteristics. They must contribute to the improvement of the production or distribution of goods, or promote technical or economic progress. The first two criteria do not often apply to services, but the last two frequently do so.

Moreover, a fair share of the benefits must be passed on to consumers and the agreement must not impose restrictions that are not indispensable for achieving these benefits or afford the parties the possibility of eliminating competition in respect of a substantial part of the products in question.

In deciding whether the share of the benefit that goes to consumers is fair, the Commission has not quantified it. Individual exclusive distribution agreements have been exempted on the ground that consumers benefit from the additional choice made possible through the existence of a local firm charged with the promotion of goods, often from another Member State that otherwise might not easily have penetrated the market.

'Consumers' is rather a misleading translation of the French '*utilisateurs*.' In most of the authentic texts other than English, the word means ultimate buyers, whether for private or business use. The 'consumers' of a bus engine, for instance, were held to be bus companies and tour operators, not commuters or tourists.[1] The other conditions are that restrictions must be indispensable to obtaining the benefits and not eliminate competition.

There are some doubts about the validity of the Commission's recent practice of exempting recommendations of trade associations on environmental grounds. Usually the consumers of environmental benefits are far wider than consumers of the product.

In *CECED*,[2] the Commission exempted the recommendation of a trade association to discontinue models of washing machines that used electricity inefficiently. This prevented their production and sale so infringed Article 81(1). The main benefit claimed was environmental, but the Commission added that the saving in electricity would soon outweigh the additional cost of buying a more efficient machine. This avoided the doubt about the validity of such an exemption.

The Commission is now exempting by comfort letter other recommendations on environmental grounds. Protecting the environment is now a

1 *ACEC/Berliet* [1968] CMLR D35, para 15.
2 [2000] 5 CMLR 635.

Community policy, but it is not entirely clear that the Commission should promote it at the expense of competition.[3] The question may never go to the CFI. Buyers from the products boycotted are unlikely to have standing to appeal to an exemption granted to a third party (3.1.1.2 below). I have suggested (at 1.3.2.8 above) that it would be better to use Article 86(2) to reconcile conflicting Community policies in relation to bodies entrusted with a task in the general interest because competition would then give way only to the extent necessary for the performance of the task. In CECED the trade association was, however, not so entrusted.

Exercising powers granted by the Council, the Commission has granted several group exemptions of general application and several more applicable to specific sectors, namely vehicles, transport, and insurance. The special regime for beer and petrol expired in May 2000 and was not prolonged. In this book, I will describe only those of general application.

3.1.1 *Individual exceptions*

The Commission used also to adopt up to four individual exemptions a year. Since Regulation 1/2003 came into effect, the notification system has come to an end and the Commission is unlikely often to apply Article 81(3) except when important new issues arise, (chapter 7 below). Only the Commission had power to grant individual exemptions under Regulation 17 (now repealed). Notification ended in May 2004 and the procedures have changed drastically (chapter 7 below).

The ECJ held in *Consten and Grundig*[4] that the exercise of the Commission's powers under Article 81(3) necessarily involved complex evaluations of economic matters and judicial review was limited. Judge Cooke of the CFI, however has suggested that the reason for the margin of discretion allowed to the Commission is that it is the institution entrusted with the orientation of competition policy.[5]

By virtue of Regulation 1/2003, Article 1, Article 81(3) will now have direct effect (7.2 below). Article 43(1) repeals Regulation 17 and with it the system of notification. Now Article 81(3) can be applied by national courts and competition authorities. The question arises whether the Community courts will permit these institutions the same margin of discretion that it used to allow the Commission, which was responsible for the orientation of competition policy.

---

3   The Commission's guidelines on the application of Art 81(3) of the Treaty, para 84 confirm that the relevant consumers are the direct and indirect customers of the parties.
4   (56 & 58/64) [1966] ECR 299, at 347.
5   JD Cooke 'Changing responsibilities and relationships for Community and national courts,' in A Dashwood (ed) *The Modernisation of European Competition Law: the next ten years* (CELS Occasional Paper No 4, 2000).

National courts and competition authorities will not be authorised to make decisions that conflict with those made by the Commission or envisaged in proceedings that have already been initiated (Article 16 of Regulation 1/2003 and *Masterfoods*,[6] chapter 7 below).

The new regulation will make it easier to sue for breach of contract, since claims based on illegality or invalidity under Article 81(1) or (2) cannot be delayed by simply applying for an exemption. A national court will, itself, have to consider whether to apply Article 81(3). The burden of proof will be on the parties trying to justify a restriction under Article 81(3).

A declaration by a court or competition authority under Article 81(3) differ from the exemptions under Article 17. The latter used to be constitutive acts—for a specified period an agreement would not be subject to Article 81(1). It might have to be renewed. Now the institution will declare that at the date in issue Article 81 does not apply to an agreement. Conditions may change, and the declaration be of little use when they have. It is, therefore, probably wrong to refer to such clearances as exemptions: they are exceptions to the prohibition, or may be treated as limiting it.

3.1.1.1 *Right of complainant to appeal against a clearance*—Until 1996, the Community courts had never quashed an exemption granted by the Commission. Their jurisdiction under Article 230 to entertain an appeal over a decision addressed to someone else is limited. The appellant must establish that it is directly and individually concerned. This was narrowly construed by the ECJ in *Plaumann v Commission*,[7] but is being interpreted more widely these days in competition cases.

In *Métropole I*,[8] the Commission had exempted a joint venture, the European Broadcasting Union, between most European state owned television companies whereby, through the Eurovision link, the members were entitled to transmit sports and other programmes made by the others. Several private television stations were excluded from the joint venture and appealed to the CFI against the decision of exemption.

Some had taken part in the Commission's proceedings and others had not. The CFI held at paragraphs 59–64 that the appellants competed directly with the members of the EBU and were excluded from the benefits of the joint venture. So, they were individually concerned by the decision, whether or not they had complained during the Commission's proceedings. They were also directly concerned by the exemption, since there was a direct causal link between it and their exclusion from the benefits. Consequently, the CFI had jurisdiction to consider the appeal. For the first time, the CFI annulled an exemption decision:

6   (C–344/98) [2000] ECR I–1136.
7   25/62, [1963] ECR 95, at 107.
8   *Metropole I*, (T–206/99) [2001] ECR II–1059.

102. by failing to examine first whether the membership rules were objective and sufficiently determinate and capable of uniform, non-discriminatory application in order next to assess whether they were indispensable within the meaning of Article 85(3) [now Article 81(3)] of the Treaty, the Commission based its decisions on an erroneous interpretation of that provision.'

Several exemptions granted to third parties have been considered by the CFI since then.

It will now not always be possible to tell whether a clearance is based on Article 81(1) or (3), but in either case a third party damaged by an agreement should be able to appeal to the CFI when the clearance is granted by the Commission. When it is granted by a national court, a reference may be made to the ECJ under Article 234, and if granted by a national competition authority, an appeal may be possible under national law and when the case reaches a court, the court can make a reference to the ECJ under Article 234 (1.4.3.2 above). The remedy is less helpful if the clearance was granted by a national authority, as the ECJ should explain the law rather than apply it and most problems relate to the application of the law.

3.1.2 Group exemptions

Until 1965, the Commission probably had power to grant exemption only to individual agreements. By Regulation 19/65, however, the Council empowered it to make regulations exempting from Article 81(1) classes of exclusive distribution and exclusive purchasing agreements and of agreements licensing intellectual property rights. The Commission's exercise of these and of powers granted subsequently will be analysed in chapters 9, 11 and 13 below.

The old model for group exemptions was to define the kinds of agreements that can come within them(distribution, technology licences, cooperation in R & D or whatever(then provide for permissible clauses in a 'white list' and in one or two 'black lists' define the conditions or provisions that prevent the application of the exemption, even to the permissible provisions.

The new model since the exemption for agreements relating to distribution, regulation 2790/99,[9] is different. The exemption in Article 2 is widely drafted to cover all kinds of agreements between firms at a different level of production or distribution containing conditions relating to the sale or purchase of goods. There is no white list: any provisions that are not black listed are permissible.

The first black list of provisions in Article 4 of Regulation 2790/99 prevents the application of the exemption altogether, but the obligations to take most or all requirements from the same supplier and similar obligations listed in Article 5 are merely outside the exemption, they do not prevent it from applying to other provisions. In drafting agreements, it should be remembered that

---

9   OJ 1999, L336/21, reprinted with my annotations [2000] ECLR supp to May issue.

provisions to which the particular block exemption does not apply will be invalid if they infringe Article 81(1). Nevertheless, it is possible that a national court or authority might apply Article 81(3) individually.

Article 3 applies a ceiling of market share. If the party to be protected has a market share exceeding 30% the regulation will not apply, although there is no presumption that such an agreement infringes Article 81(1).

It is thought that this will be the model for subsequent group exemptions, although the ceiling for agreements between competitors, actual or potential, is lower.

3.1.2.1 *Withdrawal of group exemptions*—By virtue of Article 29 of Regulation 1/2003 the Commission may withdraw the benefit of a group exemption on its own initiative or on a complaint when it finds that in a particular case the agreement is not compatible with Article 81(3). When the collusion has effects in a Member State or part of it and that territory constitutes a distinct geographic market, the NCA of that state may withdraw the benefit of the group exemption.

The Commission has exercised similar powers under the group exemptions only once. The Commission is far more likely to threaten to withdraw an exemption, at which point the parties are under considerable pressure to modify their agreement so as to satisfy it.[10]

In *Langnese*,[11] the CFI limited the withdrawal of the exemption to agreements already entered into, and held that Langnese was still entitled to benefit from the group exemption for subsequent agreements. This severely limited the Commission's power to withdraw. The problem disappeared under the group exemption for vertical distribution agreements,[12] under which the Commission may withdraw the benefit of the exemption for a specified market by regulation where more than 50% of the market is foreclosed.

Group exemptions frequently apply to a whole series of individual agreements for instance a whole dealer network. In Regulation 1215/99, the Council has enabled the Commission to take power to withdraw a group exemption made thereunder for the future as well as for agreements already made. A similar provision is lacking in Regulation 1/2003.

3.1.2.2 *No exemption from Article 82*—It should be remembered that by their terms, the group exemptions are made under Article 81(3) and do not exempt an agreement made by a firm that is later found to be dominant from infringing Article 82.[13] The reasons that caused the Commission to consider a class of agreements sufficiently favourably to adopt the group exemption may

10   As was done in *Tetra Pak I* (88/501/EEC) [1990] 4 CMLR 47, para 58, confirmed by the CFI, *Tetra Pak Rausing SA v Commission* T–51/89) [1990] ECR II–309, para 37.
11   *Langnese-Iglo* (T–7/93) [1995] ECR II–1533, paras 208–9.
12   Reg 2790/99, OJ 1999, L339/21, Art 8(1).
13   *Tetra Pak*, (T–51/89), [1990] ECR II–309, at paras 21–25.

demonstrate that the agreement does not infringe Article 82, but the market power of the dominant firm may lead to a different conclusion.

3.1.2.3 *Advantages and disadvantages of group exemptions*—When an agreement can be framed to benefit from one of these group exemptions, the risk of illegality and nullity is avoided and the task of the parties' advisers is far easier. There is no need to analyse the market or to consider whether ancillary restraints are wider than necessary to ascertain whether Article 81(1) is infringed, either when negotiating the agreement or when enforcing it.

There are, however, disadvantages in having to bring a transaction within a block exemption. The class of agreements covered is often narrow and the older ones were adopted in reaction to the backlog of notifications to the Commission rather than on commercial or economic principles.

The black lists of clauses and conditions that prevent the application of the regulation were often wide, formalistic and not always easy to apply. So, at the time when the firms had to make investment decisions, it was not always certain whether an agreement was exempt. More recent block exemptions, however, have rather shorter black lists and have replaced many formalistic provisions with a ceiling of market share, which is economically more sensible. Nevertheless, at the time a commitment is made to invest, it is not always easy to predict what market will be selected by a competition authority or court.

Another disadvantage is that the parties may distort agreements which would make the common market more competitive and would contribute to the integration of the economies of Member States in order to fall within the terms of a group exemption. Commission Regulation 240/96 for Technology transfer, for instance applied only if an exclusive territory were granted or export bans imposed.[14] Sometimes solely to bring an agreement within the regulation such restraints were imposed. This is no longer true under the new regulation for technology transfer.

A third disadvantage is that some of these exemptions, for instance that for automobile distribution,[15] attempt to make the agreement fair for dealers by inserting clauses protecting their interests. This seems misguided. As Advocate General Verloren Van Themaat said in *Pronuptia*,[16] competition policy is not directly concerned with fair bargains, although fair competition is mentioned in the preamble to the Treaty. Moreover, the fairness of a bargain does not depend on specific terms, but on the bargain as a whole. A dealer may prefer to buy at a lower price than to be given specific forms of protection specified in general terms.

---

14   OJ 1996, L31/2, [1996] 4 CMLR 405, [1996] 4 *European Intellectual Property Review* Supp iv. There were two other possibilities.
15   Reg 1400/2002, the block exemption for motor vehicles, OJ 2002, L203/30, [2002] 5 CMLR 777.
16   (161/84) [1986] ECR 353, point 4.1.

There is no duty to bring within a group exemption agreements of the kind exempted—only a duty not to infringe the treaty.[17] In the light of their economic context an agreement may not infringe Article 81(1), the restraints may be ancillary or merit individual application of Article 81(3). Many licences of intellectual property rights, such as software protected by copyright, could not be brought with Regulation 140/96,[18] but the parties have used it as a guide as to what would probably be accepted by the Commission.

3.1.2.4 *Effect of group exemption on national competition law*—Citizens used to be required to comply with both their national and EC competition rules subject only to the priority of Community law. National competition rules could, however, not restrain an agreement that had been individually exempted. Under Regulation 1/2003, however, the double barrier theory is true only of Article 82 (7.3.1 and 7.3.3 below). If there may be an effect on trade between Member States, national courts and competition authorities are not permitted to apply national competition rules without also applying Article 81 or 82. They may not forbid as anticompetitive an agreement that is not forbidden by Article 81 as a whole.

Rather than further analysing the provisions of Article 81(3) in the abstract, it is proposed to discuss the particular kinds of contracts and clauses that have been exempted in practice in chapters 9, 11 and 13 below.

3.2 Bibliography

Commission notice on the application of Article 81 (3) of the Treaty, OJ 2004, C101/97.
Stephen Kon, 'Article 81, para 3: A Case for Application by National Courts' (1982) 19 *CML Rev* 541.
Michel Waelbroeck, 'Antitrust Analysis Under Article 85(1) and 85(3)' [1985] *Fordham Corporate Law Institute* 973, 702.

---

17   *VAG France SA v Établissements Magne SA*, case 10/86, [1986] ECR 4071, para 12.
18   OJ 1996, L31/2, [1996] 4 CMLR 405. Copyright in software is now exempt under Regulation 772/2004, OJ 2004, L1223/11.

4. Dominant Position

4.1 Introduction

Article 82 prohibits, as incompatible with the common market, the abusive exploitation by one or more undertakings of a dominant position within the common market or a substantial part of it in so far as it may affect trade between Member States.

In this chapter the varying objections to market power will be considered first: whether Article 82 is intended to protect consumers and the economy as a whole or to protect competitors of the dominant firm? On the first view efficiencies and incentives to investment of all sorts should be balanced against detrimental effects, on the second view that is not so. The case law demonstrates the tension between the two possible objectives.

Secondly, the case law on the meaning of a dominant position and the two-stage analysis required by the ECJ will be analysed. What is the relevant market and does the firm alleged to be dominant have a wide range of choice over prices and other conditions of contract within the market as defined?

The two kinds of abuses—exclusionary conduct that makes it more difficult for other firms to compete with it and unfair conduct that directly harms those dealing with the dominant firm will be analysed in chapter 5, as will the condition that the abuse must affect trade between Member States.

4.2 Objections to economic strength

As explained at 1.3 above, the most important objection to market power expressed by classical economists is that a firm insufficiently constrained by competitive pressures may be able to operate inefficiently for long periods or earn high profits through charging prices higher than would be possible in more competitive conditions. The higher prices would reduce demand below the competitive level and lead to too little of the monopolised product being supplied and to resources being used to make things less wanted by consumers. This concern is often referred to as 'power over price.'

The emphasis of modern economics is even more general, but is still focused on the wide discretion enjoyed by firms with market power to pursue a variety of goals and choose a range of productive means, within wide limits unconstrained by market pressures. In most markets, many firms enjoy some discretion over their production and marketing strategies, but this is not the general independence that enables high profits or inefficiency to be maintained over long periods without risk.

Chicago economists and the enforcement authorities in the United States during the Reagan era were not concerned with protecting competitors: only with protecting from exploitation those dealing with a dominant firm. To further this objective, it is necessary to control the behaviour only of firms which are protected from competition by equally efficient firms. Consequently, the only entry barriers relevant to the assessment of the relevant market and a dominant position therein are those that would keep out or harm equally efficient firms.

It is widely agreed that entry barriers include government licensing requirements and, in some circumstances, a minimum scale of operation that is large in relation to the market (1.3.3–1.3.3.2 above). It is less clear that inferior access to capital or a distribution network or lack of reputation would keep out equally efficient firms.

In the EC, however, there is concern also that large firms may make it hard for smaller firms to compete, even if the latter are less efficient (1.3.2.2–1.3.2.8 above). The preamble to the Treaty refers to many factors other than efficiency, such as social policy, fair competition, small and medium-sized undertakings, peace and liberty. To protect small firms that are less efficient, it may be necessary to control the conduct of firms that have no power over price. To serve these objectives, which may detract from efficiency, entry barriers may be perceived as pervasive, including all the investments to be made by the new entrant, even if the incumbent had to make similar investments.

Article 82 provides:

> Any abuse by one or more undertakings of a dominant position within the common market or in a substantial part of it shall be prohibited as incompatible with the common market in so far as it may affect trade between Member States. Such abuse may, in particular, consist in:
>
> (a) directly or indirectly imposing unfair purchase or selling prices or other unfair trading conditions;
> (b) limiting production, markets or technical development to the prejudice of consumers;
> (c) applying dissimilar conditions to equivalent transactions with other trading parties, thereby placing them at a competitive disadvantage;
> (d) making the conclusion of contracts subject to acceptance by the other parties of supplementary obligations which, by their nature or according to commercial usage, have no connection with the subject of such contracts.

The treaty was influenced by theories of workable competition current in the 1930s to 1950s and based on the paradigm of the structure of the market, which affects the conduct of firms, which affects their performance. Later it was seen that each of these elements affects the other two.

Scholars of the Freiburgh school of ORDO Liberals[1] which started in the 1930s, conceived a free market as a necessary ingredient of a liberal economy, although not sufficient in itself. They attributed the horrors of the Weimar republic and Nazi Germany in part to the failure of the legal system to control and, if necessary, to disperse private economic power. They advocated an

---

1   D Gerber, *Law and Competition in Twentieth Century Europe: Protecting Prometheus*, (Oxford, Clarendon Press, 1998), chapter VII.

economic constitution to constrain the economic power of firms without giving government unconstrained power over their behaviour. Governmental power could also be pernicious. Small was beautiful and small and medium sized firms would need protection.

Their views had a direct influence on the leading figures involved in the establishment of the European Communities. The freedom to enter a market of one's choice was recognised as a fundamental freedom. Not all firms would succeed, but they should be able to try. On this basis, barriers to entry were pervasive and exclusive agreements restrained freedom.

The early case law reflected these views, and it has been only with hesitation that the Commission has accepted that efficiencies from which consumers may benefit may outweigh the freedom of citizens.

Article 82 is not expressed to prohibit uncompetitive structures or conduct that leads to them: the existence or acquisition of market power. It is expressed to restrain conduct by a dominant firm that harms those with whom it deals. The examples of abuse given also all relate to holding those dealing with the dominant firm to ransom, although paragraph (d) may also cover extending market power from one product to another.

It will be seen (5.2–5.2.7.4 below), however, that the ECJ has interpreted the notion of abuse widely to include some kinds of conduct by a firm already dominant that extend or consolidate its market power by restricting the remaining competition, even minimally. Hence, conduct that adversely affects the structure of the market may be forbidden under Article 82.

4.3 Undertakings in a dominant position

Given the fluidity of the indications of dominance, it is not easy, especially for jurists, to determine how dominant a firm may be, and both the Commission and Community courts have failed to make many clearly and cogently reasoned decisions.

In its decision in *Continental Can*,[2] the Commission defined the concept of a dominant position in much the same terms as would an economist. It focused on the discretionary power of the monopolist to set its prices and make other market decisions without being tightly constrained by competitive pressures:

> 3. Undertakings are in a dominant position when they have the power to behave independently, which puts them in a position to act without taking into account their competitors, purchasers or suppliers. That is the position when, because of their share of the market, or of their share of the market combined with the availability of technical knowledge, raw materials or capital, they have the power to determine prices or to control production or distribution for a significant part of the products in question. This power does not necessarily have to derive from an

2 (6/72) [1972] CMLR D11, para II.3.

absolute domination permitting the undertakings which hold it to eliminate all will on the part of their economic partners, but it is enough that they be strong enough as a whole to ensure to those undertakings an overall independence of behaviour, even if there are differences in intensity in their influence on the different partial markets.

The Commission referred to the need for capital and technology, although such barriers to entry could be surmounted in the long run by many firms if monopoly profits would be earned thereby. On appeal, Advocate General Roemer approved the Commission's definition[3] and the Court[4] accepted it by implication.

Later, it became clear that a dominant position in the EC differs from the economists' concept of power over price: it is a legal concept developed by Commission and courts. In virtually all its judgments since *United Brands*, the ECJ has defined a dominant position as

> a position of economic strength enjoyed by an undertaking which enables it to prevent effective competition being maintained on the relevant market by giving it the power to behave to an appreciable extent independently of its competitors, customers and ultimately of consumers.[5]

The power to behave independently sounds like the economists' concept of power over price. A monopolist, unconstrained by competitive pressures, enjoys a discretion in its pricing and other market decisions. The application of competition policy to the conduct of such a firm may protect those with whom it deals.

The concept of 'economic strength . . . which enables a firm to impede effective competition', however, may indicate a different idea: the ability to foreclose: to keep other firms out of the market. Such strategic behaviour may be restrained by the Commission to help a firm's competitors. Such strength does not necessarily imply power over price. The case law has not been helpful in reconciling the two ideas. Richard Whish[6] suggests that the idea of preventing effective competition is merely descriptive and not prescriptive: that the essential idea is the ability to act independently on the market. I hope he proves right.

In *United Brands*, the Commission found[7] and the ECJ confirmed[8] that United Brands was dominant in a market where it was unsuccessfully fighting a price war with its chief competitor and had made losses in four out of the last five years. It had no power to harm those dealing with it, but it did prevent independent dealers buying the bananas at the ports of entry and selling them on.

3   (6/72) [1973] ECR 215, at 257.
4   Paras 33–36.
5   (27/76) [1978] ECR 207, para 65.
6   Richard Whish *Competition Law*, 5th edn (London, Lexis/Nexis-Butterworths, 2003, P) 179.
7   [1976] 1 CMLR D28, para 76.
8   (27/76) [1978] ECR 207, paras 125–29.

Article 82 is as much concerned with buyer power as with selling power. The CFI confirmed that *British Air*[9] was dominant over the acquisition of services from travel agents.

4.3.1 *Market definition*

In *Continental Can*,[10] the ECJ insisted on the Commission analysing a firm's market power in two steps: first, it should define the relevant market and give reasons for its selection. Then it should assess the firm's dominance therein. This has been accepted by Commission and courts.

The relevant market has two dimensions: the product or service and the geographic area affected. Markets do not always have clear limits, and the insistence on definition rather than analysis may be misleading. There may be substitutes that are not perfect, in which case selecting a narrow definition will overstate the market power of a firm supplying a large proportion of the defined product. It may not be able to raise prices above the competitive level without losing too many sales for it to be profitable. A wide definition will usually indicate a smaller market share which understates the firm's market power.

Competition from close substitutes may constrain the firm's conduct closely and in the short term, while that from more remote substitutes only in the longer term when customers have time to adapt to the new product. Both, however, may be expected to affect its conduct. It is important that remoter substitutes should be considered when appraising dominance within the market defined. Market definitions are often arbitrary and should not determine whether the firm has market power but they do focus attention on the factors relevant to appraising market power.

4.3.1.1 *Relevant product market*—The relevant market is defined by substitutes on both the demand and supply side of the market. In *Continental Can v Commission*,[11] the Commission condemned, as an abuse of its dominant position in North West Germany, the acquisition of a potential competitor in the Netherlands in the production of cans for packing meat and fish and of metal closures. The ECJ required the Commission to define the relevant market and give reasons for its definition.

It quashed the Commission's finding that Continental Can was dominant over the supply of cans used for meat and fish products and for metal closures other than crown corks. The Commission had to some extent considered substitutes on the demand side of the market, the possibility for meat and fish suppliers to use plastic and glass containers.

9   T–219/99, [2004] 4 CMLR 1018, (5.2.2 below).
10   (6/72) [1973] ECR 215, paras 32 and 37.
11   *Europemballage Corporation and Continental Can Co. Inc. v Commission* (6/72), [1973] ECR 215.

It had not considered substitutes on the supply side: how easily the makers of cylindrical cans could start making the more complex shapes traditionally used for meat and fish. If it were easy to switch production in this way, Continental Can would have had little discretion. If it were to raise prices significantly above costs (including a normal return on capital), it would pay one of the other can makers to enter a profitable market by making cans for meat and fish. Continental Can would foresee the likelihood of such entry, so would be constrained from initiating the price rise which would not pay except in the very short term. Hence, it would be constrained even in the short term by potential competition.

The ECJ however, did not consider the possibility of a completely new entrant obtaining a technology licence from another can maker, but only of the makers of cylindrical cans making the irregular shaped ones traditionally used for meat and fish, or of a canner starting to make its own cans. The ECJ has since been referring to substitutes on both sides of the market.[12]

Where there are competitive pressures from outside the market as defined, the definition may not be very helpful to an assessment of power over price, but the difficult questions are postponed until a second stage and if there are such pressures the firm accused can bring them to the attention of the competition authority or court to show that it is not dominant even within the narrow market. The bifurcation of the analysis can be avoided under the newer hypothetical monopolist test (4.3.1.1–4.3.1.6 below).

In *Atlantic Container Line and others*[13] the CFI upheld the Commission's finding in *TACA* that the market was container shipping on particular routes. Although shippers did switch from bulk shipping to container, they did not switch the other way, so bulk shipping did not constrain their competitive behaviour.

In *British Plasterboard*,[14] before the development of the hypothetical monopolist test (4.3.1.1 below), the Commission considered the availability of substitutes, not when defining markets, but at the later stage when assessing market power.

Markets have been very narrowly defined, mainly from the demand side. In *United Brands*,[15] the ECJ upheld the Commission's choice of bananas as the relevant market:

22. For the banana to be regarded as forming a market which is sufficiently differentiated from the other fruit markets it must be possible for it to be singled out by special factors distinguishing it from other fruits that it is only to a limited extent interchangeable with them and is only exposed to their competition in a way that is hardly perceptible.

12   *E.g.*, *Michelin I* (322/81) [1983] ECR 3461, para 37.
13   T–191 and 212–214/98, judgment 30 September 2003, paras 790–95.
14   [1990] 4 CMLR 464, para 108, where the Commission said that the possible substitution of wet plaster could be taken into account when considering whether a dominant position exists. Confirmed on appeal (T–65/89) [1993] ECR II–389.
15   (27/76) [1978] ECR 207, para 22.

The ECJ confirmed that oranges were not interchangeable with bananas, and apples only to a limited extent, despite evidence of the easing of banana prices and a reduction in the quantities sold during the seasons for summer fruit and oranges, perhaps because of a finding in a report by the Food and Agriculture Organisation in 1975 that 'the price of oranges in all cases had no significant impact on banana consumption.'

In its decision, the Commission was concerned about the need of the young, the old and the infirm who may have difficulty eating other fruit. The interests of the toothless, however, are sufficiently protected by the inability of the dominant firm to discriminate against them. They rarely do their own shopping and United Brands would lose so much market share from the rest of the population that it would not be worth raising prices to exploit the weak.

Few economists would define a market so narrowly and if the hypothetical monopolist test described below is used, the Commission would not do so these days. Indeed, when considering under Article 90 of the EC treaty whether a tax imposed on bananas by Italy protected Italian soft fruit, the Court held that:

bananas must be regarded as being in partial competition with such fruit.[16]

In its group exemptions, the Commission has taken the view that the relevant product market comprises all those products and/or services which are regarded as interchangeable or substitutable by the consumer, by reason of the products' characteristics, their prices or intended use.[17]

In the cases discussed at 6.2 below under Article 82 in combination with Article 86, a dominant position has been held to follow automatically from an exclusive right conferred by government. This does not apply, however to intellectual property rights such as a patent. They may constitute a barrier to entry but will confer a dominant position only if there are no substitutes.[18] Moreover, an exclusive right may be granted for less than the whole of the relevant market. An exclusive right to run a rail service may compete with car, coach or air. It is not unusual for exclusive rights to generate gas and produce electricity or to transport them to be given to different bodies. It may be argued that neither has a dominant position given the competition from the other.[19] This may not often arise as exclusive rights are often given for an entire market, and markets are defined narrowly under EC law (4.3.1–4.3.1.6).

16   *Commission v Italy* (184/85) [1987] ECR II–2013, para 12.
17   See, *e.g.*, Reg 2790/99 on vertical distribution agreements, Art 9.
18   *Parke, Davis & Co v Probel* (24/67), [1968] ECR 55 and other cases.
19   *Ahmed Saeed Flugreisen and Silver Line Reisebüro GmbH v Zentrale zur Bekämpfung Unlauteren Wettbewerbs eV* (66/86), [1989] ECR 803, paras 39–41 and Jose Luis Buendia Sierra, *Exclusive Rights and State Monopolies under EC Law: Article 86 (former Article 90) of the EC Treaty* (Oxford, OUP, 1999).

More recently, the Commission has expressed the test more abstractly in its notice on the definition of the relevant market.[20] The Commission will consider what would happen if the alleged monopolist were to raise the price of the products affected by 5% or 10% and this were perceived to be a permanent relative change. If so many customers would then switch to other products that the original price rise would be unprofitable, those substitutes would constrain the monopolist's power over price and they should be included in the market.

15. The assessment of demand substitution entails a determination of the range of products which are viewed as substitutes by the consumer. One way of making this determination can be viewed as a speculative experiment, postulating a hypothetical small, lasting change in relative prices and evaluating the likely reactions of customers to that increase. The exercise of market definition focuses on prices for operational and practical purposes, and more precisely on demand substitution arising from small, permanent changes in relative prices. This concept can provide clear indications as to the evidence that is relevant in defining markets.

16. Conceptually, this approach means that, starting from the type of products that the undertakings involved sell and the area in which they sell them, additional products and areas will be included in, or excluded from, the market definition depending on whether competition from these other products and areas affect or restrain sufficiently the pricing of the parties' products in the short term.

17. The question to be answered is whether the parties' customers would switch to readily available substitutes or to suppliers located elsewhere in response to a hypothetical small (in the range 5% to 10%) but permanent relative price increase in the products and areas being considered. If substitution were enough to make the price increase unprofitable because of the resulting loss of sales, additional substitutes and areas are included in the relevant market. This would be done until the set of products and geographical areas is such that small, permanent increases in relative prices would be profitable. The equivalent analysis is applicable in cases concerning the concentration of buying power, where the starting point would then be the supplier and the price test serves to identify the alternative distribution channels or outlets for the supplier's products. . . .

The test, sometimes called 'the hypothetical monopolist test,'[21] was developed by the enforcement agencies in the US[22] and adopted in practice also by the merger task force in the competition department of the Commission. The Commission's notice (paragraph 11) states that it will in the future be used also under Articles 81 and 82. The Commission, however, considers substitutes on the supply side, only if entry would be as fast and effective as substitutes on the demand side (paragraphs 20 and 23). Where supply side substitution entails

20   OJ 1997, C372/5, [1998] 4 CMLR 177, paras 39–41.
21   In the US, it is called the SSNIP test, an acronym for a small but significant non-transitory increase in price.
22   US Department of Justice and Federal Trade Commission Horizontal Merger Guidelines, June 14 1992.

adjusting existing tangible and intangible assets significantly, new investment, strategic decision or delay, it will be considered only at a second stage when appraising dominance within the narrower market.

In *Atlantic Container Line*,[23] the CFI said that:

834. Although potential competition and supply-side substitution are conceptually different issues, . . . those issues overlap in part, as the distinction lies primarily in whether the restriction of competition is immediate or not.

The notice then goes on to describe some of the factors that have been taken into account when defining relevant markets, for instance what happened in response to market shocks when a substitute product ceased to be available for a time or a shortage developed or a new brand was introduced. The Commission is sceptical of market surveys prepared *ad hoc*. These days, however, one can obtain a great deal of objective information from the bar coding techniques now widely used in large retail chains and surveys based on them should be reliable.

The test is flawed when it is applied to Articles 81 or 82 (4.3.1.6 below). The notice does not bind the courts and has not yet been applied by the ECJ or CFI. So the older case law is also relevant. In decisions since the adoption of the notice, the Commission has tended to use the older more concrete test. This is important as the CFI and ECJ allow it a considerable margin of appreciation and are likely to accept the result of its analysis. The Commission's view may be less important if the initial appreciation is made by a national court or competition authority (chapter 7 below).

On occasion, complementary products[24] have been held to be in the same market: for instance, in *Tiercé Ladbroke, v Commission*,[25] the CFI treated the supply of live film of horse races by satellite as part of the market for supplying betting services. This is not consistent with either the Commission's notice or the earlier case law. Admittedly, some complements are treated as a single product, for instance a left and right shoe, since most customer want their shoes to match, but there must be uses of live film of horse races, other than as a supplement to betting shops—for instance television news or sports programmes.

In *American Container Line* (paragraphs 797–800), the CFI confirmed that when there is only minimal demand substitution, it can be ignored in defining the market, because demand substitutes constrain conduct only if the demand is fairly stable.

4.3.1.2 *Relevant geographic market*—The geographic market must be wide enough to include 'a substantial part of the common market,' (4.3.6 below).

---

23   T–191 and 212–214/98, judgment 30 September 2003.
24   Products A and B are complementary when the more of A that is sold, the more of B will be demanded. If less of B will be demanded, the products are substitutes. See Glossary below.
25   (T–504/93) [1997] ECR II–923.

Moreover, it is the abuse of the dominant position only within the common market that infringes Article 82. For some products, economists might say that the relevant market is worldwide, as the sole producer of a substance in the common market would have no monopolistic discretion were the market liable to be swamped by imports.

In the first judgment in *Wood Pulp*,[26] the ECJ treated the relevant market under Article 81 as global. In *Filtrona*,[27] a complainant appealed against the dismissal of its complaint by the Commission which argued that cigarette filters could be sold worldwide and that, consequently, the only buyer in Spain did not enjoy a dominant position over their acquisition. In its decisions on mergers, the Commission often says that the market extends at least to the whole of the EEA, without deciding whether it is global.

In *United Brands*,[28] the ECJ excluded from the relevant market three Member States where tariff preference was given to bananas from their former colonies because the applicants argued that the relevant geographic market 'should comprise only areas where the conditions of competition are homogenous.' Although this phrase has frequently been repeated by the ECJ,[29] competition from areas where the conditions of competition are not homogenous may constrain the conduct of a firm that might otherwise enjoy market power. Paragraph 8 of the Commission's notice also refers to conditions being homogenous. The idea is, however, ignored thereafter. It is hoped that this indicates that the Commission may ignore this factor unless trade from other areas is ineffective.

In *Michelin I*,[30] the Commission fined the Dutch subsidiary of a French company for abusing its dominant position over the supply of tyres for heavy vehicles to dealers in the Netherlands without enquiring whether the dealers' customers could easily have bought Michelin tyres outside that country. If they could have done so, Michelin's Dutch subsidiary, Michelin NV, could not have earned a monopoly profit from dealers without driving them out of business to its own disadvantage.

The ECJ[31] confirmed the Commission's selection of the Netherlands as the relevant market on the ground that the decision was addressed to the Dutch subsidiary, since (i) its activities were concentrated in the Netherlands; (ii) its main competitors also carried on activities there through local subsidiaries; (iii) the alleged abuse related to discounts given to dealers there; and (iv) dealers there obtained their supplies only from suppliers operating there.

---

26   (89, 104, 114, 116–117 and 125–129/85) [1993] ECR 1307, paras 12–13.
27   (T–125/89) [1990] ECR II–393. See also *Bayer/Gist* [1976] 1 CMLR D98, where the Commission looked to world markets (excluding countries then behind the iron curtain for which no statistics were available); and *KEWA* [1976] 2 CMLR D15, where it looked to the whole of Europe.
28   (27/76) February 14, 1978, [1978] ECR 207.
29   *E.g.*, *Michelin I* (322/81) [1983] ECR 3461, para 26.
30   [1982] 1 CMLR 643.
31   (322/81) [1983] ECR 3461, paras 23–28.

The ECJ held that the Commission was right to take the view that the competition facing Michelin NV was mainly on the Dutch market and that was the 'level at which the objective conditions of competition are alike for traders.' It added, however, that this did not exclude the position of the Michelin group and its competitors as a whole and a much wider market being relevant to the existence of a dominant position on the relevant product market.

The Michelin group may have been equally dominant in the areas outside the Netherlands, but this was not established. It may also be objected that it is for the Commission to establish the existence of a dominant position, and I regret that no analysis was made of competitive forces from outside the Netherlands either when defining the relevant market or when finding that Michelin was dominant within it. Earlier, in *Continental Can*,[32] Advocate General Roemer pointed out that metal closures for glass containers came to Germany from as far away as Poole in the UK, and this indicated that the relevant market for closures was far wider than North West Germany.

In *European Night Services v Commission*,[33] the CFI quashed a Commission decision under Article 81(1) for failure to give reasons for its definition of the product market and for its appraisal of the appropriate geographic market. Some chambers of the CFI are inducing the Commission to give better reasons for its decisions. This may improve their quality.

Recently, in *Michelin II*,[34] the Commission has fined the French company in the group for similar rebates without addressing the question whether France was the relevant geographic market. Michelin may have had no incentive to advocate a wider market if it was equally dominant in other Member States and the court has no jurisdiction to consider issues of substance that were not pleaded (1.4.3.2 above).

Where a narrow market is taken as relevant, the firm alleged to be dominant should take the initiative to defend itself and prove that competitive pressures from outside the market defined as relevant are so strong that it is futile to concentrate only on it. As in the case of product markets, it does not greatly matter whether this is done at the stage of defining the relevant market or when the dominant position is being assessed, as long as it is done.

Both ECJ and Commission have, however, selected narrow markets where they fear that a firm granted a special or exclusive right by the government of a Member State controls an essential facility. The port of Genoa, for instance, was considered a substantial part of the common market in view of its importance to trade into and out of Italy.[35] The Commission has been accepting even narrower markets, such as rather less important ports in Denmark.

32   (6/72) [1973] ECR 215, at 259.
33   T–374/94 and others, [1998] ECR II–3141.
34   [2004] 4 CMLR 923.
35   *Merci Convenzionali Porto di Genova v Siderurgica Gabrielli* (C–179/90) [1991] ECR I–5889, para 15.

In some cases, the criteria for defining the market have been based on the nature of the complaint. As there is no complainant in merger investigations, control of concentrations has been based on the future structure of the market. Will the dominant position persist? Consequently, rather broader markets have often been the starting point for the analysis of mergers under the regulation (12.2.6.2 below). The economic expertise of the merger task force is spreading to other parts of the Competition Department and influences the analysis under Article 82.

The Commission's notice applies the same 'hypothetical monopolist' test (4.3.1.1 above) to the definition of the geographic market. If a non-transitory relative price rise of 5–10% would cause so many consumers to buy elsewhere as to make the rise unprofitable, then the geographic market should be extended. The Commission takes into account the continuing process of market integration. As barriers to cross-border trade have been abolished under the internal market programme, many markets have become geographically wider. Many, however, remain national, especially at the retail level.

The relevant geographic market may be wider than the Community, but it is only an abuse within 'a substantial part of the common market' that is forbidden (4.3.6 below).

4.3.1.3 *Previous definitions not binding*—In *Coca-Cola Company and Coca-Cola Enterprises Inc. v Commission*,[36] the CFI held that the Commission could not automatically apply market definitions from earlier decisions under Article 82. Markets may have changed meanwhile, and a fresh analysis should be made each time an infringement is alleged. Moreover a national court is not bound by previous definitions of the Commission relating to the same product (paragraph 85). An actual decision finding an infringement may however serve as a basis for an action for damages by a third party, even when the Commission's decision did not impose a fine.

4.3.1.4 *Time scale*—In *Michelin I*,[37] the ECJ accepted that the Commission should assess the cross elasticities of supply and demand, but it assessed the alleged barriers to entry on a shorter time scale than would usually be used by economists in Europe as well as America. The ECJ observed that it takes time to build or to modify a factory or for customers to assess the quality of a new brand of heavy tyres. So the creation of new capacity could be ignored. Yet Michelin could not have exploited its position for long, if at all, if Goodyear could profitably have built a factory in the Netherlands. The desire to discourage it from doing so would constrain Michelin's conduct meanwhile (1.3.3.2. above).

36   (T–125 & 127/97), [2000] ECR II 1733, para 82.
37   (322/81) [1983] ECR 3461, para 41.

On the shorter time scale, which is used in many decisions of the Commission and judgments of the ECJ, entry barriers are pervasive. They include the need to invest in plant, an established reputation, a good commercial network, access to technology and many other assets of existing firms which do not give them power to maintain high prices for any length of time without the risk, or even the certainty, of losing market share. Unlike the American position, views in Europe have not been firmly and universally based on protecting consumers, and if competitors of the firm alleged to be dominant are to be protected, a wider definition of entry barriers is appropriate at the cost of undermining incentives to investment.

The Commission's notice on market definition does not indicate over what period switching by customers to other products is relevant. The US merger guidelines speak of one or two years. Paragraph 17 of the Commission's notice on market definition refers to a permanent relative price increase. Presumably if so many would switch so fast that the initial price rise would be unprofitable, the additional products should be included in the relevant market.

4.3.1.5 *Wider markets suggested by the ECJ*—In the late 1980s, the ECJ became less willing to confirm a finding of dominance. In *Ahmed Saeed*,[38] it suggested that charter, rail or road transport might be substitutes for scheduled flights for a particular route. In *Alsatel v Novasam*,[39] it suggested that the whole of France might be the relevant geographic market since the licences granted by regional authorities to provide the telephonic installations were valid for the whole country and not merely for a particular region. The ECJ also rejected the Commission's narrow definition of the market as that for the hire of telecommunications equipment. Consumers had the option of buying the equipment from other suppliers, and the ECJ ruled that this was also relevant. Nevertheless, in a merger decision,[40] over a year later, after considerable analysis, the Commission treated cola drinks in Great Britain as the relevant market.

In *AKZO*,[41] the ECJ treated the organic peroxides market as single, although there were very different uses to which the chemicals could be put. This must be right, since producers for one use could sell for another. There would be no cost in switching supply, save that of finding customers in the unfamiliar section of the market.

---

38 (66/86) [1989] ECR 803, para 39.
39 (247/86) [1988] ECR 5987, paras 14 and 15.
40 *Coca Cola/Amalgamated Beverages*, M 794, OJ 1997, L218/15, [1997] CEC 2226, confirmed in *The Coca-Cola Company and Coca-Cola Enterprises Inc v Commission*, (T–125 & 127/97). [2000] ECR II–1733
41 (62/86), [1991] ECR I–3359, para 58.

4.3.1.6 *The fallacy of defining markets to assess market power*—One of the drawbacks of assessing market power by reference to substitutes on the demand and supply sides is that a firm with power over price is likely to have raised prices above the competitive level to the point where, if it raised them a little further, it would lose substantial sales. Consequently, even a firm with considerable market power and charging far more than it would have been able to do had the market been more competitive, will usually face competition from substitutes at the prices it is actually charging. If the market power is already being exploited, the firm will probably be subject to competitive pressures. In America, this is often called the '*Cellophane* fallacy,' because the Supreme Court considered that there were substitutes for cellophane, without considering whether there would have been had its price been competitive.[42]

In theory the test works well enough for mergers where it was developed, because the Commission considers the effect of the additional market power. The fallacy occurs only when the test is extended to Articles 81 and 82. At paragraph 19 of its notice, the Commission says that its starting point is usually the prevailing market price, but that where the existing price has been determined in the absence of sufficient competition, the fact that it may be above the competitive level will be taken into account. This will not be easy, because in the absence of close competitors, it is often impossible to tell what the competitive price would have been. The ECJ and CFI have not addressed this problem.

A practical problem is that it is difficult to assess the extent to which higher prices of product A would cause customers to buy other products or new firms to enter the market for A, especially the latter. Unless there is excess capacity in the market for the substitutes, which I shall call B, the price of B would rise as suppliers of B switched to make A. How many buyers of B would switch to A as the price of B rose? The series of questions about substitutes may be endless.

This is not to suggest that there is a better test that might be used, merely that defining markets is at least partly arbitrary and that market shares cannot always be identified meaningfully. It has been suggested that the hypothetical monopolist or SSNIP test is an unnecessary and misleading element in the search for market power.[43]

4.3.2 *Exclusive rights granted by government*

Where special or exclusive rights are granted by government, national or local, the ECJ has repeatedly held in proceedings under Article 86 in combination with Article 82 that there is no need to establish dominance in

---

42   *Cellophane—US v EI Du Pont de Nemours & Co*, 351 US 377 (1956).
43   David Harbord and Georg Von Graevenitz, 'Market Definition on Oligopolistic and Vertically Related Markets: Some Anomalies,' (2000) 21 *European Competition Law Review*, 151.

view of the exclusive right.[44] Intellectual property rights, however, are treated differently.[45]

Governments will rarely grant exclusive rights over part of a market, as they would not confer much protection to the grantee, so the need for market analysis may not often be important. Nevertheless, it is possible, for instance, that the holder of exclusive rights over electricity is subject to competition from gas.[46]

4.3.3 *Customer dependence*

In 1977, an extension to the concept of dominant position was made by the Commission in two decisions that were subject to appeal. In *ABG*,[47] the Commission decided that during a period of acute shortage after the closure of the Suez canal, when a maximum price for petrol had been imposed by the Dutch government at a level that did not permit suppliers to cover the cost of replacing it, the customers of the oil companies:

> 76. . . . can become completely dependent on them for the supply of scarce products. Thus while the situation continues, the suppliers are placed in a dominant position in respect of their normal customers.

On appeal, Advocate General Warner recommended that this should be rejected by the Court:

> In a temporary emergency of the kind here in question, a trader cannot distribute his scarce supplies regardless of the attitude of his customers. He must have it in mind that, once the emergency is over, they will have memories of the way in which they were treated by him during the period of scarcity. Contractual customers will expect the favourable treatment to which their contracts entitle them, both as a matter of law and as a matter of commercial honour. . . .

He considered that the case was about the allocation of supplies, not about pricing, so did not consider whether a supplier can have market power when he is not allowed to sell at a price that would enable him to cover his replacement costs. The ECJ did not address the question whether BP enjoyed a dominant position.

In *Hugin/Liptons*,[48] the Commission found that Hugin, which supplied 12% of the cash registers in the common market, did not enjoy a dominant position in respect of cash registers. The spare parts for these, however, were

---

44   *E.g., Höfner and Elser v Macrotron* (C–41/90), [1991] ECR I–1979, (6.2 below).
45   *Parke, Davis & Co v Probel* (24/67), [1968] ECR 55 and a long line of cases.
46   For the development of the law under Article 82 in combination with Article 86 and under Article 82 on its own, see José Luis Buendia Sierra, *Exclusive Rights and State Monopolies under EC Law*, (Oxford, OUP, 1999) 5.26–5.35, who suggests that there should be no more than a rebuttable presumption.
47   [1977] 2 CMLR D1, para 76; quashed on appeal: *BP v Commission* (77/77) [1978] ECR 1513, at 1538.
48   [1978] 1 CMLR D19, para 62.

mostly not interchangeable with those of other cash registers. Hugin cash registers could therefore not be maintained, repaired or rebuilt without Hugin parts, and Hugin was found to enjoy a dominant position over such spares throughout the world and, consequently, in the common market. Hugin therefore:

> has a dominant position for the maintenance and repair of Hugin cash registers in relation to companies which need a supply of Hugin spare parts. It follows, therefore, that Hugin AB and Hugin UK hold a dominant position for these products and services in that substantial part of the Common Market consisting of England, Scotland and Wales. Such dominant position extends to the business, such as Liptons carried on, of reconditioning and repairing used Hugin cash registers which also depends upon a supply of Hugin spare parts.

In *Hugin v Commission*,[49] the Commission found that Hugin enjoyed a dominant position in relation to such owners. Hugin was not large, yet was subject to control under Article 82.

Later, in *Hilti v Commission*,[50] the CFI and ECJ confirmed that Hilti was dominant over the supply of nails that were compatible with its power activated tool for affixing them.

The notice on market definition (4.3.1.1 above) which is based on the idea of the constraints on the dominant firm rather than on the power to impede competition does not refer to the concept of customer dependence now that the influence of the ORDO Liberals is waning.

In the United States, the Supreme Court in *Eastman Kodak*[51] held that a firm might have market power over spare parts for the equipment it produced even if it was subject to competitive constraints in the equipment market. Consequently, a refusal to supply parts to independent maintainers amounted to monopolisation contrary to Article 2 of the Sherman Act. There was evidence that when first buying imaging equipment, some customers did not calculate the cost of maintaining it over its useful life. Indeed, Kodak had changed its practice, and those buying the equipment earlier must have expected to obtain the spare parts more cheaply from independent suppliers. The Supreme Court, therefore, referred the case back for further findings of fact.

The Commission remains concerned that intellectual property rights over spare parts that must match the original equipment may enable the holder to prevent third parties from supplying repair and maintenance services. When negotiating Directive 98/71/EC it was impossible to achieve a consensus, and whether design protection should be allowed was left to Member States.

49   (22/78) [1979] ECR 1869, paras 7–10, although the Commission decision was quashed on the ground that Liptons operated only within a radius of 30 miles from London, and the abuse did not affect trade between Member States.
50   (T–30/89) [1991] ECR II–1439, paras 64–77, confirmed (C–53/92P) [1994] ECR I–666.
51   *Eastman Kodak v Image Technical Services, Inc*, 504 US 451 (1992). The precedent has been narrowly applied by the lower courts.

Seven provided a 'repair exception' to such design protection. Four alternative sets of legal rights are now being considered by the Directorate-General for the Internal Market, but no legislation has yet been adopted or proposed.[52]

4.3.4 *Appraisal of dominant position*

In *Continental Can*,[53] the ECJ impliedly accepted the Commission's definition of a dominant position based on the economists' concept of power over price (4.3 above). This has also been accepted in the Commission's recent notice (4.3.1.1 above): a monopolist, unconstrained by competitive pressures, enjoys a discretion in its pricing and other market decisions. The application of competition policy to the conduct of such a firm protects those with whom it deals.

Since *United Brands*,[54] the ECJ has also stressed the concept of economic strength which enables an undertaking to impede effective competition: which enables it to exclude other firms, efficient or otherwise: the power to foreclose (4.3.1.1 above). This may lead to protecting a firm's competitors, whether or not they be as efficient as the dominant firm. The ECJ has not expanded in its judgments on the reasons for its definition of a dominant position, but has concentrated on developing a list of relevant factors.

4.3.4.1 *Factors found relevant by the Commission and courts*—The Commission and ECJ commonly look to barriers to entry as well as to market shares in order to assess the existence of a dominant position in the market as defined. The Commission's notice[55] clearly states that conditions of entry will be analysed when appraising the dominant position in the relevant market. It is not important whether entry barriers are considered at this stage or when defining the relevant market provided that they are taken into account at some stage.

Even if potential competition exists on the supply side, competitors may not be able to enter the market if customers are locked in to an existing product by the costs of switching, lack of information, contractual commitments etc. A brand owner that faces competition in the primary market for the product as a whole, may enjoy a dominant position in the after market—for spare parts, servicing etc. (4.3.3 above).

Not all the difficulties that competitors might face when entering a market are treated by most economists as entry barriers. In some cases (4.3.1.4

---

52   'Impact assessment of possible options to liberalise the aftermarket in spare parts', Final report to DG Internal Market by EPEC. See also *Magill* (5.2.5.2 below).
53   (6/72) [1973] ECR 215.
54   (27/76) [1978] ECR 207.
55   (4.3.1.1 above) paras 20–24. It distinguishes supply substitution which expands the market only if the effects are as immediate and effective as substitution on the demand side from potential competition, which is taken into account only when appraising market power.

above), the Commission and ECJ have treated as entry barriers short-term factors that would not be so treated by economists who are interested in efficiencies and in incentives to investment being in the right place, although paucity of assets may deter smaller firms.

Frequently, the Commission has pointed to the size of investment needed, although this would not exclude other large firms from a profitable market unless the minimum size of an efficient operation is very large in relation to the market or its expected expansion. Only in that case would a potential new entrant be deterred by the expectation that its investment would lead to excess capacity and unprofitable prices.

In *United Brands*,[56] the Commission found that United Brands enjoyed a dominant position over the supply of bananas in six Member States, although the barriers to entry listed by the Commission do not appear to have been high and, before the ECJ, United Brands stated that it had made losses for four out of the last five years.

It sold some 45% of the bananas supplied in Benelux, the Federal Republic of Germany, Denmark and Ireland, more than twice as many as its nearest rival. It had been active in plant research and developed a more prolific and disease-resistant variety of bananas, although others were free to plant or multiply that variety.

It owned plantations in different parts of the tropics, which gave it an advantage in regularity of supply when natural disasters hit a particular part of the growing area. Nevertheless, competitors could also buy or establish plantations in diverse areas and some planters had surplus bananas for sale. United Brands itself produced only half the bananas it sold on the relevant market.

United Brands owned enough refrigerated vessels to ship over half the bananas it sent to Europe through the ports of Rotterdam and Bremerhaven; but there is a charter market for such ships and ownership can be a disadvantage when freight rates slump. It had also arranged for very careful quality control and extensive promotion of the bananas it had packed in the tropics already bearing the Chiquita mark. Chiquita bananas were found by the Commission to fetch some 30–40% more than unbranded ones, and by the ECJ 7% more than rival brands.

The ECJ pointed out that United Brands supplied between 41% and 45% of the market it had defined as relevant, several times as much as that supplied by the next largest banana company.

From the cumulative advantage of all these factors the Commission found, and the ECJ confirmed, that United Brands was dominant, without finding any one of the advantages vital, or considering the possibility of new entrants coming in at one level only, buying bananas and chartering ships, etc. or of existing competitors expanding the scale of their business. United Brands,

---

56   [1976] 1 CMLR D28, paras 76–82; on appeal (27/76) [1978] ECR 207, paras 125–29.

which claimed it had made losses in 4 out of the previous 5 years, seems to have had no power over price (4.3 above), but was found to be dominant.

In *Vitamins*,[57] the ECJ again stressed the importance of market shares:

41. Furthermore although the importance of the market shares may vary from one market to another the view may legitimately be taken that very large shares are in themselves, and save in exceptional circumstances, evidence of the existence of a dominant position.

An undertaking which has a very large market share and holds it for some time, by means of the volume of production and the scale of the supply which it stands for—without those having much smaller market shares being able to meet rapidly the demand from those who would like to break away from the undertaking which has the largest market share—is by virtue of that share in a position of strength which makes it an unavoidable trading partner and which, already because of this secures for it, at the very least during relatively long periods, that freedom of action which is the special feature of a dominant position.

Later in its judgment in *Vitamins*, the ECJ confirmed a finding of dominance solely on the basis of market percentages in the eighties, although it held that further indications were necessary to establish dominance over other kinds of vitamins where the market shares were in the forties. By stressing market shares that endure and barriers to expansion, it is hoped that the ECJ was presupposing barriers to entry, without which market power cannot exist.

In *AKZO*,[58] the ECJ considered that a stable market share of 50% or more raised a rebuttable presumption of dominance, although it added that the Commission was right to consider other factors.

Economists interested in protecting consumers say that, in the absence of entry barriers, even very high market shares do not indicate a dominant position on either definition of a dominant position: freedom from competitive constraints or ability to exclude—efficient production excludes only less efficient firms.

According to the report of the UK Monopolies Commission on *the supply and export of Cigarette Filter Rods*,[59] Cigarette Components Ltd supplied almost all the cigarette filter rods in the UK with the aid of a technology licence from Courtaulds. It remained very profitable for decades. Courtaulds was prepared to grant a royalty-free licence to any of the cigarette makers. These must have considered frequently whether they could make the rods more cheaply, but continued to buy from Cigarette Components.

It seems that the latter was very efficient but enjoyed little market power. Had it increased its prices above the level at which customers thought they could produce, it would have lost its market. The Commission concluded that the monopoly was not contrary to the public interest—potential competition was working.

---

57 *Hoffmann-La Roche & Co. AG v Commission* (85/76) [1979] ECR 461, para 41.
58 (62/86) [1991] ECR I–3359, paras 59–61.
59 23 July 1969, HCP 335.

There is now rather less concern than previously that in a competitive market—and there was considerable evidence of competition in the sale of bananas—a firm with a large market share that is considerably larger than its competitors' may be found to enjoy a dominant position, especially if competition is possible only from large firms or from those operating on a different basis from the existing suppliers.

4.3.4.2 *Factors found relevant in mergers*—The Commission has been concerned whether a merger will create or strengthen a dominant position as a result of which competition will be significantly impeded. So, it is concerned with a longer time frame (12.2.6 below).

There are seldom any complainants, so the Commission does not look to conduct alleged to be abusive: the enquiry is initiated by notification of the event. The appraisal is prospective and focused on market structure.

Nevertheless the concept of a dominant position is used also under Article 82, and consideration of merger cases may be instructive. The Commission's analysis of whether a merger leading to oligopoly is likely to impede competition significantly has been more sophisticated than many of its decisions under Article 82.[60]

In *Airtours*,[61] the CFI quashed the Commission's decision because it had not established that if was possible for the remaining firms to retaliate against a competitor which increased its capacity to reduce prices, nor that competition from smaller firms would not constrain the pricing of the oligopolists. The criteria developed by the Commission are described below (at 12.6–12.6.4).

4.3.4.3 *Conduct*—The Commission also stressed United Brands' behaviour, from which dominance in some part of the area might have been inferred: geographical price discrimination coupled with the restriction on the sale of bananas while still green, from which it seems that monopoly profits may have been earned in some countries in some weeks. Once ripe, bananas cannot be shipped far without being bruised. The Commission interpreted the restriction as restraining export and insulating the high price areas.

In *Atlantic Container Line*,[62] the CFI said that a discriminatory price structure:

> is normally found only in market situations where one or more undertakings has a substantial degree of market power.

---

60   Art 2(4) and (5) of Reg 139/2004, OJ 2004, L24/1. Art 2(4) & (5) are new provisions supposed to clarify that concerns about co-ordination should be taken into account. This is not relevant to Art 82, but the case law before 2004 is.
61   T–342/99, [2002] ECR II–2585, paras 195, 261.
62   (T–191, 212–214/98),30 September 2003, para 904.

Since it is usually impossible to tell whether a firm is earning monopoly profits, however, it is hoped that the level of prices or charges will seldom be used as an indication of a dominant position because of the impossibility of determining to what level of prices competition would have led.

4.3.5 *Collective dominance*

Article 82 refers to an abuse 'by one or more undertakings' of a dominant position. In its decision in *Italian Flat Glass*,[63] the Commission condemned under Article 81 agreements between three firms allocating quotas and fixing prices and also condemned the same firms for abusing a collective dominant position because they presented themselves on the market as a single entity.

On appeal, the CFI[64] accepted that collective dominance might exist when, for instance, two independent undertakings shared a technological lead, perhaps through a technology licence, enabling them to behave to an appreciable extent independently of their competitors. It denied, however, that the Commission could 'recycle the facts' from which it had established an agreement contrary to Article 81(1) to establish abuse of a dominant position. It also observed that, before finding a dominant position, the Commission would have to define the relevant market realistically and establish a lack of imports from outside the geographical area accepted.

The Commission continued to allege joint dominance under the merger regulation or enjoyed, for instance, by the members of a shipping conference.[65] The Council has granted a block exemption to liner shipping conferences, which prevents the Commission from attacking most of their collusion under Article 81(1).[66] So, it has found that various shipping conferences were collectively dominant over the particular routes sailed by its members.[67]

The Commission also wanted to establish its competence over mergers that make a market more concentrated, and which may reduce price competition without leading to a single undertaking being dominant.

In *Gencor/Lonrho*,[68] a merger case, the Commission and CFI analysed the factors that might lead to two companies each supplying about 40% of the market not competing aggressively on price. The Commission described the market as oligopolistic.

> 141. (a) on the demand side, there is moderate growth, inelastic demand and insignificant countervailing power. Buyers are therefore highly vulnerable to a potential abuse,

---

63 [1990] 4 CMLR 535, paras 60 and 79.
64 (T–68, 77 and 78/89) [1992] ECR II–1403, para 358.
65 *E.g., French–West African Shipowners' Committees* [1993] 5 CMLR 446, para 67.
66 Council Reg 479/92, OJ 1992, L55/3.
67 *E.g., Atlantic Container Line*, The Commission first found that there was insufficient competition between the members to prevent collective appraisal, para 741–49.
68 (IV/M.619), [1999] 4 CMLR 1076, confirmed on appeal *Gencor Ltd v Commission* (T–102/96) [1999] ECR II–753.

(b) the supply side is highly concentrated with high market transparency for a homogenous product, mature production technology, high entry barriers (including high sunk costs) and suppliers with financial links and multi-market contacts. These supply side characteristics make it easy for suppliers to engage in parallel behaviour and provide them with incentives to do so, without any countervailing checks from the demand side.

The Commission has also relied in some cases on excess capacity which enables each firm to punish the other if it reduces prices or decreases supply. In relation to a merger, in *Airtours*,[69] (12.2.6.1.3 below) the CFI went further and quashed a Commission finding of collective dominance because the Commission had failed to establish a mechanism for retaliation, and had not adequately considered competition from smaller firms that might expand.

In *CEWAL*,[70] the Commission found that a shipping conference enjoyed a collective dominant position owing to the close economic links between the ship owners who met in the committees of the conference. They acted to a large extent as a single entity.

The CFI concluded on appeal by *Compagnie Maritime Belge*[71] that it is settled law that a dominant position may be collective only when the undertakings are linked in such a way that they adopt the same conduct on the market. Nevertheless, the members of CEWAL intended to act in the same way. So, the Commission had sufficiently shown the existence of a collective dominant position.

The need to establish economic links would make it difficult for the Commission to use the concept of joint dominance where it is most needed—where there are no links of ownership, contract or concerted practices, but each of a very small number of suppliers realises that if it cuts its price, its competitors will have to match the cut rapidly or lose most of their market share and the few suppliers always change prices within a day or two of each other, and always have the same list prices, although they may compete in discounts (2.2.4.1 above).

In *Gencor v Commission*,[72] the CFI expanded the concept of oligopolistic dominance in the context of a merger in two ways by holding 1) that it was not necessary to establish links between the firms in an oligopoly and 2) that oligopolistic inter-dependence amounted to a link that would make it easier to establish joint dominance (paragraphs 273–76). It also spelled out the circumstances that make it more likely that oligopolists will not compete aggressively.

In *Compagnie Maritime Belge*,[73] the ECJ applied the same test to Article 82.

---

69   T–342/99, [2002] ECR II–2585, [2002] 5 CMLR 317, paras 195, 261.
70   [1995] 5 CMLR 198.
71   [1997] 4 CMLR 279, paras 59–68, citing *Almelo* (C–393/92) [1994] ECR I–1477 and other cases that did not establish the proposition.
72   (T–102/96) [1999] ECR II–000.
73   (C–395/96P) [2000] ECR I–1365.

45. The existence of a collective dominant position may therefore flow from the nature and terms of an agreement, from the way in which it is implemented and, consequently, from the links or factors which give rise to a connection between undertakings which result from it. Nevertheless, the existence of an agreement or other [legal links][74] is not indispensable to a finding of a collective dominant position: such a finding may be based on other connecting factors and would depend on an economic assessment and, in particular, on an assessment of the structure of the market in question.

At paragraph 40 it stated that to establish joint dominance, the Commission must find that the undertakings acted as a single entity, that together they enjoyed a dominant position and that it had been abused.

In *France v Commission*,[75] the *Kali und Salz* case, where the merging undertakings had a 60% market share, the ECJ held that the presumption of single firm dominance at 50% established in *AKZO Chemie BV v Commission*[76] did not apply to joint dominance, but in *Atlantic Container Line*,[77] when a shipping conference supplied more than 60% of the market, the CFI rejected this view under Article 82.

In *Irish Sugar*,[78] the CFI held that a subsidiary, SDL, and Irish Sugar, which owned 51% of the shares in SDL, were jointly dominant on the retail sugar market—there was evidence that they adopted a single policy on the market, although, at that time, Irish Sugar did not take SDL's day to day decisions. One might have thought they constituted a single undertaking, but this is not what the CFI held. Joint dominance was confirmed by the CFI and the ECJ. The CFI also held that Irish Sugar was singly dominant, so its conclusions on joint dominance were not necessary to its judgment and the question arises whether they would be followed in the absence of common control.[79]

Irish Sugar and SDL operated in vertically related markets and were held to be jointly dominant—a new concept that was not discussed. The vertical relationship does not increase market shares directly, although it makes it easier to discriminate.

For the reasons given (at 2.2.4.2 above) it is important that parallel pricing should not be treated as abusive, but mergers of competitors with a large share of the same market should be subject to control.

It is sensible policy to apply Article 82 when each of two large firms in a concentrated market takes action to deter new entrants (5.2 below) or adopts facilitating devices that make it easier to ensure that competitors follow a

---

74   The court's version in English is links in law, but this is ambiguous. The French version reads 'liens juridique.'
75   (C–68/94 and 30/95) [1998] ECR I–1375, para 226.
76   (62/86), [1991] ECR I–3359, paras 59–61.
77   T–191 & 212–214/88, September 30 2003, para 907.
78   T–228/97, [1999] ECR II 2969, appeal C497/99R, [2001] ECR I–5332.
79   See note 57 above.

price rise when they lead to oligopolistic inter-dependence. Facilitating devices include promising many customers most favoured customer treatment, which makes it more difficult to grant secret discounts that might break down oligopolistic interdependence; or announcing price rises months in advance, which reduces the risk of announcing an initial price rise. Standardisation of the products supplied also makes it easier to monitor each other's conduct.

4.3.6 'Substantial part of the common market'

Article 82 prohibits an abuse of a dominant position within a substantial part of the common market. Even if dominance is established in a global market, abuse only within the common market is forbidden. It is not entirely clear how large an area, or what proportion of the supply amounts to 'a substantial part of the common market.' In *Suiker Unie*,[80] the ECJ stated that:

> 371. . . . . the pattern and volume of the production and consumption of the said product as well as the habits and economic opportunities of vendors and purchasers must be considered.

This is not a precise test. Precedents relating to different products will not be of much assistance. In his opinion in *BP v Commission*,[81] Advocate General Warner treated the qualification as a *de minimis* rule. He concluded that the fact that BP's customers in the Netherlands took less than 5% of the motor spirit supplied in the common market did not prevent them from amounting to a substantial part of the common market.

He seemed to assume that the limitation need not be purely geographic, provided that there is some other factor dividing customer. Yet, in *Pigs and Bacon Commission v McCarren*,[82] he said that a particular current of trade, such as the export of Irish bacon to Great Britain, did not constitute a 'part of the common market.'

In *La Crespelle*,[83] the ECJ held that where insemination centres required governmental authorisation throughout France, and were each granted an exclusive licence for a small area, the national provisions created a dominant position in a substantial part of the common market.

In *Merci v Gabrielli*,[84] the ECJ ruled that the port of Genoa was a 'substantial part of the common market' because of the important trade between Italy and the rest of the Community passing through that port. The Commission has treated as dominant in 'a substantial part of the common

---

80   (40/73 and others) [1975] ECR 1663, para 371.
81   (77/77) [1978] ECR 1513, at 1537.
82   (177/78) [1979] ECR 2161, at 2216.
83   *Société Civile Agricole du Centre d'Insémination de la Crespelle v Coopérative d'Elevage et d'Insémination Artificielle du Département de la Mayenne* (323/93) [1994] ECR I–5077, para 17.
84   *Merci Convenzionali Porto di Genova v Siderurgica Gabrielli* (C–179/90), [1991] ECR I–5889.

market' the operators of far less important ports that controlled particular shipping routes such as the operator of the port of Holyhead[85] and required them not to discriminate in favour of their own shipping organisation.

4.3.7 *Abuse in linked market*

In *Tetra Pak II*,[86] the Commission condemned an abuse in a market over which Tetra Pak was not found to be dominant when the market was linked to one over which it was found to be dominant. Tetra Pak was found to be dominant over the supply of cartons for keeping milk and fruit juice fresh for 6 months and over the machinery for filling them—the aseptic sector. It also supplied some 55% of the cartons for pasteurised milk and fruit juice and machinery for filling them—the non aseptic sector—but was not found to be dominant over it, although in *AKZO* the ECJ held that there is a rebuttable presumption of dominance at 50%.

The ECJ confirmed[87] that there were four separate markets: for aseptic cartons and equipment and for non-aseptic cartons and equipment. The CFI had correctly found that they were not substitutes for each other. The CFI had confirmed that Tetra Pak was dominant over the aseptic sector, and had a very strong position in the non-aseptic sector strengthened by associative links between the two. The ECJ upheld the fine imposed largely for abuses in the non-aseptic sector.

At paragraphs 24–33 the ECJ added:

> 27. It is true that application of Article 82 presupposes a link between the dominant position and the alleged abusive conduct,[88] which is normally not present where conduct on a market distinct from the dominated market produces effects on that distinct market. In the case of distinct, but associated, markets, as in the present case, application of Article 82 to conduct found on the associated, non-dominated market and having effects on that associated market can only be justified by special circumstances.

The ECJ went on to indicate that Tetra Pak was the leading firm in the non-aseptic markets and concluded that 'the relevance of the associative links which the CFI thus took into account cannot be denied.' The alleged links were that dairies needed equipment and cartons for both markets and 35% of Tetra Pak's customers bought both systems. It is important to note, however, that the ECJ confirmed the judgment of the CFI only on the basis of cumulative factors. Where there is less market power in the linked market, it is hoped that the result would be different.

---

85   *Sea Link/- & I Holyhead*, interim measures, [1992] 5 CMLR 255, para 40.
86   OJ 1991, L72/1, [1992] 4 CMLR 551, On appeal, *Tetra Pak Rausing SA v Commission (No 2)* (T–83/91), [1994] ECR II–755 (CFI). *Tetra Pak International SA v EC Commission* (C–333/94P), [1996] ECR I–5951 (ECJ).
87   Paras 7–20.
88   This was denied by the ECJ in *Continental Can* (6/72), [1973] ECR 215, para 27.

It is difficult to see how the alleged link increased the market power of Tetra Pak in either market. In the same month as the decision, in *Tetra Pak/Alfa Laval*,[89] the Commission cleared a merger although each firm supplied the dairies and each was dominant over supplies of certain kinds of equipment. The Commission obtained evidence from the dairies that they had no propensity to buy from a single source. So it concluded that dominance in neither market would be strengthened by the merger.

In *Tetra Pak II* the ECJ extended the earlier case law. There was no earlier judgment condemning the abuse in a linked market not vertically related to that dominated, although a refusal to supply a raw material or component may affect competition downstream. In that event a firm supplying raw materials may be dominant also over the final product, if there are no substitutes for making the input.[90]

4.3.8 *Special responsibility of dominant firms not to abuse*

It is frequently said that it is not illegal to enjoy a dominant position, but since *Michelin I*,[91] the ECJ has repeatedly said that a firm in a dominant position 'has a special responsibility not to allow its conduct to impair undistorted competition on the common market.' There are many things that a dominant firm may not do to compete aggressively. Often, there is tension between the protection of consumers and of competitors, although the ECJ has recently stated several times that Article 82 is intended to protect consumers rather than particular competitors.

Now that the ECJ has confirmed that several firms may enjoy a collective dominant position where each is in a position to retaliate if the others supply more than expected, firms with market shares in the range between 20 and 30% may be found to be jointly dominant. It is hoped that far more discretion will be left to such firms than to those found to be singly dominant with a higher market share. It is important that competition by dominant firms should not be chilled by fear of fines for infringing Article 82. Indeed, I would like to see Article 82 applied to such firms only in relation to devices facilitating tacit collusion. It is too soon after the cases considered at 4.3.5 above to be able to advise on this.

4.3.9 *Super-dominant position*

It may be that when a firm is super-dominant—when it has a very strong position in the market—it may be subject to an even greater responsibility to help its competitors. In *Compagnie Maritime Belge Transports SA v Commission*,[92]

89   (IV/M 068) OJ 1991, L290/35, [1992] 4 CMLR M81 para 30–34.
90   *Commercial Solvents* (6 & 7/73), [1974] ECR 223.
91   (322/81), [1983] ECR 3461, [1985] 1 CMLR 282, para 57.
92   (C–395/96P), [2000] ECR I–1365, paras 132 and 137. The concept of super-dominance was invoked by the UK Competition Commission Appeal Tribunal in *Napp Pharmaceutical Holdings Limited Subsidiairies v Director General of Fair Trading*, 15 January 2002.

Advocate General Fennelly said that different considerations may apply when an undertaking enjoys a position of dominance approaching a monopoly. In confirming that selective price cutting not found to be below cost but intended to drive out their only competitor amounted to an abuse, the ECJ (paragraph 119), observed that the dominant conference supplied over 90% of the market when the abuse started. In *Tetra Pak II*,[93] the ECJ stated that the CFI was correct in stating at paragraph 115 that the scope of the special responsibility imposed on a dominant undertaking must be considered in the light of the specific circumstances of each case which show a weakened competitive situation (5.2.3.10 below).

4.3.10 *Conclusion*

On the basis of these precedents, it is not easy to advise a client what the relevant market may be. The Commission has considerable discretion in selecting it. It is arguable that this does not matter since the key question is the extent of the competitive pressures on the firm. Provided that pressures from outside the market selected as relevant are taken into account at some stage, few firms that do not have power over price will be found dominant. Unfortunately, this final step is not always taken by the Commission or courts.

In *Italian Flat Glass*,[94] the CFI insisted on the Commission establishing that Italy was the relevant market, given a considerable quantity of imports from France. In *European Night Services* it quashed a decision under Article 81(1), *inter alia*, for not giving sufficient reasons for its definition of the market. When national courts and competition authorities take a larger part in controlling the abuse of a dominant position (7.3–7.3.4 below) will the CFI and ECJ allow as much discretion as they have accorded the Commission?

A greater cause for concern than the uncertainty implicit in applying such a fluid criterion as dominance is the short time scale over which the ECJ and Commission have considered barriers to entry. If, as the ECJ stated in *Michelin*,[95] it takes too long to build a new plant for new entry to be relevant to the definition of the market, firms that have substantial market shares but are subjected to intense competitive pressures may be held to be dominant and substantially constrained by Article 82 in their market behaviour while their competitors are not.

Even in *Continental Can*,[96] the ECJ treated as within the relevant market only firms that could start making the relevant kinds of cans with only a slight adaptation of their business. The Commission and, perhaps, the ECJ are concerned about the effects of market power during the period before the harsh treatment of customers or suppliers induces entry.

93 (C–333/94P), [1996] ECR I–5951, para 24.
94 (T–68, 77 & 78/89) [1992] ECR II–1403, paras 161–65 and 364–65.
95 (322/81) [1983] ECR 3461, para 41, (4.3.1.4 above).
96 (6/72), [1973] ECR 215.

A major theoretical uncertainty is the status of the notice on the relevant market (4.3.1.1 above). It is based on the concept of a firm that is not subject to competitive constraints on its conduct and which can make high profits from suppliers and customers. This derives from *Continental Can*, from the experience of the merger task force and from the economic advice it has received. Most of the cases after *Continental Can* mention the idea of an ability to impede competition without much explanation. Unless the phrase is merely descriptive, it may protect competitors and not only those dealing with the dominant firm.

Under the merger regulation, the Commission is looking concretely to see which firms might enter if the merged firms were to increase prices. In *Alcatel/Telettra*,[97] although the combined market share of the two firms for transmission equipment in Spain was 81% and for microwave equipment 83%, the Commission concluded that the market was contestable.

It observed that Telefonica, the only customer in Spain, where the Commission found the merged firm would become dominant, had a policy of buying from more than one source and had said that it would be prepared to buy abroad. The Commission indicated specific firms that might well compete. Consequently, it decided that the merger was not likely to create a dominant position as a result of which effective competition would be significantly impeded. This is in marked contrast to most of the Commission's decisions under Article 82. Had the Commission used the 'hypothetical monopolist' test to define the relevant geographic market, however, a world market might have been considered and the market shares would have been far lower.

Under Article 86 (6.2 below) the ECJ has assumed a dominant position from the fact that a firm is granted an exclusive right by state measures, without examining whether there was competition from other products. An exclusive producer or transporter of electricity might, for instance, be subject to pressures from a free market in oil or natural gas. This has not been considered. Where the exclusive right amounts to intellectual property, however, the ECJ has often ruled that it does not necessarily confer a dominant position—that depends on the existence of substitutes.[98]

When he was the Director General of Competition at the Commission, Dr Ehlermann took steps to help the greater economic content of the merger decisions spread to other directorates. This policy is being extended these days. Officials who have worked for the merger task force are joining the policy directorate of the Competition Department as well as the directorates dealing with current cases. The merger task force has been disbanded, and its officials moved to the other operating directorates. Their influence may be reinforced by collaboration with American antitrust officials in cases that give rise to problems in both jurisdictions. The current Commissioner and

---

97   IV/M 042, [1991] 4 CMLR 778, at paras 37–49.
98   *Parke, Davis v Probel* (24/67), [1968] ECR 55, 72, and many later judgments.

Director General are both trying to focus the attention of their secretariat on economics. An International Competition Network has been established more widely between competition authorities and may prove influential. Publications and meetings of the OECD with considerable economic contributions have also been influential.

4.4 Bibliography

Charles Baden Fuller, 'Article 86 EEC: Economic Analysis of the Existence of a Dominant Position' [1979] 4 *EL Rev* 423.

Maureen Brunt, *Economic Essays on Australian and New Zealand Competition Law*, (The Hague, Kluwer Competition Law Monographs, 2003).

Franklin M Fisher, 'Monopolization v Abuse of Dominant Position: An Economist's View, (2004) 2003, *Fordham Corporate Law Institute*.

Enrique Gonzalez-Diaz, 'Recent development in EC Merger Control Law—The *Gencor* judgment,' (1999) 22 *World Competition Law and Economics Journal* 3.

Thomas E Kauper, 'The problem of Market Definition under EC Competition Law,' [1996] *Fordham Corporate Law Institute*, 239 and the following papers by Cornelis Canenbley, 307, and panel discussion at 315.

Valentine Korah, 'Concept of a Dominant Position within the Meaning of Article 86' (1980) 17 *CML Rev* 395.

——, 'Compagnie Maritime Belge, II' in *Liber Amicorum Michel Waelbroeck*, (Brussels, Bruylant, 1999) 1101.

——, 'Gencor v Commission' case note [1999] *European Competition Law Review*, 337.

John Tillotson and Angus MacCulloch, 'EC Competition Rules, Collective Dominance and Maritime Transport,' (1997) 21 *World Competition Law and Economics Review*, 51.

5. Abusive exploitation

5.1 Introduction

Article 82 gives four examples of 'abusive exploitation,' which seem to refer to using the dominant position to harm directly those who have to deal with the dominant firm:

(a) directly or indirectly imposing unfair purchase or selling prices or other unfair trading conditions;
(b) limiting production, markets or technical development to the prejudice of consumers;
(c) applying dissimilar conditions to equivalent transactions with other trading parties, thereby placing them at a competitive disadvantage;
(d) making the conclusion of contracts subject to acceptance by the other parties of supplementary obligations which, by their nature or according to commercial usage, have no connection with the subject of such contracts.

The list of examples seems to refer to exploitative abuses—holding to ransom those with whom the dominant firm deals, rather than monopolisation—excluding competitors. Head (a) refers to charging customers too much, paying too little, or imposing other inequitable terms. Head (b) seems to be the other side of the same coin—limiting production or markets, which will enable the dominant firm to impose unfair terms. Either would make it easier for new firms to enter the market.

Head (c) seems to reflect an objection to unfair terms—it refers to discrimination that harms the disfavoured customers or suppliers down- or upstream rather than to discrimination that enables the dominant firm to exclude a competitor.

Head (d), however is ambivalent—it refers to tying which some people think enables a dominant firm to extend its dominance from the tying product to that in the tied market—but it is also harsh on buyers who may not want to buy the tied product from that firm.

The case law, however, has extended the prohibition from one forbidding unfair terms of dealing to one forbidding conduct that makes it more difficult for other firms to compete with the dominant firm, which may indirectly harm those dealing with the dominant firm. Conduct by a dominant firm of the kind exemplified in Article 82 is forbidden generally.

Article 82 is not expressed to prohibit the existence or acquisition of a dominant position, but only its abusive exploitation. The authentic English text of the Treaty uses the single word 'abuse,' but most of the other languages use the double concept of 'abusive exploitation,' which might be thought to forbid harsh treatment of those with whom the dominant firm deals. Since the ECJ's judgment in *Continental Can*,[1] however, it has become

---

1   (6/72) [1973] ECR 215.

clear that conduct by a dominant firm that reduces such competition as remains in the market is also treated as abusive.

In the judgments given since *United Brands*[2] and concerned with attempts by a firm found to be dominant to increase market share or extend its power to another market, such as *Vitamins*,[3] the ECJ said:

> 91. . . . . The concept of abuse is an objective concept relating to the behaviour of an undertaking in a dominant position which is such as to influence the structure of a market where, as a result of the very presence of the undertaking in question, the degree of competition is weakened and which, through recourse to methods different from those which condition normal competition in products or services based on the basis of commercial operators[4] has the effect of hindering the maintenance of the degree of competition still existing on the market or the growth of that competition.

The sentence quoted is difficult to understand. Yet, unless some meaning can be extracted, we are left only with a list of practices that have already been held to be abusive or otherwise, and no means of advising what further practices may also be condemned or approved.

John Kallaugher[5] traced the sentence quoted, through the idea of undistorted competition referred to in Article 3(1)(g), to theories of workable competition current from the 1930s to the 1950s, according to which the structure of the market affects the conduct of firms, which in turn affects their performance. It has since been recognised that in fact each of these aspects may affect the other two.

Kallaugher analyses the passage quoted to establish that the concept of abuse is objective as opposed to subjective. It does not depend on the ill will of the dominant firm, or even on an intention to foreclose. The conduct must be likely to influence the structure of the market through recourse to methods different from those that condition normal competition on the basis of performance. Only anti-competitive foreclosure is forbidden and this requires a market analysis.

The concept of competition based on performance is familiar in German law. In the law of unfair competition it is used to describe the kind of conduct that is expressly permitted, even if it harms competitors. It has also been applied under section 22 of the German Competition Act as a criterion for assessing the abuse of a dominant position. The classic forms of competition on the basis of performance include price competition (if not predatory);

---

2   (27/76) [1978] ECR 207.

3   (85/76) [1979] ECR 461, para 91.

4   This is a poor translation of the German authentic text which speaks of 'competition on the basis of performance.' In *AKZO* (62/86) [1991] ECR I–3359, para 70, in the French version, the Court used the term 'competition on the merits.'

5   At a talk organised by ESC some 20 years ago. More recently, see John Kallaugher and Brian Sher, 'Discounts as Exclusionary Abuse under Article 82' [2004] *European Competition Law Review*, 263.

improvement in quality, R & D, in services to customers and even advertising. However much such competition may exclude competitors, it is lawful.

Competition on the basis of performance is not identical with the US concept of economic efficiency; nor does it include such 'normal' conduct as mergers and acquisitions, exclusive dealing agreements or loyalty discounts, which are not necessarily illegal under US law.

Kallaugher rejected the relevance of proportionality, which has been advocated by some authors and judgments,[6] as the main criterion for abuse. However much competition on the basis of performance excludes others, it is permitted. Where foreclosing conduct is justified, proportionality may have a role to play,[7] but the role is subsidiary.

In cases dealing with predation and discrimination, the ECJ in the mid-90s seems to have taken less care to permit dominant firms to compete on the merits. In *Compagnie Maritime Belge*,[8] the CFI and ECJ confirmed the prohibition of fighting ships, without requiring the Commission either to establish that the charges were below cost or to develop any theory in relation to charges above cost (5.2.6.5 below). In *Tetra Pak II*,[9] the ECJ confirmed a finding of predation without requiring the Commission to establish that the dominant firm could recoup the lost income by raising prices in the future. Nor did it say why there was no need for the Commission to establish a possibility for recoupment, the only matter relating to predation that economists are agreed is relevant.

Luc Gyselen,[10] then a senior Commission official writing in his personal capacity 20 years after Kallaugher, advocates a two step approach in the exclusionary pricing cases. He does not define foreclosure, but at paragraph 11 states that:

> The first question [is] what degree of foreclosure the Commission must demonstrate to justify its intervention. The second question is what type of efficiencies the dominant firm can invoke as an objective justification for whatever foreclosure its pricing practices may create.

This implies that the person alleging abuse must establish actual or probable effects. For instance do pricing schemes operated by dominant firms influence

---

6 Some of these are cited and followed in the opinion of Judge Kirchner, acting as AG, in *Tetra Pak I* (T–51/89) [1990] ECR II–309, from para 69. The CFI did not address the question. See also *Hilti*, (C–53/92P), [1994] ECR I–666, where the safety justification was dismissed because safety could have been achieved by less restrictive means, such as warning customers of the dangers.

7 *United Brands*, considered at 5.2.4.3 below. It also has a role to play in relation to tying (5.1.3 below).

8 (T–24, 26 & 28/93) [1997] 4 CMLR 279, confirmed by ECJ, (C–395/96P) [2000] ECR I–1365.

9 (C–333/94P) [1994] ECR II–755 (5.2.6.3 below).

10 'Rebates, Competition on the Merits or Exclusionary practice?' forthcoming in Ehlermann and Atanasiu (eds) *[2003] European Competition Law Annual*, (Oxford, Hart Publishing, 2004).

the switching costs or artificially raise the barriers to entry for the dominant company's competitors? There is concern, however, that the Commission and CFI now treat a scheme that in theory might discourage rivals as abusive, without showing that it does actually foreclose them or is very likely to do so (5.2.2.1 below). The burden of proof of appreciable foreclosure should be on the person alleging abuse, but justification is for the dominant firm, which has to show that it is proportionate to the foreclosure (7.1 below).

The differing objectives of Article 82, freedom for potential competitors to enter a market, and efficiency for the benefit of consumers, have given rise to tensions and there is a widespread movement to attempt to persuade the Commission to clarify its policy. The senior official in DG Competition, Mr Philip Lowe, has announced that the Commission has launched an enquiry into the appropriate policy under Article 82,[11] On May 10 2004 he devoted a whole keynote speech at the annual conference of the BIICL to emphasising that the function of competition policy was to protect consumers and the role that consumers should play in enforcing the competition rules.

Many of the cases since *United Brands* have been concerned with steps taken by monopolists to increase their market share. The unfair abuses considered at 5.3–5.3.4 below are less likely to affect the structure of the market unfavourably, and in these cases[12] the ECJ has not used the kind of definition of abuse that I have quoted from *Michelin I* at 4.3.8 above, 'a special responsibility not to allow its conduct to impair undistorted competition on the common market.' High prices may attract new entry to the market and improve its structure. The requirement that structure be affected may apply only to exclusionary practices.

5.2 Reduction of competition prohibited by Article 82

The ECJ in *Continental Can v Commission*[13] construed Article 82 as prohibiting conduct by a dominant firm that substantially reduces competition. Continental Can held 85% of the shares in Schmalbach, a company found to enjoy a dominant position in North West Germany over the supply of cans for meat and fish products and of metal closures for glass containers other than crown corks. It caused another of its subsidiaries to make a bid for all the shares of Thomassen, a company that made a large proportion of all such cans and nearly half the metal closures in the Netherlands. The Commission condemned this as eliminating potential competition in respect of these products.

---

11   [2003] Fordham Corporate Law Institute, (2004) chapter 10.
12   *E.g.,*in *Ahmed Saeed* (66/86) [1989] ECR 803, at paras 42–46, the Court refers to unfair prices, which may be excessively high or excessively low. In *Bodson v Pompes Funèbres* (30/87) [1988] ECR 2479, paras 30–35, and *Lucazeau v SACEM* (110/88) [1989] ECR 2811, paras 21 *et seq.*, the Court considered only *indicia* as to whether prices were excessive. It did not give a basic definition of 'abuse' in these preliminary rulings.
13   (6/72) [1973] ECR 215.

The Community Court quashed the decision on its facts, since the Commission had not established its findings that the makers of other kinds of can could not easily start making fish and meat cans, nor had it given reasons for excluding crown corks from the market in metal closures. Nevertheless, in the light of the basic Articles of the Treaty—2 and 3(1)(g)—it concluded that, in principle, conduct that substantially reduces competition is prohibited by Article 82:

> 26. . . . the provision is not only aimed at practices which may cause damage to consumers directly, but also at those which are detrimental to them through their impact on an effective competition structure, such as is mentioned in Article 3(1)(g) of the Treaty. Abuse may therefore occur if an undertaking in a dominant position strengthens such position in such a way that the degree of dominance reached substantially fetters competition, i.e. that only undertakings remain in the market whose behaviour depends on the dominant one.

Although the Commission's decision was quashed on the facts, the ECJ clearly interpreted Article 82 to prohibit anti-competitive conduct by a firm that already enjoys a dominant position in the common market. In this case, the merger reduced the number of existing competitors, but the ECJ's reasoning has been applied to other practices thought to bar the entry or expansion of other firms such as loyalty rebates given to its largest customers by a dominant firm (5.2.2.1 below). The ECJ stated in *Michelin I* that a dominant firm bears 'a special responsibility not to allow its conduct to impair genuine undistorted competition on the common market.'[14] The ECJ has held that Article 82 forbids conduct by a dominant firm that excludes competitors otherwise than by competition on the merits.

Continental Can argued that it had not used its dominant position to harm the shareholders in Thomason whose shares it bought, but the ECJ (paragraph 27) held that a link of causality was not relevant. It is illegal for a dominant firm to strengthen its position even if it does not use its market power to do so. This widens the prohibition of Article 82 substantially.

In *Continental Can*, the ECJ stated that conduct leading to a substantial reduction of competition might infringe Article 82. In *Vitamins* (5.2.2.1 below), however, the amount of foreclosure for some vitamins was small. Hoffmann-La Roche granted loyalty rebates to only 22 of its largest customers and, for some vitamins, I am told that less than 2% of the market was foreclosed—not enough for the agreement to infringe Article 81(1). At paragraph 123, however, the ECJ ruled that:

> since the course of conduct under consideration is that of an undertaking occupying a dominant position on a market where for this reason the structure of competition has already been weakened, within the field of application of Article 82 any further weakening of the structure of competition may constitute an abuse of a dominant position.

14   *Michelin v Commission* (322/81), [1983] ECR 3461, para 57.

Consequently, even a small reduction of competition may infringe Article 82.

In *Tetra Pak II*,[15] the Commission went further and alleged that conduct in a non-dominated market which restricted competition in that market also amounted to the abuse of a dominant position held in another associated market (4.3.7 above). Some of the abuses found by the Commission were predatory pricing and tying in the non-aseptic markets and Tetra Pak argued that these could not amount to the abuse of a dominant position in the aseptic markets.

Since the confirmation by both courts in Luxembourg of the possibility of collective dominance (4.3.5 above) firms with little market power may be found to be dominant when each is in a position to retaliate if one of its competitors takes steps to increase its market share. It is hoped that the ECJ will rein back the application of Article 82 to the conduct of firms with small market shares.

From 5.2 I shall consider abuses thought to reduce competition first, then from 5.3 abuses that are unfair to those dealing with the dominant firm, and at 5.3.4.1 discrimination on the basis of nationality or residence and other abuses that interfere with market integration.

5.2.1 *Control of mergers*

Although the judgment in Continental Can gave the Commission power under Article 82 to control acquisitions by firms already dominant when these substantially reduced competition, it has not since exercised that power in any formal decisions. A few important mergers were restrained over the decade following Continental Can by threat of intervention.

At the end of 1989, the Council finally adopted a regulation requiring pre-notification of mergers and concentrative joint ventures between firms with very large turnover, enabling the Commission to prohibit those that create or strengthen a dominant position as a result of which competition is significantly impeded (12.2 below).

5.2.2 *Discrimination*

Article 82 expressly lists as a possible abuse:

> (c) applying dissimilar conditions to equivalent transactions with other trading parties, thereby placing them at a competitive disadvantage;

It does not include the kind of discrimination that would enable a dominant firm to extend its market power, such as favouring the customers of rivals.

---

15   [1992] 4 CMLR 551, On appeal, *Tetra Pak Rausing SA v Commission (No. 2)* (T–83/91), [1994] ECR II–755 (CFI). *Tetra Pak International SA v EC Commission* (C–333/94P), [1996] ECR I–5951 (ECJ).

Nevertheless, since *Continental Can*, it has been clear that the list in Article 82 is not exhaustive and prohibits exclusionary conduct.

To an economist, it is discriminatory to treat firms equally, when it is less costly to deal with one than the other, as well as to treat firms unequally when the costs of supply are identical. Differential profit margins earned from different classes of client are discriminatory.

They also believe that discrimination is not always undesirable. When a firm needs to incur heavy overhead expenses that have no other use, it will not enter the market unless it expects to recover these from someone. Consequently, sales at prices exceeding average variable cost must be allowed, even if some customers are charged more than others to cover the overheads. Where higher prices are obtainable in one market than in another, it is desirable that sales that do not reflect the full overhead cost should be made (5.2.2.4 below).

Often, everyone is better off as the result of discrimination. Buyers in the low price market get the product at a price they are willing to pay, and they may make some contribution to the overhead, making the practice desirable even to those customers who are charged more. The practice is called 'Ramsey pricing' (5.2.2 below).[16] Neither the Court nor the Commission has accepted this justification in a formal judgment or decision.

Various discriminatory practices may infringe Article 82. The imposition by a dominant firm on its customers of exclusive purchasing obligations may make it harder for rivals to compete. So may a price squeeze (5.2.2.2), although this might be better treated as a constructive refusal to supply (5.2.4–5.2.5.4 below). Sometimes a dominant firm may discriminate as between Member States and firms granted special or exclusive rights by governments may seek to ensure that national companies, or undertakings that used to be nationalised but are now in the private sector receive more favourable treatment than others. The institutions also look to an intention to exclude, although abuse is said to be an objective concept.

5.2.2.1 *Single branding to exclude competitors of the dominant firm*—The extreme example of single branding is agreeing to obtain a product only from a single supplier or to handle only a single brand, but attenuated versions include fidelity rebates offered or given to customers who take a large proportion of their requirements from the dominant firm or agree to do so and other foreclosing practices.

In several cases, the ECJ has confirmed the condemnation of discount systems which the court considered made competition by smaller competitors more difficult. These have been considered discriminatory and, when *ad hoc*, unfair (5.3.3 below) or, when systematic, anti-competitive. At this point, only

---

16   FP Ramsey,'A Contribution to the Theory of Taxation,' (1929) 37 *Economic Journal* 47–61.

the second objection will be considered. An agreement to buy a large proportion of its requirements from a designated source may also infringe Article 81(1), but only in a narrow range of circumstances (2.4.3 and 9.6.5 below).

Single branding may foreclose smaller competitors of the dominant firm and make it harder for them to compete on the merits. A buyer expecting or entitled to an extra 1% discount on all its purchases if it buys, say, 70% of its requirements from the dominant firm will require a very much lower price before it buys more than 30% from other firms. It will lose the 1% not merely on the extra amount bought elsewhere, but also on the amount that is actually bought from the dominant firm.

Where a buyer is dependent on the dominant firm for a substantial part of the range of products it needs or where some of its customers favour the dominant firm's brands, it will have to buy part from the dominant firm. Loyalty discounts may lead to other suppliers being foreclosed not only from those parts of the demand which can be supplied only by the dominant firm, but also from the other products beyond 30%.

Progressive rebates, such as an extra 1% on total purchases during the year for every 100 tons bought, may have a similar foreclosing effect. The dominant firm's customer is unlikely to buy elsewhere until he is sure that he will attain the maximum discount bracket or has no hope of attaining the next one.

Various other provisions have been treated as abusive, such as 'top slicing:' a discount for quantities ordered beyond what the customer was expected to order anyway.[17] At the beginning of the period over which the rebate is earned, the customer of the dominant firm may not know whether it will achieve its target, and may, therefore, feel compelled to buy more than the agreed part of its requirements from it.

Discounts that reflect the savings to the dominant firm of delivering a container or barge full may also exclude competitors, but may be justified: they encourage customers to organise their business so as to enable the supplier to adopt low cost methods of delivery. Other kinds of cost savings, however, are less easy to quantify and, consequently, to justify.

The concern about foreclosing others reflects the desire in the ECJ to protect the interests of traders wanting to enter a market as well as competition between suppliers in the interest of consumers. There is considerable tension between these objectives and the case law has not been consistent.

After the ECJ had condemned conduct that substantially reduced potential competition in *Continental Can*, it confirmed the condemnation of requirements that customers should buy only from a dominant firm and loyalty

---

17 *Solvay SA v Commission* and *ICI v Commission*) OJ 1991, L152/21 and 40, the Commission condemned top slicing: giving rebate only on marginal purchases beyond the amount expected to be bought. The subsequent appeals were not concerned with this, but with formal issues.

discounts promised to those buying most of their requirements from it in *Suiker Unie & others*.[18]

This was confirmed in *Hoffmann-La Roche v Commission (Vitamins)*[19] on two grounds. First, obligations to buy a firm's total requirements or a large part of them and loyalty discounts foreclose competition. They may make it harder for smaller makers of vitamins, who cannot supply a large percentage of a large customer's requirements, to compete. Secondly, they come within the examples of abuse listed in Article 82.

89 An undertaking which is in a dominant position on a market and ties purchasers—even if it does so at their request—by an obligation or promise on their part to obtain all or most of their requirements exclusively from the said undertaking abuses its dominant position, within the meaning of Article 82 of the Treaty, whether the obligation in question is stipulated without further qualification or whether it is undertaken in consideration of a rebate.

Their effect is:

90. . . . to apply dissimilar conditions to equivalent transactions with other trading parties in that two purchasers pay a different price for the same quantity of the same product depending on whether they obtain their supplies exclusively from the undertaking in a dominant position or have several sources of supply.

This seems to be a reference to Article 82(c):

applying dissimilar conditions to equivalent transactions with other trading parties, thereby placing them at a competitive disadvantage;

It might be argued, first, that where one buyer agrees to take a percentage of its requirements from the dominant firm, it is not party to a transaction equivalent to that with a buyer who buys the same quantity without such a commitment. Secondly, Roche's customers used the vitamins for different purposes, and it was not shown that they were competing downstream. Paragraph (c) deals with discrimination that harms customers of the dominant firm, whereas Roche's discounts harmed its competitors. These qualifications in paragraph (c) seem to have been ignored.

Recently, Luc Gyselen,[20] speaking in his private capacity and not as spokesman for the Commission, has advocated that to infringe Article 82 the discounts must place competitors of the dominant firm at an appreciable disadvantage: the conduct must foreclose actually or potentially.

At paragraph 111 of its judgment in *Vitamins*, the ECJ pointed out that loyalty discounts granted across the board on the proportion of all vitamins bought also had a tying effect contrary to Article 82(d): a customer who needed some vitamins that only Roche produced would have to buy part of

18 (40–48, 50, 54–56, 111, 113 & 114/73) [1975] ECR 1663, paras 517–28.
19 (85/76) [1979] ECR 461, para 90.
20 Cited note 10 above.

its requirements from Roche and would have an incentive to buy its other requirements from Roche in order to earn the higher discount on the vitamins for which it was dependent on Roche.

The ECJ referred to Article 82(c) and (d), and it may be that conduct listed in Article 82 should be assumed not to constitute competition on the merits, although where overhead costs are large and variable cost low, economists advocate recovering the overhead mainly from the customers whose demand is less elastic, as more will then be supplied (5.2.2 above).

The judgment was rigid in that the ECJ assumed fidelity discounts would foreclose without requiring any market analysis, and it specifically said at paragraph 123 that there was no *de minimis* rule for Article 82, given the distortion of competition caused by the dominant position. Indeed, it has never cleared fidelity rebates, although in *Michelin I* it said that target rebates based on specific quantities might be cost justified.

It is not easy to distinguish competing on the merits from artificially making business more difficult for competitors. Nor is it always possible to distinguish price-cutting, which should be encouraged, from exclusionary rebates, which are prohibited. In *Hoffmann-La Roche v Commission*, the ECJ distinguished quantity discounts, which it considered were legal, from loyalty rebates that were not. A quantity discount is based on the volume of products bought from the same firm, and a loyalty discount on the proportion of requirements bought from it. Quantity discounts may also foreclose small firms which cannot supply large quantities, but may lead to efficiencies.

In *Michelin I*,[21] however, the ECJ confirmed the Commission's condemnation of incentive rebates given to dealers who had met their individual targets and had sold more than they had in a previous year. Target rebates are frequently given in order to encourage dealers to try harder. It may be easy to maintain last year's turnover but expanding it often takes more effort. The rebates were based on the quantities sold, yet a fine was imposed, despite the statement in *Vitamins* that quantity discounts are permissible.

The Commission's treatment of rebates given to dealers who achieve a target follows the German practice. In *Fertigfutter (Pet Foods)*,[22] the Berlin Court of Appeal found an annual rebate system abusive, but suggested that a system with shorter reference periods would be legal. The Federal Cartel Office subsequently accepted (under protest) a rebate system by the same firm based on quarterly reference periods.

This solution would enable a dealer to qualify in the first quarter, keeping in stock such products as it could not sell, and then to buy from other firms during the second quarter, once it had disposed of its stocks. That would not be so effective in encouraging a distributor to improve its performance, but would make sales easier for competing firms.

21   (322/81) [1983] ECR I–3461, para 71.
22   WuW (OLG) 2463 [1980].

In *Coca-Cola/Amalgamated Beverages*,[23] the Commission's Merger Task Force decided to clear a merger under stage II only when Coca-Cola Enterprises made several commitments, one of which was not to impose target rebates lasting more than three months. The view that loyalty rebates and quantity discounts should be granted for only 3 months has never been approved by CFI or ECJ. The Commission stated in *Michelin II*,[24] without any citation, that the ECJ had accepted fidelity rebates lasting less than three months, but this is not true. In *Michelin II*, The CFI denied that all loyalty discount schemes with a reference period exceeding 3 months were abusive, but added that the longer the period of reference the more the scheme was likely to foreclose (paragraph 85). If the discount for additional sales applied to total sales, again the foreclosure was likely to be greater. It rejected the argument that a scheme with higher discounts applying only to the additional sales could have similar effects (paragraph 87).

Another single branding practice is freezer cabinet exclusivity. In *Van den Bergh Foods Ltd.*[25], a supplier dominant in the manufacture and supply of impulse ice creams—those that are individually packed—supplied small retailers in Ireland with freezer cabinets free of charge, but required them to be used only for its brands of individual ice creams. The Commission considered that this foreclosed other suppliers of impulse ice cream, such as Mars, from many retail outlets. Few shops in country areas would have the space or incentive to install a second freezer. *De facto* exclusivity creates concern as well as direct contractual provisions.

Originally the Commission sent a comfort letter permitting the practice to continue, provided that the dominant firm allowed retailers to buy their cabinets on reasonable hire purchase terms and thereby become be free of the tie.

When Mars failed to make much headway in Ireland, the Commission changed its mind and prohibited the practice by decision. An appeal was lodged before the CFI, but the procedure was suspended while the ECJ considered a preliminary ruling from the Irish Supreme Court as to the legality of enforcing an injunction granted by an Irish court before the conflicting decision of the Commission. The ECJ ruled that the national court should not do so. The judgment of the CFI was delivered only at the end of 2003.[26]

Under Article 81, the CFI confirmed that the Commission's decision had adequately established the extent of foreclosure (paragraphs 75–144). It referred to many of the points made by the Commission in its decision: the existence of other networks of single branding agreements, the large share HB enjoyed in the relevant market, the popularity of its brands, the inability of

23   (IV/M.794) OJ 1997, L218/15, [1997] CEC 2226 para 213, n 9.
24   [2002] 5 CMLR 388.
25   [1998] 5 CMLR 530. See comment on this and other ice cream cases by Aidan Robertson and Mark Williams, cited in bibliography at 5.8 below. The promised sequel has not yet been written, as the authors were awaiting the judgment of the CFI.
26   T–65/98, 23 October 2003. The CFI refers to the incumbent as HB, its name at the time of the Commission's decision.

retailers with little space to use more than one cabinet. HB's conduct raised rivals' costs since they would also have to provide and service freezers without charge, which would be proportionately more onerous since they had fewer brands and smaller shares of the market.

The CFI found that HB enjoyed a dominant position (paragraphs 154–58). Single branding constitutes a standard practice and is acceptable in a competitive market but not when competition is already restricted by the presence of a dominant firm. At paragraph 160 it quoted from *Hoffman- La Roche* and said:

> 160. The fact that an undertaking in a dominant position on a market ties de facto—even at their own request—40% of outlets in the relevant market by an exclusivity clause which in reality creates outlet exclusivity constitutes an abuse of a dominant position within the meaning of Article 86 of the Treaty. . .

The CFI seems to be saying that once a dominant firm forecloses 40% of the market, single branding practices are abusive. It does not repeat, even by reference, the facts mentioned under Article 81(1) that established the extent of foreclosure. I hope we can read paragraph 160 in the light of those facts. Otherwise freezer exclusivity, which enabled small shops to sell ice creams and thereby benefited consumers, will be treated as abusive even when it does not foreclose competitors of the dominant firm. Economists have pointed out that freezer exclusivity may foreclose, not that it will necessarily do so. That depends on the facts.

Michelin II,[27] concerned a system of non-individualised, linear volume rebates offered by Michelin on the French market. As an extra bracket of discount was reached, the higher discount was applied to all the dealer's sales over the period, including those made months before. For the first time, the CFI upheld the condemnation of non-discriminatory discounts which it considered were unfair on dealers, induced loyalty and divided the common market. They were unfair in that when ordering, dealers did not know what amount they would have to pay until their total sales for the period were known and they could work out which bracket their sales had achieved. Since margins were slim, dealers might trade at a loss until the rebate was paid. Remember that Article 82 refers expressly to unfair prices and trading conditions. The discounts also induced loyalty *per se*, without it being necessary to establish that other manufacturers were foreclosed; and any national quantity discount system automatically divides the common market.

The Commission was concerned that the performance discounts applied not only to the additional sales achieved above the previous bracket, but to all sales achieved. The marginal discount might be very large.

The CFI also confirmed the condemnation of Michelin's practice of giving a bonus point to dealers who returned to it worn tyres for re-treading. Yet it appears from the judgment in *Michelin I* that not all used tyres are suitable

---

27   T–203/1, 30 September 2003, [2004] 4 CMLR 923.

for re-treading and this practice enabled Michelin to protect its reputation by not using those that were not. Most important was the refusal of the CFI to consider whether the discounts had anticompetitive effects: it is necessary to show only that the discounts were granted, not that they foreclosed. After citing *Vitamins, Michelin I, AKZO* and *Irish Sugar*, it said,

> 239. The effect referred to in the case law cited . . . does not necessarily relate to the actual effect of the abusive conduct complained of. For the purposes of establishing an infringement of Article 82 EC, it is sufficient to show that the abusive conduct of the undertaking in a dominant position tends to restrict competition or, in other words, that the conduct is capable of having that effect.

The Court went on to compare its views on Article 81 and treated agreements that might foreclose as necessarily having that object.

This appears inconsistent with *British Plasterboard Industries,*[28] where the CFI described promotional payments made by the dominant manufacturer as a 'standard practice forming part of commercial cooperation between a supplier and its distributors' that 'cannot, as a matter of principle, be prohibited,' but rather assessed in the light of their effects on the market. It is also difficult to reconcile with Article 82 protecting the interest of consumers rather than of particular competitors. (5.1 above and 5.2.5.4 below, paragraph 58 of AG Jacobs' opinion in *Oscar Bronner*).

The CFI added that justifications of any discounts must be objective. Some of the criteria used to grant benefits to Michelin's dealers depended on the quality of their service and this was not objectively ascertainable. The bonus depended on the judgment of the Michelin representative. Cost savings due to taking a barge load are real enough, but it is hard to quantity them as several dealers close to each other may be able to share in the cost saving. It is becoming very difficult to reward effective dealers in Europe.

In its *Quarterly EC Competition Report* for July–September 2003,[29] the law firm Cleary Gottlieb infer a series of practical principles from the judgment, which they criticise. It may be difficult to estimate the amount of foreclosure necessary to constitute an abuse. Many European legal systems are used to rigid, formalistic rules which are easy to apply, but the CFI seems to have lost track of the notion of competition on the merits. It is not thinking *ex ante* or at the margin. Manufacturers are under pressure to do as much as possible of their own distribution, even when collaboration with an independent firm familiar with the market would be more efficient.

Other recent cases were decided by different chambers of judges and are less formalistic.

In *British Airways v Commission,*[30] the Commission condemned another system of discounts where the incentives increased exponentially if a travel

---

28   (T–65/89) 1993] ECR II–389.
29   www.clearygottlieb.com.
30   T–219/99, 17 December 2003, [2004] 4 CMLR 1008 para 23.

agent increased it sales over those in an earlier period, because the additional bonus would apply not just to the additional sales, but to all the sales (paragraph 272). The travel agents promised to treat no customer more favourably in relation to discount or priority on their screens than BA. Again the CFI looked only to the structure of the discount scheme, not to actual foreclosure:

> 293. . . . It is sufficient . . . to demonstrate that the abusive conduct of the undertaking in a dominant position tends to restrict competition, or, in other words, that the conduct is capable of having, or likely to have, such an effect.

Nevertheless, the view expressed is less rigid than in *Michelin II*. It may be possible to establish that a discount system is not capable of foreclosing or likely to have such an effect.

The third recent case relating to foreclosure is *Van den Bergh Foods v Commission*,[31] a much less formalistic decision, already discussed (text to note 25 above). It confirmed that the Commission had carried out considerable market analysis in finding actual foreclosure when applying Article 81(1). It expressly said:

> 80 . . . Judicial review of Commission measures involving an appraisal of complex economic matters must be limited to verifying whether the relevant rules on procedure and on the statement of reasons have been complied with, whether the facts have been accurately stated and whether there has been any manifest error of assessment or a misuse of powers . . .

It added:

> 82. When examining the correctness of the Commission's assessment of the existence and degree of market foreclosure, the Court cannot confine itself to looking the effects of the exclusivity clause, considered in isolation, referring only to the contractual restrictions imposed by HB's distribution agreements on individual retailers.

It went on to consider the cumulative effect of other single branding agreements made with other manufacturers. The Commission had found that only 17% of the outlets were free of a tie. Nevertheless, it denied that the benefits of the agreement to provide freezers should be balanced against the anti-competitive effect:

> 106. As regards HB's argument relating to the application of the rule of reason in the present case, the Court would point out that the existence of such a rule in Community competition law is not accepted. An interpretation of Article 81(1) of the Treaty, such as suggested by HB, is moreover difficult to reconcile with the (bifurcation of Article 81).

When it came to considering Article 82, however, the judgment was very short. The court spoke at paragraph 160 in terms that looked as if a clause, which in reality creates outlet exclusivity, automatically constitutes an abuse.

---

31   Supported by *Masterfoods*, T–65/98, 23 October 2003.

It is thought, however, that this should be read in the light of what it had already said under Article 81(1) about a firm with a very large share of the market excluding its competitors. It would be anomalous if under Article 81 market analysis is required,[32] yet condemnation under Article 82 is possible without much market analysis.

Sher and Ojala suggest[33] that the difference between this case on the one hand and *Michelin II* and *BA* on the other is that there was a considerable objective justification for requiring the freezers to be used only for HB products. HB had paid for the freezers and made it possible for small shops to sell ice cream.

The Commission is reconsidering its policy under Article 82 and in so far as its treatment of vertical conduct under Article 81 is being more clearly based on economic analysis, we may hope to see change.[34] At Fordham in 2003,[35] Commissioner Monti suggested that different types of abuse might require different treatment and suggested that per se treatment might be appropriate to some.

The block exemption for vertical distribution agreements (9.6.5 below), prevents the Regulation exempting from Article 81(1) single branding, including fidelity rebates, only when the rebates cover at least 80% of requirements and last for more than 5 years, but the test may be stricter under Article 82 owing to the market power of a firm found to be dominant. Under the Regulation, there is ceiling to the supplier's market share of 30%.

5.2.2.2 *Discrimination against competitors downstream*—Sometimes a firm dominant in the upstream market, A, competes with its customers downstream in market B. In *Irish Sugar*,[36] the very dominant supplier of industrial sugar in market A gave a discount to customers who did not compete with it downstream in selling retail sugar but did not give the discount to its competitors in market B. The CFI held that Article 82(c) applied and quoted a passage from its judgment in *Tetra Pak II*,[37]

> 167. The case law holds that for an undertaking with a dominant position on a given market to reserve for itself, without objective need, an auxiliary or derivative activity on a neighbouring but distinct market on which it does not occupy a dominant position, at the risk of eliminating all competition on that market, falls within Article 82.

In fact, owing to the common agricultural policy, Irish Sugar was virtually a monopolist on market A and supplied over 80% on market B, but the words

32   *Delimitis,* (C(234/89) [1991] ECR I(935.
33   (2003) 12 *Competition Law Insight* 7.
34   Gyselen, note 10 above.
35   Papers in [2003] *Fordham Corporate Law Institute.*
36   [1997] 5 CMLR 666, appeals T–228/97, [1999] ECR–II 2969 and C497/99R, [2001] ECR I–5332.
37   (T–83/91), [1994] ECR II–755, paras 115 and 186.

of the judgment are not limited to very dominant firms. Tetra Pak also had a very dominant position over the aseptic sector and considerable market power over the non-aseptic sector.

Irish Sugar also gave various other discounts that were condemned, loyalty rebates, border discounts and other incentives to buy from it.

5.2.2.3 *Discrimination by firms enjoying special or exclusive rights*—At 6.2 below, I will explain how undertakings that have received special or exclusive rights from government are subject to the Treaty including its competition rules. In several decisions the Commission has found that the practices of such firms infringe Article 82 in combination with Article 86.

I am less concerned about intervention under Article 82 combined with Article 86 when an undertaking has been protected from competition, often for decades, or its investments have been paid for by tax revenue. It is particularly difficult for a newcomer to compete with such a firm, and when government funds are available, the need for incentives to investment is less great. Such firms may remain super-dominant (4.3.9 above) for years or decades even after they have been privatised.

There has been a series of cases concerning airports, where the Commission has condemned a discount structure under which only the national airline could qualify. The Commission pointed out there were no economies of scale justifying high discounts only for the national carrier. The unit cost of enabling a aircraft to land and take off only a few times a week is no greater than that for planes that came many times each day.

The ECJ upheld the decision on *Portuguese Airports*.[38] It accepted that quantity discounts might be acceptable, but added:

> 52. Nonetheless, where as a result of the thresholds of the various discount bands, and the levels of discount (or additional discounts) are enjoyed by only some trading parties, giving them an economic advantage which is not justified by the volume of business they bring or by any economies of scale they allow the supplier to make compared with their competitors, a system of quantity discounts leads to the application of dissimilar conditions to equivalent transactions.

> 53. In the absence of any objective justification, having a high threshold in the system which can only be met by a few particularly large partners of the undertaking occupying the dominant position, or the absence of linear progression in the increase of the quantity discounts, may constitute evidence of such discriminatory treatment.

The Court noted that only the two Portuguese carriers could benefit from the discounts and concluded that they were discriminatory and infringed Article 82. The ECJ did not repeat the Commission's statement that,

---

38   *Landing fees* [1999] 5 CMLR 103.

There must be an objective justification for any difference in treatment of its various clients by an undertaking in a dominant position.

5.2.2.4 *Justifications*—The language of paragraphs 89 and 90 in *Hoffmann-La Roche (vitamins)* and in *Michelin II* (5.2.2.1 above) suggests that loyalty discounts are a per se offence, but some judgments and decisions[39] have said that where exclusive or near exclusive supply has neither an actual or potential effect on the market, it is not abusive. Unless those discriminated against compete with others who get a more favourable bargain, Article 82(c) does not apply and competition on the market is not reduced. Moreover, target rebates enabling the dominant firm to achieve efficiencies may be justified, provided they are proportionate—no larger than reasonably necessary.

In *Irish Sugar*,[40] the CFI accepted that reducing competition downstream is relevant as well as efficiencies in dealing not only with target rebates, but also with discounts more generally. It said:

> 114. . . . The case law shows that, in determining whether a pricing policy is abusive, it is necessary to consider all the circumstances, particularly the criteria and rules governing the grant of the discount and to investigate whether, in providing an advantage not based on any economic service justifying it, the discount tends to bar competitors from access to the market, to apply dissimilar conditions to equivalent transactions with other trading parties or to strengthen the dominant position by distorting competition. The distortion of competition arises from the fact that the financial advantage granted by the undertaking in a dominant position is not based on any economic consideration justifying it, but tends to prevent the customers of that dominant undertaking from obtaining their supplies from competitors. One of the circumstances may therefore consist in the fact that the practice in question takes place in the context of a plan by the dominant undertaking aimed at eliminating a competitor.' (citing *Vitamins*, *Michelin I* and *AKZO*)

The fact that a selective border discount policy was unsuccessful in foreclosing, however, does not prevent it from being an abuse if foreclosure was intended (paragraph 191)

In *Virgin/British Airways*,[41] the Commission stated that,

> The *Hoffmann-La Roche* and *Michelin*[42] cases establish a general principle that a dominant supplier can give discounts that relate to efficiencies, for example discounts for large orders that allow the supplier to produce large batches of product, but cannot give discounts or incentives to encourage loyalty, that is for avoiding purchases from a competitor of the dominant supplier

The distinction is not easy to draw. It may be argued that the cases suggesting that loyalty rebates are abusive per se are not always being followed[43] and

---

39 *Virgin/BA* (5.2.2.1 above).
40 T–228/97, [1999] ECR II–2969.
41 OJ 2000, L30/1, [2000] 4 CMLR 999, para 101.
42 Para 73.
43 *Eg Van den Bergh* (5.2.2.1 above).

that assessment of foreclosure and efficiencies is required before establishing even that fidelity rebates amount to an abuse.

In *Portuguese Airports*,[44] the ECJ accepted that quantity discounts are permissible provided that they are not contrary to Article 82(c) and went on to suggest that they should be roughly limited to reflect the cost savings they make possible. A bracket that only one or two customers can attain is abusive unless justified by efficiencies.

It is, however, often not possible to quantify a cost saving accurately, especially the kind of saving that results from long production runs. It is hoped that some leeway will be allowed to the dominant firm to estimate the saving.

The most important justification is Ramsey pricing. Economists generally accept that where overheads are high and variable or marginal costs low, it is desirable to recover the overhead more from those whose demand is less elastic.[45] That will result in more being supplied and everyone will be better off. Those not prepared to pay a high price will obtain the product, which harms no one, provided the price to them recovers the variable cost of supply. Those charged a higher price will benefit because the low price buyers may contribute to the overhead, although less than proportionately.

Recovery of overheads may be the main reason behind the discounts in many of the cases discussed. *ICI* and *Solvay* (5.2.2.1 above) may have been recovering their overheads on the first 80% of a customer's orders and the final 20% made only a small contribution to overheads. Indeed, in *Hoffmann-La Roche*, one of the large customers agreed to buy large quantities from Roche in order to encourage Roche to build a plant to supply them. Ramsey pricing has never been accepted by the Commission to justify foreclosing discounts, still less to justify a barrier to parallel trade in order to enable discrimination to endure.

Charging more to some customers than others presupposes that there are barriers preventing those paying more from buying from those paying less. When such barriers are imposed by a supplier and restrict trade between Member States, these have been perceived as incompatible with the principles of free movement and agreements with export deterrents have attracted heavy fines.

The case for Ramsey pricing is particularly strong in the pharmaceutical market, as the prices of medicines are restrained by different legislative and administrative means and at different levels by different national laws. The ECJ has confirmed the judgment of the CFI in *Bayer*[46] (2.2.2.1 above).

The matter will soon come before the ECJ. In *Sifait and others v Glaxowellcome*,[47] the Greek Competition Commission requested a prelimin-

---

44   *Portugal v Commission*, C163/99, [2000] ECR I–2613, paras 50–60.
45   FP Ramsey,'A Contribution to the Theory of Taxation,' (1929) 37 *Economic Journal* 47–61.
46   C–2 & 3/01 P, C2004/653, [2004] 4 CMLR 653.
47   OJ 2003, C–53/03, C101/18, [2003] 4 CMLR 925.

ary ruling: when the refusal of a dominant undertaking fully to meet orders received from pharmaceutical wholesalers is due to its intention to limit their export activity, does it constitute a *per se* abuse within the meaning of Article 82? Is an NCA under a duty to apply the competition rules in the same way to markets that function competitively and those in which competition is distorted by state intervention? If not *per se* abusive, how should abuse be assessed? Other interesting sub-questions were asked.

The reference assumes that there was no export ban, that the conduct was unilateral and that there is no express acquiescence by dealers. To treat such quotas as abusive would extend the existing case law. The patentee may not control all substitute medicines and not be dominant. It is arguable that a firm that is forbidden by law to charge a price that covers its average total costs is not dominant—it cannot charge more than a competitive price. I doubt whether the essential facilities doctrine applies. The ECJ has stated that the doctrine applies only in exceptional circumstances. The reference tells us that ultimate consumers are affected but little. Immediate consumers, wholesalers of medicaments, can switch to other drugs, not only to other medicines performing the same functions.

The questions are wide enough to enable the court to consider whether discrimination is anticompetitive when there are very significant sunk costs, low incremental costs, and prices are limited at different levels by Member States. Does the Ramsey pricing argument apply within Europe, or only in relation to the US, where the price of most medicines is very much higher than anywhere in Europe? The Greek authority, by making a reference, has speeded up the Commission's idea of making a decision under Article 82 and has also spelled out some reasons why the pharmaceutical industry may be a special case.

Surcharges, reduction of discount or other deterrents to trade between Member States will be treated with hostility especially if they confer absolute territorial protection. They are difficult to justify (5.4 below).

Obvious justifications for single branding include training schemes organised by the supplier, on which its competitors might take a free ride, or a minimum efficient scale necessary to enter a market. The guidelines on vertical restraints[48] consider some of the relevant factors.

It is particularly important that Article 82 should not lightly be applied to such arrangements adopted by firms enjoying only collective dominant positions. Loyalty and quantity rebates are an efficient way of encouraging a dealer to run the last mile and increase its sales.

---

48   OJ 2000, C–291/1, [2000] 5 CMLR 1074 (chapter 9 below).

5.2.3 *Tying*

The last example of an abuse listed in Article 82 is tying:

> making the conclusion of contracts subject to acceptance by the other parties of
> supplementary obligations which, by their nature or according to commercial
> usage, have no connection with the nature of such contracts.

The Commission's guidelines on vertical restraints[49] state that tying by a
dominant firm may be an abuse if not justified by commercial usage or the
nature of the product. It does not state that unjustified ties are necessarily
abusive. In *Tetra Pak II*, the ECJ interpreted commercial usage very narrowly—it is not enough that most firms in the market tie, if some do not. It
seems to treat commercial usage as a justification, the burden of establishing
which rests on the dominant firm, rather than as part of the definition of
abuse, where the burden is on the Commission.

Economists agree that whether ties are anti-competitive depends on
whether market power over the tying product forecloses others from selling
the tied product and on whether there are sufficient countervailing
justifications. Foreclosure pre-supposes that the dominant firm has substantial market power and there is not much other use for the tied product. The
EC case law does not contain much market analysis to see if the tie forecloses.

Tying occurs all the time—each section of this book is tied to the rest—and
often results in efficiencies. Economic theory explains in what ways tying
could be anti-competitive, not that it usually is.

There is nothing wrong in supplying more than one product to the same
buyer if the buyer wants both. If, however, a dominant firm refuses to supply
goods or services over which it has a dominant position (the tying product)
without requiring the buyer to acquire something else (the tied product) from
him, it may be able to restrict competition by excluding firms from the second
market. The basic objection is to forcing customers or licensees to buy the tied
product. In tying, the foreclosure is of firms in a different market from that
dominated, whereas in single branding (5.2.2 above), firms in the same market are foreclosed.

As the recent decision in Microsoft (5.7 below) shows, the EC Commission
has been more hostile to tying than the US Agencies because of its concern
that firms should not be excluded from markets. It fears that a tie will enable
the firm dominant over one product to extend its market power to another,
excluding suppliers of the second product.

5.2.3.1 *What is tying? Extending market power to another market*—Ties may
take forms other than requiring the purchaser to buy the tied product from a
nominated source as a condition for obtaining the tying product. Two or
more products may be supplied at less than the sum of the stand-alone price

---

49   Guideline 215, [2000] 5 CMLR 1074.

for each or a guarantee or other benefit may be given to a buyer who buys both. The Commission treated this as tying and persuaded Digital to abandon the practice,[50] sometimes called 'mixed bundling.' The possibility of mixed bundling was one of the reasons why the EC Commission refused to authorise the merger between *GE* and *Honeywell*.[51]

In *Microsoft* (5.7 below) The Commission used a wide definition of tying. Microsoft did not contest that it was dominant in the market for client PCs and the Commission found that it had abused that position by selling its PCs with a streaming media player already built in. This foreclosed other makers of streaming media players, which are different products from operating systems. The Commission did not consider that the efficiencies alleged by Microsoft outweighed the competitive harm. It ordered Microsoft to propose a remedy within 80 days and either to offer a version of Windows with the Windows Media Player or a 'must carry' provision, or to carry other brands of media player.

There is another difficulty in defining the concept of tying. Most people like their shoes to match, so we think of a pair of shoes as being a single product, rather than as a tie of the left shoe to the right. Guideline 216 in the notice for vertical restraints states that the test is whether most buyers want both products. This may be an indirect way of seeing if there are efficiencies. Buyers will want both if it is efficient to supply the package.

Unfortunately, this does not justify tying that leads to some sorts of efficiency. Where the same expensive overhead is used to make two products, Ramsey's pricing theory may apply, and discrimination in favour of the customers more sensitive to price may be desirable, such as a rebate for those buying a large proportion of their requirements of more than one product from a firm dominant over one of the products (5.2.2 and 5.2.2.4 above).

Since it is for the person alleging illegality to establish that there has been an abuse, the onus of establishing the existence of a tie must be on it. The vertical guidelines state that efficiencies will often lead to a commercial practice that justifies a tie. Unfortunately, this works badly in the most dynamic industries, such as information technology, because it takes time for a commercial practice to develop. Where the product is new and a commercial practice has not yet developed, policy requires that the efficiencies of tying should be achievable even by a dominant firm. At least, once a commercial practice has developed, tying should cease to be treated as abusive according to the wording of Article 82(d), but this is difficult to reconcile with *Hilti* (5.2.3.8 below) or *TetraPak II* (5.2.3.10 below).

Remember that the abuse need not be in the market over which the accused is dominant (4.3.7 above). Indeed, the tied product is unlikely to be in the same market as the tying one, since the concept is of extending dominance over one market to another.

50   *Digital*, Commission's annual report for 1997, 153.
51   M 1601, [2001] 5 CMLR 229 (IP).

In the early days it was thought that tying was abusive per se, but courts and Commission have recognised that there are many justifications for tying, some of them considered at 5.2.3.2–5.2.3.6 below. The onus of showing that a tie forecloses other firms is on the person alleging illegality. The onus of justifying it is on the dominant firm (Article 2 of Regulation 1/2003). It must be shown that the tie is effective, necessary and proportionate—that the benefits invoked outweigh the competitive harm caused by the practice.

5.2.3.2 *Compatible consumables*—Since the seventies the Commission has accepted that it is not abusive to preserve the reputation of complex machinery by ensuring that it is used only with compatible consumables. Ties to ensure a technically satisfactory exploitation of licensed technology are not contrary to Article 81(1) as is made clear in the former group exemption for technology transfer.[52] Neither current group exemptions for distribution or technology transfer black lists tying. Below the ceilings of market share, tying is exempt if there are no black listed provisions. It is widely assumed that this is true also under Article 82. The argument was rejected on the facts in *Tetra Pak II*[53] (5.2.3.10 below.) and in *Hilti* (5.2.3.8 below) but not in principle. There were less restrictive means of ensuring safety, such as informing customers of the dangers, or persuading the national government to introduce safety legislation. The technical need to tie must be established by the dominant firm and sometimes it may be sufficient to specify the appropriate consumables as the Commission ordered in *TetraPak I*, permitting the licensee or customer to select its source.

5.2.3.3 *Measuring usage*—One of the most frequent reasons for tying is to measure the use of some input. A royalty for the use of a machine, technology or marketing know-how is accepted as legitimate,[54] but it is not always possible to prevent the licensee from cheating and not disclosing all the use made of the input. Sometimes, therefore, the supplier may require its licensee to buy some consumable only from a designated source as a means of measuring use. This argument does not seem to have been put in *Vaessen/Moris*.[55]

5.2.3.4 *Full range of products*—Another reason for tying is to ensure that a dealer stocks a full line of products, and not merely those for which demand is greatest. This was treated in the old group exemption for exclusive distribution as an obligation which does not prevent the application of the Regulation, and tying is not black listed in the group exemption for vertical distribution agreements (9.6.5 below), although the Regulation does not

52   Reg 772/2004 OJ 2004, L123/11, which came into effect on May 1 2004.
53   (92/163/EEC) [1992] 4 CMLR 551, confirmed (T–83/91) [1994] ECR II–755, paras 138–41 and (C–333/94P) [1997] 4 CMLR 662, para 36.
54   *Coditel II* (262/81), [1982] ECR 3381.
55   [1979] 1 CMLR 511.

apply where the supplier's market share exceeds 30%. Where the supplier is dominant, it will be necessary to balance the efficiency of providing the full range in a single outlet against foreclosure.

5.2.3.5 *Economies of scope and complementary products*—Sometimes there are economies of scope in producing or delivering two products together. If demand for each is not proportional to these efficiencies charging a single price for both which is below the stand alone price for each may enable the dominant firm to discriminate and recover more of its costs from the product most in demand. This is sometimes called 'mixed bundling' and is an example of Ramsey pricing (5.2.2 above). The Commission has not yet been satisfied about its benefits.[56]

Where products are complementary—when the more of A that is sold the more of B will be demanded, such as paper and toner or hardware and software—the price of a package may be less than the stand alone price of each. A reduction in the price of A will increase demand not only for A, but also for B and vice versa. Mixed bundling is likely to result in lower prices and increased production. In *Michelin I*, the Court accepted that where the buyer performs services for the dominant seller, rebates might be acceptable, but this does not come within that verbal formulation. Moreover, in *Digital*,[57] the Commission closed its file only after mixed bundling was ended.

5.2.3.6 *Avoiding regulation*—Some monopolists have their charges regulated and may have to take any monopoly profits available in the tied market. For them, tying may extend market power to an unregulated activity. Whether this is desirable depends on whether the regulation itself is desirable. The regulator may well prevent this avoidance device.

5.2.3.7 *Excluding smaller firms*—In Europe, with its early focus on freedom to enter any market, there is considerable concern over tying and other refusals to supply which may exclude smaller firms from supplying the tied product. Profit maximisation has not been such a strong motivating force in Europe, where governments constantly try to persuade private firms to reduce national unemployment and dominant positions may be supported by exclusive rights given by law, sometimes protected by a golden share held by the government even from the market for corporate control—from being acquired by other firms—so their managers do not need to maximise profits to stay in business. The attitude to tying is changing, now that many markets are being liberalised.

---

56 *Digital*, Commission's annual report for 1997, 153.
57 Commission's annual report for 1997, 153.

5.2.3.8 *Hilti*—In *Hilti*,[58] the Commission condemned unilateral tying under Article 82. It alleged that the nail gun (equipment for inserting fastenings in the construction industry) the nails and the cartridges that enabled them to be inserted easily were in three distinct markets and that Hilti had extended its dominance over the gun to the nails and cartridges. The CFI confirmed the decision, but on further appeal Hilti conceded that if it was in a dominant position tying was illegal, so the issue was outside the jurisdiction of the ECJ (1.4.3.2 above). Dominance was alleged only over the nail gun, not over the consumables: nails or cartridges, although there was copyright protection over the cartridges in the UK.

5.2.3.9 *Télémarketing*—Shortly after the decision in *Hilti* was adopted, the ECJ gave a preliminary ruling in *Télémarketing*.[59] The Compagnie Luxemburgeoise de Télédiffusion (CLT) stopped accepting spot advertisements that indicated a telephone number to be used by the public to obtain further information, unless the number given for Belgium was that of its own subsidiary. The ECJ ruled that:

> . . . an abuse within the meaning of Article 82 is committed where, without any objective necessity, an undertaking holding a dominant position in a particular market reserves to itself or to an undertaking belonging to the same group an ancillary activity which might be carried out by another undertaking as part of its activities on a neighbouring but separate market, with the possibility of eliminating all competition from such undertaking.

CLT's alleged conduct can be analysed as a tie. The ECJ relied on its judgment in *Commercial Solvents*,[60] where it had held that an unjustified refusal by a dominant firm to supply raw materials to a former competitor downstream in order to reserve for itself the market for a final product may infringe Article 82. Similarly, a refusal by a firm dominant over the transmission of advertisements to Belgium to transmit telemarketing spots unless its own answering service were used may be an abuse of a dominant position in the absence of a technical or commercial justification.

The ECJ did not indicate whether it was guided by the desire to make the market for telemarketing in Belgium more competitive, or to enable a firm to stay in the market when it had not been shown to be less efficient than CLT's subsidiary.

5.2.3.10 *Tetra Pak II*—In *Tetra Pak II*,[61] the Commission imposed a fine of 75 million ECUs, then the highest ever on a single firm, for various items of conduct by a very dominant firm, including tying. The Commission found

---

58   (88/138/EEC) [1989] 4 CMLR 677, confirmed by the CFI (T–30/89) [1991] ECR II–1439.
59   (311/84) [1985] ECR 3261, at para 27.
60   (6 & 7/73) [1974] ECR 223 (and 5.2.4.1 below).
61   [1992] 4 CMLR 551, para 184 and Art 2 of the decision. For critical comments see Jones, Korah and Levy (cited 5.8 below).

that Tetra Pak was dominant over cartons for long life milk and fruit juice as well as the equipment for filling them aseptically, but did not find that it was dominant over the cartons or equipment used for pasteurised liquids, although it supplied more than 50%, at which level there is a presumption of dominance. Tetra Pak's market power over the tied product may have coloured the views of the ECJ.

I would like to think that the precedent applies only to super dominant firms, with significant market power over the tied product.

Tetra Pak required the customers to whom it supplied machines to use only Tetra Pak cartons and to obtain them from the Tetra Pak subsidiary within the Member State where the customer was operating. Sometimes the obligation was limited to the cartons needed for a specific machine, sometimes it was general (paragraphs 116-21).

Even in relation to machines for filling cartons non-aseptically, over which Tetra Pak had not been found to be dominant, the ECJ confirmed that tying cartons to the supply of the equipment was an abuse of its dominant position over aseptic cartons and equipment.[62] This is difficult to reconcile with the ECJ's statement at paragraph 37 that:

> the application of Article 82 presupposes a link between the dominant position and the alleged abusive conduct.

It had earlier referred to the associative links between the markets for aseptic and non-aseptic machines, but did not explain how this led to the use of a dominant position to exclude competition (4.3.7 above). The ECJ also said (paragraph 37) that even if the tie was in accordance with commercial usage, or there is a natural link between them, tying is abusive if some competitors supply only one of the products.

5.2.3.11 *Conclusion*—In the US, fear of foreclosure has decreased substantially as it will rarely pay a monopolist to tie for this reason. It is usually free to charge the monopoly profit for the item over which it has market power and, to the extent that it charges more than a competitive price for the tied product, it will be able to obtain less for the monopolised product. Usually there is only one monopoly profit to be gained. Ties may well, therefore, have other objectives that may increase efficiency and do not necessarily amount to monopolisation.[63]

Nevertheless, the theory is not robust when the market for the tied product is not perfectly competitive, for instance when there are economies of scale in the tied market. Outcomes are very sensitive to the assumptions made. The game theoretic models of post-Chicago economists do not provide a universally valid set of conditions that could be used by competition authorities to

---

62　(C–333/94P) [1996] ECR–I 5951, [1997] 4 CMLR 662, paras 24–33.
63　*Jefferson Parish Hospital Dist. No. 2 v Hyde*, 466 US (1984).

tell whether tying is anti-competitive. At most, they provide a set of screens or filters for deciding whether a practice should be investigated. The most important is market power.

In the absence of significant market power in the tying market and of imperfect competition in the tied market, tying cannot be anti-competitive. There are many other factors to be considered and a fact intensive analysis is required.

Many economists think that tying is seldom anti-competitive, in which case a per se rule against tying seems inappropriate. Apart from *Tetra Pak II*, the Commission has clearly become less hostile over the last 25 years.

5.2.4 *Refusals to deal*

Refusals to deal may also be perceived both as unfair and as reducing competition. The two objections have not been clearly distinguished by the ECJ and are considered together here. The earlier cases seem to have been primarily based on the notion of protecting competitors, but recently, the CFI and ECJ have been stressing that the function of competition law is to protect consumers rather than a particular competitor (5.2.5.4 below). Consequently, they have narrowed the obligation of a dominant firm to deal.

5.2.4.1 *Commercial Solvents*—In *Commercial Solvents v Commission*,[64] the ECJ upheld the Commission's decision that Commercial Solvents enjoyed a dominant position in the common market. It was the only producer in the world on an industrial scale of raw materials from which ethambutol, an important drug for curing tuberculosis, could be made.

The ECJ confirmed that it was abusive to refuse to supply the raw material to Zoja, one of three makers of ethambutol in the common market. The basis of the decision is not entirely clear. Zoja had asked to be released from its contract to buy the raw materials, but when it became impossible to buy them elsewhere, Zoja complained to the Commission that it could no longer obtain them from Commercial Solvents or its subsidiary. In an interim decisions the Commission ordered that minimum quantities be supplied, but it is not clear whether it was protecting the interest of Zoja in carrying on a profitable business which it had developed, or whether it was protecting the interests of those who paid for the drug.Advocate General Warner treated the refusal to supply as an extreme example of discrimination contrary to Article 82(d)— there was no price at which Zoja could obtain supplies of the drug. Nevertheless, he suggested that there might be a justification for not supplying a product over which a firm is dominant. He suggested that it might be lawful never to supply a new product, but to manufacture the derivative product oneself from the beginning. Such a possible justification would increase the incentive to invest in the original innovation.

64   (6 & 7/73) [1974] ECR 223 (decision at [1973] CMLR D50).

There were competitive reasons for objecting to the elimination of Zoja as an independent maker of ethambutol. Commercial Solvents was the only maker of the raw materials in the world and barriers to entry, consisting of know-how since the expiry of the patent, seem to have been high. Zoja was one of only three makers of the derivative in the common market and had partially overcome the barriers to entry into the ethambutol market created by patents: there was no injunction against it. Its demand for supplies of the raw material would make it easier for a new entrant at the level of the raw materials to use its capacity profitably, but this argument was not urged and the ECJ did not explore it.

The ECJ confirmed the Commission's decision but did not distinguish between free and fair competition, although one of the judges, Pescatore, has stated in public that the ECJ had to come to the help of a small producer, Zoja. The precedent was extended by the Commission in the 1970s and 1980s to cases where dominance was less marked, even transitory, and the customer far less important.

5.2.4.2 *ABG*—In *ABG*,[65] BP had refused to supply petrol to a Dutch co-operative that had chosen to cease being BP's regular customer some months before a shortage of crude oil developed in 1973 when OPEC first closed the Suez canal, raised prices and boycotted the Netherlands. The Commission alleged that in a period of crisis, buyers could obtain petrol only from their former suppliers. Such a supplier, therefore, enjoyed a dominant position over its former customers which had become dependent on it (4.3.3 above). The Commission reasoned that BP should have supplied all its customers with the same proportion of the amounts it had supplied in an earlier period, which, it suggested, might be 12 months.

However, Advocate General Warner said on appeal:[66]

> In my opinion such a rule, which manifestly is not expressed in Article 82, could be held to be implicit in the terms of that Article only if it were equitable, practical and generally accepted. It appears to me that it would be none of these things.

It would be unfair to contractual and regular customers. It would be impractical, in that suppliers would not know when the duty to supply arose, as it is seldom possible to tell how long a crisis will last. Moreover, no such rule is generally accepted—the Rijksbureau, the Dutch government body set up to help those with insufficient supplies of petrol, used different formulae at different times when it was supporting ABG and others under Dutch law.

The ECJ quashed the decision, holding on cumulative grounds that the reduction of supplies to ABG was not an abuse. Its judgment is so specific that it is unlikely to be a precedent in future, so Mr Warner's opinion is important.

65 [1977] 2 CMLR D1, on appeal *BP v Commission* (77/77) [1978] ECR 1513.
66 At 1539 (ECR).

5.2.4.3 *United Brands*—In *United Brands*,[67] the ECJ confirmed the Commission's condemnation of the reduction in supplies to Olesen, one of United Brands' distributors in Denmark. United Brands' ripener/distributors were allowed to handle competing goods, and in 1969 Olesen had become the only Danish distributor for a rival brand 'Dole' supplied by the Standard Fruit Company. Four years later, Olesen had taken part in an advertising campaign for Dole bananas, and United Brands argued that Olesen was selling fewer and fewer Chiquita bananas, while deliberately pushing Dole bananas. United Brands then reduced its supplies to Olesen.

The ECJ's attitude to this reduction in supplies to a customer, far less important than was Zoja in *Commercial Solvents*, by a firm with no power over price was strong:

> 182. . . . it is advisable to assert positively from the outset that an undertaking in a dominant position for the purpose of marketing a product—which cashes in on the reputation of a brand name known and valued by consumers—cannot stop supplying a long standing customer who abides by regular commercial practice, if the orders placed by this customer are in no way out of the ordinary.

This view reflects the French law on refusal to sell, which is based on fair shares for all, rather than on a free market. The ECJ went on to consider whether United Brands' conduct was justified and held that a dominant firm can take only reasonable steps to ensure that its produce is properly sold.

If Olesen was spoiling the bananas, presumably United Brands should have complained to Olesen and kept records of its complaints before cutting off supplies, instead of doing nothing for four years. This might have been costly.

The ECJ considered also that United Brands' conduct had interfered seriously with the independence of small and medium-sized firms. It would discourage independent conduct by other ripener/distributors, and this may explain its concern. It had earlier observed that the restriction on selling green bananas prevented Olesen from obtaining Chiquita bananas from other ripener/distributors.

5.2.4.4 *Hugin*—In *Hugin/Liptons*,[68] the Commission condemned Hugin, which it found was in a dominant position over the spare parts for the cash registers it made, for ceasing to supply its former exclusive distributor in the United Kingdom with the spares it needed to repair and maintain the large number of Hugin cash registers it had bought to rent out.

To British lawyers and businessmen, the decision came as a surprise. Liptons could have protected itself by entering into a long-term contract for the supply of spares before investing in repairing the machines. The Commission provided it with a windfall gain. In France, Belgium, Italy and other civil law countries, however, exclusive dealers are protected against

---

67   (27/76) [1978] ECR 207.
68   (76/68/EEC) [1968] 1 CMLR D19 (see 5.4 generally).

termination of their contracts, so such protection must seem natural in some Member States.

The refusal to supply might be seen as anti-competitive in that it restricted Lipton's ability to rent out Hugin registers. Hugin, however, was not dominant in the supply of registers, and we are not told there was any scarcity of registers to hire.

Despite an export ban accepted by another dealer, which prevented Liptons from obtaining supplies indirectly (paragraph 15), the ECJ quashed the Commission's decision finding an infringement of Article 82, on the ground that the refusal to supply a firm that operates only locally does not affect trade between Member States (paragraph 19). It did not address the question whether the refusal to supply was abusive.

5.2.4.5 *Sea and airports*—In many cases concerning sea and airports, the Commission has decided that the operator must give access to third parties. It has defined geographic markets narrowly to include only a single port. The ECJ ruled in *Merci Convenzionali Porto di Genova v Siderurgica Gabrielli*,[69] that Genoa amounted to 'a substantial part of the common market' because of its importance to trade between Italy and the rest of the common market, but the Commission has gone far further in applying Article 86 in combination with Article 82 to far less important ports.[70]

5.2.5 *Obligation to licence*

It was feared that, where intellectual property rights confer a dominant position on the holder, the latter might be under an obligation to grant a licence to anyone prepared to pay a reasonable royalty. Any such obligation would reduce the value of the intellectual property right. Usually, higher profits are to be made by exploiting intellectual property rights oneself, so technology licences are usually granted voluntarily only where, for some reason, the holder is unable efficiently to exploit the rights itself.

Moreover, there is no obvious way of deciding what amounts to a reasonable royalty (5.2.5.4 below). Refusals to license have been treated by the institutions as an example of refusal to supply.

5.2.5.1 *Volvo*—The judgment in *Volvo*[71] came as a considerable relief to those investing in innovation and their advisers. Independent repairers wanted to import from Italy spare body parts for Volvo cars, but Volvo held a registered design in the UK and was not prepared to grant a licence for a royalty. Advocate General Mischo concluded that the holder of intellectual property rights is dominant over the products they protect only if it is in a position to

---

69   (C–179/90), [1991] ECR I–5889.
70   E.g., *Sea Link/B & I Holyhead*, interim measures, [1992] 5 CMLR 255.
71   (238/87) [1989] 4 CMLR 122.

prevent the maintenance of effective competition over a considerable part of the relevant market. He added, however, that since there were no substitute parts, Volvo enjoyed a dominant position over the body parts once it began to exercise its design rights, a view slightly narrower than that in *Hugin*,[72] which was not mentioned by the ECJ.

The ECJ did not expressly decide whether Volvo enjoyed a dominant position over the spare parts for its vehicles but, even if it did, followed Advocate General Mischo in holding that the right to restrain third parties from exploiting the design 'constitutes the very subject-matter of his exclusive right.' Consequently, to order the proprietor to grant a licence would deprive it of the substance of its exclusive right and a refusal to license did not constitute an abuse of the right. Nevertheless, it added that the exercise of a holder's exclusive right might be prohibited by Article 82 if it involves,

> certain abusive conduct such as the arbitrary refusal to supply spare parts to independent repairers, the fixing of prices for spare parts at an unfair level or a decision no longer to produce spare parts for a particular model even though many cars of that model are still in circulation, provided that such conduct is liable to affect trade between Member States.

It seems then that the proprietor of an exclusive right who is held to enjoy a dominant position may be required either to license third parties, or to supply them with the protected product on terms that are not 'unfair,' whatever that may mean (see 5.3.1 below).

5.2.5.2 *Magill*—The Commission and courts limited intellectual property rights further in *Magill*.[73] The three television stations transmitting programmes that could be received in Ireland and Northern Ireland each published its own weekly guide of programmes in advance. When Magill started to publish a comprehensive guide to the three stations, each sued it successfully for copyright infringement. The Commission adopted a decision stating that this amounted to an abuse of a dominant position and required each to grant Magill a copyright licence. This was confirmed because of the special circumstances of the case by the Court of First Instance and the ECJ.

The ECJ confirmed that mere ownership of an intellectual property right does not confer a dominant position (paragraph 46), but that since the stations were the only source of programme information to a company publishing a comprehensive guide to television programmes, they each enjoyed a dominant position over that information.

---

72   *Hugin Kassaregister AB v Commission* (22/78) [1979] ECR 1869, paras 9 and 10, and 5.2.4.4 above.
73   *ITP, BBC and RTE v Commission* [1989] 4 CMLR 757, On appeal, *Radio Telefis Eireann and Others v Commission* (T–69, 70, 76–77 & 91/89), [1991] ECR II–485 *et seq.*, and (C–241 & 242/91P), [1995] ECR I–743.

The ECJ also confirmed (in paragraph 49) that in the absence of standard-isation or harmonisation, the scope of intellectual property rights was a matter for national law, but added that

> the exercise of an exclusive right by the proprietor may, in exceptional circum-stances, involve abusive conduct.

It then went through the various criteria mentioned by the CFI and found that the exercise of copyright against Magill was abusive. There were no sub-stitutes for the information, the CFI had found that the weekly highlights and daily programmes or the individual guides published by the stations were not sufficient substitutes. The ECJ has no jurisdiction on questions of fact.

The producer of a comprehensive weekly guide was dependent on the sta-tions:

> 54. The appellants' refusal to provide basic information by relying on national copyright provisions thus prevented the appearance of a new product, a compre-hensive weekly guide to television programmes, which the appellants did not offer and for which there was a potential demand. Such refusal constitutes an abuse under heading (b) of the second paragraph of Article 82 of the Treaty.

The refusal was not justified, and enabled the stations to reserve the market for weekly television guides to themselves. In the light of all these circum-stances, the ECJ held that the CFI had not erred in law.

How far the judgment went was controversial. What was exceptional? Were the three conditions of paragraph 54 cumulative, as indicated by the conjunction 'and', or alternative? Were they exhaustive or could other cir-cumstances be special?

Few Member States grant copyright in information. Such copyright gives too broad an exclusive right. The stations needed consumers to be aware of their programmes and needed no copyright protection to induce them to pub-lish their own guides.[74] The United Kingdom law of copyright was changed in 1988 to require a statutory licence.

Nevertheless, it is questionable whether competition law should limit intellectual property law on grounds of policy. Do judges and competition authorities have the right background for the task? It would lead to great uncertainty, and intellectual property rights might not induce enough invest-ment were their validity subject to so vague a test.

In *Magill*, it might have been argued that there was no market downstream, since no-one could produce a comprehensive television guide to the three sta-tions. The ECJ did not address the point, which it is thought is bad. It is worse for consumers if there is no-one producing than if there are only a few. What

---

74 Hugh Hansen's comment on Ian Forrester's speech on *Magill* in Hugh Hansen (ed), *International Intellectual Property Law and Policy*, vol II, (New Jersey, Juris Publishing and London, Sweet & Maxwell, 1998) at 36–1. See also Jacobs AG in *Oscar Bronner GmbH & Co. KG v Mediaprint Seitungs-und Zeitschriftenverlag GmbH & Co. KG and others* (C–7/97) [1998] ECR I–7817, para 63 (5.2.5.4 below).

matters should be whether the dominant firm controls an input needed to satisfy potential demand downstream. This has been accepted by the High Court of Australia, its Supreme Court, in *Queensland Wire Industries Pty Ltd v Broken Hill Pty Ltd* and by the ECJ in *IMS* (5.2.5.5 below)[75]

5.2.5.3 *Tiércé Ladbroke*—The Commission's Legal Service has been construing the precedent narrowly as have the CFI and ECJ. In *Tiércé Ladbroke v Commission*,[76] the CFI held that the judgment in *Magill* did not apply to the refusal by the copyright holders in horse races to enable Ladbroke to screen the films in its Belgian betting shops. Ladbroke was not endeavouring to enter a market: it was the largest operator of betting shops in Belgium (paragraph 130). A licence was neither essential nor were betting shops a new product (paragraph 131). Nevertheless, the CFI construed paragraph 54 of *Magill* (5.2.5.2 above) to contain alternative rather than cumulative conditions. This was not necessary to its judgment, nor argued, so is but a weak precedent as the CFI has no jurisdiction to go beyond the pleadings (1.4 above).

Moreover, the CFI observed that the copyright holders were not protecting their own activities in Belgium, where they were not exploiting their copyright. This hostility to discrimination downstream seems to amount to the protection of competitors. Consumers, those betting on the horse races, would be better off with one firm providing the excitement of live films than with no one.

5.2.5.4 *Oscar Bronner*—The duty to supply under Community law is not often referred to by the courts as the essential facilities doctrine, but the ECJ has narrowed the duty to supply to an essential facility. In *Oscar Bronner v Mediaprint*,[77] after considering the US case law on a requirement to give to competitors access to an essential facility, Advocate General Jacobs gave several classic reasons why any duty to provide access should be narrowly construed.

First, an obligation to supply, even when it is possible for two undertakings to use a facility, reduces the incentive to make the original investment (paragraph 57). Secondly, it reduces the incentive to duplicate the facility when this is practicable (paragraph 57) and, thirdly, since the holder does not want to grant access, someone will have to establish the amount of compensation (paragraph 69). This is difficult for a regulator who is likely to have a great deal of information about the regulated market. It would be even more difficult for a court or general competition authority.

---

75   (1988) 83 ALR 577. The court of appeal had held that there was no duty to supply because there was no market downstream: no transactions could take place because the monopolist refused to supply. In a famous judgment, this was reversed by the High Court.
76   T–504/93, [1997] ECR II–923, paras 130–31.
77   (C–7/97) [1998] ECR I–7817.

The Advocate General suggested that it was only when there is a serious bottleneck and no competition downstream (paragraph 58) that there should be a duty to supply.

At paragraph 58 he said:

> . . . the primary purpose of Article 82 is to prevent distortion of competition—and in particular to safeguard the interests of consumers—rather than to protect the position of particular competitors. It may therefore, for example, be unsatisfactory, in a case in which a competitor demands access to a raw material in order to be able to compete with the dominant undertaking on a downstream market in a final product, to focus solely on the latter's market power on the upstream market and conclude that its conduct in reserving to itself the downstream market is automatically an abuse. Such conduct will not have an adverse impact on consumers unless the dominant undertaking's final product is sufficiently insulated from competition to give it market power.

Like Advocate General Fennelly in *Compagnie Maritime Belge,* Advocate General Jacobs suggested that where the dominant position is particularly strong, there may be wider duties to help its competitors (4.3.9 above).

Oscar Bronner wanted access to Mediaprint's national home delivery service for its paper, *Der Standard* the circulation of which would not warrant such a service, but its case was particularly weak. The ECJ held it is not enough to show that use of the facility would be desirable, it must be necessary. *Der Standard* was enjoying spectacular growth and could be sold in kiosks by mail and other methods. The facility for home delivery might be desirable but was not necessary.

The ECJ suggested that where the facility was essential, there was a duty to supply unless the refusal was justified. This is disputed; it would result in patents for important inventions being of little value as licences would have to be given. The Court also suggested that once two undertakings enjoyed the facility, further supply would not be required.

5.2.5.5 *Other recent cases*—In other recent cases[78], the CFI has required the Commission to find that the essential facility is really necessary. It is arguable that where a facility has been paid for by the state, it would be particularly difficult for a new entrant to duplicate the facility.[79] So, a duty to supply might be greater than for firms in the private sector. Moreover, the need to protect incentives to investment is less important for investment by the government or aided by exclusive rights. This distinction may account for the Commission's use of the doctrine in relation to sea and airports which have often been developed by the public sector.

---

78 *E.g., European Night Services v Commission* (T–374, 375, 384 & 388/94) [1998] ECR II–3141.
79 See AG Jacobs in *Oscar Bronner*, para 66.

Interesting issues arise in *IMS*. An interim decision of the Commission required *IMS* to license its copyright in what was claimed to be a de facto industry standard, a set of maps on the basis of which it provided localised data to its pharmaceutical laboratories.[80] The President of the CFI issued an interim order[81] suspending the obligation to license so that the whole chamber dealing with the case could decide. The new comers did not intend to provide an entirely new service. They wanted to provide data which they bought independently to the pharmaceutical laboratories electronically. Were the conditions set out in paragraph 54 of *Magill* cumulative and were they were exhaustive?

The hearing on the Commission's interim order has been held, but the Commission has withdrawn its interim decision[82] prospectively because an appellate court in Germany subsequently held that IMS could not sue for copyright infringement, only for slavish imitation. Consequently IMS could not exclude new entrants. In no way did it suggest that its interim decision might have been excessive when adopted.

Since he suspended the obligation to license, the President of the CFI did not have to decide the criteria for quantifying the royalty. Should it compensate for the loss of the monopoly profit on the basis of which the original investment may have been made? If so, the duty to license would have little effect. Or should it cover only the cost of issuing the licence, thereby reducing the incentive to invest in the original facility. Where, in between these figures should it be set?

Should it be set at a level that enables the newcomer downstream to make a profit? This would act as an umbrella protecting the newcomer even if inefficient. If it be set on the basis of the costs of the incumbent including a normal profit, multiplied by a premium for successful risk taking, the incumbent would have an incentive to increase its costs!

Meanwhile the ECJ received a request for a preliminary ruling from the German trial court and the ECJ followed *Magill*.[83] It said that the duty to supply arises only if there are separate markets, one up-stream and the other down-, but it followed AG Tizzano (paragraphs 56–59) adding that 'it is sufficient that a potential market or even hypothetical market can be identified:' a question for the national court to answer. It was also for the national court to decide whether access to the brick structure was essential and whether,

> the undertaking which requested the licence does not intend to limit itself essentially to duplicating the goods or services already offered on the secondary market by the owner of the copyright but intends to produce new goods or services not

80   [2002] 4 CMLR 58.
81   *IMS Health v Commission* (T–184/01R II), 26 October 2001, [2002] CMLR 58. See V Korah, [2002] *Anuario di competentia.*.
82   *NDC HELTH v IMS HELTH*, [2003] 5 CMLR 820.
83   C–418/01, opinion October 2, 2003.

offered by the owner of the right and for which there is a potential consumer demand.' (paragraph 49)[84]

This confirms the narrow view of paragraph 54 of the judgment in *Magill*. For an obligation to supply to arise the potential licensee must be introducing a new product not offered by the holder of the right. Case law will have to work out how different and superior the product demanded is from that already supplied.

In *Microsoft*,[85] the Commission imposed the highest fine ever, nearly 500 million euros, partly for refusing to provide interface information to its competitors. Microsoft did not contest that it was dominant over operating systems for PCs and the Commission objected that it had extended its dominance to neighbouring markets. It ordered Microsoft to make available the necessary interface information to its competitors in low-end servers on reasonable and non-discriminatory terms. Some of the interface information was protected by copyright. The Commission followed *Magill*.

The remedy is far reaching and goes far beyond those imposed in the US. The decision is based on the concept that Microsoft has the opportunity to spread its near-monopoly in PC client operating systems to adjacent markets. If it be allowed to continue, it may become impossible for a new entrant to compete for the next generation of IT.

Requiring Microsoft to charge no higher price than that charged within M's group of wholly owned companies or divisions is not a long term solution. M could raise that price. It is unlikely to care which department makes profits. No one knows what is a reasonable return for a risky, innovative investment, or even the criteria for deciding. Yet if access to an essential facility is ever sensible, this may be the case. I understand that domination of the entire IT industry would make entry into any part of it virtually impossible. The Commission requires that a trustee be appointed to monitor compliance and he will have to take many decisions that will be criticised as arbitrary.

M has said that it will appeal, although employees say that it intends to be cooperative.

5.2.6 *Predatory pricing*

The general concept of predatory pricing is that a dominant firm may sell at a price, even below its own cost, in order to drive other firms from the market with the expectation of raising the price again above the competitive level. There are several more sophisticated versions of this scenario.

5.2.6.1 *Economics*—There is a large literature on predatory pricing in the United States. For fear of chilling price competition, the courts there have

---

84   C–418/01, opinion Oct. 2 2003.
85   OJ 2004, L, (5.7 below).

treated as predatory only prices that are very low indeed: they have mostly accepted the Areeda/Turner[86] test of predation, which is based on a criterion of efficiency: sales below average variable cost are usually predatory. Various cost concepts are described in the glossary below. Which is appropriate to measure predation?

The cost of producing and marketing an extra unit of output is its marginal cost. Marginal costs as a test of abuse, however are unsatisfactory. The cost of selling the last seat on a flight may be close to zero, but if taking the next passenger requires the use of an extra plane, the marginal cost may be large.

Avoidable costs are those that can be avoided by producing one less unit of output. Incremental cost is the cost of producing one extra unit of output. The two concepts are very similar unless the costs of producing one extra unit differ greatly from producing one less. Average variable cost embraces both ideas, but takes an average, to avoid the arbitrary and volatile result of marginal cost pricing.

Average variable cost is the average cost of taking on a new customer, not just the final passenger to board a plane which is close to zero, nor the passenger for which a new plane has to be provided, but the cost of providing a plane divided by the average number of passengers likely to take it.

Provided that the dominant firm can cover its average variable costs, it is not inefficient for it to sell additional units even if the sales do not fully cover overheads. The cost of plant is seldom variable, save in the very long term, when a new one may have to be built.

On the basis of this very low level of costs, economists from Chicago argued that there cannot be much predatory pricing. The dominant firm would lose on each sale it makes, and to drive out a competitor it would have to supply the increased quantities demanded at a low price. This would seldom pay if, after a period of price cutting when the predator tried to recoup its loss of income, the new entrant were to re-enter the market or the person who bought its plant from the liquidator did so. Only a firm more concerned with turnover or market share than with profits would think it worthwhile.

In some circumstances, however, sales below average variable cost may be commercially sensible. If there are high barriers to entry, recoupment may be possible. Moreover, where a firm is dominant in more than one market, it may find it sensible to predate in the one with lower turnover, in order to gain a reputation for competing aggressively in the bigger market and discouraging new entrants from entering that market.

Other possible concepts of predation are based on average *total* cost. The disadvantage of this is that sales below average total costs, including overheads, are common. When there is excess capacity, as happens in cyclical markets and others, any sensible firm would sell a bit more even if the addi-

---

86   Philip Areeda and Don Turner, 'Predatory Pricing and Related Practices under Section 2 of the Sherman Act', (1975) 88 *Harvard Law Review* 697.

tional sales make only a small contribution towards overheads. Such sales make commercial sense even with no intention or likelihood of excluding a rival and then raising prices again. To forbid them would result in less being produced to the detriment both of consumers and the dominant firm.

Some economists fear that lowering prices where it might most hurt actual or potential competitors may be prevalent and effective, irrespective of cost. In *Concrete Roofing Tiles*,[87] the UK Monopolies and Mergers Commission accepted that the dominant firm, Redland, did not sell at below average variable cost. Its market was local and it reduced prices locally whenever a new firm started to supply. Indeed, even its most heavily discounted prices were not clearly below the full costs of using the plant at a high level of capacity. Yet the Monopolies Commission concluded that:

> 10.57. . . . the established suppliers are able to contain new entrants' market penetration and accompanying price competition at relatively low cost to themselves by means of selective discounting. We regard Redland's behaviour as an indication of how deep selective discounting may be used by established firms as a means of preserving their dominant position. Such behaviour which operates as a barrier to entry may in the circumstances of this industry be expected to operate against the public interest.

The criterion used to define predation in that report was selective price cutting just where a new competitor entered the market with an intent to exclude it and discourage others. This may be far more common than sales generally below the incumbent's average variable cost. Reliance on intention has the disadvantage, however, that most competitors would like their rivals to disappear. Sophisticated firms are advised not to send threats or produce memoranda alleging an intent to exclude for inspectors to find. The less sophisticated may be caught.

Economists frequently use the words 'intent to exclude' to refer to conduct that would not be commercially sensible unless it excluded, and this interpretation has the advantage of being objective and avoiding chasing for documents with macho statements.

Many American courts have followed the Areeda/Turner test and treated sales as predatory only if below average *variable* costs, on the basis that such sales make no commercial sense without the expectation of recoupment: of eliminating a competitor and raising prices later.

It is particularly difficult to know what to do about network industries: those where the more people are added to the network, the more valuable it is to be a member. There is no point in having the only phone in the world, but as more people are added to the network, the phone becomes more useful. In such industries, there is often a race to be the first to develop a large network, and a tendency to charge very low prices, often below average total

---

87 *Report of the Monopolies and Mergers Commission on the Supply of Concrete Roofing Tiles* (1981–1982) HC 12, 1981–1982 HC 120.

cost. Competitors who expand slowly may find that the market is tipped against them and everyone has bought the low cost product. Sometimes the market tips so that the superior technology loses out to inferior technology which got a head start. Often it is very expensive to set up the network: there are large overhead costs, but once it is set up, it is virtually costless to supply new customers. In that circumstance, initial prices even below incremental cost may make sense, because it is likely that both overhead and variable costs will be reduced as the technology improves and the network expands. The low price makes commercial sense even without any hope of raising prices later.

There is danger that if low prices are treated as abusive, price competition will be chilled. There is no satisfactory definition of predation, of distinguishing competition on the merits from excluding others by illegitimate means, and there is significant room for judges and officials to get the answer wrong. The only factor on which economists are agreed is that unless predation can be followed by a period when the lost profits are recouped, there is no threat to competition. Consumers will benefit from the low prices during predation, and if the firm has insufficient market power to recoup later, consumers will not be hurt.

5.2.6.2 *AKZO*—In *AKZO*,[88] the Commission condemned predatory pricing largely on the basis of internal memoranda and threats by AKZO to deter a smaller firm, ECS, from supplying organic peroxides for making plastics. It imposed a fine of 10 million ECUs, high in comparison with other fines imposed at that time.

AKZO produced organic peroxides for use in the plastics industry, and supplied compounds of benzoyl peroxide, one of the organic peroxides, also for use as a whitening agent for flour. ECS, a small company operating in the UK, made nearly a full assortment of flour additives, including organic peroxides, which it sold to flour millers in the UK.

In 1979, when ECS began to sell organic peroxides to the makers of plastics, AKZO made direct threats to ECS in meetings with the aim of persuading ECS to withdraw from the plastics sector. Thereafter, AKZO systematically offered and supplied organic peroxides to ECS's customers at abnormally low prices while maintaining its prices to other customers.

On appeal, after repeating the definition of abuse given in *Vitamins* (5.2 above), the ECJ said:

> 70. It follows that Article 82 prohibits a dominant undertaking from eliminating a competitor and thereby strengthening its position by using methods other than those which come within the scope of competition on the basis of quality. From that point of view, however, not all competition by means of price can be regarded as legitimate.

88   [1986] 3 CMLR 273.

71. *Prices below average variable costs* (that is to say, those which vary depending on the quantities produced) *by means of which a dominant undertaking seeks to eliminate a competitor* must be regarded as abusive. A dominant undertaking has *no interest in applying such prices except that of eliminating competitors so as to enable it subsequently to raise its prices* by taking advantage of its monopolistic position, since each sale generates a loss, namely the total amount of the fixed costs (that is to say, those which remain constant regardless of the quantities produced) and, at least, part of the variable costs relating to the unit produced [my emphasis].

72. Moreover, *prices below average total costs*, that is to say fixed costs plus variable costs, but above average variable costs, must be regarded as abusive if they are determined as *part of a plan for eliminating a competitor*. Such prices can drive from the market undertakings which are perhaps as efficient as the dominant undertaking but which, because of their small financial resources, are incapable of withstanding the competition waged against them.

73. These are the criteria that must be applied to the present case.'

(author's emphasis added)

Paragraph 71 implies that there can be predation only when the dominant firm expects to raise prices later and recoup the loss of profit due to the price reduction. Nevertheless, the rules of thumb are worrying. A stricter test is to be applied in the context of a plan to drive out a competitor, although competition on the merits may drive out competitors. A rule based on intent leads to lawyers preventing sophisticated clients from making threats or leaving memoranda about intent for Commission inspectors to find. Perhaps the *AKZO* rule is a little narrower than one based just on intent; it is only when a *plan* is discovered that the stricter test applies.

In cyclical industries it is normal to sell at below average total costs during the downturn of the business cycle, and recoup during the upturn. It would be absurd to impose fines on the ground that the former prices are predatory and the latter excessive. Recoupment must amount to making more than a normally competitive profit over the cycle.

There are fewer problems with the test of average *variable* cost as these are usually lower. Nevertheless, it is often not possible to determine average variable costs, especially where there are economies of scope. Suppose the cost of an additional unit of product X is 10, and of a Y is 10, but an extra X + Y is 15, what is the variable cost of X: 10, 5 or 7.5? Moreover, what is variable depends on the time scale. Most costs, even labour, are usually fixed in the short term, but little is fixed when considering a period long enough to build a new plant. Labour is often a fixed cost in Europe as redundancy payments are large and labour cannot be shed without substantial cost, except over long periods.

Furthermore, if judged on a historic basis, the sale of products that are either technically obsolescent or out of fashion might be predatory. That problem did not arise as AKZO continued to make organic peroxides, but it may be argued that one should take into account the words I have italicised in paragraph 71 of the judgment in *AKZO*, that sales below average variable cost could have no object other than that of driving out a competitor and recouping later. Sales below historic cost when their purchase was mistaken or excessive make commercial sense without the hope or expectation of charging excessive prices later, as do low promotional prices.

Another way of treating the disposal of obsolescent products so as to avoid the danger of predatory pricing would be to take into account the opportunity cost rather than historical cost. If the value of a product is less than was paid for it, the cost of the opportunity to sell would be below the historical cost of acquisition.

Average variable costs are very low in some markets. Once telephone wires and switches have been installed, the cost of carrying additional calls is close to zero: so is the cost of taking additional passengers or freight if a plane or ship has been designated for a particular journey and has spare space.

5.2.6.3 *Tetra Pak II*—Unfortunately, the Commission followed the statement that prices below average variable costs are predatory in *Tetra Pak II*,[89] without taking into account the reasons for the rule. First it condemned Tetra Pak for refusing to supply the aseptic equipment over which it enjoyed a dominant position to dairies and suppliers of fruit juice without also supplying the cartons, in the supply of which there was more competition (5.2.3.10 above). It went on (in paragraph 157) to object to the sale in the UK of non-aseptic machinery at prices below average variable cost, without taking into account the profits from the tied cartons. At least this amounted to double counting.

It also condemned the sale of machinery in Italy as being below average variable cost when the purchase was made from a fellow subsidiary, but we are not told the cost to that subsidiary. Only if the sale price and other associated income fall below the variable cost to the corporate group should the Commission infer an intent and likelihood of later charging excessive prices.

5.2.6.4 *Recoupment*—An important issue in cases on predatory pricing is the possibility of 'recoupment.' The issue was raised for the first time before US Supreme Court in *Matsushita*.[90] The Supreme Court stated that any realistic theory of predation recognises that the predator incurs losses that it considers as an investment for obtaining future monopoly profits. The expected future flow of profits, appropriately discounted, must then exceed the present size of losses for predation to be sensible.[91]

---

89   *Elopak Italia Srl v Tetra Pak* [1992] CMLR 551 (5.1.3.10 above).
90   *Matsushita Electric Industrial Co., Ltd. et al. v Zenith Radio Corporation et al.*, 475 US 574, (1986).
91   See also R Bork, *The Antitrust Paradox: A Policy at War With Itself* (New York, Basic Books, 1978), 145; and F Easterbrook, 'Predatory Strategies and Counter Strategies' (1981) 48 *University of Chicago Law Review* 263, 268.

Therefore, the plaintiff in a predatory pricing claim must prove that the predator will be able to maintain monopoly power for long enough both to recoup the losses and to harvest some additional gain. Otherwise it will expect new entrants will bring the price down again or prevent it from rising.

The same approach was followed by the Supreme Court in *Brook Group v Brown and Williamson*[92] where there was insufficient market power to enable recoupment, there could be no possibility of predation. American antitrust these days is intended to protect those dealing with dominant firms, and not their competitors. Customers benefit from the immediate lowering of price, and will not have to pay for it if prices cannot be raised later. Economists are not agreed as to the definition of predation, but are agreed that without recoupment, consumers cannot be harmed.

The defence based on the impossibility of recoupment may have been rejected by the European Court of Justice in *Tetra Pak II*.[93] There it was argued that, since Tetra Pak was not dominant over the non-aseptic market, it would not be able to recoup its losses. The ECJ concluded that:

> it would not be appropriate in the circumstances of the present case to require in addition proof that Tetra Pak had a realistic chance of recouping its losses. It must be possible to penalize predatory pricing whenever there is a risk that competitors will be eliminated.

This begged the question of what amounts to predation. It is unfortunate that the ECJ did not consider how predation might work. Some scholars interpret the passage as affecting only the onus of proof. It is for the dominant firm to establish that it cannot recoup as it has better information than the Commission. This view reduces the concern over the judgment, but it is widely accepted that the onus of establishing an abuse is not on the dominant firm.

5.2.6.5 *CEWAL*—In *CEWAL*,[94] the Commission was unable to challenge under Article 81 most of the exclusionary practices operated by the members of a liner shipping conference because of a group exemption granted by the Council. So, it alleged that the members were jointly dominant (4.3.5 above) and challenged their practices under Article 82. This was confirmed by the CFI and ECJ.

One of the practices condemned was 'fighting ships'. Whenever the new-comer, G & C, announced a sailing the freight rate for the conference sailing nearest in date on the same route was reduced to the same price as G & C's at the collective expense of the members of the conference. The Commission did

---

92   *Brook Group Ltd v Brown and Williamson Tobacco Corp*, 405 US 209, 113 Sup Ct. 2578, (1993).
93   (C–333/94P) [1997] 4 CMLR 662, paras 41–45. Some of the facts were described at 5.1.3.10 above.
94   [1995] 5 CMLR 198, On appeal, *Compagnie Maritime Belge* (T24 /93 and others) [1996] ECR II 1201, further appeal (C–395/96P) [2000] ECR I–1365.

not allege that this was below any level of cost, but it condemned the practice. It is unfortunate that it did not spell out its reasons better. The decision was confirmed by the CFI and by the ECJ.

Advocate General Fennelly took economic theory into account and stressed the importance of not chilling price competition even by a dominant firm

> 117. . . . Price competition is the essence of free and open competition which it is the objective of Community policy to establish on the internal market. It favours more efficient firms and it is for the benefit of consumers both in the short and the long run. Dominant firms not only have the right but should be encouraged to compete on price.

He refused to distinguish collective from unilateral action (paragraph 116). He considered that it was established that the intention of the conference members was to exclude, but did not discuss what this meant nor whether it should be relevant. In the absence of selectivity, however, he thought it would have been far harder to treat the price cuts as not amounting to competition on the merits (paragraph 120). This is the first occasion on which the ECJ has tried to indicate what competition on the merits may be.

After analysing the case law, he concluded that non-discriminatory price cuts at a level above costs by a dominant firm should not be treated as abusive even if they were for a very short period. It did not follow that all prices above average variable costs should be allowed. Average variable costs can be very low, especially when a sailing has been announced, but there is additional space in the hold.

The Advocate General also pointed out that CEWAL, the shipping conference, enjoyed almost a monopoly. He suggests, as did Advocate General Jacobs in *Oscar Bronner v Mediaprint*,[95] that there may be a greater responsibility for very dominant firms not to exclude competitors (paragraph 135) (5.2.5.4 above).

At paragraph 136, he confirmed that there cannot be predation without a chance of recoupment, as had been held in *AKZO*. In *Compagnie Maritime Belge*, the parties were able to recoup, because the price cut was absorbed collectively.

For all these reasons he considered that the CFI had not erred in failing to quash the Commission's decision. The ECJ followed its Advocate General on the result, but refused to lay down general principles for deciding whether low prices were abusive. It said:

> 117. . . . where a liner conference in a dominant position selectively cuts its prices in order deliberately to match those of a competitor, it derives a dual benefit. First, it eliminates the principal, and possibly the only, means of competition open to the competing undertaking. Second it can continue to require its users to pay higher prices for the services which are not threatened by that competition,

95   (C–7/97) [1998] ECR I–7817, para 65.

118. It is not necessary, in the present case, to rule generally on the circumstances in which a liner conference may legitimately, on a case by case basis, adopt lower prices than those of its advertised tariff in order to compete with a competitor who quotes lower prices. . . .

Does paragraph 117 amount to requiring recoupment as a condition for abuse? Does paragraph 118 indicate that discrimination is not necessarily abusive? I would like to think so. The judgment did not spell out the reasons as fully as the Advocate General, but it did not disagree with him.

In *Deutsche Post*,[96] the Commission condemned sales below average incremental cost. Deutsche Post enjoyed a monopoly over the postal service for parcels and was required by law to provide a universal service. It had invested in the necessary infrastructure. This it used also for delivering mail order parcels, an activity in which it faced competition. In deciding that it had predated in the private sector the Commission said it had priced below average incremental cost—it ignored the cost of the infrastructure, which would have been incurred anyway.

Wanadoo,[97] a subsidiary of France Telecom, was fined 10.35 million euros for predatory pricing in the ADSL market, originally below average variable cost, but later at average variable cost, but well below average total cost. It is not clear on what basis the Commission found a plan.

In *Deutsche Telecom*,[98] the Commission treated a margin squeeze as abusive, although access on unfavourable terms was ensured by the regulation of telecoms. How far will this involve second guessing the regulator's requirements? Should those regulated not be entitled to rely on the decisions of the regulator?

Both cases raise issues on how to define costs.

5.2.7 Other exclusionary conduct

The list of exclusionary practices is not limited to the examples given in Article 82 and is not closed. It did not impose a fine because the level at which prices become predatory was not clear at the time the low charges were made.

5.2.7.1 *Raising rivals' costs*—In the US, there has been concern that even if predatory pricing is seldom a problem outside the regulated sectors, a more important form of predation is to raise rival's costs.[99] An obvious example might be obligations imposed on buyers to buy their total requirements or a large part of them from a dominant firm. This was considered at 5.2.2.1

---

96   [2001] 5 CMLR 99.
97   IP/03/1025.
98   [2004] 4 CMLR 16.
99   T Krattenmaker and S Salop, 'Anticompetitive Exclusion: Raising Rivals' costs to Achieve Power over Price,' (1986) 96 *Yale Law Journal* 209.

above. Refusals to deal, (5.2.4–5.2.4.5 above), might force competitors to acquire their own facilities, raw materials and so on, thereby increasing the minimum capital required to enter a market downstream.

A simpler example is persuading government to license the incumbents to supply, while forbidding everyone else, perhaps on environmental grounds.

In *Van den Bergh Foods Ltd*,[100] (5.2.2.1 above) the CFI observed under Article 81(1) that HB's provision and maintenance of freezer cabinets would force its rivals to do the same, but under Article 82, it did not address the question.

5.2.7.2 *Vexatious litigation*—In *Boosey & Hawkes*,[101] the Commission found that when its distributor started to make its own brass band instruments, Boosey & Hawkes abruptly ceased supply, started vexatious litigation and adopted other harassing tactics while the distributor's production arrangements were still vulnerable. The Commission adopted a decision under Article 82 imposing interim measures requiring supplies to be provided. This is a remedy that may work in the short term to cover a temporary emergency, but the determination of the price over a longer period would be arbitrary (5.2.5.4 above). In *Promedia, ITT v Commission*,[102] the Commission repeated that:

> in principle the bringing of an action, which is the expression of the fundamental right of access to a judge, cannot be characterised as an abuse [unless] an undertaking in a dominant position brings an action (i) which cannot reasonably be considered as an attempt to establish its rights and can therefore only serve to harass the opposite party, and (ii) which is conceived in the framework of a plan whose goal is to eliminate competition.

Promedia did not challenge this view, only its application. At paragraph 17, the CFI confirmed the Commission's cumulative tests. The question is not whether the right being claimed existed, but whether the undertaking might reasonably think it did. The criterion is based on a concept of fundamental rights—the right of access to a judicial decision. The US courts permit litigation started in good faith,[103] but Judge Posner prefers a test based on the probability of the benefit of litigation in the short term exceeding its cost. Since the Commission's criteria were not challenged, the CFI did not consider any other criteria.

5.2.7.3 *Price squeeze*—In *Napier Brown/British Sugar*,[104] the Commission

---

100   T–65/98, 23 October 2003, para 113.
101   [1988] 4 CMLR 67. Boosey & Hawkes submitted, so no final decision on the merits was required.
102   (T–111/96) 17 July 1998, [1998] ECR II–2937.
103   *Professional Real Estate Investors v Columbia pictures Industries*, 508 US 49 (1993), p 56.
104   [1990] 4 CMLR 196, paras 64, 81 and Art 2 of the decision. See also *Irish Sugar*, C497/99R, [2001] ECR I–5332, paras 150–72.

imposed fine of 3 million ECUs on British Sugar for refusing to supply a
former customer who wanted to sell in a market downstream and for imposing a price squeeze. It sold industrial sugar in large quantities at the same
price as it charged for sugar in kilo packages, leaving no margin for competitors at the wholesale level to break bulk. The CFI confirmed the abusive
nature of a price squeeze in *Irish Sugar*,[105] where the very dominant supplier
gave a discount only to those that did not compete with it downstream in the
retail market.

Should a price squeeze be treated more harshly than a refusal to supply? In
a sense it amounts to refusal to supply at a commercially acceptable price. The
problem is that fixing the price at which supply is required is arbitrary. In the
case of a price squeeze care must be taken to ensure that the buying price is
not so low that the dominant firm is being required to hold an umbrella over
an inefficient competitor.

5.2.7.4 *Acquiring the only competing technology*—In *Tetra Pak I*,[106] the
Commission condemned a dominant firm for acquiring a company that
enjoyed an exclusive licence for rival technology that was being developed
and having the licence assigned to it. This was confirmed by the CFI.

5.3 Unfair competition

As explained at 5.1 above, Article 82 forbids the abusive exploitation of a
dominant position. A dominant firm may not charge too much, pay too little
or do other things that directly harm those with whom it deals, even though
overcharging might operate as a signal to attract other firms into the market
and so attract competition. The Commission and ECJ used to be concerned
as much with fair competition as with free competition, although attitudes are
now changing.

5.3.1 *Unfair prices*

Now that anti-competitive conduct adopted by dominant firms is illegal, the
Commission has avoided the difficulties of deciding when prices and other
terms are fair. In two early decisions, it attempted to protect those dealing
with dominant firms directly, by reference to the practices listed in Article 82.

In *General Motors Continental*,[107] the ECJ confirmed in principle that it is
an abuse to charge prices that are excessive in relation to the 'economic value'
of a service. In that case, it was not necessary to decide on what criteria prices
should be held to be excessive, since the firm had already reduced them very

---

105   T–228/97, [1999] ECR II–2969.
106   [1990] 4 CMLR 47, confirmed (T–51/89) [1990] ECR II–309, para 45–46.
107   (26/75) [1975] ECR 1367, para 15.

substantially before the Commission intervened. On this ground, and because of other mitigating circumstances, the ECJ ruled that GMC's dominant position had not been abused.

In *United Brands*,[108] the Commission found that United Brands' prices for bananas in Germany, Denmark and Benelux were excessive on three grounds: first, they exceeded prices in Ireland, on which it considered that profits were being earned; secondly, they were 20–40% higher than the prices of unbranded bananas, and only about half of this differential could be justified by differences in quality and advertising costs; and thirdly, prices for Chiquita bananas were higher than for other brands. On appeal, the ECJ confirmed that:[109]

> 248. The imposition by an undertaking in a dominant position directly or indirectly of unfair purchase or selling prices is an abuse to which exception can be taken under Article 82 of the Treaty.

> 249. It is advisable therefore to ascertain whether the dominant undertaking has made use of the opportunities arising out of its dominant position in such a way as to reap trading benefits which it would not have reaped if there had been normal and sufficiently effective competition.

This is reminiscent of the approach adopted by the German Cartel Office, the Bundeskartellamt, of comparing the prices of the dominant firm in Germany with those in more competitive markets. It has, however, been accepted by the German Federal Supreme Court with reserve because of its unreliability. That court has insisted on a considerable additional margin being allowed to the dominant firm.[110]

In *United Brands*, the ECJ quashed the Commission's decision that UBC's prices were excessive because the Commission should at least have asked United Brands about its costs. It also suggested, without specifying them, that there might be other ways of objectively determining whether prices were too high.

In *United Brands*, the ECJ added that the 7% premium enjoyed by Chiquita bananas over rival brands did not necessarily show that the price of Chiquita bananas was excessive. It is uncertain whether a larger premium might have done so. The comparison with unbranded bananas was not considered by the ECJ.

Recently, in cases where the Community Court was giving a preliminary ruling and did not have to decide itself whether charges were unfair, it has suggested comparisons with charges made in other markets.

In *Lucazeau v SACEM*,[111] the operators of discotheques in France com-

108   [1976] 1 CMLR D28, paras 100–102.
109   (27/76) [1978] ECR 207, paras 248–49.
110   *Vitamin B12*, WuW/E (BGH) 1435 [1976] and *Hoffmann-La Roche*, WuW/E (BGH) 1445 [1976].
111   (110/88) [1989] ECR 2521. See also *Bodson v Pompes Funèbres* (30/87) [1988] ECR 2479, para 31. See also *Avis* No 93-A-05 of 20 April 1993, of the French Cour de Cassation to the Conseil de la Concurrence. In answer to questions, the court considered what criteria were relevant to deciding whether SACEM's charges were excessive.

plained that SACEM, the French copyright collecting society, was charging more for licences of performing rights than were the similar collecting societies in other Member States. The discotheques wanted licences mainly for English-language works, but were not able to obtain from a copyright society elsewhere a licence confined to these at a lower royalty. SACEM replied that different methods of calculation were used in different Member States and that the results were not comparable. The ECJ concluded that:

> 25. When an undertaking holding a dominant position imposes scales of fees for its services which are appreciably higher than those charged in other Member States, and where a comparison of the fee levels has been made on a consistent basis, this difference must be regarded as indicative of an abuse of a dominant position. In such a case it is for the undertaking in question to justify the difference by reference to objective dissimilarities between the situation in the Member State concerned and the situation prevailing in all the other Member States.

The ECJ's statement is welcome in that it admits of justifications. The limit to the usefulness of such a test is that the basis of comparison is rarely uniform. Quite apart from different methods of calculation, conditions are frequently so varied in different parts of Europe that foreign experience is of limited value. In one country labour costs may be higher, but fuel costs lower and so forth. Nevertheless, the onus of proof is on the dominant firm to analyse and establish reasons for price differences where the basis of comparison is homogeneous.

It seems from *United Brands*, that if prices do not exceed costs, including a reasonable profit on the capital used, they cannot be excessive, but in *Lucazeau v SACEM*, the ECJ added that if the dominant firm's costs were higher than those of firms providing the same service in other Member States, prices might be excessive, even if profits were not. If prices exceed reasonable costs, it may be necessary to consider whether they are fair, presumably by comparing prices elsewhere.

Although the ECJ is prepared to consider justifications, its acceptance that excessive prices may infringe Article 82 is disturbing, although this should be blamed on the wording of the Treaty rather than on the ECJ. How is the economic value of a product to be determined if the market does not constrain pricing decisions? A firm may be condemned and fined for having charged a price which the Commission later decides exceeds the economic value of the product. Moreover, the cost plus approach ignores the function of pricing as a signal encouraging new entrants. If prices and profits are high, new firms may be attracted into the market over, at least, modest entry barriers.

Many people think that only if natural barriers to entry—those not imposed by state measures—are very high, should this 'invisible hand' of competition be sacrificed to price regulation. Because of the impreciseness of the legal criteria, price regulation *ex post facto*—the condemnation of excessive prices in the past—is even more worrying than regulation for the future. It is seldom possible to tell what level prices would have reached in a more competitive market.

Moreover, price regulation is a far cry from the liberal inspiration of the treaty, and made more serious where, as in *United Brands*, the ECJ treated as dominant a firm subject to substantial competition and with no power over price.

The Commission has been loathe to decide whether prices are excessive and has left the question of SACEM's pricing policy to the French courts. SACEM's pricing has been condemned by the French competition authority, the Conseil de la Concurrence.[112] Since *United Brands*, the Commission has rarely been condemning excessive prices. The cases have come to the ECJ under Article 234 from national courts, not on appeal from the Commission. It did, however, bring pressure on mobile telephony prices in nine Member States, although it has closed some of the files, because of the procedures initiated by national competition authorities or regulators.[113]

The Commission has, however, challenged the prices charged for connection to mobile phones.[114]

5.3.2 *Other unfair terms*

In *BRT v SABAM*,[115] the ECJ condemned restrictions imposed on the authors, composers and publishers who were members of a performing rights society, in so far as these were not justified by the need for the society to strengthen its bargaining power when negotiating with national radio and television stations, etc. over copyright licences.

Unfair buying terms for services are also prohibited by Article 82. In *British Air*,[116] the CFI confirmed that British Air was dominant over the acquisition of services from travel agents. In *CICCE v Commission*,[117] the ECJ confirmed the possibility of dominant buyer power, although it quashed the Commission's decision on the facts.

Public sector buying power is now important and in *FENIN*[118] the CFI confirmed the Commission's rejection of a complaint on the ground that hospitals buying from the private sector were not undertakings when acting in the exercise of public activities. They did not resell what they bought, but used it to perform a public function (2.2.1 above). The Court did not have to consider whether FENIN's buying prices were abusive. An appeal has been

---

112   Avis 93-A-05, 20 April 1993.
113   IP/98/707 and 1036.
114   IP/00/111.
115   (127/73) [1974] ECR 51 and 313.
116   T–219/99, 17 December 2003, paras 101 and 191. British Air conceded that this is so.
117   C–298/83 [1985] ECR 1105.
118   T–319/99, [2003] ECR 000; Lauro Montano and Jane Jellia, 'The Concept of Undertaking in Competition Law and Application to Public Bodies: Can you buy your way into Article 82?' (2003) 2 *Competition Law Journal*, 110.

launched.

In *AOK and others v Ichthyl-Gesellsschaft Cordes and others*,[119] where *FENIN* was distinguished, Advocate General Jacobs treated the fixing of buying prices as falling within Article 81(a). There is no significant difference between buying and selling power in the wording of 82(a).

5.3.3 Ad hoc *discriminatory pricing*

The prohibition of discriminatory pricing to maximise profits has not been confined to geographical discrimination backed by territorial protection, which shows up the lack of unity of the common market (5.4 below). Despite the ECJ in *AKZO*[120] carefully going through the various discriminatory prices to see whether they were predatory, in *Tetra Pak II*, the Court of First Instance[121] and ECJ[122] objected to non-geographical discrimination.

In the United States, the Robinson Patman Act, which prohibits price discrimination generally, has been very seriously and cogently attacked in the literature, by both White House task forces and in 1977 the Department of Justice,[123] for interfering with price competition.

Many markets, especially for components, are served by few suppliers, and in such markets overt price competition is unlikely, even in the absence of collusion. Each firm knows that it will not gain market share by charging less than its competitors. Overt price cuts will be matched immediately, so it will not increase its market share. In such markets, the only sort of price competition likely is in secret discounts to important buyers who bargain toughly (2.2.4.1 above). It is hoped that this will not be discouraged by fears of Article 82.

5.3.4 *Refusal to deal*

There is considerable case law on refusals to deal, but it is not always possible to discern whether the ECJ has been protecting consumers or competitors, although the recent cases clearly protect consumers and competition. Both reasons for condemning refusals to deal were considered at 5.2.4–5.2.4.5 above.

5.3.4.1 *Refusals to deal based on nationality*—Refusals to deal have been condemned not only when they were thought unfair or restrictive of competition, but also when based on nationality or country of residence. In *GVL*,[124] the ECJ confirmed that it was abusive for the only collecting society in Germany for a particular kind of copyright to be prepared to collect royalties for artists

---

119   C–264, 306 & 355/01, opinion 22 May 2003, para 67. The judgment did not address the issue.
120   (62/86) [1991] ECR I–3359.
121   See, *e.g.*, *Tetra Pak II* (T–83/91) [1994] ECR II–755, para 160.
122   (C–333/94P) [1996] ECR I–5951, para 41.
123   US Department of Justice, *Report on the Robinson-Patman Act* (1977), based on hearings conducted in December 1975.
124   (7/82) [1983] ECR 483.

established outside the Federal Republic only if they were of German nationality. Article 7, as it then was, prohibited discrimination on grounds of nationality and Article 82 has been used to implement it.

5.4 Integration of the common market

A frequent reason for discouraging cross frontier trade is to recover overhead costs when these are large. Provided customers in each region pay enough to cover the average variable cost of supply, no one is harmed if some regions are supplied more cheaply than customers elsewhere. They may even make some contribution to the overhead cost and result in buyers in the high priced regions paying less than they would if the low priced region were not supplied (5.2.2.4 above).[125] Nevertheless, the Commission has never accepted Ramsey pricing as a justification for export deterrents, even when it was well made out.[126]

In *United Brands*,[127] the ECJ confirmed the condemnation of the kind of *ad hoc* price discrimination that enables a firm held to be dominant to maximise its profits by charging what each geographic market will bear. This is an example of the unfair or exploitative practices which Article 82 was originally intended to control. In *United Brands*, a supplier charged different prices for identical boxes of bananas delivered free on rail at the same ports, according to the Member State to which the boxes were going. The ECJ stated that:

> 217. The price in any given week is calculated so as to reflect as much as possible the anticipated yellow market price in the following week for each national market.

It was simple to prove discrimination in this market since boxes of identical branded bananas were delivered free on rail at the two ports of Rotterdam and Bremerhaven, to which the freight cost was virtually identical. Local VAT charges and freight from the ports were paid by United Brands' customers. Prices were set when the bananas were already at sea in answer to offers from the distributor/ripeners. At that time, the supply for the following week was fixed by the quantity of bananas at sea and it might have been argued that price discrimination encouraged United Brands to give priority to those areas where bananas were most strongly wanted. To this the ECJ objected:

> 229. The interplay of supply and demand should, owing to its nature, only be applied at each stage where it is really manifest.

---

125   See Korah, *Cases and Materials on EC Competition Law*, 2nd edn, (Oxford, Hart Publishing, 2001). Pricing and the reasons why it may be efficient and result in more being supplied than would occur under more uniform pricing.
126   *DaimlerChrysler*, [2003] 4 CMLR 95. See also, the ECJ in *Merck & Co Inc v Primecrown Limited* (C–267 & 268/95), [1996] ECR I–6285.
127   (27/76) [1978] ECR 207.

230. The mechanisms of the market are adversely affected if the price is calculated by leaving out one stage of the market and taking into account the law of supply and demand as between the vendor and the ultimate consumer and not as between vendor (UBC) and the purchaser (the ripener distributors). . . .

232. These discriminatory prices, which varied according to the circumstances of the Member States, were just so many obstacles to the free movement of goods and their effect was intensified by the clause forbidding the resale of bananas while still green and by reducing the deliveries of the quantities ordered.

UBC claimed that the weekly variations in price were due to various factors that were hard to predict when a decision was taken on the number of bananas to be shipped from the tropics, more than two weeks before the banana ship could arrive. Demand in Europe depended on the weather which affected the development of other fruit, holidays, strikes, government measures and currency fluctuations.

One might think that these factors, leading to a temporary local shortage in some weeks, would lead to short-term monopoly rents to be taken by either United Brands, its distributor/ripeners or the retailers. In other weeks, there might be a surplus of fruit of which United Brands would have difficulty in disposing and prices might not cover average total costs.

The ECJ's view that it should not be United Brands that took the risk of these fluctuations does not seem to be based on Article 82(c). Since distributors were prohibited from selling the bananas while they were still green and were capable of distant travel, the distributors in places where the prices were low were not able to sell to distributors for places where they were higher. They did not compete with each other. The ECJ, however, condemned the restriction on selling bananas while still green on the ground that it operated as an export deterrent.

There is an interesting reference from the Greek competition authority in *Sifait* raising the question whether it is an abuse per se for a dominant firm to reduce supplies in countries where it is not permitted to sell at a price that covers its average variable cost and, if not, what criteria are relevant.

One problem of controlling vertical relationships strictly is that the dominant firm may integrate: the ECJ gave United Brands an incentive to do its own distribution and ripening.

Without discussing these considerations, the ECJ spoke of adverse effects on the mechanism of the market, but did not spell out what these were.[128] It ignored the function of prices in signalling to suppliers the markets in which their services are most valued.

In *Tetra Pak II*,[129] the Commission condemned vertical integration—Tetra Pak's policy of supplying the market by wholly owned subsidiaries that it

---

128   The best criticism of this aspect of the Judgment was by William Bishop, 'Price Discrimination under Article 86: Political Economy in the European Court' (1981) 44 *Modern Law Review* 282
129   [1992] 4 CMLR 551.

controlled. This made it easier to charge different prices in different Member States.

Several other cases already discussed may well have been motivated by division of the common market. The type approval relevant in *General Motors Continental* (5.3.1 above) was needed by residents in Belgian who bought vehicles in other Member States. *Irish Sugar*[130] also granted border rebates to discourage retailers near Northern Ireland from importing. This the CFI also found infringed Article 82.

5.5 That may affect trade between Member States

As described at 2.3–2.3.5 above, this condition of the application of Article 82 has been treated similarly to that under Article 81.

5.6 Conclusion

Cases decided under Article 82 until the late 1990s gave rise to concern that firms with no power over price might be held dominant and be discouraged from competing on the merits. Recent judgments and opinions of Advocates General, however, have been stressing that the Article is intended to protect consumers rather than competitors (5.2.5.4 above).

From the ECJ's judgment in *United Brands*,[131] it seemed that firms meeting substantial competition might be treated as dominant if they supplied over 45% of the market and considerably more than its largest competitor. Firms with no power over price might be treated as enjoying a dominant position under this test and responsible for helping their competitors. With the 'hypothetical monopolist' test now adopted in the Commission's notice (4.3.1.1 above) the Commission would probably not now consider that United Brands was dominant and both courts allow the Commission a considerable margin of appreciation, so its views are important.

When the effects of the conduct are structural, as in the case of mergers, the precedents have developed wider concepts of a relevant market than under Article 82. Indeed, in the last two decades the ECJ has been suggesting that markets may be wider than seemed likely earlier. The Commission's notice has moved further in the same direction. In the past, small markets have been investigated for dominance, for example Hugin spare parts,[132] and the certification of Opel cars bought abroad by residents as being fit to be driven on Belgian roads.[133]

Now that the ECJ has confirmed the concept of joint dominance, many oligopolists may find their conduct is limited by Article 82. It is becoming

---

130   (C–497/99R), [2001] ECR I–5332, paras 173–93.
131   (27/76) [1978] ECR 207.
132   *Hugin v Commission* (22/78), [1979] ECR 1869, 1874, para 30.
133   *General Motors Continental* (26/75) [1975] ECR 1367, 1370, para 26.

more important to assess the extent of a firm's market power, before intervening under Article 82.

Once dominant, a firm may not discriminate. It may, and probably should, charge more for supplying in small quantities or at a distance, when freight charges, etc., are borne by the supplier, but it seems not to be permitted to earn substantially higher profits in one Member State than in others. Nevertheless, I hope that dominant firms may still be allowed to give secret discounts to important customers to secure an order. If not, the competitive process would be considerably impaired in concentrated markets. Where market conditions are very different, we have to argue that it is not discriminatory to treat them differently. I would also like Commission and courts to accept Ramsey pricing (5.2.2 above).

Mainstream economists, such as JS Bain,[134] working in the 1950s, were concerned that entry barriers were pervasive, and feared systematic price discrimination, such as loyalty discounts, might inhibit entry. The UK Monopolies and Mergers Commission articulated this theory cogently in its Report on *The Supply of Metal Containers*.[135] Given the European interest in protecting competitors and its associated fear of entry barriers that would keep out only less efficient firms, it is not surprising that loyalty discounts have been attacked under Article 82.

Economists have indicated ways in which various practices, such as fidelity rebates, may restrict competition. They insist, however, that whether they do so is a question of fact, which should be investigated before the practice is condemned. There is considerable concern that price competition is being chilled by treating the possibility of foreclosing rivals as abusive without investigating whether they are foreclosed, or are likely to be. Moreover, vertical integration is more likely to lead to efficiencies than horizontal relationships.

It is particularly important that the incentive to the original investment should not be chilled in network markets,[136] where the importance to consumers of many outlets being connected to the same network leads to concentrated markets and it is efficient to make the entry of late comers difficult. Competition in relation to such markets is for the market rather than in it. Suppliers race to acquire the innovative technology that will enable them to supply the next generation (1.3.3.2.3 above).

It is, however, difficult to advise an important firm how to compete effectively without incurring the risk of being fined. Commissioner Monti has threatened to impose high fines for well-established infringements of Article 82.

---

134 Joe Bain, *Barriers to New Competition: Their Character and Consequences in Manufacturing Industries* (1956).
135 1970 HCP 6.
136 See Christian Ahlborn, David S Evans and Atilano Jorge Padilla, 'Competition Policy in the New Economy: Is the European Competition Law up to the Challenge? [2001] *European Competition Law Review*, 156.

Exclusive or partly exclusive agreements with customers may be avoided by vertical integration: by buying one's customers, or starting to operate at another level by natural growth. This was one of the practices condemned in *Tetra Pak*, but the reasoning was not very clear.

The prohibition of overcharging by firms with only slight market power is also worrying. Article 82(a) forbids unfair prices, but does not set up any machinery for determining what prices are fair. The problems are particularly acute where there are intellectual property rights encouraging innovation by enabling the holder to charge more than a competitive price. The Commission, however, is taking few initiatives to control excessive prices: the cases come to the ECJ through preliminary rulings.

The requirement that a dominant firm should supply third parties has been narrowed considerably by ECJ and CFI in the last few years.

My concern is that the competition rules have been used not to enable efficient firms to expand at the expense of the less efficient but to protect smaller and medium sized firms at the expense of efficient or larger firms. I am concerned that the interests of consumers, and the economy as a whole, in the encouragement of efficiency by firms of any size has been being subordinated to the interests of smaller traders.

The Competition Department of the Commission was staffed until the end of the 1980s largely by jurists to whom justice between two parties seemed important, especially in the light of some of the Continental laws protecting existing traders. Their education had not encouraged them to think at the margin, to look to the effects of a ruling on the operation of the economy as a whole, nor to ensure that incentives to efficient performance could be provided. The attitude of many officials however, is becoming far more sensitive to economic arguments, largely under the influence of experience in controlling mergers.

The ECJ and CFI too, have been absorbing economic theory, perhaps through their legal secretaries, many of whom nowadays learned some economics in their LLM courses on competition law and more from their clients before coming to the courts.

The importance of economic analysis is now being recognised at the top of DG competition.[137] The appointment of a chief economist at the level of director should make a difference to the Commission's decisions. The Commission has started a study on the appropriate policy to be adopted under Article 82. Attention is increasingly being focused on the interests of consumers and the need to induce dominant firms to invest in expensive and risky projects by enabling them to reap where they have sown.

---

137   See the Commission's *XXXI Report on Competition Policy*, at 3, where it refers to wider consumer choice, technological innovation and price competition for the benefit of European citizens. Commissioner Monti usually starts his speeches by saying how important economics is, *e.g,* 'The New Shape of European Competition Policy,' Tokyo, Nov 20, 2003.

At a political level the distinction between benefits to competitors and to consumers is less clear. The Lisbon Summit,[138] concluded:

> 5. The Union has today set itself a ***new strategic goal*** for the next decade: *to become the most competitive and dynamic knowledge-based economy in the world, capable of sustainable economic growth with more and better jobs and greater social cohesion. . . .'* (italics and bold in the original)

At paragraphs 14–15 the Council concluded that it should create a climate favourable to small and medium sized firms. It continues to urge many divergent aims.

5.7 Postscript—*Microsoft*

Software is a network industry with an applications barrier to entry. Microsoft licenses some 93.8% of the operating systems for personal computers (PCs). Consequently, there is a big incentive for consumers to use Microsoft operating systems, so that they can communicate with more people. Moreover, firms writing application programmes to be used with an operating system will target the most popular system so as to increase their potential client base. It is costly in time and money to design an application to be compatible with additional operating systems. Consequently more applications are written to be compatible with Microsoft Windows and, in turn, this increases the inducement for consumers to take a license to use Windows (1.3.3.2.3 above).

Once an undertaking has achieved a very large share of a network market, it becomes very difficult for competitors to challenge it, even if their technology is superior, as fewer applications are designed to be used with the new operating system and there are fewer clients with whom to communicate. The market is 'tipped' in favour of the incumbent.

If only part of an industry is a natural monopoly, it may be possible to keep the rest of the market competitive. A competition authority has a strong incentive to act to prevent the monopolist of one part of the system extending its market power to other parts before those markets tip, too. If all the adjacent markets are supplied mainly by the same firm, it will be very difficult for a newcomer to challenge the original monopoly.

A possible way out of the dilemma is the creation of middle ware: a platform designed to be compatible with several operating systems, which can support many applications software. In that way, the applications compatible with the middleware can be 'ported' or used with any operating system.

The Commission's decision in *Microsoft*[139] is controversial, as was expected, and Microsoft has announced that it will appeal against it. The

---

138 Presidency Conclusions, Lisbon European Council, 23 and 24 March 2000, http://europa.eu.int/comm/off/index_en.htm.
139 Decision of 24.03.2004, appeared on the Commission's web site 21.04.2004, expected to be published, OJ 2004, L000/00

Commission took great care over its preparation and the file was subject to peer review.

The decision objected under Article 82 to Microsoft leveraging its dominant position over operating systems for client PCs into the market for work group servers, and to Microsoft tying its streaming media player to the Windows operating system. The remedies are to require Microsoft to make available the necessary interface information to its competitors in work group servers on reasonable and non-discriminatory terms, and either to offer a version of Windows without the Windows Media Player or a 'must carry' provision, whereby it would offer competing media players with Windows. It has given Microsoft 60 days to make proposals to the Commission and 120 days to make the interface information available and 90 days to cease bundling the media player. It also imposed the largest fine ever on a single firm—497 million euros—more than for any one firm condemned even for price fixing, although at the time the conduct took place it was not clear that it constituted an abuse.

5.7.1 *Dominant position*

Microsoft does not deny that with Windows, it enjoys a dominant position over operating systems for PCs. At para 435, the Commission said:—

> Microsoft, with its market shares of over 90%, occupies almost the whole market— it therefore approaches a position of complete monopoly, and can be said to hold an overwhelming dominant position.

It cited the opinion of AG Fennelly in *Compagnie Maritime Belge*,[140] suggesting that the special responsibility of an overwhelmingly dominant firm might be greater than of a less dominant undertaking.

It did not rely only on massive market shares, but went on to point to two connected barriers to entry. First, Microsoft operates in a network industry where it is particularly difficult to challenge the position of the firm with the largest market share. Secondly, there is the applications barrier to entry. The suppliers of applications software will work to make their product compatible with the most popular operating system, which gave Microsoft a large advantage over other providers of operating systems.

The Commission also found that Microsoft was also dominant over work group server operating systems. Its shares of the various products averaged at least 60%. Moreover, applications software could be run on work group servers, so the applications barrier to entry existed, although not as strongly as for operating systems. It also found other network effects, such as the ease of finding support officers skilled in the leading system. The finding of a dominant position was not important for the finding of abuse.

---

140   (C–395/96P), [2000] ECR I–1365, paras 132 and 137.

5.7.2 *Interoperability*

The Commission alleged two specific abuses: Microsoft had extended its dominant position over Windows to adjacent markets in work group servers and streaming media players. Work group servers allocate everyday tasks within a computer network of an organisation. They enable users to sign on or share files. They route jobs to printers etc.

Withholding the information necessary to design competing programmes for work group servers compatible with Windows was found to be an abuse, although much of it was protected by intellectual property rights. It foreclosed other firms from designing work group servers compatible with Windows. At paragraphs 548–59, the Commission shortly considered several of the judgments on refusals to supply or license discussed at 5.2.4.1–5.2.5.5 above. It relied on special circumstances and the *Magill* case.[141] It decided that the special circumstances mentioned in *Magill* (5.2.5.2 above) were not exhaustive (paragraph 555).

The Commission found several circumstances that in combination made the case special. Microsoft's refusal was part of broader conduct of not supplying interoperability information to vendors of work group servers (paragraphs 573–77). It involved disruption of previous patterns of cooperation (paragraphs 578–84). At this point the decision did not spell out the motivation for Microsoft's change of practice. Until the introduction of Windows 2000, Microsoft had given considerable interface information to the providers of work group servers. It had only just started to compete on the work group server market so may have seen that market as complementary to its Windows operating systems (paragraph 734): as helping it to sell the operating system. Once Microsoft introduced Windows 2000 it was competing effectively also to provide work group servers and may have perceived the other providers as competitors to be squeezed out.

Microsoft's conduct created a significant risk of eliminating competition in the supply of work group servers (paragraphs 585–692) and harming consumers. Since Sun and other providers of work group servers were unable to compete, their incentive to innovate was lost. In the past they had introduced new features that customers bought. If they are finally squeezed out of the market, the only innovations will be those introduced by Microsoft and its incentive to innovate will be reduced if it faces no competition (paragraph 725).

Microsoft's justification for refusing the interface information was that it was the result of massive research and development, much of it protected by intellectual property rights (paras 709–78). In rejecting this defence, the Commission adopted a new concept of the function of intellectual property rights:

---

141   *ITP, BBC and RTE v Commission* (C–241 & 242/91P), [1995] ECR I–743.

711. The central function of intellectual property rights is to protect the moral rights in a right-holder's work and ensure a reward for the creative effort. But it is also an essential objective of intellectual property law that creativity should be stimulated for the public good. A refusal by an undertaking to grant a licence may, under exceptional circumstances, be contrary to the general public good by constituting an abuse of a dominant position with harmful effects on innovation and on consumers.

The focus on moral rights is not in the common law tradition, but is widely accepted in civil law systems. The reward for creative effort comes from the early cases on exhaustion (10.4.1 below) and the civil law justification for intellectual property rights. The essential objective of stimulating creativity for the general good may come from the judgment in *Thetford Corporation v Fiamma SpA*[142] (10.4.2 below), but it begs the question as to how this should be done. The decision, however, merely asserts that copyright will not prevail in exceptional circumstances and this had already been decided in *Magill*. The exceptional circumstances in this case, however, were different from those in *Magill*.

Since access to the source code is not being required, Microsoft's fears of cloning were not justified (paragraphs 713–29). So, requiring access would not reduce Microsoft's incentives to innovate. This statement seems to me to be too broad, but a considerable incentive must have remained. The Commission observed that disclosure of interoperability information is not exceptional (paragraphs 730–35 and 1004).

5.7.3 *Tying media player to Windows*

A streaming media player enables users to enjoy audio and visual media without having to wait to download. The Commission found that since 1999 Microsoft had tied the Windows Media Player (WMP) to Windows, by providing it without additional charge contrary to Article 82(d).

794. Tying prohibited under Article 82 of the Treaty requires the presence of the following elements: (i) the tying and tied goods are two separate products, (ii) the undertaking concerned is dominant in the tying product market, (iii) the undertaking concerned does not give customers a choice to obtain the tying product without the tied product; and (iv) tying forecloses competition.

The Commission found that the WMP and operating systems were separate products, although the WMP was integrated into the software (paragraphs 800–25). The test adopted by the ECJ in *Hilti*[143](5.2.3.8 above) and *Tetra Pak II*[144] (5.2.3.10 above) was not integration. It sufficed that independent

142   (35/87), [1988] ECR 3585.
143   (C–53/92P),[1994] ECR I–666.
144   (C–333/94P),[1996] ECR I–5951.

companies provided the tied product separately from the tying product, which indicated separate demand.

The Commission added that Microsoft gave customers no choice to obtain Windows without the WMP (paragraphs 826–34). By its standard licence to manufacturers of computers, they were required to pre-install the WMP when licensing Windows. They were free to install other media players only in addition. So their customers in turn were unable to choose whether to have the WMP,

The fourth element of tying is foreclosure (835–954). The Commission considered the judgments on loyalty inducing rebates (analysed at 5.2.2.1 above) and, while noting that the CFI in *BA* and *Michelin II* had stated that conduct that tends to foreclose is abusive whether or not it has such an effect, went on, in some detail, to analyse the foreclosure in this case.

With a share of the operating system market of 93.8%, the WMP was ubiquitous. In 2002, 121 million client operating systems were shipped and on 114 million the player was pre-installed (paragraphs 843–48). The Commission analysed the possibility of selling media players through the internet and other channels and found that they were far less satisfactory than pre-installation.

Just as most software applications are designed by third parties to work on the most popular operating system, the content providers tend to target the most popular media player as their platform (paragraphs 879–96). Microsoft's share of the player market increased hugely after it started to tie its player to its operating system. The Commission did not accept that this was the result of competition on the merits. It compared various commercial reviews, which often concluded that other media players were better.

It concluded (paragraph 978) that Microsoft had used Windows to distribute the MWP leaving its competitors at a disadvantage. Tying raises the content and applications barriers to entry that protect Windows and will facilitate the erection of such a barrier for WMP. A position of strength in a market with network effects is sustainable. This shields Microsoft from effective competition from potentially more efficient vendors of media players. It reduces the talent and capital invested in media players, including its own. Moreover, tying enables Microsoft anti-competitively to expand its position in adjacent media-related software markets. It sends messages that deter innovation in any technologies in which Microsoft could conceivably take an interest and tie with Windows in the future.

The Commission did not consider whether investing massive amounts in designing the WMP and then giving it away free amounted to predation. It seems to consider that sales above long run incremental costs (lric) are not predatory. The cost of licensing the WMP is virtually nil, so was little below lric. In any event, it had mounted a powerful challenge to tying and did not need to consider predation.

The more important objection to tying, that Microsoft has the opportunity to spread its near-monopoly in PC operating systems to adjacent markets, was mentioned only to justify the timing of the remedy for tying, when the Commission said the tying must be prevented before the market tips (paragraph 1016). It did not add that if tying is allowed to continue, it might be impossible for a new entrant to compete for the next generation of information technology.

5.7.4 *The remedies*

The remedies are far reaching and have been carefully drafted. For refusing to disclose the interface information it is only the protocols needed to design compatible work group servers that must be disclosed, not the source code. The disclosure must be on reasonable and non-discriminatory terms. Consequently, any information used for the Microsoft work group server must be made available to competitors.

Tying of the WMP to Windows is defined in terms of effects, which should prevent formalistic avoidance of the order. It has been broadly drafted to cover not only the versions of Windows and WMP current when Sun made its complaint, but also versions later to be released.

If this had been all, there might have been disputes as to the extent of the unbundling required, how much information is necessary and the price that may be charged by Microsoft. So, the Commission is arranging for the appointment of a monitoring trustee to be paid by Microsoft to whom disputes can be submitted. He will also have to decide the charge Microsoft may make for the interface information. The decision makes clear that this will be less than its monopoly value, but the requirement of non-discrimination is not helpful in deciding the fee or royalty in the long term. Microsoft is free to impose a charge to its own subsidiary or department responsible for licensing work group servers.

The large fine may not be as disproportionate as alleged by some critics when compared to the amount that Sun will receive to settle its litigation against Microsoft. The amount was doubled because of Microsoft's substantial financial resources and the need to deter.

5.7.5 *Comment*

By the time this book is published, there will doubtless be comments in the *ECLR*, *World Competition Law and Economics Journal* and elsewhere.

The existence of a dominant position over PC operating systems was not challenged, only its extension to neighbouring markets. It seems to me that the decision has been carefully drafted and considered, but I would have liked to see a longer discussion of the earlier cases on refusal to supply or license and more economic theory.

The interface information is to be given to anyone prepared to pay a reasonable and non-discriminatory price for it in order to provide work group servers. It seems that it is not enough to provide access to a single firm. The facility must be essential, but how many firms must be given access? In *Oscar Bronner v Mediaprint*,[145] the ECJ suggested that once two undertakings operated a national delivery service, compulsory access would not be justified.

Would access to interface information have been required had Microsoft been less dominant, or if it had not already achieved a dominant position in the work group server market?

Much remains to be decided about the duty to grant access. The Commission still fails to decide the criteria on the basis of which a charge for access may be made, but provides a mechanism for someone else to set the price in case of dispute.

5.8 Bibliography

Christian Ahlborn, David S Evans and *Atilano Jorge Padilla*, 'Competition Policy in the New Economy: Is the European Competition Law up to the Challenge? [2001] *European Competition Law Review*, 156.

Philip Areeda, 'Essential Facilities: an Epithet in Need of Limiting Principles,' (1989) 58 *Antitrust Law Journal*, 841.

William Bishop, Cristina Caffarra, Kai-Uwe Kühn and *Richard Whish*, 'Liberalizing Postal Services: On the Limits of Competition Policy Intervention,' first Occasional Paper of the European Law Centre, King's College London, obtainable from Professor Whish.

William Bishop (May 2004) 16 *Competition Law Insight*.

Timothy F Bresnahan in 'Competition, co-operation and predation in innovative industries,' *Konkurrensverket, (Swedish Competition Authority)*. *Fighting cartels— why and how;* The 3rd Nordic Competition Policy Conference in Stockholm, September 2000.

Maureen Brunt, *Economic Essays on Australian and New Zealand Competition Law*, (The Hague, Kluwer Competition Law Monographs, 2003).

Mauritz Dolmans, 'Tying under EU law', paper delivered at the BIICL Competition Law Forum, Sept 10, 2003.

Frank H Easterbrook, 'Monopolization: Past, Present, Future' (1992-3) 61 *Antitrust Law Journal* 99.

Franklin M Fisher, 'Monopolization v Abuse of Dominant Position: An Economist's View, (2004) *Fordham Corporate Law Institute*, Chapter 9.

Eleanor Fox, 'Abuse of a Dominant Position under the Treaty of Rome—a Comparison with US Law,' in [1983] *Fordham Corporate Law Institute*; also reply by V Korah, 367 and 423.

D Gerber, *Law and Competition in Twentieth Century Europe: Protecting Prometheus*, (Oxford, Clarendon Press, 1998), chapter VII.

Enrique Gonzalez-Diaz, 'Recent development in EC Merger Control Law—The *Gencor* judgment,' (1999) 22 *World Competition Law and Economics Journal* 3.

Luc Gyselen, 'Abuse of Monopoly Power Within the Meaning of Article 86 of the EEC Treaty: Recent Developments' [1989] *Fordham Corporate Law Institute* 597.

---

145   (C–7/97) [1998] ECR I–7817 (5.2.5.4 above).

Luc Gyselen, 'Rebates, Competition on the Merits or Exclusionary practice?' in Ehlermann and Atanasiu (eds) *2003 European Competition Law Annual*, (Oxford, Hart Publishing, 2004).

Per Jebsen and Robert Stevens, 'Assumptions, Goals and Dominant Undertakings: The Regulation of Competition under Article 86 of the European Union' (1996) 64 *Antitrust Law Journal* 443.

René Joliet, *Monopolization*, cited in general Bibliography.

Alison Jones, 'Distinguishing Predatory Prices from Competitive Ones' [1995] *European Intellectual Property Review*, 252.

Thomas E Kauper, 'Whither Article 86? Observations on Excessive Prices and Refusals to Deal' [1989] *Fordham Corporate Law Institute* 651.

Valentine Korah, 'Interpretation and Application of Article 86 of the Treaty of Rome: Abuse of Dominant Position within the Common Market', (1978) 53 *Notre Dame Lawyer*, 768.

——, Case note on *Michelin I* (1982) 7 *European Law Review*, 130.

——, 'The paucity of Economic Analysis in the EEC decisions on competition—*Tetra Pak II*,' (1993) 46 *Current Legal Problems*, 148.

——, '*Tetra Pak II*: Lack of Reasoning in Court's judgment' [1997] *European Competition Law Review*, 98.

——, 'The Ladbroke Saga,' [1998] *European Competition Law Review*, 169

——, *Compagnie Maritime Belge, II* in *Liber Amicorum Michel Waelbroeck*, (Brussels, Bruylant, 1999), 1101.

——, *Gencor v Commission* case note [1999] *European Competition Law Review*, 337.

N Levy, 'Tetra Pak II: Stretching the Limits of Article 86' [1995] *European Competition Law Review*, 109.

Forrest Miller, 'Predatory Pricing in deregulated Telecommunication Markets, (1997) *World Competition Law and Economics Review*, 65.

FP Ramsey,'A Contribution to the Theory of Taxation,' (1929) 37 *Economic Journal* 47-61.

Richard Rapp, 'Predatory pricing and entry deterring strategies: the economics of *AKZO*' [1986] *European Competition Law Review*, 233.

Derek Ridyard, 'Exclusionary Pricing and Price Discrimination: Abuses under Article 82—An Economic Analysis, [2002] 23 *European Competition Law Review*, 286.

Aidan Robertson and Mark Williams, 'An Ice Cream War: the Law and Economics of Freezer Exclusivity,' [1995] *European Competition Law Review*, 7.

John Temple Lang, 'Some Aspects of Abuse of Dominant Positions in European Community Antitrust Law' (1979) 3 *Fordham International Law Forum*, 1.

——, 'Monopolisation and the Definition of "Abuse" of a Dominant Position under Article 86 EEC Treaty' (1979) 16 *Common Market Law Review*, 345.

Michel Waelbroeck, 'Price Discrimination and Rebate Policies under EU Competition Law,' [1997] *Fordham Corporate Law Institute*, 147.

Lucio Zanon, 'Price Discrimination and Hoffmann-La Roche' (1981) 15 *Journal of World Trade Law*, 305.

——, 'Price Discrimination under Article 86 of the EEC Treaty: A Comment on the *UBC* Case' (1982) 31 *International and Comparative Law Quarterly*, 36.

6. State measures to protect firms from competition

6.1 Introduction

Although later chapters of this book are confined to analysing Articles 81 and 82 and the Merger Regulation, which apply only to undertakings, it may well be that the most important distortions to competition are caused by state intervention. Without state protection, cartels seldom survive for long. State subsidies are illegal under Articles 87–89 of the EC Treaty in so far as they may affect trade between Member States (6.5 below), although there are some exceptions and more discretionary exemptions. Taxation that discriminates in favour of locally produced goods is controlled under Article 90, and some distortions of trade between Member States caused by the buying practices of state monopolies can be controlled under Article 31.

These provisions are often not perceived as part of the competition rules, and the control of discriminatory taxation is not dealt with by the Competition Department of the Commission in Brussels, but by the department responsible for the Internal Market.

More generally, Article 3(1)(g) provides for the institution of:

a system ensuring that competition in the common market is not distorted.

The Treaty is neutral as between public and private property and the public sector of several Member States is large. It is hardly surprising that the Community should have wished to control anti-competitive state measures. On the other hand, curbing state powers is a highly sensitive political act, and the ECJ was more activist in the early 1990s than it has been since.

Articles 81 and 82 are not addressed to Member States directly, but to undertakings. Article 10 requires Member States to refrain from any measure which could jeopardise the attainment of the objectives of the Treaty. From this very general provision, the ECJ has ruled in a series of cases that effect should not be given by national courts to measures which encourage, require or reinforce the effects of an agreement that infringes Article 81(1) (6.2 below). In theory Article 10 also supports Article 82 but Article 86 is usually invoked for that purpose (6.2 below). In *Consorzio Industries Fiammiferi (CIF) v Autorità Garante*[1] (6.3 below) the ECJ ruled that the direct effect and priority of Community law obliges a national administrative authority which is authorised to apply Articles 81 and 82 to disapply national legislation that requires undertakings to act so as to restrict competition when this may affect trade between Member States. Consequently, NCAs may disapply the illegal national law for the future. Although if the legislation required firms to enter

---

1   C–198/01, [2003] 5 CMLR 829.

into an agreement that infringed Article 81, it will be a defence for the past. If the law merely encouraged an infringement, it would be no defence.

6.1.1 *Government encouragement or persuasion is no defence to Article 81*

It is clear that non-binding action such as mere persuasion or encouragement by a government to enter into an anti-competitive agreement is no defence— hardly even mitigation—under the competition rules. In the French bovine cartel,[2] after the scare about mad cow disease, the French farmers complained to the minister about imports from England and went as far as vandalising the equipment of the slaughterers. The minister did not arrange for legislation, but told the farmers to go ahead and arrange a cartel. They agreed on minimum prices and suspending imports into France. The agreement was against the interest of the slaughterers, who joined only after the minister encouraged the cartel. These facts were no justification for the farmers, but 30% of the fine the slaughterers would have been charged was forgiven.

In *BNIC v Clair*,[3] the ECJ stated that the recommendation by a private trade association of minimum prices for cognac and the *eaux de vie* from which it is distilled infringed Article 81, although the association was set up by ministerial order. The minister appointed the members of the board and sent a nominee to its meetings. The ECJ added that the recommendation was not excused by a subsequent ministerial order that made the prices binding on non-members.

The minister initiated and supervised the cartel and ensured its success by making it illegal for outsiders to undercut it. The ECJ has limited the effect of this judgment by subsequently finding in other industries that traders consulted by the minister were operating on his behalf and not that of the industry (6.1.4 below). Consequently, there was no agreement between undertakings.

6.1.2 *State measures reinforcing the effects of anti-competitive agreements*

In *BNIC v Aubert*,[4] the ECJ ruled that the ministerial order extending the effect of the same anti-competitive agreement to bind all traders in *eaux de vie* was itself subject to Articles 3(1)(g), 10 and 81 in combination. The national measure could not be relied upon as a basis for prosecuting a trader who exceeded maximum quotas fixed by the agreement. The national law itself was ruled to be subject to Community law, which takes priority.

Similarly, in *Belgian Travel Agents*[5] the ECJ ruled that the Belgian state should not prosecute a travel agent for sharing its commission with a cus-

---

2   *Federation Nationale des Syndicats Exploitatants Agricoles and others*, OJ 2003, L209/12, [2003] 5 CMLR 891.
3   (123/83) [1985] ECR 391, paras 22–23.
4   (136/86) [1987] ECR 4789.
5   *Vlaamse Reisbureaus* (311/85) [1987] ECR 3801.

tomer when sharing commission was prohibited by a royal decree of 1966. The decree gave legal effect to the rules of professional conduct recommended by a trade association that forbade such price competition. The original re-commendation had expired—it had become unnecessary once the national law of 1966 took its place. This judgment was less controversial in that the government had not encouraged and supervised the restrictive agreement as the minister had done in *BNIC*—it merely reinforced the agreement that had been freely made.

6.1.3 *State measures that delegate the fixing of prices to citizens*

In *Leclerc v Au Blé Vert*,[6] Leclerc operated a supermarket chain with a policy for price cutting. The French Lang Act, however, required publishers or importers of books to fix minimum retail prices for the books they published or imported, and it was made a criminal offence for retail sales to be made at a discount of more than 5%. Provision was made for competitors and various kinds of trade associations to seek an injunction or damages, as well as for criminal prosecutions to be brought.

Leclerc sold various titles below the permitted level, and at the suit of several competing booksellers was ordered to comply with the law. The Court of Appeal at Poitiers, however, asked the ECJ for a preliminary ruling whether the French law infringed the EC rules of competition in the light of Articles 3(1)(g) and 10.

Leclerc argued that the law was not simply price control by the state, since the prices could be fixed freely by publishers and importers. In effect, Leclerc argued that the Lang Act set up a resale price maintenance system which it would be illegal for the undertakings to arrange. The Commission, however, asked the Court to distinguish state measures from agreements between undertakings, since Article 81 applies only to the conduct of undertakings.

The ECJ referred at paragraph 15 to a principle it had established in somewhat obscure terms in 1977 and which underlies its later judgments:

> Whilst it is true that the rules on competition are concerned with the conduct of undertakings and not with national legislation, Member States are none the less obliged under the second paragraph of Article 5.2 (now Article 10) of the Treaty not to detract, by means of national legislation, from the full and uniform application of Community law or from the effectiveness of its implementing measures; nor may they introduce or maintain in force measures, even of a legislative nature, which may render ineffective the competition rules applicable to undertakings (cf. judgment in *Wilhelm v Bundeskartellamt*,[7] and judgment in *Inno v ATAB*[8]).

The ECJ observed that the French law did not restrain the conclusion of agreements, but only unilateral conduct. It then went on to consider whether

6   (229/83) [1985] ECR 32.
7   (14/68) [1969] ECR 1.
8   (13/77) [1977] ECR 2115, at para 31.

the Lang Act deprived the competition rules of their effectiveness by making collusion unnecessary. It mentioned that the French measure protected book prices on cultural grounds, that the resale prices of books are maintained in many Member States and that the Commission had, so far, attacked only one system of resale price maintenance for Dutch-language books embracing two Member States, and never a national system.

The ECJ concluded at paragraph 20 that, as Community law then stood, Article 10, combined with Articles 3(1)(g) and 81, was not sufficiently well defined to prevent Member States from enacting legislation such as that in issue.

6.1.4 *Anti-competitive state measures making agreements between undertakings unnecessary*

Judge Joliet has since argued[9] that the ECJ objected in principle to national measures, such as the Lang Act, for depriving Article 81 of its effect. A private firm should not be able to dictate the terms on which other firms deal. Nevertheless, he says that the Court declined to strike down the Act as unconstitutional on grounds of legal certainty. The tide of thought in the ECJ seems to have shifted since then in favour of state rights, so whether he was right at the time or not, it is less clear that the ECJ would now strike out such legislation.

The argument, based on the failure of the Commission to challenge resale price maintenance of books, may well mask a compromise. It was not accepted in relation to package tours in *Belgian Travel Agents*.[10] Nevertheless, more Member States permit an exception to prohibitions of resale price maintenance for books than for travel agents. In all these cases, the government had enabled existing traders to fix the prices at which others were allowed to trade.

In *Cullet v Leclerc*,[11] however, where the French government itself had fixed minimum prices for petrol, there was no question of delegating its discretion to firms that might want protection from outsiders, and the ECJ held that Article 81 was not deprived of its effectiveness. This view was formalistic since, in the absence of inter-brand competition, the law was even more anti-competitive than the Lang Act.

In *Van Eycke*,[12] the ECJ went out of its way to rule that Article 10 forbids governments to delegate to associations of private banks decisions on rates of interest. It seems that the government did not delegate its powers, so the legislation was presumably valid. Some commentators consider that this was a strong *dictum*, in as much as interest rates were closely allied to monetary

9   René Joliet, 'National Anti-competitive Legislation and Community Law,' in Barry Hawk (ed) [1988] *Fordham Corporate Law Institute*, chap 16.
10   *Vlaamse Reisbureaus* (311/85) [1987] ECR 3801, paras 25–27.
11   (231/83) [1985] ECR 305, paras 17–18; Luc Gyselen, 'State Action and the Effectiveness of the EEC Treaty's Competition Provisions' (1989) 26 *CML Rev* 33.
12   (267/86) [1988] ECR 4769, paras 16, 19–20.

policy which, before Maastricht, was reserved to Member States by title 2 of the Treaty. What the Court objected to, however, was the delegation of the government's discretion to a particular group of undertakings that might operate in its own interest.

It has been argued[13] that the judgment in *Van Eycke* should have persuaded the ECJ to reconsider its judgment in *Au Blé Vert*, where the setting of the resale price was delegated to publishers but was not found to be contrary to Article 10 combined with Article 81. In *Échirolles Distribution SA v Association de Dauphiné and Others*,[14] however, *Van Eycke* was not cited and the ECJ followed *Au Blé Vert* since the rules for free movement and competition had not been amended by legislation. The Court has no jurisdiction to consider points not raised in the pleadings (1.4.3.2 above), although it sometimes does so. It is thought, therefore that the ECJ should reconsider *Au Blé Vert* should an opportunity arise.

Luc Gyselen argued[15] that the ECJ's alternative rulings in *Van Eycke* were incompatible: first it said that for a measure to infringe Article 10 there must also be an agreement between undertakings. Secondly, it suggested that the delegation of discretion would infringe Article 10, presumably in the absence of any such agreement. There seems to be a dual possibility of infringement.

Where, as in the case of books, the products are heterogeneous, the government cannot set a mandatory price. Consequently, it must delegate the price fixing to individual producers. The ECJ ruled in *Leclerc v Au Blé Vert*[16] that this may infringe Article 10. Where, like petrol, the products are homogeneous, however, the government may impose controls directly. The Court has not addressed this argument. It has not articulated the reasons for distinguishing measures where the right to fix the prices is delegated to businessmen. It seems unlikely that governments would fix the price at a more desirable level than would individual suppliers who would suffer from giving more market power to their dealers.

Without articulating its reasons, the ECJ held in 1993 that national measures that make it unnecessary for undertakings to agree, such as a national legislative prohibition on an agent sharing his commission with his customer, do not infringe Articles 3(1)(g), 10 and 81[17] even though a horizontal agreement between the agents would certainly restrict competition and might well affect trade between Member States. It also distinguished the *BNIC* cases in *Reiff*[18] by treating the members of the industry as representing the minister and not their own interests. Such legislation may well be more anticompetitive than that which has been condemned under Articles 3(1)(g), 10

13   By Luc Gyselen, 'Anticompetitive State Measures under the EC Treaty: Towards a Substantive Legality Standard' [1994] *EL Rev* competition checklist for 1993, CC 55–65.
14   (C–9/99) [2000] ECR I–8207.
15   Cited note 13 above.
16   (229/83) [1985] ECR 1, para 31.
17   *Meng* (C–2/91) [1993] ECR I–5751 and *Ohra* (C–245/91) [1993] ECR I–5851.
18   (C–185/91), [1993] ECR I–5801.

and 81, but by 1993 the ECJ ceased to be willing to cut back state power. A cynic might object to the findings of fact,[19] but the ECJ has become loathe to interfere with ministerial discretion conferred by national law. Price control is a matter for Member States rather than the Community. Nevertheless, the ECJ may strike down similar schemes in future and the proposition that encouragement by the government remains no defence to an infringement of Article 81(1) can stand[20] although it may not be applied frequently.

In *Arduino*,[21] AG Léger argued that Articles 3(1)(g), 10 and 81 would not apply if the public authority exercises effective control, follows a legitimate aim in the public interest and the measure is proportionate to the need. At paragraphs 35–37 the ECJ was less specific when approving pricing conditions drawn up by the Bar Association at the request of the minister who maintained some control over the draft tariff.

In *Wouters*,[22] the Dutch Bar, exercising statutory powers, drew up rules which restrained lawyers from becoming partners of accountancy firms. The ECJ observed that the drafting committee was composed solely of members of the Bar elected by members of the profession, that the government had not laid down criteria in the public interest and that drawing up the rules of professional conduct was an economic activity. It was irrelevant that the rules formed part of public law. Consequently, in principle, Articles 3(1)(g) and 10, excluding from the prohibition of Article 81 price fixing by committees of experts in the public interest, were not applicable.

The ECJ accepted that competition was restricted in that the rule prevented the emergence of a 'one-stop-shop' for clients with both legal and accountancy requirements. Trade between Member States might be affected.

On the facts, however, the ECJ considered that the rule was important for the independence of the Bar in that it helped to avoid conflicts of interest and:

> 107. . . . could therefore reasonably be considered necessary the proper practice of the legal profession as it is organised in the Member State concerned.

It concluded that the rule did not infringe Article 81.

The judgment in *Wouters* is not easy to classify. It lays down criteria for deciding whether a professional body is operating on behalf of government or of its members which seem to be more exacting than the criteria in *Reiff.* Yet it goes further in accepting a new justification excluding the operation of Article 81, possibly on the ground that the control of the Bar is a matter for Member States.

Even in a fully federal system a supreme court must not act too strongly when expanding federal law at the expense of state rights. The Member States

---

19   The ECJ should not make findings of fact when making preliminary rulings. The application of the law is for the national court.
20   *Commission v Italy*, (C35/96) [1998] 1 ECR 3851.
21   (C–35/99) 19 February, [2002] 4 CMLR 866, para 91.
22   C–309/99, [2002] ECR I–1577, paras 56–71.

transferred rather little of their sovereignty to the European Communities. Taking more power to the centre is a sensitive political matter. The Community Courts have no physical powers and must rely on the courts of Member States to apply their rulings. If such courts are outraged, the application of Community law may be prejudiced and the ECJ has trodden warily in the last few years when considering state action that makes anti-competitive agreements unnecessary.

6.1.5 *State measures are subject to the rules for free movement of goods*

Some government intervention to protect local traders may infringe Article 28, which prohibits quantitative restrictions on imports, including measures that bear more heavily on imports than on domestic production. Such action can be restrained by the Commission operating under Article 226 and, since it has direct effects, Article 28 can be used by citizens as a defence to prosecution under the offending law.

In *Leclerc v Au Blé Vert*,[23] the ECJ found that the provisions relating to books imported from other Member States infringed the rules for the free movement of goods, which are addressed to Member States. The French law required the importer, not the publisher, to fix the resale prices. So a dealer could prevent its competitors from undercutting it and thereby reduce demand for imported books. The law did not apply to imported books the same regime as for those published in France. The law was later amended and became valid.[24]

6.1.6 *Conclusion on Article 10*

There is considerable regulation in Europe that might interfere with 'undistorted competition,' but the ECJ has become cautious in applying Article 10. It has not accepted that government persuasion is a defence to an agreement that infringes Article 81. It has condemned as contrary to a combination of Articles 3(1)(g), 10 and 81 government measures that require, favour or reinforce agreements that infringe Article 81. It has gone further and condemned national measures that delegate to a private firm or trade association the fixing of terms on which outsiders may trade.

It has, however, drawn back from ruling that a government measure might be invalid when there had never been any agreement between undertakings restricting competition in the common market. Where prices are fixed by government on the basis of advice from industry, the ECJ no longer states that that amounts to collusion between undertakings. It examines whether the advisors were looking to criteria set by the state rather than to their own

---

23   (229/83) [1985] ECR 32, paras 25–30.
24   *Librairies de Normandie v L'Aigle Distribution, Centre Leclerc* (254/87) [1988] ECR 4457, paras 4 and 12.

interest. Further action against anti-competitive regulation must probably be left to measures of harmonisation under Articles 94 and 95 of the treaty, and to Article 86, which empowers the Commission to take action against state monopolies (6.2 below).

6.2 Special and exclusive rights (Article 86)

Until 1992, the DG Comp devoted considerable resources to enforcing Article 86. It provides:

> 1. In the case of public undertakings and undertakings to which Member States grant special or exclusive rights, Member States shall neither enact nor maintain in force any measure contrary to the rules contained in this Treaty, in particular to those rules provided for in Article 12 and Articles 81 to 89.
>
> 2. Undertakings entrusted with the operation of services of general economic interest or having the character of a revenue-producing monopoly shall be subject to the rules contained in this Treaty, in particular to the rules on competition, in so far as the application of such rules does not obstruct the performance, in law or in fact, of the particular tasks assigned to them. The development of trade must not be affected to such an extent as would be contrary to the interests of the Community.
>
> 3. The Commission shall ensure the application of the provisions of this Article and shall, where necessary, address appropriate directives or decisions to Member States.

Paragraph 1 is addressed to states, but indirectly restrains public undertakings and undertakings to which the state has granted special or exclusive rights from acting contrary to the rules of the treaty, expressly mentioning the competition rules.

Paragraph (2) provides derogation for revenue producing monopolies or undertakings entrusted with services of general economic interest. The provision has been narrowly construed. It applies only if the measure is reasonably necessary to the performance of its task and is proportionate.

The third paragraph enables the Commission to enforce the provisions of Article 86 by directives and decisions. Without going through the Council or European Parliament, the Commission cannot legislate on state measures conferring exclusive rights by invoking Article 86(3) in combination with some other provision in the Treaty, but it can make clear what was already illegal—a narrow distinction!

Article 86 has been treated by the ECJ as a special instance of Article 10.[25] The ECJ stated that it is not illegal for a Member State to grant special or exclusive rights to an undertaking, but when it has done so, the undertaking may be liable under Articles 81 or 82 if the undertaking infringes Article 86 in

---

25 *Merci Convenzionali Porto di Genova v Siderurgica Gabrielli* (C–179/90), [1991] ECR I–5889, para 16 and many other judgments.

combination with Article 81 or 82[26] and the government may be liable under Article 86.

6.2.1 *Undertakings*

The ECJ construed Article 86 very broadly in the early 1990s. The derogation in paragraph (2) was narrowly construed and, in *Italy v Commission*,[27] the ECJ upheld a decision that British Telecom had infringed Article 82 before it was privatised. It was then an undertaking carrying on commercial activities although it was owned by the government. It enjoyed exclusive rights and the terms on which it forwarded telex messages from Europe did not obstruct the performance of the task of providing a universal telephone service assigned to it.

There remains considerable doubt about what public bodies amount to 'undertakings.' The ECJ has tried to distinguish state measures of a regulatory nature from its commercial activities, but has used different criteria in different cases.

The German state labour exchange was held to constitute an undertaking in *Höfner and Elser v Macrotron*,[28] because it carried on an economic activity finding jobs, although it operated under statutory powers, was funded by government, made no charges for its service and could not make profits. The ECJ said that any body carrying on an economic activity is included, irrespective of the way it was financed. The critical factor was the kind of activity, not the formal legislative basis of the activity. This went very far and would subject the furnishing of most goods or services by the state to Articles 81 and 82 coupled with 86(1). Any derogation would have to be permitted under Article 86(2) as necessary and proportionate to enable the undertaking to fulfil a public interest task entrusted to it.

In *Poucet*,[29] however, it was held that the office for dispensing national insurance and health payments in France was not an undertaking for various reasons: the social security system performed a social function, was based on the principle of solidarity and those with bad health were subsidised by the more fortunate. The office enjoyed no discretion. A private firm could not afford to compete without favouring the better risks. The ECJ looked also to the office not being for profit. These criteria differ from those listed in *Höfner*, but the Court did not explain its thinking. Instead of stating that the funds were undertakings to which a social task had been entrusted and holding that Article 86(2) permitted a derogation provided that the rules went no further than necessary, it ruled that the social function and solidarity prevented the

---

26 *La Crespelle*, (323/93), [1994] ECR I–5077, paras 24–26.
27 (41/83) [1985] ECR 873, paras 17–20.
28 (C–41/90) [1991] ECR I–1979, paras 20–23.
29 *Poucet and ors v Assurances Générales de France and ors.* (C–159 & 160/91) [1993] ECR I–637, paras 18–20.

funds from being undertakings. This takes away the limitation in Article 86(2) that the measures must go no further than necessary. Many bodies granted special or exclusive rights contain an element of solidarity. Letters posted to an address within the same town subsidise those sent to a remote or distant destination. From *Poucet* it seems that such an element is sufficient to take the rules out of Article 86(1).

In *FFSA v Commission*,[30] the Court limited what it had decided in *Poucet*. The CCMSA managed a voluntary additional pension scheme for agricultural workers. The scheme enjoyed tax advantages and supplemented a compulsory scheme. Some private insurers challenged the French legislation that established the scheme on the basis that it had an effective monopoly— the premiums the private firms received were subject to income tax while those of CMMSA were not.

The ECJ ruled that CCMSA was an undertaking. It distinguished *Poucet* on the grounds that the CCMSA scheme was voluntary and benefits depended on the amount of contributions (para 17). The element of solidarity was narrowly limited (para 19). The CCMSA carried on an economic activity in competition with other pension funds and in much the same way (para 17). The fact that it was non-profit making was not enough to prevent its being an undertaking (para 21).

There have been several other judgments on whether statutory insurance funds carry on an economic activity. The line between them is narrow and unclear but it seems to depend on whether the fund was set up to promote public or private objectives, whether the body enjoys discretion or whether it is bound by statutory criteria, whether joining it is voluntary, whether there is considerable cross-subsidisation and on whether it is operated in the same way as competing funds in the private sector. The distinction between public and private objectives is not obvious to me.

Advocate General Jacobs tried to clarify the law in *AOK and others v Ichthyl-Gesellsschaft Cordes and others:*–[31]

> 32. It seems to me clear that compulsory state social security schemes such as those at issue in *Cisal* and *Poucet and Pistre* are not classified as economic activities because they are incompatible, even in principle, with the possibility of a private undertaking carrying them on. Such schemes entail such an element of redistribution in the interest of social solidarity that little or no scope remains for the various actuarial, investment and intermediary services which private pensions and insurance can and do supply on the market.

This would have left the justification on social grounds to Article 86(2) with the need to establish that the measures were necessary and proportionate.

The ECJ in *AOK*, however, preferred to follow *Poucet* and treated a social security system performing an exclusively social function based on solidarity

---

30   C–224/94. [1995] ECR I–4013.
31   C–264, 306 & 355/01, opinion 22 May 2003, 16 March 2004.

as not constituting an undertaking and being outside Article 86 altogether, whether or not the rules went further than required to enable it to perform its task in the public interest (paras 51–57).

6.2.2 *Unable to avoid infringing*

In *Höfner*, the ECJ said:

> 27. . . . [A]ny measure adopted by a Member State which maintains in force a statutory provision that creates a situation in which a public employment agency cannot avoid infringing Article 82 is incompatible with the Treaty.'

This is important because in Europe there are many state undertakings that provide subsidised services, for which the demand exceeds the supply, as in *Höfner*. In *Höfner* it is clear that the employment office could not satisfy the demand for head hunting services, but it could have hired more head hunters, unless the government limited its resources or activities.

6.2.3 *Mere exercise of exclusive right infringes*

In some cases, the ECJ has held that there must be an abuse by the undertaking with an exclusive right, and in others that it suffices if the exclusive right confers the potentiality of abuse.

In *Merci v Gabrielli*,[32] the exclusive right to unload and trans ship cargoes was entrusted under Italian legislation to co-operatives of workers in the port of Genoa. When a cargo of steel arrived, the workers in the co-operatives were on strike, and the ship was not permitted to use its own tackle to unload. The cargo owner sued in Italy and the ECJ was asked to make preliminary rulings under Article 234.

The co-operatives were ruled to be undertakings (paragraph 9). The port was considered a substantial part of the common market within the meaning of Article 82 because of the large amount of trade from other Member States that passed through it (paragraph 15). The statutory exclusive right led to the co-operatives enjoying a dominant position (paragraph 14). The ECJ also ruled that Italy infringed Article 86 if the mere exercise of the exclusive right by the co-operative infringed Article 82, or if the exclusive right were capable of creating a situation in which the undertaking was caused to commit an abuse, by one of four acts (paragraph 19):

—requiring payment for services that were not requested;
—charging disproportionate prices;
—refusing to use modern technology; or
—price discrimination.

---

32 *Merci Convenzionali Porto di Genova v Siderurgica Gabrielli* (C–179/90) [1991] ECR I–5889, paras 9, 15, 19, 23.

The Court added that even in the context of Article 86, Article 82 was directly effective and created rights for individuals, which national civil courts were required to protect (paragraph 23). The cargo owner may be able to sue the co-operatives for infringing Article 82 and also the Italian government for infringing Article 86, although it may be harder to quantify the damage than it was in *Francovich*.[33]

In *Corbeau*,[34] a former postman was prosecuted for infringing the Belgian postal monopoly by carrying on a business of collecting mail within the city of Liège and promising to deliver it by next morning for a charge of one Belgian franc less than the cost of a stamp. He was skimming the cream — delivering the letters that took little effort and not those to distant or sparsely populated parts of the country. The ECJ ruled that although the obligation of universal service imposed on the post office came within the derogation of Article 86(2), to refuse permission to others to compete by providing a superior service on any terms was contrary to Article 86 in combination with Article 82.

It is not clear what the petty criminal court in Liège should do. Should it work out how great a profit the post office needs on each letter within a substantial town in order to subsidise delivery at a distance or to areas where few people live? Such a task would be difficult for a regulatory Commission and virtually impossible without one. If the national court does not do this, would the postal service have to decide the matter itself, subject to review by the Commission which could make a decision under Article 86(3)?

Since *Höfner*, the ECJ has frequently stated that the holder of special or exclusive rights automatically enjoys a dominant position within the meaning of Article 82. Usually this will be so, as governments are unlikely to grant rights over only part of a market. Nevertheless, a monopolist of gas may suffer competition from wind power or electricity. It is hoped that where there is significant competition, even a firm with special or exclusive rights will not be treated as dominant (4.3.2 above).

While Member States were having difficulty ratifying the treaty of Maastricht, the Commission hesitated to use its power under Article 86(3) to adopt by directive or make individual decisions against Member States although, earlier, it had adopted two directives[35] on terminal equipment for telephones and on value added services. The Commission has since adopted several other directives to liberalise the telecommunications market. After considerable difficulty and delay, it has adopted directives liberalising the supply of energy under Article 95, which requires a regulation in the Council.

---

33   *Francovich v Italy* (C–6 & 9/90) [1990] ECR I–5357.
34   (C–320/91) [1993] ECR 2533.
35   Dir on Terminal Equipment, Dir 88/301, OJ 1988, L131/73. The Community ECJ upheld the Dir in *France v Commission* (202/88) [1991] ECR I–1223. See also the Services Dir, Dir 90/388, OJ 1990, L192/10.

6.2.4 *Extension of market power to another activity*

The ECJ has objected under Article 82 to the extension by a private firm of market power to an ancillary activity. This reflects its hostility to tying (5.2.3–5.2.3.11 above).

In several cases relating to sea and air ports, where the holder enjoyed special or exclusive rights, the ECJ has objected to discounts, usually in favour of the operator's own subsidiary or the national carrier, as being contrary to Article 82(c). Where a subsidiary is wholly owned, this seems formalistic. The transfer price to its own subsidiary is only an accounting entry. It does not matter whether profits are earned in the one company or the other: they enure to the group.

Discrimination in favour of the national carrier is more obviously contrary to Article 82(c) and treats the common market as not being integrated (5.2.2–5.2.2.3 above). In these cases, the operator was a natural monopoly and so super-dominant (4.3.9 above). It may be that discrimination by a less powerful undertaking that did not isolate parts of the common market would not be treated so strictly.

The categories of infringement under Article 86 in combination with Article 82 are not closed. The ECJ has been asked by national courts to interpret Article 86 and it may well be that complainants harmed by the failure of some liberalisation initiatives may take the matter before the ECJ through suit in a national court followed by a reference under Article 234. In the last few years, several requests for preliminary rulings have been made to the ECJ by Italian courts, and the ECJ has followed the law it created earlier, but it has not extended it.

Community law under Article 86 developed rapidly in the early 1990s at the expense of state regulation. Significant progress has been made since on telecommunications. At some point, the ECJ may relent and give greater recognition to state rights as it has done under Article 10.

6.2.5 *Derogation under Article 86(2)*

In *AOK and others v Ichthyl-Gesellsschaft Cordes and others*,[36] in an attempt to limit the cost of the national health scheme, a German statute required sickness funds to agree the maximum price they would reimburse for medicinal products. A patient might pay more, but the excess would not be reimbursed. Advocate General Jacobs had concluded that the sickness funds might well be undertakings and that they would infringe Article 81(1) if they enjoyed some autonomy in setting the price at a high level.

It was not disputed that the sickness funds were entrusted with the operation of a service of general economic interest (para 87). To escape liability under Article 81 for damages (para 104) by virtue of Article 86(2), they would

---

36 C–264, 306 & 355/01, opinion 22 May 2003, judgment 16 March 2004.

have to show also that fixing the maximum prices that they would reimburse was necessary to enable them to perform their general interest task of providing general health insurance. It would suffice to show that the task could not be performed in economically acceptable conditions or in conditions of financial stability (para 88).

To qualify under Article 86(2), the agreement on maximum prices must be proportional. It did not matter that the agreement had not been notified under Article 81(3). The derogation under Article 86(2) is separate from that under Article 81(3). The main disagreement was whether there were alternative institutional arrangements to contain the costs of medicinal products. It was not necessary to show that alternatives were inconceivable (para 94). Community law allows national authorities considerable freedom in organising their social security systems. The derogation would now be applicable only if the measures were manifestly disproportionate. Other states had adopted more invasive controls. The ECJ never reached this issue, as it ruled that the funds were not undertakings subject to Article 81.

In *Albany*, the ECJ had looked to four relevant factors when applying Article 86(2):

1–the specification of criteria by the minister,
2–the complexity of evaluating the effects of particular decisions on the financial equilibrium of the undertaking,
3–the state's margin of appreciation in relation to social security and
4–the existence of adequate national judicial review to prevent arbitrary decisions.

Whether those conditions prevailed would be a question for the national court to determine.

6.3　Undertakings infringe only by autonomous conduct

Articles 86 and 10 may be used in conjunction with both Article 81 and Article 82. Undertakings infringe these Articles, however, only if their conduct is autonomous. In *Commission and France v Ladbroke Racing*,[37] the ECJ, following considerable case law, said:

> 33. Articles 85 and 86 (now Articles 81 and 82) of the Treaty apply only to anti-competitive conduct engaged in by undertakings on their own initiative. . . . If anti-competitive conduct is required of undertakings by national legislation or if the latter creates a legal framework which itself eliminates any possibility of competitive activity on their part, Articles 81 and 82 do not apply. In such a situation, the restriction of competition is not attributable, as those provisions implicitly require, to the autonomous conduct of the undertaking.

37　C–359 and 379/95P, [1997] ECR I–6265, citations omitted in the following quotations. National competition authorities as well as courts may declare national legislation incompatible with Articles 81 or 82 in combination with Articles 11 or 86 (7.3.2 below).

34. Articles 81 and 82 may apply however, if it is found that the national legislation does not preclude undertakings from engaging in autonomous conduct which prevents, restricts or distorts competition.

35. When the Commission is considering the applicability of Articles 85 and 86 of the Treaty to the conduct of undertakings, a prior evaluation of national legislation affecting such conduct should therefore be directed solely to ascertaining whether that legislation prevents undertakings from engaging in autonomous conduct which prevents, restricts or distorts competition.'

In *Consorzio Industries Fiammiferi (CIF) v Autorità Garante della Concorrenza e del Mercato*[38] and other cases, the ECJ applied these paragraphs. Italian legislation conferred a fiscal and commercial monopoly on CIF to manufacture and sell matches for consumption in Italy. CIF was a consortium of match manufacturers whose operations were governed by agreements between CIF and the Italian state.

The legislation was amended several times. At first membership was limited and compulsory. As required by this legislation a quota allocation committee of CIF allocated production and sales quotas. The Committee consisted of an official of the State Monopolies Board, who acted as chairman, a representative of the CIF and three representatives of the member undertakings. Its decisions were taken by simple majority, so the chairman could be outvoted. As described at 6.1.4 above in relation to Article 10, this committee was representing the interests of the members rather than the state.

This agreement was held unconstitutional by the Italian Constitutional Court as new manufacturers were excluded. So a ministerial decree of 1983 made provision for new members to be included. The latest version of the decree in 1992 still required production quotas to be allocated and retail prices to be fixed.

A match manufacturer in Germany complained to the Italian competition authority that it was still having difficulty distributing its products on the Italian market.

The Autorità distinguished three kinds of conduct among the CIF's activities:

1. conduct required by legislation,
2. conduct facilitated by legislation and
3. conduct attributable to CIF's own initiatives.

It found that legislation shielded the first category of conduct, but that it should be disapplied for the future by any court or public administrative body because of the direct effect and priority of Community law. Conduct that was not required, such as the actual way the quotas were handled was subject to Article 81, because the CIF had some discretion. Finally once CIF's fiscal and commercial monopoly was terminated, Article 81 clearly applied.

38   (C–198/01), 9 September 2003, [2003] 5 CMLR 829.

An appeal was brought against the decision of the Autorità and the national court made a reference to the ECJ, asking whether Article 81 requires or permits a national competition authority to disapply a state measure and to penalise anti-competitive conduct of undertakings, and if so with what legal consequences. It also asked whether compulsory membership of a body with power to allocate production and fix retail prices precluded undertakings from engaging in autonomous conduct that may affect trade between Member States and prevent, restrict or distort competition.

The ECJ cited many of the cases considered at 6.1–6.1.6 above, and others and concluded:

> 49. The duty to disapply national legislation which contravenes Community law applies not only to national courts but also to all organs of the state including administrative authorities (. . . .), which entails, if the circumstance so require, the obligation to take all appropriate measures to enable Community law to be fully applied (. . .). [citations omitted]

> 50. Since a national authority such as the Authority is responsible for ensuring, *inter alia* that Article 81 is observed and that provision, in conjunction with Article 10 EC imposes a duty on Member States to refrain from introducing measures contrary to the Community competition rules, those rules would be rendered less effective, if in the course of an investigation under Article 81 (EC) into the conduct of undertakings, the authority were not able to declare a national measure contrary to the combined provisions of Article 10 EC and 81 EC and if, consequently, it failed to disapply it.

Since May 2004 all Member States have been required to empower their competition authorities to apply Article 81 and 82 (7.3.2 below). Consequently, paragraph 50 will become of wide application.

The ECJ also ruled (paras 52–54) that where the undertakings had no autonomy under national law, they should not be penalised for activities before the national legislation was disapplied because of the general principle of legal certainty. For conduct after the disapplication of the legislation becomes definitive, however, penalties may be imposed.

Where the legislation merely encourages or facilitates anti-competitive conduct, however, penalties may be imposed for activities preceding the decision of disapplication, although the conflict of legislation may mitigate the penalty.

The ECJ made it clear that it is for the national court to find the facts, but it suggested that the freedom of the members of the CIF to buy and sell quotas might be autonomous conduct of the members contrary to Article 81. In my view, however, it would not be anti-competitive (see para 34 of *Ladbroke Racing*, quoted 6.3 above). As the Advocate General observed in *CIF*, (para 16), agreements on quotas favour the survival of inefficient firms, but it is less inefficient to enable the higher cost firms to sell part of their quotas to those that can use them more efficiently.

6.4 State monopolies of a commercial character (Article 31)

Article 31 provides that:

> Member States shall adjust any State monopolies of a commercial character so as to ensure that no discrimination regarding the conditions under which goods are procured and marketed exists between nationals of Member States.
>
> The provisions of this Article shall apply to any body through which a Member state, in law or in fact, either directly or indirectly supervises, determines or appreciably influences imports or exports between Member States. These provisions shall likewise apply to monopolies delegated by the State to others.
>
> 2. Member States shall refrain from introducing any new measure which is contrary to the principles laid down in para 1 or which restricts the scope of the Articles dealing with the prohibition of customs duties and quantitative restrictions between Member States.

Paragraph 3 makes a special provision for agriculture.

Article 31 does not require the abolition of such monopolies, only that they be adjusted to prevent discrimination against nationals from other Member States. It is part of the rules for free movement. The Commission continues to monitor the conduct of Member States under Article 31 and may proceed against infringements under either Article 226 or under Article 86(3). If proceedings are started under Article 226, the Commission must give the ECJ the information required to enable it to decide whether there has been an infringement. If the proceedings are brought under Article 86, the Member State may establish that the conduct was necessary to its special task under Article 86(2). Article 31 has direct effect. Consequently, a national from another Member State that suffers discrimination may sue in a national court.[39]

6.5 State aids (Articles 87–89)

Possibly the most important way for states to distort trade is by the grant of aid. Politicians are subject to strong temptation to be seen to decrease unemployment in a marginal constituency by subsidising failing firms, even if the inefficiency leads in the longer run to greater unemployment through the need to raise taxes to pay for the aid and to loss of work to international competitors once the aid is reduced. Aids are controlled by the Competition department under Articles 87–89 of the treaty. Article 87(1) provides that:

> . . . any aid granted by a member state or through state resources in any form whatsoever which distorts or threatens to distort competition by favouring certain undertakings or the production of certain goods shall, in so far as it affects trade between Member States, be incompatible with the common market. . . .

---

39   *Commission v Netherlands*, C–157/94, [1997] ECR I–5699.

The concept of an aid from state resources is very broad and covers not only grants, loans at a low rate of interest and deferment of tax liabilities, but also schemes of aid financed by compulsory contributions by all traders including those who do not benefit and, in general, any gratuitous advantage such as a state guarantee of the firm's debts.

The worst sufferers from state aids may be firms in the same industry locally that have to meet subsidised competition, profitable firms in the same country that have to pay taxes higher than they might otherwise be in order to provide the state resources and the workers that these would otherwise employ. These effects, however, are not on trade between Member States so are not restrained by Article 87. The Commission can control aids only in so far as firms in another Member State suffer too.

Since the Commission has discretion to authorise aids, Article 87 is not directly applicable until the Commission makes an individual decision refusing to authorise an aid. All new state aids are illegal, however, unless notified by the government to the Commission and approved by it, and this provision does have direct effect. The Commission may, and normally does, require the state to recover at least part of the aid illegally paid even if it has been spent. So there is danger in accepting the aid, unless the government has notified it.

State aids increased as the unemployment statistics deteriorated in the early 1980s and again in the mid-1990s. The Commission has taken more decisions condemning them and the ECJ has confirmed its powers, but condemned some decisions of the Commission for failing adequately to state the reasons on which they were based. The Commission's later decisions have set out its reasons better, and it has been clarifying its practice on the control of aids. Appeals from decisions on state aids that are not brought by Member States now go before the CFI, which may well require the Commission's practice to be more open.

Nevertheless, the limitation of state aids is a highly political exercise, and many very large ones have been permitted, subject to conditions and, allegedly, 'for the last time.' Yet further aids have been permitted to the same firms subsequently. This has been criticised and actions are being brought by competitors to quash the decisions permitting them.

Interesting remedies may be available. Previously, if a firm's competitor obtained a state aid, the natural reaction was to seek one too. Now the firm may complain to the Commission, and it is strongly arguable that a firm that suffers can recover damages from the state.[40] This field is also developing. The Member of the Commission responsible for competition policy has been spending more time on government measures than on the activities of firms in

---

40   The ECJ's language in *Francovich v Italy* (C–6 & 9/90) [1991] ECR I–5357, was far broader than necessary to deal with a directive which the Italian government failed to implement. The ECJ made it clear that national courts must provide an effective remedy for infringements of Community law.

the private sector. The Commission's work on state aids is described annually in its Reports on Competition Policy.

6.6 Anti-dumping duties (Article 133)

Anti-dumping duties may be imposed by the Commission where imported products are sold within the Community at prices below the comparable prices in the country of export plus the cost of freight, customs duties etc., if a Community industry is harmed. These duties must then be confirmed by the Council. Countervailing duties may also be imposed on imports that have been subsidised abroad by the government.

The task of imposing anti-dumping duties is performed by the department responsible for foreign affairs, not that responsible for competition, and the Commission has delegated power to the Commissioner responsible to make decisions binding the Commission. The calculations of the price in the country of export are not always transparent. Sometimes the goods are not sold there, sometimes the country of export is not a market economy, and a price is constructed based on a price somewhere else.

Duties have sometimes led to an importer operating a 'screwdriver' operation within the Community, importing parts, and assembling them here. Firms downstream, which require the imports, complain that they are being made to bear the cost of the antidumping duty and cannot remain competitive in world markets if they continue to produce in Europe. Some control of such duties is now being exercised by the World Trade Organisation in Geneva, and this may be more effective than the old GATT panels.

It is not easy for an outsider to estimate either the economic effects of anti-dumping and countervailing duties. It is said that it is hard for the importers to challenge whether Community interests have been harmed. The procedures are not very transparent, but this is another area where the CFI is beginning to intervene effectively. The subject is important, but will not be considered in this book.

6.7 Conflict between competition rules and other Community policies

Some Community policies, such as the principle of free movement and competition were adopted in the original EEC Treaty. Others were added at Maastricht. The Treaty does not provide which should prevail over others. To the extent that one policy can be restricted and conflict avoided, doubtless that will be done as in *Albany* (6.7.2 below) but in some factual circumstances, they are entirely inconsistent and it has to be decided which should prevail.

6.7.1 *Free movement and intellectual property*

An early clash came between intellectual property rights and free movement of goods and the doctrine of exhaustion was created (10.4 below). The specific subject-matter of the intellectual property right was accepted, but the ECJ ruled that it could not be exercised to restrict free movement. One can sue someone for fraudulently infringing a mark to which he has no right at all, but not someone who had the right to sell in one Member State and tried to take advantage of it in another. In *Centrafarm BV and de Peijper v Sterling Drug Inc.*[41] the ECJ stressed that Article 30 was an exception to one of the fundamental principles of the Treaty, and limited its protection of intellectual property rights significantly despite the express exception in Article 30 of conduct justified on grounds of the protection of industrial and commercial property.

6.7.2 *Social policy and competition*

Where a task of general interest has been entrusted to an undertaking, Article 86(2) provides that the limitation of the competition or other rules shall be proportionate. Unfortunately, in several but not all cases, the ECJ has tended to say that a social purpose and solidarity takes measures entirely outside the competition rules, because the institutions are not undertakings, and then there is no mechanism for applying the doctrine of proportionality.

In *Albany*,[42] Dutch law required the members of various professions to contribute to pensions through a single public fund. The rules favoured those with ill health over the healthy, so there was considerable solidarity and private schemes would not be able to compete. The ECJ told the referring court that:

> 59. It is beyond question that certain restrictions of competition are inherent in collective agreements between organisations representing employers and workers. However, the social policy objectives pursued by such agreements would be seriously undermined if management and labour were subject to Article 81(1) of the Treaty when seeking jointly to adopt measures to improve conditions of work and employment.

> 60. It therefore follows from an interpretation of the provisions of the Treaty as a whole which is both effective and consistent with agreements concluded in the context of collective negotiations between management and labour in pursuit of such objectives must, by virtue of their nature and purpose, be regarded as falling outside the scope of Article 81(1).

At paragraphs 103–4, under Article 86(2), the ECJ took into consideration the national interest in using an undertaking, particularly in the public sector, as an instrument of economic or fiscal policy. Article 86(2) is probably more appropriate than Article 81(3) to reconciling a conflict of Community policies, since the need to perform the public interest task rather than the benefit to consumers would be weighed against the anti-competitive effects of the

---

41   (15/74), [1974] ECR 1147, para 8.
42   *Albany International BV v Stichting, Bedrijfspensioenfonds Textielindustrie and others,* (C–67/96, C–115–117 and 219/97) [1999] ECR I–5751, paras 102–3.

agreement. It leaves the difficult issue how far state rights should escape the competition rules to national courts.

Social policy was narrowly defined in *Albany*, but completely trumped considerations of competition.

6.7.3 *The environment and competition*

In *CECED*,[43] the Commission exempted under Article 81(3) the recommendation of a trade association of firms making electrical equipment to discontinue production of machines that used excessive amounts of electricity. The problem is that one of the conditions of Article 81(3) is that a fair share of the benefit must be passed onto the consumers of the product affected. This recommendation was motivated by environmental considerations, but the Commission added that consumers of the equipment would benefit from the saving in electricity, which would compensate for the greater expense within months.

In this decision, the commission could not take advantage of Article 86(2) because no task in the general interest had been entrusted to the trade association or its members.

Sometimes, such a benefit to consumers of the products may not be available to validate an exemption. Of more general application is the end of notification from May 2004.

This should make it easier for national judges to make decisions under Article 81(3). They will not be required to balance the value of different policies.

6.7.4 *Other Community policies and competition*

Judge Joliet argued in *Leclerc v Au Blé Vert*,[44] that the Court may have been influenced by cultural policy (6.1.4 above).

6.8 Conclusion

There is a continuing tension between state rights to intervene in the economy and Community competition law. Community legislation is adopted in part by the Council of Ministers, which is sensitive to state rights, so the battle for state control may be won in the Council as well as in the courts. Politicians must be seen to do something about unemployment and pollution and are tempted to raise barriers to entry and expansion in that endeavour.

The law considered in this chapter has fluctuated over time. Social policy is important when unemployment is high and increasing. Environmental policy has become important since Maastricht. Often the conflict between policies is

---

43   OJ 2000, L187/47, [2000] 5 CMLR 635.
44   (229/83) [1985] ECR 32.

hidden under the guise of defining legal terms, such as 'undertaking'. This and the unwillingness of the courts to give separate or dissenting decisions make it dangerous to rely on older case law and difficult to give firm advice.

6.9 Bibliography

Guiliano Amato, *Antitrust and the Bounds of Power: the Dilemma of Liberal Democracy in the History of the Market*, (Oxford, Hart Publishing, 1977).

Jose Luis Buendia Sierra, *Exclusive Rights and State Monopolies under EC Law: Article 86 (former Article 90) of the EC Treaty*, (Oxford, OUP, 1999).

Luc Gyselen, 'Anticompetitive State Measures under the EC Treaty: Towards a Substantive Legality Standard' [1994] *EL Rev* competition checklist for 1993, CC 55–65.

Allan B Hoffman, 'Anti-competitive State Legislation Condemned under Articles 5, 85 and 86 of the EEC Treaty: How Far Should the Court Go' [1990] *ECLR* 11.

René Joliet, 'National Anti-competitive Legislation and Community Law,' in Barry Hawk (ed) [1988] *Fordham Corporate Law Institute*, chap 16.

7. Enforcement after Regulation 1/2003

7.1 Introduction

If the competition rules are to be effective in helping to integrate the common market and improve efficiency for the benefit of consumers, they must be enforced. Enforcement by the Commission and by national competition authorities (NCAs) under Regulation 2001/03 will be described at 7.3.1 and 7.3.2 below. Enforcement by national courts through the law of tort or a refusal to enforce provisions in a contract that have been made illegal and void by Article 81 and 82 will be considered mainly at 7.3.4 below. The Regulation entered into force on 1 May, 2004. The references in this chapter, mostly in brackets, to Articles or recitals are to those in Regulation 1/2003, unless otherwise specified.

In 1962, Regulation 17[1] was adopted by the Council and gave considerable powers to the Commission to design and implement competition policy. Only it was empowered to grant individual exemptions under Article 81(3). The Commission treated any restriction of conduct important on the market as infringing Article 81(1). Consequently, the difficult decisions as to whether an agreement infringed Article 81 were reserved to it and it hoped to achieve a coherent competition policy throughout the Common Market.

To obtain an individual exemption it was necessary to notify an agreement to the Commission. This was not simple, but required a written analysis of the market and a statement of the reasons why the agreement might infringe Article 81(1) as well as why it merited exemption. The Commission had to allocate staff to monitoring the notifications, which rarely revealed any serious infringements of Article 81(1). If granted, exemptions were constitutive: for a specified period Article 81(1) did not apply to an agreement, unless and until the exemption was withdrawn by a formal decision on a limited number of grounds.

The system of enforcement is very different from that in the USA, where the agencies detect infringements and then prosecute offenders before the courts. The tasks of detection and prohibiting or punishing an infringement are in different hands. Enforcement by the Commission has been described as Kafkaesque in that it operated as policeman, judge and jury.

By the 1990s the notification system in Europe was perceived as cumbersome: as creating unnecessary work for both the Commission and the parties. The regulatory approach, with the Commission granting dispensations subject to conditions was also inconsistent with the liberal concept of a free market.

The Commission's exclusive power to exempt also created difficulties when enforcing a contract. Before litigating in a national court the parties to

---

1   Main implementing regulation, OJ Spec Ed., 1959–62, 87, JO 1962, 204.

a contract had to notify the agreement and wait for the Commission to grant an exemption, which in most cases could be retrospective only to the date of notification. The Commission lacked the resources to grant many exemptions. So this created delays in enforcing contracts and made it more difficult to settle disputes.

Moreover, the defendant to an action had only to ask the Commission for an exemption for a national court to have to adjourn an action to enforce a contract or an NCA to suspend proceedings under Article 81. An analysis of these the procedural rules for exemption can be found in any competition book published before 2003.

The Commission now wants to devote its scarce resources to controlling:

—international cartels, which would be easier for it than for a national authority, since the evidence and parties may be in several different countries.
—state aids and
—the conduct of nationalised industries and other undertakings granted special or exclusive rights, which only it has power to control by decision or directive.

The Commission therefore proposed and the Council adopted Regulation 1/2003,[2] which came into force on 1 May 2004 when the candidate countries from Eastern and Southern Europe joined the Community. It repeals Regulation 17, thereby abolishing the system of notification.

Mergers are controlled under Council Regulation 4064 on merger control[3] (chapter 12 below) and Regulation 1/2003 does not apply to concentrations as defined in the merger regulation including full function joint ventures. Only the Commission can control those where the turnover of the undertakings concerned exceeds the thresholds prescribed in the merger regulation, and for those, notification remains obligatory. NCAs may apply national law to mergers below those thresholds.

Article 81(3) will now have direct effect in the courts and before the NCAs of Member States (Articles 1(2), 5 and 6).

Article 2 provides that the burden of establishing an infringement of Article 81(1) rests on the person alleging illegality, but the justification for the application of Article 81(3) must be established by the parties.

In the old case of *Consten and Grundig v Commission*,[4] the ECJ said that:

59. The undertakings are entitled to an appropriate examination by the Commission of their requests for 81(3) to be applied. For this purpose the Commission may not confine itself to requiring from undertakings proof of

---

2   OJ 2003, L1/1, [2003] 4 CMLR 551.
3   Council Regulation 139/2004, on the Control of concentrations between undertakings, OJ 2004, L24/1, [2004] 4 CMLR 000.
4   (56 & 58/64), [1966] ECR 299, [1966] CMLR 418, CMR 8046.

the fulfilment of the requirements for the grant of an exemption but must, as a matter of good administration, play its part, using the means available to it, in ascertaining the relevant facts and circumstance.

Article 2 provides that the burden of proof under Article 81(1) is on the person alleging that it is infringed, but that under Article 81(3) it is on the party alleging legality. This seems to override the judgment in *Grundig* and enable to Commission merely to leave it to the parties to establish a justification for a restraint on competition. The distinction between Article 81(1) and (3) may not be easy to draw as, unless the justification is based on environmental protection, social policy, or other non-competition grounds, the same arguments may be used under both paragraphs of the Article. If the parties cannot defend their conduct with the benefit of the burden of proof under Article 81(1), they are not very likely to justify it under Article 81(3). There may be little scope for Article 81(3) where the justification is based on competitive grounds.

The provisions of the EEA treaty are similar. By virtue of Article 56 (EEA), where the agreements affect trade only between the EFTA states, the EFTA Surveillance Authority (ESA) is competent. Where trade between only EC Member States is affected, the EC Commission is competent. In other cases where trade between an EFTA and one or more EC Member States are affected, the ESA has competence only if one third of the turnover of the undertakings concerned is in the EFTA area. Even before the accession of Austria, Finland and Sweden to the EC this was rarely the case. Now that the EEA members consist only of Norway, Iceland and Lichtenstein, the ESA is rarely competent.

In order to ensure uniform standards, the two authorities are required by Article 58 (EEA) to co-operate with each other. If the wrong authority is notified, for instance, the file will be passed to the other. Only the EC Commission has power to control mergers over the thresholds provided by the EC Regulation.

The existing EC regulations were adopted in Annex XIV to the EEA treaty, and more recent ones are adopted some months later by the ESA and are then incorporated into the national laws by national legislation (see Article 105 (EEA)). In accordance with Article 105, the EFTA Court and the ESA deliberately interpret the law in the same way as the EC institutions. The concept of the two pillars works better than might have been expected.

Under Article 105(3) (EEA) where differences in case law or any other dispute concerning the interpretation of the law arise which the EEA Joint Committee cannot resolve, the dispute settlement procedure may be invoked by a Member State. If the dispute concerns provisions of the EEA Agreement that correspond in substance to the EC provisions, the EFTA states may authorise their national courts to request a binding ruling from the ECJ on the interpretation of the relevant rules.

If no ruling is requested and the Joint Committee fails to reach a solution, the Contracting Parties may consider taking unilateral safeguard measures where 'serious economic, societal or environmental difficulties of a sectorial or regional nature liable to persist are arising'.[5]

Whatever institution is considering legality, the burden of establishing that Article 81(1) applies to an agreement falls on the undertaking or institution alleging illegality, but the burden of justifying the application of Article 81(3) rests on the party alleging it (Article 2). Often the same matters are critical under both parts of Article 81, so there may not be many applications of Article 81(3), save where non-competitive factors are relevant, such as protection of culture or the environment.

7.2 Articles 81 and 82 are directly applicable in national courts and authorities

Even before the adoption of Regulation 1/2003, in *BRT v SABAM*,[6] The ECJ ruled that Articles 81(1) and (2) and 82 have direct effect in national courts. Infringements give rise to an action for non-contractual liability. In *Consorzio Industries Fiammiferi (CIF) v Autorità Garante della Concorrenza e del Mercato*[7] (6.1 above) the ECJ ruled that the direct effect and priority of Community law obliges a national administrative authority which is authorised to apply Articles 81 and 82 to disapply national legislation that requires undertakings to act so as to restrict competition when this may affect trade between Member States. If the national legislation left no room for competition it may impose penalties for conduct taking place after the decision of disapplication has become final. If there was some scope for the undertakings not to infringe Article 81, it could impose penalties even for conduct predating the decision of disapplication.

During the 1990s, the ECJ held that national courts must provide adequate remedies for breach of Community law, although most of the cases have been against governments. It is for national law to establish procedural rules such as which court has jurisdiction, but the remedy must be proportionate, efficacious, and no worse than that available for infringement of national law. A person harmed by a breach of community law must be able to sue for damages and this must not be made impossibly difficult.

In the UK the House of Lords held in *Garden Cottage Foods v Milk Marketing Board*[8] that the appropriate action would be for breach of statutory duty. In *Peterbroeck*,[9] the ECJ ruled that a national court cannot be pre-

---

5   Art 112 *(EEA)*.
6   *BRT v SABAM* (127/73) [1974] ECR 51, paras 16 and 17; *Ahmed Saeed* (66/86) [1989] ECR 803, para 33.
7   (C–198/01) [2003] 5 CMLR 829.
8   [1984] AC 130.
9   *Peterbroeck, Van Campenhout & Cie v Belgian State* (C–312/93) [1995] ECR I–4599 and *Van Schijndel*, 430/90, [1995] ECR 1–4705, paras 17 & 19 and Commission's notice on cooperation between the Commission and the National Courts, OJ 1993, C39/6 paras 18–23.

vented by domestic rules of procedure from considering of its own motion whether a measure of domestic law is compatible with a provision of EC law.

In *Leclerc v Commission*,[10] the CFI stated that according to consistent case law, national courts can apply Article 81(1) as a result of its direct effect. Consequently, a dealer wrongly excluded from a selective distribution system can bring action before national courts or before national authorities.

In *Courage v Crehan*,[11] the tenant of a pub was sued by Courage for rent and other breaches of contract. It pleaded in an English court that the agreement, which included a beer tie, infringed Article 81(1) and had caused it damage in that it had to pay more than a free house would have done for its beer. Under English law, if the tie infringed Article 81 it would be illegal and *ex turpi causa non oritur actio*: the party to an illegal contract cannot obtain help from the courts.

The ECJ ruled that the national court must provide a remedy for someone harmed by an infringement of Article 81, although it might be proper to deny relief when the claimant was significantly responsible for the breach. The absolute ban on recovery under English law had, therefore, to be set aside.

Moreover, where an agreement infringes Article 81(1) and does not merit exemption, the provisions that restrict competition will be void by virtue of Article 81(2). This used to give rise to problems in that either party could apply to the Commission for an exemption, and proceedings would be delayed, possibly for years, while the Commission decided whether to grant one. Now, by virtue of Article 1 of Regulation 1/2003, a national court may itself consider whether it is appropriate to apply Article 81(3). So there will be no need to adjourn to let the Commission consider the issue.

7.3 Community powers of NCAs, Commission and national courts

Only national courts are concerned with Article 81(2) which renders void contractual provisions, but all three institutions may be concerned with Article 81(1) and (3) and with Article 82. The Regulation provides procedural rules and remedies only for proceedings before the Commission. In proceedings before a national authority or court, procedure and remedies are a matter for national law even when dealing with an infringement of Community law. Member States are, however, required by Article 35 to designate NCAs. These may well consist of a general competition authority, but may also include sector regulators, for instance of telecommunications, energy or other pubic utilities.

---

10 (*Yves Saint Laurent*) (T–19/92), [1996] ECR II–1851, para 128 and (*Givenchy*) (T–88/92) [1996] ECR II 1961, para 22.

11 (C–453/99) [2001] ECR 1–6297. Thereafter, the English court considered the Community case law on beer ties carefully and found that in its economic context the agreement did not infringe Article 81(1); Rob Merkin, 'A Survey of Recent Judgments, Decisions, Legislation and other Legal Developments in UK Competition Law,' *Competition Law Insight*, (October 2003).

7.3.1 *National powers of NCAs and courts—Article 3*

NCAs have the responsibility for enforcing national competition laws most of which are copies of Articles 81 and 82, save that there is no requirement that trade between Member States be affected (a concept considered at 2.3–2.3.4 above). They are also empowered by Article 5 to enforce Articles 81 and 82.

Until now, NCAs have usually preferred to operate under national law as

1) they had no power to apply Article 81(3) and
2) might lose their powers to enforce Article 81(1) or 82 should the Commission decide to take up the case or
3) should the undertaking being pursued request an individual exemption from the Commission.

The first reason for not applying Community law no longer applies as NCAs have power to apply Article 81(3) (Articles 1 and 6). Nor does the third reason remain valid as notification to the Commission requesting an individual exception will no longer be possible and an NCA may, itself, apply Article 81(3) (recital 6). The second reason is no longer strong as the Commission does not intend to intervene frequently unless several Member States are affected significantly. Then it will do so only after consultation through the network of competition authorities.

If all NCAs and courts apply the same criteria, substantially different practice in different Member States is less likely to develop. So, to ensure uniform application throughout the common market, Article 3 of Regulation 1/2003 provides that if there may be an effect on trade between Member States[12] NCAs and courts that apply their national competition law to an agreement must also apply Article 81. Recital 8 states that agreements may not be forbidden under national competition law if they are not also prohibited by Community competition law. Nevertheless, recital 8 adds that unilateral action can be prohibited under national law, even if it also infringes Article 82. This was inserted to preserve the German law on unfair competition (Article 3(3) and recital 9). The double barrier theory, according to which citizens must comply with both Community and national competition law, is retained in relation to unilateral action (7.3.4 below), but not for collusion. National competition rules cannot forbid agreements that may affect trade between Member States and that either escape Article 81(1) or qualify under Article 81(3). NCAs and courts may, however, apply prohibitions that are not related to concerns for competition, such as infancy, fraud or duress.

NCAs and courts may also apply national laws controlling anti-competitive mergers that are below the thresholds of turnover set by the merger regulation (Article 3(3) of Regulation 1/2003).

---

12   (2.3–2.3.5 above). See Commission's guidelines on the effect on trade concept, O.J. 2004, C101/81 G 9 *et seq.*

7.3.2 *Community law powers of NCAs and Commission—Articles 5 and 7–10*

Article 43 of Regulation 1/2003 repeals Regulation 17 and this terminates the provisions for notification and the exclusive power of the Commission to apply Article 81(3), although some of the case law under Regulation 17 will continue to apply under the new Regulation. Article 5 provides that NCAs shall have power to apply Articles 81 and 82 in individual cases. This required an amendment of the law in several Member States.

Article 1 together with recital 4 confirms that the doctrine of direct effect applies to administrative action and provides:

1. Agreements, decisions and concerted practices caught by Article 81(1) of the Treaty which do not satisfy the conditions of Article 81(3) of the Treaty shall be prohibited, no prior decision to that effect being required.
2. Agreements, decisions and concerted practices caught by Article 81(1) of the Treaty which satisfy the conditions of Article 81(3) of the Treaty shall not be prohibited, no prior decision to that effect being required.
3. The abuse of a dominant position referred to in Article 82 of the Treaty shall be prohibited, no prior decision to that effect being required.

Although the Article, drafted in the passive voice, does not make it clear who can declare that conduct is or is not forbidden, recital 4 clarifies that this may be done by the Commission, an NCA or national court. Article 1 is supported by Articles 4–10 which confer powers on all three.

Article 5 confers powers on NCAs to make decisions, whether acting on their own initiative or on complaint:

—requiring that an infringement be brought to an end,
—ordering interim measures and
—accepting commitments (i.e. undertakings from the parties),

NCAs may also impose fines, periodic penalty payments or any other penalty provided for in their national law. The Commission also has power to impose fines and periodic penalties (Articles 18–21 (7.6 below)).

By virtue of Article 5, NCAs may also certify that on the basis of the facts in their possession there is no ground for action on their part. The Commission may do so by virtue of Article 10, but only in exceptional circumstances where the public interest of the Community so requires (recital 14). The Community public interest may require such a negative clearance when divergent interpretations have been given in different Member States (recital 14). Such clearance may also be sought when the agreement will be the basis of substantial sunk cost.

The nature of a declaration under Article 81(3) will change. Collusion will no longer be exempted by a constitutive act of the Commission for a specified period. The Commission, NCAs or national courts will be able to declare

Article 81(1) inapplicable on the grounds set out in Article 81(3), but the declaration will apply only at the time it is made. It will not continue for a specified period. Circumstances may change and the declaration not be of much use for a later period.[13] The treatment of Article 81(3) is the most radical change to the Community competition rules in 40 years. The substantive bifurcation of Article 81(1) and (3) has gone.

Similar powers are conferred on the Commission in rather more detail by Articles 7–10. In ordering termination of an infringement, the Commission is expressly empowered to impose structural remedies, where there is no equally effective behavioural remedy, or where such a remedy would be more burdensome. In the case of a joint venture that does not fall within the merger regulation (chapters 12 and 13 below), the Commission might order that the some of the assets of one of the firms be sold, when the other has competing activities. Since the remedies available to NCAs and national courts are a matter for national law, this has not been provided for them.

The Commission can order interim measures only in cases of urgency due to the risk of serious and irreparable harm, and on the basis of a prima facie finding of infringement.

Such a decision will apply for a specified period of time, but may be renewed if necessary and appropriate. The powers of national authorities will depend on national law and this may give rise to forum shopping.

Where the Commission intends to order that an infringement be terminated and commitments are offered by the parties, the Commission may make these binding (Article 9 and recital 13).[14] Such a decision may be adopted for a specified period and shall state that there are no longer grounds for action by the Commission. On request or on its own initiative, the Commission may reopen the proceedings if there has been a material change in the facts, where an undertaking acts contrary to its commitments or where it was based on incomplete, incorrect or misleading information provided by the parties. No such power is provided for NCAs, since their procedural rules and remedies are governed by national law.

The Commission has been given power by other Council regulations to adopt group exemptions (3.2 above). Article 29(1) of Regulation 1/2003 provides that the Commission may withdraw the benefit of a group exemption in a particular case, if it finds that the agreement has effects contrary to Article 81(3). Where an agreement benefitting from a group exemption has effects contrary to Article 81(3) in the territory of a Member State or part thereof, which constitutes a distinct geographic market, the NCA of that state may withdraw the benefit of the exemption in respect of that territory.

---

13   *The Coca-Cola Company and Coca-Cola Enterprises Inc v Commission*, T–125 & 127/97, [2000] ECR II 1733, para 82.
14   John Temple Lang, 'Commitment Decisions under Regulation 1/2003: Legal Aspects of a New Kind of Competition Decision, (2003) 24 *European Competition Law Review*, 347.

There is no provision, as there is the Regulation 2790/99 (9.6.6 below) for the Commission to adopt a regulation withdrawing the exemption for a sector of the economy. The new group exemption for technology transfer includes such a power.[15] It seems that such powers will now be included when the power to grant a group exemption is exercised.

7.3.3 Co-operation between competition authorities—Articles 12–14

Similar powers have been given to the Commission and NCAs and it is necessary to decide who does what. Article 11(1), therefore provides for close co-operation between the Commission and the NCAs.[16]

Commission and NCAs are required to give the other notice of proceedings and copies of the most important documents (Article 11). Article 12 enables NCAs to use as evidence, even confidential documents, provided by the Commission to establish a breach of the Community competition rules, or a breach of national competition law when that is being alleged in parallel with EC competition law and does not lead to a different result.

This reverses the earlier case law of the ECJ in *Spanish Banks*[17] where it was held that an NCA might not use confidential information obtained from the Commission in order to establish an infringement of either Spanish or Community law. Subject to Article 12, however, the information may not be used as evidence for other purposes.[18]

Article 14(1) requires the Commission to consult an Advisory Committee composed of representatives of NCAs before it takes any substantive decision. The competition network will be organised through the Advisory Committee which will cooperate through its intranet. The Commission has a power of pre-emption. If it initiates proceedings, NCAs cease to be competent (Article 11(6)). It will be able to reconcile conflicting practices of different authorities and to adopt the important new precedents.

In order to avoid multiple proceedings relating to the same alleged infringement (recital 17), when more than one NCA is proceeding against the same agreement or practice, each has power to suspend its proceedings or dismiss a complaint. The Commission may also suspend its proceedings when the matter is being dealt with by an NCA (Article 13).

In relation to fines for hard core infringements, the principle *ne bis in idem* developed under the European Convention on Human Rights (ECHR) may prevent multiple litigation.[19] The Community is not party to the Convention,

---

15   Reg 772/2004, OJ 2004 L123/11, Art 7.
16   Guidelines on co-operation within the network of Competition Authorities, OJ 2004. C101/43, *passim.*
17   *Dirección General de Defensa de la Competencia v Associatión España de la Banca Privada (AEB) and Others* (C–67/91), [1992] ECR I–4785.
18   *PVC II*, (C–238/99P and others) [2002] ECR I–835, [2003] 4 CMLR 10, paras 298–307, citing *Dow Benelux*, (97–99/87) 1989 ECR 3137.
19   Wouter Wils, 'The principle of *ne bis in idem* in EC Antitrust Enforcement: a legal and economic analysis.'(2003) 26 *World Competition Law and Economics Review*, 131.

but all the Member States are. The Community Court often develops fundamental principles of Community law on the basis of the provisions and case
law of the Convention.

Under Article 4 of protocol 7[20]

> 1. No one shall be liable to be tried or punished again in criminal proceedings
> under the jurisdiction of the same State for an offence for which he has already
> been finally acquitted or convicted in accordance with the law and penal procedure
> of that State.

The concept of 'criminal' has been widely construed by the Court of Human
Rights in relation to Article 6 to include administrative fines.

It is not enough to take into account the punishment in the first proceedings when imposing a fine in the second.[21]

Article 50 of the Charter of Fundamental Rights, solemnly proclaimed by
the Community Parliament, Council and Commission,[22] implements this
broadly to treat the Community as a single state for this purpose and provides:

> No one shall be tried or punished again in criminal proceedings for an offence for
> which he has been finally been acquitted or convicted within the Union in accor-
> dance with the law.

This seems to prevent more than one competition authority or court from
imposing fines in respect of the same anti-competitive conduct, although
interim measures might be available in more than one Member State.
Moreover, the Commission considers that fines imposed outside the
Community relate to the effects of the conduct there, and do not mitigate the
fines under Community law. The double barrier theory remains only under
Article 3 (7.3.1 above). Unilateral action may be attacked under national
unfair competition law or Article 82.

The question arises whether proceedings for which a fine is not likely or
where the likelihood of a fine has not been stated in the statement of objections should be treated as criminal. Fines are not infrequently imposed for
infringement of Article 82.

The authorities intend to operate one-stop-shops, and avoid multiple proceedings.[23] If several Member States are materially affected, the one that is
best placed will start proceedings, with co-operation from any other affected.
If more than three NCAs are materially affected by conduct, it is thought that
the Commission will be the prime authority, but it will still have a discretion
whether to take a case.

---

20   Only 9 Member States have ratified protocol 7.
21   *Franz Fischer v Austria*, 29 May 2001, application No. 37950/97.
22   OJ 2000, C364/1.
23   Draft Guidelines on co-operation within the network of competition authorities, OJ 2003
C243/11, [2003] 5 CMLR 1044

In order to ensure the uniform application of Community law, Article 16(2) and recital 22 provide that NCAs and courts may not take a decision that runs counter to a decision taken by the Commission. This enables the Commission to pre-empt NCAs, for instance, when it wants to establish some particular policy or when NCAs from different Member States have been reaching different results.

Consequently, the Commission may remain the institution charged with the orientation of competition policy and be allowed by the CFI a wider discretion on policy matters than are courts. This remains to be seen.

It is thought that considerable effort will be spent by legal advisors deciding where to complain. The rights of a complainant will depend on national procedural laws which vary considerably from each other, from the Commission's and as between courts and NCAs.

Large firms of lawyers will have expertise in relation to many systems of law as to the ease with which an interim order can be obtained and the ease with which it can be overturned *inter partes*. It may be harder for individual lawyers, or those in small firms to compete unless they have a network of associations with lawyers from other Member States. Firms in the new Member States may well find it convenient to occupy the same building in Brussels as lawyers from other accession countries, as was done to some extent before when new countries first joined the Community.

There is no equivalent as between competition authorities to the Brussels[24] and Lugano Conventions, which provide for the enforcement of foreign judgments and prevent multiple actions. Even as between courts, those Conventions are of little use as they relate only to actions between the same parties and relating to the same matter. A judgment in France as to the validity of the agreement with one's French distributor will not have effect when suing a German distributor in Germany.

7.3.4 *Powers of national courts*

The doctrine of direct effect was explained at 1.5.2 and 7.2 above, and it clearly applies to Articles 81 and 82 (Articles 1 and 6 of Regulation 1/2003). A national court, like a competition authority, is required to apply Articles 81 and 82. It may also have to enforce decisions taken by the Commission under Articles 7–10 in so far as they are sufficiently clear, precise and unconditional to have direct effect, but not orders of other NCAs unless national law so provides.

It is clear that national courts may now apply Article 81(3) as well as Articles 81(1 and 2) and 82 EC (Articles 1 and 6). Where an agreement may affect trade between Member States, Article 3 provides that a national court

---

24   Brussels Convention 1968 on jurisdiction and the enforcement of judgments in civil and commercial matters OJ 1978, L304/1, amended several times, most recently OJ 2001, L12/1. It is now a regulation, not a convention.

must apply Article 81 EC if it applies national law and may not forbid an agreement under national competition law if it escapes the prohibition of Article 81, whether or not by virtue of Article 81(3) (7.3.1 above). It may, however apply national unfair competition law to unilateral conduct even if it is not prohibited by Article 82. Agreements may also be void and illegal on non-competition law grounds, such as fraud or duress.

Procedural rules, including remedies, are to be governed by national law, subject to the rules relating to direct effect (1.5.2 above). Consequently, Community law will govern the substantive questions and national law those of procedure. No measures of procedural harmonisation have been proposed by the Commission, so there will be considerable scope for forum shopping.

In Europe there is no indication whether plaintiffs may recover damages only for anti-competitive harm as is the position in the US. In *Brunswick Corp v Pueblo Bowl-O Mat*,[25] the US Supreme Court held that a plaintiff for treble damages must show that its injury resulted from anti-competitive effects. Several owners of small bowling alleys objected to a competitor buying several bankrupt competitors, which it would keep open, thereby reducing the plaintiff's profits. A similar rule applies to injunctive relief.

Nor is there any EC case law relating to recovery by indirect buyers from an infringer, or whether the damages payable to immediate purchasers should be reduced on the ground that they may be able to pass on the overcharge.[26] These questions are probably to be decided by national law, as relating to procedure and remedies. If indirect buyers cannot recover, there is less force in the argument made by Mario Monti, the Member of the Commission responsible for competition, that private actions in national courts should be welcomed as helping to enforce the competition rules.[27] Those who suffer from their breach may not be the persons who can recover.

I know of no Member State that encourages civil litigation as much as the US. There, damages are often set at very high levels by a jury and then trebled; the successful plaintiff can recover reasonable attorney's fees, although the successful defendant cannot. The English concept of joint plaintiffs is nothing like as extensive as the certification of a class action in the US, and the possibility of contingency fees according to which the plaintiff may arrange for its lawyer to obtain a proportion of whatever damages are recovered in lieu of normal fees are narrowly limited in Europe.

The plaintiff in the US has wide powers of discovery to obtain documents from the defendant, and the mere cost of finding and producing the documents may cause the defendant to come to a voluntary settlement. Moreover, there is no contribution between joint defendants, so a plaintiff can often

---

25   429 US 477, 97 Sup Ct 690, 50 L Ed 2d 701.
26   Mark Brealey,' Adopt *Perma Life*, but follow *Hanover Shoe* to *Illinois Brick*? Who can sue for damages for breach of EC Competition Law? (2002) 2 *Competition Law Journal*, 127.
27   Wouter Wils, 'Should Private Antitrust Enforcement be Encouraged in Europe', (2003) 26 *World Competition Law and Economics Review*, 473.

recover a comparatively small sum when the first defendant settles—enough to pay the legal fees for suing the others, creating a huge incentive for defendants to settle early. The last firm to settle may have to pay mammoth damages.[28]

Partly for these reasons, until recently few actions for an injunction or damages were brought before European national courts. There are many problems facing a plaintiff. It may establish that the only three firms in a market each refused to supply it, but it may be harder to show that they did so as the result of collusion. Even if that is established, it may be difficult to quantify the damage for which compensation is sought if the plaintiff was unable to obtain supplies and test the market.

Analysis of conduct in the context of the relevant market is a task unfamiliar to many judges and counsel. Until May of 2004, national courts have not had to consider Article 81(3), which may require a court to balance a restriction of competition against a justification based not on competitive factors but, for instance, those of the environment. Many lawyers think that such issues of policy are not appropriate to a court. Now national judges will have to apply Article 81(3) as well as Article 81(1).

This may well be the reason why the Commission said in paragraphs 10 and 38 of its draft guidelines on the application of Article 81(3) of the Treaty[29] that Article 81 is concerned only with effects, actual or potential, on competition and not with other public interest issues (1.3.2.8 and 3.1.1 above). This statement has, however, disappeared from the actual guidelines.[30] The Commission may not have decided how to deal with conflicting policies.

Article 82 raises problems quite as difficult as Article 81(3) and courts have long been able to enforce Article 82. In common law countries, there is a specialist Bar, well educated in the economics of competition and it is the task of the Bar to educate the judges in the economics of competition and, since barristers manage the case, they can select an economist to provide a written report and address the court. It is important that economists may be hired at an early stage, so that the whole presentation of the case is centred around the theory they advance.

My impression is that far more control is exercised by the judge in civil law countries and that the judge will decide whether to call in an economist and if so, which one. Doubtless, civil law counsel will address the courts on these issues, but they may not know which economist will be called until a late stage in the case.

A disincentive to litigation that will continue, results from the Commission's dominance over competition policy. A national court is not permitted to give judgment contrary to a decision already taken by the

28   E.g. William Andersen & Paul Rogers, *Antitrust Law: Policy and Practice,* 3rd edn,(*LexisNexis, 1999*), 803–04.
29   OJ 2003, C243/62, [2003] CMLR 1127.
30   OJ 2004, C101/97.

Commission or one contemplated in proceedings already opened (Article 16 and recital 22). Moreover, a court may not enforce an injunction if it is contrary to a decision of the Commission even if adopted after the national injunction was granted.

In *Masterfoods Ltd and HB Ice Cream v Commission*,[31] the facts were extreme. The Commission opened proceedings against HB, which it alleged enjoyed a dominant position, for supplying freezer cabinets to small retailers in Ireland on terms that they be used to stock for sale only HB impulse ice creams. These proceedings were compromised without a formal decision. HB changed its contracts in accordance with the settlement to enable the retailers to free themselves of the tie if they bought the freezers, even on reasonable hire purchase terms. It obtained an injunction from an Irish Court to restrain retailers placing Mars ice creams in the freezers without buying the freezers from HB.

When a further complaint that few retailers were freeing themselves from the tie was made by Mars, the Commission changed its mind and adopted a formal decision prohibiting the freezer tie. When HB's successor in title tried to enforce the injunction granted by the Irish court, the ECJ ruled that the court should not enforce an injunction that was incompatible with a decision of the Commission even if adopted subsequently.

The number of cases based on the competition rules may increase as a result of *Courage Ltd v Bernard Crehan and others*[32] (7.2 above) and the direct effect of Article 81(3). A court will usually be able to proceed to judgment, although when the Commission has opened proceedings, a national court may adjourn until a decision has been adopted.

Recently, more cases for damages have been brought before English courts. Where the Commission has adopted a decision, the issues of fact cannot be reopened in an English court: the proper appeal is to the CFI. In *Iberian*[33] the Commission, upheld by the CFI and ECJ in most respects, had condemned BHP's conduct as contrary to Article 81. When Iberian sued BHP for damages, the High Court held that it was under a duty to avoid conflicting decisions with the Commission and that, although the Commission's proceedings were not *res judicata*, the facts found by it, in so far as they were not reversed on appeal, could not be re-opened (paragraph 44). Proceedings are most likely to be brought when the Community authorities have already intervened.

Litigation will be simpler now that the court can apply Article 81(3). It will no long be necessary to adjourn if the defendant notifies the agreement requesting an exemption.

As actions in national courts are made easier by the new Regulation, there will be less discretion in the competition rules. Currently, if the Commission

---

31   C–344/98, [2000] ECR I–1136.
32   C–453/99, [2001] ECR 1–6297.
33   *Iberian v BHP* [1996] 2 CMLR 601 (Eng HC).

sees merit in some kind of conduct, it does not have to open proceedings. Prosecutorial discretion disappears as plaintiffs, possibly more interested in damages than in a competitive market, decide what actions are brought.[34]

7.3.4.1 *Nullity* Contracts that infringe Article 81 as a whole are nullified by Article 81(2). Some agreements prohibited by Article 81(1) have no legal effects to nullify, but nullity is important for vertical contracts where the respective interests of the parties may diverge as one or other makes investments.

As early as 1966, the Court held in *Société La Technique Minière v Maschinenbau Ulm*[35] that it is only those provisions that have the object or effect of restricting competition that are void and that it is for national law to decide whether enough remains for the rest of the contract to be enforceable. It has repeated this view several times, for instance in *Delimitis*.[36] Consequently, even if the amount at issue is trifling, a national court may have to make a complex market analysis before enforcing a contract.

In *Delimitis*, at paragraph 13, the Court concluded that an exclusive purchasing obligation accepted by the tenant of a single beer house provided benefits to both parties and did not have the object of restricting competition. In deciding whether it had that effect, the national court should enquire whether there were barriers to entry by retailers and whether so many bars were tied for so long to one or other of the breweries that it would be difficult for another brewer to find enough outlets to enter the market (paragraphs 13–23). The national court should also consider possibilities of a new entrant opening new cafés or buying a chain of them.

Even if there were significant foreclosure, it would be only the ties that made a significant contribution to it that would be illegal and void (paragraphs 24-26). The cost of such an enquiry may be large in relation to the small loan in issue. In my view, it should suffice to prove that a new firm could enter the market in any one of these ways to establish conformity with Article 81.

7.3.4.2 *Effect of comfort letters*—In *Guérlain*,[37] the Court ruled that a national court may take into account any view expressed by the Commission in a comfort letter, although it is not binding as either a negative clearance or an exception. The ruling probably created no great difficulties for the parties in the case, since the letter implied that the vertical selective dealing agreement made by a firm supplying a small proportion of the perfumes and toilet preparations in the common market had no significant effect on competition or trade between

---

34   See Diane Wood, 'The Courts in private antitrust actions' in Barry Hawk (ed) [2002] *Fordham Corporate Law Institute*, (Juris Publishing and Sweet & Maxwell, 1997), 400, and Wouter Wils, 'Should private enforcement be encouraged in Europe?' (2003) 26 *World Competition Law and Economics Review*, 473, 480–84.
35   (56/65) [1966] ECR 235, 250.
36   (C–234/89) [1991] ECR 935, para 48.
37   (253/78) [1980] ECR 2327.

Member States once the dealers were permitted to sell to authorised outlets outside their area. Problems might arise, however, should a firm's market share increase.

It is hoped that in future when the Commission considers that an agreement does not infringe Article 81 and is sufficiently moved to send a comfort letter, it will be prepared to do so formally under Article 10, in which event it will be binding. An informal clearance may be taken into account by a national court but is not binding.

7.3.4.3 *Assistance from the Commission*—Regulation 1/2003 provides for the Commission to help national courts.[38] Recital 21 and Article 15 provide that, in the interests of consistency, national courts should be able to ask the Commission about the application of competition law. Within the framework of national procedural rules, the Commission and NCAs may make observations on the application of Articles 81 or 82 to a national court. At the request of the court these may be oral, otherwise only written.

The national court will not have to adjourn if the issue has already been decided by the Commission or on appeal from it. If it does adjourn, the national court may grant interim relief.

In *Postbank v Commission*,[39] the CFI held that by virtue of Article 10 of the EC Treaty (6.1–6.1.6 above), the Commission and national courts owe each other a duty of sincere cooperation and the Commission is required to pass confidential information to a court that requests it. A national court is bound by the duty of confidentiality imposed by Article 287 EC not to disclose confidential information and business secrets, so transmitting the information or documents is not a breach of the Commission's obligation of confidentiality. Such disclosure is pursuant to Article 10 EC and not Article 15 of Regulation 1/2003,[40] so the provisions relating to confidentiality in the Regulation do not apply.[41]

Questions about the state of the Commission's procedure, such as whether it has opened proceedings or contemplates doing so and, if so, what is or will be alleged in the statement of objections, should not give rise to much trouble, but a question relating to an assessment of conduct that does not amount to a hard core restraint with the object of restricting competition may require assessment of complex facts in the context of a market analysis.

Almost certainly, its legal service will monitor the final text sent to a national court or appear orally. Problems are more likely to relate to matters, such as the definition of the relevant market, than to pure points of law, and it is doubtful whether members of the legal service would have time to go far

---

38   Commission's notice on cooperation between the Commission and the National Courts OJ 2004, C101/43.
39   *Postbank v Commission* (T–353/94), [1996] ECR II–921, [1997] 1 CMLR 33, [1997] CEC 454, paras 62–65.
40   Which applies only to NCAs not courts.
41   *Postbank*, paras 66–70.

into the facts. The notice does not state at what level in the hierarchy of DG Competition the observations will be finalised.

The procedure for asking the ECJ for a preliminary ruling (1.1.4.3.2 above) applies to competition cases and a national court may grant interim relief pending an answer, but since such rulings should be limited to points of law and the major difficulties are likely to be in appraising the facts, this will be helpful only occasionally. Some rulings that have been given by the ECJ are extremely important.

7.3.4.4 *Forum shopping*—The Brussels[42] and Lugano conventions provide for the enforcement of foreign judgments and prevent multiple actions in different jurisdictions, but they are of little significance in most competition scenarios as they relate only to actions between the same parties and on the same matter. A judgment in France as to the validity of the agreement with one's French distributor will not have effect when suing its German distributor in Germany on a virtually identical contract. There will be considerable scope for forum shopping and litigating first in a country where the procedural rules are favourable. The ease with which a preliminary injunction is obtainable and the difficulty of dislodging it may be the most important consideration.

7.4 The Commission's powers to obtain information (Articles 17–22)

There is no need for the regulation to empower NCAs to obtain information, since their procedure is governed by national law. Member States may have to adopt implementing legislation to provide for this. Article 22 of Regulation 1/2003 provides that an NCA may carry out an inspection in its own territory, using national powers on behalf of itself or for the account of another NCA.

Markets change over time and updating information is sometimes required. In *Coca-Cola v Commission*,[43] the CFI made it clear that market definitions and market power have to be reassessed and reasons given each time: it is not enough to cite earlier case law.

Frequently, the Commission starts proceedings on the basis of a complaint, in which case the complainant may provide information voluntarily both about the market and the conduct of the firm suspected of an infringement. It may even provide a memorandum prepared by consulting economists. The complainant may, however, request that it remain anonymous, in which event the Commission may seek other sources of information to use as evidence.

The Commission may receive replies to informal enquiries, sometimes to a trade association, complaints from Members of the European Parliament, or may read the information in the press. It also has two ways in which it may obtain information under Regulation 1/2003.

---

42   Brussels Convention 1968, Convention on jurisdiction and the enforcement of judgments in civil and commercial matters OJ 1978, L304/1, amended several times, most recently OJ 2001, L12/1. It is now called 'the Brussels regulation.'
43   22 March 2000, T–125 & 127/97, paras 81–93.

7.4.1 *Requests for information (Article 18 and recital 23)*

Article 18 provides that:

> (1) In order to carry out the duties assigned to it by this Regulation, the Commission may, by simple request or by decision, require any undertakings and associations of undertakings to provide all necessary information.

Such requests may be addressed to third parties as well as to the person thought to have infringed Article 81 or 82. NCAs and governments are also required to supply all necessary information (Article 18(6)). There is probably no duty for undertakings to comply with a request for information unless made by decision, but if the information be supplied in answer to a simple request, it must be prepared carefully as it may be difficult to convince officials later that the information was inaccurate. If a mistake is made, it should be corrected in writing as soon as possible.

If no information is supplied, or not as much as is requested and even if the Commission has not made a request by mandate, the Commission may take a formal decision, in which case, if the information requested is not supplied within the time allowed, the Commission may impose a fine under Article 23(1)(b) or daily penalties under Article 24(d). This procedure involves two decisions, one under Article 18 requiring the information to be furnished and another under Article 23 or 24 imposing the fine or penalty. The amount of the fine under Article 23(1) has been increased to 1% of total turnover for intentional or negligent infringements. The daily penalty under Article 24 has also been increased: to 5% of the average daily turnover of the undertaking.

The Commission may not know how firms keep their files, and it may ask precise questions which would take time to answer. Often a prompt telephone call or email to Brussels analysing the difficulties will result in the case handler agreeing to accept information more readily available that will serve his purpose. Sometimes, the official may ask for the information that can easily be provided to be sent within the deadline but give a longer period to answer other questions. The deadlines for answering questions are short, seldom more than six weeks, less if the questions are simple and short. In merger investigations, where the parties usually want the procedure finished fast, the request is often made informally by fax and replied to the same day.

Priority should be given to answering requests for information and the task of supervision should be given to someone intelligent. He may have to delegate a good deal of his normal work to devote time and thought to this. Preliminary estimates should not be lightly given as, if they are later retracted, the Commission may believe the first statement as it did in *United Brands*.[44] More important they may colour the attitude of the official handling the file.

---

44 [1976] 1 CMLR D28, para 100. The retraction is made clear by the Court on appeal (27/76) [1978] ECR 207, para 243.

False information can easily be given through carelessness. One firm, asked for its share of the market in the whole EC and in each Member State, produced figures for its share of sales from America in each area, as those were the figures readily available. These far larger market shares made its conduct appear much more serious. Fortunately, the error was spotted and corrected before the information was sent. It is vital to ask of whoever answers the questions supplementary questions about the sources from which information was obtained.

The Commission's power is to obtain all 'necessary information.' The Commission has wide discretion to decide whether particular information is necessary. It is difficult to establish that information required is not necessary. A mere relationship between a document and an infringement is not enough. The Commission must reasonably suppose that the document would help it to decide whether an infringement had been committed.[45] If some utterly irrelevant information is requested, one may refuse to provide it, giving reasons. The Commission may accept these, but if not, may compel the information by a decision as it did in *RAI/UNITEL*.[46] An appeal under Article 230 EC can be taken to the Court of First Instance against this, but would be advisable only in an extreme case.

Since the information supplied to the Commission may be passed on to the NCAs and used by them in making formal decisions that are published, care must be taken to ensure the confidentiality of some information. Usually the Commission asks informants, especially complainants, to provide it with full and accurate information, but to supply a non-confidential version that may be shown to outsiders.

Under the Commission's inquisitorial procedure the firm being investigated is required to assist it effectively. In *Orkem*,[47] the Court held that the Commission may compel an undertaking to provide information concerning facts known to it, even if the information may be used to establish anti-competitive conduct. It would, however, be contrary to the rights of the defence (7.5.1 below) for the Commission to compel an undertaking to answer questions which might constitute an admission of an infringement which it is for the Commission to establish.[48] The distinction between the two propositions is not always clear, but has been confirmed by the ECJ.[49]

---

45 *SEP* C36/92 P, 19 May 1994, [1994] ECR 1–1911, para 21, referring to paras 21–42 of the opinion of Advocate General Jacobs.
46 [1978] 3 CMLR 306.
47 (374/87) [1989] ECR 3343, para 27, confirmed in *PVC II—Limburgse Vinyl and others v Commission*, (C–238/99P and others), [2002] ECR I–8375, [2003] 4 CMLR 10 paras 273–93, referring also to more recent case law of the European Court of Human Rights.
48 See generally, Wouter Wils, 'Self-incrimination in EC Antitrust enforcement: A legal and economic analysis,' (2003) 26 *World Competition Law and Economics Review*, 567.
49 *PVC II-Limburgse Vinyl and others v Commission* (C–238/99P and others), [2002] ECR I–8375, [2003] 4 CMLR 10, paras 267–93. The cases were joined for the purposes of the judgment.

It has been argued that the case law under the European Convention does not permit compulsion to answer even purely factual questions. The recent judgments of the ECJ have not had to address the issue.[50]

The privilege against self-incrimination may induce addressees of a request for information by simple mandate to wait for the Commission to make a decision compelling it to reply. If the Commission does not give way, an appeal may then be taken to the CFI.

7.4.2 Inspections (Articles 19–21)

Often the Commission starts an investigation informally or by requesting information under Article 18 but, by virtue of Articles 19–21 it also has powers of inspection: to enter the premises of an undertaking, or other premises including directors' homes, examine and copy books and other business records and ask for oral explanations on the spot. These need not now be limited to questions about the documents. It will now also have power to seal premises when it cannot finish an inspection on the same day.

The Commission does not attempt to download all the contents of a computer on an inspection as this would exceed its mandate, but some of the documents of which it takes a copy may be electronic.

By virtue of Article 19, the Commission may also interview any legal or natural person who consents to be interviewed for the purpose of collecting information on the subject matter of an investigation. It has no power to compel such evidence nor, to punish those giving misleading or false answers. So the power does not give rise to issues of self-incrimination. A secretary might be asked where particular types of files are kept, or the languages used in a particular office, so that the right office can be raided by officials able to speak the appropriate language.

The power is broader, however, and includes much loose talk. For instance, a secretary who heard one side of a conversation might tell the inspectors what she thought the conversation was about. Those drafting compliance programmes should consider whether to tell staff not to answer such questions.

There was a furore when the Commission's proposal for what became Article 20(2) of Regulation 1/2003 provided power to inspect homes, and the power to inspect premises other than those of the undertaking has been limited in Article 21(2) and (3) by requiring that the decision to inspect be based on specified reasons and that the inspection should be authorised by a national judge who must check that the coercive measures are not arbitrary or excessive having regard to the seriousness of the suspected infringement, to the importance of the evidence sought and other specified matters. This follows the ECJ's judgment in *Roquette Freres*.[51]

---

50   See Wils, above n 48, 567.
51   (C94/00), [2003] 4 CMLR 46, a case when Regulation 17 was in operation.

Article 22 enables the Commission to request an NCA to conduct an inspection in its own territory, or send an official or other person to assist the Commission officials. The latter may be important when investigating a cartel when many offices have to be inspected simultaneously by officials conversant with the appropriate languages.

Simultaneous inspections in several countries may take place without prior notice to the undertakings if the Commission suspects an international cartel to fix prices or allocate markets. Usually the inspectors are accompanied by officials from the national competition authority, but their function is to assist the Commission rather than protect the firm being inspected. Nevertheless, preventing illegal pressure may assist the Commission. The procedures under Articles 17 to 22 are independent of each other and the Commission may request additional documents after it has carried out an inspection of the premises.[52]

There is a two-step procedure,[53] as under Article 18, but no need to make a request under Article 20(3) before making a decision to inspect the premises under paragraph (4).[54] Under paragraph (3), an inspector may come with a simple mandate, but there is no duty to admit him. Where inspectors arrive without warning they will probably be armed with a decision adopted under paragraph (4), and if this is not complied with, the Commission has power to impose a fine under Article 23(1)(c) or daily penalties under Article 24(1)(e) in much the same way as for non-compliance with a request for information made by decision.

There is, however, no direct power under Community law to enter premises.[55] Therefore, Article 22(2) requires Member States to assist the inspectors and in the United Kingdom the Crown has obtained an injunction from the Commercial Court to assist an inspection when the inspectors have been refused admission. Its terms were similar to an Anton Piller order obtainable to discover breaches of copyright law.[56] The Commission will usually ask the OFT to apply for an injunction only after a tentative inspection has taken place and the undertaking has denied access to the premises. Otherwise it would have to bring evidence to the Court of a substantial likelihood of refusal to admit inspectors.[57]

It is seldom sensible to refuse entry to Commission inspectors. The Commission may not unreasonably infer that the undertaking has something to hide and may make adverse findings of fact on the basis of such information

---

52   *Orkem v Commission* (374/87) [1989] ECR 3343, para 14.
53   The two-step procedure was considered by the Court in *Hoechst* (46/87 & 227/88) [1989] ECR 2859, paras 55–56.
54   *National Panasonic v Commission* (136/79) [1980] ECR 2033.
55   *Hoechst AG and Others v Commission* (46/87 & 227/88), [1989] ECR 2859.
56   See annex to the House of Lords' report of 1982, cited in the bibliography to this chapter (7.8 below).
57   *Roquette Frères v Director General for Competition*, C–94/00, 22 October 2002, [2003] 4 CMLR 46. This is repeated in Art 20(8).

as it may have. Indeed, inspectors are usually admitted when only a mandate under Article 20(3) is produced.

When, however, mandates are drawn very widely asking for documents which may enable the Commission to ascertain whether an infringement of Article 81 or 82 has been committed in relation to a specified product, there is an argument for refusing admittance until a decision is produced, as it is subject to appeal. Once a firm agrees to submit to an investigation by mandate, it cannot bring the investigation to an end unilaterally.

Officials making an inspection habitually bring with them a memorandum setting out the rights of the firm being inspected, *inter alia*, to bring in its lawyer, although the inspection will not be long delayed to enable a specialised lawyer to come.[58]

It is important to arrange in advance for an appropriate committee to meet the inspectors from the Commission. This should include a lawyer, a manager of sufficient seniority to release confidential documents and good shorthand secretaries to take a record of what is asked for, provided or refused, and the reasons given for any refusal, what documents and rooms have been seen by an inspector and which were examined carefully. There may be more than one inspector, and a separate secretary may be needed to follow each around the building. The Commission does not normally make its record available to the parties. There should be sufficient alternative names on the committee to cover for absences.

The lawyer will, doubtless, inspect the mandate, though it is unlikely to be insufficient, and he may wish to advise his client not to provide certain documents, for instance, on the ground that they are privileged (7.4.4 below) or irrelevant.

A lawyer may object to complex oral questions on the spot, as these deprive individuals of the time to think or check that is allowed by a request for information. The Commission considers that it is entitled to demand to see an individual who is, for instance, shown by the documents to have attended a meeting with competitors.

In *Orkem v Commission*,[59] the ECJ confirmed the Commission's view that the undertaking has a duty to cooperate actively. It must provide the documentation required by the inspectors. They usually ask to inspect the documents where they are normally kept and decide themselves which documents or parts of documents are necessary. The undertaking is advised to bring out factors in its favour. The inspectors are said to have no power of search, but are entitled to demand to see particular documents of which they already know, or files which they can see.

It is usual for a firm to make its photocopier available to the inspectors and to take a second copy of each document for itself, so that it knows at least

---

58   The memoranda for inspection both by simple mandate and those made by virtue of a decision are appended to the *XIIIth Report on Competition Policy*, 270–72.

59   (374/87) [1989] ECR 3343, para 27.

some of the evidence the Commission has, and can later send explanations of documents that might look suspicious if read out of context. The Commission usually agrees to pay for its copies. The alternative may be to have the inspectors for days taking longhand notes, or they may leave before the firm has established points in its favour. The inspectors are not entitled to copy the whole of a firm's hard disk, because they have to inspect specific documents, but they may copy specified parts of it.

It is dangerous to refuse documents on the grounds that they have been destroyed unless a good reason can be given for their destruction. In *German Machine Blacksmiths*[60] documents were refused on the ground that the directors had ordered their destruction, and the Commission issued a decision under Article 14(3) of Regulation 17 requiring the firm to submit to an investigation, at its Düsseldorf offices, into various classes of documents including those relating to its joint office in Zurich, outside the Community.

If the firm fails to produce the documents, the Commission may require it, by decision made under Article 24(1)(d), to pay penalties of up to 5% of its daily turnover *per* day indefinitely. If the firm does produce them, it will have difficulty in persuading the Commission of its honesty in view of its earlier statement that they had been destroyed. In *Pioneer*,[61] the failure to take minutes of a meeting between a supplier's dealers to discuss cross-frontier trading was treated by the Commission as evidence of a concerted practice to restrain parallel trade.

The destruction of records on an *ad hoc* basis is dangerous, although, in order to save storage space, many firms legitimately arrange for systematic destruction of old documents that national law does not require should be kept. In these days when emails are used to circulate between many people, it is very difficult to conceal the existence of a document even if the original has been destroyed.

It is important to realise that the procedure is inquisitorial and not adversarial. One must try to find out what the Commission officials suspect as clearly as possible. If it is wrong, do not merely deny the suspicions but produce evidence to demonstrate or at least suggest the correct facts. The Commission recommends that the firm being investigated should take the initiative and use the inspection to bring out points in the firm's favour and not merely respond passively to questions asked. This may be difficult if the inspection is not announced in advance and may give rise to loose talk.

It may be sensible to arrange a meeting of managers concerned with the matter being investigated shortly after an inspection in case there are points in the firm's favour that can be forwarded to Brussels which were overlooked in the strained atmosphere of the inspection. Any misconceptions should be corrected before they have time to colour the case handler's approach to the situation.

60   [1978] 1 CMLR D63.
61   [1980] 1 CMLR 457.

Those present at an inspection must keep their wits about them and remember cultural differences. On one occasion, a junior Japanese employee was asked by inspectors to read and translate a document and turned white when he did so. The reason was that no one so junior should have seen such a document. It was not at all damning.

Information obtained in answer to a request for information or an inspection cannot be used for any other purpose. It may be shown to officials of competent authorities and may be used by them to establish liability under Community law or under both Community and national law where the outcomes are the same (Article 12).

The Commission has taken slightly wider powers to obtain information than it had under Regulation 17, but less than the American agencies enjoy. Irish and UK law also provide greater powers to obtain information.

7.4.3 Sector enquiries (Article 17)

The Commission has power to make enquiries into a whole sector of the economy, such as brewing in Belgium or the supply of margarine to the Continent. The provisions of Articles 18 to 22 apply also to such enquiries. Few have been made.

7.4.4 Confidentiality (Articles 12 and 28)

Information obtained by requests or inspections may be used only for the purpose of the relevant request (Article 28(1)). There is no express restriction on the use of information obtained from informal chats with officials. Officials of the Commission and of the Member States are not, however, allowed to disclose confidential information obtained under any of the provisions of the Regulation (Article 28(2)). For the use of information received by one NCA from another, see 7.3.3 above.

Article 287 of the EC Treaty provides that the institutions and officials of the Community shall not disclose information of the kind covered by the obligation of professional secrecy. It is not clear exactly what this means. Under the laws of some Member States such words cover all information obtained by a Commission official by virtue of his functions, and are not confined to business secrets. Probably that concept is too wide for this purpose. Guideline 28(a) of the notice on co-operation within the network of competition authorities[62] gives the examples of 'business secrets or other confidential information.'

In *AKZO*[63] the ECJ objected when the Commission gave a copy of a document that may have been secret to the complainant, without giving AKZO an opportunity to object to its decision to hand the document over, and

---

62   OJ 2004, C101/43.
63   (53/85) [1986] ECR 1965, paras 26–30.

ordered the Commission to recover the document. This prevented the complainant from using it as evidence in national proceedings.

In *Postbank v Commission*,[64] the Commission had sent the statement of objections without its annexes to firms bringing actions in a national court in order to enable them to prepare for the Commission's hearing in proceedings concerning an agreement. It expressly required that the statement should not be used in a national court and refused to release the plaintiffs from this restriction.

The CFI held that the Commission had no power to forbid such use. It was under a duty of sincere co-operation with national courts imposed by Article 10 of the Treaty and must help them to apply the direct effect of Article 81. Moreover, there is a presumption that a national court would guarantee the protection of confidential information.

If the Commission requires the production of highly sensitive information, such as a document containing valuable know-how, try to persuade its official that it is not necessary for its purposes.

It was established in *AKZO*[65] that some documents are privileged under Community law, but the extent of the privilege has not been fully defined. The concept applies to documents provided to or from lawyers inscribed in a Bar of a Member State seeking or giving legal advice. The ECJ held, however, that it does not cover in-house counsel or lawyers employed by a firm of lawyers, since in many Member States employed lawyers are disbarred and not subject to professional discipline. There is a move to provide privilege for in house counsel.[66]

The Commission may make a decision requiring a particular document to be produced, as it did in *AM&S*.[67] The decision enables the undertaking to appeal against it to the ECJ. This is the procedure to settle a dispute whether the Commission is entitled to it.

In *AM&S*, the ECJ held that a firm being investigated enjoys what in England is called 'legal professional privilege,' and in France, '*le secret professionnel*:' concepts that are not identical. The undertaking need not produce correspondence with a lawyer entitled to practice in a Member State and not permanently employed by his client if it was written in order to obtain or give legal advice.

Since 1985, and in reaction to the judgment of the ECJ in *AM&S*, officials have placed confidential information in a separate annex to a file, so the Commission knows what to withhold from a complainant. It is sensible to draft a less precise version of confidential information for the Commission to

---

64   (T–353/94) [1996] ECR II–921, (7.3.4.3 above).
65   *AKZO Chemie BV v Commission* (62/86), [1991] ECR I–3359. See Theofanis Christoforou, 'Protection of Legal Privilege in EEC Competition Law: The Imperfections of a Case' (1985–1986) 9 *Fordham International Law Journal*, 1, for the extent of privilege.
66   (7.4.2 above).
67   *AM&S v Commission* (155/79) [1982] ECR 1575. See Christoforou, above n 55, at 1.

show other people. Even if a document marked 'confidential' is shown to a complainant, an adverse decision may not be quashed. In *FEDETAB*,[68] the Court did not decide whether the information disclosed to a complainant was covered by '*le secret professionnel*,' but refused to quash the adverse decision on the merits on the ground that the improper disclosure had not affected the result—hardly the relevant consideration!

Files should be kept with privileged documents tagged, as thousands of pages may be required by the inspectors in a single day.

At one time, it was hoped that the Commission would not demand to see advice given by in-house lawyers in order to enable them to assist their clients to comply with the law. In *Deere (John)*,[69] however, the Commission relied on such advice to show that the firm knew it was infringing Article 81, and deserved a heavier fine. This makes it more difficult and expensive to arrange a compliance programme. Some firms go to outside lawyers, but this may be less efficient than using in house counsel who is more conversant with the business and which employees are likely to infringe the competition rules unless restrained.

The American Bar Association has made great efforts to secure the client's privilege for its attorneys but legislation has not been adopted. Some American law firms include counsel qualified under European law, and they may sign the documents for which privilege is desired.

Privilege for such in house lawyers as are subject to professional discipline is in issue in *AKZO Nobel Chemicals Ltd and another v Commission* as are some of the other rules governing legal privilege and the President of the CFI has envisaged the possibility of these rules being altered by the full chamber.[70] He observed at paragraph 167 that:

> the purpose of professional privilege is not only to protect a person's private interest in not having his rights of defence irremediably affected but also to protect the requirement that every person must be able, without constraint to consult a lawyer.

He objected that the Commission should not have taken even a cursory glance at papers claimed to be privileged, but should have placed them in a sealed document so that the CFI could decide.

Now that more Member States are subjecting in house lawyers to professional discipline and extending privilege to them, the CFI in the main proceedings may enlarge its scope.

7.5 The Commission's Procedure (Article 27)

It is for the Commission to establish an infringement, although the burden of establishing a justification under Article 81(3) EC is on the parties (Article 2).

---

68   (209–215 & 218/78) [1980] ECR 3125, paras 41–47.
69   OJ 1985, L35/58, [1985] 2 CMLR 554, confirmed, (C–7/95P), [1997] ECR I–3111.
70   (T–125 & 253/03 R), [2004] 4 CMLR 744.

The CFI is being stricter nowadays in requiring the Commission to establish the factual basis of its decisions. For instance in three merger decisions[71] (12.2.6.1.2 below), the CFI made it clear that it must get simple facts, such as the contents of a letter, right but it has more discretion on complex issues such as the likelihood of joint dominance being created.

It is not enough for the Commission to rely on economic theories without showing that the conditions for their application prevail. Once the Commission has some evidence, however, it may be for the parties to show that it is inadequate or that the conclusions drawn from it are not necessarily correct.[72]

Where the Commission alleges that the established facts can be explained only by inferring illegal collusion, it is enough for the undertakings to suggest other possible explanations of their conduct. Where the Commission's finding is based on more than parallel conduct, however, the burden of proof shifts to the undertaking.[73]

When adopting a decision about a complex cartel which may include a series of meetings, some attended by some firms and some by others, the Commission is not required to decide whether each party adhered to a particular part of an agreement or concerted practice. Several judgements of the CFI holding that it may treat the cartel as a whole as an agreement and/or concerted practice[74] were approved by the ECJ in *PVC II.*[75] A firm that has attended only some of the meetings and said nothing may be found to have been party to the whole cartel for the period when it knew the purpose of the meetings. Its attendance record might be material to the extent of its participation, not to whether it has infringed at all.

7.5.1 *Rights of the defence*

The European Community is not a party to the European Convention on Human Rights 1950 (ECHR), but the Member States are, and the ECJ respects its provisions under Community law as being part of the general principles of law accepted by Member States. Article 6 of the Convention, which protects the right to a fair hearing when fines or penalties may be

---

71   *Air Tours/First Choice* T–342/99, [2002] ECR II–2585, [2002] 5 CMLR 317, *Tetra Laval BV v Commission* (T–5/92) [2002] ECR II–4381, [2002] 4 CMLR 1182 and *Schneider/Legrand* (310/01) 22 October 2002, [2002] ECR II–4071, [2003] 4 CMLR 768.
72   See Marc van der Woude, 'Hearing Officers and EC Antitrust Procedures: The Art of Making Subjective Procedures more Objective' (1996) 33 *CML Rev*, 531.
73   The CFI in *PVC II*, T–305 and others, [1999] ECR II–931, [1999] 5 CMLR 303, paras 725–29. The burden of proof is not relevant on appeal as the ECJ does not decide factual questions.
74   *E.g., PVC II-Limburgse Vinyl and others v Commission*, T–305 and others, [1999] ECR II–931, [1999] 5 CMLR 303, paras 696–99.
75   *PVC II-Limburgse Vinyl and others v Commission*, (C–238/99P and others), [2002] ECR I–8375, [2003] 4 CMLR 395, paras 508–12. The cases were joined for the purposes of the judgment.

imposed, has often been invoked by parties to EC competition proceedings, for example, when claiming access to the Commission's file under Article 27(1).

In *Friedrich Kremzow v Austria*,[76] for instance, the ECJ ruled:

> . . . fundamental rights form an integral part of the general principles of Community law whose observance the Court ensures. For that purpose, the Court draws inspiration from the constitutional traditions common to the Member States and from the guidelines supplied by international treaties for the protection of human rights on which the Member States have collaborated or of which they are signatories. The [European] Convention has special significance in that respect.

This case law was broadly enshrined by the Treaty of European Union (Maastricht) in Article 6:

> 1. The Union is founded on the principles of liberty, democracy, respect for human rights and the fundamental freedoms, and the rules of law, principles which are common to the Member States.

> 2. The Union shall respect fundamental rights, as guaranteed by the European Convention for the Protection of Human Rights and Fundamental Freedoms signed in Rome on 4 November 1950 and as they result from the constitutional traditions common to the Member States, as general principles of Community Law.

The fundamental rights recognised by the CFI may exceed those of the ECHR, but cannot be narrower. It is not always easy to predict what principles will be found common to Member States. In *Orkem* (7.4.1 above) the ECJ failed to find a general principle against self-incrimination in the law of Member States, but in *Hoechst* it found a common principle to provide protection against arbitrary or disproportionate intervention in the course of an investigation. In an attempt to clarify the rules, the Charter of Fundamental Rights[77] lists various fundamental rights, including the right to access to documents (Article 42), the rights of defence (Article 48), and the principal against double jeopardy (Article 50). The Charter is not binding but has been cited by Advocates General. In future it may be incorporated into the EC Treaty.

Article 6(2) of the Treaty of Maastricht affects only Community law and not the law of Member States. So it does not apply to the procedure of NCAs. By and large, however, they recognise similar principles under national law, although the detail may differ.

In several cases, the ECJ and CFI have held that proceedings in the Commission are administrative and that the Commission is not a tribunal within Article 6 of the European Convention on Human Rights.[78] As explained at 7.4.1 above, however, proceedings that may end in the imposi-

---

76   C–229/95, [1997] ECR I–2629.
77   OJ 2000, C 364/1.
78   *E.g.*, *Shell v Commission (polypropylene)* (T–11/89) [1992] ECR II–757, para 39.

tion of fines are treated as criminal within the meaning of Article 6, and the right to a fair hearing requires a full review on the merits by a court. The question arises, therefore, whether the CFI can provide a fair hearing on appeal from the Commission.

This is now questionable as a result of the decision of the Commission of Human Rights in *Stenuit v France*.[79] Stenuit appealed unsuccessfully from an administrative decision of the French Conseil de la Concurrence to the Minister and to the Conseil d'Etat. The European Commission of Human Rights upheld its argument that the administrative decision had not been reviewed by a court with full jurisdiction. So, contrary to the Convention, it had not been heard by an impartial tribunal.

The CFI's jurisdiction is only to review Commission decisions to ensure that they are not in manifest error and that they adequately state the reasons on which they are based. It does not have jurisdiction to rehear the case on the merits (1.4.3.2 above). It is arguable, therefore, that there is no tribunal and that the Commission's procedure does not provide a fair trial.[80] The counter-argument is the jurisdiction of the CFI goes beyond 'manifest error'. This may encourage the CFI to review Commission decisions as fully as possible.

On factual matters, the CFI requires the Commission to establish its case. Only on issues of policy or of economic evaluation does it respect the Commission's discretion. While the courts in Luxembourg do not accept that they are subordinate to the European Court in Strasbourg, which hears cases on fundamental rights under the European Convention, they are clearly familiar with and influenced by its judgments. They would not want to give a judgment that conflicts with those from Strasbourg.

Until now the Community courts have themselves tried to ensure that the rights of the defence are protected as part of the general principles of Community law and have drawn their inspiration from the experience under the European Convention. In *Polypropylene*,[81] the ECJ recognised as a fundamental right a presumption of innocence based on Article 6 of the European Convention.

7.5.2 *Statement of objections and hearing*

Article 27 provides that the parties shall be given an opportunity to present their views before the Commission makes a decision on the merits. This right is further protected by the hearing regulation, No 2842/98.[82] The

---

79   (A/232) (1992) 14 EHRR 509, paras 72–74.
80   The arguments are complex. See D Waelbroeck and D Fosselard, 'Should the Decision-making Power in EC Antitrust Procedures be left to an Independent Judge? The Impact of the European Convention on Human Rights on EC Antitrust Procedures' (1995) 14 *Yearbook of European Law*, 111.
81   C–51/92P, [1999] ECR 4235.
82   OJ 1998, L354/18.

Commission may not impose a fine or prohibit an infringement unless the Commission notified its allegations to the parties and gave them a chance to answer (Article 27(1)).

If the Commission intends to adopt a decision under Article 9 or 10 (to take commitments, or clear conduct as not infringing) it must publish an outline of the case and the main elements of the commitments or conduct to be cleared, having regard to the confidentiality of business secrets (Article 27(4)).

The Commission's practice is to prepare a document, known as the statement of objections, to which the parties are invited to reply within a time limit which varies, but is frequently about two months, sometimes longer. Extra time is allowed over major holiday periods. The short deadline may create problems, and if a survey is likely to be important, work should be put in hand well in advance and before the case against the undertaking is known. Lawyers who have been dealing with requests for information or inspections try to find out what is troubling the Commission and arrange for any fact finding likely to be important to be put in hand even before receiving the statement of objections.

The time for the 'hearing' is usually fixed for soon after the deadline for the reply to the statement of objections and since a room and interpreters have to be hired well in advance, it is very difficult to persuade the Commission to delay the hearing, although an extra few weeks may be given for the written reply.

Not only the parties to the agreement, but also others showing a sufficient interest, such as complainants, have the right to make their views known in writing and may also request an oral hearing (Article 27(3)). The rights of complainants are however less than those of the parties.

The ECJ held in *Transocean Marine Paint II*,[83] that if parties are to be able to present their views effectively, they must be told the case against them and the substance of any conditions which may be attached to an exemption with some particularity. Article 27(1) provides for this expressly not only in relation to a decision to stop infringing or to impose a fine, but also when the Commission intends to accept commitments.

A hearing officer presides over the hearing and sets deadlines. His or her task is to ensure that the case of the firm whose conduct is being investigated is understood and taken into account: that the procedural rights of the parties are respected. The hearing officer does not inspect the file to see that privilege has been respected and so forth: his functions start with the hearing, although he may meet the parties first to organise it.

The mandate of the hearing officers was extended in 1994[84] to enable them, on application by the parties, to determine whether sufficient access has been

---

83   (17/74), [1974] ECR 1063.
84   Commission decision 94/810/ECSC, EC on the terms of reference of hearing officers in competition procedures before the Commission [1995] 4 CMLR 115.

given to Commission's evidence. In May 2001, their mandate was further modified.[85] Their reports will now be published at the same time as the decision—too late to cure any deficiencies in their rights without the costs of an appeal. The reports have traditionally been extremely short, although recently they have become a little longer. In the hope of making the officer more independent, the hearing officer is no longer attached to the secretariat of DG Competition, but directly to the Member of the Commission. The resources of the hearing officers have recently been increased.

The hearing takes place in Brussels and often lasts only one day and, as the afternoon may be left for questions from the representatives of Member States, there may be only a morning for the parties to take the initiative. Where there are many parties or the issues are complex two to five days are not uncommon. In large cartel cases the hearing may last three weeks or more. The hearing on the *Cement Cartel* took a full month.

The hearing usually starts with the case handler stating the facts and issues as seen by the Commission. Even the remaining time may not all be available to the parties to the agreement. If there is a complainant he also has a right to be heard, and to hear such of the evidence as is not confidential. Consequently, the parties must divide their address into the parts with no confidential evidence, and those from which the complainant may be excluded.

The Advisory Committee consisting of NCAs must be consulted before a decision is made on the merits but, except for merger cases, its opinion is not made public, and its procedure remains a mystery to outsiders. Its members, or their substitutes, attend the hearing and may ask questions.

The hearing is attended by the team of officials who have dealt with the case and the Advisory Committee of NCAs. Some officials, and even the Commissioners themselves, may alter the draft decision, without having attended the hearing. They are, however, unlikely to alter the factual part of the decision without consulting the case team.

The Commission may accept further evidence after the formal hearing while drawing up a draft decision. Since the hearing and any further evidence may cause the Commission to change its mind, the final decision may not be identical with the statement of objections, but it may not go beyond what was alleged in the statement of objections. If the Commission develops further objections, it may serve a supplementary statement of objections at any time provided that the undertakings are given time to consider their reply.[86]

---

85   OJ 2001, L162/21.
86   (T–305 and others) *PVC II, Limburgse Vinyl v Commission*, [1999] ECR II–931, [1999] 5 CMLR 303, para 497 and Reg 2842/98, Art 2(2). The ECJ confirmed most of the judgment of the CFI.

7.5.3 *Access to the file*

After receipt of the statement of objections, parties must have access to all the documents in the Commission's file apart from the categories of documents identified in the *Hercules* judgment[87]—business secrets, Commission's internal documents[88] and other confidential information.

The Commission notice on access to the file is unhelpful about what this includes. For example, it refers to the decisions of the hearing officer to determine what constitutes a business secret (at point IA(1)), but these decisions were not public documents. Secrets are protected as long as they remain commercially important or are unknown outside the firm or group or association of firms. I hope that when only some people outside the firm know them and are subject to a duty of confidence, secrets will still be protected. Confidential documents are subject to rather less protection and may be disclosed if necessary to prove an alleged infringement or in favour of the person accused (see point IA(2)).

Article 27(2) provides that the right of access to the file does not entitle the parties to see confidential information.

In practice the Commission has done more to help the parties than has been required by the Court. When the Commission has promised to make items available, the CFI has held it to its promise, (*Hercules*, para 53). It is now customary to append to the statement of objections a list of the documents that the Commission has. With the exception of those that are confidential or prepared by officials for the purpose of the case, the parties are entitled to inspect these before completing the answer to the statement of objections. The Commission has stated that in future it will send copies of all the documents necessary to the defence.

The documents disclosed should include those favourable to the defence. In *Italian Flat Glass*,[89] the Court of First Instance objected when a passage favourable to one of the firms was deleted from a document that was used. Dr Ehlermann, when Director General in charge of the competition department, informed the House of Lords Select Committee that safeguards had been introduced to prevent a repetition. He also accepted a duty to give access to documents that are manifestly exculpatory.[90]

If they want documents not to be disclosed to their competitors, undertakings should state specifically and in writing which documents commun-

---

87 (T–7/89) *Hercules v Commission*, [1991] ECR II–1711, paras 53 and 54. The appeals were confined to other problems.

88 Point II A(2c) of the notice on access to the file, [1997] 4 CMLR 490.

89 (T–68, 77 & 78/89) [1992] ECR II–1403, and see also (T–7/89) *Hercules v Commission* [1991] ECR II–1711, para 54.

90 Minutes of Evidence to House of Lords Select Committee on the European Communities, *Enforcement of Community Competition Rules*, 7 December 1993, HL paper 7, from question 419, at 106.

icated to the Commission or obtained during an investigation[91] are confidential and ask for this to be respected. They are habitually asked to supply a non-confidential version which may be disclosed to complainants or the parties to an agreement (see point IIA(1.3)).

In proceedings under Article 82, care will be taken to ensure the anonymity of a complainant against whom the dominant firm might retaliate (point IID(2)). Furthermore, parties will not be given access to the internal documents of the Commission. The Commission notice applies only to those alleged to have infringed the competition rules, not complainants or third parties who are entitled to access to somewhat less information than the parties to a notification.

Giving access to a large file is very time consuming for the Commission, since thousands of documents may have to be checked to exclude confidential information. The practice of officials, who were brought up under different legal systems, on how much disclosure should be given varies.

In *Soda Ash*[92] the CFI concluded that the principle of 'equality of arms' required that the firms accused should know as much about the file as does the Commission. In *PVC II*,[93] the CFI confirmed that the Commission cannot be permitted to decide on its own whether to use documents against the applicants, where the latter had no access to them, and could not decide whether or not to use them in their own defence, even if the Commission officials acted in good faith. The Commission cannot send only those documents used against a particular undertaking leaving it to obtain further documents from other undertakings, who may be its competitors. The decision should be quashed, however, only if access to the documents might have affected the result.

7.5.4 *Subsequent steps*

After the hearing, the case team will draft the decision, taking into account the statements of parties and the views of the Advisory Committee. The draft decision will be checked by the handler's immediate superiors, by Directorate A and by the legal service of the Commission. The file may be subject to peer review, in which case someone from the team of the chief economist will be involved. Parts may be read by the Director and Director-General of the Competition Department to check policy matters. Any of these persons may suggest changes to the decision even if they have not attended all the meetings with the parties or read the complete file. Nevertheless, the factual parts of the decision are unlikely to be changed without being put back to the case team. Eventually, the draft decision will be sent to the Member of the Commission

91   Point IIA(1.2) of the Notice on access to the file, [1997] 4 CMLR 490.
92   *Solvay v Commission* (T–30/91) [1995] ECR 1775, para 83 and *ICI v Commission*, *ibid*,1847, para 93 (appeals from the *Soda Ash* decisions).
93   (T305/*PVC II, Limburgse Vinyl v Commission*, T–305 and others, [1999] ECR II–931, [1999] 5 CMLR 303, paras 1012–14.

who will submit it to his colleagues. The *Chefs du cabinet*—the senior officials attached to each of the Members—will consider the draft, and only when they have approved it, possibly in an amended form, will it normally go before the Members at one of the weekly meetings of the Commission. The draft decision will not be put to the parties or complainants.

Decisions adopted under Articles 7–10, that is, to clear, forbid, or accept commitments must be published (Article 30). They appear in the twenty official languages in the Official Journal of the Communities, 'Legislation' (L) series.

Under the new procedure for dealing with structural joint ventures within two months, the Commission publishes a few facts in the OJ as soon as possible after receiving the notification in order to encourage third parties to submit evidence, without indicating whether its decision will be favourable. Decisions to impose fines or daily penalties are not required to be published, but if they are, they appear in the Legislation series.

7.5.5 *Appeals*

No appeal is possible against preliminary steps taken by the Commission, but they can be raised after a formal decision on the merits has been adopted.[94] This is expensive for the parties, who have to pursue the complaint all the way through to an appeal.

Most appeals to the CFI are brought by the addressees of Commission decisions, but as explained at 3.1.1.2 above, in *Métropole I*,[95] it was held that a person with a sufficient interest to be permitted to take part in the procedure, even if it has not done so, is entitled to appeal against an exemption granted to a competitor which excludes it from the benefit of the agreement. Under Regulation 1/2003, individual exemptions will no longer be adopted. A clearing declaration under Articles 5 or 10 will not be binding in so far as conditions may change. In so far as they remain the same, neither a NCA nor a court is allowed to decide contrary to a Commission decision, so the right to appeal against a clearing decision granted to someone else may remain important.

I see no reason why *Métropole I* should not still apply. Where the clearance is contained in a Commission decision, an appeal will lie to the CFI under Article 230 EC. Where it is granted by an NCA, no reference is possible under Community law unless the NCA is a court, but an appeal under national law may lie to a court and that court may ask the ECJ for a preliminary ruling under Article 234 EC.[96]

---

94   *IBM v Commission*, C–60/81, [1981] ECR 2639.
95   *Métropole Télévision SA and others v Commission I* (T–528/93 and others) [1996] ECR II–649.
96   There are some doubts: Marie Demetriou, 'Preliminary References and Competition Law,' (2002) 1 *Competition Law Journal*, 345. She considers that it is clear that where the NCA is bound to apply Community law, a reference lies, and where it is not bound but encouraged to do so, it probably lies.

The jurisdiction of the CFI on appeal from the Commission under Article 230 EC is limited to judicial review (1.4.3.2 above). The court does not decide whether the Commission's decision was correct, but whether it was manifestly contrary to the requirements of the Treaty and its subordinate legislation. Nevertheless, in some of its recent decisions, the CFI has been quashing the Commission's decisions for not giving adequate reasons as is required by Article 253 EC. It is hoped that this will lead to decisions that are more cogently reasoned. When considering individual exemptions, the CFI recognises that the decisions are based partly on policy, and does not constrain the Commission tightly. The ECJ refers to the Commission's margin of appreciation.

An appeal from the CFI lies to the ECJ only on questions of law and it has interpreted this concept narrowly. Mixed questions of law and fact are treated as outside its jurisdiction. Again, the ECJ does not rehear the issues, but decides only whether the CFI judgment was wrong.

The Commission's decision finding a cartel and fining the parties was annulled on appeal in *PVC I*, for formal reasons—it had not been signed by the appropriate people, although it had been adopted by the College of Members of the Commission. The Commission readopted the decision, without issuing a new statement of objections or giving the parties a further opportunity to state their views. The CFI and ECJ held that the annulment of the decision left the preparatory steps valid and, therefore, upheld the new decision which had been properly taken through the formal steps of authentication.[97]

7.6 Fines and penalties (Articles 23–26)

Article 23(2) provides for fines of up to 10% of the undertaking's turnover for the previous year, for intentional or negligent infringement of Article 81 or 82, or for infringing a decision ordering interim measures under Article 8 or failing to comply with commitments it gave to the Commission under Article 9.

In fixing the fine, the Commission shall have regard to the gravity and duration of the infringement (Article 23(3)).

The fines are said not to be of a criminal law nature (Article 23(5)) but, as explained at 7.5.1 above, the jurisprudence of the European Court of Human Rights has treated proceedings leading to administrative fines under French competition law as being criminal, and subject to the provisions of Article 6 (ECHR) which ensures a fair hearing.

Smaller fines of up to 1% of an undertaking's turnover the previous year may be imposed for not supplying correct information under Articles 17 or 18, or for responding inadequately to an inspection (Article 23(1)). One per cent of the previous year's turnover will almost always be far heavier than the

---

97 *PVC II-Limburgse Vinyl and others v Commission*, (C–238/99P and others), [2002] ECR I–8375, [2003] 4 CMLR 395. The cases were joined for the purposes of the judgment.

small absolute sums that could be required under Regulation 17, which have been further reduced by inflation.

Article 23(2) provides that where an infringement by an association of undertakings relates to the conduct of its members, the fine shall not exceed 10% of the turnover of each member active on the relevant market. If it is not solvent, Article 23(4) requires the association to seek contributions from its members. If the contribution is not made, the Commission can collect the fines directly from the members which participated in the infringement.

The level of fines has been increased from time to time. In *Pioneer*,[98] the ECJ confirmed that the Commission was entitled to change its policy and impose a fine far heavier than under its previous practice without giving any prior warning. The Court confirmed that the basis for the 10% was the entire turnover of the group of companies on all products, worldwide, but where the infringement concerned only one item of business, among others, the Commission habitually reduced the proportionate fine. Often the Commission imposed a fine based on the turnover of the group in the product to which the illegal conduct related, but it has a wide discretion about what to take as its base. Turnover is habitually excised from the public decisions, and it is not easy to read into them what weight was given to the various factors stated to be relevant. This gives the Commission considerable discretion.

Although the CFI has full jurisdiction over fines and can increase or reduce them, it has made it difficult for itself to exercise this in cases where multiple infringements are alleged. In *Tetra Pak II*,[99] it held that the Commission was under no duty to apportion the fine as between the different infringements alleged. Faced with a large fine, there is little a firm can do to show it is excessive, although the CFI is entitled to reduce a fine when the party shows that one or more of the findings in a complex infringement is unjustified. The courts have also reduced fines, less than proportionately, on the ground that the infringement was established only for part of the period found by the Commission.

Care must be taken when acquiring a company to ensure that it has not infringed the competition rules, as the new company will be liable for the fines imposed in relation to conduct before the acquisition.[100]

7.6.1 *Notice on the method of setting fines*

The Commission has been concerned that the fines it imposed were insufficient to deter firms from committing infringements of the competition

---

98   (100–103/80), [1983] ECR 1825.
99   *Tetra Pak II* (T–83/91) [1994] ECR II–762, para 236.
100   See Laurent Garzaniti and Giuseppe Scassellati-Sforzolini, 'Liability of Successor Undertakings for Infringements of EC Competition Law Committed Prior to Corporate Reorganisations' (1995) 16 *European Competition Law Review*, 348. See also *Daimler Chrysler* 10 Oct 2001, [2003] CEC 2003.

rules. In January 1998, it announced a policy of imposing far higher fines:[101] in future it will start its fining calculation for minor infringements—usually vertical agreements with limited impact on the market and covering only part of the common market—at between a thousand to a million euros. For serious infringements, usually between competitors, with wider impact, the fine would start at between 1 and 20 million euros. For very serious infringements such as cartels, practices dividing the common market and clear cut infringements of Article 82 at 20 million euros. If the duration exceeds a year, a 10% surcharge per annum might be added. Aggravating or mitigating circumstances, such as the size of the firm, whether it was a ring leader, and so on, may also affect the level of the fine.

Following the notice, the Commission has spelled out in most of its decisions the calculations it has used, and the fines have been very much greater than previously. The CFI and ECJ have largely approved the Commission's calculations on the grounds that it is the institution in charge of the orientation of competition policy.

Very high fines were imposed on firms that operated the cartel for lysine and appeals were brought to the CFI. In *Kyowa Hakko Kogyo and another v Commission*,[102] for example, the CFI confirmed a long line of cases stating that the Commission has a margin of discretion when fixing fines and that it may change its policy without prior notice. It treated the notice as binding the Commission:

> 62. In setting the amount of the fine which it imposed on the applicants in the decision the Commission used the calculation method which it imposed on itself in the Guidelines. According to settled case-law, the Commission may not depart from rules which it has imposed on itself (see Case T–7/89 *Hercules Chemicals v Commission* [1991] ECR II-1711, paragraph 53, confirmed on appeal in Case C–51/92 P . . . [1999] ECR I-4235, and the case law cited). In particular, whenever the Commission adopts guidelines for the purpose of specifying, in accordance with the Treaty, the criteria which it proposes to apply in the exercise of its discretion, there arises a self-imposed limitation of that discretion in as much as it must then follow those guidelines.

Guidelines stating how the Commission intends to exercise its discretion give rise to legitimate expectations in contrast to guidelines on the scope of the law, which do not, and which do not bind the Commission (2.4.9 above), although it may well follow them.

In failing to consider the market power of the appellant, however, the Commission had departed from the notice (paragraphs 72-77). The CFI proceeded to consider whether this had led the Commission to breach the principle of proportionality in setting fines (para 78) and concluded that it had not and, in the exercise of its unlimited jurisdiction over fines, the CFI rejected the complaint.

101   [1998] 4 CMLR 472.
102   T–223/00, 9 July 2003, paras 61 ff.

The factors that aggravate infringement include recidivism, but in the *Carbon Graphite Cartel*,[103] the Commission did not increase the fine on a firm that had joined several cartels broadly contemporaneously and reduced the fine on another firm because it had already been fined for two other cartels and was in a difficult financial position.

In Its decision on the *Organic Peroxides Cartel*,[104] the Commission fined AC Treuhand for organising a cartel in which it did not participate, although the amount was reduced because of the novelty of this approach.

7.6.2 *Notice on the reduction of cartel fines*

Even earlier, the Commission endeavoured to increase the risk of exposure for firms engaged in cartel activities. The Department of Justice in the US has had huge success in discovering cartels by introducing a leniency programme. The first carteliser to inform the Department will not be fined or sent to prison, although this is no protection from a treble damage action by customers, suppliers or other persons harmed by the cartel.[104a]

In *Cartonboard*,[105] the Commission fined Stora only one third of what it would have done had Stora not come to the Commission and given it information about the cartel at a time when the Commission did not know about it. In 1996, the Commission stated the conditions under which it would reduce fines[106] and revised its notice in 2002.[107] The earlier notice had provided less security than the US system. The Commission has had remarkable success in pursuing cartels, often but not always, on the coat-tails of US prosecutions.

In 2002, the Commission increased the incentive for undertakings to blow the whistle on secret cartels fast by promising not to fine the first firm to give it sufficient evidence of a secret cartel to find an infringement or authorise an inspection when it was not previously in a position to do so. There are three further conditions:

a) the undertaking must cooperate fully, on a continuous basis and expeditiously throughout the Commission's administrative procedure and remain at the Commission's disposal to answer swiftly any request that may help to establish the facts;

b) the undertaking must end its involvement in the suspected infringement when it submits evidence; and

---

103   IP (03) 1651, [2004] 4 CMLR 257.
104   IP (03) 1700, [2004] 4 CMLR 259.
104a   A bill to detreble damages for a person benefitting from leniency has been introduced.
105   [1994] 5 CMLR 547.
106   [1996] 5 CMLR 362.
107   Commission notice on immunity from fines and reduction of fines in cartel cases, OJ 2002, C 45/3, [2002] 4 CMLR 906. See Wouter Wils, 'Self-incrimination in EC Antitrust enforcement: A legal and economic analysis,' (2003) 26 *World Competition Law and Economics Review*, 567. See also *Bertus Van Barlingen*, 'The European Commission's 2002 Leniency Notice after one year's operation,' (2003) 2 *Competition Policy Newsletter*, 16.

c) it must not have coerced other undertakings to participate in the infringement.

Under the more recent notice, it will give the first qualifying firm a certificate entitling it to complete immunity. It will also reduce by 30–50% the fine on the second undertaking to provide information and smaller proportions on those that inform it later, provided there is sufficient added value to the information it has. It has retained its discretion to reduce fines for an undertaking that provides evidence of facts not known to the Commission relating to the gravity or duration of suspected cartel. The Commission is devoting more resources to finding cartels. The more generous leniency programme produced immediate results.

In former times, if it was discovered that one's client had been engaged in fixing prices or allocating markets, one advised it to stop doing so and to arrange an effective compliance programme. There is no duty to notify a cartel: only not to infringe. Five years after termination of the infringement, the limitation regulation would save the firm from being fined (7.6.3 below).

Nowadays there is the fear that one of the other members of the cartel may try to obtain the benefits of the leniency programme and urgent consideration should be given to being the first to inform the Commission. If a different employee of one of the members of a cartel attends a meeting where prices are discussed, one of the conspirators may claim leniency fast.

7.6.3 *Limitation periods*

Periods of prescription are provided by Articles 25 and 26. The Commission cannot impose fines more than five years after the termination of conduct infringing Article 81 or 82, or more than three years in relation to requests for information or inspections. Fines have been imposed for continuing cartels going back far more than 5 years. The period of prescription begins to run only when the conduct ceases.

It is not always easy to establish when an old or illegal agreement ceases. The *Soda Ash* cartel[108] to divide the world market was formally determined by a letter in 1973 when the UK acceded to the Community, but the parties did not invade each other's previous territory, so the Commission found that tacit agreement continued (paragraphs 53–59), although once markets have been divided territorially, it makes sense for each firm to refrain from selling in the traditional territory of the other, as it would expect retaliation. The Commission mentioned, however that the firms continued close commercial relationship and alleged that they exchanged detailed information in alternate months about their production costs until the mid-seventies (para 30).

It is difficult to refute such an allegation when the two major producers met each other for various legitimate purposes.

---

108   *ICI and Solvay et Cie*, [1994] 4 CMLR 454, paras 26–29.

7.7 Conclusion

The procedure is still very centralised, although substantial work has been outsourced to NCAs and courts. The Commission has power to forbid various kinds of conduct without having to prosecute before a court. It still remains both detective and judge. The German and Italian NCAs argued strongly for an independent tribunal before which the Commission might act as prosecutor.

The Commission, with the power of pre-emption, retains its control of policy, although the formation of the policy may be preceded by discussions with NCAs through the Advisory Committee and the intranet. If the Commission opens proceedings, NCAs are required to terminate theirs (Article 11(6)), and both courts and NCAs are required not to adopt decisions incompatible with a particular decision of the Commission, or one envisaged under proceedings that it has already initiated (Article 16). The Commission also retains powers to grant group exemptions, and the power to withdraw the benefit from individual agreements.

Its powers to obtain information by compulsion have been slightly widened—homes can now be inspected provided a warrant is obtained from a court, and seals may placed when an inspection is not completed. Nevertheless, the sanctions are far less than in some jurisdictions. Some NCAs, such as those in the UK and Ireland can prosecute cartelisers before the courts and argue for a term of imprisonment. This is true in the US and Canada, where the agencies have wider powers of search and opportunities for extensive discovery.

In the USA, tort actions can be brought for treble damages with other important rules favouring the plaintiff (7.3.4 above). In most Member States, only single damages will be granted.

I welcome the end of the substantive bifurcation of Article 81(1) and (3). The two paragraphs require much the same analysis of competitive factors, and it is desirable that whoever considers the application of Article 81(1) should be the person responsible for applying Article 81(3). Many lawyers think that courts will have great trouble applying Article 81(3).

Where the policy being pursued is not competition, but another policy such as the environment or employment, the balancing of that policy against an anticompetitive restraint may not be an appropriate task for a court. Common lawyers may be less concerned than civil lawyers about the need for economic analysis because there are specialist lawyers well educated in economic analysis, they manage their cases, can select economic consultants, and educate the judges.

With the accession of ten new Member States, many of them with little experience of competition law, it was clear that the Commission lacked the resources to manage competition in the way it has done until now. Something had to change. We have spent 42 years educating the Commission and now that it is adopting a more economic approach, it might have been better to have made more resources available to it. Now we will have to educate national authorities and courts in many of the 25 Member States. Many of the new ones are too small to have a competition authority large enough to allow specialisation.

7.8 Bibliography

Bertus Van Barlingen, 'The European Commission's 2002 Leniency Notice after one year's Operation,' (2003) 2 *Competition Policy Newsletter*, 16.

Theofanis Christoforou 'Protection of Legal Privilege in EEC Competition Law; the Imperfections of a Case,' (1985–6) 9 *Fordham International Law Journal*, 1.

Marie Demetriou, 'Preliminary References and Competition Law,' (2002) 1 *Competition Law Journal.*

Claus Dieter Ehlermann, *The Modernisation of European Competition Law: the Next Ten Yars, CELS Occasional Paper No 4.*

Claus Dieter Ehlermann, 'The European Administration of Member States with Regard to Competition Law' [1995] *European Competition Law Review*, 454.

——, **and** *Isabela Atanasiu* (eds) *European Competition Law Annual 1999: The Modernisation of EC Antitrust Policy*, (Oxford, Hart Publishing, 2000).

——, **and** *Atanasiu* (eds) *European Competition Law Annual 2000* (Oxford, Hart Publishing, 2001).

——, **and** *Berend Jan Drijber*, 'Legal Protection of Enterprises: Administrative Procedure, in particular Access to Files and Confidentiality' [1996] *European Competition Law Review,* 375.

Ian Forrester **and** *Christopher Norall*, 'The Laicization of Community Law—Self-help and the Rule of Reason: How Competition Law is and could be applied,' [1983] *Fordham Corporate Law Institute*, chapter 8, from 305.

Walter van Gerven, 'The Genesis of EEA Law and the Principles of Primacy and Direct Effect,' (1982–3) 16 *Fordham International Law Journal,* 955.

Luc Gyselen, 'Le Juge national face aux règles de concurrence communautaires applicables aux entreprises,' *Journal des tribunaux*, Droit européen, of 23 October 1993, (no 2), 25–33.

D Jarret Arp **and** *Cristof RA Swaak*, 'A Tempting Offer: Immunity from Fines for Cartel Conduct under the European Commission's New Leniency Notice,' (2002) 16 (no 3) *Antitrust* 59

Celia Hampton, 'EC Competition Law: cooperation within the European Competition Network, Proposals by the Competition Law Forum,' [September 2003] *Competition Law Insight* 11.

Barry Hawk (ed) [1993], [2001] and [2002] *Fordham Corporate Law Institute;* many papers consider the problems and limitations of enforcement by national courts and national authorities.

House of Lords, Select Committee on the European Communities, *Competition Practice*, 23 February 1982 (paper 91).

——, Select Committee on the European Communities, *Enforcement of Community Competition Rules*, 7 December 1993, HL paper 7.

——, Select Committee on the European Communities, *Reforming EC Competition Procedures* with evidence, Session 1999–2000, 4th Report. (These are significant

critical reports and the minutes of evidence by officials, academics and practitioners are of exceptionally high quality. The first report resulted in several reforms to
Competition Department's procedure and the others may well do so.)

C S Kerse, *EEC Antitrust Procedure* 4th edn (London, Sweet & Maxwell, 1999). The
5th edition expected late in 2004.

——, 'The Complainant in Competition Cases: a progress report,' (1997) 34 *Common
Market Law Review*, 213.

Louis Ortiz Blanco, *EC Competition Procedure* (Oxford, OUP, 1996).

Alberto Pera **and** *Mario Todino*, 'Enforcement of EC Competition Rules—Need for a
Reform' in Barry Hawk (ed) [1996] *Fordham Corporate Law Institute* (Juris
Publishing and Sweet & Maxwell, 1997.)

Russell Richardson, 'Guidance Without Guidance—A European Revolution in Fining
Policy; The Commission's Guidelines on Fines.' [1999] *European Competition Law
Review* 360.

John Temple Lang, 'Commitment Decisions under Regulation 1/2003: Legal Aspects
of a New Kind of Competition Decision, (2003) 24 *European Competition Law
Review*, 347.

James S Venit, 'Brave New World: the Modernization and Decentralization of
Enforcement under Articles 81 and 82 of the EC Treaty,' (2003) 40 *Common Market
Law Review*, 545.

Bo Vesterdorf, 'Complaints Concerning Infringements of Competition law within the
Context of European Community law,' (1974) 34 *Common Market Law Review*, 77.

Marc van der Woude, 'Hearing Officers and EC Antitrust Procedures: The Art of
Making Subjective Procedures more Objective' (1996) 33 *Common Market Law
Review*, 531.

——, *and Valerie Landes* (2003), 'The Procedural rules for the Application of the
Articles 81 and 82 EC Special Alert', Chapter 10A, pp 10A.01–10A 07 in Valentine
Korah (ed), *Competition Law of the European Community*, (LexisNexis). This will
be superceeded by a longer analysis in September 2004, to be followed in later years
by consideration of procedure for competition cases before national courts and
authorities.

Philippa Watson, 'Fundamental Rights and Competition Law,' (2003) 2 *Competition
Law Journal*, 36.

Wouter Wils, 'The Commission's New Method for Calculating Fines in Antitrust
Cases,' (1998) 23 *European Law Review*, 252.

——, 'The Commission Notice on the Non-Imposition or Reduction of Fines in Cartel
Cases: a Legal and Economic Analysis,' (1997) 22 *European Law Review*, 125.

——, 'Self-incrimination in EC Antitrust enforcement: A Legal and Economic
Analysis,' (2003) 26 *World Competition Law and Economics Review, 567.*

——, 'Should Private Enforcement be Encouraged in Europe' (2003) 26 *World
Competition Law and Economics Review, forthcoming,* 473.

——, 'The Principle of *Ne Bis in Idem* in EC Antitrust Enforcement: A legal and
Economic Analysis. (2003) 26 *World Competition Law and Economics Review,* 131.

(These and other Articles by Wouter Wils are reproduced in a volume published by
Kluwer. Another will be published by Hart Publishing in 2005).

8. Classes of Agreement Clearly Prohibited

8.1 Distinctions between hard core and ancillary restrictions of competition and between horizontal and vertical agreements

The Sherman Act 1890 in the United States prohibits all agreements, combinations and conspiracies in restraint of trade. This prohibition is as broad as that in Article 81(1), and might have been construed to render all important commercial transactions illegal: if traders satisfy their needs for supply or demand with particular traders, fewer opportunities remain available to others. To avoid holding all important contracts void and illegal, the judges early read into the Act a qualification, foreshadowed by the common law doctrine of restraint of trade, that only unreasonable restraints are illegal.

8.1.1 *Hard core restraints illegal* per se

Interpreting the same statutory language, the US courts condemned hard core cartels: agreements between competitors to reduce supply or raise price. They give rise to the result that consumers who would like to buy at a price that covers expenses, including a return on capital not being able to do so. Consumers are worse off and no one but the cartelisers are better off (1.3.1 & 2.2.4.1 above). US courts did not permit parties to justify price fixing cartels or collective boycotts by competitors on the ground that the prices fixed were reasonable, or that a collective boycott was agreed for justifiable purposes, such as restraining infringement of copyright for which the civil remedies were considered to be too weak.

In his famous judgment in *US v Addyston Pipe and Steel*,[1] Judge (later President) Taft distinguished a naked cartel between competitors to keep up the price of steel, which was illegal however reasonable the prices set, from restraints ancillary to a wider lawful purpose. In the absence of a competitive market, there is no way of knowing what level prices would have reached but for the cartel. Even if prices were reasonable yesterday, it does not follow that they are today. Judge Taft refused to 'set sail on a sea of doubt' and permit the justification of a cartel on the ground that the prices fixed were reasonable. The issue was not one that courts could resolve.

In this condemnation of hard core cartels that are not justified as necessary to make viable a pro-competitive transaction, the European Commission and Court have followed the American case law. Agreements about prices and production are listed in Article 81(1). Price-fixing agreements between competitors and collective boycotts have attracted heavy fines and rarely been exempted. The economic objections to market power are explained at 1.3–1.3.2.7 above and to cartels at 2.2.4–2.2.4.3 above.

---

1   85 Fed 271 (6th Cir 1898), affirmed by the Supreme Court on other grounds.

In its notice on the application of Article 81(3) of the Treaty,[2] G 21, the Commission treats the restrictions black listed in the various group exemptions (chapters 9, 11 and 13 below) as restricting competition by object and infringing Article 81(1) without it being necessary to investigate their effect, although no agreements are utterly incapable of exemption.

Other restraints are illegal only if their actual or potential effects are likely to restrict competition appreciably.

8.1.2 *Ancillary restraints may be justified*

As an illustration of the kind of agreement that might be lawful as being reasonably necessary to make the main transaction viable, Judge Taft instanced covenants not to compete with the buyer of one's business or with a partner or former partner.

Permitting the sale of goodwill may be pro-competitive. It encourages the proprietor of the business to build up goodwill to sell later, and enables him to move on or retire and a younger person to take over. No one would pay for goodwill if next day the former proprietor could legally canvass his former customers. The reasonableness of the restraint can be judged by the amount of protection needed to enable the goodwill sold to keep its value. Under US law, as under the English common law, the restraint must be limited in relation to the products and area for which the business had achieved a reputation and for the period reasonably necessary to secure the goodwill to the buyer.

A very similar analysis of covenants on the sale of a business was adopted by the Commission in *Nutricia*[3] and confirmed by the ECJ in *Remia and Nutricia v Commission*.[4] The Court said that the Commission was right to assert that such covenants do not, in themselves, infringe Article 81(1). The situation with the restriction should be compared with that which would have prevailed without it: no one would have bought the business without some protection. Perceived *ex ante*, from the time the contact was made, no competition that was possible was restrained: only perceived *ex post*, after the sale was complete, was competition reduced. The protection must, however, be limited in time, space and product to what is necessary to make the transaction viable. Moreover, the Commission decided in *Quantel*[5] that the vendor may not protect itself territorially from the buyer of one of its subsidiaries, with whom it had previously not been competing. If followed, this decision may deter management from selling off parts of a business that could be better managed by third parties and so may reduce efficiency and competition rather than increase it.

---

2   OJ 2004, C101/97, [2004] 4 CMLR 000.
3   [1984] 2 CMLR 165, paras 26–30.
4   (42/84) [1985] ECR 2545, paras 17–20.
5   [1993] 5 CMLR 497, paras 41–42.

Article 81(3), unlike US antitrust law, provides a possibility for exemption, and in many situations where US courts may now hold that competition is not restricted, the Commission has held to the contrary but granted an exemption under Article 81(3). In this way it has centralised control in its own hands, as only the Commission had power to grant exemptions (2.4.5 above).

The main drawback has been that the Commission had insufficient resources to grant many exemptions and national courts asked to enforce a contract had no power to exempt. This is no longer the law. Articles 1 and 6 of Regulation 1/2003 (7.2 above) provide that Articles 81 and 82 have direct effect in the courts and NCAs of Member States. They may now apply Article 81(3) as well as Article 81(1) and (2).

We will return to the concept of ancillary restraints (2.4.5. above) in the specific context of a franchising agreement when dealing with the ECJ's judgments in *Pronuptia*[6] and *Nungesser*,[7] which adopted the ancillary restraints doctrine (9.5.1, 11.3 and 13.2.1.5 below).

8.1.3 *Horizontal and vertical relationships*

A slightly different distinction from that between hard core and ancillary restraints has been developed by Chicago economists. Horizontal agreements are made by firms that would otherwise compete with each other at the same level of trade or industry—between manufacturers, between retailers or between licensees of competing products. Relationships between firms at different levels of trade or industry, such as a supplier and his customer or a licensor of technology and his licensee are vertical, where the firms could not have competed but for the agreement in question.

Each party to a horizontal agreement has an interest in the other producing less and charging more, whereas each party to a vertical agreement will benefit from increased demand if the other supplies more at a lower price. Vertically related products are complementary—the more of one that is produced the greater the demand for the other—whereas those provided by competitors are substitutes.

Although some joint ventures between actual or potential competitors may be necessary if economies of scale or scope are to be realised or other pro-competitive developments are to take place, horizontal restraints are suspect. Competitors are likely to want to raise prices collectively and, if not exposed to substantial competition, may be able to do so.

A supplier or technology holder normally has no interest in protecting its dealers or licensees from competition between each other. The lower the price they charge the more will be sold and, other things being equal, the greater the profit of the firm upstream. If there is any monopoly profit to be reaped the firm upstream can achieve that through the price or licence fee it charges:

6   (161/84) [1986] ECR 353, paras 15–22.
7   (258/78) [1982] ECR 2015.

there is no reason why it should be shared with dealers or licensees. It is in its interest to protect dealers or licensees from each other only to the extent necessary to induce investment that would not otherwise occur.

Not only are vertical agreements and mergers less likely to restrict competition than are horizontal arrangements—those between competitors—they may lead to various kinds of efficiencies which may benefit consumers. First, they may protect investment from others taking a free ride on it, secondly, they may overcome a hold up problem and thirdly, reduce transaction costs: where the interaction of two businesses is too complex, vertical integration through merger or contract may be the only way of synchronising them The first two pro-competitive functions are mentioned in the guidelines (Gs) on vertical restraints[8] The first three indents of G 116 describe free rider situations that may be overcome by a vertical restraint. The fourth and fifth describe a solution to hold up problems.

A dealer might not be prepared to advertise goods, enable the public to inspect them or provide technical advice that might increase the popularity of the brand, if a discount house, not having borne similar costs, could take a free ride on the investment and undercut the dealer investing in the service. For this sort of reason, the US Supreme Court held in *Continental TV v GTE Sylvania*[9] that location clauses, whereby each retailer agreed to sell only from a specified address in order to protect dealers in a different city, were not necessarily illegal. Such a clause may make competition between brands possible, by restricting competition between dealers in the same brand.

Sylvania's market share increased after adopting the practice; it was not encouraging dealers to sell less on higher margins, but encouraging them to perform pre-sales services wanted by consumers. Similarly, a patentee may have to protect a licensee if the latter is to develop a market, and tool up to operate a system that may not even have been tried on an industrial scale. The first licensee might consider the investment too risky if it feared that when it got the system to work smoothly and began to trade profitably, another licensee with lower costs, because of the development of a market and improvements to the technology which were passed on to it, could reap where it had sown.

To protect a dealer from free riding by others, the ECJ ruled in *Société La Technique Minière v Maschinenbau Ulm*[10] that to grant it an exclusive territory does not infringe Article 81(1) if exclusivity is necessary to penetrate a new market. An agreement should be appraised in its legal and economic context. Similarly, in *Nungesser*[11] it held that, in view of the investment by both the patentee and licensee, an open exclusive licence does not, in itself, infringe Article 81(1). In *Pronuptia*,[12] many restrictions of conduct necessary to make

---

8   OJ 2000, C291/01, Gs 115–18.
9   433 US 36 (1977) (US Sup Ct).
10   (56/65) [1966] ECR 235, 250.
11   (258/78) [1982] ECR 2015, paras 56–58 (11.3 below).
12   (161/84) [1986] ECR 353, paras 15–22 (9.5.1 below).

distribution franchising viable were ruled not, in themselves, to restrict competition.

The second problem that can justify a vertical restriction is called by economists 'the hold up problem.' Where investment in more than one asset is required to bring a product to market, the person investing later can hold up the first to invest. If A, a component manufacturer sets up a production line to serve a particular customer, B, B can hold A up by offering a price for the component that covers only the incremental costs of production and delivery, without enabling A to benefit from its capital investment. A would be stupid to make the investment unless it could make a valid long term contract with B ensuring that B buys from A.

There is a hold up problem only if A's production line cannot be exploited as efficiently otherwise than for B. In other words, there must be no equally profitable use for the asset in which A invests except in collaboration with B's. Moreover A must not be able to exploit its production line by carrying on the activity that B was to have carried on (see: glossary, costs—sunk costs, below). Within these limits, however, the Commission's vertical guidelines 115–19 stress the efficiencies that can arise from vertical relationships. Similar efficiencies can also result from vertical or conglomerate mergers.

Nevertheless, the Community Court has not embraced the American doctrine wholeheartedly. It has rarely accepted what it calls 'absolute territorial protection' and, apart from *Remia* (8.1.2 above),[13] its judgments seem to have been confined to exclusive agreements.

The Commission has followed the Court to some extent, especially in some of the block exemptions mostly for vertical agreements, which permit exclusivity and some territorial protection under Article 81(3).[14] Until recently, however, it has rarely cleared agreements as outside the prohibition of Article 81(1) on this ground.

The Commission often defines vertical agreements to mean those between firms 'at a different level of the production or distribution chain'[15] without considering whether the parties are also actual or potential competitors and this has led to complications when drafting group exemptions for vertical agreements. The US agencies treat an agreement as vertical only if the parties were not actual or potential competitors in a relevant market when the agreement was made and the commitment to investment undertaken. Until recently, the Commission used to treat a relationship as horizontal once both parties were producing or marketing similar products, but it has recently been persuaded that, by then, the inducement to invest is water under the bridge (11.5.2.1 below). In G17 on the application of Article 81(3) of the Treaty the Commission cites *La Technique Minière*[16] and says:

---

13   (42/84) [1985] ECR 2545.
14   See chaps 9, 11 & 13 below.
15   Article 2(1) of Reg 2790/99 granting a group exemption for vertical distribution agreements.
16   (56/65) [1966] ECR 235.

The assessment of whether an agreement is restrictive of competition must be made within the actual context in which competition would occur in the absence of the agreement with its alleged restrictions.

The American agencies are right to think *ex ante* and consider whether the relationship is horizontal or vertical at the time commitments to invest are undertaken.

Recently, the Commission has stressed the distinction between horizontal and vertical restraints and treated the latter more leniently in the notice on minor agreements (2.4.9 above) and by granting a wide block exemption for vertical agreements (9.6 below). Article 81 does not refer in so many words to horizontal or vertical agreements. The distinction is relevant only indirectly because the effects of each on competition differ according to the relationship between the parties in the absence of the transaction. Similarly, Article 81 does not distinguish in words between hard core and ancillary restraints.

In *FEDETAB*[17] the Court clearly distinguished vertical from collective exclusive dealing in holding that provisions it had cleared in a vertical context were forbidden when adopted by competitors, but expressed no reasons for adopting the distinction. In *SSI*,[18] it confirmed that high fines were appropriate for a horizontal, hard core cartel to maintain dealers' margins even if the agreement was capable of being exempted.

Unfortunately, in *Salonia v Poidomani*,[19] it later advised a national court under Article 234 to apply the rule it had developed for vertical agreements also to a horizontal agreement.

Professor, now Judge, Posner in the US has gone much further and suggested that, owing to the interest of the supplier or licensor in not raising the prices of the goods to the public, vertical restraints should be *per se* legal. This remains controversial even in the United States. For some products, many buyers do not need pre-sales advice from the retailer. If a few marginal customers do, however, it may pay the brand owner to encourage the dealer to provide it, by promising him an exclusive territory or maintaining resale prices even if this raises resale prices and does not benefit all consumers.

Where the supplier or licensor is subject to strong competition there is no need for competition authorities to intervene. The market will drive out those who confer too much protection.

An argument in favour of intervention is that it is not always easy to detect a horizontal agreement between dealers to which effect is given vertically in supply contracts. Moreover, in Europe, efficiency is not the only aim of the competition rules; the well-being of small and medium-sized firms is mentioned in the preamble to the Treaty. This concern is not limited to those that produce efficiently what consumers want to buy. The preamble refers also to

---

17   (209/78 and others) [1980] ECR 3125, paras 135–41.
18   (240/82 and others [1985] ECR 3831, para 82.
19   (126/80) [1981] ECR 1563, paras 14–27. 8.3 below.

'fair competition,' which some perceive as including the right of those that have not made the investment to share in its benefits (1.3.2.2 above).

Neither the distinction between hard core and ancillary restraints nor that between horizontal and vertical agreements solves all the problems, although each helps. The ancillary restraint doctrine may apply both to vertical and to horizontal agreements.

In *Topco v US*[20] some small supermarket chains had collaborated through a trade association to develop the Topco mark, and only one shop in any locality was allowed to join the association and use the mark. The Supreme Court treated it as a horizontal agreement between the supermarkets rather than as a vertical licence. Was the development and licence of the mark to be thought of as ancillary to a market sharing agreement or *vice versa*? Probably the association increased competition by helping small supermarket chains to compete with larger but, unfortunately, it was condemned as being an unreasonable restraint of trade.

In *Rothery Storage & Van Co. v Atlas Van Lines,*[21] Judge Bork suggested that to the extent that *Topco* stands for the proposition that all horizontal restraints are automatically illegal even if ancillary to a pro-competitive transaction, it must be regarded as effectively overruled by various subsequent decisions of the American Supreme Court.

An agreement, rather similar to that in *Topco*, made through an association of small grocers was cleared by the EC Commission in *SPAR*,[22] but only because its effects were not appreciable, not because it enabled small grocers to compete with supermarket chains by combining their purchases.

8.2 Hard core horizontal cartels affecting price and allocating markets or customers

If one discovers that one's client or firm has entered into a horizontal cartel to restrict production or raise price it is no longer safe to ensure that it is terminated forthwith. Consideration should be given to informing the Commission before anyone else does so.[23]

To be forbidden, collusion must be capable of affecting trade between Member States and have the object or effect of restricting competition within the common market. The list of practices set out in Article 81(1), although not exhaustive, exemplifies agreements likely to restrict competition. The most immediate and effective competition between suppliers of goods or services satisfying similar needs is in price, and Article 81(1)(a) expressly lists agreements which 'directly or indirectly fix purchase or selling prices or other

---

20   405 US 596 (US Sup Ct, 1972).
21   792 F 2d 210 (DC Cir, (1986) 224–30.
22   [1975] 2 CMLR D14.
23   See the Commission's leniency notice (7.6.2 above).

trading conditions' as falling within the prohibition. Commissioner Monti[24] has frequently explained the increased priority given to the fight against cartels.

The *Quinine Cartel* decision[25] was the first to condemn a hard core cartel to raise prices by restricting production. Undertakings in the Netherlands, France and Germany agreed not only on the prices they would charge, but also to keep out of each other's national markets. Quotas were also allocated for countries with no national producer. These restrictions are listed in Article 81(1)(a)–(c). The decision that these restrictions contributed to the division of national markets and denied consumers the benefit of competition was upheld by the Court in *ACF Chemiefarma NV v Commission*.[26] The *Dyestuffs* case[27] is an example of a simpler concerted practice affecting the levels of prices in different Member States.

Recently, the Commission has devoted considerable resources to detecting such agreements and has been imposing heavy fines. In the appeals from the decision against the lycine cartel, for instance, *Kyowa Hakko Kogyo and another v Commission*,[28] the CFI confirmed its earlier case law establishing that the Commission should follow the guidelines it published on fining policy (7.6.1 & 7.6.2 above). Unlike guidelines relating to questions of law, those stating how the Commission will exercise its discretion raise legitimate expectations and bind the Commission. The guidelines themselves still allow considerable discretion.

There has been a substantial number of appeals to the CFI on the level of fines, and the CFI has for the most part followed the Commission, although it has occasionally reduced a fine less than proportionately if it found the infringement established only for a shorter period.

An agreement may be condemned as having the prohibited effects even if the parties do not always abide by it,[29] although in some decisions by the Commission this has been found to reduce the gravity of the infringement and lead to lower fines.

These decisions and others have been upheld by the CFI and ECJ, except that fines on a few firms have been reduced on the ground that the Commission had not established the full duration of the infringement alleged.

In the appeals from *PVC II*, the ECJ confirmed many of the propositions accepted by the CFI in earlier case law. It confirmed that it is not necessary for the Commission to establish an actual effect on the market if the object of the cartel is to restrict competition. In *Enichem's* appeal from PVC the ECJ confirmed:

24   *E.g.*, Brussels, 11 September 2002, speech to EMAC.
25   [1969] CMLR D41.
26   (41/69) [1970] ECR 661, (2.2.4.2 above).
27   (48/69) and others [1972] ECR 619 (2.2.4.2 above).
28   T–223/00, 9 July 2003, paras 61 *et seq.*
29   *PVC II—Limburgse Vinyl and others v Commission* (C–238/99P and others), [2002] ECR I–8375, para 508. The cases were joined for the purposes of the judgment.

508. It is sufficient that the aim of an agreement should be to restrict . . . competition, irrespective of the actual effects of that agreement. . . . and

509. . . .the liability of a particular undertaking in respect of the infringement is properly established where it participated in those meetings with knowledge of their aim, even if it did not proceed to implement any of the measures agreed. . . .

513. . . . given the absence of pricing documentation to prove the actual participation of every producer in concerted price initiatives, . . . the Commission has . . . considered in relation to each expected participant whether there is sufficient reliable evidence to prove its adherence to the cartel as a whole rather than proof of its participation in every manifestation thereof.

518. the frequency of an undertaking's presence at the meetings did not affect the fact of its participation in the infringement but rather the extent of its participation.

8.2.1 Indirect influences on pricing policies

Restrictions inhibiting price competition indirectly are also prohibited. In *Re IFTRA Rules for Producers of Virgin Aluminium*,[30] the Commission treated the rules of a producers' association as an agreement between the members who signed them. They were found to have at least the object of restricting competition although they had not been enforced. Indeed, the excess supply which led to their introduction had been reduced by an increase in demand so soon that the rules had never come into play but they had been retained as a safety net.

The Commission considered that their existence, supported by an arbitration clause, was likely to discourage any action contrary to their letter and spirit. It added that their object would be to restrict competition if that was a reasonably foreseeable consequence of the application of the rules. Labelling the rules as being 'against unfair competition' did not prevent the application of Article 81. The members agreed not to make 'destructive sales below cost.' Not only did this go beyond the law of unfair competition in some Member States; it was so vague and difficult to apply that it was likely to discourage some commercial initiatives.

The parties agreed not to sell below their published prices and to exchange information about the prices charged. The Commission found that the restrictions had the object and effect of restricting competition. It confirmed that firms that do not enjoy a dominant position within the meaning of Article 82 must be allowed to give secret discounts and that these might be necessary to obtain a foothold in a new market.

Other provisions for the exchange of information about costs were also condemned as they enabled each firm to predict the others' pricing policy with greater certainty. They might be called 'facilitating devices' making it easier for the firms to act together without expressly agreeing to do so.

---

30 [1975] 2 CMLR D20, para 12.

8.2.2 *Information agreements*

From the 1960s, Commission officials have considered that agreements to exchange information about prices that have been charged or paid might infringe Article 81. They may have two anticompetitive effects. First, they might be the visible tip of the iceberg: they may operate to monitor an illegal price fixing cartel to reduce cheating. Secondly, they may help to stablise an oligopoly where sellers rapidly follow each other's price changes by reducing each member's uncertainty about the prices being charged by the others.

According to the notice it issued in 1968 on Co-operation Agreements,[31] however, collaboration in producing joint statistics is permitted. The exchange of information about competitors is most likely to restrict competition when there are few of them, it takes place very rapidly, perhaps by email or through a trade association, when it gives sufficient detail to identify specific contracts and enables competitors to react. In the *IFTRA Rules on Glass Containers*,[32] the Commission stated that:

> 43. It is contrary to the provisions of Article 81(1) . . . for a producer to communicate to his competitors the essential elements of his price policy such as price lists, the discounts and terms of trade he applies, the rates and dates of change to them and the special exceptions he grants to specific customers.

Where information about a discount that has been made to obtain an important order by one of only a few suppliers must be disseminated immediately to competitors, there is little incentive to make the price cut. Competitors are likely to make a similar cut when the next big order comes along, even if they do not actively retaliate against a firm that has rocked the boat. Consequently the initial discounter is unlikely to obtain additional turnover in the long run.

In *COBELPA*,[33] the Commission stated that there is no objection to national trade associations collecting and disseminating statistical information indicating the industry's output and sales, provided that individual firms cannot be identified. Under that agreement, however, the output of and prices charged by individual companies were disseminated, and the Commission proceeded to condemn the agreement although the parties had amended it to comply with the Commission's suggestions:

> 29. The only possible explanation of the exchange of this information is again the desire to co-ordinate market strategies and to create conditions of competition diverging from normal market conditions, by replacing the risks of *pricing* competition by practical cooperation. The undertakings concerned in this naturally worked out their export prices policy in the light of the conduct of firms which, in by and large the same conditions, were also manufacturing for sale in the country of destination and which had the natural advantage of being closer to the user and having long-standing ties with national distributors.

31   OJ 1968, C84/14.
32   [1974] 2 CMLR D50.
33   [1977] 2 CMLR D28, paras 25–30.

The Commission objected even to the agreement to exchange published price lists, on the grounds that it was easier to get them directly from competitors, and was an indication that they were not competing normally (paragraph 30). In its decision on *Vegetable Parchment*,[34] the Commission added that sending invoices to a trade association, etc., on an individual basis would be evidence of a concerted practice, since individual information is not necessary for the preparation of trade statistics.

In the special circumstances of the Italian market for insuring engineering risks, however, the Commission exempted an arrangement whereby, on the basis of information given to it about members' risk experience, *Nuovo Cegam*,[35] their association, prepared a common tariff of standard premiums for each kind of risk. The Commission required that members should individually set their final premium to include a margin for costs and profit.

Since it is difficult to ensure that cheating does not break down an old fashioned cartel, it is unlikely that an agreement to exchange information about prices will for long keep prices much above the level they would reach in its absence. Nevertheless, the exchange of information may help to stabilise consciously parallel conduct, since a member realises that if it is caught cheating even once it will be treated as untrustworthy and may expect retaliation.

In *UK Agricultural Tractor Registration Exchange*,[36] there was no opportunity to cheat, since the UK ministry of transport provided detailed figures of tractor deliveries within each of a large number of small areas with exact figures of sales by each member of each model. The Commission stressed that there were high entry barriers and that the market was concentrated. It is hardly surprising that it condemned the agreement although no information on price levels was exchanged. The decision is useful in setting out the kinds of information that may safely be exchanged.

The agreement was implemented for 12 years before it was notified, so it was somewhat surprising that the Commission did not consider the possibility of fines.

8.2.3 *Joint sales organisations*

In the days before the establishment of the common market when cartels were lawful, one of the most effective forms was a joint sales organisation. Members gave up their own marketing resources and could sell only through the joint organisation. This prevented cheating. Chiselling has always been a problem to those organising cartels. If the price is maintained above cost, including a normal return on capital, it pays each member to sell below the price agreed if it can thereby increase its turnover. Such price cutting,

---

34   [1978] 1 CMLR 534, paras 63–67.
35   [1984] 2 CMLR 484.
36   [1985] 2 CMLR 554, confirmed (34/92) [1994] ECR II 957, (C–7/95P), [1998] ECR I–3111.

however, leads to sales at lower prices, and conflicts with the interests of other members. Joint sales organisations have long been condemned by the Commission as hard core cartels.

In *Dutch Nitrogenous Fertilisers*,[37] a joint sales organisation, confined to a single Member State and sales outside the common market and where quotas were allocated to the parties, was condemned as restricting competition and affecting trade between Member States on the grounds that the two members' co-operation within their joint venture in the Netherlands affected their whole production and sales policy and so affected trade between Member States. The Commission added that parallel imports might also be discouraged by the joint operations of firms supplying three-quarters of the Dutch market. There were various other circumstances deterring the parents from competing in other Member States, such as joint ventures with foreign firms in which each participated.

In *Floral*,[38] the parties shared the profits of the joint sales organisation through their equity holding, and this was condemned. A firm that benefits from a substantial part of the profits earned by another member has less incentive to compete aggressively.

In *Finnpap*,[39] before Finland joined the common market, the Commission issued a notice stating that it did not intend to take action against a joint sales organisation of producers of newsprint in Finland on the ground that it had no appreciable effect on trade between Member States. Finnpap was smaller than several of its competitors. The Commission stated that there was no second-hand market in newsprint, which is cut to the size used by a particular client. It required the parties to alter their agreement, however, so as to permit buyers to meet unsolicited orders. It is at least possible that the decision was affected politically by the hope that Finland would join the EEA and, eventually, the EC.

In *UIP*[40] the Commission granted an exemption to a joint sales organisation for films—a heterogenous product—that achieved substantial cost savings. There were no quotas and profits could not be shared since each parent agreed to pay for the individual costs attributable to its products, and share only overhead costs. The joint sales organisation was established in such a way as not to make any profit.

It is thought that the favourable conclusions in both these later cases are sensible. Finnpap lacked market power, so could not increase prices by restricting output, but this was not the reason given, and there was no way

37   *CSV* [1979] 1 CMLR 11.
38   [1980] 2 CMLR 285, paras 40–44.
39   [1989] 4 CMLR 413.
40   [1990] 4 CMLR 749. The Commission decided to take a favourable review of its extension when it expired, in view of the heterogeneous nature of the product, the efficiencies the joint venture makes possible and commitments offered by the parties. Some of these were overtly political—adding to the functions of the joint venture distribution of EEA films as well as American: [1999] 5 CMLR 732.

that the parents in UIP could restrict production profitably to raise price. The producer of a popular film would not restrict licences to facilitate the showing of less popular films. I am unhappy about the reasoning and would have been happier had UIP been cleared rather than exempted.

Where there are substantial savings in costs to be made through a joint sales organisation, one should be organised with these two cases in mind— avoid both quotas and the possibility of the sales organisation earning profits to be shared between the members.

There have been several decisions clearing joint sales and buying organisations between small firms on the ground that joint operations enabled them to compete with large firms and had no appreciable effects on trade or competition.[41] The Commission did not decide that these strengthened competition although may well have done so.

8.2.4 *Agreements about standard conditions of sale*

Agreements between competing suppliers not to sell a product in bulk, or to sell only on prescribed conditions of sale, have been condemned, but in its Notice on Co-operation Agreements,[42] the Commission has stated that the issue of standard printed forms is unobjectionable, provided that firms are free not to use them and there is no tacit agreement or understanding on prices, discounts or conditions of sale.

If all the firms supplying a particular product in a concentrated market adopt the same conditions of sale, it may be easier for them not to compete on price and conditions as it is easier to compare prices. Commodity exchanges, however, operate sales by description, and must prescribe conditions of sale. Some commodity exchanges, such as the London Metal Exchange are concentrated.

8.2.5 *Market allocation*

Agreements between competitors to fix prices are often supported by quotas, so that each party can maintain its share of the demand, which is likely to be reduced if they are successful in raising prices. *Quinine*[43] concerned an agreement whereby quotas as well as prices were fixed.

Indirect market sharing is also prohibited. In *White Lead*[44] an agreement fixing quotas in an attempt to prevent prices falling still further was replaced in 1971 by an agreement under which quotas were fixed only for countries outside the EC, but members were required to notify all export deliveries broken down by country to a central office for distribution.

---

41   *SPAR-Re Intergroup Trading BV*, [1975] 2 CMLR D 14.
42   [1969] CMLR D41.
43   [1969] CMLR D41, confirmed in *ACF Chemiefarma* (41/69) [1970] ECR 661 (8.2 above).
44   [1979] 1 CMLR 464.

The common market was excluded from this at the end of 1972, but the parties continued to notify the central office of their deliveries in each Member State, and the Commission concluded that the quota system was intended to apply to the common market. It condemned the exchange of information as a concerted practice: it was not normal statistical information, since sellers were identified. The Commission also condemned a quota scheme despite cheating, as having the object of restricting competition.

8.2.6 *Maximum buying prices*

Agreements to combine buying power are equally prohibited.[45] There have been several cases on buying power in 2003, for instance, *FENIN*.[46]

8.3 Collective discrimination—boycotts and reciprocal exclusive dealing

In Benelux it has been traditional for traders to collaborate through a trade association. There may well be half a dozen classes of members: manufacturers, importers, wholesalers, retailers, repairers, itinerant traders, restaurants and so forth. Rules or recommendations will determine with which classes of members each class may deal on trade terms. Importer and manufacturer members are entitled to sell only to wholesalers and wholesalers to buy only from them, and so on down the chain.

A non-member at any level of trade will be unable to deal on trade terms with members at any level. Except when there is a substantial part of the trade outside the association, an outsider will be unable to operate unless it can make the products or import them and sell at the retail level itself; frequently, multiple retailers are excluded from membership or are not permitted to undercut other retailers.

In *FEDETAB*[47] the Commission condemned many such restrictions, although some of them had ceased to operate three years earlier. The restrictions included:

(1) the approval and classification of wholesalers and retailers into categories, with different profit margins provided for each category;
(2) the collective maintenance of resale prices during periods when price competition was compatible with the restrictive Belgian tax system;
(3) the criteria for approving traders and the collective boycott of those not approved;
(4) the standard terms of payment; and
(5) the requirement that some retailers should stock a minimum number of brands.

---

45   Press release [1976] 1 CMLR D11.
46   T 319/99, [2003] ECR 000, [2003] 5 CMLR 34, an appeal has been lodged.
47   [1978] 3 CMLR 524.

The decision was confirmed by the ECJ in 1980.[48] Even though the Court accepted that government measures made it impractical for manufacturers and importers to compete in ways that would affect retail sale prices, it condemned the collective fixing of margins which prevented price competition at intermediate stages. The Court clearly distinguished its case law on selective distribution, whereby an individual brand owner may restrict dealers from selling to traders who lack appropriate premises and staff (see 9.4 below) from collective agreements, whereby all manufacturers collectively set and apply the criteria, although later judgments such as *Salonia v Poidomani*[49] have ignored this important distinction. In confirming the decision of the Commission not to grant an exemption in *FEDETAB*,[50] the Court denied that increasing the number of outlets necessarily improved distribution:

184. . . . The quality of a distribution sector may be judged above all by its commercial flexibility and capacity to react to stimuli both from manufacturers and consumers.

The Court stressed the importance of adaptation to new purchasing habits. Sales by supermarkets had increased, although they no longer stocked, as previously they were required to do, such a wide range of brands as did the specialist trade. This must have reduced their costs and enabled them to compete in price and freshness with more traditional outlets.

In *APB*[51] the Commission intervened in a collective boycott organised by a trade association of pharmacists in Belgium. Pharmacists there are legally responsible for the products they sell and the association organised a testing facility to ensure that products corresponded to the claims made for them by their manufacturers. They seem to have carried on the testing without charge, and the manufacturers were then entitled to use the association's stamp on the product and required not to sell the product save to pharmacists. This seems to have been a serious restriction of competition, aggravated by the government licensing system, which limited the number of pharmacists permitted to operate.

The association altered its scheme so that manufacturers were entitled to sell tested products to other retailers in the same packaging, but without the stamp. The Commission decided that the restriction of competition was no longer appreciable. The association was providing a service, on which it could not let other retailers take a free ride. The Commission did not discuss the free rider problem in its decision, so it did not consider other ways of solving it. Nor did it say why a collective reciprocal arrangement like this did not have appreciable effects. It admitted that pharmacists charge more than other retailers. It is regretted that the reasons for the decisions were suppressed.

48   (209/78 and others) [1980] ECR 3125.
49   (126/80) [1981] ECR 1563, paras 14–27 (8.3 above).
50   (209–215 & 218/78) [1980] ECR 3125, paras 135–41.
51   [1990] 4 CMLR 176.

8.4 Collective aggregated discounts

In *Re German Ceramic Tiles*,[52] an aggregated discount scheme was con-demned. Most German manufacturers agreed through their trade association to grant to buyers quantity discounts based on the total quantities bought by each during the year from all German producers. This deterred buyers from buying a small quantity of such tiles from Italy. Where that additional quan-tity would enable the firm to obtain a higher discount, an outside competitor would have to match that discount not only on the quantities it sold, but also on all the quantities bought from those whose sales were counted when cal-culating the amount of discount.

This effect was magnified by the uncertainty: most customers would not know during the year whether at the end they would have bought just under the amount needed to obtain a better rate of discount if they were to buy a particular lot of tiles from outsiders. The scheme had effects similar to a collective loyalty rebate. The Commission added that collectively agreed dis-count rates also inhibited almost the only form of price competition possible in an oligopolistic market.

The foreclosing effect is similar to progressive discounts offered by a dominant firm, as in *Michelin*,[53] but a dominant firm cannot be expected to compete with itself in price, so the second reason does not apply to unilateral conduct. Aggregated discounts are unlikely to generate any cost savings, but they help small suppliers to compete with larger ones.

8.5 Agreements to tie the sale of one item to another

In *FEDETAB*,[54] the Commission objected to the minimum range of brands that supermarkets were required to stock by the manufacturers' association. The general tenor of the Court's judgment,[55] and its observation that the requirement might increase costs, demonstrate its support for that view, although it did not find it necessary to deal with the question of tying specifically.

The Commission has condemned individual tying agreements as contrary to Article 81. In *Vaessen/Moris*,[56] it objected to a patent licensee being required to buy from the patentee all the casings into which he packed *Saucissons de Boulogne* with the aid of a patented device, on the ground that this extended his market power over the device to the market for casings. Lucio Zanon has sug-gested,[57] however, that the more significant effect was that the patentee was

---

52   [1971] CMLR D6.
53   (322/81) [1983] ECR 3461 (5.2.2.1 above).
54   [1978] 3 CMLR 524, paras 163–64 (8.3 above).
55   (209–215 & 218/78) [1980] ECR 3125, para 184.
56   [1979] 1 CMLR 511.
57   L Zanon, 'Ties in Patent Licensing Agreements' (1980) 5 *EL Rev,* 391.

able to obtain more from those processors who used the device more intensively and to whom it was worth more. Had the patentee required payment of a royalty instead it might have been difficult to control cheating.

In *Tetra Pak II*,[58] the Commission imposed the highest fine ever imposed at that time, 75 million ECUs, on a Swiss firm that was very dominant over the supply of machinery for making and filling cartons with milk, fruit juice and the like in such aseptic conditions that the liquid would last for six months without refrigeration. Among other practices, Tetra Pak required those to whom it supplied machines to buy their cartons from it. The Commission considered that the tie would extend its dominance to the supply of the cartons.

It did not address the question how Tetra Pak would be able to exploit its market power over the machines more effectively. To the extent that licensees disliked buying the licensor's cartons, they would pay less for the patented machines. Tetra Pak does not appear to have suggested that it was trying to extract more revenue from those who most used the machinery. So one cannot criticise the Commission for not taking the point. The decision was confirmed by the Court of First Instance and the Court.[59]

8.6 Export bans

The Commission habitually imposes heavy fines on firms that have engaged in classic cartels, often supported by provisions that none shall sell in the home territory of the others. These are horizontal agreements between competitors and not ancillary to any pro-competitive transaction. So they are clearly anti-competitive.

The Commission has, however, taken a further more questionable step in habitually condemning export bans and deterrents accepted in vertical agreements between a single brand owner and its dealers. In the absence of a cartel at the level of either dealers or manufacturers, a brand owner usually has an interest in letting its dealers compete with each other, as the lower the margin on which they operate, the more they are likely to sell. As described at 8.1.3 above, Chicago economists argue that if a supplier does protect its dealers from each other, it is likely to be because the dealers have to invest in pre-sales services, for which it is difficult to charge, and which promote the brand generally.

If poaching were permitted, one dealer could take a free ride on the services of another. Buyers could make their selection in an expensive shop providing the services, but buy in a discount shop that does not. This would deter any shop from providing services that might be worthwhile for the brand as a whole.

---

58 [1992] 4 CMLR 551, paras 116–20.
59 Case (T–83/91) [1994] ECR II–755, paras 134 and 136–41 (CFI); (C–333/94P) [1996] ECR I–5951, paras. 67–71 (ECJ).

The contrary argument is that cartels at both dealer and producer level are more likely in Europe than the United States, and that the Commission lacks the resources to discover them all, so is more hostile to agreements even if they appear to be vertical.[60] It is also possible that only a few marginal customers require the services, in which case it may be undesirable that those who do not should have to pay to encourage them.

It was the absolute territorial protection given to Consten and the sole distributors in other Member States that prevented the Commission from exempting the exclusive dealing agreement in *Grundig*.[61] We will see in chapter 9 that the exclusivity would probably have been exempted otherwise. If competition policy is seen as a buttress to the principle of the free movement of goods, services and other resources, and businessmen's strategic reactions to public control are ignored, then any artificial restrictions on imports or encouragement to exports interferes with the functioning of the common market, and is very unlikely to be tolerated.

Subject to the *de minimis* rule accepted by the Court in *Völk v Vervaecke*,[62] export restrictions have always been treated as prohibited by Article 81 and not capable of exemption. The very large fine imposed on *Tetra Pak* under Article 82 was due in part to its attempt to maintain different prices in different Member States.

In *Miller International Schallplatten*,[63] the Court confirmed the condemnation of a no-poaching clause without making any market analysis beyond stating that Miller supplied about 5% of the German market for records and without enquiring whether dealers would have been reluctant to incur sunk costs in the absence of protection.

> 7. . . . it must be held that, by its very nature, a clause prohibiting exports constitutes a restriction on competition, whether it is adopted at the instigation of the supplier or of the customer since the agreed purpose of the contracting parties is to endeavour to isolate a part of the market.
>
> Thus the fact that the supplier is not strict in enforcing such prohibitions cannot establish that they had no effect since their very existence may create a "visual and psychological" background which satisfies customers and contributes to a more or less rigorous division of the markets.

The Commission treats bans on trade between Member States as *per se* contrary to Article 81(1), although it may exempt a restriction on active sales in the territory of another dealer or licensee. Yet, even when export bans led to absolute territorial protection, the Court held in two cases on licences of

---

60   See M Waelbroeck 'Vertical Agreements: Is the Commission right not to follow the current US policy?' (1985) 25 *Revue Suisse de Droit de la Concurrence Internationale (now World Competition)* 45.

61   [1964] CMLR 489, (and 2.3.1 and 2.4.1 above).

62   (5/69) [1969] ECR 295, (2.4.9 above). The new bagatelle notice OJ 2001, C368/13, [2002] 4 CMLR 699, does not apply to absolute territorial protection.

63   (19/77) [1978] ECR 131.

performing and plant breeders' rights in 1982[64] that export bans do not in themselves infringe Article 81(1).

8.6.1 *Export deterrents*

The Commission looks not only to the form of the agreement, but also to the substance. Distillers sold many brands of spirits in the UK and continental Europe and faced very different markets in the two areas. The sale of whisky responded acutely to price in the UK. So there was no money with which to promote. On the continent there were discriminatory taxes and Distillers could not compete on price. It was illegal to advertise whisky in France; so more expensive kinds of promotion were required. These rules had been condemned by the Community Court but had not then been abrogated by the French state and were enforced. In *Distillers*[65] the Commission condemned the export deterrent created by Distillers' dual pricing system as well as the absolute export ban which it replaced. It refused to exempt the Distillers Company's conditions of sale, under which rebates worth some £5 per case were denied on the quantity of whisky exported. The Commission rejected the argument that this was needed to protect Distillers' exclusive distributors on the Continent who spent considerable sums on promotion from which parallel importers would benefit.

On appeal,[66] however, Advocate General Warner strongly rejected the Commission's view. He accepted that the markets in the United Kingdom and on the Continent were very different, and that promotion was needed on the Continent if whisky was to be sold there. He added that Distillers could not afford to raise its prices in the United Kingdom to cover the overseas promotional costs in view of the evidence given of the extreme elasticity of price there.

The dual pricing system had not eliminated parallel exports as had the *Grundig* agreements (2.3.1 and 2.4.1 above). Three hundred and forty thousand cases had been sold at the higher price for export to the Continent. He would, therefore, have recommended that the decision should be quashed had Distillers notified its agreement. The Court did not deal with the points of substance, but merely confirmed that an exemption could not be granted as the agreement had not been properly notified. Mr Warner's opinion on the substance was cogent. Distillers reacted to the decision by raising the price of some brands in the United Kingdom, and those almost ceased to sell there. It also ceased to sell Johnny Walker Red Label Whisky in the UK. The other brands ceased to be promoted on the Continent.

---

64   *Coditel II* [1982] ECR 3381 and *Louis Erauw-Jacquéry* (27/87) [1988] ECR 1919 (see 11.3 below).
65   [1978] 1 CMLR 400.
66   (30/78) [1980] ECR 2229, paras 89–21.

The result was that the Distillers' brands sold in the United Kingdom differed from those sold on the Continent. This splitting of the brands and the Commission's decision that led to it must have retarded the integration of the common market once the discriminatory taxes and other disadvantages imposed on the sale of whisky on the Continent were abrogated.

I am told that the year after it split its brands, Distillers' turnover on the Continent for those brands, the price of which in England had not been raised and which ceased to be worth promoting on the Continent, increased less than its turnover for those that suffered no parallel imports and whose price was higher. In 1983, the Commission announced that it was considering an exemption for a dual pricing scheme for Red Label, provided that the additional price charged in the UK to dealers for the quantities exported was used for promotion.[67] No such decision was ever adopted.

The Court has confirmed the condemnation of export bans and the imposition of fines even where there was governmental price control leading to artificially low prices in the country of export in *BMW Belgium v Commission*,[68] and the Commission continues to condemn such bans, without considering whether the effects of governmental price controls in one country should be spread in this way throughout the common market, or whether it would pay a firm to refuse to supply a country subject to such control thereby dividing the common market more severely.[69]

Even mild deterrents that may be important to people who move around the common market, such as military personnel and diplomats, have been prohibited. In *Zanussi*,[70] the Commission objected to a system of after-sales guarantees that did not apply to washing machines used in a different Member State from that where they had been bought. This view was accepted by the Court in *Hasselblad v Commission*.[71] In the first *Transocean* case,[72] however, members were allowed to agree to pass over part of the profit on exports to other Member States, on the ground that the product was new and required promotion in many ports if it was to compete with marine paints from larger competitors. The agreement has been exempted again three times, but without the previous profit passover clause.

The Commission adopts simply argued decisions imposing fines for vertically imposed export bans, for instance in *Polistil/ Arbois*,[73] although it has recognised the free rider argument and permitted limited territorial protection in its group exemptions (see chapters 9 and 10 below).

---

67   [1983] 3 CMLR 173.
68   (32/78 and others) [1979] ECR 2435.
69   *Adalat* [1996] 5 CMLR 416. The Commission's decision was reversed by the CFI and ECJ in *Bayer v Commission* (C2 & 3/01P) 6.1.2004.
70   [1979] 1 CMLR 81.
71   (86/82) [1984] ECR 883, paras 32–35.
72   [1967] CMLR D9.
73   [1984] 2 CMLR 594.

Export deterrents are also condemned very easily under Article 82 unless justified.

8.6.2 *Export boosters*

Export boosters are just as incompatible with the concept of a common market as import deterrents. In *Cimbel*,[74] the Commission condemned the arrangements whereby Belgian cement producers encouraged exports by collectively paying for the freight beyond the Belgian border. Freight was a large proportion of the delivered value of cement. The Commission concluded that:

> 42c. The result of the agreement regarding the equalisation of receipts in Market A is an artificial raising of export receipts and it is capable, for this reason if for no other, of deflecting trade between Member States from its natural channels. . . . the fact that the export receipts are calculated on the basis of a single free-at-frontier price for each country supplied eliminates, in addition, to a large extent, the advantages resulting from geographical situation. This also artificially distorts trade between the member-states because exports, which, if the agreement did not exist, would not take place or would be made to a country situated at a more favourable distance, are deflected from their natural channels.

It added that the subsidisation of exports by domestic sales injures consumers within the home country. Since the Commission said that the arrangement helped to absorb surplus capacity, the writer would have enquired whether average export prices exceeded variable costs before concluding that there was a cross-subsidy. Similar examples are *Milchförderungsfonds*[75] and the *EATE Levy*.[76]

8.7 Conclusion

Subject to a *de minimis* rule the Commission has habitually condemned horizontal and vertical agreements fixing buying or selling prices, directly or indirectly, or allocating markets. The ECJ treats such restrictions on conduct as restrictions of competition 'by their very nature', although they may not infringe Article 81(1) where their effect on trade is not appreciable. The Commission no longer applies the *de minimis* rule to them. Collective boycotts and provisions that isolate part of the market, such as export boosters, import deterrents or aggregated discounts, have also habitually been forbidden and are excluded from the de *minimis notice*.

Vertical agreements will be considered at chapters 9 and 11 below.

Heavy fines may be expected for those joining hard core cartels or imposing export bans or deterrents. If a client has already done so, it should consider fast taking advantage of the leniency programme (7.6.2 above).

---

74 [1973] CMLR D167.
75 [1985] 3 CMLR 101.
76 [1988] 4 CMLR 677.

The following chapters will describe the kinds of agreement that may well enjoy exemption.

8.8 Bibliography

Charles Baden Fuller, 'Price Variations—the Distillers Case and Article 85 EEC' [1979] *International and Comparative Law Quarterly*, 128.

——,'Economic Issues Relating to Property Rights in Trademarks: Export Bans, Differential Pricing, Restrictions on Resale and Repackaging' (1981) 6 *European Law Review*, 162.

Ivo Van Bael, 'Heretical Reflections on the Basic Dogma of EEC Antitrust: Single Market Integration', (1980) 10 *Revue Suisse de Droit de la Concurrence Internationale* (*now World Competition*) 39.

Frank H Easterbrook, (1984) 'The Limits of Antitrust', 63 *Texas Law Review*, 1.

——, 'Vertical Arrangements and the Rule of Reason' (1984) 53 *Antitrust Law Journal*, 135.

Konkurrensverket, (Swedish Competition Authority). *Fighting cartels—why and how*, The 3rd Nordic Competition Policy Conference in Stockholm, September 2000.

Valentine Korah, 'Goodbye Red Label: Condemnation of Dual Pricing by Distillers' (1978) 3 *European Law Review*, 62.

Richard Posner, 'The Next Step in the Antitrust Enforcement treatment of Restricted Distribution: *per se* Legality' (1981) 48 *University of Chicago Law Review*, 6.

Michael Reynolds, 'Trade Associations and the EEC Competition Rules' (1985) 23 *RSDIC*, 49.

Patrick Rey and James S Venit, 'Parallel trade and pharmaceuticals: a policy in search of itself,' (2004) *European Law Review*, 153.

F Scherer and *D Ross*, *Industrial Market Structure and Economic Performance* 3rd edn, (1990), 542–48.

Michel Waelbroeck, 'Vertical Agreements: Is the Commission right not to follow the current US policy?' (1985) 25 *Revue Suisse de Droit de la Concurrence Internationale* (*now World Competition*) 45.

9. Distribution Agreements

9.1 Former exemptions of individual agreements

In its first decisions from the beginning of 1964, the Commission granted individual exemptions under Article 81(3) to several exclusive distribution agreements. It decided that agreements whereby a manufacturer agrees to sell to a sole distributor for a large area, often the whole of a Member State, had at least the object of restricting competition, in that they restrained the manufacturer from supplying any other distributor directly, thus having the object of restricting competition between its distributors.

This reasoning, confirmed by the ECJ in *Consten & Grundig v Commission*,[1] was criticised at 2.4.1 and 2.4.2 above. If Grundig would not have been as successful in extending its marketing to France without the help of Consten and if Consten would not have invested enough without protection from free riders, the exclusive territory may have increased competition by enabling Grundig to penetrate a new Member State. The Advocate General recommended that the decision be quashed for lack of reasoning on this point. To use the language explained at 8.1.2 above, the exclusive provisions were ancillary to the pro-competitive transaction and may have been necessary to enable Grundig to penetrate the French market. Moreover, Consten remained subject to competition from other brands.

The Commission, however, saw exclusive distribution agreements as dividing the common market although they usually provide by far the easiest way for a manufacturer to start exporting to another Member State and increase competition by adding to the number of brands available.

The Commission took the view also that agreements by a distributor not to handle competing goods made the entry of competing manufacturers into the industry or the expansion of existing suppliers more difficult. Subject to the *de minimis* rule (2.4.9 above), the Commission considered that most exclusive agreements infringed Article 81(1) and granted, first, individual exemptions and, later, a series of group exemptions (9.2 below).

Much later, in *Delimitis*,[2] the ECJ observed that this would be so only if it were difficult for a new dealer to enter the market, and if so many of the existing ones were tied for so long that those remaining free could not absorb the output of a plant large enough to produce and promote economically.[3]

1 (56 & 58/64), [1966] ECR 299.
2 (C–234/89), [1991] ECR I–935,(2.4.3 above).
3 Paras 13–27.

In *Van den Bergh Foods Ltd.*[4] (5.2.2.1 above) the CFI confirmed the need for market analysis and that the extent of foreclosure had to be established under Article 81(1).

> 84. It follows that, contrary to HB's submission, the contractual restrictions on retailers must be examined not just in purely formal manner from the legal point of view, but also by taking into account the specific economic context in which the agreements in question operate, including the particular features of the relevant market, which may, in practice, reinforce those restrictions and thus distort competition on that market contrary to Article 81(1) of the Treaty. . . .

> 89. The Court finds that, in the circumstances set out in paragraphs 85–88 above, the provision of a freezer without charge, the evident popularity of HB's [the incumbent's] ice cream, the breadth of its range of products and the benefits associated with the sale of them are very important considerations in the eyes of retailers when they consider whether to install an additional freezer cabinet in order to sell a second, possibly reduced, range of ice cream or, a fortiori, to terminate their distribution agreement with HB in order to replace HB's freezer cabinet either by their own cabinet or by one belonging to another supplier.

Nevertheless, it added at paragraph 106 that the ECJ had not accepted that there was a rule of reason under Article 81(1) and that it would be difficult to reconcile such a rule with the bifurcation of the Article.

The CFI took into account HB's 89% share of the relevant market. When it began to enforce the injunction on stocking other brands in its freezers, Mars and Nestlé lost market share. In the supermarkets, which did not use HB's freezers, other producers had much greater market shares.

HB's practice raised rivals' costs, as they would have to provide and service freezers free of charge (paragraph 113). With a smaller range of products to place in them, this would be relatively costly for them. Wholesaling was relatively undeveloped. HB enjoyed a first mover advantage. This part of the judgment on Article 81(1) was far less formalistic than the recent judgments of the CFI on Article 82 (5.2.2.1 above).

9.2 Former group exemptions for exclusive distribution and exclusive purchasing agreements

The Commission received about 30,000 notifications requesting exemption of exclusive distribution agreements soon after Regulation 17[5] was adopted. In an attempt to escape from such a load of paper and concentrate its resources on more serious restrictions of competition, the Commission obtained from the Council of Ministers, under regulation 19/65,[6] power to exempt by cate-

---

4 [1998] 5 CMLR 530. See comment on this and other ice cream cases by *Aidan Robertson* and *Mark Williams*, cited in bibliography at 5.8 above. The promised sequel has not yet been written. The authors have awaited the judgment of the CFI.

5 Repealed, but described shortly at 7.1 above.

6 OJ Spec Ed, 1965, 35, amended by Council Reg 1215/95, OJ 1999, L148/1. Powers have since been granted by the Council to exempt joint ventures, (13.2.4 below).

gory exclusive distribution and purchasing agreements and agreements licensing intellectual property rights.

It first exercised this power by adopting Regulation 67/67[7] which exempted both exclusive distribution and exclusive purchasing agreements. This expired and was replaced by Regulations 1983/83 and 1984/83[8]. It also granted a group exemption for franchising agreements.[9] These all expired in 2000 and have been replaced by Regulation 2790/99.[10] Little of the case law under the earlier regulations remains relevant.

9.3 Clearance of exclusive distribution agreements

The CFI and ECJ are less likely to hold that exclusivity requires exemption than the Commission has been. In *Société La Technique Minière v Maschinenbau Ulm*,[11] the ECJ ruled that an exclusive distribution agreement without export bans would not have the effect of restricting competition, if there were no other way of penetrating a new territory. Agreements should be appraised in their legal and economic context. (2.4.2, 2.4.3 and 8.1.2–8.1.3). It also held that selective distribution did not infringe Article 81(1) (9.4 below).

The Commission cleared a few agreements, mostly those whereby a common market manufacturer had appointed an exclusive distributor for a territory outside the common market. In *Grosfillex*[12] the Commission found that an agreement did not come within the prohibition of Article 81(1), despite an export prohibition, on the ground that re-exports from the Swiss distributor to the common market were unlikely in any event, owing to the double customs barrier at that time. The Commission also mentioned the number of competing suppliers and competition at the distribution level. The restrictions were, therefore, not appreciable.

The precedent must, however, now be applied with caution. For most products and countries that belong to the EC or EEA or with which the Community has a free trade or association agreement the argument no longer applies as customs duties have been reduced or eliminated.

9.4 Selective distribution

The ECJ cleared what are often called 'selective distribution agreements.' These form part of distribution networks where the brand owner wants to

---

7   OJ Spec Ed, 1967, 10.
8   OJ 1983, L173/1, corrections OJ 1984, C101/2, and OJ 1983, L173/5, corrections OJ 1984, C101/2.
9   Commission Reg 4087/88, [1989] 4 CMLR 387.
10   OJ 1999, L336/21, [2000] 4 CMLR 398, [2000] ECLR supp. to May issue. The guidelines were published in OJ 2000, C291/1.
11   (56/65) [1966] ECR 235, 249–50 and 2.4.2 above.
12   [1964] CMLR 237.

control the outlets from which its product is sold to the public. The brand owner supplies only approved dealers, usually retailers, and tells those dealers to supply only the general public or other authorised dealers. Non-authorised dealers are unable to obtain supplies.

The term 'selective distribution' is a misnomer. A supplier that does not enjoy a dominant position is entitled to deal with whom it likes and to refuse supply to anyone else without having any justification. The Commission and ECJ have been concerned that once a dealer owns the goods, an unjustifiable restriction on selling to whomever it wants may infringe Article 81(1), although they are becoming less formalistic.

In *AEG Telefunken v Commission*,[13] the ECJ stated that:

> it has always been recognised in the case law of the Court that there are legitimate requirements, such as the maintenance of a specialist trade capable of providing specific services as regards high-quality and high technology products, which may justify a reduction of price competition in favour of competition relating to factors other than price. Systems of selective distribution, in so far as they aim at the attainment of a legitimate goal capable of improving competition in relation to factors other than price, therefore constitute an element of competition which is in conformity with Article 81(1).

The Court specified in *Metro v Commission*[14] that such systems are permissible,

> provided that resellers are chosen on the basis of objective criteria of a qualitative nature relating to the technical qualifications of the reseller and his staff and the suitability of his trading premises and that such conditions are laid down uniformly for all potential resellers and are not applied in a discriminatory fashion.

In the second paragraph quoted, the Court distinguishes what are called 'quantitative criteria.' As soon as the supplier attempts to protect the investment of approved dealers from other qualified traders by limiting the number of approved dealers in its area, the ECJ and Commission consider that Article 81(1) is infringed, although such restrictions have occasionally been exempted.

The test given by the Court in *AEG* and other cases was interpreted narrowly by the Commission in *Ideal-Standard's distribution system*,[15] where it doubted whether plumbing fittings can be considered as technically advanced products justifying selective distribution. It also doubted whether limiting wholesalers rather than retailers to those technically qualified escapes the prohibition of Article 81(1).

In *Binon*,[16] however, the Court went the other way and considered that selective distribution of newspapers did not infringe Article 81(1) provided there was no quantitative criterion. The judgment was not very cogent as the

13   (107/82) [1983] ECR 3151, from ground 33 onwards.
14   (26/76) [1977] ECR 1875, para 20.
15   [1988] 4 CMLR 627, para 15.
16   (243/83) [1985] ECR 2015, para 34.

justification for limiting retail outlets was the need to deliver quickly in the morning, and for that, a quantitative restriction would be appropriate.

In *Leclerc v Commission*,[17] the Court confirmed that a supplier of prestigious fine fragrances is permitted to limit re-sellers to those able to provide an aura of luxury. Nevertheless, the criteria must not go further than necessary (paragraphs 116 and 117) and hypermarkets must not be excluded. It may be difficult to reconcile these statements, but some hyper-markets have a series of small shops at the edge of the premises and some of these may offer service and an elegant ambiance.

In *Grundig II*,[18] the Commission held that requiring retailers to make a substantial sales effort is caught by Article 81(1), and it exempted but did not clear the obligation of such retailers to stock and display as full a range as reasonable and a requirement that the goods be demonstrated in suitable premises and attractively displayed.

In 1992, the Commission required perfume manufacturers to set up a system whereby those wanting approval would be inspected within a maximum of six months and an average of four months, and permitted to receive products from other dealers within the year.[19] More important, when the CFI confirmed the decision it stated that the criteria must be applied without discrimination, but did not mention the inspections or time periods required by the Commission.

The Commission submitted to the Community Court in *Demo-Studio Schmidt*[20] that there is no duty to supply all approved dealers. The Court accepted this in *Metro II*.[21] The infringement of Article 81(1) consists in prohibiting dealers admitted to the distribution network from supplying other resellers who are qualified but not admitted. Even a unilateral refusal to supply a dealer on grounds other than those specified by the ECJ may lead to a finding that the supplier was tacitly colluding with the dealers he was protecting by not supplying retailers likely to operate on very slim margins, contrary to Article 81.[22]

Even where the criteria for choosing retailers lower down the chain are justifiable, it is seldom possible to come within the Court's definition. Normally it is expensive to comply with the criteria. Consequently, a manufacturer or trade mark owner may also have to adopt quantitative criteria, promising not to select any other retailers within 50 kilometres or in an area with a population of half a million or some such limitation. The Commission and Court have treated such criteria as restricting competition contrary to Article 81(1), although individual exemptions have occasionally been granted by the Commission.

17   (T–88/92), [1996] ECR II 1961, paras 109–15.
18   [1988] 4 CMLR 865, paras 20–25 and 28.
19   *Parfums Yves Saint Laurent* [1993] 4 CMLR 120, paras 11–12 and 33.
20   (210/81) [1983] ECR 3045, 3056.
21   (75/84) [1986] ECR 3021, para 12.
22   *AEG* (107/82) [1983] ECR 3151, para 38.

In *FEDETAB*,[23] the Court stated that its ruling that selective distribution based on qualitative criteria does not infringe Article 81(1) applies only to the conduct of an individual brand owner and not to collective agreements. This was forgotten in *Salonia v Poidomani*,[24] where the Court ruled on a collective system between competitors for distributing newspapers in Italy. It is thought that not only is *FEDETAB* more sensible, it is a stronger precedent since the judgment was on an appeal from the Commission under Article 230 rather than on a preliminary ruling under Article 234, where the Court may be less familiar with the facts.

The Court's view that some restrictions of conduct imposed on dealers do not restrict competition is welcome, but the narrowness of the tests was regretted. The rules are nonsense commercially and economically speaking. It is very difficult for the holder of a prestigious brand to become master of its retail outlets. The rules encouraged a firm that was concerned about the services offered by retailers to integrate forward, and sell as far down the distribution chain as it could manage. This policy did not increase competition and may well have reduced efficiency. Moreover, it could not be adopted by small firms.

In *Villeroy & Boch*,[25] the Commission relented. A selective distribution scheme was operated for ceramic tableware. Villeroy & Boch insisted on its approved retailers also selling other brands, so that customers could choose effectively. The Commission cleared a restriction on selling to non-approved retailers, and an obligation to promote the goods, in view of the competitive nature of the market and the large number of retailers—some 17,000—which made a dealers' cartel impossible.

This decision represented a change of view by the Commission. As Professor Demaret suggested,[26] it was difficult to reconcile the decision with *Grundig II*. For some years there were no further decisions on selective distribution. Unfortunately, different officials took charge later, and the Commission returned to ignoring market conditions, and applying the rules formalistically.[27] Consequently, it was almost impossible for brand owners to control the retail outlets where their products were sold to consumers and compete on pre-sales services rather than on price.

9.5 Franchising

Franchising was hardly known in Europe in the 1960s but spread rapidly from the United States and is now a common way to distribute goods and services in the common market when considerable control over retailers is

23   (209–215 & 218/78) [1980] ECR 3125, paras 139–41 and 146.
24   (126/80) [1981] ECR 1563.
25   [1988] 4 CMLR 461, paras 30–32.
26   See bibliography, 9.9 below.
27   *Parfums Yves Saint Laurent* [1993] 4 CMLR 120; *Parfums Givenchy* [1993] 5 CMLR 579; and the CFI in *Vichy* (T–19/91) [1991] ECR II–265.

desired. The word, franchising, is a chameleon, and when it is referred to, it is usually worth asking what is meant. Some people use it to mean exclusive distribution—I will sell only to you. I shall use it to describe a system that enables a firm that has developed a sales formula to license its trademark and provide marketing assistance to firms that remain independent of it, but exploit the formula, usually for a royalty.

Franchisors may exercise substantial control over their licensees in order to maintain the identity of the network.

Franchisors do not, necessarily, supply the franchisee with the products they sell, in which case it is hardly a method of distribution.

9.5.1 *The ECJ's judgment in Pronuptia*

In *Pronuptia*,[28] the ECJ was asked to give a preliminary ruling. Pronuptia de Paris and its subsidiaries franchised various retailers to sell wedding gowns according to its instructions in shops that looked as if they were owned by Pronuptia, but which in fact were owned or rented by the franchisee. Pronuptia promised that it would franchise only Frau Schillgalis in three cities in Germany, the franchised territories, and she agreed to sell gowns only from the contract premises. When sued for non-payment of royalties, she argued that the franchise agreements were anti-competitive and that, by virtue of Article 81(2), the duty to pay royalties was void.

The Court confined its remarks to what it called 'distribution franchising' (paragraph 13)—in the USA usually referred to as 'retail format franchising.' It observed at paragraph 15 that franchising has desirable characteristics. It is not so much a method of distribution as a method for a firm that has found a good way to sell things to exploit its formula without using much of its own capital. It also permits firms without the necessary experience, but some capital, to enter the market with the aid of the instructions, assistance and the established reputation of the franchisor.

Only a small proportion of firms survive on the market for more than five years from formation, but the insolvency statistics for franchisees are considerably better.

The Court did not conclude that the transaction increased competition, merely that it did not, in itself, restrict it, contrary to Article 81(1) (paragraph 15). It then observed that for such a transaction to be viable, the franchisor must be able to ensure that the assistance it gives to its franchisees does not benefit competitors even indirectly; and it must preserve the identity and reputation of the network.

On the first ground, it cleared a restriction on a franchisee opening a competing shop, or selling its shop without the franchisor's approval (paragraph 16). On the second ground, it cleared many methods of control (paragraphs

28   (161/84), [1986] ECR 353.

17–22). The franchisee may be required to sell only from premises laid out and decorated according to instructions; not to change its address without consent; to follow the franchisor's business methods; where it is not possible to specify the goods to be sold, or there are too many franchisees to monitor, to buy goods only from designated sources, provided they may also be bought from other franchisees; and to obtain the franchisor's consent for the nature of any advertising, although the franchisor may not control the prices at which goods are advertised.

Up to this point in its judgment, the Court adopted the doctrine (2.4.5 and 8.1.2 above) that ancillary restraints needed[29] to support a transaction that is not anti-competitive do not restrict competition. Nevertheless at paragraph 24 it added that the obligation to sell only from the contract premises restrained the franchisees from opening a second shop without consent and, coupled with an exclusive territory, gave each franchisee absolute territorial protection which, in accordance with the Court's judgment in *Consten and Grundig v Commission*,[30] would infringe Article 81(1) once the network was widespread. Nevertheless,

> 24. It is of course possible that a prospective franchisee would not take the risk of becoming part of the chain, investing its own money, paying a relatively high entry fee and undertaking to pay a substantial annual royalty, unless he could hope, thanks to a degree of protection against competition on the part of the franchisor and other franchisees, that his business would be profitable. That consideration, however, is relevant only to an examination of the agreement in the light of the conditions laid down in Article 81(3).

It is true that in *Consten and Grundig* (2.4.1 and 2.4.2 above) the Court mentioned that the brand was well known, but that was not true in France when the distributorship was negotiated. In *Pronuptia* the Court looked *ex ante* to the time when the franchisee agreed to undertake commitments and not *ex post* when it hoped to benefit from its investment. The Court's statement goes further than *Consten and Grundig* in one further way: it suggests that the Commission should exempt even absolute territorial protection if that were necessary to induce the franchisee to make commitments.

The Court added, in its summary at paragraph 27, that the agreement must be judged in the light of the particular provisions in the contract and their economic context. It may be that, as Advocate General VerLoren van Themaat had suggested, even an exclusive territory does not infringe Article 81(1) if there is a great deal of competition from other brands, whether franchised or not.

The Commission did not wish to discourage franchising and this part of the judgment placed considerable pressure on it to grant a group exemption. Few franchisees would make commitments without at least a small exclusive

---

29   The CFI says 'directly related and directly necessary' (2.4.5 above).
30   (56 & 58/64) [1966] ECR 299.

territory. This and the group exemptions for exclusive distribution and purchasing finally expired in May 2000.

9.6 Group exemption for vertical agreements

The former group exemptions were formalistic and not based on economic
principles. They were concerned largely about export restraints and assumed
that any restraint on conduct that could have appreciable effects on a market
were anti-competitive. Some officials even believed that vertical restraints
were more serious than horizontal restraints, as they were likely to divide the
common market.

More recently, the Commission has accepted that vertical restraints can
do little harm to competition in the absence of market power. It has been
concerned rather that where the firm being protected enjoys market power,
anticompetitive agreements may be treated as legal, at least until the
Commission withdraws the block exemption.

It has also accepted that complaints by business that the block exemptions
operated as strait jackets and discouraged agreements that did not harm competition and might well have enhanced it. Sometimes restraints had to be
tightened for an agreement to qualify.

Officials observed[31] that with developments in information technology,
passing an object under the bar coding machine at a franchisee's outlet, would
not only create the invoice for the customer, but also re-order an identical
item, perhaps from a distance. The control over retail outlets required to
achieve delivery 'just in time' resulted in considerable saving of idle capital
and also the waste of obsolescent or unfashionable goods at the end of the
selling season. In the absence of market power, these savings would be passed
on to consumers. Treating any restriction of conduct as anticompetitive was
a mistake.

After much soul searching, the Commission adopted a single umbrella
block exemption that embraces many ways of bringing goods or services to
market, but will not apply when the party being protected has a market share
exceeding 30%.

Regulation 2790/99[32] exempts vertical agreements as defined in Article 2.
Unlike the earlier regulations, there is no white list of restrictions or obligations that may be included, only black lists in Article 4 of provisions that
prevent the application of the Regulation even to other provisions and in
Article 5 of provisions that are not exempted, but do not prevent the application of the Regulation to other provisions. Any other provisions are permissible. The absence of a limiting white list substantially increases the scope

31   David Deacon, 'Vertical restraints under EU competition law: new directions', [1995]
Fordham Corporate Law Institute 307, 320.
32   Regulation 2790/1999 on the application of Art 81(3) of the Treaty to vertical agreements
and concerted practices, [2000] 4 CMLR 398.

of the exemption and is being repeated in later group exemptions. It reflects the greater focus of the Commission on economic analysis at the expense of formalism.

Another important change from the former regulations is the ceiling of market share. The Regulation will not apply when the party protected has a market share exceeding 30%, although there is some marginal relief when market shares have recently increased. The Commission has been concerned that the block exemptions should not apply when the party protected enjoys market power, but considers that the concept of market share it is easier to apply in a block exemption than that of market power.

The drawback is that a firm with a high market share may have little market power when conditions of entry are easy, and, in defining the relevant market, the Commission attaches little weight to potential entry unless possible new entrants have effects as immediate and effective as substitutes on the demand side (4.3.1.1 above).

Business complains that it would like to have a single system of distribution throughout the common market, but it may have a large market share in some states only, and from those it cannot protect dealers where it has less market power under the block exemption if the relevant geographic market is national. This limitation is anomalous—it is the dealer in the area with the high market share that it should not be possible to protect.

The Regulation is due to expire at the end of 2010.

The Commission has published a notice giving its interpretation of many aspects of the Regulation.[33] This will not bind anyone other than the Commission (2.4.9 above) but is helpful in indicating the Commission's far more economic approach.

There are considerable advantages to be derived from bringing a contract within the terms of the new Regulation. Such a contract enjoys exemption from Article 81(1), although not from Article 82,[34] unless and until the Commission makes a decision withdrawing the exemption for the future (9.6.6 below). Consequently, the agreement can be enforced in national courts without the need for a market analysis.

9.6.1 *The exemption (Article 2)*

The single Regulation applies to exclusive distribution, non-exclusive distribution, exclusive purchasing, franchising and selective distribution. For the first time in decades one chapter of a book on EC competition law has become shorter, although there are some differences between the different categories of contract.

Franchising is not specifically mentioned except in the guidelines, but comes within the definition of Article 2(1) at least when products are supplied

33   Guidelines on Vertical Restraints, OJ 2000, C291/1, [2000] 5 CMLR 1074.
34   *Tetra Pak I* (T–51/89) [1990] ECR II–309, para 25 and recital 16.

by the franchisor or a designated source. It may also come within the definition of 'selective distribution' when franchisees are chosen on the basis of specified criteria even when the criteria are not qualitative, proportionate and applied without discrimination (9.4 above).

9.6.1.1 *'Vertical agreements'*— Article 2(1) provides:

1. [1] Pursuant to Article 81(3) of the Treaty and subject to the provisions of this Regulation it is hereby declared that Article 81(1) shall not apply to agreements or concerted practices
[2] entered into between two or more undertakings
[3] each of which operates, for the purposes of the agreement, at a different level of the production or distribution chain, and
[4] relating to the conditions under which the parties may purchase, sell or resell certain goods or services ("vertical agreements").
[5] This exemption shall apply to the extent that such agreements contain restriction of competition falling within the scope of Article 81(1) ("vertical restraints").'

(*Single paragraph divided for ease of reference.*)

The terms in [1] and [5] of 'vertical agreement' and 'vertical restraints' are somewhat misleading. The Commission states that the Regulation does not apply to vertical technology licensing agreements generally, but mainly only to various kinds of distribution.

9.6.1.2 *Two or more parties*—Unlike its predecessors, the new Regulation applies where there are more than two parties ([2]). It is often sensible to have registered user agreements to deal with the trademark rights between a brand owner, a supplier and a distributor. This no longer prevents the application of the exemption. The problem of tripartite agreements between an oil company, the operator of a garage, and the licensee to operate it in Italy will disappear. As long as the parties are not actual or potential competitors, there is no reason to exclude multipartite agreements.

9.6.1.3 *Agreement between actual or potential competitors*— [3] To be exempt, the parties must be operating at different levels, such as a producer and its distributor, or a distributor and a retailer it supplies.

The definition of 'vertical agreements' is not the same as that used in the US, which would treat an agreement as vertical only if the parties did not and could not easily have competed at either level without the agreement. Article 2(4), however, excludes most agreements between actual or potential competitors. The definition of 'competing undertakings' in Article 1(b) includes potential suppliers. So the exclusion may be wide and is unclear in scope.

Nevertheless, the regulation may apply when the buyer is small, has a turnover not exceeding 100 million ECUs, or the supplier is a manufacturer and distributor of goods, and the buyer does not manufacture. The first exception to the limitation is derived from the earlier group exemptions and the second enables the manufacturer to organise showrooms in large towns from which some items may be sold. There is a similar provision for services.

The exclusion of agreements between competitors is important. It brings the exemption more in line with economic and US thinking by excluding horizontal agreements (8.1.3 above). They may qualify under the stricter provisions for joint ventures (chapter 13 below).

Article 2(2) provides for small retailers, who have concentrated their buying through a trade association, to take advantage of the Regulation when they buy from the association or the association buys from third parties. This is not very helpful as the horizontal agreement between the retailers is not covered, although it may escape Article 81(1), especially when the association has little market power. Under Article 81(1), the ECJ has cleared many such agreements between retailers or farming cooperatives with modest market shares.[35] They may need to combine to compete with nation-wide chains of supermarkets or large independent farmers.

The buyer may operate as the agent of another firm (Article 1(g), but if the agreement with its supplier infringes Article 81(1) it may benefit from the block exemption.[36]

9.6.1.4 *Subject to conditions*—The final words of Article 2(1) at [4] defining a vertical agreement are controversial: to qualify, the agreement must relate 'to the conditions under which the parties may purchase, sell or resell certain goods or services.' It seems to me clear that this would cover an agreement by an author granting a copyright licence to a publisher, under which the publisher agreed not to publish and sell other works on the same topic. That is a condition relating to sale or purchase by the licensee. The Commission, however, denies this in guideline 32 and states that, subject to Article 3(2) it is only agreements for sale or purchase of goods or services between the parties that are covered.

9.6.1.5 *Other group exemptions*— Article 2(5) provides:

> This Regulation shall not apply to vertical agreements the subject matter of which falls within the scope of any other block exemption.

These words seem at first sight to have no effect. If an agreement falls within another group exemption it is irrelevant whether it falls within this one. Article 2(5) refers, however, to subject matter rather than the agreement falling within another group exemption.

---

35   *E.g. Gottrup Klim*, (C–250/92) [1994] ECR–1 5641. Contrast *Stremsel v Commission*, (61/80) [1981] ECR 851, where the co-operative had a virtual monopoly over the supply of rennet in the Netherlands.
36   Art 1(g). For the draft guidelines on agency, 9.7.1 below.

It seems, for instance, that Article 2(5) prevents Regulation 2790/99 from applying to any agreement that qualifies as a technology transfer agreement within the meaning of the introductory words of Article 1(1), Regulation 140/96,[37] and not only to agreements that are exempted by the latter. One cannot avoid the black list of the technology transfer regulation by using that for vertical agreements.

9.6.1.6 *Intellectual property rights*—Article 2(3) extends the exemption to:

> vertical agreements containing provisions which relate to the assignment to the buyer or use by the buyer of intellectual property rights, provided that those provisions do not constitute the primary object of such agreements and are directly related to the use, sale or resale of goods or services by the buyer or its customers. . . . on condition that, in relation to the contract goods or services, those provisions do not contain restrictions to competition having the same object or effect as vertical restraints which are not exempted under this regulation.

The qualification about primary object of the agreement may give rise to difficulty. If one needs both the electronic disk plus the licence to open it, which is the primary object of the licence or assignment? They are complementary. We will have to argue that the primary object was the dissemination of the software rather than the licence, and that the provision has no application otherwise.[38]

Fortunately, the new technology transfer group exemption includes licences of software, so this gap in the vertical regulation ceased to be very important.

There is a helpful list in Guideline 44 of clauses that may be inserted in a trademark license to a franchisee on the ground that they are necessary to protect the franchisor's intellectual property rights.

9.6.2 *No white list*

There is no limiting white list to this regulation. Any provisions are permitted in an agreement that fulfils the conditions of Article 2, provided that there is no provision black listed by Article 4 or 5 and provided that the ceiling of market share is not exceeded.

9.6.3 *30% ceiling of market share—(Article 3)*

If the firm being protected has a market share of over 30%, the Regulation will not apply. Law reform groups and industry have objected that the ceiling should be higher. With such a low ceiling, should more provisions be allowed?

---

37   Now, within the meaning of Art 2 of Reg 772/2004, OJ 2004, L123/11.
38   See Guideline 40, which applies only when the intermediary acquires no licence, but a shrinkwrap licence is imposed on the end user. From May 2004, this ceased to be important as copyright licences for software can now be brought within the technology transfer regulation, (11.5.1 below).

Problems will arise in defining the relevant market. They seem to me particularly acute when appraising agreements to supply traders, since peas or fish fingers may compete with ice cream for space in a trader's freezer cabinet, container or vehicle. In Guideline 91, the Commission suggests that where a buyer acquires an entire portfolio from a single supplier that portfolio may constitute the relevant market.

There is a trade off between legal certainty and a more economic approach to block exemptions. The former formalistic regulations exempted some anti-competitive agreements.

Article 9 provides criteria for defining the relevant market in the concrete terms used by the ECJ, rather than in the abstract SSNIP test also used in the notice on market definition (4.3.1.1)—substitution on the demand side 'by reason of the products' characteristics, their prices and their intended use.' Indeed, the Commission has been using the concrete tests in most of the non-merger decisions adopted since the adoption of its notice on market definition.

Guideline 80 also refers to the geographic market being homogenous. Although the reason for that limitation escapes me, it is mentioned by the ECJ in several judgments. Usually it is the market share of the supplier that is relevant, but that of the buyer when he is given an exclusive territory covering the whole of the common market (Article 3(2)) as that is the firm protected.

Firms with market shares exceeding 30% in some geographic markets may find that their agreements do not infringe Article 81 when entry is easy or when efficiencies outweigh the anti-competitive effect, but there will be no safe harbour.

9.6.4 *Hard core restraints (Article 4)*

There are two black lists. Where minimum prices are maintained (rpm), there are excessive territorial restraints and in some other circumstances, Article 4 prevents the exemption applying even to other provisions of the agreement. Rpm, territorial restraints and the other provisions listed do not infringe Article 81(1) and need no exemption unless they may have an appreciable effect on trade between Member States.[39] When the supplier does not have a market share in excess of 30%, these provisions may well not have appreciable effects on inter-state trade or competition. Nevertheless, the exemption will not apply to other provisions, such as an exclusive territory.

The introductory words of Article 4 are very broad, including 'directly or indirectly, in isolation or in combination with other factors in control of the parties.' This includes deterrents as well as prohibitions.

---

39   *Javico International and Javico AG v Yves Saint Laurent Parfums SA* (C306/96), [1998] ECR I–1983.

9.6.4.1 *Resale price maintenance (Article 4(a))*—The maintenance of resale prices is black listed by Article 4, but not maximum or recommended prices. There was some fear that franchisees might not qualify. They usually benefit from advertising that includes an indication of price and few depart from it. Under earlier drafts of the article, this might have been treated as a fixed price. The final version of Article 4(a), however, excluded from the black list recommended prices, provided they do not amount to minimum prices 'as a result of pressure from, or incentives offered by, any of the parties'. Where the franchisor merely indicates a price, and does not discipline those operating on narrower margins, the exemption may still apply, although few retail franchises have enough market power to infringe Article 81(1).

There are economic justifications for rpm. It is one way of protecting sellers who have had to incur sunk costs in bringing the products to market. The maintenance of maximum resale prices may enable a vendor with any market power to prevent its exclusive dealer exploiting it. It is not black listed.

On the other hand, rpm may lead to a proliferation of services required only by marginal buyers and increase the cost to others. Moreover, historically, rpm was often initiated by dealers who asked their suppliers to impose minimum prices. Economists generally agree that when there is a cartel between dealers, rpm is likely to lead to higher prices without any countervailing benefits. Rpm may also make it easier for suppliers not to compete aggressively on price.

9.6.4.2 *Territorial restraints (Article 4(b))*—The other major black listed provisions are those conferring protection on others by restraining further sale by the buyer outside its exclusive territory or customer group. To this there are four exceptions. Article 4(b), first indent, permits restraints on active sales (undefined, save in draft Guideline 50 about internet advertising) imposed on dealers only to protect other dealers or the supplier, not to protect a technology licensee which manufactures the product invented by the supplier in parts of the common market it does not supply itself. This is anomalous. Licensees that have to set up a production line are likely to have more rather than less sunk cost than dealers (11.5.3.2.2 below).

The protection permitted may be substantial where goods are sold for incorporation into other items by the buyer. Where, however, the product is traded, very little protection is given as customers from the buyer cannot be restrained, and intellectual property rights will be exhausted once the goods have been sold by or with the consent of the holder in any Member State (10.4 below).

The second indent excludes from the black list, and enables the regulation to apply where wholesalers are restrained from combining the retail function and selling to consumers. I assume that this is in recognition of the German law of unfair competition. In my view it is misguided. Huge economies have resulted from multiple chains confusing the wholesale and retail function, but there is no need to insert such a clause.

The second indent excludes from the black list a restraint on members of a selective distribution system supplying unauthorised distributors. 'Selective distribution' is defined in Article 1(d) more broadly that in the case law under Article 81(1) (9.4 above):

> "Selective distribution system" means a distribution system where the supplier undertakes to sell the contract goods or services, either directly or indirectly, only to distributors selected on the basis of specified criteria and where these distributors undertake not to sell such goods or services to unauthorised distributors;

It is not limited (as under the case law of the ECJ) to systems where the specified criteria are qualitative, proportionate and applied without discrimination. So some protection can be given to encourage investment by the dealer. The definition includes franchise agreements where the criteria for selection are specified.

The second indent to Article 4(b) also excludes from the hard-core restraints that prevent the application of the Regulation, a restriction imposed by the supplier of components sold for incorporation into something else to sell the components to someone who would use them to manufacture the same kind of goods sold by the component maker.

Where a producer of components supplies them for incorporation in a larger item, the Regulation will not apply if the component supplier is restrained from selling the components as spare parts to end-users or repairers or other service providers not entrusted by the buyer with the repair or servicing of its goods. Guideline 56 indicates that this prevents the buyer from being the only seller supplying its main dealers and restraining the component maker from selling to other repairers. Suppose that C, a maker of diesel engines and fuel injection pumps, supplies them to T, a maker of trucks which makes its own pumps for another model of diesel engine. C may restrain T from selling the pumps to a competing maker of diesel engines or pumps, but may not restrain T from selling to dealers.

Since sales of the complete product are often very price sensitive, manufacturers often want to recover their sunk costs largely from the replacement market. This provision makes that more difficult when the component is bought in. The Commission is not persuaded that Ramsey pricing is acceptable (5.2.2 above).

9.6.4.3 *Selective distribution (Article 4(c))*—By virtue of Article 4(c), for the block exemption to apply, retailers in a selective distribution system, as widely defined in the Regulation, must be allowed to sell to end users anywhere, but they may be limited to selling from a specified place of establishment. Retailers and wholesalers in a selective distribution system must be allowed to sell to any other approved dealers, even when operating at a different level of trade. Where prices are very different in different Member States, it may pay a wholesaler in the expensive area to buy from a retailer in the area where the products are cheaper.

9.6.4.4 *Cross supplies* (Article 4(d)—Article 4(d) black lists restraints on cross sales between dealers, which is the main mechanism for the equalisation of prices throughout the EC.

9.6.5 *Single branding (Article 5)*

The second black list in Article 5 does not affect the validity of other terms of the agreement. Article 5 limits the duration of covenants not to compete with the supplier. Remember that a non-compete obligation infringes 81(1) and requires exemption only if there are barriers to entry downstream and so many outlets are tied for so long that a new firm cannot enter the market at an efficient scale or an existing firm expand—*Delimitis (Stergios) v Henninger Bräu.*[40]

Where the black listed provision does not infringe Article 81(1) the black list in Article 5 does not deprive other provisions of the exemption. Given the ceiling of market share at 30%, and the possibility of the Commission or a national competition authority withdrawing the exemption one wonders why Article 5 is necessary.

Article 5 prevents the exemption applying to non-compete clauses imposed on buyers for more than five years or after the term of the agreement. Article 1(b) defines 'non compete obligation' widely as a direct or indirect obligation to take at least 80% of the buyer's total purchase of the contract goods and their substitutes from the supplier or a source designated by it. Tacitly renewable contracts are still treated as being of excessive duration even if either party can terminate the agreement by short notice. The contract goods may include more than one group of products. Where several products groups are supplied a supplier might require all of a new product to be sourced from the same supplier, provided that other products, for which the supplier has a stronger reputation, may be bought elsewhere.

Franchisors are very concerned by Article 5. Five years may be too short a period where the buyer gains a reputation through dealing with the products of the supplier and wants to use it to promote competing products. In *Pronuptia* (9.5.1 above), however, the ECJ stated that for franchising to be viable the franchisor must be able to provide its formula without the franchisee being able to open a similar shop to compete with a member of the network during or for a reasonable period after the expiry of the franchise. Moreover to control the quality of the products sold, the franchisee may be required to buy them from a designated source where it is otherwise not practicable to monitor quality.

These provisions in a franchise do not infringe Article 81(1) and require no exemption. Since this black list does not affect other provisions in the agreement, the Commission's limitations are not so important. The question arises

---

40   (C–234/89), [1991] ECR I–935 (2.4.3 above).

whether *Pronuptia* applies outside the context of franchising. Probably not. It depends on the protection of the seller's marketing formula, and the need for uniform presentation of franchised outlets. The argument for clearance is less strong where the retailer does not operate under its supplier's trade mark.

Where the buyer is operating from premises provided by the supplier, non-compete provisions are permitted for as long as the premises are occupied, provided that they cannot last more than a year after the expiry of the agreement. The non-compete provision is subject also to other limitations.

9.6.6 *Withdrawal of exemption (Articles 6–8)*

In only one reported case has a group exemption been withdrawn,[41] and with the low ceiling of market share, one might expect fewer withdrawals in future. Nevertheless, the provision for withdrawal is important as it enables the Commission to persuade the parties to amend their agreements.

The provisions are complex. Article 6 provides for the Commission to withdraw the benefit of the exemptions where the agreement does not merit it. A national competition authority also has power to withdraw it where an agreement has effects within a state where there is a distinct geographic market.

The Commission may also withdraw the benefit by regulation where parallel networks of similar vertical restraints cover over half the relevant market. This provision avoids the difficulty faced by the Commission after the appeal from its decisions on ice creams in Germany. It could condemn existing agreements, but had no power to restrain the firms from taking advantage of the group exemption for the future (*Langnese*).

9.6.7 *Transitional provisions (Article 12)*

The Regulation came into force at the beginning of 2000 to extend the former group exemptions. It has applied from 1 June, 2000 to grant the new exemption. Old agreements, for instance by manufacturers with large market shares, made before 1 June, 2000 were exempt until the end of 2001 if they complied with the former regulation.

9.7 Ways of bringing goods and services to market

This single Regulation applies to various ways of bringing products to the market. We used to have separate regimes for exclusive distribution—I will sell only to you within a territory, exclusive purchase, you will buy only from me—and franchising. Some selective distribution agreements were not subject to a group exemption, but Article 81(1) did not apply when the criteria for selecting approved dealers were proportionate, of a qualitative nature and applied without a discrimination.

41   *Langnese-Iglo GmbH & Co KG, v Mars GmbH* [1994] 4 CMLR 51, paras 208–9.

These classifications are now less important. Selective distribution as defined in the case law of the courts is not contrary to Article 81(1) and needs no exemption. When, however, the criteria for approving dealers are not qualitative, proportional and applied without discrimination, the Regulation may apply. We need to be familiar with both the case law applicable to clients with large market shares, and with the exemption, when the selection is quantitive.

Exclusive distribution and attenuated restraints are not exempt if accompanied by any of the hard core restraints listed in Article 4: rpm and post-sale restrictions, especially territorial protection. Exclusive purchasing is subject to the limitations on non-compete clauses listed in Article 5, but often will not infringe Article 81(1). In *Van den Bergh Foods Ltd v Commission*,[42] the CFI confirmed that a proper market analysis must be made as to the existence and extent of foreclosure (paragraphs 75–100). Much is relevant. It confirmed the Commission's adverse finding when a dominant firm supplying over 75% of the market and enjoying a large first mover advantage foreclosed about 40% of the market by requiring that only ice creams bought from it should be placed in freezers it supplied for free. The exclusivity raised rivals' costs (paragraph 113) as they would have to provide freezers on similar terms.

Franchising will usually amount to selective distribution as defined in the Regulation. In the absence of either an exclusive territory or a location clause, however, it is not likely to infringe Article 81(1). Moreover, although many franchises have famous marks, few have significant market power.

9.7.1 *Agency*

In 1962, when there was no case law and the Commission feared more notifications under Regulation 17 than it could handle, it issued a notice on exclusive agency agreements and said that, in its view, exclusive distribution agreements between principal and agent, including a *del credere* guarantee, do not infringe Article 81(1). Vertical integration to avoid making an agreement between independent undertakings that is subject to Article 81(1) may, therefore, take the form of appointing agents instead of dealers.

The ambit of this possibility is, however, very narrow. In several cases such as *Pittsburg Corning Europe*[43], *Suiker Unie*,[44] and *Belgian Travel Agents*[45] both the Commission and the ECJ have made it clear that for an agreement to come within this exception, the agent must be integrated into the undertaking of the principal. It need not be an employee, but it must take its instructions in detail from the principal and, according to the Commission, not be a firm capable of acting in its own name and on its own behalf, nor

---

42   T–65/98, 23 October 2003.
43   [1973] CMLR D2, paras 8–11.
44   (40/73 and others) [1975] ECR 1663, paras 543–47.
45   (311/85) [1987] ECR 3801, paras 19–20.

must it act much on behalf of other principals. A travel agent which acts as agent for several tour operators is not sufficiently integrated into the organisation of any of its principals for its agreement automatically to escape Article 81.[46]

The test adopted by the Court—the agent being integrated into the undertaking of the principal—is very difficult to apply as it is based on a common characteristic of independent dealers: many are closely integrated into the supplier's business. It is not enough to ensure that title to the goods should remain with the principal until it passes to a third party, since an agent is defined by reference to its commercial functions and not merely by reference to its legal position.

The Commission has been working on a notice giving its views on when an agreement with an agent infringes Article 81(1). At last these appear in the guidelines on vertical restraints (Guidelines 12–20). Limitations on the scope of the agent's authority do not infringe Article 81(1) (G.13). It remains free to exceed these when operating on its own behalf.

The main test of an integrated agent is that it does not bear the financial and commercial risks of the transaction, not only the risk of unsold stocks as under the previous notice (Guidelines 13–17). It will be treated as an independent trader if it contributes to advertising budgets, maintains stocks at its own risk, or organises a distribution network with market specific investment in equipment, premises or personnel. This last narrows the exclusion from Article 81 in the old Christmas message.

The guidelines include agents who negotiate or conclude contracts (paragraph 12). It is doubtful whether these infringe Article 81(1). The notice differs from the draft that circulated in 1990 in that qualifying agency agreements are entirely outside Article 81. Bans on even passive sales may be imposed. Guidelines 13 states that when an agency infringes Article 81, the block exemption may apply. This was unclear under the earlier block exemptions.

9.7.2 *Collective exclusive distribution*

This chapter has been concerned only with vertical agreements between one supplier and each of its dealers. Collective agreements between competitors do not fall within the group exemption, and are unlikely to receive exemption.[47]

9.8 Conclusion

If an undertaking supplies over 30% of the market, it should avoid any black listed provisions and it is then unlikely that its agreement will infringe Article

46   *Van Vlaamse Reisbureaus,*(311/85) [1987] ECR 3801.
47   *FEDETAB, Heintz van Landewyck Sàrl, Fédération Belgo-Luxembourgeoise des Industries du Tabac Asbl v Commission* (209–215 & 218/78), [1980] ECR 3125, para 184 (9.4 above).

81(1). So it is not as important as it seems at first sight to ascertain the relevant market. Moreover, if in some market the market share limit is exceeded, any institution, court or competition authority dealing with the agreement has power to apply Article 81(3).

9.9 Bibliography

Ivo Van Bael, 'Heretical Reflections on the Basic Dogma of EEC Antitrust: Single Market Integration' (1980) 10 *RSDIC* 39.

J S Chard, 'The Economics of the Application of Article 81 to Selective Distribution Systems' (1982) 7 *EL Rev* 83.

David Deacon, 'Vertical restraints under EU competition law: new directions' in Barry Hawk (ed), [1995] *Fordham Corporate Law Institute* 307.

Paul Demaret, 'Concurrence et Distribution en Droit Communautaire' [1984] *Juris Classeurs* 1–37.

——, 'Selective Distribution and EEC Law after the *Ford, Pronuptia* and *Metro II* judgments' in Barry Hawk (ed) [1986] *Fordham Corporate Law Institute* 151.

European Commission, *Proceedings of the European Competition Forum*, Ehlermann and Laudati (eds) (Wiley, EC Office for Official Publications, 1995).

Joanna Goyder, *EU Distribution Law*, 3rd edn (London, Palladian Law Publishing, 2000)

Frances Hanks and *Philip Williams*, 'The Treatment of Vertical Restraints under the Australian Trade Practices Act' (1985) 15 *Australian Business Law Review* 147.

Barry Hawk '*System Failure: Vertical Restraints and EC Competition Law*' (1995) 32 *CML Rev* 973.

Valentine Korah and *Denis O'Sullivan*, *Exclusive Distribution and the EC Competition Rules*, (Oxford, Hart Publishing, 2002).

Stephen C Salop, 'Analysis of Foreclosure in the EC Guidelines on Vertical Restraints,' in *Barry Hawk*, (ed) [2000] *Fordham Corporate Law Institute* 117.

Richard Whish, 'Regulation 2790/99: The Commission's "new Style Block Exemption for Vertical Agreements,' 37 *CML Rev*, 887.

10. Intellectual Property Rights and the Free Movement of Goods

10.1 Intellectual property rights and competition

In order to encourage and reward investment in innovation, the law of most countries enables inventors or their employers to apply for patents. If these are granted, the patentee or holder may, generally, sue anyone who, within that country's territory, uses the patented process, or who makes, sells or imports protected products without a licence, for a period, usually, of 20 years from filing. The patentee is protected from competition by others using the invention.

Copyright lasts longer: in the EC, for the lifetime of the author and 70 years thereafter,[1] and enables authors, or their successors in title, to sue those copying their work.

Trade marks may last indefinitely, as long as goods or services continue to be supplied under the mark. They enable the holder to identify goods and services as deriving ultimately from the same controlling source. It may or may not make them, itself, but may specify the goods to which the mark may be attached by others. It may change the specification, but has an interest in preserving any goodwill adhering to a mark and, consequently, has an incentive not lightly to reduce quality.

On an analysis *ex post*, as perceived after an investment has been made in innovation, incentives to innovate are no longer required. Exclusive intellectual property rights are anti-competitive since they restrain other people from taking advantage of innovation or reputation without the consent of the holder: they constitute barriers to entry. For this reason, German economists and political scientists after the Second World War were distrustful of intellectual property rights and of restrictive clauses in licences. This attitude influenced the thinking of Commission officials dealing with licensing in the 1970s and may well have influenced the Court.

On the other hand, when analysed *ex ante*—from the time when the decision to invest or create was made—such rights encourage some kinds of investment that otherwise might not be worthwhile and so lead to a more competitive economy. Some inventions, once available, can be easily copied and, without protection, it would not be worth investing in making them. This is particularly true of pharmaceutical products that are costly to develop and take through their clinical trials, but can often be cheaply copied from the specification required for their marketing authorisation. Many artistic works can be copied and, without copyright, authors and artists might have little chance to earn a living.

---

1   Under the harmonisation directive (10.5.1 below).

Trade marks enable the holder to sue those who confuse buyers into thinking that their products emanate from him. They make possible competition in qualities that are not immediately obvious to shoppers, such as the taste of packaged food. They do not prevent others from selling competing goods unbranded or under their own mark. In the long term, protection of such rights may increase efficiency as well as consumer choice and so make the economy more competitive.

10.2 Birth of the distinction between the existence of rights and their exercise

The national limitations of intellectual property rights, however, are difficult to reconcile with the concept of a common market. A French patent extends only throughout France and a UK one only throughout the UK. Exploitation of the invention in Belgium would not infringe either. Benelux— Belgium, the Netherlands and Luxembourg—have regional trade marks and designs that apply throughout the three Member States. Until the mid-1960s, it was widely believed that, for goods protected by such rights, the common market could be divided along frontiers through the use of national intellectual property rights (iprs).

Consten and Grundig v Commission[2] was the beginning of a development preventing this. The way Grundig enabled its exclusive distributors for all Member States except Germany to register the trade mark Gint, which it placed on all the apparatus made at that period, was described at 2.3.1 and 2.4.1 above. This enabled Consten to sue the parallel importer UNEF under French law for trade mark infringement in addition to unfair competition. Advocate General Roemer considered merely that this was an abuse of trade mark law, since the Grundig mark which was also placed on the equipment adequately indicated the origin of the goods, that is, who was responsible for their specification.

The ECJ went further and distinguished the existence or ownership of such rights under national law, which is protected under Article 295 of the Treaty, from their exercise, which is subject to the Treaty provisions. In legal theory, it is impossible to draw the line between existence and exercise, except at the extremes. Analytically, the existence of a right consists of all the ways in which it may be exercised. In ruling that an important difference rests on a distinction which cannot be drawn by logical analysis, the Court created a very flexible instrument for it to develop the law and reduce the possibilities of dividing the common market through the use of national or regional intellectual property rights.

---

2   (56 & 58/64) [1966] ECR 299.

10.3 Free movement of goods

The principle of the free movement of goods mentioned in Article 3a of the EC Treaty is crystallised in Articles 28–30. Article 28 provides:

> Quantitative restrictions on imports and all measures having equivalent effect shall be prohibited between Member States.

The ECJ has interpreted this provision, implementing one of the fundamental principles of the common market, very widely. 'Quantitative restrictions' is a term referring to customs quotas—only so many widgets shall be imported from state A each year. An extreme quantitative restriction is a nil quota—no widgets shall be imported thence. The right of a patent or trade mark holder to restrain imports has been perceived as a measure of equivalent effect to a nil quota—no protected articles shall be imported without its consent. Article 29 makes similar provision for quantitative restrictions on exports.

Exceptions are provided in Article 30 for measures *justified* on various grounds, including the protection of 'industrial or commercial property', but its provisions derogate from a fundamental principle of the Treaty and have been narrowly construed. Moreover, there is a sting in the tail:

> The provisions of Articles 28 and 29 shall not preclude prohibitions or restrictions on imports, exports or goods in transit justified on grounds of . . . the protection of industrial and commercial property. Such prohibitions or restrictions shall not, however, constitute a means of arbitrary discrimination or a disguised restriction on trade between Member States.

Article 30 confirms that the authors of the treaty thought that industrial and commercial property rights could be of equivalent effect to quantitative restrictions.

10.4 Exhaustion of intellectual property rights when a product has been sold by or with the consent of the holder in another Member State

10.4.1 *Early cases on exhaustion*

The ECJ developed the concept of the 'specific subject matter' of the particular kind of industrial or commercial property, in the light of which protection may be justified. In *Centrafarm v Sterling*,[3] it stated:

> 9. As regards patents, the specific subject matter of the industrial property is the guarantee that the patentee, to reward the creative effort of the inventor, has the exclusive right to use an invention with a view to manufacturing industrial

---

3 (15/74) [1974] ECR 1147. For comment, see Michel Waelbroeck, 'The Effect of the Rome Treaty on the Exercise of National Industrial Property Rights' (1976) 21 *The Antitrust Bulletin*, 99.

products and putting them into circulation for the first time, either directly or by the grant of licences to third parties, as well as the right to oppose infringements.

'The specific subject matter' includes both the nature of the right—the right to restrain others from using the invention or selling goods made through its use—and the reason the law grants it—the reward to those investing in innovation.

Sterling owned patents in the UK, the Federal Republic, the Netherlands and elsewhere. Centrafarm had bought the drug in England and Germany where Sterling had obtained some recompense; but the UK price for the drug was half the Dutch price, partly because of fluctuating currencies, and partly because of the buying power of the UK government (it pays for most medicines used in the UK and had a right to exploit patented inventions for its own use in return for a royalty under the Crown use provisions of the Patents Act 1949).

The Court does not seem to have been concerned about the size of the reward, and was not prepared to allow the national patent laws to divide the common market in order to permit Sterling to have a second bite of the cherry when its drug entered the Netherlands, where it was more highly valued:

> 11. Whereas an obstacle to the free movement of goods of this kind may be justified on the ground of protection of industrial property where such protection is invoked against a product coming from a Member State where it is not patentable and has been manufactured by third parties without the consent of the patentee
>
> and in cases where there exist patents, the original proprietors of which are legally and economically independent,
>
> a derogation from the principle of the free movement of goods is not, however, justified where the product has been put onto the market in a lawful manner, by the patentee himself or with his consent, in the Member State from which it has been imported, in particular in the case of a proprietor of parallel patents'

[The sentence has been divided into three for ease of reference].

The Court did not address the issue of direct sale by a licensee outside its territory. It made clear the possibility of restraining parallel traders at the two extremes, but there is some intermediate ground which it left open, part of which has been clarified by later cases. Later judgments applied ground 11 literally and treated a patent as exhausted by any sale in another Member State by or with the consent of the holder, whether or not a monopoly profit could be earned in the country of export.

For some years, little attention was given to the need for a monopoly profit—the reward for creative effort mentioned in paragraph 9 of the judgment which provides the incentive to invest in innovation. This is unfortunate and surprising in view of the teleological approach the Court claimed to adopt in the 1970s. The Court may have been influenced by the ordo liberal distrust of intellectual property rights, which were percieved as entry barriers depriving others of their freedom.

Sterling had argued that it should be allowed to protect the Dutch market because the price differences were due to different government policies in the two countries. The Court answered:

> 23. It is part of the Community authorities' task to eliminate factors likely to distort competition between Member States, in particular by the harmonization of national measures for the control of prices and by the prohibition of aids which are incompatible with the Common Market, in addition to the exercise of their powers in the field of competition.

It added (at paragraph 24) that the different national policies did not justify the exercise of the patent rights: it was for the Community institutions to prevent such distortions. Since then, the Commission has not proposed legislation to limit national price control, where it does not bear particularly hardly on imports, and has used the competition rules to make export limitations illegal. Even if the Commission were to propose a directive to the Council, it is unlikely that the Member States that constitute the Council would be prepared to give up their freedom to reduce the cost of medicines.

In *Merck v Stephar*,[4] Merck had sold or consented to the sale in Italy by its subsidiary of a drug called 'Moduretic.' It held patents for this in other Member States, but at the time of the discovery it was not possible to obtain a patent for pharmaceutical products in Italy. Although the law preventing the grant of patent protection for drugs had since been held unconstitutional by the highest Italian court, no transitional provisions were enacted for drugs discovered during that period, which cannot now be patented because they are no longer novel.

Prices for the drug were very different in different Member States. In the Netherlands, Germany and Belgium, the patent law was strong and the price was high; in the UK, where the main purchaser was entitled to a compulsory licence under the Crown use provisions, the price was less than half the Dutch price. In Italy the price was still lower, but it was lowest of all in France, where there was patent protection. The French government, however, imposed maximum price controls, restricting the returns on the drug even more tightly than did the lack of patent protection in Italy.

Although neither Merck nor its subsidiary had had any possibility of earning a monopoly profit in Italy, the Court ruled that Merck could not rely on its Dutch patent to keep out a drug that had been sold in a Member State by it or with its consent.

The Advocate General had pointed out that not all patentees make a monopoly profit—they have only a chance of doing so. One might reply that there are always commercial constraints. Some patents have little value because there are cheaper substitutes on the market or a drug is found to produce disastrous side effects. The Italian law, however, ensured that no

---

4   (187/80) [1981] ECR 2063.

inventor of pharmaceutical products who sold them in Italy could prevent firms taking a free ride on its investment in innovation for medicines.

The Court's only apparent reason for preventing Merck from using its Dutch patent to protect one of the countries where it could make a monopoly profit was that Merck must take the consequences of its conduct in selling the product in Italy. That is not a reason, but a conclusion. To discourage the patentee from selling in countries where it can obtain no protection may in theory lead to the products being sold only where they are protected by patent, and this might divide the market even more seriously than does differential pricing. It may be that patents for pharmaceutical products are weak in too many countries for this to be worthwhile.

The Court's judgment must have reduced the returns in Europe from R & D, and may have marginally reduced that activity although pharmaceutical companies also exploit their R & D mainly in the US and other developed countries outside the EEA.

The only policy reason which in my view might justify the Court's decision is that it encouraged private firms to persuade their governments not to control a patentee's profit margin too tightly. I am told that after the judgment, French pharmaceutical firms persuaded the French government to raise the maximum prices at which they were permitted to sell in France on the ground that this would enable them to make higher profits on exports to other Member States. This had the advantage of bringing the national laws closer together.

It is, however, tough for a firm in the private sector to be squeezed between the desire of the Government in some countries to keep down the cost of medicine and the Community rules for free movement, which seem to extend to the whole common market the rules of the Member State giving least protection to innovators. It is also hard on the countries which provide strong patents because of their desire to encourage innovation.

Hugh Hansen of Fordham Law School argued in a lecture that neither the Treaty nor the principles of free movement require international exhaustion between Member States. Exhaustion expands the number of people selling products that are already on the market in Member States. It does not increase the amount of different products moving across Europe. In fact, it decreases the amount of such products because exhaustion acts as a barrier to entry as parallel trading will be expected to prevent the recovery of the costs of introducing a new product onto the market.[5]

The doctrine of exhaustion limits the extent to which holders of intellectual property rights can discriminate geographically. At 5.2.2, I explained that when overhead costs were high, everyone would be better off if they were recovered from the customers whose demand is less responsive to price.

5   Hugh Hansen, 'International exhaustion: an economic and non-economic policy analysis', in *International Intellectual Property Law and Policy*, vol 6, (New Jersey, Juris Publishing, 2001), 114–1, 114–10.

In several subsequent cases the ECJ has drawn back somewhat from the erosion of intellectual property rights and has stressed the need for the holder's consent if the doctrine of exhaustion is to apply.

Under the Benelux uniform law on designs, the first person to apply for a design is granted an exclusive right to sell goods that conform to it against anyone save the author or his assigns.

In *Keurkoop v Nancy Kean Gifts*,[6] Nancy Kean Gifts registered the design for a handbag in 1978. Apparently, it was similar to an earlier design filed in the US, but this did not affect the validity of the Benelux rights unless the original innovator objected. Nancy Kean had the bag made in Taiwan and despatched directly to the Netherlands. The following year, Keurkoop was found to be offering a bag of the same design, also made in Taiwan. Some items came directly from Taiwan and some were put on the market in Germany.

When Nancy Kean Gifts tried to exercise its design rights to restrain commercial imports into the Netherlands the ECJ stated that, at the present stage of Community law, where national intellectual property rights have not been harmonised, it is for national law to define their scope and ruled that a design law protecting persons other than the inventor does come within the class of industrial and commercial property rights mentioned in Article 30.

Not only can the design right be invoked to restrain direct imports from Taiwan which are not subject to Article 28 since they do not constitute trade between Member States, but also against those items first sold in the Federal Republic of Germany without the consent of the Benelux holder, which enjoyed no exclusive right in Germany. It must follow that, had Moduretic been sold in Italy by a third party without Merck's consent, Merck could have prevented exports from there to other Member States.

In *Pharmon v Hoechst*,[7] the Court held that a patent in the Netherlands can be exercised to keep out goods exported there by a compulsory licensee in the United Kingdom. The ECJ did not address the problem of direct sales by a licensee outside its territory. It treated manufacture or putting on the market by a compulsory licensee as being carried out without the consent of the holder. The licence was a state measure, not a voluntary one. So whether direct sales by a licensee exhaust the right was not relevant and not considered.

The Commission used to allege that the grant of a licence exhausted a patent and that direct sales by the licensee into another Member State cannot be restrained. It has clearly changed its view. In *PMI/DSV*,[8] the Commission rejected a complaint against a licence limited territorially on the ground that such a licence did not infringe either Article 81 or the rules for free movement. At paragraph 12, the Commission said:

---

6 (144/81) [1982] ECR 2853.
7 (19/84) [1985] ECR 2281.
8 [1996] 5 CMLR 320.

Such a clause could not be caught by Article 85 (now Article 81), since the licensor remains free, under such Community rules, to choose his licensee and the size of the territory which he grants him. If such a clause were not included, the licence would become a European licence under which the licensor would no longer be free, in particular, to choose his sub-licensee for the other Member States for business or financial reasons, or on the grounds of honesty. The omission of such a clause might also deprive the licensor of the right to check the subcontractor's technical capacities, such as his capacity to relay properly the sound and pictures sent to him, bearing in mind in particular the fact that the authorisation conferred on FCR (the licensee for Germany) for the relay of such sound and pictures stops at the boundaries of the territory granted under the agreement. . . . If such a clause were not included, therefore, the licensor would be unable to co-ordinate the management of all the relays of sound and pictures to the other Member States. . . .

This view was confirmed by the CFI in *Tiercé Ladbroke v Commission*,[9] an appeal from the rejection of another complaint that was never published.

A patent can be exercised to inhibit parallel trade, however, only if the law does not discriminate against imported goods contrary to the second sentence of Article 30. In cases against the UK[10] and Italy, the Court held that national provisions for granting compulsory patents when the patent was worked in another Member State rather than locally were contrary to the principle of free movement.

10.4.2 *Copyright—the ECJ emphasises the need for rewards and incentives*

A problem rather similar to that in *Merck v Stephar*[11] had arisen earlier in *Musik-Vertrieb Membran v GEMA*,[12] a reference for a preliminary ruling to the ECJ made by the German courts. Under section 8 of the UK Copyright Act 1956, once records of a musical work have been made in or imported into the United Kingdom for the purpose of retail sale, by or with the consent of the holder, any other manufacturer may make records of the work for sale by retail on giving notice to the holder and paying a royalty of 6.25% of the retail price. Consequently producers normally consent to such manufacture at that rate of royalty.

Advocate General Warner said there could be no exhaustion of a right when there was no power to prevent exploitation by others, and that GEMA, the performing rights society in Germany acting on behalf of the copyright holders, should be allowed to charge the importer of records from England to Germany the difference between the UK statutory 6.25% and the royalty that would have been obtainable in England but for section 8—a difficult test to apply!

   9   (T–504/93) [1997] ECR II–923, paras 151, 160
  10   *Commission v United Kingdom* (C–30/90) [1992] ECR I–B829.
  11   (187/80) [1981] ECR 2063.
  12   (55 & 57/78) [1981] ECR 147.

The Court accepted that copyright is included in the term 'industrial and commercial property' in Article 30 of the Treaty which provides the exception to Article 28, although Article 30 does not refer to artistic property rights. The Court referred, however, to paragraphs 22–25 of the judgment in *Centrafarm v Sterling*[13] (10.4.1 above) and, without discussing the amount of the reward, repeated that the existence of differences in national law that may distort competition between Member States cannot justify the protection by a Member State of the practices of a private organisation that are incompatible with the free movement of goods.

Anticipating its later judgment in *Merck v Stephar* (10.4.1 above), it added that the holder can choose in which state to market its records. Where there is some protection in the country where the goods were first sold, the common market is not divided.

The ECJ has treated far more favourably copyright in the exhibition of films, broadcasts and other performing rights—the right to reproduce the protected work in public. In *Coditel v Ciné Vog Films*,[14] a Belgian cable television company picked up the transmission of a film from Germany and relayed it to clients in parts of Belgium. The exclusive licensee in Belgium objected and sued the cable company to protect itself.

The ECJ distinguished broadcast diffusion rights from copyright in a physical disk or cassette (paragraph 12). The former are governed by the rules for the free movement of services—Articles 45 and 50 (EC), rather than for goods. It implied something like Article 30 into the rules relating to services, but went considerably further.

It stated at paragraph 13 that a copyright holder and its assigns have a legitimate interest in calculating royalties on the basis of the number of performances by the licensee and that exploitation of copyright involves various methods, including television. It ruled that the holder was entitled to rely on its copyright to restrain Coditel from relaying the film transmitted with consent in another Member State (paragraph 18). Consequently, broadcast diffusion rights are not exhausted by a performance in another Member State.[15]

The distinction between the mechanical rights, subject to the rules for the free movement of goods and performing rights, subject to those for the provision of services was commercially artificial, although they are governed by different parts of the treaty. A film producer is induced to invest because of a series of exploiting acts. There are royalties to be obtained from cinemas downtown charging high prices, then from general release and television—all these derive from services. Now, an increasing proportion of the revenue

---

13   (15/74) [1974] ECR 1147, paras 22–B24.
14   (62/79) [1980] ECR 881.
15   Subsequently, the Court found for the same reasons that exclusive licences to different broadcasters in different Member States do not infringe Art 81(1), although Reischl AG observed that such a conclusion would result in absolute territorial protection. See *Coditel II*, at 11.3 below.

comes from the sale and, more recently, the hire of video cassettes and DVDs. This is subject to the free movement of goods, but the Court has not relied on the distinction.

Warner Bros & Metronome v Christiansen[16] was concerned with the hiring out of video cassettes. Christiansen bought some in England with the consent of the copyright holder and imported them into Denmark for the purposes of hiring them out from his shop. Under Danish law, sale and hire are separate infringing acts. Under UK law at that time, copyright holders were able to oppose the sale but not the hire of the cassettes.

Citing *Keurkoop* (10.4.1 above) for the proposition that it is still for national law to define the scope of industrial and commercial property rights and *Coditel II*, the ECJ stressed the need for the holder to make an adequate return on its investment. The Danish law was not discriminatory. Had the cassettes been bought in Denmark, hiring them would still have infringed the copyright. The Court refused to follow its Advocate General, and its ruling that an injunction might be granted came as a great surprise to experts.

I welcome the Court's emphasis on the need for adequate remuneration, although it is not possible to say how much remuneration is needed to induce the producer's investment. That should be determined by the market—by the amount that producers can extract from the licensees and buyers of the protected goods.

Thetford v Fiamma[17] concerned a patent, rather than copyright, but has brought together the ideas of reward and incentives for investment. Under UK law, it was possible to obtain a patent if an inventive idea had not been anticipated by any patent specification or other publication in the preceding 50 years, although it was not novel in the absolute sense. Following Advocate General Mischo, the Court recognised at paragraph 19 that the doctrine of relative novelty was adopted in the UK:

> *to foster creative activity* on the part of inventors in the interest of industry. To that end the "fifty year rule" aimed to make it possible to give a reward, in the form of the grant of a patent, even in cases in which an "old" invention was "rediscovered." In such cases the UK legislation was designed to prevent the existence of a former patent specification which had never been utilised or published from constituting a ground for revoking a patent which had been validly issued.

> 20. Consequently, a rule such as the 'fifty year rule' cannot be regarded as constituting a restriction on trade between Member States' [my emphasis].

The Court perceived the matter *ex ante*, at the time the commitment to investment in research is made, and not *ex post*. It brought together the concept of reward for the inventor, introduced in *Centrafarm v Sterling* and stressed in the *Coditel* and *Warner* judgments, and that of incentives. The expectation of a reward is the incentive to investment: it 'foster[s] creative activity.' On this

16   (158/86) [1988] ECR 2605.
17   (35/87) [1988] ECR 3585.

basis, the exercise of the right is not anti-competitive. Nor does it impede free movement. But for the hope of reward, there might have been no product to import.

The Court confirmed in *Thetford* that where the national law discriminates against imports from another Member State, this will amount to 'a disguised restriction of trade between Member States' within the second sentence of Article 30, and its exercise would infringe Article 28.[18]

10.4.3 *Law of unfair competition*

The ECJ has treated the national laws of unfair competition very much like industrial and commercial property rights, although it may be directly interpreting Article 28 rather than Article 30 which does not mention unfair competition as a possible justification. In *Béguelin*,[19] the ECJ ruled that an exclusive distributor cannot rely on national laws of unfair competition to exclude imports from another Member State when such parallel trade, in itself, is alleged to amount to unfair competition.

In *Dansk Supermarked v Imerco*,[20] however, it distinguished the use of rules for unfair competition to control the circumstances and methods in or by which the imported goods are put on the market. Imerco, a Danish retailing co-operative, ordered from an English firm sets of a special dinner service decorated with pictures of Danish castles to celebrate its fiftieth anniversary. It stipulated high quality standards but, to save cost, permitted the sale of seconds in parts of England not much visited by tourists. One of Imerco's competitors, Dansk Supermarked, bought some 300 of the 1,000 sets of seconds and started to sell them in Denmark without any indication that they were seconds.

As it happened, the Danish Supreme Court, applying the ruling of the ECJ, held that Imerco was saved from competition in its home market because the indication that the sets were seconds had been removed, although not by Dansk Supermarked. Had they not been, members of Imerco would have been faced with competition in their home market.

The ECJ's reasoning may be criticised as formalistic. The ruling could have been avoided with the aid of sophisticated advice. Imerco could have bought the seconds itself and sold them to retailers at a distance from Denmark and in small quantities, but if it was not organised for such an operation its costs would have increased substantially; or it could have sold them in Sweden before the EEA was established (10.4.6.1 below). In eradicating obvious restrictions on inter-state trade, the ECJ has ignored the probable strategic

---

18   In *Warner*, the Court reached the same conclusion by stating that the exercise of copyright would not then be justified by the first sentence of Art 30.
19   (22/71) [1971] ECR 949.
20   (58/80) [1981] ECR 181. See Karen Dyekjaer-Hansen '*A/S Imerco v Dansk Supermarked A/S*—Parallel Import of Branded Seconds' [1982] *European Intellectual Property Review* 85.

reactions of intelligent businessmen to its ruling and may have reduced efficiency and consumer choice and even helped to segregate the common market.

10.4.4 *Rights in reputation—trade marks*

Trade marks may similarly be treated as quantitative restrictions on imports, the use of which is prohibited by Article 28, unless justified on grounds of trade mark law. At first, in cases such as *Sirena v Eda*,[21] the ECJ was scathing about the value of marks. The Italian trade mark for a brand of saving cream was assigned long before the establishment of the common market. Decades later, when shaving cream lawfully bearing the mark in Germany was exported to Italy, the Italian mark was used to restrain the commercial importation. Three years before the development of the doctrine of exhaustion in *Centrafarm v Sterling*, the ECJ ruled that the exercise of the national mark might infringe Article 81

> each time it manifests itself as the subject, the means or the result of a restrictive practice, when a trade mark right is exercised by virtue of assignments to users in one or more Member States, it is thus necessary to establish in each case whether such use leads to a situation falling under the prohibitions of article 85 (now 81).

In the much criticised case of *Van Zuylen v Hag*,[22] Hag's Belgian subsidiary was seized as reparations after the war and the Belgian mark came, by public act, to be owned separately from the German mark.

The ECJ decided that where the same trade marks are held by different firms in different Member States but were once of common origin, neither holder can prevent goods bearing the mark from being sold in other Member States where it owns the right by either the other holder itself or by purchasers from it if the goods were genuinely put on the market, bearing the mark, in the area where the other has the right. The case was greatly criticised as the common origin had been rendered asunder by a government decree.

The judgment was firmly reversed by the ECJ, following Advocate General Jacobs, in *Hag II*.[23] The Court ignored the scathing remarks it had made about trade marks in early cases and, at paragraph 13, referred to rights in a mark as being:

> an essential element in the system of undistorted competition which the Treaty aims to establish and maintain. In such a system enterprises must be able to gain customers by the quality of their products or services, which can be done only by virtue of the existence of distinctive signs permitting identification of those products and services. For a trade mark to be able to play this part, it must constitute a guarantee that all the products bearing it have been manufactured under the

21   (40/70) [1971] ECR 69.
22   (192/73) [1974] ECR 731.
23   (C–10/89) [1990] ECR I–3711.

supervision of a single enterprise to which responsibility for their quality may be attributed.

The Court went on to hold that the holder in Germany was entitled to use the mark 'Hag' to restrain the sale of coffee made by the successor in title from the Belgian sequestrator.

Some controversy remained, in that the judgment was based on both the lack of consent by the German holder (paragraph 15) and on the possible confusion of the public (paragraph 16). In *Ideal Standard*[24] a single firm owned two businesses, one in France and one in Germany. The insolvent business in France was sold by the liquidator as a going concern with the French trade mark, but the Court ruled that its products had not been sold with the consent of the German holder. The Court stressed that the function of a trade mark is to save consumers from confusion (paragraph 45). Where there is no continuing relationship between the vendor and purchaser of a business, there is no guarantee that the specification of the products in the two areas will be the same. So, consumers may be confused.

Consequently the holder of the mark 'Ideal Standard' in Germany was entitled to restrain direct sales by the French assignee in Germany. The Court ruled that the sale of the business with the French mark was not the kind of consent required for the doctrine of exhaustion to apply, and that before finding that:

a trade mark assignment can be treated as giving effect to an agreement prohibited under Article 81, it is necessary to analyse the context, the commitments underlying the assignment, the intention of the parties and the consideration for the assignment.' [paragraph 59].

10.4.4.1 *Repackaging and relabelling of trade marked goods*—In *Hoffmann-La Roche v Centrafarm*[25] a trade mark holder had packed pills in different quantities in different Member States. A parallel importer bought some in England where they were far cheaper and repacked them so as to follow the practice of German hospitals of buying in larger containers. Both the original mark and Centrafarm's name had been placed on the packaging. The Court ruled that the exercise of German trade mark rights in such circumstances to oppose import and sale was justified within the meaning of the first sentence of Article 30.

The specific subject matter of trade mark rights is to protect the holder against competitors who would abuse the reputation protected by the mark. The essential function of a mark is to guarantee to buyers or final users the original identity of the marked product, so as to avoid confusion. This implies that the goods have not been tampered without the holder's authorisation.

Nevertheless, the Court added that the sale of the pills in smaller packages in England than in Germany, coupled with the exercise of the trade mark

24 (C–9/93) [1994] ECR I–2789, paras 46–51.
25 (102/77) [1978] ECR 1139.

right, might constitute 'a disguised restriction of trade between Member States' within the second sentence of Article 30, if it had the *effect* of dividing the market.

To avoid an injunction, however, the repackager, Centrafarm, would have to establish that the repacking was not of a nature to affect the original state of the product. This might be possible if it removed only an outer packing, leaving the inner packing untouched, or repacked subject to the control of a public authority. The Court added that the repackager, to rely on the provision to Article 30, would have to give the holder advance warning, and indicate clearly on the final package that the goods had been repacked by it.[26] It made it clear that its judgment extends beyond the pharmaceutical industry.

In *Centrafarm v American Home Products*[27] the Court ruled on a similar problem, but said that relabelling would be a disguised restriction within the second sentence of Article 30 if the *intention* was to divide the market. The change of emphasis by the Court from the *effect* on inter-state trade in the *Roche* case to the *purpose* of the holder enabled Roche to defeat Centrafarm's Euro-defence to the German proceedings. Packaging in different quantities may have had the effect of dividing the common market, but it was difficult to show that Roche adopted different packages for this purpose. Hospitals in Germany habitually order pills packed in larger quantities than do those in England and this may have explained Roche's method of packaging.

In *Bristol-Myers Squibb and Others v Paranova*,[28] the ECJ reverted to 'effect' as the connecting factor (paragraph 57). Various pharmaceutical companies sold their trade marked pills in the quantities customary in each Member State. There are vast differences in the prices at which they are sold owing to national measures, such as the control of maximum prices. Parallel traders bought these in the countries where they were cheap, and cut the blister packs or changed the quantities in ampoules etc. so as to contain the appropriate amount of medicine for the country of destination and replaced the outer packaging in such a way that the original trade mark could be seen.

The Court held (paragraph 55) that repackaging would not prevent the doctrine of exhaustion from applying where it was necessary to enable the parallel trader to conform to rules about the quantities to be marketed, reimbursement of medical expenses, or well established medical prescription practices. The Court went on to confirm the conditions under which repackaging did not prevent exhaustion that it had specified in *Hoffmann-La Roche* and added that untidy, defective or poor quality outer packaging should not be permitted to detract from consumers' confidence (paragraph 75). It was for the national court to decide whether the original condition of the goods was

26 *Pfizer v Eurimfarm* (1/81) [1981] ECR 2913 para 13.
27 (3/78) [1978] ECR 1823, paras 19–23.
28 (C–427/93 and others), [1997] 1 CMLR 1151, [1996] 1 CEC 716. The cases was decided under the trade mark directive, 89/104/EEC, OJ 1989, L40/1, CMR 5826, but that was construed in the light of the case law under Art 30 (paras 38–41), so must be relevant to that provision.

affected by the repackaging (paragraphs 58–66). In *Boeringer Ingelheim v Swingward*,[29] it applied the same criteria under the trade mark directive (10.5.2 below).

10.4.5 *Merck v Stephar remains the law*

The pharmaceutical and agricultural chemicals industries need patents more than most. Much is spent on R & D, and on the safety tests needed to obtain marketing authorisation. The life of the patent is shortened by the safety testing required before marketing is authorised. This has been recognised by regulations introducing supplementary protection certificates, conferring exclusive rights when the patents for these products expire (10.5.3.1 below). It was hoped that some of the more recent cases ruling that there would be no exhaustion if this would undermine the specific function of the intellectual property right, stressing the importance of rewards and incentives and that consent is given to marketing in the low price country only when it is voluntary might result in *Merck v Stephar* being reversed by the Court.

In Spain and Portugal, before their accession, it was not possible to obtain product patents for pharmaceutical products. Under their Acts of Accession, Spain and Portugal were required to alter their law and also to join the European Patent Convention[30] under which national product patents can be obtained. When the inventions of Merck were novel, however, it could not have obtained a product patent in Spain or Portugal and when product patents became available, it was too late to do so.

The inability to obtain a patent was aggravated by the control of maximum prices at levels very much lower than in some Member States and other distortions caused by the reimbursement rules for medical insurance etc. In *Merck v Primecrown*,[31] the English patent court asked the ECJ whether it would reverse its ruling in *Merck v Stephar*, but the Court refused to do so.[32]

Advocate General Fennelly spelled out with great care the reasons of policy for reversing the earlier judgment. In the light of some excellent articles which he cited, he indicated the poverty of the court's reasoning and its failure to take into account the need for a reward which the Court has said was part of the specific subject matter of a patent. He went on to analyse the later case law with its emphasis on not undermining the specific function of each kind of intellectual property right.

Mr Fennelly suggested a compromise to the Court. He recommended that where Merck had been unable to obtain patent protection, there should be no exhaustion, but where it had been able to obtain a patent, price control that

29 C–143/00, [2002] 2 CMLR 623.
30 Convention for the European Patent, 5 October 1973, CMR 5795.
31 [1996] 3 CMLR 724.
32 *Merck v Primecrown* and *Beecham v Europharm of Worthing Ltd* (C–267 & 268/95) [1997] 1 CMLR 83.

deprived it of a monopoly profit should not prevent exhaustion. This was not a satisfactory compromise, since price control can deprive an inventor of its chance of reward as effectively as lack of a patent.

The Court rejected the views of its Advocate General with very little reasoning and refused to depart from *Merck v Stephar*. At paragraphs 30 and 31 it accepted that the reward for creative effort was a justification within the meaning of Article 30, but added that a patent does not guarantee a reward. This may be true. Many drugs fail their safety tests, others are soon overtaken by better medicines, but if Merck were not to be allowed to exercise its patent to protect the higher priced markets, it would have no chance of gaining a monopoly profit on the items it sold in Spain or Portugal.

The Court thereafter considered only the nature of the right and concluded that if Merck chose to sell in a country where it had no patent, it must take the consequences of its choice. This is not a reason, but a conclusion. The only qualification it made was that if Merck were under a legal duty under national or Community law to market the product in Spain, it would have no choice in putting it on the market there, and its right would not be exhausted. It was for the English court to decide that question, but the case was settled.

10.4.6 *Sales outside the EEA do not exhaust intellectual property rights*

The rules relating to the free movement of goods relate only to imports and exports between Member States. So in *EMI v CBS*,[33] the Court held that where the mark had lawfully been affixed to the goods in the United States by the holder there, the holder in various common market states could rely on national law to prevent the import of records bearing the mark, although the marks were of common origin.

Goods bearing a mark may be imported from outside the common market to a Member State where no similar mark is held, but they can be kept out of any other Member States where the mark might be confused with one held independently in that state.[34] There is no doctrine of international exhaustion (10.6 below) in relation to goods sold with the holder's consent outside the common market.

In *Hauptzollamt Mainz v Kupferberg*,[35] the Court ruled that the provisions on the free movement of goods between Member States of the common market and countries with which it has entered into free trade or association agreements do have direct effect. Nevertheless, it held earlier, in *Polydor v Harlequin Records*,[36] that they should be construed far more narrowly than the EC rules since they are not intended to create a common market.

33   (51, 86 & 96/75) [1976] ECR 811.
34   This follows from *Keurkoop* (144/81) [1982] ECR 2853 (10.4.1) above, and from *EMI v CBS and others*, (51/75 and others), [1976] ECR 811.
35   (104/81) [1982] ECR 3641.
36   (270/80) [1982] ECR 329.

Consequently, an exclusive licensee of the copyright holder in the UK was entitled to exercise the copyright to restrain the import of records sold with the consent of the holder in Portugal, before its accession to the common market. The Court's reasoning is based on general considerations that apply equally to marks, patents and other intellectual property rights.

This rule will continue to apply to the association agreements the EC has made with some third countries. Holders of intellectual property rights will be able to sell cheaply in those countries and prevent the goods from undermining the price in the common market. This will not continue after they accede to the EC treaty.

10.4.6.1 *Exhaustion applies to goods sold anywhere in the EEA*—Protocol 28 of the EEA Agreement provides for exhaustion throughout the European Economic Area. Exhaustion is to be understood in accordance with the case law of the ECJ. Goods sold by or with the holder's consent in Norway cannot be kept out of the common market by exercising intellectual property rights or vice versa.

10.5 Harmonisation of intellectual property rights

The existence of intellectual property rights in only some of the Member States may divide the common market. Free riders can sell where there are no rights but not export to countries where there are.

The problem caused by differences in national patent and price control law remains. Pharmaceutical products can now be protected by product patents throughout the common market, since all Member States have joined the European Patent Convention.[37] Nevertheless, there remain patents in some Member States that are undermined by the lack of patentability in others at the time when they were novel and by maximum price control at low levels.

10.5.1 *Copyright*

Copyright protection used to last for different periods in different Member States, and in *EMI v Patricia*,[38] the Court held that where copyright had expired in the country of origin but not where the goods were sold, copyright might be invoked. This followed from *Keurkoop*,[39] but divided the common market.

---

37 The new Member States that acceeded in 2004 were required to accede to the Convention on the European Patent 1973.

38 (341/87) [1989] ECR 79, para 12. See Gerald Dworkin, 'Authorship of Films and the European Commission Proposals for Harmonising the Term of Copyright' [1993] *European Intellectual Property Review* 151.

39 *Keurkoop BV v Nancy Kean Gifts BV* (144/81), [1982] ECR 2853.

As part of the programme for the internal market in 1992, therefore, the Commission proposed directives to the Council[40] to harmonise intellectual property rights where the differences were capable of dividing the common market. In the field of copyright, this has been done largely by raising the level of protection to the highest in any Member State. For instance, copyright has been extended throughout the Community from the life of the author plus 50 years in most Member States to the German period of life plus 70 years[41] so as to avoid the division of the market exemplified in *EMI v Patricia*.

Some Member States protected software by copyright, and now all have been required to do so by the software directive[42] which determines the scope of the right. The rights of third parties to decompile programmes sufficiently to permit one programme to work with another are now recognised throughout the EC and the directive is appended to the EEA treaty, which will, therefore, confer the same rights since it has been incorporated into the national law of the three Member States within the EEA.

The need for a high level of protection of copyright and related rights in the information area led to the adoption of the directive on the legal protection of databases.[43] Nevertheless, legislation by directive suffers from the drawback that the Member States tend to implement the directives differently, adding them to what was law before, so the effects may not be entirely uniform. The Court has tried to minimise this disadvantage by construing the national law in the light of the directive it was intended to implement and the directive in the light of the case law under Article 30.[44]

10.5.2 *Trade marks*

The first trade mark directive[45] requires national laws to be adapted to comply with its provisions. The Community trade mark regulation was finally adopted in 1993[46] and a Community trade mark office, the Office for Harmonisation in the Internal Market (Trade Marks and Designs), in Alicante in Spain, started to accept filings in 1996. National marks continue and honest concurrent user of independent marks will still give rise to difficulties and divide the market. Community marks will be effective throughout the EEA in those countries

---

40   Under Art 95 of the EC Treaty. *E.g.* Council Dir 92/100/EEC of 19 November 1992 on rental right and lending right and on certain rights related to copyright in the field of intellectual property, OJ 1992, L346/61.
41   Council Dir 93/98/EEC of 29 October 1993, Harmonising the term of protection of copyright and certain related rights, OJ 1993, L290/9.
42   Dir 91/250, OJ 1991, L122/42.
43   Dir 96/9, OJ 1996, L77/20.
44   *Bristol-Myers Squibb v Paranova* (C–427, 429 and 436/93) [1996] ECR I–3457, paras 30–37, following the opinion of Jacobs AG, paras 54–58.
45   Dir 89/104 to approximate the laws of the Member States relating to trade marks, OJ 1989, L40/1.
46   Council Reg 40/94 of 20 December 1993 on the Community trade mark, OJ 1994, L11/1.

where they are not challenged on the basis of confusion with a local mark. So many appeals from the trademark office Board of Appeals have been heard by the CFI and ECJ that, pursuant to the Treaty of Nice, serious consideration is being given to setting up a new court, attached to the CFI, to deal with trade marks.

10.5.3 *Patents*

The Community Patent Convention was signed in 1976, but has not yet been fully ratified, so has not yet come into force. The European Patent Convention was not adopted by the Community as such, but all the Member States and some others have joined. It has worked well, although there are complaints about the high fees and translation cost. The cost is still very much less than that of obtaining multiple national patents, but higher than that of obtaining a unitary US patent.

If patents in two or three states that have joined the Convention are desired, it is cheaper to have a single international search made thereunder. This will result in patents being granted under the laws of those Member States for which they are requested, valid only if the applications and claims have been translated into those languages within a short period after grant. Additional fees are required for each additional country for which a patent is requested, but the bigger deterrent to multiple applications is the cost of technical translations.

10.5.3.1 *Supplementary protection certificates*—For the two products that are required to undergo extensive safety tests, medicines and plant protection products such as herbicides, an additional exclusive right under a supplementary protection certificate may be sought.[47] This may prolong the patent protection for up to five years to compensate for the expense and time lost when undergoing the tests.

10.6 No international exhaustion

The ECJ has held that the doctrine of exhaustion expressly adopted in the trade mark directive is not international, even if the Member State of import has adopted a concept of international exhaustion. This has since been extended to other intellectual property rights.

Article 5 of the directive prescribes the rights of the holder of a trade mark registered under the directive and Article 7 of the directive provides:

---

47   Council Reg 1768/92 concerning the creation of a supplementary protection certificate for medicines, OJ 1992, L1982/1. Reg 1610/96 of the European Parliament and of the Council concerning the creation of a supplementary protection certificate for plant protection products, OJ 1996, L198/30.

1. The trade mark shall not entitle the proprietor to prohibit its use in relation to goods which have been put on the market in The Community under the trade mark by the proprietor or with his consent.

2. Paragraph 1 shall not apply where there exist legitimate reasons for the proprietor to oppose further commercialisation of the goods, especially where the condition of the goods is changed or impaired after they have been put on the market.

In *Silhouette Internationale Schmied GmbH & Co. KC v Hartlauer Handellshaft mbh*,[48] elegant sun-glasses of an out of date model were sold by the holder of the trade mark in Sofia for sale in Bulgaria. The glasses were, however, found on sale in Austria and the holder sought an interim injunction. Under Austrian national law, there was a doctrine of international exhaustion so the mark was exhausted by the sale in Bulgaria outside the Community and an injunction would not be obtainable.

There had been much controversy about international exhaustion when the directive was being debated. So the directive, which represented a compromise, is not clear about it.

As the ECJ observed at paragraph 27, the doctrine of international exhaustion, adopted only in Sweden and Austria, would divide the common market, as goods sold outside the common market with the consent of the holder would be able to circulate in those two member states but not in the rest. So the ECJ interpreted the directive as precluding international exhaustion under national law. It did not consider whether it would have been desirable for the Council to have provided for such a doctrine, but held that it had not done so. Nor did it consider Article 81.

In *Javico*,[49] There were contractual restrictions forbidding a distributor in Eastern Europe selling trade marked products into the common market. The ECJ held that such a ban did not necessarily have the object or effect of restricting competition within the common market. The legal and economic context was important. Such a restraint might have an effect in the common market when the market was oligopolistic or where there was a significant difference in price between products inside and outside the common market. It was for the national court to decide the facts.

In *Davidoff (Zino) SA & A & G Imports Ltd.* (C–414/99) and *Levi Strauss & Co and another v Tesco*,[50] on a reference under Article 234, the ECJ ruled that consent to sale within the common market by an intermediary outside could not be implied:

> consent [to market the goods within the Community] must be so expressed that an intention to renounce [trade mark] rights is unequivocally demonstrated. (para 45)

Consequently an injunction could be obtained.

48   (C–355/96) [1998] ECR I–4799, paras 23–31.
49   (C–306/96), [1998] ECR I–1983, [1998] 5 CMLR 172, [1998] CEC 813.
50   (C–415/99) [2001] ECR 1–8691, [2002] 1. CMLR 1, [2002] CEC 154; comment by Thomas Heide, 'Trade Marks and Competition Law after *Davidoff*,' [2003] *European Intellectual Property Review*, 163.

The ECJ did not consider Article 81. On its ruling on free movement, however, it is not necessary to insert a bans on marketing within the common market, although it might be easier to sue the dealer for breach of contract in relation to a large batch of items rather than claim trademark rights once the goods had been distributed around the common market.

Davidoff, however, created problems relating to the burden of proof. In *Van Doren v Lifestyle*,[51] the parallel trader could not prove that the items he had bought in the common market had been sold there with the consent of the American brand owner. According to the German law applicable, the burden of proof was on it. It did not know where its supplier had obtained the goods, and even if it had, disclosing their provenance would have probably caused the supply to dry up. In its preliminary ruling, the ECJ accepted that according to the general rule, the burden of proof is a question of procedural law to be determined by national law. At paragraphs 37 and 38, it added, however, that the German rule of evidence would require qualification as a result of the principle of free movement of goods, in particular if it allowed the holder to partition national markets and ruled that if the parallel trader could establish a real risk of market partitioning if he bore the burden of proof as to where the goods were first placed on the market with the holder's consent, the burden should shift to the holder.

In *Micro Leader Business*, certain French language software was cheaper in Canada than in France. The Commission dismissed a complaint by Micro Leader Business that charging a higher price in France while relying on its copyright to exclude imports amounted to the abuse of a dominant position. The CFI[52] confirmed (paragraphs 27–39) that the sale into Canada did not exhaust the copyright and that there was no evidence that the holder had discouraged its Canadian distributor from exporting to France.

It added, at paragraph 34, that even if the holder had discouraged such trade into the common market, any agreement or concerted practice would have done no more than enforce the holder's copyright, and unilateral action is not contrary to Article 81. The language is not clear, but suggests that such an agreement would not have had any appreciable effects within the common market. If followed by the ECJ in subsequent cases this could be very helpful to those seeking to charge higher prices within the common market. The contractual restriction may be relied upon at the earlier stage when a batch of products has not been divided.

The complaint also alleged that the higher price in France amounted to the abuse of a dominant position. The Commission dismissed this complaint on the grounds that the complainant had not brought sufficient evidence, nor had it proposed a remedy. The CFI observed that the higher price seemed to show discrimination contrary to Article 82(c). The holder had issued bulletins

---

51 C–240/00, judgment 8 April 2003.
52 T–198/98, [1999] ECR II–3989.

to its dealers in France that suggested that the imported products were in direct competition with those sold in France. Enforcement of intellectual property rights may, in exceptional cases, amount to an infringement of Article 86.[53] So the Commission was wrong to dismiss the complaint under Article 82 without further investigation.

Conditions outside the common market may be very different from those within. A firm that has spent large sums on R & D may want to sell the results at lower prices in some countries and this make sense as long as it covers its incremental costs. There are moves to persuade the pharmaceutical companies to make cures or paliatives for AIDS available in Africa at prices that would not enable them to recover much of their investment in R & D.

Would a patent holder infringe Article 82 if it relied on its unexhausted patents to keep out of Europe the drugs sold cheaply in undeveloped countries?[54] Everyone is better off if a monopolist engages in Ramsey pricing (5.2.2 above). Unless the cheaper medicines can be kept out of the most developed countries, they are unlikely to be made available at prices that even the richer people in the less developed world can afford. The DG Competition shows no signs of being convinced that Ramsey pricing is desirable or even permissible. On the other hand, it can be argued that conditions in the less developed countries are very different from those in Europe, when such medicines would mostly be paid for out of tax revenue.

10.7 Conclusion

In its determination to prevent limited national intellectual property rights dividing the common market, the Court developed the doctrine of exhaustion in the 1970s and applied it even when the right holder had not been able to earn a monopoly profit because of national state measures. Its judgments during the following decade stressed the importance of not undermining the specific function of intellectual property rights, and demonstrated an awareness that rewards and incentives are important, but the Court has become more loath to reverse its earlier judgments and confirmed *Merck v Stephar*.[55]

Since intellectual property rights may impede inter-state trade where the right holder in the country of import had no rights in the country of export and the protected product was put on that market by a third party without consent, the Council has been adopting directives to ensure that differences in the law should not divide the common market. The process has been a gradual one and has usually led to greater protection than under former national law.

53   *Magill, Radio Telefis Eireann and Others v Commission* (C–241 & 242/91P), [1995] ECR I–743.
54   See Eleanor Fox 'Parallel Imports, and the Intrabrand/interbrand Competition Paradigm and the Hidden Gap between IP Law and Antitrust', (2002) 25 *Fordham International Law Journal*, 982.
55   (187/80), [1981] ECR 2063, (10.4.5 above).

I am concerned that the life of copyright has been extended to life plus 70 years, whether or not that extra protection is required to induce the creation of artistic and useful work, solely to limit restraints on inter-state trade. One of the most important functions of the Commissioner responsible for competition should be advocacy against the creation of entry barriers by Council directives.

Problems remain where protection is greater in the country of import than in that of export, and right holders will have to consider carefully before themselves marketing the goods where the protection is weak, for instance because of maximum price controls. Where large price differences are caused by governmental measures, this may divide the common market far more severely than would the exercise of patents.

It seems that any restrictions on inter-state trade will have to be imposed by contract, and be subject to the application of Articles 81 and 82. Until 2004, when such an agreement was notified, fines could not be imposed for a period before the Commission takes a decision, but now that notification is over, this safe haven has disappeared (7.2 above). Despite paragraphs 21–25 of the judgment in *Centrafarm v Sterling*,[56] the Commission has been hostile towards restraints on exports or on parallel trade but some limited protection is permitted by the group exemptions for exclusive distribution and technology transfer. Another possibility is to ration the dealers in the Member States where prices are low, being careful not to ask them not to sell in other Member States (*Bayer*,[57] 2.2.2.1 above).

Charging what the market will bear is an efficient way of recovering overhead costs, (5.2.2 above) but requires some barrier to prevent arbitrage. The Community institutions have refused to consider justifications, but assume that restrictions on trade between Member States disintegrate the market. They may do so, but not always.

It seems to me anomalous that the Council, on a proposal from the Commission, should be increasing intellectual property protection when the ECJ is reducing it through the doctrine of exhaustion even when the market is distorted by state measures, such as price control, or where there are no rights in the country of export. The Commission remains hostile to export bans and deterrents that might confine government distortions to the member state that creates it.

10.8 Bibliography

Charles Baden Fuller, 'Price Variations—the Distillers Case and Article 85 EEC' [1979] *International and Comparative Law Quarterly* 128.

——, 'Economic Issues Relating to Property Rights in Trademarks: Export Bans, Differential Pricing, Restrictions on Resale and Repackaging' (1981) 6 *European Law Review*, 162.

56   (15/74) [1974] ECR 1147, (10.4.1 above).
57   C2 & 3/01, *Bundesverband der Arzneimittel-Importeure eV and Commission v Bayer* (C–2 & 3/01P) 6 January 2004, [2004] 4 CMLR 653.

Ivo Van Bael, 'Heretical Reflections on the Basic Dogma of EEC Antitrust: Single Market Integration, (1980) 10 *RSDIC*, 39.

W R Cornish, *Intellectual Property: Patents, Copyright, Trade Marks & Allied Rights* 5th edn, (London, Sweet & Maxwell, 2003), See, especially, chapters 3.4—'Justifying the Patent System' and 7.3—'Exhaustion in the Common Market'.)

——,'The definitional stop aids the flow of patented goods' [1975] *Journal of Business Law*, 50.

Paul Demaret, (see main bibliography).

Georges Friden, 'Recent Developments in EEC. Intellectual Property Law: The Distinction between Existence and Exercise Revisited' (1989) 26 *CML Rev*, 193.

Laurence W Gormley, *Prohibiting Restrictions of Trade within the EEC: The Theory and Applications of Articles 30-36 of the EEC Treaty* (Elsevier Science, 1985).

Hugh Hansen (ed), *International Intellectual Property Law and Policy*, (New Jersey, Juris Publishing Inc), annual since 1996, the proceedings of the intensive annual conference held at Fordham Law School the week after Easter.

René Joliet, 'Patented Articles and the Free Movement of Goods within the EEC' [1975] *Current Legal Problems*, 15.

——, 'Trademark Licensing Agreements under the EEC law of Competition' (1983) 5 *North Western University Journal of International Law and Business*, 755.

——, 'Territorial and Exclusive Trademark Licensing under the EEC Law of Competition' [1984] *IIC*, 21.

David T Keeling, *Intellectual Property Rights in EU law: Vol 1—Free Movement and Competition Law,* (Oxford, OUP, 2003).

Valentine Korah, 'Dividing the Common Market through National Industrial Property Rights' (1972) 35 *Modern Law Review*, 634.

——,'National Patents and the Free Movement of Goods' (1975) 38 *Modern Law Review*, 333.

Derek Ridyard and David Lewis, 'Parallel Trade in Patented Medicines—Economics in Defence of Market Segmentation,' [1998] *Int TLR* 14.

Andreas Reindl, [1998] 'Emerging Conflict of Laws issues on the Global Information Structure,' *International Intellectual Property Law & Policy*, vol 5 (New Jersey, Juris Publishing, 2000).

Warwick A Rothnie, *Parallel Trade* (London, Sweet & Maxwell, 1993).

—— 'Hag II': Putting the Common Origin Doctrine to Sleep' [1991] *European Intellectual Property Review*, 24.

Nicholas Shae, 'Parallel Importers' Use of Trade Marks: The Liabilities,' [1997] *European Intellectual Property Review,* 103.

Concepión Fernández Vicién, 'Why Parallel Imports of Pharmaceutical Products Should be Forbidden' [1996] *European Competition Law Review,* 219.

Denis F Waelbroeck, 'Les Conventions de Délimitation des Marques Face au Droit Communautaire' [1985] *Cahiers de Droit Européen*, 402.

11. Licences of Industrial and Commercial Property Rights

11.1 Introduction: rationale for the grant of patent protection

As explained at the beginning of chapter 10, under national law a patent confers the exclusive right to prevent others from exploiting an invention within its territory. Often innovating firms obtain patents, sometimes called 'parallel patents,' in many countries. These may or may not confer a monopoly. The protected product may meet acute competition from substitutes, or be capable of being produced by a process that does not infringe, in which event the patent may provide little or no market power. Where there are no substitutes, however, and the exclusive right operates as an entry barrier, a patent may confer significant market power.

A patent does not confer any right to use an invention otherwise illegal. It enables the holder to restrain others from using it. The holder of an improvement patent may not be entitled to exploit it at all unless the holder of the basic patent grants it a licence, but the improvement patent may enable the holder to negotiate such a licence in return for a cross licence under the improvement patent.

Patents are based on a competitive philosophy: they may encourage investment in research into kinds of innovation that are easily copied and which might otherwise not be worthwhile for any individual firm. Perceived *ex post*, when the investment in innovation has been successful, valuable patents may be perceived as barriers to entry. Perceived *ex ante*, from the time when the future holder decides whether to commit resources to innovation, however, the hope of obtaining a patent may be necessary.

Common lawyers tend to stress that patents operate as incentives. Civil lawyers emphasise that patents are the reward for creative effort. A third rationale is that to obtain a patent, the inventor has to disclose secret know-how which may legally be used for research purposes even during the life of the patent. The patent may be perceived as the price of disclosure. Without a patent system, more know-how might remain secret indefinitely. Fourthly, the exclusive right makes it easier for inventors to negotiate licences—once they have applied for a patent, they can disclose the invention to potential licensees without fear of plagiarism

The holder of a patent is called the patentee. It may decide not to exploit the invention itself, but to license someone else to do so. An individual inventor can rarely raise the capital to finance the development of his ideas and set up production. In *Velcro/Aplix*,[1] the inventor's company did not start itself to manufacture until the basic patents had expired, presumably because it needed to accumulate licence fees to pay off its debts and finance a factory.

1   [1985] 4 CMLR 157.

A licence merely permits the licensee to do something that would otherwise be unlawful, so clearly does not infringe Article 81(1) unless it is coupled with other obligations that have the object or effect of restricting competition in some way. In the absence of an agreement or concerted practice, it is not contrary to Article 81 to refuse to grant a licence.

Nevertheless, in *AEG*,[2] the Court stated that *tacit* collusion with authorised dealers to protect them from dealers operating on low margins might infringe Article 81(1). In that case, there seems to have been sufficient evidence of actual collusion mentioned in the Commission's decision, but the reference to tacit collusion is worrying. In what circumstances a refusal by a dominant firm to grant a licence infringes Article 82 is an interesting question, considered at 5.2.5–5.2.5.5 above.

Most systems of antitrust law have had difficulty in distinguishing permissible clauses from those that confer undue protection. In 1995, the Department of Justice and Federal Trade Commission in the United States took the view that a patentee is entitled to a property right granted by Congress and that any monopoly power conferred by the exclusive right provides the incentive for the innovative effort required to create the property.[3] Antitrust authorities should intervene only when agreements increased that market power. For instance, agreements between competitors to pool their patents are suspect unless justified by blocking patents. This is accepted by the Commission in Guideline 17 of the Commission's notice but ignored in later guidelines (11.6 below).[4]

It is arguable, moreover, that no public control is needed when the parties could not have competed without the agreement, since the patentee has an interest in its licensees being subject to competition and earning the minimum margin. The licensor has no incentive to share any market power it may enjoy with its licensee. It is likely to protect each licensee from the others only in so far as it thinks necessary to induce them to accept the risks of investing in plant, development and establishing a market (8.1.2 above). It is more likely to get the balance right than is an official enforcing the law since it is in the business and the decision will affect its profits.

This argument, however, has not been accepted in the Community where the fear of isolating national markets is strong. Moreover, it is not always easy to tell whether the licensee would have been likely to enter the market independently or with less protection. Agreements restricting competition between actual or potential competitors may require control.

---

2   (107/82) [1983] ECR 3151, para 38, (2.2.2.1, above).
3   *Antitrust Guidelines for the Licensing of Intellectual Property*, cited in bibliography at 11.9 below, para 2.0.
4   Commission Notice: Guidelines on the application of Article 81 of the EC Treaty to technology transfer agreements , OJ 2004, C101/2.

11.2 The Commission's view of exclusive licences

By 1972, the Commission had taken the view that, subject to a *de minimis* rule of unclear ambit, any significant licence other than a non-exclusive one for the whole common market was caught by the prohibition of Article 81(1). This was not always so. In 1962, the Commission published a notice on patent licences,[5] since withdrawn, in which it accepted that where a licence for part of a Member State was granted, it was the patent that restrained sales in the other parts. Consequently, there was little need for no poaching clauses.

Many people read the notice carelessly and assumed that a licence limited to a whole Member State did not restrict competition, and that one could rely on another national patent to keep the product out of the second Member State. It has, however, been clear at least since *Centrafarm v Sterling*[6] that a sale by a holder or his licensee in one member state exhausts the patent throughout the common market by virtue of the rules for the free movement of goods. So a customer anywhere in the common market cannot be restrained from trading across frontiers. The grant of a licence, however, does not exhaust the right (10.4.1 above.)

As a result of its experience with exclusive dealing agreements, the Commission took the view in 1972 that, subject to a *de minimis* threshold, granting an exclusive territory infringes Article 81(1) and requires exemption, even if it were necessary to persuade the licensee to take a licence and commit itself to tooling up and developing a market for the product.

In *Davidson Rubber*,[7] three licensees were each allocated an exclusive manufacturing and sales territory, one in France, one in Germany and one in Italy (multiple parallel licensing). The Commission found that this infringed Article 81(1), since it restrained Davidson from licensing, say, another manufacturer in France who might have exported to Germany. When the restrictions on sales to other Member States were abrogated by the parties and the exclusivity confined to manufacture, however, the Commission exempted the agreement on the ground that, without the protection of exclusive manufacture, the Davidson process would not have been available in Europe.

Perceived *ex post*, after the technology had been introduced and a market created, the European market would be more competitive if further licensees were permitted in the territory. Perceived *ex ante*, however, this was not the case: when considering Article 81(3) the Commission accepted that without the exclusive territories the Davidson process would not have been made available by third parties in Europe, presumably because no licensee would have invested in tooling up and making a market without protection from free riders.

---

5   JO 1962, C139/2922.
6   (15/74) [1974] ECR 1147, (10.4.1, above).
7   [1972] CMLR D52 (paras 39 and 40).

It is difficult to reconcile the Commission's view that a restriction without which the process would not have been introduced in Europe infringed Article 81(1) with the Court's ruling in *Société La Technique Minière*[8] and later judgments that Article 81 is infringed only where competition that could have taken place is restricted (8.1.2, above, and 11.3 and 11.5.3.1, below).

Nevertheless, in its later decisions on know-how licences granted shortly before adoption of the group exemption in 1988, the Commission seems to have accepted that exclusive licences, even if 'open,'[9] always infringe Article 81(1), unless they are *de minimis*.

The Commission condemned and refused to exempt manufacturing exclusivity for the first time in *AOIP v Beyrard*.[10] In *Bronbemaling v Heidemaatschappij*,[11] it adopted a decision under regulation 17, Article 15(6), terminating the freedom from fines obtained by notification (a procedure no longer possible now that notification has been abrogated) when proceedings in the patent office to oppose the grant of a patent were compromised by the grant of licences with an element of exclusivity. These licences, however, were granted to competitors. So the relationship was horizontal.

The Commission exempted exclusive territories in several individual decisions, although it would have been arguable in a national court that such an agreement was not caught by Article 81(1) and the court should enforce the provisions without waiting for the Commission to grant an exemption.

11.3 The Court's view of exclusive licences

In contrast to the Commission's practice, the ECJ held in the *Maize Seed* case, *Nungesser v Commission*,[12] that an 'open exclusive licence' is not in itself contrary to Article 81(1). INRA, a research institute financed by the French Minister of Agriculture, developed a commercially important F1 hybrid maize seed that could be grown in the colder climate of Northern Europe. For a few years the variety was a great success, but was finally superseded by other varieties. INRA was not permitted by French law to exploit its discoveries commercially, so it licensed various farmers in France to grow certified seed to be placed on the market.

To exploit the German market, INRA made contracts in 1960 and 1965 with Eisele and later his firm, Nungesser, enabling Eisele to acquire the plant breeders' rights in the Federal Republic of Germany. It promised him that it would try to prevent the seed grown in France from being exported to Germany, save to Nungesser, and there were various other restrictions

---

8   (56/65) [1966] ECR 235, p 250.
9   Contrast *Nungesser*, (11.3 below).
10   [1976] 1 CMLR D14. The parties were in dispute, so there was no question of altering the provisions of which the Commission disapproved.
11   [1975] 2 CMLR D67.
12   (258/78) [1982] ECR 2015, paras 56–67.

condemned by the Commission, such as minimum prices to be charged by Nungesser on the German market and an obligation to take two-thirds of its requirements of basic seed from the French growers.

Nungesser arranged for the seeds to be grown and tested in Germany, and approved by a public authority for general sale. By 1972, the variety was already being superseded in France, and two dealers in Germany bought surplus quantities of certified seed from dealers in France. Long before *Centrafarm v Sterling*[13] was decided, Eisele persuaded a German court to restrain one of them from doing so, although it would now appear that any intellectual property rights must have been exhausted by the French grower's sale of the certified seed to a dealer.

With the advantage of hindsight, it might have been better had Eisele sued for unfair competition, on the ground that the imported seed was over two years old. That would reduce its germinating capacity considerably and harm the reputation of the INRA mark under which Nungesser was selling the newer seed.

The Commission condemned the agreement without analysing the transaction to ascertain whether INRA could have arranged for the sale of its seed in Germany without granting what the Commission and Court treated as an exclusive licence. The ECJ, however, distinguished an open exclusive licence from one where absolute territorial protection is conferred. An 'open exclusive licence' is a novel term coined by the Court. It means an agreement:

> 53. . . . whereby the owner merely undertakes not to grant other licences in respect of the same territory and not to compete himself with the licensee in that territory.

The Court quashed the decision in so far as it condemned:

> an obligation upon INRA or those deriving rights through INRA to refrain from having the relevant seeds produced or sold by other licensees in Germany, and an obligation upon INRA or those deriving rights through INRA to refrain from producing or selling the relevant seeds in Germany themselves.

It is not clear whether a licence remains open if the licensee in one territory is restrained from selling in another—paragraph 53 of the judgment is inconsistent on that point. The Commission held in *Boussois/Interpane*[14] that it does not. It is clear that intellectual property rights are exhausted only when the licensee sells the protected goods within the terms of the licence, and not by the grant of the licence itself (10.4.1 above).

To a significant extent the ECJ expressly accepted the sunk cost argument in relation to both parties when considering Article 81(1). First, at ground 56, it referred to INRA's years of research and experimentation to justify the exclusivity. Presumably, a firm in the private sector would invest more in

---

13   (15/74) [1974] ECR 1147, (10.4.1 above).
14   [1988] 4 CMLR 124, para 16a.

innovation if it expected to be able to earn the higher royalties to be obtained from an exclusive licence. The ECJ added:

> 57. In fact, in the case of a licence of breeders' rights over hybrid maize seeds newly developed in one Member State, an undertaking established in another Member State which was not certain that it would not encounter competition from other licensees for the territory granted to it, or from the owner of the right himself, might be deterred from accepting the risk of cultivating and marketing that product; such a result would be damaging to the dissemination of a new technology and would prejudice competition in the Community between the new product and similar existing products.

> 58. Having regard to the specific nature of the products in question, the Court concludes that, in a case such as the present, the grant of an open exclusive licence, that is to say, a licence which does not affect the position of third parties such as parallel importers and licensees for other territories, is not in itself incompatible with Article 81(1) of the Treaty.

Despite the Court's concern in relation to Article 81(1) that the Commission should investigate the effects of exclusivity and consider whether INRA's varieties could have been sold in the Federal Republic without protection from the French licensees, it was much more rigid when discussing the possibility of exemption. INRA had not granted open exclusivity; it had tried to prevent the French licensees from exporting, and Eisele had succeeded in restraining parallel imports by two dealers. Without giving reasons, the Court concluded that:

> 77. As it is a question of seeds intended to be used by a large number of farmers for the production of maize, which is an important product for human and animal foodstuffs, absolute territorial protection manifestly goes beyond what is indispensable for the improvement of production or distribution or the promotion of technical progress. . . .

It is anomalous that the Community Court adopted a *per se* rule for an important licence under Article 81(3), while not doing so in relation to Article 81(1). In *Consten and Grundig v Commission*,[15] the Community Court had stressed the complex economic appraisal needed in deciding whether to grant an exemption, which necessitates a wide discretionary power being exercised by the Commission.

In both *Consten & Grundig*[16] and *Nungesser*,[17] however, the Court adopted a *per se* rule against absolute territorial protection.[18] It did not articulate its reasons. The rule is arbitrary in its application: open exclusivity gives considerable protection from parallel imports of goods of low value in relation to the cost of freight, but virtually no protection for more valuable products.

15   (56 & 58/64) [1966] ECR 299, 347, (2.4.1 above).
16   (56 & 58/64), [1966] ECR 299.
17   (258/78), [1982] ECR 2015.
18   Compare the ECJ in *Miller International Schallplatten GmbH v Commission* (19/77), [1978] ECR 131, (7.6 above).

In its decisions made before adopting a block exemption for know-how, the Commission distinguished the concept of 'open exclusivity' on the ground that the product was not new, even when it was better than anything else on the market.[19] Nevertheless, a national court should follow the Court's precedents rather than those of the Commission.

The Court went much further in relation to a licence of performing rights in *Coditel II*.[20] It ruled that even absolute territorial protection may not infringe Article 81(1) in the light of the commercial practice in the particular industry and the need for a film producer to obtain an adequate return. The Court went further still in relation to plant breeders' rights in basic seed in *Erauw-Jacquéry*.[21] It referred to *Nungesser* and the investment needed to develop basic seed. It should be remembered that plant breeders' rights remain valid only so long as the variety is distinct, uniform, stable and useful. The Court ruled that the holder of the plant breeders' rights that result:

> must be allowed to protect himself against improper handling of those varieties of seeds. To that end the breeder must have the right to reserve propagation for the propagating establishments chosen by him as licensees. To that extent the clause prohibiting the licensee from selling and exporting basic seeds does not come within the prohibition laid down by Article 81(1) of the Treaty.

In *Erauw-Jacquéry*, the Court distinguished the basic seed supplied to propagators from the certified seed sold to farmers. Even absolute territorial protection for the basic seed sent to propagating establishments for multiplication before sale to farmers was cleared, whereas in *Nungesser* such a clause in relation to certified seed was held to go too far even for an exemption.

The Court's remarks in *Erauw-Jacquéry* were confined to basic seed, but the reference to investment is of wide application, so the judgment might be extended to other protected products that need careful handling, such as software. The Commission, however, is construing the precedent more narrowly to relate only to basic and certified seed. Moreover, once a plant variety ceases to be distinct, uniform and stable, the intellectual property right is lost. This is not true of most other kinds of intellectual property right.

11.4 The former group exemptions for patent, know-how and mixed licences

A group exemption for exclusive and other pure patent or mixed patent and know-how licences was eventually adopted by the Commission in 1984.[22] After being renewed retroactively twice, it expired at the end of 1996. In 1989

19   *Rich Products/Jus-Rol*, [1981] 4 CMLR 527. In *Nungesser*, the ECJ rejected the Commission's view that INRA maize seed was not new, because the variety was better than what preceded it. See my monograph on technology transfer (cited in the bibliography at 11.9 below) at pp 47–48.
20   (262/81) [1982] ECR 3381, paras 15–20.
21   *Erauw-Jacquéry (Louis) v La Hesbignonne* (27/87) [1988] 4 CMLR 576.
22   Reg 2349/84 OJ 1984, L219/15, corrections OJ 1985, C113/34, [1984] 2 CLE 389.

another group exemption for pure know-how, or mixed patent and know-how licences that permitted rather more provisions was adopted.[23] The third group exemption, that for technology transfer agreements[24] expired at the end of April 2004. They will not be analysed here, but licences exempted by the last group exemption continue to be exempt under the new technology transfer regulation for eighteen months. Agreements made after 1 May 2004 will be group exempted only if they qualify under the new criteria.

11.5 The group exemption for technology transfer—Regulation 772/04[25]

In April 2004, the Commission adopted the fourth group exemption for technology transfer and adopted guidelines both on the Regulation and on agreements outside its scope. Sometimes these go further that the Regulation. Sometimes they even conflict with it. Now that the Commission is unlikely to deal with many individual technology-licensing agreements the question arises how far they will be observed by NCAs and courts—the institutions most likely to deal with licensing agreements. The Commission will liaise with the NCAs through the network (7.3.3 above), so many NCAs may follow them, at least where they are not inconsistent with the Regulation. National courts may refer questions of construction to the ECJ. Courts are less likely than NCAs to follow the guidelines (2.4.9 above). Doubtless, differences will develop. The structure of the new Regulation is similar to that for vertical distribution agreements (9.6 above). Article 2 exempts:

> technology transfer agreements entered into between two undertakings permitting the production of contract products.

They are exempt as long as the last intellectual property right has not expired and the know-how remains confidential. The simplicity is only apparent. There are complex definitions in Article 1 to which we will return.

Article 3 provides ceilings of market share above which the exemption does not apply: 20% of the combined market share of the parties if they are competing undertakings and 30% each if they are not. Both the market for the products and the technology market are relevant, but potential competition is not relevant to the technology market. This makes the application of the Regulation more predictable, as almost anyone in an industry might be looked upon as a potential entrant. The Commission states at Guideline 131 that in the absence of hardcore restraints, it will rarely consider that Article 81 is infringed if there are at least four other undertakings independent of the parties that can be substituted for the licensed technology.

Article 4(1) contains the black list of hard-core restrictions that prevent the application of the exemption if the parties are competing undertakings, and

---

23   Reg 556/89, [1989] 4 CMLR 774.
24   Reg 240/96, [1996] 4 CMLR 405.
25   [2004] OJ 2004, L123/11.

Article 4(2) a list (adapted from Regulation 2790/99 exempting vertical distribution agreements (9.6.4–9.6.4.5 above)) of restrictions that prevent the application of the Regulation if the parties are not competing.

Article 5 lists provisions to which the exemption does not apply, although they are severable and do not prevent the Regulation applying to other provisions.

Articles 6 and 7 provide for withdrawal of the exemption.

11.5.1 *The exemption—Article 2*

The technology transfer agreements exempted by Article 2(1) of the Regulation are defined in Article 1(1):

> (b) "technology transfer agreement" means a patent licensing agreement, a know-how licensing agreement, a software copyright licensing agreement or a mixed patent, know-how or software copyright licensing agreement,

The coverage of this group exemption is wider than that of 1996 in that it embraces licences not only of patent and know-how but also of copyright in software and designs as well as mixed agreements. The definition of 'patent' in Article 1(1)(h) is broad. It covers, *inter alia*, applications for patents, plant breeders' certificates and designs. Designs were not previously covered. The Commission was advised that it did not have power to include more traditional kinds of copyright and it did not want to wait, probably for about two years, to obtain broader powers from the Council. It states [G 51] that as a general rule it will apply to them the principles set out in the Regulation and guidelines. This device for exceeding its powers is controversial. On the one hand it goes clearly beyond the Regulation, and even the Commission's power to regulate. The Commission is not likely to deal with many licences, but NCAs and national courts can now apply Article 81(3) and may follow the guideline without relying on the Regulation.

Not only licences, but also assignments are covered provided that some of the risk associated with exploitation remains with the assignor, for instance where royalties rather than a lump sum are payable.

Article 4(1)(b) continues:

> including any such agreement containing provisions which relate to the sale and purchase of products or which relate to the licensing of other intellectual property rights or the assignment of intellectual property rights, provided that those provisions do not constitute the primary object of the agreement and are directly related to the production of the contract products;

Provided the licensee is permitted to produce contract products, as required by Article 2(1), restraints on how it may buy or sell products, not only contract products, are also exempted: restrictions applying to purchases, sales or licences by the licensee or licensor are exempt. This accounts for Article 4(2), which lists as hardcore restraints between non-competing undertakings adapted from the hardcore list in the exemption for vertical distribution agreements. Restraints on licensing other intellectual property rights, such as trademarks, to third parties, are also exempt.

They are, however, exempt only if they are ancillary. They must not constitute the primary object of the agreement and must be directly related to the production of the contract products. This is the test of ancillary restraints now habitually given by the Commission and by the CFI in *Métropole Télévision (M6) v Commission II*[26] (2.4.5 above). I am not sure how strong the qualification 'directly related' is. It may be that if the relationship is close, an indirect relationship will qualify.

11.5.2   *Ceilings of market share—Article 3*

The group exemption does not apply if the market shares of the parties exceed the ceilings imposed by Article 3. Nevertheless, there is no presumption that their licences infringe Article 81(1). They are outside the safe harbour of the Regulation, that is all.

The ceilings of market share have been very controversial for two reasons. First, it is difficult to predict what market will be identified as relevant by a court or NCA in the future. In the case of medicines it will probably be all the drugs used for treating a particular ailment. In other industries the selection may be more difficult (4.3.1–4.3.1.6 above). For medicines, the alternative criterion of four independent poles of research (G 131) is likely to work well, as the long period needed for clinical trials enables us to know what new drugs are in the pipeline. They may work less well for other products, but it is the pharmaceutical companies who really need their patents and licences, because it is so easy to copy a medicine once the exact formulation is disclosed in accordance with safety rules.

The second objection is that the permissible market shares are low. Where R & D are expensive, they may be commercially worthwhile only if a large part of the market can be supplied. Consequently many technology markets are concentrated. The only possible licensors and licensees may have large market shares. Many fear that in the pharmaceutical industry these limitations to the safe harbour of the Regulation will cause firms to carry on their R & D and production outside Europe, supplying Europe by export. This may endanger many good quality jobs in the Common Market.

There are some provisions concerning the rules about market share in Article 8.

Article 10 provides for a very short transitional period. Agreements that came within the old group exemption before 21 May, 2004 will remain valid for 18 months after 1 May, those made after 30 April will enjoy no option for coming within Regulation 240/96. This left very little time for business to become familiar with the new regime and apply it to agreements being

26   (T–112/99), [2002] ECR II–2459.

negotiated. It may be particularly unfortunate for firms in the new Member States, who receive no transitional relief under the Act of Accession other than 6 months in which to bring their agreements within a group exemption.

11.5.2.1 *'Competing undertakings'—Article 1(1)(j)*—Until 2004, the Commission treated undertakings as competing once both parties are producing. This was to look *ex post*, after the technology has been successfully undertaken. Consequently, the lower market share was appropriate according to the version of the Regulation published for comment in October 2003. It is at the time the commitment is made to invest in it, however, that the American agencies decide whether parties are competing. When the intellectual property right is being licensed, the need to induce the investment in R & D is usually water under the bridge. So the main justification for restrictive terms has ceased to be relevant.

There is a new definition of 'competing undertakings,' however, in Article 1(1)(j). It describes undertakings as competing only if they could have done so in the absence of the licence without infringing the other's intellectual property rights. The result is that most licences will now be treated as vertical, subject to the higher ceiling of market share and to the less stringent list of hard-core restraints in Article 4(1)(2). The question is being raised whether this definition can be transposed to decisions under Article 81 or the group exemption for R & D, which decides whether undertakings are competing *ex post*. The Commission's notice on the application of Article 81(3)[26a] of the Treaty, (G 18) states that there are two questions to be answered when deciding whether an agreement infringes Article 81(1)—does it restrict actual or potential competition that would have existed without the agreement and does it restrict actual or potential competition that would have existed without the restriction. So it seems that the radical change in perception is general and not confined to licensing.

There are two markets to be considered when applying Articles 3 or 4. Potential competition is relevant to defining the product market: not only firms making close substitutes, but also firms that might be induced to do so if the price of the product were to rise by 5% or 10% and be expected to stay high. It is often difficult enough to know who are potential competitors on the product market. It is impossible on the technology market. So only actual competitors on the technology market are taken into account.

11.5.3 *Hard-core restraints—Articles 4(1) and (2)*

The first three black listed clauses are the classic cartel provisions, which most antitrust systems condemn between competitors: price fixing, limitation of output and the allocation of markets. A hard-core restraint is not only illegal

26a   OJ 2004, 101/96.

and void in itself, but it prevents the application of the block exemption to other provisions in the licence (2.4.2 above).

Article 4 now distinguishes between licences between competitors, which are dealt with by Article 4(1), and those between non-competitors. The new definition of competing undertakings in the absence of a licence (11.5.2.1 above), is very important, as most licences become horizontal when looked at *ex post*.

The introductory words to both Article 4(1) and (2) are very broad and blacklist agreements which 'directly or indirectly, in isolation or in combination with other factors under the control of the parties, have as their object' the classic cartel provisions.

11.5.3.1 *As between competing undertakings—Article 4(1) and Guidelines 77–95*—There are several exceptions to limitation of output or the allocation of markets where the licence is not reciprocal. Guideline 78 states that they are less likely to lead to the restriction of output.

'Reciprocal agreement' is defined in Article 1(1)(c) as the situation where A licences B and B licenses A, in the same or separate contracts, to exploit a patent, know-how or software copyright, where the technology is competing or can be used for competing products. A grant back clause does not make the licences reciprocal, but a licence may become reciprocal if at a later date a cross licence is granted.

11.5.3.1.1 *Price fixing*—The first black listed provision is terms 'that have as their object' the fixing of prices for products sold to third parties. It does not prevent the parties from agreeing the royalty to be paid for the licence, unless this varies according to whether suggested prices to third parties are complied with. Guideline 79 makes it clear how wide the introductory words are.

Where royalties are calculated on the basis of all product sales whether or not the licensed technology is used, the agreement is caught by Article 4(1)(a) and (d). It raises the cost of making competing products and discourages the licensee from using its own technology or that of someone else. Nevertheless, such an agreement might merit the individual application of Article 81(3), for instance when there is no available method of monitoring use (Gs 81, 95).

11.5.3.1.2 *Output limitation*—Limitations of output are forbidden only if the restriction is reciprocal and, even then, not if it is imposed in relation to the licensed product on only one licensee. One way restrictions are less likely to result in lower output. Remember the wide introductory words.

11.5.3.1.3 *Market allocation*—The allocation of markets or customers excludes the agreement from the Regulation, irrespective of whether the licensee is free to use its own technology. The Commission is concerned by the cost of setting up separate production facilities for different areas or customers.

To this item there are many exceptions where the licence is not reciprocal. For instance, under Article 4(1)(c)(ii) the holder may grant an exclusive licence or a licence for a particular field of use or product. This may give the licensee an incentive to invest. For this reason too, Article 4(1)(c)(iv) allows non-reciprocal agreement not to sell actively or passively into the exclusive territory or customer group reserved for the other party.

11.5.3.1.4 *Restriction on using others' technology*—A restriction on the licensee using its own technology is treated as hard-core. Both parties must be free to carry on their own R & D, whether or not in the field covered by the licence. They may, however, agree to provide each other with future improvements. They may restrict R & D with third parties when necessary to preserve the secrecy of know-how, but not to ensure that the technology is not stultified. If a Chinese wall will preserve confidentiality, the exemption will not apply if collaborative R & D is restricted (Gs 95 and 95).

11.5.3.2 As between non-competing undertakings—The black list of Article 4(1) does not apply when the parties are not competing undertakings. Article 1(1)(b) provides that a technology transfer agreement may include provisions relating to the sale or purchase of products (11.5.1 above). The contracts of sale or purchase may come within the group exemption for vertical distribution agreements, but the limitation by one party to a licence of the other's sales or purchases are exempted under this Regulation. In Article 4(2), therefore, the Commission has adapted the black list from the vertical restraints regulation (9.6.4–9.6.4.5) with some changes.

As in the regulation for vertical restraints, the introductory words are very broad:

> agreements which, directly or indirectly, in isolation or in combination with other factors under the control of the parties, have as their object:

11.5.3.2.1 *Price restrictions*—The first item, Article 4(2)(a), is similar to that for vertical agreements (9.6.4.1 above), a restriction on a party's ability to determine its prices when selling products to third parties. Again maximum prices are permitted, as are recommended prices, provided that they do not amount to fixed or minimum prices as a result of pressure or incentives by the parties.

11.5.3.2.2 *Restrictions on passive sales*—Article 4(2)(b) blacklists territorial restrictions on the licensee making passive sales but not the licensor. The licensee may not be restrained from responding to unsolicited orders. Whereas in the distribution regulation all territorial restrictions are black listed and only a few restrictions on active sales allowed (9.6.4.2 above), the technology transfer regulation blacklists restrictions only on passive sales, exempting all restraints on active sales, and some restrictions on passive sales. The exemption of restrictions on active sales in licences is justified by the greater sunk costs normally accepted by a licensee (G 99) which has to establish a production line as well as a market. 'Passive sales' are not defined in the Regulation or guidelines, but are widely described in the guidelines on vertical agreements[27] to exclude an advertisement on the internet with various languages on which to click. The licensor may accept restrictions on active or passive sales until one of the parties reaches the market share ceiling of 30%.

The first two exceptions to the black listed item are:

(i) the restriction of passive sales into an exclusive territory or to an exclusive customer group reserved for the licensor;

(ii) the restriction of passive sales into an exclusive territory or to an exclusive customer group allocated by the licensor to another licensee during the first two years that this other licensee is selling the contract products in that territory;

So, the licensor may protect its own exclusive territory or customer group from even passive sales, or that of another licensee for two years from the time when the licensee protected first put the product on the market. Probably it can protect the territory of an exclusive distributor. If no licence has been granted for the territory protected, it may be reserved for the licensor. It is anomalous that a licensee can be kept out of the territory of a distributor indefinitely, but that a licensee can be protected only for two years after it starts to market. Moreover, under the vertical restraints regulation, a dealer cannot be kept from even actively selling into the exclusive territory allocated to a licensee. In principle, the free rider argument is stronger for licensees, since usually they have to set up a production line as well as develop a market. The Commission seems to assume that the holder will either license for the whole Common Market, or will produce enough itself to supply the whole. This is not always the case and with enlargement will become less common.

The next two items protect component makers who license their technology to makers of products that incorporate them:

(iii) the obligation to produce the contract products only for its own use provided that licensee is not restricted in selling the contract products actively and passively as spare parts for its own products;

(iv) the obligation to produce the contract products only for a particular customer, where the licence was granted in order to create an alternative source of supply for that customer;

Guidelines 102 and 103 explain: a component maker, C may want to persuade a vehicle maker, V, to use C's technology to make fuel injection pumps, an important component in diesel engines. It may want to restrain V from selling to Ci, a competitor of C.

---

27   OJ 2000, C291/1, Gs 50 and 51.

Component makers may spend a great deal on R & D, but not be able to charge enough on initial equipment to cover those costs. It is efficient for a component maker to supply as long as it covers its incremental costs. Manufacturers find the demand for a vehicle or diesel engine very sensitive to price, but the demand for spare parts far less sensitive. So, component makers often charge little for initial equipment but recover their overheads mainly from replacement parts. This cannot be done under the Regulation, as C may not restrict V from selling to repairers. The Commission has provided a compromise. If C licenses V cheaply, it can restrain it from selling to C but not from selling to the repairers. The Commission is hostile to discrimination even when it is justifiable and customers may all be better off (5.2.2 above).

The fourth item is similar except that C may license a third party to make the pumps for V. Under this provision, the licensee, but not V, may be restrained from selling to repairers.

The fifth item is like Article 4(b), second indent, of the vertical group exemption. It excepts a restriction on wholesalers supplying end users. This probably reflects the German view that it is unfair for a dealer to earn both a wholesale and a retail margin even if it performs both functions. There is, however, no need to take advantage of the freedom to impose the restraint.

The sixth item treats the ECJ's case law on selective distribution (9.4 above) as applying to licensing. The licensor may restrict its licensee from selling to dealers who have not been authorized. Article 4(2)(c), however, prevents a restriction on active or passive sales to end users by a licensee who also sell by retail.

Article 4(3) provides that if the parties to the licence were not competing when the licence was granted but later come to be 'competing undertakings' the licence is subject to the list in Article 4(2) rather than that in Article 4(1). This provision applies only to Article 4 and not to Article 3.

11.5.4 *Provisions that are not exempt*

Article 5 lists the restrictions that are not exempted by this Regulation, but which do not prevent the Regulation applying to other provisions. These restrictions may or may not infringe Article 81(1). If they do not, they create no problem. Article 5 is more important than the similar list of conditions in the vertical distribution regulation, because the provisions in this regulation are more likely to infringe Article 81(1).

The introductory words to each item are as broad as the introductory words of Article 4(1).

The first two items are:

(a) any direct or indirect obligation on the licensee to grant an exclusive licence to the licensor or to a third party designated by the licensor in respect of its own severable improvements to or its own new applications of the licensed technology

(b) any direct or indirect obligation on the licensee to assign, in whole or in part, to the licensor or to a third party designated by the licensor, rights to its own severable improvements to or its own new applications of the licensed technology [Gs 109–111].

The Commission has long been concerned about strong grant back clauses of intellectual property rights. It has permitted an obligation to feed or grant back non-exclusively when it is reciprocal, but not an exclusive licence or to assign the rights. Article 5(1)(a & b) is concerned with exclusive grant back or assignment to the licensor of severable improvements of the licensed technology or new applications. An improvement is severable if it can be exploited without infringing the licensed technology. Strong grant back clauses reduce the incentive for the licensee to innovate, since they restrain it from exploiting the results through licensing. Non-exclusive grant back is, however, permitted. If the licensor grants a package licence it has no chance of getting a technical lead over its licensees, and cannot afford to let them gain a lead on it. There would be less licensing if grant back obligations were not permitted.

The payment of compensation for grant back is not relevant under the Regulation, but Guideline 110 states that it may be relevant under Article 81, as it may increase the incentive to innovate.

The third item is:

(c) any direct or indirect obligation on the licensee not to challenge the validity of intellectual property rights which the licensor holds in the common market, without prejudice to the possibility to provide for termination of the technology transfer agreement in the event that the licensee challenges the validity of one or more of the licensed intellectual property rights.

The Commission has long objected to no challenge clauses on the ground that they stifle innovation. It has been hard to persuade it that without limitations on challenge, a smaller inventor cannot afford to licence a large, aggressive firm, often the only possibility for smaller innovators to exploit their innovations. The Commission has given way to the extent of permitting the possibility of withdrawing the licence once the intellectual property right is challenged. It permits, however, a clause protecting know-how because of its fragility.

The final provision is contained in Article 5(2). Under Article 4(1)(d) restrictions on the licensee using its own technology are blacklisted as between competitors. As between non-competitors they are merely not exempt, they do not prevent the regulation from applying to other provisions.

11.5.5 *Miscellaneous provisions* (Articles 6–11)

The provisions for withdrawal are the same as those for the vertical distribution block exemption (9.6.6 above). Article 6(1) provides that the Commission may withdraw the exemption when a technology transfer agreement has effects that do not merit exemption. An NCA may do so only where an agreement has effects incompatible with Article 81(3) in its territory or part of it, which has all the characteristics of a distinct geographic market. It may do so only in respect of that territory.

By virtue of Article 7, where parallel networks of similar technology transfer agreements cover more than half of the relevant market, the Commission may disapply the exemption by regulation.

The transitional provisions are very short—18 months for those agreements made before 1 May which qualified under Regulation 140/1996, nothing for agreements made after April. Some undertakings negotiate thousands of licences every year and 18 months is not very long. The revised licences will require negotiation, as important terms will need to be changed. With the Regulation becoming public only on 7 April, three weeks for lawyers to become familiar with it and for businessmen to negotiate within its terms is extremely short. Many licences granted by companies with important market shares will cease to be exempt. Lawyers and businessmen in the accession countries will be even more taxed. The only help they get under the Accession Agreement is six months to renegotiate agreements to come within the group exemption for maritime shipping to or from a Community port.[28]

11.6 Conclusion on the Regulation

The version published for comment was so much narrower than the US guidelines on technology licensing that there was substantial fear that R & D in Europe would be chilled. It would be commercially sensible to conduct the R & D and produce the products outside Europe and export to Europe. The version finally adopted has the same structure, but the redefinition of 'competing undertakings' in *ex ante* terms results in the higher ceiling of market share applying to most licences, and the black list of Article 4(1) not applying. This is a huge improvement, because under the earlier version, once both parties were producing the protected product, they would have been treated as competitors.

Nevertheless, the ceilings of market share are very low. Where R & D is expensive, markets tend to be concentrated. There may be no one to whom a licence can be granted that qualifies under the ceilings.

Application of the ceilings depends on uncertain definition of the relevant market. Clarity is important when large sums are being invested in R & D. The Commission seems to use the guidelines to amplify the Regulation. Will NCAs and courts follow the guidelines when they go further than the Regulation, such as applying the principles of the Regulation and guidelines to traditional copyright. It may be easier now that courts and NCAs have jurisdiction over Article 81(3).

---

28   The Treaty of Accession 2003, Annex II, 5 Competition Policy p 1101.

No challenge clauses are very important if a smaller licensor faces a larger licensee, financially more capable of managing patent litigation. Merely to determine the licence and put the licensee on risk for suit may not be sufficient protection.

There have been notable improvements since the draft published for comment, but I still fear some migration of R & D from Europe with the loss of high quality jobs.

11.7 Other guidelines

The antitrust authorities in the US accept that the holder of an intellectual property right should be able to earn any monopoly profit made possible by its rights and that agreements should be subject to antitrust only if they increase that market power. Intellectual property rights are given to induce investment and should not be undermined *ad hoc* by antitrust law. If the rights are too broad, they should be modified by legislation taken in response to thorough analysis of the likely effects of any proposed change, not by arbitrary decisions of antitrust authorities. This view has gained wide acceptance by economists.

The Commission's guidelines start by saying that:

> The aim of Article 81 as a whole is to protect competition on the market with a view to promoting consumer welfare and an efficient allocation of resources (G 5)

It adds at Guideline 7 that there is no inherent conflict between intellectual property rights and competition and says:

> 8. In the assessment of licence agreements under Article 81 it must be kept in mind that the creation of intellectual property rights often entails substantial investment and that it is often a risky endeavour. In order not to reduce dynamic competition and to maintain the incentive to innovate, the innovator must not be unduly restricted in the exploitation of intellectual property rights that turn out to be valuable. For these reasons the innovator should normally be free to seek compensation for successful projects that is sufficient to maintain investment incentives, taking failed projects into account. Technology licensing may also require the licensee to make significant sunk investments in the licensed technology and production assets necessary to exploit it. Article 81 cannot be applied without considering such *ex ante* investments made by the parties and the risks relating thereto. The risk facing the parties and the sunk investment that must be committed may thus lead to the agreement falling outside Article 81(1) or fulfilling the conditions of Article 81(3), as the case may be, for the period of time required to recoup the investment.

It adds that there is no presumption that licences outside the block exemption infringe Article 81(1), perhaps because the ceilings of market share are exceeded (Gs 9 and 130). Guideline 17 lists the ways in which licensing can increase competition: it may enable innovators to earn returns to cover at least part of the costs for R & D; it may lead to the dissemination of technologies and reduce the production costs of the licensee.

At Guideline 15 it lists the restrictive effects a licence may have, but balances the two only under Article 81(3) (G 146), where the onus is on those who claim that the licence does not infringe.

When it deals with licences outside the Regulation, the pro- and anti-competitive effects must be balanced. The Commission will look to the market affected by the agreement and it is not clear whether it will consider the disincentive that antitrust intervention will have on investment by others in other markets. It does take into account the initial sunk investments, the risk and the need to recoup (G147). Is this sufficient? Large firms may be able to produce within the corporate group and avoid making agreements that are subject to Article 81. Smaller firms that are unable to exploit the whole of the Common Market through sales may have to leave the technology idle in some areas, or sell their entire rights to larger firms, in which case restrictive clauses may not be necessary. These possibilities may be less valuable than granting, say, exclusive licences for parts of the Common Market.

When dealing with exclusive licences between non-competitors it places on the positive side the inducement the licensee needs to invest in the licensed technology (G 165), without considering the need to induce the investment in the original investment, or the investment of others in R & D.

The guidelines explain the Commission's attitude to many specific kinds of agreement.

11.8 Licences of other kinds of commercial and industrial property rights

The group exemption applies only to pure patent, know-how or copyright software licences and to mixed licences, not to traditional copyright or trade mark licences, unless these are ancillary to qualifying licensed technology (11.5.1 above). Pure trademark or traditional copyright licences clearly cannot qualify.

Regulation 2790/99[29] exempting vertical distribution agreements applies to:

> vertical agreements containing ancillary provisions on the assignment or use of intellectual property rights' (recital 3).

This is implemented by Article 2(3), which extends the exemption to:

> vertical agreements containing provisions which relate to the assignment to the buyer or use by the buyer of intellectual property rights, provided that those provisions do not constitute the primary object of such agreements and are directly related to the use, sale or resale of goods or services by the buyer or its customers.

The drafting, copied in Article 1(1)(b) of the technology transfer Regulation is unfortunate: is the primary object of an agreement to distribute disks i) the copyright licence or ii) the distribution of the physical disk?

---

29   OJ 1999, L336/21.

Maurits Dolmans has suggested[30] that software licences to end-users will not infringe Article 81(1) when the end-user operates in a different market from the holder. Where the licensee is to make modifications, however, it may well be a software company and at least a potential competitor, and there may be problems. These he analyses. Now that software copyright may come within the group exemption, this does not matter if the licence qualifies under the ceilings of market share.

It is not clear how far the technology transfer Regulation is a good guide to the Commission's thinking about other kinds of intellectual property rights apart from traditional copyright which Guideline 51 states will be treated according to the principles of the Regulation and guidelines. Nevertheless, the Commission frequently states how concerned it is to encourage R & D, and it must take care not to discourage it through unduly strict control over the transfer of technology.

There were a few informal decisions on copyright other than software reported many years ago in the *Competition Policy Reports* but the law and policy had not yet been worked out. Where licences of other intellectual property rights are granted, the best advice probably is to establish a file to show that only the minimum of restrictive provisions necessary to ensure that the transaction is viable has been accepted and hope that a national court or the Community Court might decide that the licence promotes rather than restricts competition, at least in the absence of significant market power.

11.9 The subcontracting notice

The Commission issued a notice on subcontracting[31] stating that in its view certain restrictions on the conduct of those to whom work is given out, and which are required to ensure the continued value of the technology and equipment, do not come within the prohibition of Article 81(1). This is an interesting and early example of the Commission adopting a flexible approach under Article 81(1). If the person requiring the work could not protect its technology, it would probably do it itself, and the result might be less competitive. The person undertaking the manufacture of the product is, therefore, not to be treated as an independent undertaking.

In so far as the technology or equipment is necessary to carry out the work under reasonable conditions, and the undertaking carrying it out could not reasonably obtain access to it otherwise, it may promise not to use it except for the purpose of carrying out the agreement, not to make it available to others, nor to supply the goods resulting from its use to anyone else. Either

---

30   Maurits Dolmans, 'Software Licensing in Europe—Do we need a group exemption?' in Hugh Hansen (ed), *I International Intellectual Property Law and Policy* (Juris Publishing and Sweet & Maxwell, 1996), 409.
31   OJ 1979, C1/2.

party may also agree not to disclose secret know-how, and the person doing the work may agree not to use secret manufacturing processes or know-how even after the agreement has expired, until they become public knowledge. It may also agree to a feed- and grant-back clause, which must usually be non-exclusive.

This notice has proved to be very useful. The official who drafted it listened carefully to comments from industry and it is not too tightly circumscribed to be of use. This is one of the few examples of the Commission using the adjective 'reasonable' rather than 'directly related.' The Commission was going to abrogate it, but the actual text of the guidelines leaves it alone.

11.10 Bibliography

Maurits Dolmans, 'Software Licensing in Europe—Do we need a group exemption?' in Hugh Hansen (ed), *I International Intellectual Property Law and Policy* (Juris Publishing and Sweet & Maxwell, 1996), 409.

Eleanor Fox, 'Maize Seed: A Comparative Comment', Chap 6 of Barry Hawk (ed) [1982] *Fordham Corporate Law Institute* 151.

Hugh Hansen (ed), vols. 1–7 *Fordham International Intellectual Property Law and Policy*, (Juris Publishing).

——, 12th *Annual Conference on International Intellectual Property Law and Policy*, CD and website www.fordhamipconference.com.

René Joliet, 'Territorial and Exclusive Trade Mark Licensing under EEC Law of Competition' [1984] *IIC* 21.

——, 'Trademark Licensing Agreements Under the EEC Law of Competition' (1983–1984) 5 *Northwestern University Journal of International Law and Business*, 757.

Christopher Kerse, 'Block Exemptions under Article 81(3): The Technology Transfer Regulation—Procedural Issues' (1996) 6 *European Competition Law Review*, 331.

Valentine Korah, *Technology Transfer and the EC Competition Rules* (Oxford, OUP, 1997).

——, 'Exclusive Licences of Patent and Plant Breeders' Rights under EEC Law after Maize Seed' (1983) XXVIII *Antitrust Bulletin*, 699.

——, 'The *Ladbroke* saga,' [1998] 19 *European Competition Law Review*, 169.

Robert C Lind, Charles River Associates, *Competition Policy Discussion Papers 8*, 'The European Commission's draft Technology Transfer Block Exemption Regulation and Guidelines: A significant departure from accepted competition policy principles,' for futher information contact JAzevedo@crai.co.uk.

US Department of Justice and Federal Trade Commission, *Antitrust Guidelines for the Licensing of Intellectual Property*, 6 April 1995, CCH, *Trade Regulation Report*, 13, 132, BNA ATRR 462.

James S Venit, 'Boussois/Interpane, the treatment of know-how licences under EEC Competition Law' [1987] *European Intellectual Property Review*, 164.

——, 'In the Wake of *Windsurfing*: Patent Licensing in the Common Market' in Barry Hawk (ed) [1986] *Fordham Corporate Law Institute*, chapter 22, from page 522.

M Waelbroeck 'The Effect of the Rome Treaty on the Exercise of National Industrial Property Rights' (1976) 21 *Antitrust Bulletin* 99.

12. Concentrations

12.1 Control under Article 81 and 82

In *Continental Can*,[1] the Community Court held that Article 82 prohibits the acquisition by a dominant firm of most of the shares in a potential competitor in the product dominated where this would virtually eliminate competition. The Commission intervened informally in a few large mergers after 1973, and either prevented or modified them,[2] but it took no formal decisions. The Commission believed that it lacked sufficient power to control anticompetitive mergers. It had no power to require firms to notify their mergers in advance. It was widely thought that it could not forbid mergers that created a dominant position. It could intervene only if at least one of the firms was already dominant and the merger strengthened its position. Nor was it clear whether Article 82 applied to small accretions of market power. The Commission even doubted whether it had power to grant interim relief to restrain a merger while it was considering the matter, and there were some doubts whether it had power to order divestiture after the event.[3]

For a decade and a half the Commission continued to propose a regulation to the Council requiring firms to notify significant mergers and giving it power to control them. Some of the Member States, however, were loath to relinquish their power to control mergers and the regulation made little progress, although the Commission continued to raise the thresholds of turnover above which it would have power to intervene.

In *BAT*,[4] the Court stated that the acquisition of a minority shareholding which led to control of a competitor might infringe Article 81 if the acquisition restricted competition. This caused great concern as it was not clear how much of the transaction might be void by virtue of Article 81(2). If the acquisition of the target company's assets was void and not merely voidable, title would not have passed and great confusion might ensue when its assets were sold by the new management to innocent third parties. There was also concern that under Article 81, any perceptible restriction of competition would be forbidden. The judgment left a very unsatisfactory situation and business came to accept the need for merger control at the Community level.

---

1   (6/72) [1973] ECR 215, (5.2 and 5.2.1 above).
2   These are summarised in the Commission's *Reports on Competition Policy* and by James Venit, 'The "Merger" Control Regulation: Europe Comes of Age or Caliban's Dinner' (1990) 27 *CML Rev*, 7.
3   Karen Banks, 'Mergers and Partial Mergers under EEC Law' in Barry Hawk (ed) [1987] *Fordham Corporate Law Institute*, chapter 17 and reply by V Korah, chapter 19, *ibid*.
4   The Commission's decision to close the file is described under the name of *Philip Morris* in its *XVIth Report on Competition Policy*, point 98. The ECJ confirmed that decision in *BAT and Reynolds v Commission* (142 & 156/84) [1987] ECR 4487, paras 37–39 and 64.

12.2 The successive merger regulations

On 21 December 1989, the Council eventually adopted a regulation[5] requiring the pre-notification to the Commission of concentrations within its scope—those where the parties' turnover exceeded the thresholds—and providing for possible prohibition by the Commission. This was amended in 1997 then repealed and replaced by Regulation 139/2004.[6]

There are five major advantages in devising transactions so as to qualify under the regulation. First, the substantive test (12.2.6 below) is far more favourable than that under Article 81(1). Secondly, the proceedings inevitably lead to a formal decision. So the need for self assessment and the ensuing uncertainty under Regulation 1/2003 are avoided. Thirdly, most transactions are cleared within 25 working days and most of those raising serious doubts within 90 working days, increased to 105 working days when commitment are offered more than 55 working days after proceedings were initiated. Fourthly, national authorities cannot apply national competition rules to mergers above the thresholds (12.2.10 below), and fifthly, the analysis of markets under the merger regulation has more often been realistic than under Article 81(1).

12.2.1 *Mergers and acquisitions of sole control*

Article 3(1) of Regulation 139/2004 provides that

a concentration shall be deemed to arise where a change of control on a lasting basis results from:

(a) the merger of two or more previously independent undertakings or parts of undertakings, or

(b) – the acquisition by one or more persons already controlling at least one undertaking, or by one or more undertakings, whether by purchase of securities or assets, by contract or by other means of direct or indirect control of the whole or parts of one or more other undertakings.

Few full mergers within the meaning of paragraph (a) occur. Most fall under paragraph (b). The definition is in terms of common control over two or more undertakings previously independent of each other, however acquired, whether by operation of law or through agreement. The Commission has clarified the definition in its notice on the concept of a concentration.[7] The acquisition of control over part of an undertaking may also constitute a merger. Control may be by law, as when all the shares are acquired, or *de*

---

5   Reg 4064/89, amended by Council Reg 1310/97 on merger control, OJ 1997, L180/1, [1997] 7 ECLR 451, [1997] 5 CMLR 387.

6   Reg 139/2004, OJ 2004, L24/1, [2004] 4 CMLR.

7   OJ 1998, C66/5.

facto. Usually some assets are acquired, but control may arise through long term supply or loan contracts (see point 9 of the notice).

A minority shareholder may also be deemed to have sole control on a *de facto* basis. In *Arjoumari-Prioux/Wiggins Teape Appleton*,[8] the Commission considered that the acquisition by Arjoumari of 39% of the shares in Wiggins Teape would enable it to exercise decisive influence over Wiggins Teape because the remainder of the latter's shares were widely dispersed. Contracts providing for an option resulting in the acquisition of control do not in themselves constitute concentrations; the concentration arises on the exercise of the option.[9]

12.2.2 *Concentrative joint ventures*

Article 3(4) of the merger regulation extends the concept of a concentration to include concentrative but not co-operative joint ventures.

4. The creation of a joint venture performing on a lasting basis all the functions of an autonomous economic entity shall constitute a concentration within the meaning of paragraph 1(b).

The Commission has long, although not entirely consistently, considered that concentrative joint ventures are not subject to Article 81.[10] It issued a *memorandum on concentrations* in 1966, after receiving the reports of two groups of professors. It thought that mergers often resulted in efficiencies and should be subject to a more lenient test than that under Article 81(1). It tried to explain what is meant by the term 'concentrative joint venture' in a notice,[11] but in practice it departed from the notice in its actual decisions, largely in order to find that more joint ventures are concentrative and came within the competence of the merger task force, which dealt more rapidly and more favourably with joint ventures than did the other directorates in the competition department.

Joint control exists where two or more undertakings or persons are able to exercise decisive influence over another undertaking. The acquisition of joint control includes changes from sole to joint control as well as a deadlock situation where more than one parent company is able to reject strategic decisions, so that they have to reach agreement. Joint control may exist through veto rights, by a sharing in voting rights or by *de facto* control.

For the joint venture to be concentrative it must 'perform on a lasting basis all the functions of an autonomous economic entity.' Under Article 3(2) of the original regulation, joint ventures were excluded where:

8   (IV/M 025) [1991] 4 CMLR 854.
9   *Elf/Retool* M 063, Merger Control Reporter, B 133, para 3.
10 See *SHV/Chevron* [1975] 1 CMLR D68, *Himont, XVIIth Report on Competition Policy*, point 69. Contrast *De Laval/Stork* [1977] 2 CMLR D69, paras 41–46.
11 Notice on the concept of concentrations between undertakings, OJ 1998, C66/5,[1998] 4 CMLR 586, paras 18–40.

they g[a]ve rise to coordination of the competitive behaviour of the parties amongst themselves or between them and the joint venture.

This provision was deleted in 1997. Coordination between the joint venture and one parent is now irrelevant, but where the merger has the object or effect of co-ordinating the competitive behaviour of the parents *inter se*, this may be investigated under Article 81 in the context of the merger investigation and within the same tight time limits under Article 2(4). This has happened mainly in the telecommunications sector.

A joint venture cannot be 'an autonomous economic entity.' It cannot be independent of its parents when they control it jointly. It performs the functions of an autonomous economic entity when it has all the resources required to carry on as if it were independent. If it carries on only one function, such as R & D which it provides for its parents, however, and has no access to the market, it will not function as an autonomous economic entity, sometimes called 'a full function joint venture.' It will be treated as auxiliary to its parents' business and its creation as subject to Article 81, although the joint venture may make some use of the distribution facilities of one or both of its parents without ceasing to act as if autonomous.[12]

The criteria for distinguishing joint ventures to be treated under the regulation from those appraised under Article 81 was always unsatisfactory. Joint ventures may lead to integration which may produce efficiencies as may mergers. The fact that a joint venture is limited in time or scope should mean that prima facie there is less cause for concern, yet cooperative joint ventures are subject to the stricter control under Article 81.

It is often unclear under what regime a joint venture comes—a fact intensive analysis of the market may be necessary to see whether the parents compete in adjacent markets and whether there would be sufficient incentives for them to coordinate their behaviour. This may require much work to be done before notification and also even during the short period allowed for an investigation under stage I (12.2.5 below).

Co-ordination may be a proper concern for the Commission, but if it causes the parents to increase the scope of the joint venture merely to avoid coordination outside the joint venture and come under the regime of the regulation, the Commission is jumping out of the frying pan into the fire. It is ensuring coordination within the joint venture. The deletion of Article 3(2)(b) is, therefore welcome. It may not have gone far enough.

If the parents transfer all the assets relating to a wide geographic and product market into a joint venture the joint venture will have the resources it needs to be full function and parties will have left the market on a long term basis. So the concentration may come within the more lenient test of the merger regulation. The parties may even covenant not to enter the relevant or

---

12   Notice on the distinction between concentrative and co-operative joint ventures, [1995] 4 CMLR 227, para 14.

neighbouring markets, to establish that they have left the market for the long term.[13] The Commission tends to treat five years as sufficient to be 'on a lasting basis.' Legal advice leads to more functions being controlled jointly than their clients would like. This cannot increase competition.

The Commission contemplated bringing production joint ventures within the merger rules even where they are not full function,[14] provided that a minimum value of assets, still to be decided, is invested and no block exemption applies. So far it has not done so.

A concentration may be invalid by virtue of Article 7(4) if not notified in the belief that a joint venture was collaborative, provided the Commission eventually finds that it is incompatible with the common market. Notification under the merger regulation used to operate also under Regulation 17, but notification ended in May 2004. Normally, the parties talk to the Commission before filing their notification, so the position is usually sorted out informally. Now the merger task force has been disbanded and its officials spread among the sectoral directorates, which will handle mergers (14.2.4 below).

12.2.3 *Thresholds*

A concentration has a Community dimension and is subject to the regulation, when the turnover of the parties exceeds the thresholds provided by Article 1(1):

2. A concentration has a Community dimension where:

(a) the combined aggregate worldwide turnover of all the undertakings concerned is more than 5000 million ECUs, and

(b) the aggregate Community-wide turnover of each of at least two of the undertakings concerned is more than 250 million ECUs

unless each of the undertakings concerned achieves more than two-thirds of its aggregate Community-wide turnover within one and the same Member State.

The high thresholds gave both industry and the Commission time to organise and recruit appropriate staff. The Commission proposed in 1996 that they be lowered, but this was rejected by the Council. The Council accepted, however, the alternative proposal[15] that, in order to extend the benefit of the one-stop-shop, the regulation should apply where turnovers are substantially lower if the requisite turnovers are achieved in more than two Member States.

The method of calculating turnover is prescribed in Article 5 of the merger regulation and explained in the Commission's notice on the calculation of

---

13   *Mitsubishi/UCAR* (IV/M.024) [1992] 4 CMLR M50, para 7. This is contrary to the usual rule that to escape Art 81(1) a covenant not to compete should be no wider than necessary to induce a transaction that is not anticompetitive.

14   *White Paper on Modernisation*, Commission programme No 99/027, para 79 & 80.

15   Published as consolidated [1997] 5 CMLR 387.

turnover.[16] Discounts and turnover taxes, transactions between parties and within groups are to be disregarded. The relevant turnover is that of the undertakings concerned, which, in a merger, are the merging corporate groups (paragraphs 36–42 of the notice on the calculation of turnover) and, in case of acquisition of sole control, the acquiring company and acquired or target company or activity.[17] Where A acquires only one of B's activities, the whole of B's turnover is not relevant, only that of the part acquired. In the case of a joint venture, however, the total turnover of all the parents is included (points 22–25).

Mergers below the thresholds may be investigated by Member States under national law, but the regulation will not apply (12.2.8 below). About half of the concentrations dealt with have been joint ventures. At first the Commission dealt with some 50 to 60 notifications a year, but the number had doubled by 1996 and according to the Commission's annual report for 2002, 345 mergers were notified in 2001. With the recession, the numbers declined in 2002 to 277, but have started to rise again.

12.2.4 *Notification*

Article 4 requires the participating undertakings to notify concentrations with a Community dimension not more than one week after the agreement, announcement of a public bid or the acquisition of a controlling interest. Since May 2004, the parties have been allowed to notify intended mergers in advance. They may not put the concentration into effect before it is notified and the Commission has completed its assessment by formal decision or should have done so (Article 7(2)). Nevertheless, with the Commission's permission (Article 7(3)), a public bid may be implemented if it was notified before its announcement, and the acquirer did not exercise the voting rights otherwise than in order to maintain the full value of its investments (Article 7(2)).

Article 7(4) provides that:

> the validity of any transaction carried out in contravention of paragraph (1) shall be dependent on a decision . . .

by the Commission on whether the concentration be compatible with the common market. It seems that if the Commission eventually approves of the concentration there will be no nullity, but that if it does not, then something will be void: it is not clear what. At least the danger of invalidity is reduced to unnotified mergers not involving quoted securities that are condemned.

---

16   Notice on the calculation of turnover under Regulation 4064/89 on the control of concentrations between undertakings, O.J 1998, C66/25, [1998] 4 CMLR 613.
17   Notice on the notion of the undertakings concerned, [1998] 4 CMLR 599, points 5–7.

The regulation that governs notification, Commission Regulation 802/2004,[18] requires a great deal of information—its predecessor was modelled on the second request under the Hart-Scott-Rodino Act of the United States. If, however, the parties informally consult the Commission in advance and it is clear that the merger is unlikely substantially to restrict competition in the common market, the Commission can and does waive the requirement of much of the information. Where the bid is friendly, or a party enters into many joint ventures, the parties often begin to put the information on to a computer in advance, but sometimes there are problems in meeting the deadline for notification of hostile take-over bids as it may be difficult for the bidder to obtain sufficient information about the target company.

12.2.4.1 *Referral to NCAs*—Under Article 9 the Commission has always had power to refer a merger or part of a merger to a national competition authority to investigate under national competition law when there is a distinct market within that Member State that will be affected by the merger. NCAs may themselves request such a reference. Not many references have been made, because often the territory of more than one Member State was involved. The Commission therefore investigated the merger itself and did not refer. If the distinct geographic market does not amount to a substantial part of the common market, the Commission is required to make a reference. The procedure is likely to be used more now that in non-merger cases NCAs will conduct so much of the investigation. The time limits for invoking the procedure have been extended which should make it easier to operate.

12.2.5 *Procedure*

The procedure under the merger Regulation is not very different from that adopted by the Commission when it deals with a case under Regulation 1/2003 save that the need for speed results in each stage taking far less time and the Commission has no discretion not to investigate. The Commission has power to obtain information under Articles 11–13, but the parties are usually so desirous of a rapid decision that any information required is usually provided voluntarily, often by fax or email the same day.

Under the cooperation agreement with the US agencies,[19] the latter provide considerable input into merger decisions when they may reduce competition within both jurisdictions. Neither agency has power to disclose confidential information to the other, but usually the parties make available to each authority any information sent to either, and provide additional information to whichever agency is less likely to understand the context. The

18   Regulation 802/2004,implementing Council Reg 139/2004 on the control of concentrations between undertakings
19   (95/145/EC), OJ 1995, L131, amended by EU-USA Positive Comity Agreement 1998, 4 June 1998, [1999] 4 CMLR 502.

parties have a significant incentive to have similar decisions in both jurisdictions, so welcome the cooperation. In *WorldCom/MCI*,[20] American officials attended one hearing in Brussels *inter vivos* and were connected to another through closed circuit TV. Nevertheless, most of the cooperation takes place by email or phone. The official of the FTC involved travels to Brussels only about once a year.

Article 10(1) provides that the Commission has only 25 working days (extended to 35 if a Member State requests a reference to it under Article 9(2)) to decide whether a merger raises significant doubts as to its compatibility with the common market. This is frequently referred to as the first stage. For stage II, it has 90 working days, extended to 105 when the parties offer commitments in an attempt to avoid the prohibition. The parties may also request a further 15 days. These time limits were increased in 2004, but are sometimes still tighter than those in cases involving also the US. The former limits sometimes gave rise to difficulties in settling congruent remedies in the two jurisdictions.

Only the Commission may implement the regulation and Member States may not normally apply their competition laws to concentrations with a Community dimension, but Article 21(3) adds that, nevertheless, Member States may take appropriate measures to protect three specified legitimate interests: public security, plurality of the media and prudential rules, and other unspecified public interests that are recognised by the Commission after notification by the Member State. They may also apply national rules that do not relate to competition, such as those that protect buyers of shares or minority interests.

If the concentration is likely significantly to impede competition, the Commission should declare that it is incompatible with the common market, which automatically results in the merger being forbidden. More often, however, the parties either hive off some overlapping activities or undertake to do so, in which event the Commission may declare, subject to conditions or commitments, that the concentration is compatible with the common market. If the criteria for prohibition are not fulfilled, the Commission must declare by decision that the concentration is compatible with the common market.

Commitments used to bind the parties only if imposed after an investigation that has progressed to stage II, but that was changed in 1997. Article 10 ensures that such undertakings are proposed well before the Commission's normal deadline expires and provides for 15 extra working days if they are not, to enable the Commission to explore their efficacy with customers and competitors.

20   [1999] 5 CMLR 876.

12.2.6 *Criterion for appraisal by the Commission*

Article 2 requires the Commission to appraise concentrations above the thresholds to see whether they are compatible with the common market.

Article 2(3) prescribes the criterion of incompatibility with the common market:

> a concentration which would significantly impede effective competition in the common market or in a substantial part of it, in particular as a result of the creation or strengthening of a dominant position, shall be declared incompatible with the common market.

In assessing whether a dominant position is created or strengthened, Article 2(1) requires the Commission to take into account:

(a) the need to preserve and develop effective competition within the common market in view of, among other things, the structure of all the markets concerned and the actual or potential competition from undertakings located either within or outwith the Community;

(b) the market position of the undertakings concerned and their economic and financial power, the alternatives available to suppliers and users, their access to suppliers or markets, any legal or other barriers to entry, supply and demand trends for the relevant goods and services, the interests of the intermediate and ultimate consumers, and the development of technical and economic progress provided that it is to consumers' advantage and does not form an obstacle to competition.

Justification on non-competition grounds was removed from an earlier draft of this Article and replaced by these provisions. The limitation to competitive criteria was controversial. Some of the matters to be taken into account under Article 2(1)(b) could be interpreted to include non-competitive criteria. 'Economic and financial power' is not the same as power over price and other matters. Considerations of industrial policy were firmly rejected by the Commission in *De Haviland*.[21] The list of factors to be taken into account, however, is not exhaustive, although the Commission is required to consider relevant matters in the list.

Since it does not act on a complaint, there is no particular conduct on which to focus. The ECJ noted in *France v Commission*,[22] that the appraisal must be prospective. Guideline 9[23] states that:

> in assessing the competitive effects of a merger, the Commission compares the competitive conditions that would have prevailed without the merger. In most cases the competitive conditions existing at the time of the merger constitute the

---

21   (IV/M 053), [1992] 4 CMLR M2.
22   (C–68/94 and 30/95) [1998] ECR I–1375, (appeal from *Kali und Salz* (IV/M 308) OJ 1993, L395/1), paras 112–21.
23   Guidelines on the assessment of horizontal mergers under the Council Regulation on the control of concentrations between undertakings OJ 2004, 31/5.

relevant comparison for evaluating the effects of a merger. However, in some circumstances the Commission may take into account future changes to the market that can reasonably be predicted. It may, in particular, take account of the likely entry or exit of firms if the merger did not take place when considering what constitutes the relevant comparison.

Often the investigation has to focus on several overlapping activities of the parties. has usually defined the relevant markets by reference to substitutes on the demand side because constraints on the supply side rarely operate as fast or effectively (4.3.1–4.3.1.5 above).

12.2.6.1 *Horizontal mergers*—Most of the mergers considered have been between competitors and have increased market shares, but some mergers have been vertical or conglomerate. The Commission has recently issued a revised set of horizontal guidelines (Gs).[24] These take into account the Commission's evolving experience and the case law of the CFI (G 4). In so far as the Commission is allowed a considerable margin of appreciation by the CFI and ECJ, it may be that the Gs are binding on the Commission (2.4.9 above). The Guidelines, however, are flexible, so that may not be important. It is the weight to be given to different factors that matters.

If actual or potential competitors merge, competition between them will cease and the question arises whether there is sufficient competition from other undertakings to constrain the pricing and other decisions of the participating parties (Gs 22(a), 24 *et seq.*). This requires appraisal of the relevant market, particularly of its definition (4.3.1–4.3.1.6). The other possible anti-competitive effect in a very concentrated market is that the merged firm and an independent competitor may start to operate as if they were colluding even if they are not (12.2.6.1.2 below).

12.2.6.1.1 *Market shares*—Where the merger is between firms that compete with each other or are likely to do so (G 2), the Commission pays considerable attention to market shares as a first indication (G 14). A concentration may well be incompatible with the common market if the aggregate market shares exceed 50% (G 17), but other factors are relevant. Where the aggregate market share is below 25% the merger is unlikely to be incompatible (G 18). The concept of a relevant market considered at 4.3.1–4.3.1.6 above works better for mergers, where the Commission is concerned with the increase in the firms' market power (4.3.1.6 above) than under Articles 81 and 82.

The Commission sometimes uses the Herfindahl-Hirschman Index for measuring concentration (HHI, Gs 17 & 19–21) so as to give greater weight to the shares of the firms that are large in the relevant market. The market share of each participant in the market is squared and then they are added up. A firm with a 40% share of the market would contribute 1600 to the HHI,

24   Cited note 23 above.

whereas two firms with 20% each would contribute 400. If the two firms with 20% merge the HHI will increase by 1200 (1600 minus 400). The Commission refers to this as 'the delta'. The market share of each firm in the market is also squared and added to find the HHI, but squaring the shares of the small firms will not increase it significantly. So it may not matter if their exact shares cannot be ascertained. The levels of the HHI and the other circumstances treated as relevant by the Commission are set out at Guidelines 19–21.

Often the Commission has to focus on several overlapping activities of the parties. It has usually defined the relevant market by reference to substitutes on the demand side because constraints on the supply side rarely operate as fast or effectively. Often there are significant switching costs and delays. When appraising whether the concentration is likely to create market power, however, it takes into account the possibility of specific firms entering the market in the near future and eroding it.

In *Alcatel/Telettra*,[25] for instance, there was concern about the Spanish market where Telefonica, the telephone monopoly, bought some 83% of some products from the parties. A market share of 50% raises a presumption of dominance within the meaning of Article 82 according to *AKZO* (4.3.1 *et seq.* above). Yet the Commission looked to specific firms outside the common market, which made similar equipment, and other makers of telephone equipment that were already operating in Spain. Although the public procurement directive was not due to apply in Spain for several years, Telefonica stated that it favoured having two sources for each item of equipment and would be willing to buy abroad. The Commission decided, therefore, that the market was contestable and that the concentration 'would not create . . . a dominant position as a result of which effective competition would be significantly impeded in the common market or in a substantial part of it.'

Had the Commission adopted a broader definition of the geographic market, however, the market shares cleared would have been far more modest.

12.2.6.1.2 *Other factors*—Market shares, however, are not determinative, particularly, where there is reason to expect them to change, for instance when the patent on a pharmaceutical product is about to expire, when market shares for a heterogeneous product have been volatile, or when entry is easy. The Commission has accepted that reliance on market shares may not be sensible in relation to markets where technology is developing rapidly, or where much of the turnover is bid for by large tenders and a newcomer may rapidly increase its market share.[26]

The Commission considers conditions of entry, but potential entry will constrain the conduct of the merging firms only if it is likely to occur soon (Gs 68–75). The Commission enquires how easily or quickly existing competitors

25 (IV/M 042) [1991] 4 CMLR 778, paras 38–43.
26 N Levy, in Valentine Korah (ed) *Competition Law of the European Community*, 2nd edn, (LexisNexis) 5.07 [4][a]–[d].

could expand production or refocus it and how easily and fast buyers could switch to other suppliers. It looks also to buyer power (G 64–67) and the relative strengths of the merging entities and their competitors, financial and in reputation. Market shares may predict the future better when the market is stable than when it is dynamic. The CFI acknowledges that the Commission has a margin of discretion. Where innovation is the main competitive force, the Commission will focus on the competitive pressure and incentives to innovate (G 38). This is important in many network markets.

Countervailing power may lessen the danger of large market shares. After the merger *Enso/Stora*,[27] the firm would have supplied 60% of liquid packaging board with two competitors having market shares of 10–20% each. The main buyer of liquid packaging board was Tetra Pak with 60–80% of total demand.

Despite this large market and the big gap between it and the next largest firm, there were two strategies that buyers might adopt if Ensa Stora should raise prices unduly. Enso Stora had high fixed costs, so even a small reduction in the use of its capacity would have a drastic effect on its profits. Tetra Pak and the other makers of carton could each switch even a small part of their demand to the two smaller firms and punish Enso Stora. Tetra Pak could also encourage new entry by agreeing to buy a large fixed quantity from the new entrant, thereby reducing the risk of entry. Since buyers had a weapon to discipline Ensa Stora's market conduct, the merger would not create or strengthen a dominant position despite the high market share.

Nevertheless, the Commission was concerned that Tetra Pak might have more buying power than its two smaller competitors, so the Commission obtained a commitment that Ensa Stora would not charge them more than it charged Tetra Pak.

12.2.6.1.3 *Collective dominant position*—There was a possible gap in the regulation of 1989. A concentration could be forbidden only if it created or strengthened a dominant position as a result of which competition would be significantly impeded. In several countries, any merger, which may substantially lessen competition, may be forbidden even if a dominant position is not obtained. The Commission has largely filled the gap by stating in particular decisions, some relating to Article 82 and some to mergers, that the two remaining firms will have large market shares and are likely to act as a single entity, the concentration leads to a collective dominant position (4.3.5 above).

The Commission several times found that a merger would lead to a collective dominant position and has considered carefully any constraints on the conduct of the merged firms due to the possibility of new entrants, and whether the remaining firms would have the incentives and possibility of behaving as if they had agreed not to compete without having to make an

---

27   (M 1225) OJ 1999 L254.

agreement. Coordination also requires that there is some mechanism for punishing the firm that starts the rot of cutting prices.[28]

In *France v Commission*,[29] the ECJ confirmed that there might be joint dominance when two firms, the merged undertaking and one independent of it, became a single entity in view of the links between them. It added however, that there was a strong burden of proof to show that the merging firms would act as a single entity with its competitors.

In *Gencor*,[30] the Commission condemned a merger that would lead immediately to the merging firms selling 30–35% in the world of the platinum and precious metals usually found in the same ore. A third party, Anglo American, would have a similar share of world supply, while the Russians, with mines considered by the Commission to be exhausted, would sell from stock and supply about 10% for the next two years, when the share of the merging parties and Anglo American would increase to about 40% each.

At paragraph 141 the Commission described the market as oligopolistic.

   (a) on the demand side, there is moderate growth, inelastic demand and insignificant countervailing power. Buyers are therefore highly vulnerable to a potential abuse,

   (b) the supply side is highly concentrated with high market transparency for a homogenous product, mature production technology, high entry barriers (including high sunk costs) and suppliers with financial links and multi-market contacts. These supply side characteristics make it easy for suppliers to engage in parallel behaviour and provide them with incentives to do so, without any countervailing checks from the demand side.

On appeal,[31] the CFI confirmed the Commission's finding of collective dominance when the two remaining firms were likely to act as a single entity, whether or not there were links between them. In *Kali und Salz*, the ECJ said that there is no presumption of joint dominance when the remaining duopolists have 60% of the market,[32] but when the Russians left the platinum market the share was expected to rise to nearly 80% with high entry barriers and other features of an oligopolistic market.

The concept of dualistic or collective dominance was ultimately accepted also in relation to Article 82 by the ECJ in *Compagnie Maritime Belge Transports SA v Commission*,[33] in terms similar to the judgment of the CFI in *Gencor*.

---

28 Cristina Caffarra and Kai-Uwe Kühn, 'Joint dominance: the CFI judgment on *Gencor/Lonrho*' [1999] *European Competition Law Review*, 355.

29 (C–68/94 and 30/95) [1998] ECR I–1375, appeal from *Kali und Salz* (IV/M 308), OJ 1993, L395/1.

30 *Gencor/Lonrho* (IV/M 619), [1999] 4 CMLR 1076.

31 (T–102/96) [1999] ECR II– 753.

32 Contrast *AKZO Chemie BV v Commission* (62/86), [1991] ECR I–3359, where the Court treated the market share of a single firm of 50% as raising a rebut table presumption of dominance.

33 On appeal (C–395/96P), [2000] ECR I–1365, para 45.

We thought that the analysis of collective dominance would be based on the factors likely to make it easier for the remaining firms not to compete such as those mentioned by the Commission in *Gencor*—on whether parallel pricing was likely even in the absence of collusion.

In *Airtours/First Choice*,[34] however, not only did the Commission extend *Gencor* from duopoly to a merger reducing the major firms from 4 to 3, it also forbade a merger in a dynamic market where the product was not homogenous and where the ways of marketing the product are changing with the advent of the internet. The tacit collusion that was feared related to the planning of capacity (airline seats and hotel bookings), although this is fixed some 18 months before the holidays are sold. Consequently, it would not be possible to retaliate promptly against a firm seen to be increasing capacity. The decision left practice in confusion. We no longer knew on what theory the Commission was working and it was impossible to advise firms whether mergers had a good chance of being cleared. Although it was too late to resume the merger, Airtours appealed.[35] The CFI held that the term 'dominant position' included a collective dominant position as explained in relation to Article 82 (4.3.5 above).

In a notable judgment the CFI confirmed the earlier theory of *Gencor*. It insisted (paragraph 62) that to find a dominant oligopoly the Commission must establish three conditions: first, an ability by each to monitor the conduct of the others. For tacit coordination to be sustainable over time, there must be an incentive not to depart from the common policy. In other words: all the members of the dominant oligopoly must be able to retaliate. Moreover, the Commission must establish that the foreseeable reaction of current and future competitors, as well of consumers, would, not jeopardise the results expected from the common policy. In other words, it is permissible to rely on economic theory, only if all the conditions for its application are established:

> 63. The prospective analysis which the Commission has to carry out in its review of concentrations involving collective dominance calls for close examination in particular of the circumstances which in each individual case, are relevant for assessing the effects of the concentration on competition in the reference market.
> . . .

> 64. Furthermore, the basic provisions of Regulation 4064/89, in particular Article 2 thereof, confer on the Commission a certain discretion, especially with respect to assessments of an economic nature, and, consequently, when the exercise of that discretion, which is essential for defining the rules on concentrations, is under review, the Community judicature must take account of the discretionary margin implicit in the provisions of an economic nature which form part of the rules on concentration.

---

34   [2000] 5 CMLR 494.
35   *Airtours/First Choice*, T–342/99, [2002] ECR II–2585, [2002] 5 CMLR 317 (CFI).

The court proceeded to consider in what ways the Commission had failed to carry out the analysis and quashed the decision.

At many points, the CFI insisted that the burden of proof was on the Commission. It must get simple facts, such as the contents of a letter, right. It has a margin of appreciation on more complex matters, such as the likely emergence of a dominant oligopoly.

The question arises whether the Commission is more likely to get its analysis wrong when the merger results in joint, rather than single, dominance. After the decision in *Gencor*, the Russians did not leave the market but continued to mine for the precious metals with the aid of improved technology. The parties' market shares did not rapidly rise as had been predicted.

In two later cases, *Tetra Laval BV v Commission*,[36] and *Schneider/Legrand*,[37] the CFI confirmed the need for the Commission to take much greater care before alleging that a merger would lead to a dominant position as a result of which competition would be significantly impeded.

12.2.6.1.4 *Unilateral effects*—The judgments in *Gencor* and *Airtours* were concerned only with a finding of joint dominance arising from of a merger that led to tacit collusion between the participating undertakings and third party, and not with mergers leading to unilateral conduct in a concentrated market. It was not clear whether unilateral conduct also qualified under Article 2.

This is the reason why the test in Article 2(2) and (3) has been altered (12.2.6 above). The Commission is now satisfied that a merger leading to collective dominance, when tacit collusion is not alleged to be likely, may be declared incompatible with the common market. Prospective unilateral effects may significantly impede competition.

Formerly the test was whether the merger 'creates or strengthens a dominant position as a result of which significant competition would be significantly impeded in the common market or a substantial part of it.' The new test (12.2.6 above) is arguably no different from the old one. Now it is clear that unilateral effects are covered. Recital 25 provides that

> The notion of "significant impediment to effective competition" in Article 2(2) and 2(3) should be interpreted as extending, beyond the concept of dominance, only to the anti-competitive effects of a concentration resulting from the non-coordinated behaviour of undertakings which would not have a dominant position on the market concerned.

This reduces the greater focus of the new test on the significant impediment to competition rather than on the concept of dominant position. A merger may be forbidden even if it does not cause the merged firms and another undertaking or others to reduce competition without acting as if there was

36   (T–5/02) [2002] ECR–II 4381, [2002] 5 CMLR 1182.
37   (310/01) [2003] 4 CMLR 678.

collusion (12.2.6.1.3 above), but a dominant position must result for a merger to be forbidden, unless unilateral effects are likely.

If the concentration is likely significantly to impede competition, the Commission should declare that it is incompatible with the common market and it may not proceed. More often, however, the parties either hive off some overlapping activities, or undertake to do so, in which case the Commission may declare, subject to conditions or commitments, that the concentration is compatible with the common market. If the criterion for prohibition is not fulfilled, the Commission must declare by decision that the concentration is compatible with the common market.

12.2.6.1.5 *Efficiencies*—One possibly perverse feature of the EC law is that efficiencies, which in the US may justify a merger that significantly lessens competition, seem to have been treated in the opposite way under the regulation. If the merged firm can reduce costs or provide a better product, the Commission seems to have thought that would help create or strengthen a dominant position.

The Commission has been persuaded to change its mind a little.[38] Efficiencies are no longer an offence, but they are a defence only when they are substantial, merger specific, verifiable and quantifiable. The burden of establishing all these characteristics is on the participating parties and will be difficult to discharge before the directors have have taken charge of the target company. It will be almost impossible in the case of hostile takeovers, which have done so much in the common law countries to create a market for corporate control.

Part of the benefit must be passed on to consumers. The Commission takes the view that that consumer welfare and not total welfare is its objective, so efficiencies which accrue to the participating entities and which will not be passed on, do not count.

The Commission tries to balance the benefits to consumers of substantial efficiencies and the significant impediment to competition. It is justified in excluding benefits that could be fully obtained short of a merger. It requires, however, that the efficiencies result directly from the merger. The parties may be able to establish this for production cost savings due to combining assets, such as using the technology of the other party. It will often not be possible for the more important dynamic efficiencies, which may occur to management when it has come to organise the assets of all the merging firms. I sympathise with the Commission's dilemma. It believes that many mergers are inefficient, and wishes to ensure that they do not pass through the control unless there is good evidence of substantial efficiencies.

---

38   Guidelines on the assessment of horizontal mergers under the Council Regulation on the control of concentrations between undertakings OJ 2004, 31/5, G76–88.

12.2.6.1.6 *Vertical or Conglomerate mergers*—Usually vertical concentration will not increase market shares and it may yield substantial economies. The competitive objection to vertical integration is that competitors at one level *may be* foreclosed if there is market power at the other. This will often not be the case: it is necessary to look carefully and see that there is not only an ability to foreclose, but also an incentive. At 2.4.3 and 9.6.5 above the narrow circumstances in which there is a risk of foreclosure were considered. There must be barriers to entry in the market that is not dominated and so few firms able to operate in it that competitors of the dominant firm will not be able to enter on a viable scale.

In *Van den Bergh Foods Ltd* (5.2.2.1 above),[39] however, where there was foreclosure of 40% of the market by a very dominant firm, the ECJ treated foreclosing conduct as abusive. I hope that in construing the judgment, we can take account of the very careful analysis performed by the CFI in finding foreclosure before applying Article 81.

As analysed at 8.1.3 above, vertical integration will not raise price, unless there is market power at one level of production or trade and competitors can be foreclosed from the other. Vertically related products are complements. The more of one that is sold, the greater the demand for the other. The incentive for the reduction of the price of one is increased by the increased sale of both products. So, vertical integration is likely to result in lower prices for the benefit of consumers. Some economists refer to this as avoiding double marginalisation.

Efficiencies were considered at 12.2.6.1.5 in relation to horizontal mergers, and more generally at 8.1.3 above. They are most likely to arise in a vertical relationship. Vertical integration avoids the cost of negotiating contracts between independent firms. This can be very important when suppliers of complementary products have complex interactions. It may avoid disincentives to investment in sunk costs due to fear of an independent supplier of complementary products taking opportunistic advantage of the sunk costs incurred—the hold up problem.

Vertical integration may however raise rivals' costs when both activities are seen as essential in a particular market because a new entrant would have to enter at both levels at once if supply or outlet were refused. It may also make it easier for the merged firm to discriminate. The participating firms will have to establish that competitors have alternative suppliers or buyers at both levels. This concern is about a horizontal effect of a vertical merger.[40]

---

39   T–65/98, [2004] 4 CMLR 14.
40   See Juan Briones Alonso, 'Vertical Aspect of Mergers, Joint Ventures and Strategic Alliances,' [1997] *Fordham Corporate Law Institute*, 129 and the following papers by Bernard E Amory at 147, Michael J Reynolds, 'Mergers and Joint ventures: the vertical dimension,' at 153, and the ensuing panel discussion at 201.

12.2.7 *Powers of the Commission*

Article 6 requires the Commission to examine notifications as soon as they are received, and if it concludes that the concentration does not fall within the scope of the regulation it is required to adopt a formal decision to that effect. If it concludes that a concentration is clearly not incompatible with the common market, it is required to declare that it is compatible with it. If it has serious doubts about the merger's compatibility with the common market it is required to initiate proceedings to investigate the matter further—often called 'stage II'. All these conclusions must be reached by formal decision, so are subject to appeal. Reasons must be given but, in view of the time constraints, these are short, especially in proceedings undertaken in stage I.

Investigations are carried out in two stages. In the first the Commission must decide whether the concentration gives rise to serious doubts about its compatibility with the common market. If it does not that is the end of the matter, although it may so find only because of commitments offered by the parties. If serious doubts remain, the investigation goes into an intensive second stage. The time frame for decisions under both stage I and stage II investigations has been lengthened. The old limits of one month and four months respectively proved too tight.

Article 10(1) provides that decisions at stage I shall be taken within 25 working days of receiving complete notification, which is increased to 35 working days if a Member State makes a request under Article 9 that the matter be referred to it or if, after notification, the parties offer commitments. The Commission often negotiates with the parties, and persuades them to agree to hive off some of the activities of one of the parties where they used to compete with each other, in which event it may declare the concentration compatible with the common market. Draft commitments are usually put to competitors and customers to ensure that they suffice, and this requires considerable extra time. Undertakings given at this stage used not to be enforceable, but are now (Article 6(2)). Most notified mergers have been cleared at the first stage.

Article 10(2) now requires the Commission to make a decision under Article 8 after an investigation that went to the second stage under Article 8, within 90 working days of initiating proceedings for stage II, or the concentration will be deemed to have been approved by virtue of Article 10(6). The period is increased to 105 working days when the parties offer commitments 55 working days or more after proceedings were initiated. The Commission needs time to take advice from customers, competitors and others as to whether the commitments offered suffice to remove the anticompetitive effects. A further 15 working days is possible, but as the parties must make the request within 15 working days of the start of stage II, this can usually be done only by the Commission with the consent of the parties.

Article 8(2) provides that the Commission can attach obligations and conditions to such a decision made at stage II, and this less drastic remedy has enabled it to prohibit outright only 10 mergers by the end of 2002. In 67 cases after stage I and in 35 after stage II, the merger was cleared with commitments. It is said that enforcement has become tougher since Mario Monti became the member of the Commission responsible for competition in the summer of 1999, but since then there have been some very large mergers with complex effects on more than one market. It is not clear that the standards have changed.

If the concentration would create or strengthen a dominant position, by virtue of Article 8(3), the Commission is required to adopt a decision that it is incompatible with the common market. If the merger has been legally implemented, for instance, under derogation from the Commission, the Commission may order divestiture. This is far more satisfactory than invalidity under Article 7(4), although the US experience of divestiture has not been very happy. The merger will not be very old by the time the Commission makes its decision and assets and activities will probably have been kept separate, so the EC experience could be more successful.

A great advantage to the parties of a concentration over cooperative joint ventures is that notification leads to a formal decision under stage I or II, within a short time. The decisions binds the parties to whom it is addressed and an appeal may lie.

Regulation 1/2003 (chapter 7 above) applies only to proceedings relating to Articles 81 or 82, and not to mergers.

12.2.8 One stop control

Concentrations including concentrative joint ventures above or below the thresholds can, apparently, not be attacked under Article 81. The dangers of nullity resulting from the *BAT* case[41] have been largely avoided. Nevertheless, it is unfortunate that business will be advised to negotiate acquisitions and concentrative joint ventures rather than co-operative joint ventures, which remain subject to Article 81. A permanent concentration which extends to joint distribution is likely to be more anti-competitive than a temporary joint venture, or one limited to production and R & D, but the latter may be attacked under Article 81 as well as under national laws while the former enjoys the five benefits of falling within the merger regulation (12.2 above).

A Council regulation cannot deprive Articles 81 and 82 of their direct effect. Nevertheless, unless the Court departs from earlier case law in the transport sector to which, also, Regulation 17 ceased to apply, agreements for concentrative joint ventures below the thresholds will enjoy provisional validity.[42] They may, however, be attacked in national courts under Article 82[43] as

41   *BAT and Reynolds v Commission* (142 & 156/84) [1987] ECR 4487, paras 37–39 and 64 (12.1 above).
42   *Ahmed Saeed* (66/86) [1989] ECR 803, para 29.
43   *Ibid*, para 33.

well as under national law. It has not been held, however, that Article 22 is not valid on the ground that Article 308, under which many provisions of the Regulation were adopted, provides for filling gaps in the Treaty, not for creating them.

The parties to concentrations above the thresholds are absolved from having to notify national authorities under national law, and sometimes an extra firm has been acquired solely to bring the concentration over the thresholds. Most Member States now have legislation requiring the notification of concentrations and providing for their control. It can be very expensive to have to supply different information, on different forms, to multiple national authorities all within differing, but short, time periods. Some national authorities have agreed to the use of a single 'best practice' form, but the information is unlikely to be the same in all the states that require notification.

The lower thresholds adopted for mergers between parties whose requisite turnover is in more than two Member States have not resulted in many additional mergers being investigated by the Commission.

Business supported the project of merger control by the Commission to achieve 'one stop control' on the basis that concentrations within the scope of the regulation would not have to be notified to the competent authorities in Member States under national law. Nevertheless, some of the smaller Member States which in 1989 could not control mergers under their national law wanted the power to control concentrations below the thresholds that were important in their national markets. Article 22(3) provides that a Member State may request the Commission to investigate under the Regulation a concentration below the thresholds.

Article 9 provides that the Commission may, by decision, refer a notified concentration to a Member State in limited circumstances (12.2.4.1 above).

Subject to Articles 9 and 22, if a concentration is above the thresholds, the Commission investigates under the merger regulation. This is true even under the EEA treaty: the ESA is not competent to apply the merger regulation. If the turnover is below one of the thresholds, the regulation normally does not apply and national authorities are competent to apply their national competition law.

12.2.9 *The Commission's power to obtain information*

Article 11 is virtually identical to Article 18 of Regulation 1/2003, allowing the Commission to request information, first without threat of sanctions, and then by decision (7.4.1 above). Article 12 provides for the Commission to request national competition authorities to undertake investigations considered necessary by the Commission. Article 13 provides the Commission to carry out inspections itself with or without other accompanying persons.

Since the parties are usually so keen to get their mergers approved, the Commission rarely has to rely on its statutory powers. The parties reply immediately to requests for information by fax or email, often the same day when the answers are simple.

12.2.10 *Fines*

By virtue of Article 14(2), the Commission may impose fines not exceeding 10% of the aggregated turnover of the undertakings concerned for intentionally or negligently failing to comply with obligations to suspend or abrogate the concentration, or for implementing a concentration that has not been notified within a week. It may impose fines of between 1,000 and 50,000 ECUs for failing to notify, or notifying incorrectly or misleadingly, and so forth.

Article 15 provides for periodic penalties.

12.2.11 *Miscellaneous*

The Community Court was given unlimited jurisdiction over the amount of a fine by Articles 16 and 21 of the Regulation and jurisdiction to review substantive decisions on the merits under Article 229 of the EC treaty by Article 21. Such cases now go to the CFI. Article 17 protects some kinds of confidential information from being used for other purposes or from being disclosed. Article 18 provides for undertakings with a legitimate interest to make their views known to the Commission. Article 19 provides for close and constant liaison with the competition authorities of Member States. The Commission must publish decisions taken after the second stage of proceedings in the Official Journal. Decisions made after stage I only are not published officially, but are loaded on the Commission's website in the original language.[44] The majority of the decisions is in English.

12.3 Conclusion

There are some unsatisfactory provisions, such as the distinction between concentrative and cooperative joint ventures, but it is not easy to suggest alternative limitations to the concept of a joint venture. Regulation 1/2003 makes the lack of a formal decision less important than it was. The Regulation will catch a few conglomerate mergers and joint ventures, even small ones, between large firms, but the Commission normally waives most of the information that it is expensive to obtain where it is clear that the merger will not significantly impede competition within the common market.

Business and its advisers seem to be happy with their experience under the merger regulation. The Commission has seldom missed a deadline and has been flexible in requiring information and finding sensible solutions. Some

---

44 Kluwer publishes all the decisions in the *EEC Merger Control Reporter* and translates into English those decisions dealt with in a different language. The CMLR and CEC publish a selection of decisions.

markets have been defined too narrowly; in the first merger that was forbidden, *De Haviland*,[45] the market for commuter planes—those able to carry up to 100 passengers—was divided into three classes according to size. It did not result in great market power. Nevertheless, sophisticated quantitative analytical techniques are frequently being used now to define relevant markets.

Problems arose in negotiating commitments in time, and rather than be caught short, legal advisers were induced to offer more than the Commission was probably entitled to receive. With the longer time limits now provided by Article 10, the problem may be reduced. The balance between the firms' need for speed and the public interest in sufficient remedies is not easy to strike and no mergers have yet been examined fully under the new regulation.

12.4 Bibliography

Juan Briones Alonso, 'Vertical Aspect of Mergers, Joint Ventures and Strategic Alliances,' [1997] *Fordham Corporate Law Institute*, 129 and the following papers by ***Bernard E Amory***, 147, ***Michael J Reynolds***, 'Mergers and Joint ventures: the vertical dimension,' 153 and the ensuing panel discussion 201.

Antonio Bavasso, 'A Judicial Review of the Commission's Policy and Practice: Many Lights and Some Shadows,' (1999) 22 *World Competition Law and Economics Review, 45.*

Pierre Bos, Jules Stuyck and ***Peter Wytinck***, *Concentration Control in the European Community* (Graham & Trotman, London, 1992). (Accurate, perceptive and doctrinal analysis of the merger regulation in the light of its history.)

Cristina Caffarra and ***Kai-Uwe Kühn***, 'Joint Dominance: the CFI judgment on *Gencor/Lonrho*' [1999] *European Competition Law Review*, 355.

John Cook and ***CS Kerse***, *Merger Control,*3rd edn, (London, Sweet & Maxwell, 2000).

Frank L Fine, *Mergers and Joint Ventures in Europe* 2nd edn, (Graham & Trotman, London 1994).

Eleanor M Fox, 'Federalism, Standards, and Common Market Merger Control' in Barry Hawk (ed) [1988] *Fordham Corporate Law Institute*, chapter 23.

Enrique Gonzalez-Diaz, 'Recent Developments in EC Merger Control Law—The Gencor Judgment,' (1999) 22 *World Competition Law and Economics Review*, 3.

Barry Hawk and ***Henry Husser***, *European Community Merger Control: A Practitioner's Guide* (Kluwer Law International, 1996) (2nd edn in preparation).

Barry Hawk, 'A Bright Line Shareholding Test to end the Nightmare under the EEC Merger Regulation' (1993) 30 *Common Market Law Review*, 115.

Valentine Korah, '*Gencor v Commission*—Collective Dominance,' [1999] *European Competition Law Review*, 337.

Jeremy Lever and ***Paul Lasok***, in M Weinberg and Blank, *Takeovers and Mergers*, (London, Sweet & Maxwell, 1990, looseleaf) chapter 3, section 2, on 'EEC Merger Law', and later releases.

N Levy, in Valentine Korah (ed), *Competition Law of the European Community*, 2nd edn, (Lexis/Nexis).

---

45   (IV/M 053), [1992] 4 CMLR M2.

Alistair Lindsay, *The EC Merger Regulation: Substantive Issues*, (London, Sweet & Maxwell, 2003).

Ernst-Joachim Mestmäcker, 'Merger Control in the Common Market Between Competition Policy and Industrial Policy' in Barry Hawk (ed) [1988] *Fordham Corporate Law Institute*, chapter 20.

Damien Neven, Robin Nuttall and *Paul Seabright*, *Merger in Daylight—The Economics and Politics of European Merger Control* (CEPR, 1993). (Analytical critique of the legislation and practice of the Commission by three economists.)

FM Scherer, 'European Community Merger Policy; Why? Why not?' in Barry Hawk (ed) [1988] *Fordham Corporate Law Institute*, chapter 24.

Panel Discussion, 'EEC Merger Policy' [1998] *Fordham Corporate Law Institute,* chapter 25.

Dieter Schwarz, 'New EEC Regulation on Mergers, Partial Mergers and Joint Ventures,' [1998] *Fordham Corporate Law Institute,* chapter 21.

Mario Siragusa and *Romano Subiotto*, 'The EEC Merger Control Regulation: The Commission's Evolving Case Law' (1991) 28 *Common Market Law Review*, 877.

Robert Strivens (ed), *Merger Control in the EEC*, 2nd edn, (Kluwer, 1993).

James S Venit, 'The "Merger" Control Regulation: Europe Comes of Age or Caliban's Dinner' (1990) 27 *Common Market Law Review,* 7.

13. Joint Ventures and Specialisation Agreements

13.1. Introduction

Joint ventures may take many forms and have very different functions. Sometimes the parents virtually merge part of their activities into a jointly owned subsidiary; sometime the joint venture is limited to a single stage of the process between research and development to marketing providing a service to its parents; sometimes there is no jointly owned subsidiary but merely cross technology licences, or a joint committee may be set up to which each parent commits resources.

Sometimes a joint venture may integrate the existing facilities of its parents or it may consist of an independent firm formed or bought jointly by the parents. Sometimes it will develop its own R & D or production facilities. *Prima facie*, the former may be more likely to restrict competition if the number of competitors will be significantly reduced. Sometimes, however, the old plant will be replaced by more effective modern installations and may add a viable competitor to the market. Sometimes, the parents may continue to produce on their own, leaving the joint venture to meet the expansion of demand.

To come within the merger regulation (12.2 above), there usually will be a joint subsidiary. A committee would probably not amount to an undertaking nor have all the resources on a long term basis to enable it to operate as if economically independent. Most of the joint ventures subject to a formal decision have been adopted under the merger regulation, but most of the joint ventures formed are subject to Article 81.

The justification given for treating full function joint ventures under the merger regulation more leniently than others (12.2 above) is that a full function joint venture may also lead to integration of the former businesses and this is as likely to provide efficiencies as are full mergers. This is formalistic. Partial function joint ventures may also lead to efficiencies. So may other forms of cooperation that do not result in a jointly controlled entity. The Commission's Chief Economist, Lars-Hendrik Roeller is not convinced that mergers always produce efficiencies, efficiencies should be considered case by case. The same can be said of joint ventures.

Where the parties do not abandon the market, one might say that efficiencies are possible without any reduction in the number of competitors and the more lenient test of the merger regulation is justified. On the other hand, cooperation in the joint venture may restrict competition with it, for instance if the joint venture was previously an existing competitor of the parents, who buy it jointly and the cooperation may also spread to other fields and dampen competition.

All joint ventures were governed by Article 81 until the merger regulation came into force in 1990. Originally only full function joint ventures, where there was no risk of the parents coordinating their market behaviour with each other or with the joint venture, came within the merger regulation. Perceived after the completion of the transaction this resulted in no likelihood of coordination. Unfortunately, it led to firms deliberately leaving the market so that their joint venture would qualify as a concentration and be considered under the more lenient test of dominance (12.2.2 above). Whether the joint venture led to greater efficiency in such circumstances is doubtful.

In 1997, when the regulation was first amended, the risk of coordination between a parent and the joint venture ceased to take a merger outside the merger regulation, and the risk of co-ordination between the parents, although still subject to Article 81 was to be considered as part of the merger investigation, subject to the same substantive tests and time limits under Article 2(4) (12.2.2 above).

In the White Paper on Modernisation,[1] the Commission said it contemplated bringing within the merger regulation partial function production joint ventures to which a certain minimum level of assets was to be contributed, but this has not yet happened. As more joint ventures are monitored under the merger regulation, Article 81 applies less often, and fewer joint ventures are subject to its more stringent control. The Commission has not been attacking many in formal decisions recently, and it will be interesting to see the practice of the national competition authorities.

13.2 Case law on co-operative joint ventures

The criteria for assessing joint ventures under Article 81(1) are stricter than those relevant under the merger regulation, having the object or effect of perceptibly restricting competition as opposed to significantly impeding competition, in particular as a result of the creation or strengthening of a dominant position (12.2.6 above). There have been few formal clearances, although many joint ventures have been exempted for a few years.

In markets where there are many suppliers or which lack barriers to entry, joint ventures are unlikely to restrict competition. Even if the parents are unlikely to compete with their venture, other firms can. Indeed, a joint venture may be able to compete more effectively than each firm operating on its own, especially when they contribute complementary resources. If the joint venture or its parents try to exercise market power, consumers can turn to competing products.

---

1   Of the Rules Implementing Arts 85 and 86 of the EC Treaty, Commission programme No 99/027, paras 79–81.

Until 1998,[2] the ECJ and CFI were not called upon to consider the merits of any of the decisions on the application of Article 81 to joint ventures,[3] largely because few have been condemned, although some were exempted subject to conditions and obligations.

In concentrated markets where there are barriers to entry such as government regulation or a minimum efficient scale that is large in relation to the expected demand, the Commission may rightly be concerned by co-ordination between competitors. Its published decisions under Article 81 have mostly related to concentrated markets, and many have been exemptions for collaboration over sophisticated R & D. Where markets are not concentrated, the Commission has saved its resources by issuing informal comfort letters, many stating that Article 81(1) is not infringed, but few of these have been published.

In this chapter it is proposed to consider first the criteria adopted in the case law of the Commission and CFI and later the guidelines on the applicability of Article 81 of the EC Treaty to horizontal cooperation agreements,[4] as well as the group exemption for R & D.

13.2.1 *Inherent effect: loss of potential competition*

Whether or not the joint venturers agree not to compete with their joint venture, the Commission used to consider that parents with a substantial equity interest will be deterred from doing so. This concern was felt whether the parties were already in the market or were merely potential competitors. Indeed, during the 1970s the Commission treated joint ventures between potential competitors in concentrated markets as requiring exemption without any realistic analysis of the markets being made to establish that Article 81(1) was infringed.

The concern about potential competition, based on the judgment of the US Supreme Court in *US v Penn/Olin*,[5] was often invoked in the 1970s, but is seldom cogent and is less likely to be invoked by the Commission these days. The Supreme Court held that even if not more than one of the parent companies would have entered the market without the joint venture, the joint venture would be anti-competitive if, in its absence, the other parent would have been in the wings waiting to enter if the first should overcharge. This possibility would constrain the performance of the entrant even if the other did not actually enter.

---

2   *European Night Services (ENS) and others v Commission*, T–374/94, [1998] ECR II–3141, (13.2.1.3.2 below).
3   The *Philip Morris* decision, the appeal from which, *BAT Cigaretten-Fabriken GmbH and Reynolds v Commission* (142 & 156/84), [1987] ECR 4487 was mentioned at 12.1 above, was merely to reject the complaint, after the transaction had been altered, so the Court did not have to consider the Commission's causes for concern.
4   OJ 2001, C3/2, [2001] 4 CMLR 819.
5   378 US 158 (1964).

Yet if one firm were to enter on a scale that would supply most of the expected increase in demand for some years, entry would be less attractive to the other, especially if the minimum scale of operation was large in relation to the demand or its expected increase, a common reason for supply being concentrated. The first entrant will recognise this and will not be constrained.

The Supreme Court's theory also ignores the pro-competitive effect of the addition to supply provided by the joint venture, often faster than either parent could manage alone. Since 1986, however, the Commission has not so lightly asserted that the parties are potential competitors.

The practice of treating anyone sufficiently interested in a project to enter a joint venture as a potential competitor enabled the Commission to attach conditions and obligations to an exemption. In *De Laval/Stork*,[6] for instance, De Laval was part of a large US group of companies just beginning to sell compressors and turbines in Europe. Stork was part of a Dutch group of companies operating under a technology licence from De Laval and with a more effective sales force in Europe. The firms were actual competitors, but had complementary strengths to contribute to their joint venture. The Commission did not clear, but exempted it for 15 years from its inception in 1971, subject to conditions that would enable Stork to operate independently thereafter.

The market was one where each order had to be specifically designed by adapting basic designs. 85% of the work was based on those contributed by De Laval. The same team of engineers had to negotiate a contract, co-operate technically with each customer to design a product, work out a production programme and carry out the after-sales service, which was an important element of competition. So, contrary to its usual practice, the Commission exempted a transaction which included joint sales as well as development and manufacture.

The Commission provided, however, that when the agreement terminated, each party should be entitled to a licence of the technology that had been available to the joint venture for longer than the three years agreed by the parties and on a most-favoured-licensee basis. Each was to be entitled to sell products made thereby not only in the common market but also throughout the world.

The Commission's condition affected the commercial balance of the agreement, since 85% of use was of De Laval's designs. Worse still, since each party provided some technology to the joint venture, each could refuse to grant any licence, so was in a position to renegotiate the entire agreement by threatening to make the exemption ineffective. When the Commission intervened long after the joint venture was negotiated, it adds to the risks undertaken by the major contributor of the technology.

6   [1977] 2 CMLR D69.

Fear of such a condition being imposed has deterred some firms from noti-fying their joint ventures to the Commission. Seen *ex post*, the changes required by the Commission may have made the market more competitive, although, as it happened, it had to renew the exemption[7] because the de Laval/Stork joint venture did not thrive during the recession. The risk of hav-ing to renegotiate when the Commission imposes obligations or conditions may deter some firms from entering into a joint venture that would otherwise have been viable. The problem is less serious now that notification has been abolished and the grant of an exemption is no longer necessary. A national court asked to award damages can itself apply Article 81(3).

In most of its joint venture cases until *BP/Kellogg*,[8] the Commission assumed that joint ventures between actual or potential competitors infringed Article 81. In few decisions did it analyse the market to see whether the parents would be likely to coordinate their market behaviour as a result of the joint venture. In *Exxon/Shell*,[9] however, the coordination effect was dis-cussed more fully. The joint venture was to produce certain grades of poly-ethylene and supply them to its parents. The joint venture would have capacity to produce 17% of these grades in the common market and its parents a further 3%. The Commission said:

> 63. . . . the flow of information between Exxon and Shell allowed by the joint ven-ture structure is the basis on which each partner can plan its polyethylene produc-tion and adapt it to the choices of the other partner. This interdependence has a direct effect on the Exxon and Shell joint venture production plans (allowing . . . a perfect equalisation of the quantities produced by the two ventures or a contem-poraneous halting of the joint venture's production), but also an indirect effect (spill-over or group effect) on the polyethylene production plans of the Exxon and Shell groups as a whole. In fact any increased reduction or halt in production decided by one partner in order to adjust its behaviour to the other partner's choices in the joint venture entails a general reconsideration of the production plans of all polyethylene sites belonging to that partner's group.

The Commission has since adopted a more realistic approach to potential com-petition (13.2.1.3 below), though the case law has not been entirely consistent. Faull and Nikpay[10] comment:

> It is not just the relative importance of the JV to the parents' activities on the mar-ket that will determine whether they will co-ordinate their behaviour. The greater the parents' combined market share on the market the stronger the incentive there is for them to co-ordinate and hence a smaller JV can be the source of anti-competitive co-ordination.

---

7   *De Laval II* [1988] 4 CMLR 714.
8   [1986] 2 CMLR 619.
9   [1994] CMLR 19, [1994] 2 CEC 2061
10   *The EC Law of Competition*, (Oxford, OUP, 1999) at 361. The chapter was written by F Enrique Gonzalez Diaz, Dan Kirk, Francisco Perez Flores, and Cécile Verkleij. The section on joint ventures is outstanding.

13.2.1.1 *Ancillary restrictions*—Clearly, the Commission is right to check that cartel agreements are not attached to a valid joint venture. The ancillary restrictions should be only as wide as can be justified as necessary to make the basic transaction viable (2.4.5 and 8.1.2 above). Under US case law, the ancillary restrictions need only be reasonably necessary, and it is irrelevant that a slightly less restrictive provision can be devised with the advantage of hindsight. Despite the stricter language in the Community decisions, I am not sure that there is a difference of substance. The Commission does not always consider whether a less restrictive alternative exists. Nevertheless, unlike the Court, it seems to consider whether the ancillary restrictions are justified mainly under Article 81(3) and rarely under Article 81(1).[11]

From the viewpoint of policy, the principle that the ancillary restraint be no wider than strictly necessary would be difficult to reconcile with the incentive to firms to covenant to leave the market of the joint venture in order to show that they have done so on a lasting basis, and come within the merger regime.

13.2.1.2 *The need for each party to appropriate the benefits of its investment*—If investment in the joint venture is to be commercially viable, it is vital that the cash investor should expect to be able to appropriate the fruits to itself. This is difficult enough for a single innovating firm, especially when patent protection is not possible or too expensive. Indeed, when the investment is first made it may be uncertain whether a patentable invention will emerge. It is even more difficult to ensure that each firm can reap where it has sown when the work is done jointly. It can be done only by contract, which must be enforceable.

When the parties need the results for different purposes, it may suffice merely to ensure that the other party keeps any results secret from the rest of the world, informs its partner of new technology and grants licences under any intellectual property rights it may acquire. Sometimes there may be field-of-use restrictions to restrain either party from entering the other's market.

When the parties want the results for the same purpose each may have to ensure also that the other does not over-exploit the market at its expense. Often it is impossible to foretell at the time the agreement is being negotiated how much the work will cost or whether it will be successful, let alone how successful. Sometimes the only possible formula for joint R & D is that A will pay for a proportion of the cost and B for the rest, and that they will benefit from the results in agreed proportions.

In that event, the protection may take the form of agreed quotas or joint sales. Alternatively, the world market may be divided territorially. The protection may take various forms, but some protection against over-exploitation by the other may be commercially necessary to induce investment.

---

11   The sub-contracting notice, 11.9 above, is a notable exception.

Should these restrictions on conduct be seen as anti-competitive or as ancillary restraints necessary to make viable co-operation that may increase competition? Is this a question of fact? For how long can they be shown to be indispensable? *Ex post*, it may be argued that such an agreement results in a single seller or imposes quotas on each party. No one minds if A and B are unimportant in the market, but if there are only a few firms, these restrictions on conduct are important.

On the other hand, without these restrictions, neither party could be sure of recovering the benefit of the investment in joint research. It might be that neither would supply its best technology if the other could use it to compete immediately or soon afterwards, so such restrictions on conduct may be necessary for several years after the investment starts to bring in profits. Perceived *ex ante,* the restrictions are ancillary and, if no wider than reasonably necessary, may be pro-competitive if they enable each party to appropriate the expected benefit of its investment and, so, make the joint venture viable.

I have complained throughout this book of the Commission's practice of exempting rather than clearing agreements containing ancillary restrictions needed to make viable some agreement that may well increase competition. If the application of Article 81(3) is required, the burden of proof is on the person alleging the agreement is valid, and it may be more difficult to enforce the term. This may deter some marginal joint ventures or cause the parties to operate them less aggressively.

13.2.1.3 *More realistic attitude to be taken to potential competition*—In its *XIIIth Report on Competition Policy* for 1983, pages 50–52, the Commission promised to look more realistically before finding an inherent anti-competitive effect in joint ventures.[12] It said that in deciding whether the parties were potential competitors the Commission would consider each party's ability to finance the operation independently, the productive capacity of each party, its familiarity with the process technology, the size of the demand and the distribution facilities of each party, as well as its ability to bear the risk.

It seemed that the Commission was prepared to analyse the situation *ex ante*, at the time the joint venture was entered into and neither party had access to the other's resources. We hoped for clearance, not exemption, of agreements between those with complementary resources, or where the risk was too great for a single firm and so forth.

In its next two decisions, the Commission did, indeed, not find that the parties were potential competitors, but in the first case, *BP/Kellogg*,[13] the

---

12 Confirmed by the Commission's notice concerning the assessment of co-operative joint ventures [1993] 5 CMLR 401, para 15, replaced by the horizontal guidelines (13.2.3 below) and more generally in Guidelines on the Application of Art 81(3) of the Treaty, OJ 2004, C101/97, Gs 17 and 18.
13 [1986] 2 CMLR 619.

Commission found that ancillary restrictions which, when dealing with Article 81(3), it described as 'reasonable and necessary' restricted competition and required exemption.

The parties had complementary technology: BP had come across a catalyst it thought would be useful for making ammonia and Kellogg designs and builds process plants. They agreed to collaborate to design a plant in which to produce ammonia using BP's catalyst. BP agreed to sell its catalyst only to Kellogg's customers, and Kellogg not to invest in ways of producing ammonia without the use of the catalyst, without first telling BP and giving it a chance to resile from the contract. This arrangement for limited exclusivity for both parties was found to infringe Article 81(1) and exempted.

In *Optical Fibres*,[14] Corning Glass had developed optical fibres which revolutionised the technology used for telecommunications networks. It entered into two joint ventures to produce the fibres, one with BICC in the United Kingdom and another with Siemens in the Federal Republic. Corning could have made the fibres in Europe, but would have had difficulty in selling them to the PTTs, most of which were state owned and tended to buy only from firms within the country. Neither Siemens nor BICC could have made the fibres without a technology licence from Corning.

There were two other joint ventures, one between Corning and a French cable maker, which was likely to be exempted once it had been renegotiated to conform to the Commission's ideas, and one which was also being negotiated by Corning with a Spanish firm. Corning had also granted licences to firms in other Member States.

The Commission found that each individual joint venture did not restrict competition, since the parties contributed complementary technology. Unaided, the cable makers could not have produced the fibres, nor Corning the cables (at paragraph 46). This was the precedent for which we had waited since the Commission's *XIIIth Report*, stating that where not more than one of the parties could enter the market, a joint venture does not have an inherent anti-competitive effect. The Commission accepted also that a licence to a joint venture is a good way to disseminate technology (at paragraph 59).

In *Optical Fibres*, the Commission added that a network of joint ventures infringes Article 81(1) when a provider of technology has a substantial interest and control over each joint venture and the market is oligopolistic (at paragraph 48). Its theory is that Corning might use its control over one joint venture to prevent its expansion in order to protect one of the others.

The Commission granted an exemption only after Corning reduced its managerial control, the technology licence ceased to be exclusive, the territorial protection was reduced below that permitted by the patent licensing regulation (presumably because of the horizontal relationship between the joint ventures), each party was entitled to expand the capacity of the joint venture,

14   OJ 1986, L235/30.

either with the consent of the other or, if that was refused, by paying for the additional capacity and taking a larger share of the benefit. There were other provisions to ensure that information about each joint venture's prices and output was not passed on to the other joint ventures.

In *BBC Brown Boveri/NGK*,[15] the Commission exempted a joint venture agreement which, in my view, should have been cleared rather than exempted. BBC was trying to develop a sodium sulphur battery for use in vehicles, but lacked technology in the ceramics required for insulation. NGK had developed the technology for ceramics, but had no access to technology relating to batteries. The Commission alleged that NGK became a potential competitor of BBC when it acquired the latter's technology through its share in the joint venture and that, consequently, its agreement not to export from the Far East infringed Article 81(1) and required exemption. The joint venture restricted no competition that would have been possible without it.

This is regretted. Impliedly, in *BP/Kellogg* and expressly in *Optical Fibres* the Commission looked *ex ante*: to the position that existed without the joint venture and licence in deciding whether the parties were potential competitors.[16] The Commission has not been consistent in clearing joint ventures.

13.2.1.3.1 *ODIN*—In 1990, the Commission adopted a decision clearing the *ODIN* joint venture between Metal Box and Elopak to develop a carton with a replaceable metal lid to contain aseptic particulate foodstuffs.[17] The Commission decided:

—First, that the venturers were not even potential competitors: the technology and other resources provided by each were complementary. Each parent lacked one element of it.

—Secondly, the joint venture was unlikely to foreclose other parties, since each party to the joint venture had important competitors in its own field.

—Thirdly, the joint venture to make a completely new product was risky and would require substantial investment, so the ancillary restrictions were also cleared as necessary for the joint venture.

—ODIN was given the exclusive right to exploit the know-how and any improvements made to it for the field of use specified which, according to the Commission, guaranteed that ODIN would concentrate its best efforts on the project. Each party would obtain access to the technology for the specified field of use, so would be able to compete in the field of the joint venture when it ended. The ancillary restrictions were very limited, but it was most encouraging that the agreement, including an exclusive right, was cleared and not exempted.

---

15   [1989] 4 CMLR 610, para 18.
16   See the notice on horizontal cooperation, G 24, second indent, (13.4 below).
17   [1991] 4 CMLR 832.

Unfortunately, most of the formal decisions on cooperative joint ventures since *ODIN* have been exemptions and not clearances, although it seems as if some of them foreclosed no competition that was possible without the joint venture.[18] Nevertheless, some provisions that might well have been treated as restrictive of competition in earlier periods have been cleared.

In *Olivetti/Digital*,[19] for instance, the Commission said that Olivetti's agreement to use only Digital's technology for its RISK architecture 'does not restrict Olivetti's competitive freedom beyond what is inherent in any choice of a specific RISK platform.' Olivetti needed such a platform and, given the investment required, would not be likely to use more than one even without a contractual commitment. Nevertheless, the Commission exempted and did not clear the obligation to buy parts from Digital rather than from its technology licensees.

13.2.1.3.2 *European Night Services*—The breakthrough came with the judgment of the CFI in *European Night Services*.[20] The CFI quashed the Commission's decision on an expensive and risky joint venture between four incumbent train operators in different Member States, each with a monopoly for its home country. The Commission decided that their agreement to provide passenger services under the Channel tunnel between distant cities at night infringed Article 81(1) and granted an exemption for only 10 years after notification and subject to conditions.

The CFI quashed the decision for failure to give adequate reasons for almost all its findings. Some chambers of the CFI are controlling the Commission's decision by quashing decisions when the Commission fails to give adequate reasons. There were serious omissions in the decision which could not be remedied later in the Commission's submissions to the CFI. For instance, it had failed to state the market shares of the parties or of its competitors. Only on a very narrow market definition, which was that most unfavourable to the parties, did their market share reach 7% or 8%. The Commission had not established any appreciable effects on the market—it was not enough to say that a joint venture between competitors might exceed the 5% threshold mentioned in the notice on minor agreements current at the time.

The CFI stressed that a realistic appraisal was required before the Commission objected that existing and potential competition was restricted between the parents, between them and ENS or vis-à-vis third parties and that they were aggravated by a network of joint ventures (paras 135–60). It

---

18 *Konsortium ECR 900* [1992] 4 CMLR 54 concerned a short term consortium for a single round of tenders and was cleared. *Iridium* [1997] 4 CMLR 1065 was cleared because of the vast scale of the investment and the technical and commercial risk. See also Guideline 24 second indent, (13.4 below).
19 OJ 1994, L309/24, para 20.
20 *European Night Services and others v Commission*, cases T–374/94, [1998] ECR II–3141.

indicated carefully the various ways in which the Commission's analysis was not realistic.

Since the Commission had not adequately established an infringement of Article 81(1), there was no need to consider the conditions imposed on the exemption—the requirement that the parents supply the special high speed locomotives, train crews and paths under the channel to any new entrant who wanted to compete with them. Nevertheless, the CFI continued its objections. The decision did not contain the relevant analytical data about the structure and operation of the market on which ENS was to operate, so the Commission was not in a position to show that access would be indispensable for a new entrant. It would have to show that it was not possible to buy or rent locomotives and train or hire qualified drivers etc. Moreover, the Commission had defined the market to include other methods of travel. The Commission's own directive provided access for third parties to paths under the Channel (205–21).

The CFI also objected that an exemption only 'for the period for which it can reasonably be supposed that market conditions will remain the same'; 10 years from the notification, was inappropriate for a 'product dependent on securing advantageous 20 year financing.'

> 230. . . . even if it is assumed that the Commission's assessment of the restrictions on competition in the contested decision were adequate and correct, the Court considers that the duration of an exemption granted under Article 85(3) (now 81(1)) of the Treaty . . . must be sufficient to enable the benefits justifying such exemption, namely, in the present case, the contribution to economic progress and the benefits to consumers provided by the introduction of new high-quality transport services, . . . Since, moreover, such progress and benefits cannot be achieved without considerable investment, the length of time required to ensure a proper return on that investment is necessarily an essential factor to be taken into account when determining the duration of an exemption, particularly, in a case such as the present, where it is undisputed that the services in question are completely new, involve major investments and substantial financial risks and require the pooling of know-how by the participating undertakings.

The CFI treated the decision like a boxer's punch ball. Technically any one of its points would have sufficed to quash the decision. It chose, however, to attack it in many ways, and this has led to the Commission making more realistic analyses. It is one of the recent judgments stressing the relevance of risk and the need to finance large risky investments.

13.2.2 The group effect—spillover

In several decisions, the Commission has been concerned that once the parties find that collaboration is fruitful in reducing competition, it may spread to other activities: they may cease to compete aggressively in other markets.

In *Wano Schwarzpulver*,[21] for instance, the Commission said that both parties had interests in explosives, explosives accessories and safety fuse. The joint venture in black powder would give 'opportunities and strong inducements' for market allocation in safety fuse.

The parties may lessen this fear by arranging that only a limited number of employees will work on the joint venture and will not come into contact with the parents' other employees more than is necessary, though this may discourage brighter employees working for the joint venture. Sometimes the parties agree that the joint venture will hire its own personnel and agree that they will not themselves employ anyone that has worked for the joint venture.

No joint venture has been prohibited solely on this ground, and in *European Night Services*,[22] the CFI, in quashing a Commission decision, rejected the Commission's argument based on other joint ventures of the parties to transport goods through the Channel Tunnel, in particular two joint ventures to transport freight and vehicles on the ground that these were related markets, whereas ENS related to passenger trains.

13.2.2.1 *Spillover under the merger regulation*—Under Article 2(4) of the merger regulation, coordination between the parents is judged according to the tests of Article 81 as part of the merger investigation and subject to the same short time limits. The Commission's case law has helped to clarify its analysis. In *Telia/Telenor/Schibsted*,[23] it identified three relevant markets and found that in none of them would the merger create or strengthen a dominant position.

When turning to analyse the possibility of coordination, it identified the markets in which coordination was possible, and then considered whether the coordination therein would be likely, appreciable and result from the merger.[24] With regard to the likelihood of coordination, the Commission focused on whether the characteristics of the market were conducive to coordination. On appreciability it seems to have gone further than the notice on minor agreements and it looked just to the creation of the joint venture and not to previous links between the parties. The test of appreciability is traditional under Article 81(1), but those of likelihood and causality are welcome new developments.

13.2.3 *Foreclosure*

The Commission should be concerned when firms with access to separate, scarce resources combine to create a monopoly, in which case it may want to

---

21   [1979] 1 CMLR 403, para 30.
22   *European Night Services and others v Commission*, T–374/94, [1998] ECR II–3141, (13.2.1.1 above).
23   IV/JV1 (1998), [1999] 4 CMLR 216, para 28.
24   Faull and Nikpay, paras 6.111–6.122.

enable others to have access to the resource. This concern is exemplified by the Commission's decision in *European Night Services*.[25] The decision was reversed by the CFI[26] on the ground that the Commission's reasoning had not established that third parties did not have access.

In *Tetra Pak I*,[27] the Commission was concerned by an acquisition which brought into the same hands two competing technologies for treating milk to be placed in cartons aseptically. It closed its proceedings under Article 82, when the technology licence acquired was made non-exclusive.

It is now clear from Guidelines 43 and 45[28] that the Commission would not treat a significant improvement in an existing product as being in the same market as the traditional version. Consequently, the parties' share of the traditional products or technologies can be ignored when there is a major breakthrough making the old technology obsolescent. Guidleline 27 to the new guidelines on technology transfer states:

> In order to determine the competitive relationship between the parties it is necessay to examine whether the parties would have been actual or potential competitors in the absence of the agreement.

This represents a radical change of mind by the Commission which applies also to other kinds of transaction:[29] if without the joint venture the parties could not have competed, the joint venture will not be treated as being between actual or potential competitors.

Another concern of the Commission is that too many firms from a particular industry may join in the joint venture, leaving no firms with which other undertakings might form a joint venture.[30]

It is for this reason that the group exemption for cooperation in R & D, (analysed at 13.5 below), applies only if the parties have a market share in the common market of under 30%.

13.2.4 *Networks of joint ventures*

A fourth concern in a concentrated market is that a single technology provider will enter into several joint ventures with different partners, and may deter the joint ventures from competing with each other (*optical fibres*, 13.2.1.3 above)

---

25   T–374/94, [1998] ECR II–3141, paras 79–89.
26   (T–374, 375, 384 & 388/94), [1998] ECR II–3141, 205–21, (13.2.2.2 above).
27   [1990] 4 CMLR 47, confirmed by CFI (T–51/89) [1990] ECR II–309.
28   Guidelines on the applicability of Art 81 to horizontal co-operation, OJ 2001, C3/2, [2001] 4 CMLR 819.
29   Gs 17 and 18 to the Notice on Article 81(3), OJ 2004, C101/97
30   See *Odin* [1991] 4 CMLR 832, para 27, (13.2.1.3.1 above).

13.2.5 *Joint sales organisations*

Joint sales organisations are seldom ancillary to a pro-competitive joint venture, and at 8.2.3 above we saw that they are usually treated by the Commission as classic cartels that enable the parties to restrict production and raise price.

The Commission cleared a joint sales organisation as not having appreciable effects in *SAFCO*[31] whereby small makers of preserves were able to penetrate the German market where they met substantial competition. In *SPAR*,[32] too, it cleared a buying group that enabled small grocers to increase their buying power towards the level exercised by multiple retailers with which they competed. Each was entitled to buy separately as much as it liked, and many bought independently. In my view that should have been cleared because individually they would not have been able to compete effectively.

The ECJ has held that co-operative buying and selling organisations with small market shares do not infringe Article 81(1), even when members agree for long periods to buy largely from or sell to the organisation and there is a penalty on leaving it, provided that the rules are proportional to the functions of the joint operation.[33] The rules of the association must be appraised in the light of their economic context.

Where the joint selling has almost a monopoly the ECJ confirmed in *Stremsel v Commission*,[34] that joint buying infringed Article 81.

Occasionally, the Commission has tolerated a joint sales organisation with market power. In *Finnpap*,[35] where the Commission thought that after the agreement had been modified, trade between Member States was unlikely to be appreciable, it granted an informal clearance. The somewhat surprising result may be explained politically, since the Commission may not have wanted to offend Finland just before it finally agreed to join the Community.

It is difficult to see how a joint sales organisation can restrict production to raise price unless the parties accept restrictions on production or agree to share profits. In *UIP*[36] (8.2.3 above) it exempted a joint sales organisation for films when very substantial cost savings were expected. There were no quotas, but the Commission perceived a slight possibility of the parties sharing profits through their dividends from the joint venture. This it prevented, so there was

31   [1972] CMLR D83.
32   [1975] 2 CMLR D14.
33   *E.g.*, *Coberco* (C–399/93) [1995] ECR I–4515, paras 9–20.
34   *StremselI* (61/80), [1981] ECR 851, confirming the Commission's decision in *Rennet*, [1980] 2 CMLR 402.
35   (8.2.3 above). The Commission published its decision under Art 19(3) to take a favourable view [1989] 4 CMLR 413. This was followed by press release IP (89) 496.
36   [1990] 4 CMLR 749, para 44. A further notification was made after the exemption expired and further undertakings were given. Because of the heterogenous nature of the product and the cost savings due to avoiding duplication, the Commission sent a favourable comfort letter.

no way the parties could restrict production to raise price. The agreement was exempted, not cleared.

Even when a joint venture extends from R & D and production to marketing, the Commission will usually object to joint sales unless they can be justified, as they were in *De Laval/Stork* (13.2.1 above).[37]

13.3 Disadvantages to industry of the Commission's refusal to clear joint ventures

Until May 2004, major difficulties in enforcing agreements arose from the Commission's unwillingness to clear joint ventures when the parties could not have competed as effectively individually, or when the joint venture created benefits to consumers. This is less serious now that NCAs and courts have power to apply Article 81(3). Nevertheless, the burden is on the parties to show that an agreement qualifies under Article 81(3). So its recent acceptance in three sets of guidelines, especially those on the application generally of Article 81(3), paragraphs 17 and 18, that where the parties could not have operated without the agreement, they are not to be treated as actual or potential competitors, is most welcome.

I am delighted that the success of a risky and expensive joint venture, resulting in a large market share, may no longer cause the ancillary restraints necessary to appropriate the benefit of investment to become invalid just when they are needed, leading the parties to invest only if the expect to earn sufficient profit before their market share becomes too high.

13.4 Guidelines on joint ventures

The Commission's guidelines on horizontal cooperation[38] define horizontal agreements as those between 'companies operating at the same level(s) in the market' without considering whether they could have operated without the agreement. Two other guidelines, however, look *ex ante*. Guideline 14, second indent, states that 'cooperation between competing companies that cannot independently carry out the project or activity covered by the cooperation' does not fall within Article 81(1) and Guideline 20 refers to the need under Article 81(1) to consider an agreement in its economic context. Nevertheless Guidelines 32 *et seq* take account of economic benefits arising from joint ventures under Article 81(3). I regret this, as the burden of proof is then on the parties. It is hoped that Guideline 27 relating to technology transfer demonstrates that the Commission will look *ex ante* and clear agreements when the parties could not have operated without the agreement.

---

37   [1977] 2 CMLR D69 (13.2.1 above).
38   Guidelines on the applicability of Article 81 to horizontal co-operation, OJ 2001, C3/2, [2001] 4 CMLR 819.

27. In order to determine the competitive relationship between the parties it is necessary to examine whether the parties would have been actual or potential competitors in the absence of the agreement. If without the agreement the parties would
not have been actual or potential competitors in any relevant market affected by
the agreement they are deemed to be non-competitors.

It is confirmed generally in Guidelines 17 and 18 of the notice on Article 81(1).

The horizontal guidelines state that joint ventures may lead to substantial
economic benefits. They may enable companies to respond to the competitive
pressures driven by globalisation and the speed of technological progress. On
the other hand they may restrict competition and a balance must be struck
between the two (Guideline 4). Greater emphasis will be placed on economic
criteria.

It then lists the kinds of agreement illegal in themselves, and the kinds that
escape Article 81(1) generally and in relation to various kinds of agreement.
And the matters, especially market power to be considered in other cases. It
will however, consider efficiencies mainly under Article 81(3).[39]

13.5 The group exemption for co-operative R & D

Although the Commission has not been prepared to exempt joint ventures
generally by regulation, since the criteria are not easy to apply, in Regulation
2659/2000,[40] it has exempted *en bloc* a limited class of joint ventures for
R & D. The Regulation is due to expire at the end of 2010, and is only a little
more useful than Regulation 418/85, which it replaces. In this edition, I shall
discuss it very shortly.

Where the parties need the results for different purposes, their joint venture
is unlikely to infringe Article 81(1), since the only restrictive provisions likely
to be needed are not to divulge secret know-how, pass on to its partner new
technology and possibly a field of use restriction. These may be imposed
under the group exemption.

Few agreements qualify under Regulation 2659/2000 when the parties need
the results for the same purpose: it does not apply when there are ancillary
provisions enabling each joint venturer to ensure that the others do not over-
exploit. Quotas are blacklisted (Article 5(1)(c)), little territorial protection is
permitted (Article 5(1)(f) and (g)), although a field-of-use restriction may
suffice when the parties need the results for different markets. Where the parties are not competitors, the exemption applies for the duration of the R & D
and joint exploitation is allowed for seven years from the time when the contract products were first put on the market and thereafter until a market share
of 25% is reached (Article 4(1) & (3)). Article 4(2) permits joint sales by competing undertakings for the seven years only if they do not have a market

---

39   Gs 32–38, but see G 24 second indent.
40   For research and development agreements, OJ 2000, L304/7, [2001] 4 CMLR 808.

share of 25% when the joint venture starts and thereafter until their market share reaches 25%. These provisions may enable each to appropriate the benefit of its investment when the market is broad, but where the results will constitute a new market it will not protect each from over-exploitation by the others after the seven years from first marketing. It is hoped that where the results are sufficiently novel, the agreement will not infringe Article 81 (Guidelines 43, 49 and 51).

The most important provision in the Regulation is recital 3 which states that joint ventures for R & D that do not continue into exploitation usually do not need exemption as generally they are not caught by Article 81(1). There is no need to tailor these to fit the Regulation. Where the market shares permitted under Article 3 are exceeded, it may be that the agreement will be found not to infringe Article 81(1) especially where there are competing centres of innovation outside the common market.

The current Regulation exempts slightly more than did Regulation 418/85 in that the ceiling of market share under Article 3 is higher than formerly. The black list has been slightly limited.

13.6 Conclusion on joint ventures

In the field of joint ventures there has been continuing tension between those who think *ex post* and those who think *ex ante*. Seen *ex ante*, substantial investment will not be made unless each joint venturer can ensure that it will be able to supply an agreed proportion of the demand, or obtain the agreed proportion of the results through dividends obtained from the joint venture, which makes the sale. Seen *ex post*, after the investments have been made, it would be more competitive for the venturers to compete with each other and others. For significant periods, able Commission officials who thought *ex ante* were in charge of joint ventures, and many comfort letters were written stating that the joint venture did not infringe Article 81(1) even when provisions enabled the joint venturers to appropriate an agreed share of the benefits.

Under Article 81(3), it may well be that the Commission has been too generous in permitting joint ventures. Few have been forbidden, but the Commission has substantial discretion when applying Article 81 and, from the published decisions it is impossible to be sure whether a prospective joint venture will infringe Article 81. It is not yet clear whether the CFI and ECJ will allow such a wide discretion to national courts and authorities.

13.7 Specialisation agreements

When the common market was established many small and medium-sized firms were too small to be able to utilise fully an automatic production line, or achieve other economies of scale or scope in either production or distribution.

The Commission encouraged specialisation agreements between such firms, often in different Member States, under which the production of one range of products was allocated to one party and another range to another and each appointed the other or others as its exclusive distributor in the other's home market.

In this way, exports became easier because there was no need to set up a new sales network, the output of each party often increased rapidly and, if this warranted the installation and full use of an automatic production line, costs were dramatically reduced, often by a quarter or a third.

One of the reasons for establishing the common market was to facilitate specialisation, so it is not surprising that the Commission favoured such agreements. Frequently, the only competition restricted was the possibility of each firm extending production into the other's range. They agreed that both firms should sell the full range, and the Commission considered this to be more competitive than a joint venture if the latter resulted in a single seller. Specialisation agreements are less frequent now than thirty years ago.

13.7.1 *Effects of specialisation agreements on competition*

Where there was a large number of firms making all the products that were subject to the specialisation agreement, any reduction of competition between the parties was unlikely to be significant, and cost savings were likely to increase the effectiveness of each to such an extent that competition was increased, not restricted. In accordance with its practice in other fields, however, and arguably inconsistently with the judgments of the Community Court (8.1.2 above), where total market shares exceed the percentage given in the notice on minor agreements, the Commission has considered only the reduction in the number of competitors under Article 81(1), the effectiveness of their competition being taken into account only under Article 81(3).

From 1970, the Commission granted individual exemptions, not clearances, to such agreements and, in 1972, it granted a group exemption, which was extended to rather larger firms in 1985 and 2001(13.7.3 below).

13.7.2 *Individual decisions*

An early individual decision was *Clima Chappée/Buderus*.[41] Each of two participants was allocated a list of air-conditioning products, which the other agreed not to make unless its turnover exceeded a level to be agreed. For those products not allocated to either party, each was to give preference to the other when buying, provided that price and quality were equal. Clima Chappée was a French firm, already established in supplying air-conditioning apparatus, while Buderus was a German firm new to this field. There were no restrictions

---

41 [1970] CMLR D7.

on sale, save in the Federal Republic of Germany, where Clima Chappée agreed to sell only to Buderus, and in France, where Buderus agreed to sell only to Clima Chappée. The Commission stated that there were a large number of undertakings which made and sold air-conditioning equipment comparable to that made by the parties.

Despite the last statement, the Commission found that the agreement had the object of restricting potential competition, in that the parties each gave up their freedom of action in various respects. Each agreed not to make the products allocated to the other, not to sell in the other's country save through the other and to give preference to the other when buying the products that were not allocated to either. Neither gave up the manufacture of any products it was already making, but the Commission held that the specialisation arrangement restricted potential competition in that each firm had the financial backing and other attributes necessary to extend its range.

The agreement was exempted on the ground that the elimination of duplication and the economies derived from passing to series production and so forth improved both production and distribution and increased consumer choice. There were other firms to compete. If, as seems unlikely, the agreement did really restrict competition, the key policy question should have been whether these benefits could have been obtained by any means that would have left possible any potential competition between the two firms. This issue was not addressed. The exemption expired in 1979.

There were several similar decisions, in some of which the Commission seems merely to have certified the matters on which it must be satisfied if it is to apply Article 81(3). An extreme example was *Fine Papers*,[42] where the specialisation between the French makers of cigarette and other very thin papers seems to have eliminated most of the competition that remained in that industry, without ensuring that any benefits were passed on to consumers.

In some decisions, the Commission ignored effective competition under Article 81(1). In *Rank/Sopelem*,[43] it held that an agreement infringed Article 81(1) because the parties were potential competitors in a concentrated market (paragraph 22) and exempted it on the ground that the restrictions were indispensable, as without them the parties could not have supplied such a comprehensive range of products. It added that other large suppliers provided effective competition (paragraph 28).

By exempting rather than clearing the agreement, the Commission was able to put pressure on the parties to ensure that each would remain capable of selling in both countries when the agreement came to an end (paragraph 17). It pointed out that the Sopelem lenses were to be sold under Rank trade marks, which would make it very difficult for Sopelem to distribute them independently when the exemption came to an end and seems to have

42   [1972] CMLR D94.
43   [1975] 1 CMLR D72.

persuaded the parties to modify the agreement, so that Sopelem would be entitled to buy the mark at the end of the period.

There is much to be said for arranging that both the manufacturer's and the distributor's mark be used, so that when the agreement comes to an end, each will have a reputation in all areas where its goods have been marketed, or where it has marketed the other's goods. On the other hand, the change in contractual terms gave Sopalem an opportunity to renegotiate the deal after Rank had invested in building up its reputation: the very evil the Commission was trying to avoid.

13.7.3 *Group exemption – Regulation 2658/2000*

In Regulation 417/85 confirmed later in Regulation 2658/2000,[44] the Commission extended the earlier group exemption for specialisation agreements to more important agreements. The specialisation group exemption applies even if the agreement is made between more than two undertakings. Article 1 exempts:

> the following agreements entered into between two or more undertakings . . . which relate to the conditions under which those undertakings specialise in the production of products:

> (a) unilateral specialisation agreements, by virtue of which one party agrees to cease production of certain products or to refrain from producing those products and to purchase them from a competing undertaking, while the competing undertaking agrees to produce and supply those products: or
> (b) reciprocal specialisation agreements, by virtue of which two or more parties on a reciprocal basis agree to cease or refrain from producing different specified products and to purchase these products from the other parties, who agree to supply them; or
> (c) joint production agreements, by virtue of which two or more parties agree to produce certain products jointly.

Article 1(2) permits ancillary provisions to be included, such as those concerning the assignment or use of intellectual property rights. Exclusive buying and marketing arrangements are also exempted by Article 3.

To revert to the facts of *Clima Chappée* (13.7.2 above) had the Regulation been in force at the time, Clima Chappée could have agreed not to make the items allocated to Buderus, to supply only Buderus in the Federal Republic of Germany and not to make similar agreements about air-conditioners with anyone else, and vice versa. Alternatively, they could have arranged for joint production and sale only by the parties.

This gives considerable protection to each party from competition from the other parties. Clima Chappée could probably be restrained from distributing the products allocated to it in the Federal Republic directly to large users as

---

44   For specialisaton agreements OJ 2000, L304/3, [2001] 4 CMLR 800.

well as to dealers. Nevertheless, buyers in France from Clima Chappée must not be deterred from selling in the Federal Republic. This would make it difficult to charge very different prices in the different areas. If there had been a third party from England, it could have been given exclusive distribution rights there by both the other parties, but would probably have had to be free to sell goods made by the other parties also in France and the Federal Republic.

Since the parties often make complementary products, they may well be potential competitors and may actually have competed before the conclusion of the agreement. It is therefore important that the Regulation should not apply if collectively the parties enjoy market power. So Article 4 provides a ceiling of the combined market share of 20%. This is lower than in the group exemption for vertical agreements because the parties may have been competitors before the agreement, and a little lower than in that for R & D because specialisation agreements are less likely to lead to improved technology.

Where the parties' market share is larger, such agreements may be treated as elements of a classic cartels and heavy fines be imposed. In *Trefileurope Sales v Commission*,[45] the CFI confirmed the Commission's view and said:

> because of its intrinsic gravity and obviousness, that [specialisation] agreement constitutes an infringement of Article 81(1) of the Treaty.

Were it not for the limitation of market share, I would be very concerned about specialisation agreements, but only when there are significant entry barriers and few competitors.

13.8 Bibliography

Joseph Brodley, 'Joint Ventures and Antitrust Policy' (1982) 95 *Harvard Law Review*, 1521; the decision in *Optical Fibres* was largely based on Brodley's thinking.

Jonathan Faull, 'Joint Ventures Under the EEC Competition Rules' [1984] *European Competition Law Review*, 358.

Barry Hawk, 'Joint Ventures under EEC law' [1992] 2 *Fordham International Law Journal*, 303.

——, **and** *Henry Husser*, 'A Bright Line Shareholding test to end the Nightmare under the EEC Merger Regulation' (1993) 30 *CML Rev*, 115.

Alexis Jacquemin **and** *Bernard Spinoit*, 'Economic and Legal Aspects of Cooperative Research: A European View,' in Barry Hawk (ed) [1985] *Fordham Corporate Law Institute*, chapter 24.

Valentine Korah, R & D Joint Ventures and the EEC Competition Rules: Regulation 418/85 (ESC, Oxford, 1986).

——, 'Critical comments on the Commission's recent decisions exempting joint ventures to exploit research that needs further development' (1987) 12 *EL Rev*, 18.

——, 'Collaborative joint ventures for research and development where markets are concentrated: the competition rules of the common market and the invalidity of contracts' [1992] 2 *Fordham International Law Journal* 248.

45   141/89, [1995] ECR II 791, para 97.

Angus Maciver, 'EEC Competition Policy in High Technology Industries' [1985] *Fordham Corporate Law Institute*, chapter 25.

John Temple Lang, 'International Joint Ventures under Community Law.' [1999] *Fordham Corporate Law Institute*.

James S Venit, 'The Treatment of Joint Ventures under the EC Merger Regulation—Almost Through the Thicket,' [1999] *Fordham Corporate Law Institute*.

14. Conclusion

My object in this chapter, written more than 40 years after the adoption of the first implementing regulation, is to assess some aspects of competition policy and of the institutions that enforce it. In the past I have complained about the paucity of economic reasoning by the Commission, and in this edition I shall discuss some of the steps the Commission and CFI have taken to meet the criticism. I will express my personal conviction that competition policy and its enforcement have improved dramatically over the last decade and the Commission's initiative to abandon its monopoly over Article 81(3) promises vast change, largely for the better.

14.1 Criticisms

14.1.1 *The paucity of economic analysis in the Commission's and Courts' public decisions*

In previous editions I complained about the lack of reasoning by the Commission to connect specific facts with the legal conclusions in its decisions. Now that the Commission is adopting virtually no decisions under Article 81(1) except in order to impose a fine on cartels, this criticism is less appropriate, although it still applies to Article 82. The Commission has explained its reasons for objecting to hard core cartels on many occasions. The reasoning in its merger decisions is of mixed quality and three decisions were quashed by the CFI last year for insufficient reasoning or manifest error of appraisal.[1]

In *Airtours* (paragraph 62) the CFI made it clear that the Commission may rely on economic theory only if it establishes the conditions necessary for its application. The CFI has been quashing decisions of the Commission for failure to give adequate reasons for its conclusions. This has had the effect of tightening the preparation of its decisions (14.2.4 below). The CFI ensures that the Commission establishes simple facts alleged such as the contents of a letter, but leaves it a substantial margin of discretion over economic analysis and policy.[2]

The ECJ also refuses to review the Commission's economic analysis.[3] The ECJ made assertions of principle and provided little economic analysis even in the cases I welcomed at 11.3 for perceiving transactions *ex ante* at the time when commitments to investment are required, such as *Nungesser*,[4]

---

1 *Air Tours/First Choice* (T–342/99) [2002] ECR II–2585, [2002] 5 CMLR 317; *Tetra Laval BV v Commission* (T–5/02) [2002] ECR–II 4381, [2002] 5 CMLR 1182 and *Schneider/Legrand* (T–310/01), [2002] ECR II–2387, II–4071 [2003] 4 CMLR 678.
2 *Airtours*, para 64 (12.2.6.1.3 above).
3 *E.g.*, *Consten and Grundig v Commission* (56 & 58/64) [1966] ECR 299; *Windsurfing* (193/83) [1986] ECR 611.
4 (258/78) [1982] ECR 2015 (11.3 above).

Coditel II[5] and *Erauw-Jacquéry*.[6] It is frequently not possible to advise businessmen what the attitude of the courts or Commission to their agreement is likely to be.

Many decisions on joint ventures (13.2.1–13.2.1.3.2 above) are also based on inadequate analysis. Few are analysed *ex ante* as promised in the Commission's *XIIIth Report on Competition Policy*.[7] Nevertheless, in *Optical Fibres*,[8] a decision I welcome, the Commission spelled out its reasoning much more clearly. It stated at paragraphs 46 and 47 that since Corning Glass was not in the cable market, nor BICC or Siemens in that for optical fibre, the parties were not even potential competitors, and each joint venture was not, in itself, caught by Article 81(1). A joint venture was an excellent way of disseminating rapidly developing technology.

Moreover, when stating at paragraphs 48–53 that the network of joint ventures with a common partner which provided the technology infringed Article 81(1), the Commission explained its theory: that the common partner might restrict production in one joint venture in order to enable one of the others to increase its prices.

In *European Night Services*,[9] the CFI insisted on a realistic analysis of contractual restraints both in the light of their economic context and the need to induce substantial and risky investment. Well analysed reasoning need not add to the length of a decision, as the Commission can limit the factual part to what is relevant for or against its conclusion. It may be easier for an official to draft a decision without articulating the appropriate economic analysis and it used to be less likely to be held invalid by the ECJ if there was little reasoning to criticise. Nowadays, however, the CFI is emphasising the requirement to give adequate reasons for the Commission's findings under both Article 81(1) and Article 81(3). A decision is now less likely to be quashed if cogent reasons are articulated. By seldom spelling out the economic and legal theory more precisely in its decisions and in the recitals to its regulations, the Commission has missed a chance to educate not only business and its advisers, but also its own officials, national authorities, national courts and the Community Courts. Wide discretion makes work easy for those who enjoy the discretion, but impossible for those who advise firms whose business decisions are affected by it.

The recitals to the Commission's regulations and its notices usually state its conclusions but rarely explain the reasons for the policy, although to some extent this is done in guidelines.

5   (262/81) [1982] ECR 3381 (11.3 above).
6   (27/87) [1988] ECR 1919 (11.3 above).
7   [1993] 5 CMLR 401, point 55 and notice on co-operative joint ventures, para 19, (13.2.1.3 above).
8   OJ 1986, L236/30 (13.2.2 above). See also *ODIN* [1991] 4 CMLR 832 (13.2.1.3.1 above), where the Commission spelled out all its causes for concern and explained why none of them applied to the joint venture.
9   (T–374/94 and others), [1998] ECR II–3141 (13.2.1.3.2 above).

In the notice on market definition[10] (4.3.1.1 above) the economic analysis is articulated. Unfortunately, the more abstract hypothetical monopolist test to which the theory relates has rarely been used by the Commission, and then, mainly in merger cases. More often it uses the more concrete test adopted by the ECJ—substitutes on the demand side—by reference to their 'characteristics, price and intended use.'

14.1.2 *The Commission's view that Article 81(1) prohibits any restriction of conduct that is significant on the market*

In the early days, the Commission obtained exclusive power to grant individual exemptions so that it could keep control over the key, difficult decisions. Otherwise, the courts or authorities in the different Member States might have come to very different decisions. By creating precedents that any restrictions on conduct of importance on the market restricted competition,[11] the Commission increased this control. It could be argued that it had virtually unfettered discretion whether to grant an exemption. None was quashed by either Community Court until *Métropole I*[12] in 1996. Since its legal conclusions are rarely related to specific facts, the Commission can justify almost any decision in the difficult area where ancillary restraints are necessary to restrain free riders and induce the investment required for some activity that may increase competition or where anti-competitive harms have to be balanced against efficiencies from which consumers may benefit.

It is often difficult to reconcile the Commission's conclusions under Article 81(1) with those under Article 81(3). Various ancillary restrictions necessary to make viable a transaction that may even increase competition have been held to restrict competition contrary to Article 81(1) because they limit the parties' freedom of action and have significant effects on the market.[13] Yet when granting the exemption the Commission describes them as 'necessary and reasonable' to make the transaction viable.

These views were not consistent. It is of the nature of contracts to restrict the parties' freedom of action. The Commission's reasoning suffices to catch all contracts that have significant effects on the market, whether they increase, decrease or do not affect competition (2.4.1 above). For instance, the Commission exempted rather than cleared limited exclusivity in *BP/Kellogg*[14]

---

10   [1998] 4 CMLR 177.
11   Helmuth Schröter, 'Antitrust Analysis under Articles 81(1) and (3)' in Barry Hawk (ed) [1987] *Fordham Corporate Law Institute*, chapter 27,at 667 *et seq*, where he cites some of the Court's judgments that support the Commission's views.
12   [1996] ECR II–649 (3.1.1.2 above).
13   Giuliano Marenco, 'La notion de restriction de concurrence dans le cadres de l'interdiction des entents', in *II Mélanges en homage a Michel Waelbroeck*, (Brussels, Bruylant, 1999) 1217, and Schröter, above note 11.
14   [1986] 2 CMLR 619 (13.2.1.1 above).

and *Mitchell Cotts/ Sofiltra*.[15] Indeed, until *ODIN*,[16] despite the Court's judgments from *Société La Technique Minière*[17] onwards, the Commission had never cleared exclusive obligations in a formal decision, save on *de minimis* grounds. It has, however, sometimes exempted exclusive territories, not supported by a restriction on passive sales, as in *Davidson*,[18] *Campari*[19] and *Delta Chemie*[20] on the ground that without an exclusive territory, the pro-competitive transaction would not be viable. How then can the obligation have had the object or effect of restricting competition?

In regulations, such as Regulation 240/1996,[21] the Commission recited that exclusive technology licences help suppliers to penetrate another Member State, yet granted an exemption rather than a negative clearance. It also recited that open exclusive licences do not usually infringe Article 81(1), although in its individual decisions, it has always distinguished the Court's judgment in *Nungesser*[22] and granted an exemption, on the ground that the product was not new even when it was the best brand on the market.

The Commission has seldom cleared a collaborative joint venture by formal decision,[23] although it has cleared some provisions, such as the obligation not to compete with the joint venture and an exclusive manufacturing territory in *Mitchell Cotts/Sofiltra*.

Exclusive technology licences have been cleared by the Commission only when, *ex post*, the licensor and licensees obtained a small market share,[24] although, after the adoption of the patent regulation, the Commission limited its prohibition in *Velcro/Aplix*[25] to the period after the basic patents had expired. Few exclusive agreements that were significant have been cleared, although many come within a group exemption.

Despite the Court's judgment in *Delimitis*,[26] ruling that exclusive purchasing agreements restrict competition only in very unusual circumstances, in

---

15   [1988] 4 CMLR 111 (13.2.1.1.above).
16   [1991] 4 CMLR 832 (13.2.1.3.1 above).
17   (56/65) [1966] ECR 235 (2.4.1 above).
18   [1972] CMLR D52 (11.2 above).
19   [1978] 2 CMLR 397.
20   [1989] 4 CMLR 535.
21   [1996] 4 CMLR 405, recital 12, now replaced by Reg 772/2004, OJ L123/11, which is more favourable to exclusive licences.
22   (258/78) [1982] ECR 2015 (11.3 above). The cases are analysed in my monograph on technology transfer cited in the main bibliography, at pp 43–51.
23   It did clear joint R & D in *ODIN*, and two joint ventures for satellite telephone systems, where the huge investment could not have been undertaken by fewer firms (13.2.1.3.1 above). It also cleared consortia in several decisions, and a concentrative joint venture in *Metal Europe* [1991] 4 CMLR 222 on the ground that the effects were not perceptible. Recently, however, clearances of joint ventures have come mainly through the merger regulation.
24   *E.g.*, *Burroughs* [1972] CMLR D67 and 72, decided before the adoption of the group exemption for patent licences.
25   [1985] 4 CMLR 157 (11.1 above).
26   (C–234/89) [1991] ECR I–935 (described at 2.4.3 above).

Langnese and *Schöller*,[27] the Commission started to analyse the freezer and outlet exclusive purchasing agreements only under Article 81(3). Both decisions were reversed in their reasoning on appeal where the analysis was carried out under Article 81(1) not Article 81(3).[28] In various cases concerning fine fragrances, a competitive market, no analysis of the market was attempted before finding that selective distribution agreements infringed Article 81(1).[29]

In two decisions, the Commission did not analyse whether there were appreciable effects on trade between Member States or appreciable restraints on competition. *Finnpap*[30] was an informal decision, but even a notice under Article 19(3) followed by a press release operates as a precedent for later transactions. So it would be helpful if the Commission had stated which of the facts led to the particular conclusion. I am glad that on occasion the Commission finds that the effects are not appreciable but, as argued at 8.2.3 above, it is difficult to see why it was necessary for the Commission to make the joint sales organisation abrogate the restriction on passive sales by members.

At 8.3, I criticised the formal decision in *APB*[31] for failing to spell out the free-rider problem that could have been overcome by less restrictive means— such as letting the producers pay for the test, and permitting them to sell the products with the stamp wherever they liked.

For many years there have been some Commission officials who refused to find that an agreement required exemption unless they could realistically establish that it was likely to lead to a loss of competition. Unfortunately, many of these proceedings did not result in a formal decision and were not publicised. With the creation in 1989 and 1990 of the Merger Task Force, which attracted respected economists into the competition department, far more attention was paid to the need for incentives to investment and generally, to a more economic approach to competition issues.

By then, it had become clear that all the Commission's ways of minimising the disadvantages of taking a wide view of Article 81(1) were unsatisfactory. The Commission was unhappy at having to devote considerable resources to monitoring notifications: it would prefer to allocate more officials to pursuing price fixing cartels, to controlling state aids and undertakings granted special or exclusive rights by Member States. Already, it was then working on a new broader group exemption in the area of distribution and the adoption

---

27   *Langnese-Iglo v Commission* and *Schöller Lebensmittel v Commission*, OJ 1993, L183/1 and 19.
28   (T–7/92) [1995] ECR II–1533, paras 95–114 and (T–9/92) [1995] ECR II–1615, paras 95–96.
29   *Parfums Yves Saint Laurent* [1993] 4 CMLR 120, *Parfums Givenchy* [1993] 5 CMLR 579, and the CFI in *Vichy* (T–19/91) [1991] ECR II–265.
30   Notice [1989] 4 CMLR 413 (8.2.3 above).
31   [1990] 4 CMLR 176.

of Regulation 1/2003, the new implementing regulation (14.2.3 below), is even more radical.

The bifurcation of Article 81(1) and (3) is far less important now that Article 81(3) has direct effect by virtue of Regulation 1/2003 and can be applied by national courts and authorities, not only by the Commission. Nevertheless, the burden of proof to justify a restriction under Article 81(3) is on the parties. The Commission may not now deal with many cases that merit exemption, but its old case law may be taken into account by national courts and authorities. I fear that many transactions that can do no harm to consumers may be forbidden. It is no longer possible to notify an agreement to the Commission with a request for an individual exemption and the burden of proof to justify the application of Article 81(3) is on the party wanting it.

14.1.2.1 *The Court's analysis has been more helpful than that of the Commission*—In *Consten and Grundig*,[32] Advocate General Roemer's opinion raised the important questions: he pointed to the need to compare the situation after the agreement with that which would have prevailed in its absence; the need to examine incentives *ex ante*; the need to appraise vertical agreements in their economic context. The ECJ has adopted two further ways of achieving realistic outcomes. In *Société La Technique Minière v Maschinenbau Ulm*,[33] the ECJ ruled that agreements must be appraised in their economic as well as their legal context, and ancillary restraints required to make a transaction viable do not infringe Article 81(1) (2.4.2 above).

The strongest support for the first proposition was in *Delimitis*[34](2.4.3 above). Single branding infringes Article 81(1) only in narrow circumstances and there is no need for an exemption. The precedent has made it far easier to enforce such contracts. Indeed, many firms, rather than distort their commercial agreements to come within one of the group exemptions, already relied on this principle and did not notify their agreements even when notification was possible.

The other proposition is less clear. As early as 1966, in *La Technique Minière,* the Court ruled that an exclusive distribution agreement would not restrict competition if an exclusive territory were necessary for the manufacturer to have its earth moving equipment sold in France. In *Remia and Nutricia v Commission*,[35] it ruled that a covenant not to compete with a business sold as a going concern would not restrict competition if properly limited in products, space and time to what was reasonably necessary to the transfer of a business with its goodwill.

In several other judgments discussed at 2.4.5 above, the ECJ went further in treating ancillary restraints as falling outside Article 81(1). It is not clear

---

32   (56 & 58/64) [1966] ECR 299 (2.3.1 and 2.4.1 above).
33   (56/65), [1966] ECR 235, at 250.
34   (C–234/89), [1991] ECR I–935, paras 13–27.
35   (42/84) [1985] ECR 2545 (8.1.2 above).

how far the guidelines of the Commission on mergers[36] or the judgment of the CFI in *Metropole II*,[37] has narrowed the concept or whether that judgment can stand with the judgment of the ECJ in *Wouters*.[38]

Nevertheless, the Court's judgments have not been uniformly favourable to investments. In *Merck v Primecrown*[39] the Court refused to reverse its early judgment in *Merck v Stephar*.[40] It held that the exercise of a UK patent was not justified within the meaning of Article 30 to restrain the importation of pharmaceutical products imported from a Member State where the innovator could not have obtained a patent when the invention was novel and where prices were limited by price control unless it was under a legal duty to sell in the country of export. The ECJ favoured parallel traders over patent holders.

14.1.3 *The need to analyse ex ante: at the time the commitments are made*

Where incentives to invest are important, competition analysis should be made *ex ante*: at the time an undertaking is considering whether or not to commit itself to investment. At that time, each party needs assurance that the contract will be performed and that it will benefit from its investment if the transaction is successful commercially.

In many situations, investment is unattractive unless the investor is protected from other undertakings taking a free ride on it. Parties to a joint venture usually promise not to derogate from their grant: to deal with the joint venture wherever practicable. Dealers who are committed to invest in marketing resources may require an exclusive territory. So may technology licensees who have to create a market and tool up to serve it.

This has been recognised by the CFI (13.2.1.3.2 above). Once the investment has been made, the market would be more competitive if free riders could compete. If, however, this happens too often, undertakings will learn, and will not make investments for free riders to share.

The analysis of joint ventures explained in the *XIIIth Report on Competition Policy* was *ex ante* (13.2.1.3 above). One should look at the ability of the parties at the date of the transaction (*Odin*, 13.2.1.3.1 above). Unfortunately, the Commission and courts do not consistently do this: they often look *ex post* and treat resale price maintenance or export restrictions as restrictive of competition 'by their very nature,' however much a firm needs protection before committing itself to sunk costs.

---

36 Guidelines on the assessment of horizontal mergers under the Council Regulation on the control of concentrations between undertakings, OJ 2004, C31/5.
37 (T–206/99) [2001] ECR II–1061.
38 *Wouters* (C–309/99) [2002] ECR I–1577 (2.4.5 above).
39 (C–267 & 268/95) (10.4.4 above).
40 (187/80) [1981] ECR 2063 (10.4.1 above).

14.1.4 *Hostile attitude to export bans and deterrents*

From the earliest days, the attitude of Commission and ECJ to restrictions on cross border trade has been hostile. Seen *ex post*, after any investment has been made, they divide the common market. They prevent parallel trade providing arbitrage, lowering prices in those Member States where the product is more expensive. Perceived *ex ante*, however, they may be necessary to induce a distributor to invest in promotion or a joint venturer to provide its contribution to the venture. The free rider argument may be made too often, but *Consten and Grundig v Commission*[41] has frequently been followed by the ECJ, even when the different price levels were due to legislation by Member States. In *Merck & Co Inc v Stephar BV*[42] the ECJ did not permit the exercise of a patent to keep a protected medicine out of the Netherlands even when it had not been capable of protection in the country of export and no monopoly profit can have been earned. At 5.2.2.4 above I discussed Ramsey pricing and the economic benefits of recovering much of the overhead of R & D from those customers prepared to pay. Not only have the Community institutions failed to prevent Member States from imposing minimum prices at different levels for medicines in different countries, the Commission has struck down export bans or deterrents imposed by firms especially when they provide absolute territorial protection. It is not clear to me that this is justified by the integration of the market. It leaves an opportunity for the distributors or their trade association to persuade Member States to pick different maximum prices.[43]

14.1.5 *Article 82 is intended to protect consumers not particular competitors*

As explained above at 1.3.2.3 in the early cases under the competition rules, the ECJ was concerned about the interests of small firms wanting to enter or stay in a market. Dominant firms were found to have abused their position if they excluded competitors. The ECJ repeated time and again, that this was true only if the conduct did not amount to competition on the merits, but in no judgment has it considered what this includes. It was difficult to advise firms that might be dominant what they might legally do to meet competition.

I regret the continued failure by the Commission in decisions adopted under Article 82 to distinguish between competition on the merits and other exclusionary conduct. In relation to Article 81, it has accepted the need to encourage investment except in relation to restraints on parallel trade, but not in relation to Article 82.

---

41   *Consten & Grundig* [1964] CMLR 489. Appeal—*Consten SA and Grundig-Verkaufs-GmbH v EEC Commission* (56 & 58/64), [1966] ECR 299 (2.4.1 above).
42   (187/80), [1981] ECR 2063.
43   Michel Paradis, one of my students at Fordham, has found an association claiming to have done exactly that.

Advocate General Fennelly tried, in *Compagnie Maritime Belge*,[44] to indicate what does not amount to competition on the merits, in that case, the selective nature of the price cuts. He thought that price reductions across the board to a level that covered costs would probably have amounted to competition on the merits (paragraph 121). Reductions across the board might not have enabled the undertakings to recoup the loss of income (paragraph 136). The ECJ did not address the issue of low pricing in general terms.

More recently the ECJ has been stressing the interests of consumers. In *Oscar Bronner v Mediaprint*,[45] a case about a refusal to supply by an undertaking assumed to be dominant, Advocate General Jacobs said:

> 58. . . . the primary purpose of Article 82 is to prevent distortion of competition—and in particular to safeguard the interests of consumers—rather than to protect the position of particular competitors.

The interest of consumers, or efficiently producing what they are able and willing to buy may be the key to the question of what amounts to competition on the merits.

Like Advocate General Fennelly in *Compagnie Maritime Belge*, paragraph 135 (5.2.6.5 above), Advocate General Jacobs suggested that where the dominant position is particularly strong, there may be wider duties to help its competitors. In *Compagnie Maritime Belge* (paragraph 119), the ECJ stressed that the appellants had a share of over 90% of the market, and only one competitor. This might indicate that very dominant firms have a greater responsibility not to exclude others.

It is arguable that the ECJ is narrowing the special responsibility of dominant firms to protect their competitors.

14.1.5.1 *Duty to supply narrowed*—In *Bronner* (5.2.5.4 above), Mr Jacobs went on to narrow the obligation to give a competitor access to a facility. He indicated the objections to requiring access: the reduction in the incentive to make the original investment (paragraph 57) the reduction in the incentive to duplicate it where this is feasible (paragraph 57), and the need to regulate the price of access (paragraph 69). Without addressing his theory, the ECJ followed him in narrowing any duty to supply. So has the Court in *IMS* (5.2.5.5 above)

14.1.5.2 *Predation illegal only if recoupment*—In *Compagnie Maritime Belge*, Advocate General Fennelly stressed the importance of not chilling price competition even by a dominant firm.[46] He added at paragraph 136 that loss of revenue in selectively reducing prices to a level not below cost would be abusive only if the Commission could establish an intention or a possibility of

---

recoupment. The ECJ refused to rule generally on the circumstances in which a liner conference may selectively cut prices (paragraph 118) but pointed out that where prices were cut selectively the dominant firm could continue to earn higher revenue elsewhere (paragraph 117). This is an important limitation to the judgment in *Tetra Pak International SA v EC Commission II*.[47]

The CFI refused to rule in general when sales above cost that departed from a price list were abusive, but observed that the discriminatory conduct of CEWAL deprived a new entrant of its only method of competing and enabled it to charge more where it did not meet competition.

14.1.5.3 *Discrimination forbidden very widely—Is the prohibition limited to Article 82 in combination with Article 86?*—Ten years ago, the Commission adopted several decisions objecting to discrimination by undertakings enjoying special or exclusive rights granted by government (6.2 above). Such undertakings usually enjoy strong market power owing to their legal rights and may be treated as super-dominant. Moreover, their investments were often financed either by the taxpayer, or other government action. Consequently, it was particularly difficult for others to compete with them. So, I am not troubled by the decisions adopted under Article 82 in combination with Article 86, or the cases where the dominant firm is heavily protected by state or Community measures. Both courts and Commission have been condemning discrimination by dominant firms enjoying exclusive rights, (5.2.2.3 above). I would be greatly concerned, however, if this case law were applied without modification to situations where the dominant firm achieved its position without government help (5.2.2.1 above).

14.1.5.4 *Rebates after Michlin II and British Air*—The recent judgments of the CFI in *Michelin II* and *British Air* (5.2.2.1 above) have been widely criticised at recent conferences. We had come to think that the CFI was rather good at dealing with competition cases, but these judgments show that not all chambers think alike. In both judgments the court objected to rebates that were capable of foreclosing—of excluding new entrants or the expansion of competitors. In *Michelin II* it went so far as to say that whether the rebates did foreclose was irrelevant if they were capable of having that effect. In *British Air,* the court was almost as rigid. In *Van den Bergh* the court made a significant analysis of foreclosure under Article 81(1) but did not refer to this, even by reference, when stating that if there was foreclosure of 40% of the market freezer exclusivity that amounted de facto to outlet exclusivity being abusive.

Economists have indicated practices that are capable of foreclosing competitors, but they stress that those practices do not necessarily have that

---

47   (C–333/94P), [1996] ECR I–5951.

effect. It is necessary to examine the facts to see whether they do so in a particular case.

14.1.5.5 *Joint dominant position*—The other major development affecting dominant firms is the acceptance of a concept of collective dominance by the CFI under the merger regulation in *Gencor v Commission,*[48] whether or not there are agreements or other legal links between the undertakings, and by the ECJ in *Compagnie Maritime Belge* (paragraph 45) (4.3.5 above). The position under the merger regulation, in the light of the new text of Article 2(2) and (3) and recitals 25 and 26, remains to be worked out. The Article seems to stress the impediment to competition more than the dominant position, but the last sentence of recital 25 seems to contradict this. It is clear that the probability of anticompetitive unilateral effects may cause the Commission to forbid a merger.

It is to be hoped that the concept of collective dominance under Article 82 will not be used to challenge parallel conduct in the absence of a concerted practice for the reasons given at 2.2.4.1 and 2.2.4.2 above. It might be helpful to use the concept to challenge facilitating practices that make it easier for the jointly dominant firms to coordinate their pricing and other policies, such as announcing price rises well in advance or telling many customers that it would extend to them any more favourable terms offered to others, as this makes it more risky to chisel.

14.2 Steps taken by the Commission to meet the criticisms

The Commission has taken various steps to increase legal certainty and to adopt a more economic approach.

14.2.1 *Old group exemptions*

To avoid the problems of legal insecurity for many kinds of agreements that are often concluded, and to reduce the backlog of notified agreements in its files, the Commission adopted regulations granting group exemptions for categories of agreements. Until 1999 they were, however, drafted in formal terms not based overtly on economic justifications and they operated as straitjackets forcing agreements into a particular mould permitted by the exemption.

First, they were drafted to fit typical agreements, or the kind of agreement being notified in large quantities, rather than on the public policy considerations being pursued. Some desirable agreements fell between the exempted categories. Large undertakings, which had readier access to expert legal advice, structured agreements artificially to take advantage of the discrepancies. Smaller firms were less able to afford the expense of such advice, although some trade associations helped.

48   (T–102/96) [1999] ECR II–753.

For example, a supplier wishing to distribute its goods through an independent firm used to be well advised to look at the group exemption for franchising[49] if it was most interested in controlling its retail outlets.

Particular group exemptions had little to do with competition policy. Whether one is trying to protect the public from extortion or competitors from foreclosure, the legal classification of the contract is irrelevant. A brand owner supplying a reseller may have as great an interest as a franchisor in the final customer being able to buy its product only in outlets providing the range of services it considers appropriate.

Advisers sometimes persuaded their clients to distort a transaction to come within the straitjacket of one of the group exemptions. This should cause concern. One great virtue of contracts is that they are infinitely variable and can be drafted to fit any possible transaction. It is so much more sensible for the Commission to develop broader rules, based on openly acknowledged economic considerations, indicating why particular provisions are or are not anti-competitive in specified circumstances.

There is widespread agreement that few vertical agreements restrict competition where markets are competitive. There was never any economic or commercial reason for separate rules for exclusive distribution, selective distribution, franchising, etc. A rule based more on economics would enable national courts to enforce agreements affecting competitive markets as being unlikely to restrict competition and which may well increase it. Where one party has market power, however, even vertical agreements make it easier to discriminate and may foreclose potential competitors from resources or outlets.

Anomalously, the best way for firms that do not enjoy a dominant position both to control their dealers and segregate the common market is not to sell to independent firms but to sell through subsidiaries and employees as far as possible down the distribution chain, so no agreements are needed between independent undertakings.[50]

The second drawback to the method of drafting narrow group exemptions was that many harmless agreements could not be brought within any of them. Not many R & D joint ventures can be brought within Regulation 2659/2000[51] (13.5 above). It is also absurd that Regulation 1983/83 that used to apply to exclusive distribution agreements did not apply to services which were not 'goods supplied for resale.'

Thirdly, some of the items in the black lists of the regulations granting block exemptions are not clear in their application and may be used opportunistically by one party to prevent the other from enforcing a contract.

---

49   Reg 4087/88, [1989] 4 CMLR 387.
50   *Viho v Commission* (C–73/95P), [1996] ECR I–5457.
51   OJ 2000, L304/7, [2001] 4 CMLR 808.

14.2.2 *New group exemptions since 1999*

The distortions to commercial transactions caused by the narrow group exemptions for the different ways of bringing goods to market have been greatly reduced by the new broader based Regulations, no. 2790/99, for vertical distribution agreements[52] and the three subsequent group exemptions that have followed a similar pattern.[53]

The first to be adopted, that for vertical agreements, is drafted simply to cover agreements between two or more undertakings operating at different levels of production or trade and relating to the conditions under which the parties may buy, sell or resell goods or services. It covers exclusive distribution, exclusive purchasing, franchising and selective distribution, but is subject to a cap of a 30% share of the market for the undertakings at the level being protected.

Market shares may not give an exact indication of market power, especially under EC law where market definition is affected by conditions of entry only when new entry would be as fast and effective as substitutes on the demand side. The Commission, however, thought that a ceiling of market power would lead to even greater legal uncertainty than a test based directly on market share.

There is no white list—any provision not black listed is exempt.

I am unhappy with the black lists: minimum resale price maintenance and territorial restraints relate only to intra-brand competition, and such restraints may be justified as necessary to protect against free riders. With a market share ceiling there should be sufficient inter-brand competition to make intra-brand competition unnecessary. The power to withdraw the benefit of the regulation provides a safety net.

Moreover, dealers cannot be restrained from selling in territories for which a firm has an exclusive manufacturing licence. In principle, technology licensees require more protection than dealers because they have to invest in setting up a production line as well as establishing a market. Where they do not, the holder of the technology has no incentive to grant them protection.

The black list in Article 5 is less worrying than Article 4, as it is only the black listed provision and not the whole agreement that falls outside the exemption. Few non-compete clauses infringe Article 81(1) according to the judgment of the ECJ in *Delimitis*.[54] They do so only if there are entry barriers downstream, and so many dealers are tied to one or other of the suppliers for so long that a new supplier would not have a real and concrete chance to enter the market on a minimum efficient scale or existing ones to expand.

---

52   Reg 2790/1999 on vertical agreements, [2000] 4 CMLR 398, (9.6–9.6.7 above).
53   Reg 772/2004 on technology transfer agreements OJ 2004, L123/11. Specialization Reg 2658/2000, OJ 2000, L304/1, and R & D, Reg 2659/2000, OJ 2000, L303/7.
54   (C–234/89), [1991] ECR I–935 (2.4.3 above).

Those conditions cannot often apply. When they do, automatic legality may be inappropriate.

The group exemption for technology transfer agreements is of wider application than its predecessor. It covers not only patent, know-how or mixed agreements, but also licences of copyright in software and designs. Pursuant to the Commission's greater interest in economics the black list is substantially more limiting when the parties are competitors than where they are not. I am delighted by the new definition of 'competing undertakings in Article 1(1)(j) as construed in Guideline 29.[55] It is now confined to 'undertakings which, in the absence of the technology transfer agreement, would compete on the relevant technology market and/or the relevant product market.' This is contrary to the previous practice of the Commission in appraising licences, but is the approach that has been adopted in the US. It corresponds to the statement by AG Roemer in *Consten and Grundig v Commission:*[56]

> 33. Properly understood, therefore, Article 81(1) requires a comparison between two market situations: that which arises after making an agreement with that which would have arisen had there been no agreement.

The ceiling of market share will be even more difficult to apply than that for distribution agreements. It is hard enough to be sure that one's definition of the product market for goods and services will be selected by whatever institution vets a licence. It is even more difficult in relation to licensing when markets are developing rapidly.

14.2.3 *Regulation 1/2003*

The Commission's objective in proposing what became Regulation 1/2003[57] was to free its resources from monitoring notifications which seldom disclosed any serious restriction of competition. It wanted to focus on large international cartels which it would be difficult for any one national authority to forbid, and on the control of state aids and undertakings granted special or exclusive rights which only it had power to control. It was also concerned that with ten new states acceding, its resources would be stretched even further.

Questions remain how far national courts and authorities will be able to adopt economic ways of thought. How many will focus on the need for inducement to investment and think *ex ante*? How many will think at the margin?

The abandonment of the Commission's exclusive power to apply Article 81(3) is warmly welcome. It removes much of the difficulty experienced in enforcing agreements or settling disputes out of court. Litigation will be far more satisfactory. National courts will be able to complete the job without

---

55   Guidelines on technology transfer agreements, OJ 2004, C101/2.
56   (56 & 58/64) [1966] ECR 299, para 33.
57   Reg 1/2003, OJ 2003, L1/1, [2003] 4 CMLR 551.

long adjournments. Litigation may take slightly longer as there will be an additional question to consider, but most of the evidence relevant under Article 81(1) will be relevant again under Article 81(3), there will seldom be need to distinguish clearance from exemptions save to determine the burden of proof, and no need to wait for the Commission to prepare a formal decision.

The direct effect of Article 81(3) does, however, leave national judges to make decisions of policy which some claim are not justiciable. It is too early to say whether the wide margin of discretion allowed by the ECJ and CFI over matters of policy will also be allowed to national courts and authorities.

Much has been done to encourage consistent decisions, but the Brussels Regulation[58] is of little use when enforcing foreign judgments relating to competition as it applies only between the same parties and in relation to the same matter. There is no equivalent for NCAs at all. Article 3 which, to increase consistency, requires NCAs also to apply Community law if they apply national law to agreements that may affect trade between Member States will be uncertain in application because the concept of affecting trade is so flexible.

The Commission hopes to save resources for more important tasks, but if it is to coordinate proceedings before national authorities and national courts it is not clear that much time will be saved. The Commission wants to keep control over the interesting decisions, and the coordination required will take time.

A major problem arises from leaving procedural rules, including remedies, to national law. Forum shopping may centre round the ease with which interim injunctions or orders can be obtained *ex parte* and how difficult it is to reverse these *inter partes*.

Many commentators are concerned about respecting the confidentiality of trade secrets. Others fear the increased powers of the Commission to enter homes to seek information in private homes, and from individuals not representing the undertakings concerned.

Nevertheless, the White Paper answers many of the criticisms I have been making in this chapter for decades. The wide interpretation given to Article 81(1) will matter less when the same institutions also apply Article 81(3). The admonition of the CFI and ECJ that a realistic and concrete economic assessment be made under Article 81 will apply equally to national competition authorities and courts.

There is some doubt as to how easily judges will be able to cope with the economic arguments appropriate to competition cases. They will, however, be educated by counsel appearing before them and may seek the advice of the Commission, although it remains to be seen what resources the Commission will devote to such a task. I am concerned about the ability of many judges at first instance in civil law countries, who may well not have learned competition

---

58 Formerly the Burssel Convention, now Council Reg (EC) No. 44/2001 on jurisdiction and the enforcement of judgments in civil and commercial matters, OJ 2001, L12/1.

law at university and not have had clients to teach them to look *ex ante* and about the need to protect incentives to investment. They will be able to seek preliminary rulings from the ECJ on questions of the interpretation of Community law, but they will have to apply the answers. This may result in more competition cases being heard by the ECJ that would formerly have been decided by the CFI, which has equipped itself with expertise on competition issues.

Under the Treaty of Nice the power to give preliminary rulings in particular areas may pass to the CFI, but the likely first candidate for this treatment is intellectual property rights. A huge backlog of such cases has built up in the CFI and soon the trademark cases will flood into the ECJ. The jurisdiction over Article 81 or Article 82 may be passed down by the end of the decade. By then, however, there may be another court attached to the CFI to hear appeals from Commission decisions. If so, the current expertise in competition may well pass down to that court and the CFI will no longer have an advantage in expertise over the ECJ in ruling on competition matters. It will, however, have the advantage that many competition cases would be decided by a chamber of three or five judges, whereas the ECJ sits in plenum on references. Persuading 11 independently minded people, with experience in different legal systems and unable to dissent or prepare an individual judgment, makes it very difficult to reach agreement. There is some hope that the 10 new judges from Eastern and Southern Europe will favour economic arguments more than some of the incumbents.

14.2.4 *Appointment of the Commission's Chief Economist—Peer Review and Reorganisation of the Directorate General for Competition*

The Commission's appointment of a chief economist for a non-renewable term of two years may have gone far to meet the criticism of its decisions for not stating cogent reasons. He has twelve economists working for him and the right to speak directly to the Member of the Commission responsible for competition and his Director-General. All stage II merger decisions, most decisions under Article 82 and some other cases (not cartels) will be considered by a second team of officials from DG Comp to see whether they come to the same decision. A member of the Chief Economist's team will join the review team. If the review team has little success in persuading senior officials to change their mind, the Chief Economist can put in a word at the top.

DG Comp has been reorganised. Officials have been redistributed among the sectoral directorates, which will now also handle mergers. Consequently there will usually be some members of the case team familiar with the relevant market. It is also hoped that the habitual speed of operation achieved by the task force will spread throughout the secretariat.

The three mergers cases of 2002 cited at note 1 above have caused the Commission to be much more careful in its findings of fact.

14.2.5 *Review of the Application of Article 82*

The Commission has announced that it will review the application of Article 82. Philip Lowe, the Director-General, said at Fordham that[59] 'a credible policy on abusive conduct must be compatible with mainstream economics.' He listed many options for change.

It remains to be seen how the Commission is able to circumvent some of the recent judgments of the courts and adopt more flexible principles. It can prepare guidelines, and the ECJ has said on several occasions that the Commission should stick to its guidelines when they relate to the way it will exercise its discretion (2.4.9 above). The Commission would, however, prefer not to handle many individual cases itself unless many Member States are involved. It is, however, likely to influence NCAs and some national courts might follow its views.

14.2.6 *Cartels and the Leniency Programme*

The Commission used to have great difficulty in establishing the existence of a cartel. It adopted few decisions and most of those were appealed. So, considerable resources were consumed and it was difficult to persuade industry that cartels were not worthwhile. Over time it increased the level of fines and, even if they were suspended during an appeal, interest had to be paid on a bank bond guaranteeing payment. The level of fines has been increased again (7.6.1 above), but is still insufficient to deter infringements.

The Commission's leniency notice (7.6.2 above) has transformed the position. Cartels have become unstable, as the parties each fear that one of the others will tell the Commission first and gain total immunity from fines. Many investigations have started with one of the parties claiming leniency, although some involving international cartels have resulted from the leniency programme in the US. The Commission now gets good evidence of many cartels and when it adopts a decision to fine the participants, any appeal is usually limited to procedural points, such as a failure to observe fundamental rights. Participants rarely contest the existence of the cartel.

Lawyers advising on compliance programmes can paint a very dark picture. Even the participant who gains total immunity from fines will be mentioned in the Commission's decision. If the cartel was international and extended to the US, there will be antitrust problems there. Not only may the Justice Department secure a fine or the imprisonment of directors from the federal courts, those harmed can sue for treble damages. Often managers compromise with the authorities and serve a term in a US jail and their employers pay a fine to avoid prosecution.

---

59 (2004) *[2003] Fordham Corporate Law Institute*, chapter 10.

If the fines went to DG Comp, its shortage of resources would be substantially alleviated, but the Community budget each year is fixed. The fines go to reduce the payments due from Member States.

The leniency programme has been hugely successful and DG Comp attaches great importance and devotes substantial resources to it. Since the introduction of criminal sanctions, such as imprisonment for individuals, is unthinkable in many Member States, the leniency programme in the US is even more effective, but this is an area where the Commission has been very successful.

14.3 Conclusion

It is always difficult to foresee the future. The Commission's initiative in Regulation 1/2003 to share its competence over exceptions from Article 81(1) with national authorities and courts is radical. The wide scope of Article 81(1) has become less important now that the same institutions that apply Article 81(1) can consider Article 81(3) and the system of notification under Article 81 is abrogated. Nevertheless, the burden of proof is on the parties under Article 81(3), which causes me concern that many agreements having no adverse effects on competition may become unenforceable.

The Commission has rejected the option of its making a full market analysis under Article 81(1) (2.4.2–2.4.4 above). I regret this.

In the USA, there is a continuum of the level of analysis required under section 1 of the Sherman Act. At the one end, horizontal price fixing, market allocation or joint sales will seldom bring attenuating efficiencies, and few cases will escape the prohibition. Most can be forbidden after only a quick look to see whether production is being restricted to raise prices.[60] At the other end of the continuum, vertical restraints in a competitive market will seldom be illegal, and only a truncated analysis is required to ensure that the market is competitive and that the parties are not actual or potential competitors. In between these extremes, a less quick look will be required.[61]

Similar levels of analysis in Europe might be more satisfactory than continued reliance on group exemptions with ceilings of market share. Nevertheless, the new group exemption for vertical agreements relating to the conditions for the purchase or sale of goods and services is far wider and less formalistic than the regulations it replaces. It is a major improvement. The same can be said of the new regulation on technology transfer with its distinction between agreements between competitors and non-competitors and

---

60   *Broadcast Music, Inc. v Columbia Broadcasting System* (BMI), 441 US 1 (1979) is an unusual case where the only way artists could enforce their performing rights effectively was through a copyright collection society. In *National Collegiate Athletic Association v Board of Regents of the University of Oklahoma*, 468 US 85, the Department of Justice argued that there is a spectrum rather than a bright line distinction between the *per se* and rule of reason approaches.
61   *California Dental Association* May 24 1999, 526 US 756, 119 Sup Ct 1604.

which favours licences between non-competing undertakings over others, especially now that 'competing undertakings' has been redefined to mean those who could have competed legally even without a licence. Guidelines 17 & 18 of the Guidelines on Article 81(3) make the same point generally.

The CFI has made a major contribution in cases like *European Night Services*[62] in requiring more analysis by the Commission before finding that agreements infringe Article 81(1). It has stressed the need not to discourage risky investments.

The ECJ has narrowed the special obligation of dominant firms towards their competitors, partly by stressing that the function of the article is to protect consumers rather than competitors and suggesting that some of the obligations of dominant firm may arise only when a firm enjoys special or exclusive rights or, otherwise, enjoys a super-dominant position. The CFI has, however, been very rigid in three recent judgments about loyalty inducing rebates (5.2.2.1 above).

14.4 Bibliography

Claus Dieter Ehlermann **and** *Loraine L Laudati*, (eds) *European Competition Law Annual 1997: Objectives of Competition Policy*, (Robert Schuman Centre at the European University Institute, Hart Publishing, Oxford, 1998).
Subsequent volumes with varying assistant editors.
Commission's White Paper on Modernisation of the Rules Implementing Articles 85 and 86 of the EC Treaty. Commission programme No 99/027.
Enrique Gonzalez Diaz, 'Some Reflections on the Notion of Ancillary Restraints under EC Competition Law' (1995) *Fordham Corporate Law Institute* 325.
Luc Gyselen, 'Vertical Restraints in the Distribution Process: Strength and Weakness of the Free Rider Rationale under EEC Competition Law' (1984) 21 *CML Rev* 648.
Barry Hawk, 'System Failure: Vertical Restraints and EC Competition Law' (1995) 32 *CML Rev* 973.
———, (ed) *Fordham Corporate Law Institute*. Annual volume.
Frédéric Jeny, 'Competition and Efficiency' in Barry Hawk (ed) [1993] *Fordham Corporate Law Institute* 185.
René Joliet, *The Rule of Reason in Antitrust Law*, (The Hague, Nijhoff, 1967).
V Korah, '*Tetra Pak II* —Lack of Reasoning in Court's Judgment' [1997] *European Competition Law Review*, 24.
———, Chapter 1 'Invalidity of Exclusive Provisions in Distribution Contracts under EC Competition Law' in L Gormley (ed) *Current and Future Perspectives on EC Competition Law*, (14 Kluwer European Monographs).
Philip Lowe, [2003] *Fordham Corporate Law Institute*, chap 10.
Patrick Massey, 'Reform of EC Competition Law: Substance, Procedure and Institutions,' [1996] *Fordham Corporate Law Institute* 91.
Warwick A Rothnie, 'Commission Re-runs Same Old Bill (Film Purchases by German Television Stations)' [1990] *European Intellectual Property Review*, 72.

---

62   T–374 and others, [1998] ECR II–3141 (13.2.2.2 above).

Helmuth Schröter, 'Antitrust Analysis under Article 81(1) and (3)' in Barry Hawk (ed) [1987] *Fordham Corporate Law Institute*, chapter 27.

Michel Waelbroeck, 'Antitrust Analysis under Article 81(1) and Article 81(3),' in Barry Hawk (ed) [1987] *Fordham Corporate Law Institute,* chapter 28, and the panel discussion in chapter 29.

Bibliography

Art, Jean-Yves and van Liedekerke, Dirk, 'Developments in E.C. Competition Law in 1994—An Overview' (1995) 32 *CML Rev*, 921, continued annually by various authors

Bael, Ivo Van and Jean-Francois Bellis, *Competition Law of the European Community*, 3rd edn, (Oxon, CCH Europe (1994), now also loose leaf. (The named authors are very good and busy practitioners. This is one of the first places I check when seeking information and comment.)

Bellamy, Christopher and Graham Child, *European Community Law of Competition*, 5th edn by Peter M Roth, (London, Sweet & Maxwell, 2001) clxx + 1339 pp (Well organized, legal practitioners' work, probably the most widely used in practice in the UK. Readable, accurate, with very condensed footnotes—more critical than earlier editions.)

Berman, George A, Roger J Goebel, W J Davey and Eleanor M Fox, *Cases and Materials on European Community* Law, 2nd edn (American Casebook Series, St Paul, Minn, West Publishing, 2002), lxxxi + 1434 pp, document supp 1998). The competition part is also marketed separately, ***Eleanor M Fox***, *Cases and Materials on the Competition law of the European Union*, 2nd edn (American Casebook Series, St Paul, Minn, West Publishing, 2002). (Outstanding analysis, comments, questions and other materials on competition by Fox, but insufficient amount of each case included for a whole LL M course, although the selection is excellent and the comments and questions outstanding.)

Carlton, Dennis W and Jeffrey M Perloff, *Modern Industrial Organization*, 4th edn, (New York, Harper Collins, 2005) (Textbook on economics).

Cook, CJ and CS Kerse, *EC Merger Control*, 3rd edn, (London, Sweet & Maxwell, 2000). (Compressed, clear, thorough and perceptive analysis of the regulation in the light of the case law. The authors also speculate about possible future developments.)

Cornish, William R, *Intellectual Property: Patents, Copyright, Trade Marks & Allied Rights* 5th edn, (London, Sweet & Maxwell, 2003), xcv + 817 pp. (A classic, accurate, lucid, perceptive and basic book, with full and critical analysis of whole area of intellectual property. See, especially, chapters 3.4—'Justifying the Patent System' and 7.3—'Exhaustion in the Common Market'.)

Ehlermann, Claus-Dieter (and various editors) *Proceedings of the European Competition Forum*, (Wiley, 1997, Kluwer, 1998 and Hart Publishing thereafter), published as *European Competition Law Annual* (The first volume contained the proceedings of the forum organized for the Commission on what should go into its draft green paper on vertical restraints. Later volumes include papers first discussed at the European University Institute near Florence. The fora are superb and influential.)

Empel, Martin Van, *Competition Law in Western Europe and the USA*, (Deventer, Kluwer, looseleaf multi-volume). (Contains the legislation relating to competition in the European communities and under national laws. Substantial and critical commentaries thereon, as well as reprints of many of the decisions of Commission and Courts of the European communities, Commission's annual reports etc)

Faull, Jonathan and Ali Nikpay (eds), *The EC Law of Competition,* (Oxford, OUP, 1999) 2nd edn in preparation. (Detailed work contributed by officials of the Commission, mostly lawyers, but the first two are economists. Sophisticated, and soundly based on theory, economic as well as legal.)

Freeman, Peter and Richard Whish (eds), *Competition Law,* (London, Butterworths), 5 vols looseleaf (an accurate, substantial and perceptive practitioners' guide to both EC and UK competition law, with legislation and extensive commentary.)

Gellhorn, E and William E Kovacic, *Antitrust Law and Economics in a Nutshell*, 4th edn, 5th ed expected Sept 2004 (St Paul, Minn, West Publishing, 1994) xliii + 520 pp. (Basic and critical analysis of American antitrust law in the light of the latest as well as earlier economic theory. A readable and perceptive contrast to EC thinking.)

Goyder, DG, *EC Competition Law*, 4th edn, (European Community Law Series, Oxford, OUP, 2003) lxix + 592 pp. (Accurate, elegant, partly historical description of the EC competition rules, with a critical appraisal in the last chapter. Rather few headings, and difficult to find a point, but accurate, easy to read, through and very interesting.)

Green, N and A Robertson, *Commercial Agreements and Competition Law: Practice and Procedure in the UK and EEC*, 2nd edn, (London, Kluwer, 1997) (A substantial and accurate practitioners' text, somewhat outdated, but fuller than many others.)

Hawk, BE and Henry L Huser, *European Community Merger Control: A Practitioner's Guide*, (Boston, the Hague, Kluwer Law International, 1996). (Full analysis in the light of the decisions of the merger task force by authors very active in mergers and acquisitions.)

Joliet, R, *The Rule of Reason in Antitrust Law: American, German and Common Market Law*, (The Hague, Nijhoff, 1967). (Classic, perceptive, clear analysis of crucial issues in English, by Belgian law professor with deep understanding of economics and of US antitrust, later a judge in the Community Court.)

——, *Monopolization and Abuse of Dominant Position: A Comparative Study of American and European Approaches to the Control of Economic Power,* (The Hague, Martinus Nijhoff, 1970)—as previous entry.

Jones, Alison and B Sufrin, *EC Competition Law: Text, Cases and Materials*, (Oxford, OUP, 2001), xcix + 1159 large pages. 2nd edn in preparation (A very well chosen selection of materials, but a very heavy book for students to carry around.)

Jones, C and M Van der Woude, *EC Competition Law Handbook*, (London, Sweet and Maxwell, annual or nearly, last edn 2003/2004). (No comment, but well conceived series of lists of relevant cases with three citations to most and text of regulations as corrected; a very quick way to find what judgments, decisions or annual reports on competition policy are relevant to a problem. Each edition improves on the last by increased coverage and new ideas for presentation.)

Keeling, David, *Intellectual Property Rights in EU Law: Free Movement and Competition Law,* (Oxford, OUP, EC Law Library, 2003), xlv + 110 pp., hardback. (Critical and perceptive analysis of the case law of the ECJ on exhaustion and Article 81, the inconsistencies and omissions.)

Kerse, CS, *EC Antitrust Procedure*, 4th edn, (London, Sweet & Maxwell, 1998). 5th edn in preparation. Superb, accurate, lucid, tightly written and full analysis. A perceptive, most useful, thoroughly, researched and practical guide.

Konkurrensverketl, *Fighting cartels–why and how*, *Swedish Competition Authority*, the 3rd Nordic Competition Policy Conference in Stockholm September 2000.

(Exceptionally thoughtful collection of talks by economists and lawyers explaining the reasons for policy decision as well as a detailed analysis of the law, with helpful references to the paragraph numbers in judgments.)

Korah, V, Cases and Materials on EC Competition Law, 2nd edn (Oxford, Hart Publishing, 2001). (Some cases reproduced with little cutting, others considerably cut, with many questions after each case, some easy to answer, others to which there is no unique correct answer.)

———, *Technology Transfer Agreements and the EC Competition Rules,* (Oxford, OUP, 1997).

———, (General Ed and contributor), *Competition Law of the European Community,* 2nd edn (Lexis/Nexis) from 1999 (One release annually about October, not all chapters revised each release, so more like a series of monographs in loose leaf format. The contributions are critical and fuller than many practitioners' books. Nick Levy's chapter on mergers is not only up to date; it is also fuller than most books on the subject. The special sector contributions are particularly full.)

———, with *Denis O'Sullivan, Distribution Agreements under the EC Competition Rules,* (Oxford, Hart Publishing, 2002. (Clause by clause critical commentary of regulation in the light of economic analysis and the earlier case law.)

Maher, Imelda, Competition Law—Alignment and Reform, (Dublin, Round Hall/ Sweet & Maxwell, 1999) (lxvii + 514 pp) (Thoughtful work covering EC and Irish law.)

Navarro, Edurne, Andres Font, Jaime Folauera and Juan Briones, Merger Control in the European Union, (Oxford, OUP 2002) 879 pp. (Significant book by highly competent authors; I have not yet used it.)

Neven, Damien, Robin Nuttall and Paul Seabright, Merger in Daylight, (London, CEPR, 1993). (Critical assessment of how mergers should be controlled and of the practice of the Merger Task Force of the Commission by three economists, supported, but not influenced, by Commission funds.)

Neven, Damien, Penelope Papandropoulos and Paul Seabright, Trawling for Minnows—European Competition Policy and Agreements between Firms, (CEPR, London 1998) (Excellent and perceptive criticism of the monitoring system of the EC Commission by economists, used to addressing lawyers.)

Ortiz Blanco, Luis, EC Competition Procedure, (Oxford, OUP, 1996) 2nd edn in preparation. (Readable translation from Spanish, analyses the practice of the Commission as well as the regulations and case law; critical, accurate and interesting.)

———, with *Ben van Houtte, EC Competition Law in the Transport Sector,* (Oxford, OUP, 1996).

Power, Vincent, Competition Law and Practice, (London, Butterworths/Lexis Nexis, 2001) clxi + 1874 pages. (A substantial work by a highly competent lawyer on Irish and EC competition law. I have not had time to use it yet.)

Ritter, L, D Braun and Rawlinson, EC Competition Law: A Practitioners' Guide, 2nd edn, (Deventer, Kluwer Law International, 2000), xcix + 1377 pp. (There is also a student edition with more print per page, xcix + 963 pp.) Accurate, detailed, well written work explaining, but not criticizing, the Commission's current practice; much easier to find answers than in the previous edition. It was originally advertised as being updated on the web, but this useful facility was lost when Kluwer was acquired by Aspen.)

Round, David K (ed) *The Australian Trade Practices Act 1974—Proscriptions and Prescriptions for a more Competitive Economy*, (London, KLI, 1994, Studies in Industrial Organization). (Collection of critical analyses of the major controversial cases in Australia and New Zealand.)

Scherer, FM and David Ross, *Industrial Market Structure and Economic Performance*, 3rd edn, (Boston, Mass, Houghton Miffin, 1990), xvi + 713 pp. (Lucid and thoughtful economic analyses of main problems arising from Antitrust.)

Subiotto, Romano and Robert Snelders, *Antitrust Developments in Europe*, (Cleary, Gottlieb and Kluwer Law International) (Annual description of the more important recent developments with apt comment.)

Swann, Dennis, *The Economics of Europe: from Common Market to European Union*, 9th edn, (London, Penguin Books, 2000), 412 pp. (A clear and helpful introduction, not specifically dealing with the competition provisions but excellent background reading.)

Tirole, Jean, *Theory of Industrial Organization*, (Cambridge, Mass, MIT Press, 1988), xii + 479 pp. (Lucid economic text by world famous economist.)

Whish, RP, *Competition Law*, 4th edn, (London, Butterworths, 2001), lxxix + 913 pp. (A lucid, interesting student text covering UK and EC law in the light of economic theory both from Chicago and its critics—more balanced than my work and far more detailed.)

Waelbroeck, Michel, with A Frignani, *European Competition Law*, Vol 4, Concurrence, 3rd edn in French and Italian (Brussels, Universitié libre de Bruxelles, 1997), (English edition, 1999). (A learned, scholarly and historical commentary, the only book regularly consulted by experts who know the law but need exciting ideas succinctly expressed. Unfortunately marred by lack of editorial discipline.)

Zoudis, J, *Les accords de distribution au regard du droit de la concurrence—droit suisse et droit communautaire dans une perspective economique*, (Publications du Centre d'Etudes Juridique Européennes, 2002) (An interesting, critical work, properly researched)

Commission of European Communities, *Reports on Competition Policy*—annual from 1971, published in the Autumn, now in two volumes, one short and a later one that is fuller.

——, *Competition News Letter*, published by Office for Official Publications 3 times a year.

European Court Reports (ECR), the official reports of the Community Courts.

Official Journal (OJ)—*Gazette of the Communities*. The L volumes contain the decisions and regulations of the Commission, the C volumes short summaries of pending decisions, and issues before the Community Court, notices and draft regulations.

Common Market Law Reports (CMLR). Law reports, cases in courts of members are now normally published in *European Commercial Cases (ECC)*. CMLR contains Commission decisions and judgments. Volume 4 of each year since 1989 and a fifth since 1995 is confined to the competition materials, including cases, legislation, draft legislation, state of Court's list etc.

Common Market Reporter (CMR). Commerce Clearing House (CCH), now Sweet & Maxwell. Useful series of looseleaf volumes replaced each year by bound volumes containing reports of the decisions of the Commission, judgments of the Court and press releases, Parliamentary questions etc., together with a comment on the treaty not confined to competition. The series has gone through two major changes. Since 1989, the judgments and decisions have been reported as CEC and bound in two volumes a year, but from 1996 in one volume. By 1997, the name of the CMR was changed to The European Union Law Reporter.

Some journals which publish commentaries on EC Competition Law

Business Law Review (Bus LR)
Cahiers de droit europeen (CDE)
Common Market Law Review (CML Rev)
Competition Law Insight (10 issues per year, very up to date)
Competition Law Journal
Europarecht (EurR)
European Competition Law Review (ECLR)
European Intellectual Property Review (EIPR)
European Law Review (EL Rev)
Fordham Corporate Law Institute, (ed) Barry Hawk, (Juris Publishing) (proceedings of outstanding annual conferences on competition law—many excellent and influential articles appear there).
International Intellectual Property Law and Policy (ed) Hugh Hansen, (Juris Publishing and Sweet & Maxwell) (similar volume of revised papers from outstanding annual conference, with some contributions on the interface between IP and Competition. New books will not be produced, but see the web site www.fordhamipconference.com).
International Review of Industrial Property and Copyright (IIC)
Journal of World Trade Law (JWTL)
Legal Issues of European Integration (LIEI)
Revue du marché commun (Rev Marché Com)
Revue trimestrielle de droit europ en (RTDE)
World Competition (World Competition Law and Economics Review), formerly called Revue Suisse du Droit International de la Concurrence.)

Glossary

Absolute territorial protection — protection given, usually to an exclusive dealer or to a licensee of intellectual property rights, from competition by sellers of goods of the same brand, or made by use of the protected innovation, not only by the supplier or licensor, but also dealers or licensees for other areas as well as from their customers. Since, however, the rules for the free movement of goods prevent either party from relying on intellectual property rights to restrain imports of goods sold in other member states by or with the consent of the holder (10.4), the protection is seldom absolute, although it may be for performing rights, basic seed and products made to a different specification for each customer **(2.4.1, 8.6, 9.5.1, 11.3).**

Active sales policy, restriction on — a restriction on the active promotion of a product outside the territory is permitted by some regulations, e.g., Article 4(b) first indent of the group exemption for vertical agreements (9.6.4.2); Article 4(2)(b) of that for technology transfer (11.5.3.2.2); or Article 4(1)(f) of that for collaboration in research and development (13.2.4). Note that the exact scope of the permitted restriction differs from one regulation to another.

Advocate General — member of the Community Court, of equal status with the judges. The opinion of the Advocate General is delivered before the judgment and may help the judges to focus on the crucial issues. Since he prepares his opinion on his own, it is more likely to be cogently analytical than the judgment, which has to accommodate the views of more than one judge. Opinions may point the way to subsequent developments. Frequently more of the issues are considered by the Advocate General than by the Court (1.4.3.1).

Agent — an undertaking which sells on behalf of its principal, without owning the stocks it sells or being responsible for unsold stocks. If it is heavily dependent on its principal and integrated into its organisation, an exclusive agent and his principal may accept restrictions without infringing Article 81 (9.7.1).

Aggregated discounts — discounts granted to classes of customers based on the total bought by each customer from all members of a trade association, or from all national manufacturers, and not just from the individual seller. They discourage buyers who hope to qualify for a larger discount from buying part of their requirements elsewhere, often in another Member State, and agreements to grant a particular scale of discounts discourage secret discounts (8.4).

Cartel — term sometimes used to refer to any agreement that infringes Article 81. I tend to confine it to an agreement between competitors intended to raise prices above the competitive level. Usually quotas have to be allocated or some other mechanism adopted to restrict production, as less will be demanded when prices are higher (2.2.4–2.2.4.3, 7.6–7.6.3 and 8.2–8.2.6).

Chiselling — selling at a price lower than that agreed with competitors in order to increase market share. The practice undermines cartels even when they are legal and few last for long without government protection (2.2.4.1).

Competing undertakings — the Commission used to consider that undertakings operating at the same level of the same trade or industry were competing, but it has now changed its mind and treats them as doing so only if they could have done so in the absence of the agreement and its restrictions (11.5.2.1).

Complementary products — the opposite of substitutes. If more of one product is sold, the more of a complement and the less of a substitute will be demanded.

Concentration — word used in the merger regulation for a merger or acquisition (12.2.1–12.2.2). Concentrations over the thresholds of turnover are subject to the regulation and not to Article 81 or Article 82. Those under the thresholds may be controlled under national competition laws or Article 82.

Concentrative joint venture — a concentrative joint venture that is subject to the more lenient criteria of the merger regulation if the thresholds are exceeded. It must be an autonomous economic entity on a lasting basis, *i.e.* have all the resources needed to operate as if it were independent of its parents. If it merely provides them with some input they need and does not sell on the market it will not usually be 'full function' and will fall to be appraised under Article 81 (12.2.2).

Concerted practice — concept used to extend the prohibition of Article 81(1) to forms of collaboration looser than a contract or agreement. It is thought that it does not extend to price leadership in the absence of some deliberate conduct reducing the risks of competition (2.2.4–2.2.4.2).

Costs — there are various concepts of costs used by economists. **Average total cost** is the average cost of providing a unit of output, including overheads, such as part of the cost of the plant. **Marginal cost** is the cost of making an additional unit of output, and in the short term may not include overheads. At some point, however, additional investment in capacity may be needed, so the marginal cost at that point includes the cost of increasing capacity and may be very high. Economists, often look, therefore to **average variable cost**, averaging the need for extra capacity. **Long run incremental cost** is a concept often used by regulators. It is forward looking. Increasing output includes the need to invest in more capacity. Where technology is improving rapidly, a regulated firm permitted to charge no more than its long run incremental cost will never be able to recover its total historic cost as for each period of regulation the cost of providing future capacity will fall. The current regime for telecommunications, however, allows a further margin for profit. **Sunk costs** are investments that have no other use. Consten could not have used its promotion of Grundig products if the promotion was not successful, for instance, if it failed to obtain sufficiently large import licences. Unless it could make profits selling Grundig products, its investment would be thrown away. Consequently, it would need to expect high profits to justify making the initial investment. The high profits would attract competition, so without the protection of an exclusive territory, it might not have been prepared to make the initial, risky investment (2.3.1 and 2.4.1).

DG Comp, formerly DGIV — abbreviation used for Directorate General of Competition, the competition department of the Commission. It deals with Articles 81 and 82 as well as with concentrations and state aids granted by national governments to industry. The senior civil servant is the Director General, now Mr Lowe. The department has been reorganised several times. Directorate A is responsible for advice on policy and the preparation of regulations and notices of general application. It is responsible also for following cases to ensure that different industries do not receive different treatment without good reason. The merger task force established to deal with merger cases has been abolished and its staff scattered amongst the sectoral directorates. They deal with individual cases and are divided according to industry. A case handler can start working on a file already knowing about the market. Two Directorates deal with state aids.

Dominant position in a substantial part of the common market, abuse of — this is a technical legal concept. It is not to be identical with the economists' idea of power over price, but under the influence of the experience in dealing with mergers the concept used by the Commission is coming closer to that idea. The ECJ habitually defines it as:

> a position of economic strength enjoyed by an undertaking which enables it to prevent effective competition being maintained on the relevant market by giving it power to behave to an appreciable extent independently of its competitors, customers and ultimately of its consumers.

The Commission has been developing the concept of a joint dominant position (4.3.5), so as to be able to control acquisitions increasing concentration to the point where firms in oligopolistic industries may act as if they had conspired without the need to enter into an agreement or concerted practice (2.2.4–2.2.4.2).

The abuse of a dominant position is defined by the ECJ in cases involving exclusionary practices:

> The concept of abuse is an objective concept relating to the behaviour of an undertaking in a dominant position which is such as to influence the structure of the market where, as a result of the very presence of the undertaking in questions, the degree of all normal competition on the basis of performance, has the effect of hindering the maintenance of the degree of competition still existing in the market or the growth of that competition. (chapter 5)

Euro — the old European currency unit, the ECU, was based on a basket of currencies. It has been replaced by the Euro, the single currency unit used in all but three of the old Member States, but not yet in Denmark, Sweden or the UK. The ten new Member States hope to use it soon. The single currency works in all the Member States that have adopted it, and one can carry currency from one Member State to another without the need for conversion into a local currency. It is the currency used by the Community institutions in making charges, imposing fines or measuring turnover etc.

Exclusionary rebates and discounts — see loyalty and other exclusionary discounts or rebates.

Exclusive dealer — independent trader who buys the stocks he later sells and is protected by the supplier's promise not to sell directly to any other dealer within his exclusive territory. Such agreements may come within a group exemption, provided that the dealer is not protected from goods coming indirectly from other dealers. They must be allowed to accept unsolicited orders from outside their territories, and their customers cannot be restrained from poaching. An exclusive dealer may agree also not to handle competing products for limited periods (9.6.4.2).

Facilitating device — practices that make it easier for the few firms in an oligopolistic market not to compete: *e.g.* announcing price changes well in advance, giving competitors time to consider whether to follow them before they are implemented, most favoured customer clauses that make it harder to discriminate (2.2.4–2.2.4.3).

Foreclosure — conduct of a dominant firm or combination of firms that excludes competitors from the market. See also loyalty and other exclusionary rebates or discounts, below. Exclusive purchasing may also foreclose in limited circumstances.

The ability of a firm to foreclose its competitors is dealt with in chapter 5.

Franchise — a method of exploiting a formula for retailing without using much of the franchisor's capital. The franchisor supplies marketing advice to franchisees in return, usually, for a royalty and down payment. The latter's shops look almost as if owned and managed by the franchisor, but are in fact operated by the franchisees. Ancillary restrictions to ensure the control necessary to maintain a common reputation and to prevent the assistance coming into the hands of competitors do not infringe Article 81(1), but an exclusive territory, coupled with a duty to sell only from specified premises within it, requires exemption once the network is widespread (9.5–9.5.1). For this there is a group exemption (9.6–9.6.7).

Production franchising consists of a licence to use a trade mark, often coupled with a licence of technology. Such a franchise does not come within the group exemption for distribution. It is thought that most franchisees face sufficient competition to prevent the application of the competition rules.

Free rider — a firm that takes advantage of another's investment. For instance, the parallel importers took advantage of Consten's promotion of Grundig products (2.4.1).

Horizontal agreement — agreement between competitors: *i.e.*, between undertakings that could have competed in the absence of the agreement. (8.1–8.1.3 and 11.5.2.1).

Information agreement — agreement to inform competitors of prices, production, capacity, etc. These are treated as restrictions on competition because they affect prices or market shares if the information is detailed and disseminated rapidly. They may facilitate oligopolistic interdependence or collusion by reducing uncertainty (8.2.2). On the other hand, dissemination of information about price and quantity makes markets work better and enables undertakings better to judge prospective investment.

Joint venture — collaboration between two or more firms in one or more areas of activity. This may take any legal form, joint subsidiary, joint committee, etc. Joint ventures may reduce the incentive for the venturers to compete with each other in those activities, and may deter competition between them in others. If more than one party could have operated alone, it may reduce the number of actual or potential competitors, etc. Joint ventures may, however, increase competition by enabling the parties to do what no one of them would have been prepared to undertake independently (chapter 13).

Concentrative joint ventures (above) are dealt with more favourably under the merger regulation (12.2.2).

Know-how — secret technical information. Its communication is nowadays treated as a technology licence for which there is a group exemption. Since national laws confer no exclusive right other than the obligation to keep the technology secret, it is more vulnerable than technology protected by patents. Exclusive know-how licences may qualify under the group exemption for technology transfer (11.5.1).

Loyalty and other exclusionary rebates or discounts — a discount is a deduction made when charging a customer, often proportional to the total bill, while the term 'rebate' is used when a repayment is made at the end of a period over which the amount is calculated. A firm may grant a rebate to those who in fact buy all or a large, specified proportion of their requirements over a period from it, or a discount or rebate to those who promise to do so. Sometimes small buyers like to be assured of supplies whatever the amount they order, and in return for such a promise will agree to buy exclusively from a single supplier.

The Commission and Court see loyalty rebates by a dominant firm as making it more difficult for smaller firms to compete with it. To compete for orders that would cause the buyer to forego the loyalty rebate, a firm would have to match the dominant firm's discounts not only on the amount bought from it, but also on the amount bought from the dominant firm. Since they cannot supply the total needs of large customers, small firms cannot compete by themselves giving such discounts unless they combine (5.2.2.1).

Similar practices may operate through a trade association where buyers agree to buy a large part of their requirements exclusively from members of the association or in fact do so (8.4).

Other kinds of discount given by a dominant firm or association may have similar effects in making it difficult for a single smaller firm to compete. The dominant firm or association may grant progressive quantity discounts or rebates so that, for instance, an extra 1% saving is made by the buyer on his total purchases for each extra thousand units taken.

Where this reflects probable costs savings in planning production on a regular basis, or enabling shipments to be made in container, car or barge lots, it encourages efficiency and should be treated as competition on the basis of performance. Where this cannot be shown, it may have a similar effect to a loyalty rebate or discount. A competitor wishing to supply the last thousand units would have to match the discount not only on what he sells but also the percentage the buyer will lose on all his other sales. The Commission and courts have not treated systematic discounts or rebates as competition on the basis of performance where they are not justified by cost savings.

Where a trade association arranges for discounts or rebates proportional to the amount bought from all its members by each firm, it may be easier for smaller firms in the association to compete in service for large buyers, but harder for outsiders. Such rebates are sometimes described as collective, because arranged between competitors, and aggregated, because the purchases from all members are relevant. They have the additional anti-competitive effect of preventing competition in discounts between the members (8.4).

Monopoly — market with a single seller. The term is often used to indicate market power and refer to the major seller in the market which is able to sell at a price exceeding its cost. Monopoly is unlikely to last unless 1) there are no substitutes to which most customers can turn, *and* 2) there are entry barriers which prevent other suppliers from entering a market.

Monopoly is not necessarily anticompetitive. The holder of an important patent may be able to charge more for the protected product than it would be able to without an exclusive right, but it might not have invested in innovation without the hope of being granted a patent.

Oligopoly — a market with few sellers. In such a market suppliers are unlikely to compete in ways that can be quickly imitated. Price competition is likely to take the form of secret discounts given to large buyers who can be relied upon to keep quiet (2.2.4.1).

Open exclusive licence — a term coined by the ECJ in *Nungesser* (see 11.3). At ground 53 it defined a licence or assignment as open where:

> the exclusivity of the licence relates solely to the contractual relationship between the owner of the right and the licensee, whereby the owner merely undertakes not to grant other licences in respect of the same territory and not to compete himself with the licensee on that territory.

It is contrasted with 'absolute territorial protection,' where the parties propose to eliminate competition from third parties such as parallel importers or licensees for other territories.

Parallel imports — mechanism on which the Commission relies to lead towards the equalisation of prices throughout the common market. If there are large price differentials between the Member States, not accounted for by differences in cost, such as freight, taxes, etc., it may pay someone to buy in the low priced area and sell in the high (8.6.2, chapters 10 and 11). Parallel trade creates great difficulty for those investing, *e.g.*, in R & D to develop products the price of which is controlled at low levels in some Member States (10.4.5). The position may become more acute now that the internet reduces the cost of parallel traders and cuts out middle men.

Passive sales policy, restriction on — a restriction on accepting unsolicited offers within the territory from those outside, as permitted by the group exemption for technology transfer for five years after the goods are first put on the market by a licensee in the common market (11.5.3.2.2). An exclusive distributor may not be so protected and the group exemption for vertical agreements treats a restriction on passive sales as automatically contrary to Article 81(1), irrespective of arguments based on free riders or of market structure (9.6.4.2).

Patent — exclusive right conferred by national law to prevent others using the invention protected by the patent, also from selling, using or importing products made by use of the invention. A United Kingdom patent is infringed only by actions in the United Kingdom, and to use a United Kingdom patent to keep out goods sold by or with the consent of the holder in France and protected by a corresponding French patent infringes the principle of the free movement of goods (chapter 10).

Patent licence — permission to do what would otherwise infringe a patent. Usually, this is contained in a contract under which restrictions on competition may be accepted. There is a group exemption for technology transfer agreements (Chapter 11).

Patents, parallel — situation where patents are obtained under the law of several Member States in respect of virtually the same invention by the same person or group of companies.

Preliminary ruling — ruling of the ECJ on the interpretation or validity of Community law, given at the request of a national court or tribunal (1.5.2).

Quantitative restrictions on imports and all measures having equivalent effect — these are prohibited by Article 28 of the Treaty. Quantitative restrictions are primarily import quotas — *e.g.*, only 100 widgets shall be imported from state X in 2004. They were very common at the time the common market was established. They include a nil quota, *i.e.*, a ban — no widgets shall be imported from state X this year. Laws granting industrial property rights, such as patents and trade marks or, possibly, their exercise have been held to be measures of equivalent effect — no widgets shall be imported without the consent of the holder.

Consequently, national courts may not allow the exercise of such rights, save so far as is justified on the various grounds listed in Article 30 and does not constitute a means of arbitrary discrimination or a disguised restriction on trade between Member States. Where a quantitative restriction applies to domestic products but bears more heavily on imports from other Member States, the Court has read into Article 28 limitations for measures that protect consumers, the revenue etc. (chapter 10).

Rapporteur or case handler — term used colloquially to describe the official in one of the sectoral Directorates of DG Comp of the Commission whose function is to prepare the Commission's case against mergers or possible infringements of Article 81 or 82. Most case handlers are lawyers, although few have practised. More economists than previously are now case handlers.

Their discretion is limited. Apart from the discipline inherent in a civil service hierarchy and exercised on grounds of policy, including co-ordination from Directorate A, certain steps, such as the draft of the final decision, must be submitted to the Legal Service. The Advisory Committee of experts from Member States must be consulted before the final draft of a decision condemning an infringement, granting an exemption or imposing a fine is submitted to the Commission itself. Decisions must be adopted by the Members of the Commission acting collegiately, although they are prepared by the case handler (chapter 7).

Resale price maintenance — practice by a supplier, usually a brand owner, of requiring that dealers should sell only at a specified price. The price may be minimum, fixed or maximum. Although this may be no more restrictive a method of restraining free riders than an exclusive territory, the Commission takes the view that the maintenance of fixed or minimum resale prices always has the object or effect of restricting competition, although it may not affect trade between Member States (9.6.4.1).

Selective distribution — policy that may be adopted by a brand owner for ensuring that his output is sold only through competent dealers. Where glamour or pre-sales service is important, for example, for jewellery, vehicles and television sets, he may restrain his dealers from selling to any retailer who does not meet objective criteria. To become approved the retailer may be required to sell from specified premises, keep stocks of spare parts and have staff with specified skills available. Provided that such requirements are objective, *i.e.*, clearly specified, reasonably necessary to ensure adequate service to the consumer and applied without discrimination, the Court and Commission do not treat this as a restriction of competition (9.4).

Where, however, to protect dealers who have invested in such staff and equipment, the brand owner also imposes quantitative restrictions — refuses to approve more retailers than he thinks the traffic will bear — Article 81(1) may well apply. There is a group exemption for distribution permitting selective distribution with quantitative protection (9.6.4.3).

Single branding – the term used by the Commission in the regulation and guidelines on vertical agreements to cover requirements contracts and exclusive purchasing. I will buy all, or a substantial percentage of my requirements from you, or I will handle only your brand of products (5.2.2.1 and 9.6.5).

SSNIP test — The acronyme stands for a 'small but significant non-transitory increase in price.' It is sometimes called 'the hypothetical monopolist test.'

To ascertain the relevant geographic and product market one assumes that the price of the obvious product in an area is raised in relation to other products and areas by a small but significant amount — in the range of 5% or 10% — and that the relative rise is perceived to be lasting. If so many buyers would switch to other products or areas as to make the rise unprofitable, the product and areas to which they would switch should be included in the relevant market.

One should also consider whether the higher price would attract other suppliers to offer the product in the area, and if so many would enter as to make the rise unprofitable, then those suppliers should be added. They also constrain price rises.

Then one should take those products and areas and repeat the test, until there is a sufficient gap in the chain of substitution to make the hypothetical price rise profitable (4.3.1–4.3.1.3)

Substitutes — A and B are substitutes if the more that is sold of A the less of B will be demanded. If additional sales of A result in more of B being demanded, they are complements.

Undertaking — includes any collection of resources to carry out economic activities: services, even professional services, as well as the supply of goods. Articles 81 and 82 are addressed to undertakings. A group of companies is treated as a single undertaking, provided that the subsidiaries are totally dependent on the parent and follow its instructions. Consequently, instructions to a wholly owned subsidiary or agreements between sister subsidiaries do not infringe Article 81(1) (2.2.1 and 6.2.1).

Unit of account — see Euros.

Vertical agreements — those between undertakings at different levels of trade or industry, for example those between supplier and customer or between licensor and licensee. Where the parties did or could have competed with each other without the agreement, it will also have horizontal elements (8.1, 8.1.3 and 11.5.2.1)

The Commission is now using the term to cover vertical agreements relating to 'the conditions under which the parties may purchase sell or resell certain goods' (9.6.1.1).

Appendix I

Excerpts from the Treaty establishing the European Community[1]

Part One

PRINCIPLES

Article 2

The Community shall have as its task, by establishing a common market and an economic and monetary union and by implementing the common policies or activities referred to in Articles 3 and 4, to promote throughout the Community a harmonious and balanced development of economic activities, sustainable and non-inflationary growth respecting the environment, a high degree of convergence of economic employment, a high level of employment and of social protection, the raising of the standard of living and quality of life, and economic and social cohesion and solidarity among member states.

Article 3

For the purposes set out in Article 2, the activities of the Community shall include, as provided in this Treaty and in accordance with the timetable set out therein:

(a) the elimination, as between Member States, of customs duties and quantitative restrictions on the import and export of goods, and of all other measures having equivalent effect;

(b)   a common commercial policy;

(c)   an internal market characterised by the abolition, as between Member States, of obstacles to the free movement of goods, persons, services and capital;

(d)   measures concerning the entry and movement of persons in the internal market as provided for in Title IV;

(e)   a common policy in the sphere of agriculture and fisheries;

(f)   a common policy in the sphere of transport;

(g)   a system ensuring that competition in the internal market is not distorted;

(h)   the approximation of the laws of Member States to the extent required for the proper functioning of the common market;

(i)   a policy in the sphere comprising a European Social Fund;

(j)   the strengthening of economic and social cohesion;

(k)   a policy in the sphere of the environment;

(l)   the strengthening of the competitiveness of Community industry;

(m) the promotion of research and technological development;

(n)   encouragement for the establishment and development of trans-European networks;

(o)   a contribution to the attainment of a high level of health protection;

(p)   a contribution to education and training of equality and to the flowering of the cultures of the Member States;

(q)   a policy in the sphere of development cooperation;

(r)   the association of the overseas countries and territories in order to increase trade and promote jointly economic and social development;

1   Almost all the Articles of the EC Treaty were renumbered when the Treaty of Amsterdam came into operation on the first of May 1999. The new numbers have been used here.

(s) a contribution to the strengthening of consumer protection;
(t) measures in the spheres of energy, civil protection and tourism.

Article 10 (ex 5)

Member States shall take all appropriate measures, whether general or particular, to ensure fulfilment of the obligations arising out of this Treaty or resulting from action taken by the institutions of the Community. They shall facilitate the achievement of the Community's tasks.

They shall abstain from any measure which could jeopardise the attainment of the objectives of this Treaty.

CHAPTER 2 — ELIMINATION OF QUANTITATIVE RESTRICTIONS BETWEEN MEMBER STATES

Article 28 (ex 30)

Quantitative restrictions on imports and all measures having equivalent effect shall, without prejudice to the following provisions, be prohibited between Member States.

Article 30 (ex 36)

The provisions of Articles 28 to 29 shall not preclude prohibitions or restrictions on imports, exports or goods in transit justified on grounds of public morality, public policy or public security; the protection of health and life of humans, animals or plants; the protection of national treasures possessing artistic, historic or archaeological value; or the protection of industrial and commercial property. Such prohibition or restrictions shall not, however, constitute a means of arbitrary discrimination or a disguised restriction on trade between Member States.

Part Three
POLICY OF THE COMMUNITY
TITLE I—COMMON RULES
CHAPTER 1—RULES ON COMPETITION
SECTION 1
RULES APPLYING TO UNDERTAKINGS

Article 81 (ex 85)

1. The following shall be prohibited as incompatible with the common market: all agreements between undertakings, decisions by associations of undertakings and concerted practices which may affect trade between Member States and which have as their object or effect the prevention, restriction or distortion of competition within the common market, and in particular those which:

(a) directly or indirectly fix purchase or selling prices or any other trading conditions;
(b) limit or control production, markets, technical development, or investment;
(c) share markets or sources of supply;
(d) apply dissimilar conditions to equivalent transactions with other trading parties, thereby placing them at a competitive disadvantage;
(e) make the conclusion of contracts subject to acceptance by the other parties of supplementary obligations which, by their nature or according to commercial usage, have no connection with the subject of such contracts.

2. Any agreements or decisions prohibited pursuant to this Article shall be automatically void.

3. The provisions of paragraph 1 may, however, be declared inapplicable in the case of:

– any agreement or category of agreements between undertakings;
– any decision or category of decisions by associations of undertakings;
– any concerted practice or category of concerted practices;

which contributes to improving the production or distribution of goods or to promoting technical or economic progress, while allowing consumers a fair share of the resulting benefit, and which does not:

(a) impose on the undertakings concerned restrictions which are not indispensable to the attainment of these objectives;
(b) afford such undertakings the possibility of eliminating competition in respect of a substantial part of the products in question.

Article 82 (ex 86)

Any abuse by one or more undertakings of a dominant position within the common market or in a substantial part of it shall be prohibited as incompatible with the common market in so far as it may affect trade between Member States. Such abuse may, in particular, consist in:

(a) directly or indirectly imposing unfair purchase or selling prices or other unfair trading conditions;
(b) limiting production, markets or technical development to the prejudice of consumers;
(c) applying dissimilar conditions to equivalent transactions with other trading parties, thereby placing them at a competitive disadvantage;
(d) making the conclusion of contracts subject to acceptance by the other parties of supplementary obligations which, by their nature or according to commercial usage, have no connection with the subject of such contracts.

Article 86 (ex 90)

1. In the case of public undertakings and undertakings to which Member States grant special or exclusive rights, Member States shall neither enact nor maintain in force any measure contrary to the rules contained in this Treaty, in particular to those rules provided for in Article 12 and Articles 81 to 89.

2. Undertakings entrusted with the operation of services of general economic interest or having the character of a revenue-producing monopoly shall be subject to the rules contained in this Treaty, in particular to the rules on competition, in so far as the application of such rules does not obstruct the performance, in law or in fact, of the particular tasks assigned to them. The development of trade must not be affected to such an extent as would be contrary to the interests of the Community.

3. The Commission shall ensure the application of the provisions of this Article and shall, where necessary, address appropriate directives or decisions to Member States.

Part Six
GENERAL AND FINAL PROVISIONS

Article 295 (ex 222)

This Treaty shall in no way prejudice the rules of Member States governing the system of property ownership.

Appendix II

Regulation No 1/2003

The headings to recitals, cross references between recitals in brackets and articles at the top of each provision are by Valentine Korah and do not form part of the regulation. They are all shown in italic. The table of contents is also by the author. Commission headings are in roman and bold.

COUNCIL REGULATION (EC) NO 1/2003
of 16 December 2002

on the implementation of the rules on competition laid down in Articles 81 and 82 of the Treaty

(Text with EEA relevance)

THE COUNCIL OF THE EUROPEAN UNION,

Having regard to the Treaty establishing the European Community, and in particular Article 83 thereof,

Having regard to the proposal from the Commission[1],

Having regard to the opinion of the European Parliament[2],

Having regard to the opinion of the European Economic and Social Committee[3], Whereas:

Replace Regulation 17—Article 43

(1) In order to establish a system which ensures that competition in the common market is not distorted, Articles 81 and 82 of the Treaty must be applied effectively and uniformly in the Community. Council Regulation No 17 of 6 February 1962, First Regulation implementing Articles 81 and 82*[4] of the Treaty[5], has allowed a Community competition policy to develop that has helped to disseminate a competition culture within the Community. In the light of experience, however, that Regulation should now be replaced by legislation designed to meet the challenges of an integrated market and a future enlargement of the Community.

Article 81(3)—Articles 1, 3, 5, 6, 11, 14

(2) In particular, there is a need to rethink the arrangements for applying the exception from the prohibition on agreements, which restrict competition, laid down in Article 81(3) of the Treaty. Under Article 83(2)(b) of the Treaty, account must be taken in this regard of the need to ensure effective supervision, on the one hand, and to simplify administration to the greatest possible extent, on the other.

---

1   OJ C 365 E, 19.12.2000, p. 284.
2   OJ C 72 E, 21.3.2002, p. 305.
3   OJ C 155, 29.5.2001, p. 73.
4*   The title of Regulation No 17 has been adjusted to take account of the renumbering of the Articles of the EC Treaty, in accordance with Article 12 of the Treaty of Amsterdam; the original reference was to Articles 85 and 86 of the Treaty.
5   OJ 13, 21.2.1962, p. 204/62. Regulation as last amended by Regulation (EC) No 1216/1999 (OJ L 148, 15.6.1999, p. 5).

Decentralisation—passim

(3) The centralised scheme set up by Regulation No 17 no longer secures a balance between those two objectives. It hampers application of the Community competition rules by the courts and competition authorities of the Member States, and the system of notification it involves prevents the Commission from concentrating its resources on curbing the most serious infringements. It also imposes considerable costs on undertakings.

Articles 81 and 82 directly applicable—Articles 1 and 6

(4) The present system should therefore be replaced by a directly applicable exception system in which the competition authorities and courts of the Member States have the power to apply not only Article 81(1) and Article 82 of the Treaty, which have direct applicability by virtue of the case-law of the Court of Justice of the European Communities, but also Article 81(3) of the Treaty.

Burden of proof—Article 2

5) In order to ensure an effective enforcement of the Community competition rules and at the same time the respect of fundamental rights of defence, this Regulation should regulate the burden of proof under Articles 81 and 82 of the Treaty. It should be for the party or the authority alleging an infringement of Article 81(1) and Article 82 of the Treaty to prove the existence thereof to the required legal standard. It should be for the undertaking or association of undertakings invoking the benefit of a defence against a finding of an infringement to demonstrate to the required legal standard that the conditions for applying such defence are satisfied. This Regulation affects neither national rules on the standard of proof nor obligations of competition authorities and courts of the Member States to ascertain the relevant facts of a case, provided that such rules and obligations are compatible with general principles of Community law.

National Competition Authorities (NCAs)—Articles 3, 5, 11–14, 19–21, 35

(6) In order to ensure that the Community competition rules are applied effectively, the competition authorities of the Member States should be associated more closely with their application. To this end, they should be empowered to apply Community law.

National Courts Articles 1, 3, 6, 9, 15 Recital 21

(7) National courts have an essential part to play in applying the Community competition rules. When deciding disputes between private individuals, they protect the subjective rights under Community law, for example by awarding damages to the victims of infringements. The role of the national courts here complements that of the competition authorities of the Member States. They should therefore be allowed to apply Articles 81 and 82 of the Treaty in full.

NCAs and Courts to apply Articles 81 and 82 as well if they apply national competition law to practices that affect trade between Member States—Article 3

(8) In order to ensure the effective enforcement of the Community competition rules and the proper functioning of the cooperation mechanisms contained in this Regulation, it is necessary to oblige the competition authorities and courts of the

Member States to also apply Articles 81 and 82 of the Treaty where they apply national competition law to agreements and practices which may affect trade between Member States. In order to create a level playing field for agreements, decisions by associations of undertakings and concerted practices within the internal market, it is also necessary to determine pursuant to Article 83(2)(e) of the Treaty the relationship between national laws and Community competition law. To that effect it is necessary to provide that the application of national competition laws to agreements, decisions or concerted practices within the meaning of Article 81(1) of the Treaty may not lead to the prohibition of such agreements, decisions and concerted practices if they are not also prohibited under Community competition law. The notions of agreements, decisions and concerted practices are autonomous concepts of Community competition law covering the coordination of behaviour of undertakings on the market as interpreted by the Community Courts. Member States should not under this Regulation be precluded from adopting and applying on their territory stricter national competition laws which prohibit or impose sanctions on unilateral conduct engaged in by undertakings. These stricter national laws may include provisions which prohibit or impose sanctions on abusive behaviour toward economically dependent undertakings. Furthermore, this Regulation does not apply to national laws which impose criminal sanctions on natural persons except to the extent that such sanctions are the means whereby competition rules applying to undertakings are enforced.

National unfair competition and other laws not based on free competition—Article 3

(9) Articles 81 and 82 of the Treaty have as their objective the protection of competition on the market. This Regulation, which is adopted for the implementation of these Treaty provisions, does not preclude Member States from implementing on their territory national legislation, which protects other legitimate interests provided that such legislation is compatible with general principles and other provisions of Community law. In so far as such national legislation pursues predominantly an objective different from that of protecting competition on the market, the competition authorities and courts of the Member States may apply such legislation on their territory. Accordingly, Member States may under this Regulation implement on their territory national legislation that prohibits or imposes sanctions on acts of unfair trading practice, be they unilateral or contractual. Such legislation pursues a specific objective, irrespective of the actual or presumed effects of such acts on competition on the market. This is particularly the case of legislation which prohibits undertakings from imposing on their trading partners, obtaining or attempting to obtain from them terms and conditions that are unjustified, disproportionate or without consideration.

Group exemptions by Commission, withdrawal by Commission or NCA—Article 29

(10) Regulations such as 19/65/EEC[6], (EEC) No 2821/71[7], (EEC) No 3976/87[8], (EEC) No 1534/91[9], or (EEC) No 479/92[10] empower the Commission to apply Article 81(3) of the Treaty by Regulation to certain categories of agreements, decisions by associations of undertakings and concerted practices. In the areas defined by such Regulations, the Commission has adopted and may continue to adopt so called "block" exemption Regulations by which it declares Article 81(1) of the Treaty inapplicable to categories of agreements, decisions and concerted practices. Where agreements, decisions and concerted practices to which such Regulations apply nonetheless have effects that are incompatible with Article 81(3) of the Treaty, the Commission and the competition authorities of the Member States should have the power to withdraw in a particular case the benefit of the block exemption Regulation.

Commission's power to forbid infringements—Articles 7, 8

(11) For it to ensure that the provisions of the Treaty are applied, the Commission should be able to address decisions to undertakings or associations of undertakings for the purpose of bringing to an end infringements of Articles 81 and 82 of the Treaty. Provided there is a legitimate interest in doing so, the Commission should also be able to adopt decisions which find that an infringement has been committed in the past even if it does not impose a fine. This Regulation should also make explicit provision for the Commission's power to adopt decisions ordering interim measures, which has been acknowledged by the Court of Justice.

6   Council Regulation No 19/65/EEC of 2 March 1965 on the application of Article 81(3) (The titles of the Regulations have been adjusted to take account of the renumbering of the Articles of the EC Treaty, in accordance with Article 12 of the Treaty of Amsterdam; the original reference was to Article 85(3) of the Treaty) of the Treaty to certain categories of agreements and concerted practices (OJ 36, 6.3.1965, p. 533). Regulation as last amended by Regulation (EC) No 1215/1999 (OJ L 148, 15.6.1999, p. 1).

7   Council Regulation (EEC) No 2821/71 of 20 December 1971 on the application of Article 81(3) (The titles of the Regulations have been adjusted to take account of the renumbering of the Articles of the EC Treaty, in accordance with Article 12 of the Treaty of Amsterdam; the original reference was to Article 85(3) of the Treaty) of the Treaty to categories of agreements, decisions and concerted practices (OJ L 285, 29.12.1971, p. 46). Regulation as last amended by the Act of Accession of 1994.

8   Council Regulation (EEC) No 3976/87 of 14 December 1987 on the application of Article 81(3) (The titles of the Regulations have been adjusted to take account of the renumbering of the Articles of the EC Treaty, in accordance with Article 12 of the Treaty of Amsterdam; the original reference was to Article 85(3) of the Treaty) of the Treaty to certain categories of agreements and concerted practices in the air transport sector (OJ L 374, 31.12.1987, p. 9). Regulation as last amended by the Act of Accession of 1994.

9   Council Regulation (EEC) No 1534/91 of 31 May 1991 on the application of Article 81(3) (The titles of the Regulations have been adjusted to take account of the renumbering of the Articles of the EC Treaty, in accordance with Article 12 of the Treaty of Amsterdam; the original reference was to Article 85(3) of the Treaty) of the Treaty to certain categories of agreements, decisions and concerted practices in the insurance sector (OJ L 143, 7.6.1991, p. 1).

10   Council Regulation (EEC) No 479/92 of 25 February 1992 on the application of Article 81(3) (The titles of the Regulations have been adjusted to take account of the renumbering of the Articles of the EC Treaty, in accordance with Article 12 of the Treaty of Amsterdam; the original reference was to Article 85(3) of the Treaty) of the Treaty to certain categories of agreements, decisions and concerted practices between liner shipping companies (Consortia) (OJ L 55, 29.2.1992, p. 3). Regulation amended by the Act of Accession of 1994.

Remedies—Articles 7& 9

(12) This Regulation should make explicit provision for the Commission's power to impose any remedy, whether behavioural or structural, which is necessary to bring the infringement effectively to an end, having regard to the principle of proportionality. Structural remedies should only be imposed either where there is no equally effective behavioural remedy or where any equally effective behavioural remedy would be more burdensome for the undertaking concerned than the structural remedy. Changes to the structure of an undertaking as it existed before the infringement was committed would only be proportionate where there is a substantial risk of a lasting or repeated infringement that derives from the very structure of the undertaking.

Binding Commitments—Article 9

(13) Where, in the course of proceedings which might lead to an agreement or practice being prohibited, undertakings offer the Commission commitments such as to meet its concerns, the Commission should be able to adopt decisions which make those commitments binding on the undertakings concerned. Commitment decisions should find that there are no longer grounds for action by the Commission without concluding whether or not there has been or still is an infringement. Commitment decisions are without prejudice to the powers of competition authorities and courts of the Member States to make such a finding and decide upon the case. Commitment decisions are not appropriate in cases where the Commission intends to impose a fine.

Declaratory Clearances—Article 10

(14) In exceptional cases where the public interest of the Community so requires, it may also be expedient for the Commission to adopt a decision of a declaratory nature finding that the prohibition in Article 81 or Article 82 of the Treaty does not apply, with a view to clarifying the law and ensuring its consistent application throughout the Community, in particular with regard to new types of agreements or practices that have not been settled in the existing case-law and administrative practice.

Network of public authorities—Article 11

(15) The Commission and the competition authorities of the Member States should form together a network of public authorities applying the Community competition rules in close cooperation. For that purpose it is necessary to set up arrangements for information and consultation. Further modalities for the cooperation within the network will be laid down and revised by the Commission, in close cooperation with the Member States. (15) The Commission and the competition authorities of the Member States should form together a network of public authorities applying the Community competition rules in close cooperation. For that purpose it is necessary to set up arrangements for information and consultation. Further modalities for the cooperation within the network will be laid down and revised by the Commission, in close cooperation with the Member States.

Confidential information—Articles 11, 12

(16) Notwithstanding any national provision to the contrary, the exchange of information and the use of such information in evidence should be allowed between the members of the network even where the information is confidential. This information may be used for the application of Articles 81 and 82 of the Treaty as well as for

the parallel application of national competition law, provided that the latter application relates to the same case and does not lead to a different outcome. When the information exchanged is used by the receiving authority to impose sanctions on undertakings, there should be no other limit to the use of the information than the obligation to use it for the purpose for which it was collected given the fact that the sanctions imposed on undertakings are of the same type in all systems. The rights of defence enjoyed by undertakings in the various systems can be considered as sufficiently equivalent. However, as regards natural persons, they may be subject to substantially different types of sanctions across the various systems. Where that is the case, it is necessary to ensure that information can only be used if it has been collected in a way which respects the same level of protection of the rights of defence of natural persons as provided for under the national rules of the receiving authority.

Avoidance of multiple administrative proceedings—Article 13

17. If the competition rules are to be applied consistently and, at the same time, the network is to be managed in the best possible way, it is essential to retain the rule that the competition authorities of the Member States are automatically relieved of their competence if the Commission initiates its own proceedings. Where a competition authority of a Member State is already acting on a case and the Commission intends to initiate proceedings, it should endeavour to do so as soon as possible. Before initiating proceedings, the Commission should consult the national authority concerned.

NCA may suspend proceedings—Article 13

(18) To ensure that cases are dealt with by the most appropriate authorities within the network, a general provision should be laid down allowing a competition authority to suspend or close a case on the ground that another authority is dealing with it or has already dealt with it, the objective being that each case should be handled by a single authority. This provision should not prevent the Commission from rejecting a complaint for lack of Community interest, as the case-law of the Court of Justice has acknowledged it may do, even if no other competition authority has indicated its intention of dealing with the case.

Advisory Committee—recital 2, Article 14

(19) The Advisory Committee on Restrictive Practices and Dominant Positions set up by Regulation No 17 has functioned in a very satisfactory manner. It will fit well into the new system of decentralised application. It is necessary, therefore, to build upon the rules laid down by Regulation No 17, while improving the effectiveness of the organisational arrangements. To this end, it would be expedient to allow opinions to be delivered by written procedure. The Advisory Committee should also be able to act as a forum for discussing cases that are being handled by the competition authorities of the Member States, so as to help safeguard the consistent application of the Community competition rules.

Advisory Committee—Article 14

(20) The Advisory Committee should be composed of representatives of the competition authorities of the Member States. For meetings in which general issues are being discussed, Member States should be able to appoint an additional representative. This is without prejudice to members of the Committee being assisted by other experts from the Member States.

Cooperation with National Courts—Recital 1, Article 15

(21) Consistency in the application of the competition rules also requires that arrangements be established for cooperation between the courts of the Member States and the Commission. This is relevant for all courts of the Member States that apply Articles 81 and 82 of the Treaty, whether applying these rules in lawsuits between private parties, acting as public enforcers or as review courts. In particular, national courts should be able to ask the Commission for information or for its opinion on points concerning the application of Community competition law. The Commission and the competition authorities of the Member States should also be able to submit written or oral observations to courts called upon to apply Article 81 or Article 82 of the Treaty. These observations should be submitted within the framework of national procedural rules and practices including those safeguarding the rights of the parties. Steps should therefore be taken to ensure that the Commission and the competition authorities of the Member States are kept sufficiently well informed of proceedings before national courts.

Uniform application—Article 16

(22) In order to ensure compliance with the principles of legal certainty and the uniform application of the Community competition rules in a system of parallel powers, conflicting decisions must be avoided. It is therefore necessary to clarify, in accordance with the case-law of the Court of Justice, the effects of Commission decisions and proceedings on courts and competition authorities of the Member States. Commitment decisions adopted by the Commission do not affect the power of the courts and the competition authorities of the Member States to apply Articles 81 and 82 of the Treaty. *Applies Delimitis*

Requests for information—Article 18

(23) The Commission should be empowered throughout the Community to require such information to be supplied as is necessary to detect any agreement, decision or concerted practice prohibited by Article 81 of the Treaty or any abuse of a dominant position prohibited by Article 82 of the Treaty. When complying with a decision of the Commission, undertakings cannot be forced to admit that they have committed an infringement, but they are in any event obliged to answer factual questions and to provide documents, even if this information may be used to establish against them or against another undertaking the existence of an infringement.

Inspections—Article 20

(24) The Commission should also be empowered to undertake such inspections as are necessary to detect any agreement, decision or concerted practice prohibited by Article 81 of the Treaty or any abuse of a dominant position prohibited by Article 82 of the Treaty. The competition authorities of the Member States should cooperate actively in the exercise of these powers.

Power to take statements—Article 19

(25) The detection of infringements of the competition rules is growing ever more difficult, and, in order to protect competition effectively, the Commission's powers of investigation need to be supplemented. The Commission should in particular be empowered to interview any persons who may be in possession of useful information

and to record the statements made. In the course of an inspection, officials authorised by the Commission should be empowered to affix seals for the period of time necessary for the inspection. Seals should normally not be affixed for more than 72 hours. Officials authorised by the Commission should also be empowered to ask for any information relevant to the subject matter and purpose of the inspection.

Inspections—Article 21

(26) Experience has shown that there are cases where business records are kept in the homes of directors or other people working for an undertaking. In order to safeguard the effectiveness of inspections, therefore, officials and other persons authorised by the Commission should be empowered to enter any premises where business records may be kept, including private homes. However, the exercise of this latter power should be subject to the authorisation of the judicial authority.

Inspections—Article 21

(27) Without prejudice to the case-law of the Court of Justice, it is useful to set out the scope of the control that the national judicial authority may carry out when it authorises, as foreseen by national law including as a precautionary measure, assistance from law enforcement authorities in order to overcome possible opposition on the part of the undertaking or the execution of the decision to carry out inspections in non-business premises. It results from the case-law that the national judicial authority may in particular ask the Commission for further information which it needs to carry out its control and in the absence of which it could refuse the authorisation. The case-law also confirms the competence of the national courts to control the application of national rules governing the implementation of coercive measures.

Inspections, network—Article 22

(28) In order to help the competition authorities of the Member States to apply Articles 81 and 82 of the Treaty effectively, it is expedient to enable them to assist one another by carrying out inspections and other fact-finding measures.

Fines and penalties—Articles 23, 24

(29) Compliance with Articles 81 and 82 of the Treaty and the fulfilment of the obligations imposed on undertakings and associations of undertakings under this Regulation should be enforceable by means of fines and periodic penalty payments. To that end, appropriate levels of fine should also be laid down for infringements of the procedural rules.

Fines and penalties–associations of undertakings—Article 23(4)

(30) In order to ensure effective recovery of fines imposed on associations of undertakings for infringements that they have committed, it is necessary to lay down the conditions on which the Commission may require payment of the fine from the members of the association where the association is not solvent. In doing so, the Commission should have regard to the relative size of the undertakings belonging to the association and in particular to the situation of small and medium-sized enterprises. Payment of the fine by one or several members of an association is without prejudice to rules of national law that provide for recovery of the amount paid from other members of the association.

Prescription—Article 25

(31) The rules on periods of limitation for the imposition of fines and periodic penalty payments were laid down in Council Regulation (EEC) No 2988/74[11], which also concerns penalties in the field of transport. In a system of parallel powers, the acts, which may interrupt a limitation period, should include procedural steps taken independently by the competition authority of a Member State. To clarify the legal framework, Regulation (EEC) No 2988/74 should therefore be amended to prevent it applying to matters covered by this Regulation, and this Regulation should include provisions on periods of limitation.

Prescription—Article 26

(32) The undertakings concerned should be accorded the right to be heard by the Commission, third parties whose interests may be affected by a decision should be given the opportunity of submitting their observations beforehand, and the decisions taken should be widely publicised. While ensuring the rights of defence of the undertakings concerned, in particular, the right of access to the file, it is essential that business secrets be protected. The confidentiality of information exchanged in the network should likewise be safeguarded.

Unlimited jurisdiction of Court of Justice re fines & penalties—Article 31

(33) Since all decisions taken by the Commission under this Regulation are subject to review by the Court of Justice in accordance with the Treaty, the Court of Justice should, in accordance with Article 229 thereof be given unlimited jurisdiction in respect of decisions by which the Commission imposes fines or periodic penalty payments.

Central role of Commission—passim

(34) The principles laid down in Articles 81 and 82 of the Treaty, as they have been applied by Regulation No 17, have given a central role to the Community bodies. This central role should be retained, whilst associating the Member States more closely with the application of the Community competition rules. In accordance with the principles of subsidiarity and proportionality as set out in Article 5 of the Treaty, this Regulation does not go beyond what is necessary in order to achieve its objective, which is to allow the Community competition rules to be applied effectively.

NCAs to apply Community competition law—Articles 1, 3

(35) In order to attain a proper enforcement of Community competition law, Member States should designate and empower authorities to apply Articles 81 and 82 of the Treaty as public enforcers. They should be able to designate administrative as well as judicial authorities to carry out the various functions conferred upon competition authorities in this Regulation. This Regulation recognises the wide variation which exists in the public enforcement systems of Member States. The effects of Article 11(6) of this Regulation should apply to all competition authorities. As an exception to this general rule, where a prosecuting authority brings a case before a separate judicial authority, Article 11(6) should apply to the prosecuting authority subject to the conditions in Article 35(4) of this Regulation. Where these conditions

---

11   Council Regulation (EEC) No 2988/74 of 26 November 1974 concerning limitation periods in proceedings and the enforcement of sanctions under the rules of the European Economic Community relating to transport and competition (OJ L 319, 29.11.1974, p. 1).

are not fulfilled, the general rule should apply. In any case, Article 11(6) should not apply to courts insofar as they are acting as review courts.

Transport—Articles 32, 36, 37, 38, 39, 41, & 42

(36) As the case-law has made it clear that the competition rules apply to transport, that sector should be made subject to the procedural provisions of this Regulation. Council Regulation No 141 of 26 November 1962 exempting transport from the application of Regulation No 17[12] should therefore be repealed and Regulations (EEC) No 1017/68[13], (EEC) No 4056/86[14] and (EEC) No 3975/87[15] should be amended in order to delete the specific procedural provisions they contain.

Charter of human rights—Article 27

(37) This Regulation respects the fundamental rights and observes the principles recognised in particular by the Charter of Fundamental Rights of the European Union. Accordingly, this Regulation should be interpreted and applied with respect to those rights and principles.

Informal guidance by Commission

(38) Legal certainty for undertakings operating under the Community competition rules contributes to the promotion of innovation and investment. Where cases give rise to genuine uncertainty because they present novel or unresolved questions for the application of these rules, individual undertakings may wish to seek informal guidance from the Commission. This Regulation is without prejudice to the ability of the Commission to issue such informal guidance,

TABLE OF CONTENTS

12   OJ 124, 28.11.1962, p 2751/62; Regulation as last amended by Reg No 1002/67/EEC (OJ 306, 16.12.1967, p 1).
13   Council Reg (EEC) No 1017/68 of 19 July 1968 applying rules of competition to transport by rail, road and inland waterway (OJ L 175, 23.7.1968, p. 1). Regulation as last amended by the Act of Accession of 1994.
14   Council Reg (EEC) No 4056/86 of 22 December 1986 laying down detailed rules for the application of Arts 81 and 82 (The title of the Regulation has been adjusted to take account of the renumbering of the Articles of the EC Treaty, in accordance with Art 12 of the Treaty of Amsterdam; the original reference was to Arts 85 and 86 of the Treaty) of the Treaty to maritime transport (OJ L 378, 31.12.1986, p 4). Regulation as last amended by the Act of Accession of 1994.
15   Council Reg (EEC) No 3975/87 of 14 December 1987 laying down the procedure for the application of the rules on competition to undertakings in the air transport sector (OJ L 374, 31.12.1987, p 1). Regulation as last amended by Regulation (EEC) No 2410/92 (OJ L 240, 24.8.1992, p 18).

THE EU COUNCIL, for these reasons HAS ADOPTED THIS REGULATION:

CHAPTER I

PRINCIPLES

Article 1

Application of Articles 81 and 82 of the Treaty [*recital 4*]

1. Agreements, decisions and concerted practices caught by Article 81(1) of the Treaty which do not satisfy the conditions of Article 81(3) of the Treaty shall be prohibited, no prior decision to that effect being required.

2. Agreements, decisions and concerted practices caught by Article 81(1) of the Treaty which satisfy the conditions of Article 81(3) of the Treaty shall not be prohibited, no prior decision to that effect being required.

3. The abuse of a dominant position referred to in Article 82 of the Treaty shall be prohibited, no prior decision to that effect being required.

Article 2

Burden of proof [*recital 5*]

In any national or Community proceedings for the application of Articles 81 and 82 of the Treaty, the burden of proving an infringement of Article 81(1) or of Article 82 of the Treaty shall rest on the party or the authority alleging the infringement. The undertaking or association of undertakings claiming the benefit of Article 81(3) of the Treaty shall bear the burden of proving that the conditions of that paragraph are fulfilled.

Article 3

Relationship between Articles 81 and 82 of the Treaty and national competition laws
[*recitals 2, 6, 8, 9, 35*]

1. Where the competition authorities of the Member States or national courts apply national competition law to agreements, decisions by associations of undertakings or concerted practices within the meaning of Article 81(1) of the Treaty which may affect trade between Member States within the meaning of that provision, they shall also apply Article 81 of the Treaty to such agreements, decisions or concerted practices. Where the competition authorities of the Member States or national courts apply national competition law to any abuse prohibited by Article 82 of the Treaty, they shall also apply Article 82 of the Treaty.

2. The application of national competition law may not lead to the prohibition of agreements, decisions by associations of undertakings or concerted practices which may affect trade between Member States but which do not restrict competition within the meaning of Article 81(1) of the Treaty, or which fulfil the conditions of Article 81(3) of the Treaty or which are covered by a Regulation for the application of Article 81(3) of the Treaty. Member States shall not under this Regulation be precluded from adopting and applying on their territory stricter national laws which prohibit or sanction unilateral conduct engaged in by undertakings. [*Not double barrier theory*]

National merger rules
3. Without prejudice to general principles and other provisions of Community law, paragraphs 1 and 2 do not apply when the competition authorities and the courts of the Member States apply national merger control laws nor do they preclude the application of provisions of national law that predominantly pursue an objective different from that pursued by Articles 81 and 82 of the Treaty.

CHAPTER II

POWERS

Article 4

Powers of the Commission [*recital 3*]
For the purpose of applying Articles 81 and 82 of the Treaty, the Commission shall have the powers provided for by this Regulation.

Article 5

Powers of the competition authorities of the Member States [*recital 3*]
The competition authorities of the Member States shall have the power to apply Articles 81 and 82 of the Treaty in individual cases. For this purpose, acting on their own initiative or on a complaint, they may take the following decisions:
requiring that an infringement be brought to an end,

- requiring that an infringement be brought to an end,
- ordering interim measures,
- accepting commitments,
- imposing fines, periodic penalty payments or any other penalty provided for in their national law.

Where on the basis of the information in their possession the conditions for prohibition are not met they may likewise decide that there are no grounds for action on their Article

Article 6

Powers of the national courts [*recital 21 & Article 1*]
National courts shall have the power to apply Articles 81 and 82 of the Treaty.

CHAPTER III

COMMISSION DECISIONS

Article 7

Finding and termination of infringement [*recital 21, Article 1*]

1. Where the Commission, acting on a complaint or on its own initiative, finds that there is an infringement of Article 81 or of Article 82 of the Treaty, it may by decision require the undertakings and associations of undertakings concerned to bring such infringement to an end. For this purpose, it may impose on them any behavioural or structural remedies which are proportionate to the infringement committed and necessary to bring the infringement effectively to an end. Structural remedies can only be imposed either where there is no equally effective behavioural remedy or where any equally effective behavioural remedy would be more burdensome for the undertaking concerned than the structural remedy. If the Commission has a legitimate interest in doing so, it may also find that an infringement has been committed in the past.

2. Those entitled to lodge a complaint for the purposes of paragraph 1 are natural or legal persons who can show a legitimate interest and Member States.

Article 8

Interim measures [*recitals 11, 14*]

1. In cases of urgency due to the risk of serious and irreparable damage to competition, the Commission, acting on its own initiative may by decision, on the basis of a prima facie finding of infringement, order interim measures.

2. A decision under paragraph 1 shall apply for a specified period of time and may be renewed in so far this is necessary and appropriate.

Article 9

Commitments [*recitals 12, 13*]

1. Where the Commission intends to adopt a decision requiring that an infringement be brought to an end and the undertakings concerned offer commitments to meet the concerns expressed to them by the Commission in its preliminary assessment, the Commission may by decision make those commitments binding on the undertakings. Such a decision may be adopted for a specified period and shall conclude that there are no longer grounds for action by the Commission.

2. The Commission may, upon request or on its own initiative, reopen the proceedings:

  (a) where there has been a material change in any of the facts on which the decision was based;
  (b) where the undertakings concerned act contrary to their commitments; or
  (c) where the decision was based on incomplete, incorrect or misleading information provided by the parties.

Article 10

Finding of inapplicability [*recital 14*]

Where the Community public interest relating to the application of Articles 81 and 82 of the Treaty so requires, the Commission, acting on its own initiative, may by decision find that Article 81 of the Treaty is not applicable to an agreement, a decision by an association of undertakings or a concerted practice, either because the conditions of Article 81(1) of the Treaty are not fulfilled, or because the conditions of Article 81(3) of the Treaty are satisfied.

The Commission may likewise make such a finding with reference to Article 82 of the Treaty.

CHAPTER IV

COOPERATION

Article 11

Cooperation between the Commission and the competition authorities of the Member States [*recitals 15, 16*]

1. The Commission and the competition authorities of the Member States shall apply the Community competition rules in close cooperation.

2. The Commission shall transmit to the competition authorities of the Member States copies of the most important documents it has collected with a view to applying Articles 7, 8, 9, 10 and Article 29(1). At the request of the competition authority of a Member State, the Commission shall provide it with a copy of other existing documents necessary for the assessment of the case.

3. The competition authorities of the Member States shall, when acting under Article 81 or Article 82 of the Treaty, inform the Commission in writing before or without delay after commencing the first formal investigative measure. This information may also be made available to the competition authorities of the other Member States.

4. No later than 30 days before the adoption of a decision requiring that an infringement be brought to an end, accepting commitments or withdrawing the benefit of a block exemption Regulation, the competition authorities of the Member States shall inform the Commission. To that effect, they shall provide the Commission with a summary of the case, the envisaged decision or, in the absence thereof, any other document indicating the proposed course of action. This information may also be made available to the competition authorities of the other Member States. At the request of the Commission, the acting competition authority shall make available to the Commission other documents it holds which are necessary for the assessment of the case. The information supplied to the Commission may be made available to the competition authorities of the other Member States. National competition authorities may also exchange between themselves information necessary for the assessment of a case that they are dealing with under Article 81 or Article 82 of the Treaty.

5. The competition authorities of the Member States may consult the Commission on any case involving the application of Community law.

6. The initiation by the Commission of proceedings for the adoption of a decision under Chapter III shall relieve the competition authorities of the Member States of their competence to apply Articles 81 and 82 of the Treaty. If a competition authority of a Member State is already acting on a case, the Commission shall only initiate proceedings after consulting with that national competition authority.

Article 12

Exchange of information [*recitals 16, 37—it reverses Spanish Banks*]

1. For the purpose of applying Articles 81 and 82 of the Treaty the Commission and the competition authorities of the Member States shall have the power to provide one another with and use in evidence any matter of fact or of law, including confidential information.

2. Information exchanged shall only be used in evidence for the purpose of applying Article 81 or Article 82 of the Treaty and in respect of the subject-matter for which it was collected by the transmitting authority. However, where national competition law is applied in the same case and in parallel to Community competition law and does not lead to a different outcome, information exchanged under this Article may also be used for the application of national competition law.

3. Information exchanged pursuant to paragraph 1 can only be used in evidence to impose sanctions on natural persons where:

the law of the transmitting authority foresees sanctions of a similar kind in relation to an infringement of Article 81 or Article 82 of the Treaty or, in the absence thereof,

the information has been collected in a way which respects the same level of protection of the rights of defence of natural persons as provided for under the national rules of the receiving authority. However, in this case, the information exchanged cannot be used by the receiving authority to impose custodial sanctions.

Article 13

Suspension or termination of proceedings [*recitals 17, 18*]

1. Where competition authorities of two or more Member States have received a complaint or are acting on their own initiative under Article 81 or Article 82 of the Treaty against the same agreement, decision of an association or practice, the fact that one authority is dealing with the case shall be sufficient grounds for the others to suspend the proceedings before them or to reject the complaint. The Commission may likewise reject a complaint on the ground that a competition authority of a Member State is dealing with the case.

2. Where a competition authority of a Member State or the Commission has received a complaint against an agreement, decision of an association or practice which has already been dealt with by another competition authority, it may reject it.

Article 14

Advisory Committee [*recitals 19 & 20*]

1. The Commission shall consult an Advisory Committee on Restrictive Practices and Dominant Positions prior to the taking of any decision under Articles 7, 8, 9, 10, 23, Article 24(2) and Article 29(1).

2. For the discussion of individual cases, the Advisory Committee shall be composed of representatives of the competition authorities of the Member States. For meetings in which issues other than individual cases are being discussed, an additional Member State representative competent in competition matters may be appointed. Representatives may, if unable to attend, be replaced by other representatives.

3. The consultation may take place at a meeting convened and chaired by the Commission, held not earlier than 14 days after dispatch of the notice convening it, together with a summary of the case, an indication of the most important documents and a preliminary draft decision. In respect of decisions pursuant to Article 8, the

meeting may be held seven days after the dispatch of the operative part of a draft decision. Where the Commission dispatches a notice convening the meeting which gives a shorter period of notice than those specified above, the meeting may take place on the proposed date in the absence of an objection by any Member State. The Advisory Committee shall deliver a written opinion on the Commission's preliminary draft decision. It may deliver an opinion even if some members are absent and are not represented. At the request of one or several members, the positions stated in the opinion shall be reasoned.

4. Consultation may also take place by written procedure. However, if any Member State so requests, the Commission shall convene a meeting. In case of written procedure, the Commission shall determine a time-limit of not less than 14 days within which the Member States are to put forward their observations for circulation to all other Member States. In case of decisions to be taken pursuant to Article 8, the time-limit of 14 days is replaced by seven days. Where the Commission determines a time-limit for the written procedure which is shorter than those specified above, the proposed time-limit shall be applicable in the absence of an objection by any Member State.

5. The Commission shall take the utmost account of the opinion delivered by the Advisory Committee. It shall inform the Committee of the manner in which its opinion has been taken into account.

6. Where the Advisory Committee delivers a written opinion, this opinion shall be appended to the draft decision. If the Advisory Committee recommends publication of the opinion, the Commission shall carry out such publication taking into account the legitimate interest of undertakings in the protection of their business secrets.

7. At the request of a competition authority of a Member State, the Commission shall include on the agenda of the Advisory Committee cases that are being dealt with by a competition authority of a Member State under Article 81 or Article 82 of the Treaty. The Commission may also do so on its own initiative. In either case, the Commission shall inform the competition authority concerned.

A request may in particular be made by a competition authority of a Member State in respect of a case where the Commission intends to initiate proceedings with the effect of Article 11(6).

The Advisory Committee shall not issue opinions on cases dealt with by competition authorities of the Member States. The Advisory Committee may also discuss general issues of Community competition law.

Article 15
Cooperation with national courts [*recital 21*]

1. In proceedings for the application of Article 81 or Article 82 of the Treaty, courts of the Member States may ask the Commission to transmit to them information in its possession or its opinion on questions concerning the application of the Community competition rules.

2. Member States shall forward to the Commission a copy of any written judgment of national courts deciding on the application of Article 81 or Article 82 of the Treaty. Such copy shall be forwarded without delay after the full written judgment is notified to the parties.

3. Competition authorities of the Member States, acting on their own initiative, may submit written observations to the national courts of their Member State on

issues relating to the application of Article 81 or Article 82 of the Treaty. With the permission of the court in question, they may also submit oral observations to the national courts of their Member State. Where the coherent application of Article 81 or Article 82 of the Treaty so requires, the Commission, acting on its own initiative, may submit written observations to courts of the Member States. With the permission of the court in question, it may also make oral observations.

For the purpose of the preparation of their observations only, the competition authorities of the Member States and the Commission may request the relevant court of the Member State to transmit or ensure the transmission to them of any documents necessary for the assessment of the case.

4. This Article is without prejudice to wider powers to make observations before courts conferred on competition authorities of the Member States under the law of their Member State.

Article 16
Uniform application of Community competition law [*recital 22*]

1. When national courts rule on agreements, decisions or practices under Article 81 or Article 82 of the Treaty which are already the subject of a Commission decision, they cannot take decisions running counter to the decision adopted by the Commission. They must also avoid giving decisions which would conflict with a decision contemplated by the Commission in proceedings it has initiated. To that effect, the national court may assess whether it is necessary to stay its proceedings. This obligation is without prejudice to the rights and obligations under Article 234 of the Treaty.

2. When competition authorities of the Member States rule on agreements, decisions or practices under Article 81 or Article 82 of the Treaty which are already the subject of a Commission decision, they cannot take decisions which would run counter to the decision adopted by the Commission.

CHAPTER V

POWERS OF INVESTIGATION

Article 17
Investigations into sectors of the economy and into types of agreements

1. Where the trend of trade between Member States, the rigidity of prices or other circumstances suggest that competition may be restricted or distorted within the common market, the Commission may conduct its inquiry into a particular sector of the economy or into a particular type of agreements across various sectors. In the course of that inquiry, the Commission may request the undertakings or associations of undertakings concerned to supply the information necessary for giving effect to Articles 81 and 82 of the Treaty and may carry out any inspections necessary for that purpose.

The Commission may in particular request the undertakings or associations of undertakings concerned to communicate to it all agreements, decisions and concerted practices.

The Commission may publish a report on the results of its inquiry into particular sectors of the economy or particular types of agreements across various sectors and invite comments from interested parties.

2. Articles 14, 18, 19, 20, 22, 23 and 24 shall apply mutatis mutandis.

Article 18

Requests for information [*recital 23*]

1. In order to carry out the duties assigned to it by this Regulation, the Commission may, by simple request or by decision, require undertakings and associations of undertakings to provide all necessary information.

2. When sending a simple request for information to an undertaking or association of undertakings, the Commission shall state the legal basis and the purpose of the request, specify what information is required and fix the time-limit within which the information is to be provided, and the penalties provided for in Article 23 for supplying incorrect or misleading information.

3. Where the Commission requires undertakings and associations of undertakings to supply information by decision, it shall state the legal basis and the purpose of the request, specify what information is required and fix the time-limit within which it is to be provided. It shall also indicate the penalties provided for in Article 23 and indicate or impose the penalties provided for in Article 24. It shall further indicate the right to have the decision reviewed by the Court of Justice.

4. The owners of the undertakings or their representatives and, in the case of legal persons, companies or firms, or associations having no legal personality, the persons authorised to represent them by law or by their constitution shall supply the information requested on behalf of the undertaking or the association of undertakings concerned. Lawyers duly authorised to act may supply the information on behalf of their clients. The latter shall remain fully responsible if the information supplied is incomplete, incorrect or misleading.

5. The Commission shall without delay forward a copy of the simple request or of the decision to the competition authority of the Member State in whose territory the seat of the undertaking or association of undertakings is situated and the competition authority of the Member State whose territory is affected.

6. At the request of the Commission the governments and competition authorities of the Member States shall provide the Commission with all necessary information to carry out the duties assigned to it by this Regulation.

Article 19

Power to take statements [*recital 25*]

1. In order to carry out the duties assigned to it by this Regulation, the Commission may interview any natural or legal person who consents to be interviewed for the purpose of collecting information relating to the subject-matter of an investigation.

2. Where an interview pursuant to paragraph 1 is conducted in the premises of an undertaking, the Commission shall inform the competition authority of the Member State in whose territory the interview takes place. If so requested by the competition authority of that Member State, its officials may assist the officials and other accompanying persons authorised by the Commission to conduct the interview.

Article 20

The Commission's powers of inspection [*recital 24*]

1. In order to carry out the duties assigned to it by this Regulation, the Commission may conduct all necessary inspections of undertakings and associations of undertakings.

2. The officials and other accompanying persons authorised by the Commission to conduct an inspection are empowered:

a) to enter any premises, land and means of transport of undertakings and associations of undertakings;

b) to examine the books and other records related to the business, irrespective of the medium on which they are stored;

c) to take or obtain in any form copies of or extracts from such books or records;

d) to seal any business premises and books or records for the period and to the extent necessary for the inspection;

e) to ask any representative or member of staff of the undertaking or association of undertakings for explanations on facts or documents relating to the subject-matter and purpose of the inspection and to record the answers.

3. The officials and other accompanying persons authorised by the Commission to conduct an inspection shall exercise their powers upon production of a written authorisation specifying the subject matter and purpose of the inspection and the penalties provided for in Article 23 in case the production of the required books or other records related to the business is incomplete or where the answers to questions asked under paragraph 2 of the present Article are incorrect or misleading. In good time before the inspection, the Commission shall give notice of the inspection to the competition authority of the Member State in whose territory it is to be conducted.

4. Undertakings and associations of undertakings are required to submit to inspections ordered by decision of the Commission. The decision shall specify the subject matter and purpose of the inspection, appoint the date on which it is to begin and indicate the penalties provided for in Articles 23 and 24 and the right to have the decision reviewed by the Court of Justice. The Commission shall take such decisions after consulting the competition authority of the Member State in whose territory the inspection is to be conducted.

5. Officials of as well as those authorised or appointed by the competition authority of the Member State in whose territory the inspection is to be conducted shall, at the request of that authority or of the Commission, actively assist the officials and other accompanying persons authorised by the Commission. To this end, they shall enjoy the powers specified in paragraph 2.

6. Where the officials and other accompanying persons authorised by the Commission find that an undertaking opposes an inspection ordered pursuant to this Article, the Member State concerned shall afford them the necessary assistance, requesting where appropriate the assistance of the police or of an equivalent enforcement authority, so as to enable them to conduct their inspection.

7. If the assistance provided for in paragraph 6 requires authorisation from a judicial authority according to national rules, such authorisation shall be applied for. Such authorisation may also be applied for as a precautionary measure.

8. Where authorisation as referred to in paragraph 7 is applied for, the national judicial authority shall control that the Commission decision is authentic and that the coercive measures envisaged are neither arbitrary nor excessive having regard to the subject matter of the inspection. In its control of the proportionality of the coercive measures, the national judicial authority may ask the Commission, directly or through the Member State competition authority, for detailed explanations in particular on the grounds the Commission has for suspecting infringement of Articles 81 and 82 of the

Treaty, as well as on the seriousness of the suspected infringement and on the nature of the involvement of the undertaking concerned. However, the national judicial authority may not call into question the necessity for the inspection nor demand that it be provided with the information in the Commission's file. The lawfulness of the Commission decision shall be subject to review only by the Court of Justice.

Article 21
Inspection of other premises [*recitals 26 & 27*]

1. If a reasonable suspicion exists that books or other records related to the business and to the subject-matter of the inspection, which may be relevant to prove a serious violation of Article 81 or Article82 of the Treaty, are being kept in any other premises, land and means of transport, including the homes of directors, managers and other members of staff of the undertakings and associations of undertakings concerned, the Commission can by decision order an inspection to be conducted in such other premises, land and means of transport.

2. The decision shall specify the subject matter and purpose of the inspection, appoint the date on which it is to begin and indicate the right to have the decision reviewed by the Court of Justice. It shall in particular state the reasons that have led the Commission to conclude that a suspicion in the sense of paragraph 1 exists. The Commission shall take such decisions after consulting the competition authority of the Member State in whose territory the inspection is to be conducted.

3. A decision adopted pursuant to paragraph 1 cannot be executed without prior authorisation from the national judicial authority of the Member State concerned. The national judicial authority shall control that the Commission decision is authentic and that the coercive measures envisaged are neither arbitrary nor excessive having regard in particular to the seriousness of the suspected infringement, to the importance of the evidence sought, to the involvement of the undertaking concerned and to the reasonable likelihood that business books and records relating to the subject matter of the inspection are kept in the premises for which the authorisation is requested. The national judicial authority may ask the Commission, directly or through the Member State competition authority, for detailed explanations on those elements which are necessary to allow its control of the proportionality of the coercive measures envisaged.

However, the national judicial authority may not call into question the necessity for the inspection nor demand that it be provided with information in the Commission's file. The lawfulness of the Commission decision shall be subject to review only by the Court of Justice.

4. The officials and other accompanying persons authorised by the Commission to conduct an inspection ordered in accordance with paragraph 1 of this Article shall have the powers set out in Article 20(2)(a), (b) and (c). Article 20(5) and (6) shall apply mutatis mutandis.

Article 22
Investigations by competition authorities of Member States [*recital 28*]

1. The competition authority of a Member State may in its own territory carry out any inspection or other fact-finding measure under its national law on behalf and for the account of the competition authority of another Member State in order to establish whether there has been an infringement of Article 81 or Article 82 of the Treaty.

Any exchange and use of the information collected shall be carried out in accordance with Article 12.

2. At the request of the Commission, the competition authorities of the Member States shall undertake the inspections which the Commission considers to be necessary under Article 20(1) or which it has ordered by decision pursuant to Article 20(4). The officials of the competition authorities of the Member States who are responsible for conducting these inspections as well as those authorised or appointed by them shall exercise their powers in accordance with their national law.

If so requested by the Commission or by the competition authority of the Member State in whose territory the inspection is to be conducted, officials and other accompanying persons authorised by the Commission may assist the officials of the authority concerned.

CHAPTER VI

PENALTIES

Article 23 Fines [*recitals 29, 30*]

1. The Commission may by decision impose on undertakings and associations of undertakings fines not exceeding 1 % of the total turnover in the preceding business year where, intentionally or negligently:

   (a) they supply incorrect or misleading information in response to a request made pursuant to Article 17 or Article 18(2);

   (b) in response to a request made by decision adopted pursuant to Article 17 or Article 18(3), they supply incorrect, incomplete or misleading information or do not supply information within the required time-limit;

   (c) they produce the required books or other records related to the business in incomplete form during inspections under Article 20 or refuse to submit to inspections ordered by a decision adopted pursuant to Article 20(4);

   (d) in response to a question asked in accordance with Article 20(2)(e),

   – they give an incorrect or misleading answer,
   – they fail to rectify within a time-limit set by the Commission an incorrect, – incomplete or misleading answer given by a member of staff, or
   – they fail or refuse to provide a complete answer on facts relating to the subject-matter and purpose of an inspection ordered by a decision adopted pursuant to Article 20(4);

   (e) seals affixed in accordance with Article 20(2)(d) by officials or other accompanying persons authorised by the Commission have been broken.

2. The Commission may by decision impose fines on undertakings and associations of undertakings where, either intentionally or negligently:

   (a) they infringe Article 81 or Article 82 of the Treaty; or
   (b) they contravene a decision ordering interim measures under Article 8; or
   (c) they fail to comply with a commitment made binding by a decision pursuant to Article 9.

For each undertaking and association of undertakings participating in the infringement, the fine shall not exceed 10 % of its total turnover in the preceding business year.

Where the infringement of an association relates to the activities of its members, the fine shall not exceed 10 % of the sum of the total turnover of each member active on the market affected by the infringement of the association.

3. In fixing the amount of the fine, regard shall be had both to the gravity and to the duration of the infringement.

4. When a fine is imposed on an association of undertakings taking account of the turnover of its members and the association is not solvent, the association is obliged to call for contributions from its members to cover the amount of the fine. Where such contributions have not been made to the association within a time-limit fixed by the Commission, the Commission may require payment of the fine directly by any of the undertakings whose representatives were members of the decision-making bodies concerned of the association.

After the Commission has required payment under the second subparagraph, where necessary to ensure full payment of the fine, the Commission may require payment of the balance by any of the members of the association which were active on the market on which the infringement occurred.

However, the Commission shall not require payment under the second or the third subparagraph from undertakings which show that they have not implemented the infringing decision of the association and either were not aware of its existence or have actively distanced themselves from it before the Commission started investigating the case.

The financial liability of each undertaking in respect of the payment of the fine shall not exceed 10 % of its total turnover in the preceding business year. 5. Decisions taken pursuant to paragraphs 1 and 2 shall not be of a criminal law nature.

Article 24

Periodic penalty payments [*recital 29*]

1. The Commission may, by decision, impose on undertakings or associations of undertakings periodic penalty payments not exceeding 5 % of the average daily turnover in the preceding business year per day and calculated from the date appointed by the decision, in order to compel them:

    (a) to put an end to an infringement of Article 81 or Article 82 of the Treaty, in accordance with a decision taken pursuant to Article 7;

    (b) to comply with a decision ordering interim measures taken pursuant to Article 8;

    (c) to comply with a commitment made binding by a decision pursuant to Article 9;

    (d) to supply complete and correct information which it has requested by decision taken pursuant to Article 17 or Article 18(3);

    (e) to submit to an inspection which it has ordered by decision taken pursuant to Article 20(4).

2. Where the undertakings or associations of undertakings have satisfied the obligation which the periodic penalty payment was intended to enforce, the Commission may fix the definitive amount of the periodic penalty payment at a figure lower than that which would arise under the original decision. Article 23(4) shall apply correspondingly.

CHAPTER VII

LIMITATION PERIODS

Article 25

Limitation periods for the imposition of penalties [*recital 31*]

1. The powers conferred on the Commission by Articles 23 and 24 shall be subject to the following limitation periods:

(a) three years in the case of infringements of provisions concerning requests for information or the conduct of inspections;

(b) five years in the case of all other infringements.

2. Time shall begin to run on the day on which the infringement is committed. However, in the case of continuing or repeated infringements, time shall begin to run on the day on which the infringement ceases.

3. Any action taken by the Commission or by the competition authority of a Member State for the purpose of the investigation or proceedings in respect of an infringement shall interrupt the limitation period for the imposition of fines or periodic penalty payments. The limitation period shall be interrupted with effect from the date on which the action is notified to at least one undertaking or association of undertakings which has participated in the infringement. Actions which interrupt the running of the period shall include in particular the following:

(a) written requests for information by the Commission or by the competition authority of a Member State;

(b) written authorisations to conduct inspections issued to its officials by the Commission or by the competition authority of a Member State;

(c) the initiation of proceedings by the Commission or by the competition authority of a Member State;

(d) notification of the statement of objections of the Commission or of the competition authority of a Member State.

4. The interruption of the limitation period shall apply for all the undertakings or associations of undertakings which have participated in the infringement.

5. Each interruption shall start time running afresh. However, the limitation period shall expire at the latest on the day on which a period equal to twice the limitation period has elapsed without the Commission having imposed a fine or a periodic penalty payment. That period shall be extended by the time during which limitation is suspended pursuant to paragraph 6.

6. The limitation period for the imposition of fines or periodic penalty payments shall be suspended for as long as the decision of the Commission is the subject of proceedings pending before the Court of Justice.

Article 26

Limitation period for the enforcement of penalties [*recital 32*]

1. The power of the Commission to enforce decisions taken pursuant to Articles 23 and 24 shall be subject to a limitation period of five years.

2. Time shall begin to run on the day on which the decision becomes final.

3. The limitation period for the enforcement of penalties shall be interrupted:

(a) by notification of a decision varying the original amount of the fine or periodic penalty payment or refusing an application for variation;

(b) by any action of the Commission or of a Member State, acting at the request of the Commission, designed to enforce payment of the fine or periodic penalty payment.

4. Each interruption shall start time running afresh.

5. The limitation period for the enforcement of penalties shall be suspended for so long as:

(a) time to pay is allowed;

(b) enforcement of payment is suspended pursuant to a decision of the Court of Justice.

CHAPTER VIII

HEARINGS AND PROFESSIONAL SECRECY

Article 27

Hearing of the parties, complainants and others [*recital 37*]

1. Before taking decisions as provided for in Articles 7, 8, 23 and Article 24(2), the Commission shall give the undertakings or associations of undertakings which are the subject of the proceedings conducted by the Commission the opportunity of being heard on the matters to which the Commission has taken objection. The Commission shall base its decisions only on objections on which the parties concerned have been able to comment. Complainants shall be associated closely with the proceedings.

2. The rights of defence of the parties concerned shall be fully respected in the proceedings. They shall be entitled to have access to the Commission's file, subject to the legitimate interest of undertakings in the protection of their business secrets. The right of access to the file shall not extend to confidential information and internal documents of the Commission or the competition authorities of the Member States. In particular, the right of access shall not extend to correspondence between the Commission and the competition authorities of the Member States, or between the latter, including documents drawn up pursuant to Articles 11 and 14. Nothing in this paragraph shall prevent the Commission from disclosing and using information necessary to prove an infringement.

3. If the Commission considers it necessary, it may also hear other natural or legal persons. Applications to be heard on the part of such persons shall, where they show a sufficient interest, be granted. The competition authorities of the Member States may also ask the Commission to hear other natural or legal persons.

4. Where the Commission intends to adopt a decision pursuant to Article 9 or Article 10, it shall publish a concise summary of the case and the main content of the commitments or of the proposed course of action. Interested third parties may submit their observations within a time limit which is fixed by the Commission in its publication and which may not be less than one month. Publication shall have regard to the legitimate interest of undertakings in the protection of their business secrets.

Article 28
Professional secrecy [*recital 16*]

1. Without prejudice to Articles 12 and 15, information collected pursuant to Articles 17 to 22 shall be used only for the purpose for which it was acquired.

2. Without prejudice to the exchange and to the use of information foreseen in Articles 11, 12, 14, 15 and 27, the Commission and the competition authorities of the Member States, their officials, servants and other persons working under the supervision of these authorities as well as officials and civil servants of other authorities of the Member States shall not disclose information acquired or exchanged by them pursuant to this Regulation and of the kind covered by the obligation of professional secrecy. This obligation also applies to all representatives and experts of Member States attending meetings of the Advisory Committee pursuant to Article 14.

CHAPTER IX

EXEMPTION REGULATIONS

Article 29
Withdrawal in individual cases [*recital 10*]

1. Where the Commission, empowered by a Council Regulation, such as Regulations 19/65/EEC, (EEC) No 2821/71, (EEC) No 3976/87, (EEC) No 1534/91 or (EEC) No 479/92, to apply Article 81(3) of the Treaty by regulation, has declared Article 81(1) of the Treaty inapplicable to certain categories of agreements, decisions by associations of undertakings or concerted practices, it may, acting on its own initiative or on a complaint, withdraw the benefit of such an exemption Regulation when it finds that in any particular case an agreement, decision or concerted practice to which the exemption Regulation applies has certain effects which are incompatible with Article 81(3) of the Treaty.

2. Where, in any particular case, agreements, decisions by associations of undertakings or concerted practices to which a Commission Regulation referred to in paragraph 1 applies have effects which are incompatible with Article 81(3) of the Treaty in the territory of a Member State, or in a part thereof, which has all the characteristics of a distinct geographic market, the competition authority of that Member State may withdraw the benefit of the Regulation in question in respect of that territory.

CHAPTER X

GENERAL PROVISIONS

Article 30
Publication of decisions

1. The Commission shall publish the decisions, which it takes pursuant to Articles 7 to 10, 23 and 24.

2. The publication shall state the names of the parties and the main content of the decision, including any penalties imposed. It shall have regard to the legitimate interest of undertakings in the protection of their business secrets.

Article 31

Review by the Court of Justice [*recital 33*]

The Court of Justice shall have unlimited jurisdiction to review decisions whereby the Commission has fixed a fine or periodic penalty payment. It may cancel, reduce or increase the fine or periodic penalty payment imposed.

Article 32

Exclusions [*recital 36*]

This Regulation shall not apply to:

(a) international tramp vessel services as defined in Article 1(3)(a) of Regulation (EEC) No 4056/86;

(b) a maritime transport service that takes place exclusively between ports in one and the same Member State as foreseen in Article 1(2) of Regulation (EEC) No 4056/86;

(c) air transport between Community airports and third countries.

Article 33

Implementing provisions

The Commission shall be authorised to take such measures as may be appropriate in order to apply this Regulation. The measures may concern, inter alia:

(a) the form, content and other details of complaints lodged pursuant to Article 7 and the procedure for rejecting complaints;

(b) the practical arrangements for the exchange of information and consultations provided for in Article 11;

(c) the practical arrangements for the hearings provided for in Article 27.2. Before the adoption of any measures pursuant to paragraph 1, the Commission shall publish a draft thereof and invite all interested parties to submit their comments within the time-limit it lays down, which may not be less than one month. Before publishing a draft measure and before adopting it, the Commission shall consult the Advisory Committee on Restrictive Practices and Dominant Positions.

CHAPTER XI

TRANSITIONAL, AMENDING AND FINAL PROVISIONS

Article 34

Transitional provisions

1. Applications made to the Commission under Article 2 of Regulation No 17, notifications made under Articles 4 and 5 of that Regulation and the corresponding applications and notifications made under Regulations (EEC) No 1017/68, (EEC) No 4056/86 and (EEC) No 3975/87 shall lapse as from the date of application of this Regulation.

2. Procedural steps taken under Regulation No 17 and Regulations (EEC) No 1017/68, (EEC) No 4056/86 and (EEC) No 3975/87 shall continue to have effect for the purposes of applying this Regulation.

Article 35

Designation of competition authorities of Member States [*recital 6 & Article 5*]

1. The Member States shall designate the competition authority or authorities responsible for the application of Articles 81 and 82 of the Treaty in such a way that the provisions of this regulation are effectively complied with. The measures necessary to empower those authorities to apply those Articles shall be taken before 1 May 2004. The authorities designated may include courts.

2. When enforcement of Community competition law is entrusted to national administrative and judicial authorities, the Member States may allocate different powers and functions to those different national authorities, whether administrative or judicial.

3. The effects of Article 11(6) apply to the authorities designated by the Member States including courts that exercise functions regarding the preparation and the adoption of the types of decisions foreseen in Article 5. The effects of Article 11(6) do not extend to courts insofar as they act as review courts in respect of the types of decisions foreseen in Article 5.

4. Notwithstanding paragraph 3, in the Member States where, for the adoption of certain types of decisions foreseen in Article 5, an authority brings an action before a judicial authority that is separate and different from the prosecuting authority and provided that the terms of this paragraph are complied with, the effects of Article 11(6) shall be limited to the authority prosecuting the case which shall withdraw its claim before the judicial authority when the Commission opens proceedings and this withdrawal shall bring the national proceedings effectively to an end.

Article 36

Amendment of Regulation (EEC) No 1017/68 [*recital 36*]

Regulation (EEC) No 1017/68 is amended as follows:

1. Article 2 is repealed;

2. 2 in Article 3(1), the words 'The prohibition laid down in Article 2' are replaced by the words 'The prohibition in Article 81(1) of the Treaty';

3. Article 4 is amended as follows:

   (a) In paragraph 1, the words 'The agreements, decisions and concerted practices referred to in Article 2' are replaced by the words 'Agreements, decisions and concerted practices pursuant to Article 81(1) of the Treaty';

   (b) Paragraph 2 is replaced by the following:

'2. If the implementation of any agreement, decision or concerted practice covered by paragraph 1 has, in a given case, effects which are incompatible with the requirements of Article 81(3) of the Treaty, undertakings or associations of undertakings may be required to make such effects cease.'

4. Articles 5 to 29 are repealed with the exception of Article 13(3) which continues to apply to decisions adopted pursuant to Article 5 of Regulation (EEC) No 1017/68 prior to the date of application of this Regulation until the date of expiration of those decisions;

5. in Article 30, paragraphs 2, 3 and 4 are deleted.

Article 37

Limitation periods relating to transport and competition

Amendment of Regulation (EEC) No 2988/74 *recital 36*

In Regulation (EEC) No 2988/74, the following Article is inserted:

'Article 7a

Exclusion

This Regulation shall not apply to measures taken under Council Regulation (EC) No 1/2003 of 16 December 2002 on the implementation of the rules on competition laid down in Articles 81 and 82 of the Treaty(*).

(*) OJ L 1, 4.1.2003, p 1.

Article 38

Maritime transport

Amendment of Regulation (EEC) No 4056/86 *recital 36*

Regulation (EEC) No 4056/86 is amended as follows:

1. Article 7 is amended as follows:

   (a) Paragraph 1 is replaced by the following:

'1. *breach of an obligation*

Where the persons concerned are in breach of an obligation which, pursuant to Article 5, attaches to the exemption provided for in article 3, the Commission may, in ordr to put an ed to such breach and under the conditions laid down in council Regulation (EC) No 1/2003 of 16 December 2002 on the implementation of the rules of competition laid down in articles 81 and 82 of the Treaty(*) adopt a decision that either prohibits them from carrying out or requires them to perform certain specific acts, or withdraws the benefit of the block exemption which they enjoyed.

(*) OJ L 1, 4.1.2003, p. 1.

   (b) Paragraph 2 is amended as follows:

   (i) In point (a), the words "under the conditions laid down in Section II" are replaced by the words 'under the conditions laid down in Regulation (EC) No 1/2003';

   (ii) The second sentence of the second subparagraph of point (c)(i) is replaced by the following:

'At the same time it shall decide, in accordance with Article 9 of Regulation (EC) No 1/2003, whether to accept commitments offered by the undertakings concerned with a view, inter alia, to obtaining access to the market for non-conference lines.'

2. Article 8 is amended as follows:

   (a) Paragraph 1 is deleted.

   (b) In paragraph 2 the words "pursuant to Article 10" are replaced by the words 'pursuant to Regulation (EC) No 1/2003'.

(c) Paragraph 3 is deleted;

3. Article 9 is amended as follows:

    (a) In paragraph 1, the words 'Advisory Committee referred to in Article 15' are replaced by the words 'Advisory Committee referred to in Article 14 of Regulation (EC) No 1/2003';

    (b) In paragraph 2, the words 'Advisory Committee as referred to in Article 15' are replaced by the words 'Advisory Committee referred to in Article 14 of Regulation (EC) No 1/2003';

4. Articles 10 to 25 are repealed with the exception of Article 13(3) which continues to apply to decisions adopted pursuant to Article 81(3) of the Treaty prior to the date of application of this Regulation until the date of expiration of those decisions;

5. in Article 26, the words 'the form, content and other details of complaints pursuant to Article 10, applications pursuant to Article 12 and the hearings provided for in Article 23(1) and (2)' are deleted.

Article 39

Sea transport

Amendment of Regulation (EEC) No 3975/87 *recital 36*

Articles 3 to 19 of Regulation (EEC) No 3975/87 are repealed with the exception of Article 6(3) which continues to apply to decisions adopted pursuant to Article 81(3) of the Treaty prior to the date of application of this Regulation until the date of expiration of those decisions.

Article 40

Empowering regulations for group exemptions

Amendment of Regulations No 19/65/EEC, (EEC) No 2821/71 and (EEC) No 1534/91

Article 7 of Regulation No 19/65/EEC, Article 7 of Regulation (EEC) No 2821/71 and Article 7 of Regulation (EEC) No 1534/91 are repealed.

Article 41

air transport

Amendment of Regulation (EEC) No 3976/87 *recital 36*

Regulation (EEC) No 3976/87 is amended as follows:

1. Article 6 is replaced by the following:

'Article 6

The Commission shall consult the Advisory Committee referred to in Article 14 of Council Regulation (EC) No 1/2003 of 16 December 2002 on the implementation of the rules on competition laid down in Articles 81 and 82 of the Treaty(*) before publishing a draft Regulation and before adopting a Regulation.

(*) OJ L 1, 4.1.2003, p. 1.

2. Article 7 is repealed.

Article 42

liner shipping

Amendment of Regulation (EEC) No 479/92 *recital 36*

Regulation (EEC) No 479/92 is amended as follows:

1. Article 5 is replaced by the following:

'Article 5

Before publishing the draft Regulation and before adopting the Regulation, the Commission shall consult the Advisory Committee referred to in Article 14 of Council Regulation (EC) No 1/2003 of 16 December 2002 on the implementation of the rules on competition laid down in Articles 81 and 82 of the Treaty(*).

———

(*) OJ L 1, 4.1.2003, p. 1.

2. Article 6 is repealed.

Article 43

Repeal of Regulations No 17 and No 141 [*recital 1*]

1. Regulation No 17 is repealed with the exception of Article 8(3) which continues to apply to decisions adopted pursuant to Article 81(3) of the Treaty prior to the date of application of this Regulation until the date of expiration of those decisions.

2. Regulation No 141 is repealed.

3. References to the repealed Regulations shall be construed as references to this Regulation.

Article 44

Report on the application of the present Regulation

Five years from the date of application of this Regulation, the Commission shall report to the European Parliament and the Council on the functioning of this Regulation, in particular on the application of Article 11(6) and Article 17.

On the basis of this report, the Commission shall assess whether it is appropriate to propose to the Council a revision of this Regulation.

Article 45

Entry into force

This Regulation shall enter into force on the 20th day following that of its publication in the *Official Journal of the European Communities*.

It shall apply from 1 May 2004.

This Regulation shall be binding in its entirety and directly applicable in all Member States.

Done at Brussels, 16 December 2002.

For the Council
The President
M FISCHER BOEL

Appendix III

Table of equivalences referred to in Article 12 of the Treaty of Amsterdam

Numbering of the Treaty on European Union and the EC Treaty *before* and *after* the entry into force of the Treaty of Amsterdam

A. Treaty on European Union (TEU)

Before	After	Before	After	Before	After
Title I	*Title I*	Art J.7	Art 17	Art K.9	Art 37
Art A	Art 1	Art J.8	Art 18	Art K.10	Art 38
Art B	Art 2	Art J.9	Art 19	Art K.11	Art 39
Art C	Art 3	Art J.10	Art 20	Art K.12	Art 40
Art D	Art 4	Art J.11	Art 21	Art K.13	Art 41
Art E	Art 5	Art J.12	Art 22	Art K.14	Art 42
Art F	Art 6	Art J.13	Art 23	*Title VIa*	*Title VII*
Art F.1	Art 7	Art J.14	Art 24	Art K.15	Art 43
Title II	*Title II*	Art J.15	Art 25	Art K.16	Art 44
Art G	Art 8	Art J.16	Art 26	Art K.17	Art 45
Title III	*Title III*	Art J.17	Art 27	*Title VII*	*Title VIII*
Art H	Art 9	Art J.18	Art 28	Art L	Art 46
Title IV	*Title IV*	*Title VI*	*Title VI*	Art M	Art 47
Art I	Art 10	Art K.1	Art 29	Art N	Art 48
Title V	*Title V*	Art K.2	Art 30	Art O	Art 49
Art J.1	Art 11	Art K.3	Art 31	Art P	Art 50
Art J.2	Art 12	Art K.4	Art 32	Art Q	Art 51
Art J.3	Art 13	Art K.5	Art 33	Art R	Art 52
Art J.4	Art 14	Art K.6	Art 34	Art S	Art 53
Art J.5	Art 15	Art K.7	Art 35		
Art J.6	Art 16	Art K.8	Art 36		

B. Treaty establishing the European Community (EC)

Before	After	Before	After	Before	After
Part One	*Part One*	Art 7	– (repealed)	Art 9	Art 23
Art 1	Art 1	Art 7a	Art 14	Art 10	Art 24
Art 2	Art 2	Art 7b	– (repealed)	Art 11	– (repealed)
Art 3	Art 3	Art 7c	Art 15	*Chapter 1*	*Chapter 1*
Art 3a	Art 4	Art 7d	Art 16	*Section 1*	*(deleted)*
Art 3b	Art 5	*Part Two*	*Part Two*	Art 12	Art 25
Art 3c	Art 6	Art 8	Art 17	Art 13	– (repealed)
Art 4	Art 7	Art 8a	Art 18	Art 14	– (repealed)
Art 4a	Art 8	Art 8b	Art 19	Art 15	– (repealed)
Art 4b	Art 9	Art 8c	Art 20	Art 16	– (repealed)

Art 5	Art 10	Art 8d	Art 21	Art 17	– (repealed)
Art 5a	Art 11	Art 8e	Art 22	Art 18	– (repealed)
Art 6	Art 12	*Part Three*	*Part Three*	Art 19	– (repealed)
Art 6a	Art 13	*Title I*	*Title I*	Art 20	–. (repealed)
Art 21	– (repealed)	Art 62	– (repealed)	Art 86	Art 82
Art 22	– (repealed)	Art 63	Art 52	Art 87	Art 83
Art 23	– (repealed)	Art 64	Art 53	Art 88	Art 84
Art 24	– (repealed)	Art 65	Art 54	Art 89	Art 85
Art 25	– (repealed)	Art 66	Art 55	Art 90	Art 86
Art 26	– (repealed)	*Chapter 4*	*Chapter 4*	*Section 2*	*(deleted)*
Art 27	– (repealed)	Art 67	– (repealed)	Art 91	– (repealed)
Art 28	Art 26	Art 68	– (repealed)	*Section 3*	*Section 2*
Art 29	Art 27	Art 69	– (repealed)	Art 92	Art 87
Chapter 2	*Chapter 2*	Art 70	– (repealed)	Art 93	Art 88
Art 30	Art 28	Art 71	– (repealed)	Art 94	Art 89
Art 31	– (repealed)	Art 72	– (repealed)	*Chapter 2*	*Chapter 2*
Art 32	– (repealed)	Art 73	– (repealed)	Art 95	Art 90
Art 33	– (repealed)	Art 73a	– (repealed)	Art 96	Art 91
Art 34	Art 29	Art 73b	Art 56	Art 97	– (repealed)
Art 35	– (repealed)	Art 73c	Art 57	Art 98	Art 92
Art 36	Art 30	Art 73d	Art 58	Art 99	Art 93
Art 37	Art 31	Art 73e	– (repealed)	*Chapter 3*	*Chapter 3*
Title II	*Title II*	Art 73f	Art 59	Art 100	Art 94
Art 38	Art 32	Art 73g	Art 60	Art 100a	Art 95
Art 39	Art 33	Art 73h	– (repealed)	Art 100b	– (repealed)
Art 40	Art 34	*Title IIIa*	*Title IV*	Art 100c	– (repealed)
Art 41	Art 35	Art 73i	Art 61	Art 100d	– (repealed)
Art 42	Art 36	Art 73j	Art 62	Art 101	Art 96
Art 43	Art 37	Art 73k	Art 63	Art 102	Art 97
Art 44	– (repealed)	Art 73l	Art 64	*Title VI*	*Title VII*
Art 45	– (repealed)	Art 73m	Art 65	*Chapter 1*	*Chapter 1*
Art 46	Art 38	Art 73n	Art 66	Art 102a	Art 98
Art 47	– (repealed)	Art 73o	Art 67	Art 103	Art 99
Title III	*Title III*	Art 73p	Art 68	Art 103a	Art 100
Chapter 1	*Chapter 1*	Art 73q	Art 69	Art 104	Art 101
Art 48	Art 39	Title *IV*	*Title V*	Art 104a	Art 102
Art 49	Art 40	Art 74	Art 70	Art 104b	Art 103
Art 50	Art 41	Art 75	Art 71	Art 104c	Art 104
Art 51	Art 42	Art 76	Art 72	*Chapter 2*	*Chapter 2*
Chapter 2	*Chapter 2*	Art 77	Art 73	Art 105	Art 105
Art 52	Art 43	Art 78	Art 74	Art 105a	Art 106
Art 53	– (repealed)	Art 79	Art 75	Art 106	Art 107
Art 54	Art 44	Art 80	Art 76	Art 107	Art 108
Art 55	Art 45	Art 81	Art 77	Art 108	Art 109
Art 56	Art 46	Art 82	Art 78	Art 108a	Art 110
Art 57	Art 47	Art 83	Art 79	Art 109	Art 111
Art 58	Art 48	Art 84	Art 80	*Chapter 3*	*Chapter 3*
Chapter 3	*Chapter 3*	*Title V*	*Title VI*	Art 109a	Art 112

Art 59	Art 49	*Chapter 1*	*Chapter 1*	Art 109b	Art 113
Art 60	Art 50	*Section 1*	*Section 1*		
Art 61	Art 51	Art 85	Art 81		
Art 109c	Art 114	*Chapter 3*	*Chapter 3*	*Part Four*	*Part Four*
Art 109d	Art 115	Art 126	Art 149	Art 131	Art 182
Chapter 4	*Chapter 4*	Art 127	Art 150	Art 132	Art 183
Art 109e	Art 116	Title *IX*	*Title XII*	Art 133	Art 184
Art 109f	Art 117	Art 128	Art 151	Art 134	Art 185
Art 109g	Art 118	*Title X*	*Title XIII*	Art 135	Art 186
Art 109h	Art 119	Art 129	Art 152	Art 136	Art 187
Art 109i	Art 120	*Title XI*	*Title XIV*	Art 136a	Art 188
Art 109j	Art 121	Art 129a	Art 153	*Part Five*	*Part Five*
Art 109k	Art 122	*Title XII*	*Title XV*	*Title I*	*Title I*
Art 109l	Art 123	Art 129b	Art 154	*Chapter I*	*Chapter I*
Art 109m	Art 124	Art 129c	Art 155	*Section 1*	*Section 1*
Title VIa	*Title VIII*	Art 129d	Art 156	Art 137	Art 189
Art 109n	Art 125	*Title XIII*	*Title XVI*	Art 138	Art 190
Art 109o	Art 126	Art 130	Art 157	Art 138a	Art 191
Art 109p	Art 127	*Title XIV*	*Title XVII*	Art 138b	Art 192
Art 109q	Art 128	Art 130a	Art 158	Art 138c	Art 193
Art 109r	Art 129	Art 130b	Art 159	Art 138d	Art 194
Art 109s	Art 130	Art 130c	Art 160	Art 138e	Art 195
Title VII	*Title IX*	Art 130d	Art 161	Art 139	Art 196
Art 110	Art 131	Art 130e	Art 162	Art 140	Art 197
Art 111	– (repealed)	*Title XV*	*Title XVIII*	Art 141	Art 198
Art 112	Art 132	Art 130f	Art 163	Art 142	Art 199
Art 113s	Art 133	Art 130g	Art 164	Art 143	Art 200
Art 114	– (repealed)	Art 130h	Art 165	Art 144	Art 201
Art 115	Art 134	Art 130i	Art 166	*Section 2*	*Section 2*
Art 116	– (repealed)	Art 130j	Art 167	Art 145	Art 202
Title VIIa	*Title X*	Art 130k	Art 168	Art 146	Art 203
Art 116 (new)	Art 135	Art 130l	Art 169	Art 147	Art 204
Title VIII	*Title XI*	Art 130m	Art 170	Art 148	Art 205
Chapter 1	*Chapter 1*	Art 130n	Art 171	Art 149	– (repealed)
Art 117	Art 136	Art 130o	Art 172	Art 150	Art 206
Art 118	Art 137	Art 130p	Art 173	Art 151	Art 207
Art 118a	Art 138	Art 130q	– (repealed)	Art 152	Art 208
Art 118b	Art 139	*Title XVI*	*Title XIX*	Art 153	Art 209
Art 118c	Art 140	Art 130r	Art 174	Art 154	Art 210
Art 119	Art 141	Art 130s	Art 175	*Section 3*	*Section 3*
Art 119a	Art 142	Art 130t	Art 176	Art 155	Art 211
Art 120	Art 143	*Title XVII*	*Title XX*	Art 156	Art 212
Art 121	Art 144	Art 130u	Art 177	Art 157	Art 213
Art 122	Art 145	Art 130v	Art 178	Art 158	Art 214
Chapter 2	*Chapter 2*	Art 130w	Art 179	Art 159	Art 215
Art 123	Art 146	Art 130x	Art 180	Art 160	Art 216
Art 124	Art 147	Art 130y	Art 181	Art 161	Art 217
Art 125	Art 148			Art 162	Art 218

Art 163	Art 219	Art 191	Art 254	Art 213a	Art 285
Section 4	*Section 4*	Art 191a	Art 255	Art 213b	Art 286
Art 164	Art 220	*Chapter 3*	*Chapter 3*	Art 214	Art 287
Art 165	Art 221	Art 192	Art 256	Art 215	Art 288
Art 166	Art 222	Art 193	Art 257	Art 216	Art 289
Art 167	Art 223	Art 194	Art 258	Art 217	Art 290
Art 168	Art 224	Art 195	Art 259	Art 218	Art 291
Art 168a	Art 225	Art 196	Art 260	Art 219	Art 292
Art 169	Art 226	Art 197	Art 261	Art 220	Art 293
Art 170	Art 227	Art 198	Art 262	Art 221	Art 294
Art 171	Art 228	*Chapter 4*	*Chapter 4*	Art 222	Art 295
Art 172	Art 229	Art 198a	Art 263	Art 223	Art 296
Art 173	Art 230	Art 198b	Art 264	Art 224	Art 297
Art 174	Art 231	Art 198c	Art 265	Art 225	Art 298
Art 175	Art 232	*Chapter 5*	*Chapter 5*	Art 226	– (repealed)
Art 176	Art 233	Art 198d	Art 266	Art 227	Art 299
Art 177	Art 234	Art 198e	Art 267	Art 228	Art 300
Art 178	Art 235	*Title II*	*Title II*	Art 228a	Art 301
Art 179	Art 236	Art 199	Art 268	Art 229	Art 302
Art 180	Art 237	Art 200	– (repealed)	Art 230	Art 303
Art 181	Art 238	Art 201	Art 269	Art 231	Art 304
Art 182	Art 239	Art 201a	Art 270	Art 232	Art 305
Art 183	Art 240	Art 202	Art 271	Art 233	Art 306
Art 184	Art 241	Art 203	Art 272	Art 234	Art 307
Art 185	Art 242	Art 204	Art 273	Art 235	Art 308
Art 186	Art 243	Art 205	Art 274	Art 236	Art 309
Art 187	Art 244	Art 205a	Art 275	Art 237	– (repealed)
Art 188	Art 245	Art 206	Art 276	Art 238	Art 310
Section 5	*Section 5*	Art 206a	– (repealed)	Art 239	Art 311
Art 188a	Art 246	Art 207	Art 277	Art 240	Art 312
Art 188b	Art 247	Art 208	Art 278	Art 241	– (repealed)
Art 188c	Art 248	Art 209	Art 279	Art 242	– (repealed)
Chapter 2	*Chapter 2*	Art 209a	Art 280	Art 243	– (repealed)
Art 189	Art 249	Part *Six*	*Part Six*	Art 244	– (repealed)
Art 189a	Art 250	Art 210	Art 281	Art 245	– (repealed)
Art 189b	Art 251	Art 211	Art 282	Art 246	– (repealed)
Art 189c	Art 252	Art 212	Art 283	Art 247	Art 313
Art 190	Art 253	Art 213	Art 284	Art 248	Art 314

Appendix IV

Useful web sites

Economic sites

energy and competition bulletins at http://www.frontier-economics.com

competition briefs at www.nera.com

competition memos at www.lexecon.co.uk and www.lexecon.com

Legal sites

In competition at www.sweetandmaxwell.co.uk, www.aspenpublishers.com or www.antitrustlaw.com/pages.asp

American Bar Association at www.abanet.org/antitrust

Competition Law Insight at http://www.informalaw.com/cli

Global Competition Review at http://www.globalcompetitionreview.com

International Competition Network at http://www.internationalcompetitionnetwork.org/index.html

OECD Competition Policy and Law Division at http://www.oecd.org/topic/0,2686,en_2649_37463_1_1_1_1_37463,00.html

UNCTAD Competition and Consumer Policies at http://www.unctad.org/en/subsites/cpolicy/index.htm

WTO Competition Policy at http://www.wto.org/english/tratop_e/comp_e/comp_e.htm

EU sites

The EU website has been recently restructured.

The front door to EU sites is now http://europa.eu.int/ and the English-language index can be found at http://europa.eu.int/index_en.htm

The home page of the ECJ and CFI are http://www.curia.eu.int/en/transitpage.htm

The activities of the European Union in the area of competition is at http://europa.eu.int/pol/comp/index_en.htm

The Commission's Competition homepage is now at http://europa.eu.int/comm/competition/index_en.html

The EC Competition Policy Newsletter is a useful resource: http://europa.eu.int/comm/competition/publications/cpn/

The Treaty, latest OJ, etc. are linked from Eur-Lex: http://europa.eu.int/eur-lex/en/index.html which also links to a search engine covering recent case law.

Other useful sites and sites with links to further resources:

http://www.publicinfo.net/

http://www.lecg.com/website/home.nsf/OpenPage/AntitrustCompetition

http://www.findlaw.com/01topics/01antitrust/index.html

http://www.cgsh.com/english/news/latestnews.aspx
http://www.freshfields.com/practice/comptrade/links/en.asp
http://www.linklaters-alliance.com/practiceareas/index.asp?navigationid=5
http://www.arnoldporter.com/practice.cfm?practice_id=1

Hart Publishing
Oxford and Portland, Oregon

Published in North America (US and Canada) by
Hart Publishing c/o
International Specialized Book Services
5804 NE Hassalo Street
Portland, Oregon
97213-3644
USA

Distributed in the Netherlands, Belgium and Luxembourg by
Intersentia, Churchillaan 108
B2900 Schoten
Antwerpen
Belgium

Hart Publishing is a specialist legal publisher based in Oxford, England.
To order further copies of this book or to request a list of other
publications please write to:

Hart Publishing, Salter's Boatyard, Folly Bridge,
Abingdon Road, Oxford OX1 4LB
Telephone: +44 (0)1865 245533 or Fax: +44 (0)1865 794882
e-mail: mail@hartpub.co.uk
WEBSITE: http//www.hartpub.co.uk

British Library Cataloguing in Publication Data
Data Available
ISBN 1–84113–397–3 (paperback)

Typeset by Hope Services (Abingdon) Ltd.
Printed and bound in Great Britain on acid-free paper by
Page Bros, Norwich

An Introductory Guide to EC Competition Law and Practice

Eighth Edition

VALENTINE KORAH LL.M., Ph.D

Professor Emeritus of Competition Law, University College London;
and a Barrister, Guildford Chambers.

·H A R T·
PUBLISHING

OXFORD – PORTLAND OREGON
2004